Library+

BTEC Level 4 HNC and
Level 5 HND in Business

We work with leading authors to develop the strongest educational materials bringing cutting-edge thinking and best learning practice to a global market.

Under a range of well-known imprints, including Financial Times/Prentice Hall, Addison Wesley and Longman, we craft high quality print and electronic publications which help readers to understand and apply their content, whether studying or at work.

Pearson Custom Publishing enables our customers to access a wide and expanding range of market-leading content from world-renowned authors and develop their own tailor-made book. You choose the content that meets your needs and Pearson Custom Publishing produces a high-quality printed book.

To find out more about custom publishing, visit www.pearsoncustom.co.uk

A Pearson Custom Publication

BTEC Level 4 HNC and Level 5 HND in Business

Compiled from:

Material specially written by Edexcel

The Business Environment
Sixth Edition
by Ian Worthington and Chris Britton

Corporate Finance
Fifth Edition
by Denzil Watson and Antony Head

Management Accounting for Decision Makers
Sixth Edition
by Peter Atrill and Eddie McLaney

Accounting for Non-accounting Students
Eigth Edition
by John R. Dyson

International Financial Reporting:
A Practical Guide
Second Edition
by Alan Melville

Management: An Introduction
Fourth Edition
by David Boddy

Management and Organisational Behaviour
Ninth Edition
by Laurie J. Mullins

Essentials of Marketing
Second Edition
by Frances Brassington and Stephen Pettitt

Essential Guide to Marketing Planning
by Marian Burk Wood

Contract Law
Seventh Edition
by Catherine Elliott and Frances Quinn

Tort Law
Seventh Edition
by Catherine Elliott and Frances Quinn

Essential Business Statistics
by Joanne Smailes and Angela McGrane

Fundamentals of Strategy
by Gerry Johnson, Kevan Scholes
and Richard Whittington

Research Methods for Business Students
Fifth Edition
by Mark Saunders, Philip Lewis
and Adrian Thornhill

PEARSON
Custom
Publishing

Pearson Education Limited
Edinburgh Gate
Harlow
Essex CM20 2JE

And associated companies throughout the world

Visit us on the World Wide Web at:
www.pearsoned.co.uk

First published 2011

Essentials of Marketing
Second Edition
by Frances Brassington and Stephen Pettitt
ISBN 978 0 273 70818 6
Copyright © Pearson Education Limited 2005, 2007

Essential Guide to Marketing Planning
by Marian Burk Wood
ISBN 978 0 273 71323 4
Copyright © Pearson Education Limited 2007

Contract Law
Seventh Edition
by Catherine Elliott and Frances Quinn
ISBN 978 1 4058 9935 2
Copyright © Pearson Education Limited 1996, 2003, 2005, 2007, 2009

Tort Law
Seventh Edition
by Catherine Elliott and Frances Quinn
ISBN 978 1 4058 9933 8
Copyright © Pearson Education Limited 1996, 2009

Essential Business Statistics
by Joanne Smailes and Angela McGrane
ISBN 978 0 273 64333 3
Copyright © Pearson Education Limited 2000

Fundamentals of Strategy
by Gerry Johnson, Kevan Scholes and Richard Whittington
ISBN 978 0 273 71310 4
Copyright © Pearson Education Limited 2009

Research Methods for Business Students
Fifth Edition
by Mark Saunders, Philip Lewis and Adrian Thornhill
ISBN 978 0 273 71686 0
Copyright © Pearson Education Limited 1997
Copyright © Pearson Education Limited 2000, 2003, 2007
Copyright © Mark Sauders, Philip Lewis and Adrian Thornhill 2009

ISBN 978 0 85776 003 6

Printed and bound in Italy by L.E.G.O. S.p.A.

Contents

CHAPTER 1

Business Environment

Unit 1: Business Environment

Unit code: Y/601/0546

QCF level: 4

Credit value: 15 credits

Aim

The aim of this unit is to provide learners with an understanding of different organisations, the influence of stakeholders and the relationship between businesses and the local, national and global environments.

Unit abstract

Organisations have a variety of purposes that depend on why they were established. Some operate for profit, whilst others do not. Organisations structure themselves and operate in ways that allow their objectives to be met. Every organisation has a range of stakeholders whose interests need to be satisfied, but stakeholders have competing interests that may be hard to reconcile.

Businesses operate in an environment shaped by the government, competitors, consumers, suppliers and international factors. Learners will understand that some influences on the business environment are direct and clear, for example taxation policies on corporate activities. Other influences are less clear, perhaps coming from the international arena and sometimes with only an oblique impact on the national business environment.

It is within this business environment that organisations function and have to determine strategies and a modus operandi that allow them to meet their organisational purposes in ways that comply with the relevant legal and regulatory frameworks. In addition, business markets take various forms and the structure of a market enables an understanding of how organisations behave. In this unit learners will consider how different market structures shape the pricing and output decisions of businesses, as well as other aspects of their behaviour.

Learning outcomes

On successful completion of this unit a learner will:

1 Understand the organisational purposes of businesses
2 Understand the nature of the national environment in which businesses operate
3 Understand the behaviour of organisations in their market environment
4 Be able to assess the significance of the global factors that shape national business activities

Unit content

1 Understand the organisational purposes of businesses

Categories of organisation: legal structure; type eg private company, public company, government, voluntary organisation, co-operative, charitable; sector (primary, secondary tertiary)

Purposes: mission; vision; aims; objectives; goals; values; profits; market share; growth; return on capital employed (ROCE); sales; service level; customer satisfaction; corporate responsibility; ethical issues

Stakeholders: owners; customers; suppliers; employees; debtors; creditors; financial institutions (banks, mortgage lenders, credit factors); environmental groups; government agencies (central government, local authorities); trade unions

Responsibilities of organisations: stakeholder interests; conflict of expectations; power-influence matrix; satisfying stakeholder objectives; legal responsibilities eg consumer legislation, employee legislation, equal opportunities and anti-discriminatory legislation, environmental legislation, health and safety legislation; ethical issues eg environment, fair trade, global warming, charter compliance eg Banking Code

2 Understand the nature of the national environment in which businesses operate

Economic systems: the allocation of scarce resources; effective use of resources; type of economic system eg command, free enterprise, mixed, transitional

The UK economy: size (gross domestic product, gross national product); structure; population; labour force; growth; inflation; balance of payments; balance of trade; exchange rates; trading partners; public finances (revenues, expenditure); taxation; government borrowing; business behaviour eg investment, objectives, risk awareness; cost of capital; consumer behaviour; propensity to save; propensity to spend; tastes and preferences

Government policy: economic goals; fiscal policy: control of aggregate demand; central and local government spending; Public Sector Net Borrowing (PSNB) and Public Sector Net Cash Requirement (PSNCR); euro convergence criteria, monetary policy; interest rates; quantitative easing; private finance initiative (PFI); competition policy (up-to-date legislation including Competition Act 1998, Enterprise Act 2002); Competition Commission, Office of Fair Trading; Directorate General for Competition; European Commission; sector regulators eg Ofgem, Ofwat, Civil Aviation Authority; Companies Acts; regional policy; industrial policy; enterprise strategy; training and skills policy

3 Understand the behaviour of organisations in their market environment

Market types: perfect competition, monopoly, monopolistic competition, oligopoly, duopoly; competitive advantage, strategies adopted by firms; regulation of competition

Market forces and organisational responses: supply and demand, elasticity of demand; elasticity of supply; customer perceptions and actions, pricing decisions; cost and output decisions; economies of scale, the short run; the long run, multi-national and transnational corporations; joint ventures, outsourcing; core markets; labour market trends; employee skills, technology; innovation; research and development; core competencies; business environment (political, economic, social, technical, legal,]environmental); cultural environment

4 Be able to assess the significance of the global factors that shape national business activities

Global factors: international trade and the UK economy; market opportunities; global growth; protectionism; World Trade Organisation (WTO); emerging markets (BRIC economies – Brazil, Russia, India, China); EU membership; EU business regulations and their incorporation into UK law; EU policies eg agriculture (CAP), business, competition, growth, employment, education, economics and finance, environment, science and technology, regional); labour movement; workforce skills; exchange rates; trading blocs (eg monetary unions, common markets; customs unions, free trade areas); labour costs; trade duties; levies; tariffs; customs dues; taxation regimes; international competitiveness; international business environment (political, economic, social, technical, legal, environmental); investment incentives; cost of capital; commodity prices; intellectual property; climate change eg Kyoto Protocol, Rio Earth Summit; third world poverty; the group of 20 (G-20); global financial stability

Learning outcomes and assessment criteria

Learning outcomes On successful completion of this unit a learner will:	Assessment criteria for pass The learner can:
LO1 Understand the organisational purposes of businesses	1.1 identify the purposes of different types of organisation 1.2 describe the extent to which an organisation meets the objectives of different stakeholders 1.3 explain the responsibilities of an organisation and strategies employed to meet them
LO2 Understand the nature of the national environment in which businesses operate	2.1 explain how economic systems attempt to allocate resources effectively 2.2 assess the impact of fiscal and monetary policy on business organisations and their activities 2.3 evaluate the impact of competition policy and other regulatory mechanisms on the activities of a selected organisation
LO3 Understand the behaviour of organisations in their market environment	3.1 explain how market structures determine the pricing and output decisions of businesses 3.2 illustrate the way in which market forces shape organisational responses using a range of examples 3.3 judge how the business and cultural environments shape the behaviour of a selected organisation
LO4 Be able to assess the significance of the global factors that shape national business activities	4.1 discuss the significance of international trade to UK business organisations 4.2 analyse the impact of global factors on UK business organisations 4.3 evaluate the impact of policies of the European Union on UK business organisations

Guidance

Links

This unit has links with other business and economics-focused units such as *Unit 3: Organisations and Behaviour, Unit 7: Business Strategy, Unit 35: European Business* and *Unit 45: Business Ethics*.

This unit also links to the Management and Leadership NOS as mapped in *Annexe B*.

Essential requirements

There are no essential or unique resources required for the delivery of this unit.

Employer engagement and vocational contexts

Centres can develop links with local employers. Many businesses look to employ learners when they finish their programmes of study and may provide information about the business environment which they operate in. They will have a view about the impact of the governmental and EU factors that shape how they behave.

Many learners are, or have been, employed and will be able to draw on their experience of employment and will have had experience of the nature of the business environment and the ways in which organisations respond to and determine the nature of that environment.

The macroeconomic environment

Introduction

By 2008 many of the world's economies were facing substantial economic problems as a result of rising oil prices, increased food and energy costs and the aftermath of the 'credit crunch' in the United States. In countries across the globe the talk was predominantly of 'recession' and the impact on the consumer, businesses and the public finances of a downturn in economic activity. In an effort to boost the US economy, the Bush administration provided a $168bn (£86bn) economic stimulus package, using tax refunds for around 130 million US households, in an effort to boost consumer spending. The evidence suggests that the US government's fiscal response had some impact on consumer behaviour, with some retailers (e.g.Wal-Mart) reporting an increase in like-for-like sales in the period after households received their refund cheques. In other areas of the US economy, however, the picture was less rosy, with many businesses experiencing extremely tough trading conditions as consumers reduced their spending to cope with higher domestic bills for food, petrol and energy and the global crisis in financial markets continued to cause considerable uncertainty about future economic prospects.

What this simple example is designed to demonstrate is the intimate relationship between business activity and the wider economic context in which it takes place, and a glance at any quality newspaper will provide a range of similar illustrations of this interface between business and economics. What is important at this point is not to understand the complexities of global economic forces or their effect on businesses, but to appreciate in broad terms the importance of the **macroeconomic environment** for business organisations and, in particular, the degree of compatibility between the preoccupations of the entrepreneur and those of the economist. To the economist, for example, a recession is generally marked by falling demand, rising unemployment, a slowing down in economic growth and a fall in investment. To the firm, it usually implies a loss of orders, a likely reduction in the workforce, a decline in output (or a growth in stocks) and a general reluctance to invest in capital equipment and/or new projects.

In this section the focus is on the broad question of the economic structure and processes of a market-based economy and on the macroeconomic influences affecting and being affected by business activity in this type of economic system. An understanding of the overall economic context within which businesses operate and its core values and principles is central to any meaningful analysis of the business environment.

Three further points are worth highlighting at this juncture. First, business activity not only is shaped by the economic context in which it takes place, but helps to shape that context; consequently the success or otherwise of government economic policy depends to some degree on the reactions of both the firms and the markets (e.g. the stock market) which are affected by government decisions. Second, economic influences operate at a variety of spatial levels, as illustrated by the opening paragraph, and governments can find that circumstances largely or totally beyond their control can affect businesses either favourably or adversely. Third, the economic (and for that matter, political) influence of industry and commerce can be considerable and this ensures that business organisations – both individually and collectively – usually constitute one of the chief pressure groups in democratic states.

Economic systems

The concept of economic scarcity

Like politics, the term **economic** tends to be used in a variety of ways and contexts to describe certain aspects of human behaviour, ranging from activities such as producing, distributing and consuming, to the idea of frugality in the use of a resource (e.g. being 'economical' with the truth). Modern definitions stress how such behaviour, and the institutions in which it takes place (e.g. households, firms, governments, banks), are concerned with the satisfaction of human needs and wants through the transformation of resources into goods and services which are consumed by society. These processes are said to take place under conditions of **economic scarcity**.

The economist's idea of 'scarcity' centres on the relationship between a society's needs and wants and the resources available to satisfy them. In essence, economists argue that whereas needs and wants tend to be unlimited, the resources which can be used to meet those needs and wants are finite and accordingly no society at any time has the capacity to provide for all its actual or potential requirements. The assumption here is that both individual and collective needs and wants consistently outstrip the means available to satisfy them, as exemplified, for instance, by the inability of governments to provide instant health care, the best roads, education, defence, railways, and so on, at a time and place and of a quality convenient to the user. This being the case, 'choices' have to be made by both individuals and society concerning priorities in the use of resources, and every choice inevitably involves a 'sacrifice' (i.e. forgoing an alternative). Economists describe this sacrifice as the **opportunity cost** or **real cost** of the decision that is taken (e.g. every pound spent on the health service is a pound not spent on some other public service) and it is one which is faced by individuals, organisations (including firms), governments and society alike.

From a societal point of view the existence of economic scarcity poses three serious problems concerning the use of resources:

1 What to use the available resources for? That is, what goods and services should be produced (or not produced) with the resources (sometimes described as the 'guns v. butter' argument)?
2 How best to use those resources? For example, in what combinations, using what techniques and what methods?
3 How best to distribute the goods and services produced with them? That is, who gets what, how much and on what basis?

In practice, of course, these problems tend to be solved in a variety of ways, including barter (voluntary, bilateral exchange), price signals and the market, queuing and rationing, government instruction and corruption (e.g. resources allocated in exchange for personal favours), and examples of each of these solutions can be found in most, if not all, societies, at all times. Normally, however, one or other main approach to resource allocation tends to predominate and this allows analytical distinctions to be made between different types of economic system. One important distinction is between those economies which are centrally planned and those which operate predominantly through market forces, with prices forming the integrating mechanism. Understanding this distinction is fundamental to an examination of the way in which business is conducted and represents the foundation on which much of the subsequent analysis is built.

The centrally planned economy

In this type of economic system – associated with the post-Second World War socialist economies of eastern Europe, China, Cuba and elsewhere – most of the key decisions on production are taken by a central planning authority, normally the state and its agencies. Under this arrangement, the state typically:

● owns and/or controls the main economic resources;
● establishes priorities in the use of those resources;
● sets output targets for businesses which are largely under state ownership and/or control;
● directs resources in an effort to achieve these predetermined targets; and
● seeks to co-ordinate production in such a way as to ensure consistency between output and input demands.

The fact that an economy is centrally planned does not necessarily imply that all economic decisions are taken at central level; in many cases decision making may be devolved to subordinate agencies, including local committees and enterprises. Ultimately, however, these agencies are responsible to the centre and it is the latter which retains overall control of the economy and directs the use of scarce productive resources.

The problem of co-ordinating inputs and output in a modern planned economy is, of course, a daunting task and one which invariably involves an array of state planners and a central plan or blueprint normally covering a number of years (e.g. a five-year plan). Under such a plan, the state planners would establish annual output targets for each sector of the economy and for each enterprise within the sector and would identify the inputs of materials, labour and capital needed to achieve the set targets and would allocate resources accordingly. Given that the outputs of some industries (e.g. agricultural machinery) are the inputs of others (e.g. collective farms), it is not difficult to see how the overall effectiveness of the plan would depend in part on a high degree of co-operation and co-ordination between sectors and enterprises, as well as on good judgement, good decisions and a considerable element of good luck. The available evidence from planned economies suggests that none of these can be taken for granted and each is often in short supply.

Even in the most centralised of economies, state planning does not normally extend to telling individuals what they must buy in shops or how to use their labour, although an element of state direction at times may exist (e.g. conscription of the armed forces). Instead, it tends to condition *what* is available for purchase and the *prices* at which exchange takes place, and both of these are essentially the outcome of political choices, rather than a reflection of consumer demands. All too often consumers tend to be faced by queues and 'black markets' for some consumer products and overproduction of others, as state enterprises strive to meet targets frequently unrelated to the needs and wants of consumers. By the same token, businesses which make losses do not have to close down, as the state would normally make additional funds available to cover any difference between sales revenue and costs. This being the case, the emphasis at firm level tends to be more on meeting targets than on achieving efficiency in the use of resources and hence a considerable degree of duplication and wastage tends to occur.

In such an environment, the traditional entrepreneurial skills of efficient resource management, price setting and risk taking have little, if any, scope for development and managers behave essentially as technicians and bureaucrats, administering decisions largely made elsewhere. Firms, in effect, are mainly servants of the state and their activities are conditioned by social and political considerations, rather than by the needs of the market – although some market activity normally occurs in planned economies (especially in agriculture and a number of private services). Accordingly, businesses and their employees are not fully sensitised to the needs of the consumer and as a result quality and choice (where it exists) may suffer, particularly where incentives to improved efficiency and performance are negligible. Equally, the system tends to encourage bribery and corruption and the development of a substantial black market, with differences in income, status and political influence being an important determinant of individual consumption and of living standards.

The free-market economy

The **free-market** (or **capitalist**) **economy** stands in direct contrast to the centrally planned system. Whereas in the latter the state controls most economic decisions, in the former the key economic agencies are private individuals (sometimes called 'households') and firms, and these interact in free markets, through a system of prices, to determine the allocation of resources.

The key features of this type of economic system are as follows:

- Resources are in private ownership and the individuals owning them are free to use them as they wish.
- Firms, also in private ownership, are equally able to make decisions on production, free from state interference.
- No blueprint (or master plan) exists to direct production and consumption.
- Decisions on resource allocation are the result of a decentralised system of markets and prices, in which the decisions of millions of consumers and hundreds of thousands of firms are automatically co-ordinated.
- The consumer is sovereign, i.e. dictates the pattern of supply and hence the pattern of resource allocation.

In short, the three problems of what to produce, how to produce and how to distribute are solved by market forces.

The diagram in Figure 1.1 illustrates the basic operation of a market economy. In essence, individuals are owners of resources (e.g. labour) and consumers of products; firms are users of resources and producers of products. What products are produced – and hence how resources are used – depends on consumers, who indicate their demands by purchasing (i.e. paying the price) or not purchasing, and this acts as a signal to producers to acquire the resources necessary (i.e. pay the price) to meet

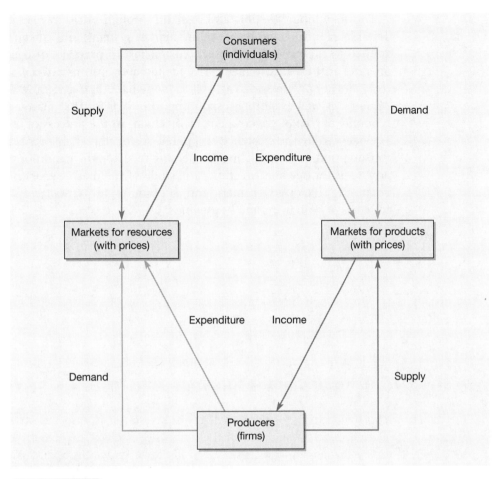

Figure 1.1   The market economy

the preferences of consumers. If consumer demands change, for whatever reason, this will cause an automatic reallocation of resources, as firms respond to the new market conditions. Equally, competition between producers seeking to gain or retain customers is said to guarantee that resources are used efficiently and to ensure that the most appropriate production methods (i.e. how to produce) are employed in the pursuit of profits.

The distribution of output is also determined by market forces, in this case operating in the markets for productive services. Individuals supplying a resource (e.g. labour) receive an income (i.e. a price) from the firms using that resource and this allows them to purchase goods and services in the markets for products, which in turn provides an income for firms that can be spent on the purchase of further resources. Should the demand for a particular type of productive resource increase – say, as a result of an increase in the demand for the product produced by that resource – the price paid to the provider of the resource will tend to rise and hence, other things being equal, allow more output to be purchased. Concomitantly, it is also likely to result in a shift of resources from uses which are relatively less lucrative to those which are relatively more rewarding.

This matching of supply and demand through prices in markets is described in detail later in the chapter (see 'The market system') and the analysis can also be applied to the market for foreign currencies. In practice, of course, no economy operates entirely in the manner suggested above; firms after all are influenced by costs and supply decisions as well as by demand and generally seek to shape that demand, as well as simply responding to it. Nor for that matter is a market-based economy devoid of government involvement in the process of resource allocation, as evidenced by the existence of a public sector responsible for substantial levels of consumption and output and for helping to shape the conditions under which the private sector operates. In short, any study of the market economy needs to incorporate the role of government and to examine, in particular, its influence on the activities of both firms and households.

Legal structures

Private sector organisations in the UK

The sole trader

Many individuals aspire to owning and running their own business – being their own boss, making their own decisions. For those who decide to turn their dream into a reality, becoming a sole trader (or sole proprietor) offers the simplest and easiest method of trading.

As the name suggests, a **sole trader** is a business owned by one individual who is self-employed and who may, in some cases, employ other people on either a full-time or a part-time basis. Normally using personal funds to start the business, the sole trader decides on the type of goods or services to be produced, where the business is to be located, what capital is required, what staff (if any) to employ, what the target market should be and a host of other aspects concerned with the establishment and running of the enterprise. Where the business proves a success, all profits accrue to the owner and it is common for sole traders to reinvest a considerable proportion of these in the business and/or use them to reduce past borrowings. Should losses occur, these too are the responsibility of the sole trader, who has **unlimited personal liability** for the debts of the business.

Despite this substantial disadvantage, sole proprietorship tends to be the most popular form of business organisation numerically. In the United Kingdom, for example, it is estimated that about 80 per cent of all businesses are sole traders and in some sectors – notably personal services, retailing, building – they tend to be the dominant form of business enterprise. Part of the reason for this numerical dominance is the relative ease with which an individual can establish a business of this type. Apart from minor restrictions concerning the use of a business name – if the name of the proprietor is not used – few other legal formalities are required to set up the enterprise, other than the need to register for Value Added Tax if turnover exceeds a certain sum (e.g. £67 000 in 2008) and/or to fulfil any special requirements laid down by the local authority prior to trading (e.g. some businesses require licences). Once established, of course, the sole trader, like other forms of business, will be subject to a variety of legal requirements (e.g. contract law, consumer law, employment law) – though not the requirement to file information about the business in a public place. For some, this ability to keep the affairs of the enterprise away from public scrutiny provides a further incentive to establishing this form of business organisation – some of which may operate wholly or partly in the **black economy** (i.e. beyond the gaze of the tax authorities).

A further impetus towards sole ownership comes from the ability of the individual to exercise a considerable degree of control over her/his own destiny. Business decisions – including the day-to-day operations of the enterprise as well as long-term plans – are in the hands of the owner and many individuals evidently relish the risks and potential rewards associated with entrepreneurial activity, preferring these to the relative safety of employment in another organisation. For others less fortunate, the 'push' of unemployment rather than the 'pull' of the marketplace tends to be more of a deciding factor and one which clearly accounts for some of the growth in the number of small businesses in the United Kingdom in the later part of the twentieth century.

Ambitions and commitment alone, however, are not necessarily sufficient to guarantee the survival and success of the enterprise and the high mortality rate among businesses of this kind, particularly during a recession, is well known and well documented. Part of the problem may stem from developments largely outside the control of the enterprise – including bad debts, increased competition, higher interest rates, falling demand – and factors such as these affect businesses of all types and all sizes, not just sole traders. Other difficulties, such as lack of funds for expansion, poor marketing, lack of research of the marketplace and insufficient management skills are to some extent self-induced and emanate, at least in part, from the decision to become a sole proprietor rather than some other form of business organisation. Where such constraints exist, the sole trader may be tempted to look to others to share the burdens and the risks by establishing a partnership or co-operative or limited company or by seeking a different approach to the business venture, such as through franchising. These alternative forms of business organisation are discussed in detail below.

The partnership

The Partnership Act 1890 defines a **partnership** as 'the relation which subsists between persons carrying on a business in common with a view to profit'. Like the sole trader, this form of business organisation does not have its own distinct legal personality and hence the owners – the partners – have unlimited personal liability both jointly and severally. This means that in the case of debts or bankruptcy of the partnership, each partner is liable in full for the whole debt and each in turn may be sued or their assets seized until the debt is satisfied. Alternatively, all the partners may be joined into the action to recover debts, unless by dint of the Limited Partnership Act 1907, a partner (or partners) has limited liability. Since it tends to be much easier to achieve the same ends by establishing a limited company, limited partnerships are not common, nor can all partners in a partnership have limited liability. Hence in the discussion below, attention is focused on the partnership as an unincorporated association, operating in a market where its liability is effectively unlimited.

In essence, a partnership comes into being when two or more people establish a business which they own, finance and run jointly for personal gain, irrespective of the degree of formality involved in the relationship. Such a business can range from a husband and wife running a local shop as joint owners, to a very large firm of accountants or solicitors, with in excess of a hundred partners in offices in various locations. Under the law, most partnerships are limited to 20 or less, but some types of business, particularly in the professions, may have a dispensation from this rule (Companies Act 1985, s 716). This same Act requires businesses which are not exempt from the rule and which have more than 20 partners to register as a company.

While it is not necessary for a partnership to have a formal written agreement, most partnerships tend to be formally enacted in a Deed of Partnership or Articles, since this makes it much easier to reduce uncertainty and to ascertain intentions when there is a written document to consult. Where this is not done, the Partnership Act 1890 lays down a minimum code which governs the relationship between partners and which provides, amongst other things, for all partners to share equally in the capital and profits of the business and to contribute equally towards its losses.

In practice, of course, where a Deed or Articles exist, these will invariably reflect differences in the relative status and contribution of individual partners. Senior partners, for example, will often have contributed more financially to the partnership and not unnaturally will expect to receive a higher proportion of the profits. Other arrangements – including membership, action on dissolution of the partnership, management responsibilities and rights, and the basis for allocating salaries – will be outlined in the partnership agreement and as such will provide the legal framework within which the enterprise exists and its co-owners operate.

Unlike the sole trader, where management responsibilities devolve on a single individual, partnerships permit the sharing of responsibilities and tasks and it is common in a partnership for individuals to specialise to some degree in particular aspects of the organisation's work – as in the case of a legal or medical or veterinary practice. Added to this, the fact that more than one person is involved in the ownership of the business tends to increase the amount of finance available to the organisation, thus permitting expansion to take place without the owners losing control of the enterprise. These two factors alone tend to make a partnership an attractive proposition for some would-be entrepreneurs, while for others the rules of their professional body – which often prohibits its members from forming a company – effectively provide for the establishment of this type of organisation.

On the downside, the sharing of decisions and responsibilities may represent a problem, particularly where partners are unable to agree over the direction the partnership should take or the amount to be reinvested in the business, unless such matters are clearly specified in a formal agreement. A more intractable problem is the existence of unlimited personal liability – a factor which may inhibit some individuals from considering this form of organisation, particularly given that the actions of any one partner are invariably binding on the other members of the business. To overcome this problem, many individuals, especially in manufacturing and trading, look to the limited company as the type of organisation which can combine the benefits of joint ownership and limited personal liability – a situation not necessarily always borne out in practice. It is to this type of business organisation that the discussion now turns.

Limited companies

In law a **company** is a corporate association having a legal identity in its own right (i.e. it is distinct from the people who own it, unlike in the case of a sole trader or partnership). This means that all property and other assets owned by the company belong to the company and not to its members (owners). By the same token, the personal assets of its members (the **shareholders**) do not normally belong to the business. In the event of insolvency, therefore, an individual's liability is limited to the amount invested in the business, including any amount remaining unpaid on the shares for which they have subscribed.[1] One exception to this would be where a company's owners have given a personal guarantee to cover any loans they have obtained from a bank or other institution – a requirement for many small, private limited companies. Another occurs where a company is limited by guarantee rather than by shares, with its members' liability being limited to the amount they have undertaken to contribute to the assets in the event of the company being wound up. Companies of this type are normally non-profit-making organisations – such as professional, research or trade associations – and are much less common than companies limited by shares. Hence in the discussion below, attention is focused on the latter as the dominant form of business organisation in the corporate sector of business.[2]

Companies are essentially business organisations consisting of two or more individuals who have agreed to embark on a business venture and who have decided to seek corporate status rather than to form a partnership.[3] Such status could derive from an Act of Parliament or a Royal Charter, but is almost always nowadays achieved through 'registration', the terms of which are laid down in the various Companies Acts. Under legislation, enacted in 1985, 1989 and 2006 individuals seeking to form a company are required to file numerous documents, including a **Memorandum of Association** and **Articles of Association**, with the Registrar of Companies. If satisfied, the Registrar will issue a Certificate of Incorporation, bringing the company into existence as a legal entity. As an alternative, the participants could buy a ready-formed company 'off the shelf', by approaching a company registration agent who specialises in company formations. In the United Kingdom, advertisements for ready-made companies appear regularly in magazines such as *Exchange and Mart and Dalton's Weekly*.

 Companies' House can be accessed at *www.companieshouse.gov.uk*

Information on how companies are created, run and wound up is contained in the 2006 Companies Act which essentially consolidates all previous legislation and case law into one Act of Parliament. As this Act shows, under British law a distinction is made between public and private companies. **Public limited companies** (PLCs) – not to be confused with public corporations, which in the UK are state-owned businesses (see below) – are those limited companies which satisfy the conditions for being a 'PLC'. These conditions require the company to have:

● a minimum of two shareholders;
● at least two directors;
● a minimum (at present) of £50 000 of authorised and allotted share capital;
● the right to offer its shares (and debentures) for sale to the general public;
● a certificate from the Registrar of Companies verifying that the share capital requirements have been met; and
● a memorandum which states it to be a public company.

A company which meets these conditions must include the title 'public limited company' or 'PLC' in its name and is required to make full accounts available for public inspection. Any company unable or unwilling to meet these conditions is therefore, in the eyes of the law, a 'private limited company', normally signified by the term 'Limited' or 'Ltd'.

Like the public limited company, the **private limited company** must have a minimum of two shareholders, but its shares cannot be offered to the public at large, although it can offer them to individuals through its business contacts. This restriction on the sale of shares, and hence on their ability to raise considerable sums of money on the open market, normally ensures that most private companies are either small or medium sized, and are often family businesses operating in a relatively restricted market; there are, however, some notable exceptions to this general rule (e.g. Virgin). In contrast, public companies – many of which began life as private companies prior to 'going public' – often have many thousands, even millions, of owners (shareholders) and normally operate on a national or international scale, producing products as diverse as computers, petro-chemicals, cars and banking services. Despite being outnumbered by their private counterparts, public companies dwarf private companies in terms of their capital and other assets, and their collective influence on output, investment, employment and consumption in the economy is immense.

Both public and private companies act through their **directors**. These are individuals chosen by a company's shareholders to manage its affairs and to make the important decisions concerning the direction the company should take (e.g. investment, market development, mergers and so on). The appointment and powers of directors are outlined in the Articles of Association (the 'internal rules' of the organisation) and so long as the directors do not exceed their powers, the shareholders do not normally have the right to intervene in the day-to-day management of the company. Where a director exceeds his or her authority or fails to indicate clearly that they are acting as an agent for the company, they become personally liable for any contracts they make. Equally, directors become personally liable if they continue to trade when the company is insolvent and they may be dismissed by a court if it considers that an individual is unfit to be a director in view of their past record (Company Directors Disqualification Act 1985).

The 2006 Act sets out in detail the duties of company directors, including the duty to promote the success of the organisation, to exercise reasonable care, skill and diligence and to give appropriate consideration to issues that go beyond the balance sheet. For example, directors of UK companies now have a duty to consider the impacts of their business operations on the environment and the community generally and quoted public companies must report on issues of social and environmental responsibility as part of an expanded review of the business.

In practice it is usual for a board of directors to have both a chairperson and a managing director, although some companies choose to appoint one person to both roles. The chairperson, who is elected by the other members of the board, is usually chosen because of their knowledge and experience of the business and their skill both internally in chairing board meetings and externally in representing the best interest of the organisation. As the public face of the company, the chairperson has an important role to play in establishing and maintaining a good public image and hence many large public companies like to appoint well-known public figures to this important position (e.g. ex-Cabinet ministers). In this case knowledge of the business is less important than the other attributes the individual might possess, most notably public visibility and familiarity, together with a network of contacts in government and in the business world.

The **managing director**, or chief executive, fulfils a pivotal role in the organisation, by forming the link between the board and the management team of senior executives. Central to this role is the need not only to interpret board decisions but to ensure that they are put into effect by establishing an appropriate structure of delegated responsibility and effective systems of reporting and control. This close contact with the day-to-day operations of the company places the appointed individual in a position of considerable authority and he/she will invariably be able to make important decisions without reference to the full board. This authority is enhanced where the managing director is also the person chairing the board of directors and/or is responsible for recommending individuals to serve as executive directors (i.e. those with functional responsibilities such as production, marketing, finance).

Like the managing director, most, if not all, **executive directors** will be full-time executives of the company, responsible for running a division or functional area within the framework laid down at board level. In contrast, other directors will have a **non-executive** role and are usually part-time appointees, chosen for a variety of reasons, including their knowledge, skills, contacts, influence, independence or previous experience. Sometimes, a company might be required to appoint such a director at the wishes of a third party, such as a merchant bank which has agreed to fund a large capital injection and wishes to have representation on the board. In this case, the individual tends to act in an advisory capacity – particularly on matters of finance – and helps to provide the financing institution with a means of ensuring that any board decisions are in its interests.

In Britain the role of company directors and senior executives in recent years has come under a certain amount of public scrutiny and has culminated in a number of enquiries into issues of power and pay. In the Cadbury Report (1992), a committee, with Sir Adrian Cadbury as chairperson, called for a non-statutory code of practice which it wanted applied to all listed public companies. Under this code the committee recommended:

- a clear division of responsibilities at the head of a company to ensure that no individual had unfettered powers of decision;
- a greater role for non-executive directors;
- regular board meetings;
- restrictions on the contracts of executive directors;
- full disclosure of directors' total enrolments;
- an audit committee dominated by non-executives.

The committee's stress on the important role of non-executive directors was a theme taken up in the Greenbury Report (1995) which investigated the controversial topic of executive salaries in the wake of a number of highly publicised pay rises for senior company directors. Greenbury's recommendations included:

- full disclosure of directors' pay packages, including pensions;
- shareholder approval for any long-term bonus scheme;
- remuneration committees consisting entirely of non-executive directors;
- greater detail in the annual report on directors' pay, pensions and perks;
- an end to payments for failure.

Greenbury was followed by a further investigation into corporate governance by a committee under the chairmanship of ICI chairman Ronald Hampel. The Hampel Report (1998) advocated company self-regulation and called for greater shareholder responsibility by companies and increased standards of disclosure of information; it supported Cadbury's recommendation that the role of chairperson and chief executive should normally be separated. A year later, the Turnbull Report (1999) considered the issue of corporate governance and information disclosure from the perspective of risk management, arguing that companies need to take steps to manage and disclose corporate risks formally.

As far as the issue of non-executive directors was concerned, this was investigated further by the Higgs Committee which was set up in 2002 and which reported the following year. In essence the Higgs Report set down a code of non-binding corporate guidelines regarding the role of non-executive directors on company boards. Like the Cadbury Report, Higgs recommended that the role of chairperson and chief executive should be kept separate and that the former should be independent, though not necessarily non-executive. As for non-executive directors, Higgs recommended that at least half the board should be independent and that non-executives should play key roles in areas such as strategy, performance, risk and the appointment and remuneration of executive directors. The latter issue, in particular, has been an area of considerable controversy in the UK in recent years and seems destined to remain so for some time.

mini case Companies under pressure

Public companies have to satisfy the conflicting demands of a range of stakeholder groups (see below), not least their shareholders who expect the organisation to operate in their interest. On the whole, individual shareholders are usually relatively quiescent, leaving the strategic and day-to-day decisions to the organisation's directors and senior executives. As an increasing number of public companies have found, however, many shareholders are becoming more actively involved in corporate decisions which they believe affect their investments and have been willing to voice their feelings at shareholders' meetings and to the media. This is particularly true of large corporate investors.

The rise of shareholder militancy at Daimler-Benz, led to shareholders expressing dissatisfaction over the company's poor performance and its effect on shareholder value. This is only one issue that has been exercising company shareholders in recent years, however. At the large UK retail chain Marks & Spencer,

for example, investors are unhappy at the decision to combine the position of executive chairman annd chief executive in contravention of City corporate governance rules; at Exxon Mobil shareholder concerns have focused on the company's environmental record, particularly with regard to its impact on climate change. At other companies, executives' pay and rewards have been the central issues that have provoked shareholder anger.

From a company's point of view, challenges such as these are not especially welcome and the board of directors may be forced to spend time and resources to justify its actions to the protestors. Apart from the negative publicity that shareholder revolts can evoke, large corporations are particularly concerned when the protests come from very large corporate investors such as pension funds, since their reactions can affect not only the current but also the future position of the organisation.

Co-operatives

Consumer co-operative societies

Consumer societies are basically 'self-help' organisations which have their roots in the anti-capitalist sentiment which arose in mid-nineteenth-century Britain and which gave rise to a consumer co-operative movement dedicated to the provision of cheap, unadulterated food for its members and a share in its profits. Today this movement boasts a multibillion-pound turnover, a membership numbered in millions and an empire which includes thousands of food stores (including the Alldays convenience chain purchased in 2002), numerous factories and farms, dairies, travel agencies, opticians, funeral parlours, a bank and an insurance company, and property and development business. Taken together, these activities ensure that the Co-operative Group remains a powerful force in British retailing into the early twenty-first century. Indeed, it is the world's largest consumer co-operative employing around 85 000 people (in 2007) following the merger of the Co-operative Group and United Co-operatives. Survey evidence indicates that in retailing it is the UK's most trusted and ethical brand name.

web link

The Co-operative Group's website address is *www.co-operative.coop*

Although the co-operative societies, like companies, are registered and incorporated bodies – in this case under the Industrial and Provident Societies Act – they are quite distinct trading organisations. These societies belong to their members (i.e. invariably customers who have purchased a share in the society) who elect Area Committees to oversee trading areas. These committees have annual elections and meetings for all members and these in turn appoint members on to regional boards and elect individual member directors to the Group Board. The Group Board also includes directors of corporate members who are representatives of other societies. Individual stores may also have member forums. Any profits from the Group's activities are supposed to benefit the members. Originally this took the form of a cash dividend paid to members in relation to their purchases, but this was subsequently replaced either by trading stamps or by investment in areas felt to benefit the consumer (e.g. lower prices, higher-quality products, modern shops, and so on) and/or the local community (e.g. charitable donations, sponsorship). The twice-yearly cash dividend was, however, reintroduced in 2006, a move which saw a significant increase in the membership of the organisation.

The societies differ in other ways from standard companies. For a start, shares are not quoted on the Stock Exchange and members are restricted in the number of shares they can purchase and in the method of disposal. Not having access to cheap sources of capital on the stock market, co-operatives rely heavily on retained surpluses and on loan finance, and the latter places a heavy burden on the societies when interest rates are high. The movement's democratic principles also impinge on its operations and this has often been a bone of contention as members have complained about their increasing remoteness from decision-making centres. Some societies have responded by encouraging the development of locally elected committees to act in an advisory or consultative capacity to the society's board of directors and it looks likely that others will be forced to consider similar means of increasing member participation, which still remains very limited.

web link

The Co-operative Commission has put forward numerous proposals for changes which are designed to improve the performance of societies. See *www.co-opcommission.org.uk*

The movement's historical links with the British Labour Party are also worth noting and a number of parliamentary candidates are normally sponsored at general elections. These links, however, have tended to become slightly looser in recent years, although the movement still contributes to Labour Party funds and continues to lobby politicians at both national and local level. It is also active in seeking to influence public opinion and, in this, claims to be responding to customer demands for greater social and corporate responsibility. Among its initiatives are the establishment of a customer's charter (by the Co-operative Bank) and the decision to review both its investments and the individuals and organisations it does business with, to ascertain that they are acceptable from an ethical point of view.

Workers' co-operatives

In Britain, workers' co-operatives are found in a wide range of industries, including manufacturing, building and construction, engineering, catering and retailing. They are particularly prevalent in printing, clothing and wholefoods, and some have been in existence for over a century. The majority, however, are of fairly recent origin, having been part of the growth in the number of small firms which occurred in the 1980s.

As the name suggests, a workers' co-operative is a business in which the ownership and control of the assets are in the hands of the people working in it, having agreed to establish the enterprise and to share the risk for mutual benefit. Rather than form a standard partnership, the individuals involved normally register the business as a friendly society under the Industrial and Provident Societies Acts 1965–78, or seek incorporation as a private limited company under the Companies Act 1985. In the case of the former, seven members are required to form a co-operative, while the latter only requires two. In practice, a minimum of three or four members tends to be the norm and some co-operatives may have several hundred participants, frequently people who have been made redundant by their employers and who are keen to keep the business going.

The central principles of the movement – democracy, open membership, social responsibility, mutual co-operation and trust – help to differentiate the co-operative from other forms of business organisation and govern both the formation and operation of this type of enterprise. Every employee may be a member of the organisation and every member owns one share in the business, with every share carrying an equal voting right. Any surpluses are shared by democratic agreement and this is normally done on an equitable basis, reflecting, for example, the amount of time and effort an individual puts into the business. Other decisions, too, are taken jointly by the members and the emphasis tends to be on the quality of goods or services provided and on creating a favourable working environment, rather than on the pursuit of profits – although the latter cannot be ignored if the organisation is to survive. In short, the co-operative tends to focus on people and on the relationship between them, stressing the co-operative and communal traditions associated with its origins, rather than the more conflictual and competitive aspects inherent in other forms of industrial organisation.

Despite these apparent attractions, workers' co-operatives have never been as popular in Britain as in other parts of the world (e.g. France, Italy, Israel), although a substantial increase occurred in the number of co-operatives in the 1980s, largely as a result of growing unemployment, overt support across the political spectrum and the establishment of a system to encourage and promote the co-operative ideal (e.g. Co-operative Development Agencies).[4] More recently, however, their fortunes have tended to decline, as employee shareholding and profit schemes (ESOPs) have grown in popularity. It seems unlikely that workers' co-operatives will ever form the basis of a strong third sector in the British economy, between the profit-oriented firms in the private sector and the nationalised and municipal undertakings in the public sector.

Public sector business organisations in the UK

Public sector organisations come in a variety of forms. These include:

- central government departments (e.g. Department of Innovation, Universities and Skills);
- local authorities (e.g. Lancashire County Council);
- regional bodies (e.g. Regional Development Agencies);
- non-departmental public bodies or quangos (e.g. the Arts Council);
- central government trading organisations (e.g. The Stationery Office); and
- public corporations and nationalised industries (e.g. the BBC).

In the discussion below, attention is focused on those public sector organisations which most closely approximate businesses in the private sector, namely, public corporations and municipal enterprises.

Public corporations

Private sector business organisations are owned by private individuals and groups who have chosen to invest in some form of business enterprise, usually with a view to personal gain. In contrast, in the public sector the state owns assets in various forms, which it uses to provide a range of goods and services felt to be of benefit to its citizens, even if this provision involves the state in a loss. Many of these services are provided directly through government departments (e.g. social security benefits) or through bodies operating under delegated authority from central government (e.g. local authorities, health authorities). Others are the responsibility of state-owned industrial and commercial undertakings, specially created for a variety of reasons and often taking the form of a **public corporation**. These state corporations are an important part of the public sector of the economy and have contributed significantly to national output, employment and investment. Their numbers, however, have declined substantially following the wide-scale privatisation of state industries which occurred in the 1980s and this process has continued through the 1990s and beyond with the sale of corporations such as British Coal, British Rail and British Energy.

Public corporations are statutory bodies, incorporated (predominantly) by special Act of Parliament and, like companies, they have a separate legal identity from the individuals who own them and run them. Under the statute setting up the corporation, reference is made to the powers, duties and responsibilities of the organisation and to its relationship with the government department which oversees its operations. In the past these operations have ranged from providing a variety of national and international postal services (the Post Office), to the provision of entertainment (the BBC), an energy source (British Coal) and a national rail network (British Rail). Where such provision involves the organisation in a considerable degree of direct contact with its customers, from whom it derives most of its revenue, the corporation tends to be called a **nationalised industry**. In reality, of course, the public corporation is the legal form through which the industry is both owned and run and every corporation is to some degree unique in structure as well as in functions.

As organisations largely financed as well as owned by the state, public corporations are required to be publicly accountable and hence they invariably operate under the purview of a 'sponsoring' government department, the head of which (the Secretary of State) appoints a board of management to run the organisation. This board tends to exercise a considerable degree of autonomy in day-to-day decisions and operates largely free from political interference on most matters of a routine nature. The organisation's strategic objectives, however, and important questions concerning reorganisation or investment, would have to be agreed with the sponsoring department, as would the corporation's performance targets and its external financing limits.

The link between the corporation and its supervising ministry provides the means through which Parliament can oversee the work of the organisation and permits ordinary Members of Parliament to seek information and explanation through question time, through debates and through the select committee system. Additionally, under the Competition Act 1980, nationalised industries can be subject to investigation by the Competition Commission, and this too presents opportunities for further parliamentary discussion and debate, as well as for government action.

A further opportunity for public scrutiny comes from the establishment of industry-specific Consumers' or Consultative Councils, which consider complaints from customers and advise both the board and the department concerned of public attitudes to the organisation's performance and to other aspects of its operations (e.g. pricing). In a number of cases, including British Rail before privatisation, pressure on government from consumers and from other sources has resulted in the establishment of a 'Customers' Charter', under which the organisation agrees to provide a predetermined level of service or to give information and/or compensation where standards are not achieved. Developments of this kind are already spreading to other parts of the public sector and in future may be used as a means by which governments decide on the allocation of funds to public bodies, as well as providing a vehicle for monitoring organisational achievement.

It is interesting to note that mechanisms for public accountability and state regulation have been retained to some degree even where public utilities have been privatised (i.e. turned into public limited companies). Industries such as gas, electricity, water and telecommunications are watched over by newly created regulatory bodies which are designed to protect the interests of consumers, particularly with regard to pricing and the standard of service provided. Ofgas, for example, which used to regulate British Gas, monitored gas supply charges to ensure that they reasonably reflected input costs and these charges could be altered by the regulator if they were seen to be excessive. Similarly, in the case of non-gas services, such as maintenance, the legislation privatising the industry only allowed prices to be raised to a prescribed maximum, to ensure that the organisation was not able to take full advantage of its monopoly power. The regulator of the gas market is now Ofgem.

An additional source of government influence has come through its ownership of a golden share in a privatised state industry which effectively gives the government a veto in certain vital areas of decision making. This notional shareholding – which is written into the privatisation legislation – tends to last for a number of years and can be used to protect a newly privatised business from a hostile takeover, particularly by foreign companies or individuals. Ultimately, however, the expectation is that this veto power will be relinquished and the organisation concerned will become subject to the full effects of the market – a point exemplified by the government's decision to allow Ford to take over Jaguar in 1990, having originally blocked a number of previous takeover bids.

The existence of a golden share should not be equated with the decision by government to retain (or purchase) a significant proportion of issued shares in a privatised (or already private) business organisation, whether as an investment and/or future source of revenue, or as a means of exerting influence in a particular industry or sector. Nor should it be confused with government schemes to attract private funds into existing state enterprises, by allowing them to achieve notional company status in order to overcome Treasury restrictions on borrowing imposed on public bodies. In the latter case, which often involves a limited share issue, government still retains full control of the organisation by owning all (or the vast majority) of the shares – as in the case of Consignia (formerly known as the Post Office). In March 2001 Consignia was incorporated as a government-owned public company. This change in legal status allowed the company more freedom to borrow and invest in the business, to make acquisitions and to enter into joint ventures and to expand internationally. The name Consignia was subsequently dropped in favour of the brand name Royal Mail.

Municipal enterprises

UK local authorities have a long history of involvement in business activity. In part this is a function of their role as central providers of public services (e.g. education, housing, roads, social services) and of their increasing involvement in supporting local economic development initiatives. But their activities have also traditionally involved the provision of a range of marketable goods and services, not required by law but provided voluntarily by a local authority and often in direct competition with the private sector (e.g. theatres, leisure services, museums). Usually such provision has taken place under the aegis of a local authority department which appoints staff who are answerable to the council and to its committees through the department's chief officer and its elected head. Increasingly, though, local authorities are turning to other organisational arrangements – including the establishment of companies and trusts – in order to separate some of these activities from the rest of their responsibilities and to create a means through which private investment in the enterprise can occur.

One example of such a development can be seen in the case of local authority controlled airports which are normally the responsibility of a number of local authorities who run them through a joint board, representing the interests of the participating district councils (e.g. Manchester International Airport). Since the Airports Act 1986, local authorities with airports have been required to create a limited company in which their joint assets are vested and which appoints a board of directors to run the enterprise. Like other limited companies, the organisation can, if appropriate, seek private capital and must publish annual accounts, including a profit and loss statement. It can also be privatised relatively easily if the local authorities involved decide to relinquish ownership (e.g. East Midlands Airport is part of the Manchester Airports Group).

Such developments, which have parallels in other parts of the public sector, can be seen to have had at least four benefits:

1 They have provided a degree of autonomy from local authority control that is seen to be beneficial in a competitive trading environment.
2 They have given access to market funds by the establishment of a legal structure that is not fully subject to central government restrictions on local authority borrowing.
3 They helped local authority organisations to compete more effectively under the now defunct system of compulsory competitive tendering (CCT), by removing or reducing charges for departmental overheads that are applied under the normal arrangements.
4 They have provided a vehicle for further private investment and for ultimate privatisation of the service.

Given these benefits and the current fashion for privatisation, there is little doubt that they will become an increasing feature of municipal enterprise in the foreseeable future. That said, local authorities are restricted in their degree of ownership of companies following the passage of the 1990 Local Government and Housing Act.

Organisational objectives

All business organisations pursue a range of objectives and these may vary to some degree over time. New private sector businesses, for example, are likely to be concerned initially with survival and with establishing a position in the marketplace, with profitability and growth seen as less important in the short term. In contrast, most well-established businesses will tend to regard profits and growth as key objectives and may see them as a means towards further ends, including market domination, maximising sales revenue and/or minimising operating costs.

Organisational objectives are also conditioned by the firm's legal structure. In sole traders, partnerships and some limited companies, control of the enterprise rests in the hands of the entrepreneur(s) and hence organisational goals will tend to coincide with the personal goals of the owner(s), whatever the point in the organisation's life cycle. In public companies, however – where ownership tends to be separated from control – the goals of the owners (shareholders) may not always correspond with those of the directors and senior managers who run the organisation, particularly when the latter are pursuing personal goals to enhance their own organisational position, status and/or rewards.

It is worth noting that the possibility of goal conflict also occurs where an individual company becomes a subsidiary of another organisation, whether by agreement or as a result of a takeover battle. This parent–subsidiary relationship may take the form of a holding company which is specially created to purchase a majority (sometimes all) of the shares in other companies, some of which may operate as holding companies themselves. Thus, while the individual subsidiaries may retain their legal and commercial identities and may operate as individual units, they will tend to be controlled by a central organisation which may exercise a considerable degree of influence over the objectives to be pursued by each of its subsidiaries. It is not inconceivable, for example, that some parts of the group may be required to make a loss on paper, particularly when there are tax advantages to be gained by the group as a whole from doing so.

Workers' co-operatives and public corporations provide further evidence of the relationship between an organisation's legal status and its primary objectives. In the case of the former, the establishment of the enterprise invariably reflects a desire on the part of its members to create an organisation which emphasises social goals (e.g. democracy, co-operation, job creation, mutual trust) rather than the pursuit of profits – hence the choice of the 'co-operative' form. Similarly in the case of the public corporation, a decision by government to establish an entity which operates in the interests of the public at large (or 'national interest') favours the creation of a state-owned-and-controlled organisation, with goals laid down by politicians and generally couched in social and financial terms (e.g. return on assets, reinvestment, job creation) rather than in terms of profit maximisation.

This apparent dichotomy between the profit motive of the private sector and the broader socio-economic goals of public bodies has, however, become less clear-cut over the last decade, as an increasing number of state-owned organisations have been 'prepared' for privatisation and successive governments have sought to bring private money into public projects by creating public/private partnerships. Equally, in other parts of the public sector – including the health service and local government – increasing stress is being laid on 'best value' and on operating within budgets – concepts which are familiar to businesses in the private sector. While it is not inconceivable that a change in government could reverse this trend, current evidence suggests that a shift in cultural attitudes has occurred and public bodies can no longer rely on unconditional government support for their activities. If this is the case, further convergence is likely to occur between state and privately owned bodies, with the former moving towards the latter rather than vice versa.

Finance

Business organisations finance their activities in a variety of ways and from a range of sources. Methods include reinvesting profits, borrowing, trade credit and issuing shares and debentures. Sources include the banks and other financial institutions, individual investors and governments, as well as contributions from the organisation's original owners.

In the context of this section it is appropriate to make a number of observations about the topic as it relates generally to the business environment:

1   All organisations tend to fund their activities from both internal (e.g. owner's capital, reinvested profits) and external sources (e.g. bank borrowing, sale of shares).

2   Financing may be short term, medium term or longer term, and the methods and sources of funding chosen will reflect the time period concerned (e.g. bank borrowing on overdraft tends to be short term and generally needed for immediate use).

3   Funds raised from external sources inevitably involve the organisation in certain obligations (e.g. repayment of loans with interest, personal guarantees, paying dividends) and these will act as a constraint on the organisation at some future date.

4   The relationship between owner's capital and borrowed funds – usually described as an organisation's **gearing** – can influence a firm's activities and prospects in a variety of ways (e.g. high-geared firms with a large element of borrowed funds will be adversely affected if interest rates are high).

5   Generally speaking, as organisations become larger many more external sources and methods of funding become available and utilising these can have implications for the structure, ownership and conduct of the organisation.

This latter point is perhaps best illustrated by comparing sole traders and partnerships with limited companies. In the case of the former, as unincorporated entities neither the sole trader nor the partnership can issue shares (or debentures) and hence their access to large amounts of external capital is restricted by law. Companies have no such restrictions – other than those which help to differentiate a private company from a public one – and consequently they are able to raise larger amounts by inviting individuals (and organisations) to subscribe for shares. Where a company is publicly quoted on the stock market, the amounts raised in this way can be very large indeed and the resultant organisation may have millions of owners who change on a regular basis as shares are traded on the second-hand market.

Organisations which decide to acquire corporate status in order to raise funds for expansion (or for some other purposes) become owned by their shareholders, who may be the original owners or may be individual and institutional investors holding equity predominantly as an investment and with little, if any, long-term commitment to the organisation they own. As indicated above, in the latter case, a separation tends to occur between the roles of owner (shareholder) and controller (director) and this can lead to the possibility of conflicting aims and objectives or differences in opinion over priorities within the enterprise – a problem discussed in more detail below under 'Stakeholders'.

A further illustration of the relationship between an organisation's legal structure and its ability to raise finance is provided by the public corporation. In this case, as a public body accountable to Parliament and the public via government, the public corporation is normally required to operate within a financial context largely controlled by government and this will be conditioned by the government's overall fiscal policy, including its attitude to the size of the Public Sector Borrowing Requirement (PSBR). One aspect of this context in Britain has been the establishment of external financing limits (EFLs) for each nationalised industry, arrived at by negotiation between government and the board running the public corporation, and used as a means of restraining monetary growth and hence the size of the

PSBR. Unfortunately this has also tended to prevent the more financially sound corporations, such as British Telecom before privatisation, from borrowing externally on a scale necessary to develop their business – a restriction which tends to disappear when the corporation becomes a fully fledged public company, either through privatisation or by some other means.

Stakeholders

All organisations have stakeholders; these are individuals and/or groups who are affected by or affect the performance of the organisation in which they have an interest. Typically they would include employees, managers, creditors, suppliers, shareholders (if appropriate) and society at large. As Table 1.1 illustrates, an organisation's stakeholders have a variety of interests which range from the pursuit of private gain to the more nebulous idea of achieving public benefit. Sometimes these interests will clash as, for example, when managers seek to improve the organisation's cash flow by refusing to pay suppliers' bills on time. On other occasions, the interests of different stakeholders may coincide, as when managers plan for growth in the organisation and in doing so provide greater job security for employees and enhanced dividends for investors.

The legal structure of an organisation has an impact not only on the type of stakeholders involved but also to a large degree on how their interests are represented. In sole traders, partnerships and smaller private companies, the coincidence of ownership and control limits the number of potential clashes of interest, given that objectives are set by and decisions taken by the firm's owner-manager(s). In larger companies, and, in particular, public limited companies, the division between ownership and control means that the controllers have the responsibility of representing the interests of the organisation's shareholders and creditors and, as suggested above, their priorities and goals may not always correspond.

A similar situation occurs in public sector organisations, where the interest of taxpayers (or ratepayers) is represented both by government and by those individuals chosen by government to run the organisation. In this case, it is worth recalling that the broader strategic objectives of the enterprise and the big decisions concerning policy, finance and investment tend to be taken by politicians, operating with advice from their officials (e.g. civil servants, local government officers) and within

Table 1.1 Organisational stakeholders and their interests

Types of stakeholder	Possible principal interests
Employees	Wage levels; working conditions; job security; personal development
Managers	Job security; status; personal power; organisational profitability; growth of the organisation
Shareholders	Market value of the investment; dividends; security of investment; liquidity of investment
Creditors	Security of loan; interest on loan; liquidity of investment
Suppliers	Security of contract; regular payment; growth of organisation; market development
Society	Safe products; environmental sensitivity; equal opportunities; avoidance of discrimination

the context of the government's overall economic and social policies. The organisation's board of management and its senior executives and managers are mainly responsible for the day-to-day operations of the business, although the board and the person chairing it would normally play a key role in shaping overall objectives and decisions, through regular discussions with government and its officials.

One important way in which public sector organisations differ from their private sector counterparts is in the sanctions available to particular groups of stakeholders who feel that the organisation is not representing their best interests. Shareholders in a company, for example, could withdraw financial support for a firm whose directors consistently disregard their interests or take decisions which threaten the security and/or value of their investment, and the possibility of such a reaction normally guarantees that the board pays due attention to the needs of this important group of stakeholders. The taxpayer and ratepayer have no equivalent sanction and in the short term must rely heavily on government and its agencies or, if possible, their power as consumers to represent their interest *vis-à-vis* the organisation. Longer term, of course, the public has the sanction of the ballot box, although it seems highly unlikely that the performance of state enterprises would be a key factor in determining the outcome of general or local elections.

The relative absence of market sanctions facing state-owned organisations has meant that the public has had to rely on a range of formal institutions (e.g. parliamentary scrutiny committees, consumer consultative bodies, the audit authorities) and on the media to protect its interest in areas such as funding, pricing and quality of service provided. As these organisations are returned to the private sector, the expectation is that the sanctions imposed by the free market will once again operate and shareholders in privatised utilities will be protected like any other group of shareholders in a privately owned enterprise. To what extent this will occur in practice, of course, is open to question, while the newly privatised public corporations face little, if any, competition. Government, it seems, prefers to hedge its bets on this question, at least in the short term – hence the establishment of regulators with powers of investigation into performance and some degree of control over pricing.

mini case   Big Mac gets bigger and more selective

Growth through franchising has become a preferred option for many organisations, typified by McDonald's, which is the world's biggest fast food chain. Established in 1955 when Raymond Croc opened his first burger restaurant, McDonald's was estimated to have had in excess of 20 000 outlets spread across the globe by the end of 1996. Contrary to popular predictions, the organisation continued to expand at a significant rate and benefited from the opening of new markets in eastern Europe and the Far East. In the mid-1990s, for example, it was estimated that at its current rate of growth, a new McDonald's was opening somewhere in the world every three hours.

When considering applicants for a coveted McDonald's franchise the company has always been concerned to ensure that its reputation for quality and service is maintained. Potential franchisees have to demonstrate not only a successful track record in a previous occupation, but also that they have the necessary financial resources and a willingness to commit themselves to the organisation. Individuals making the grade have traditionally been offered two kinds of franchise scheme. The conventional franchise involves a 20-year agreement between the franchisee and the company under which the latter buys and develops the site which the former takes over and operates for an agreed price, as well as paying McDonald's a royalty fee based on a pre-agreed percentage of turnover. Under the other option – the business facilities lease – the individual leases the restaurant normally for a three-year period, prior to being offered the opportunity to convert to a conventional franchise if funds permit.

Like any business, McDonald's fortunes have fluctuated over time. In late October 2002 McDonald's announced its intention of sharply cutting back on its expansion plans and redirecting its efforts towards supporting its existing chain of restaurants (see the *Guardian*, 23 October 2002). By 2005, McDonald's claimed to have over 30 000 local restaurants serving nearly 50 million people each day in more than 119 countries. Adverse publicity, following the documentary *Super Size Me* appears to have led to a consumer backlash in recent years and the company has closed some stores, while opening new ones. McDonald's strategy is to undertake a programme of worldwide restructuring coupled with more careful targetting of the market. This includes getting the 'right restaurants' in the 'right places' and responding to local requirements (e.g. Kosher outlets in some Israeli branches of McDonald's).

 The website for McDonald's is *www.mcdonalds.com*

Politico-economic synthesis

The economic problem of resource allocation, described above, clearly has a political dimension, given its focus on the ownership, control and use of wealth-producing assets within society. This allows links to be made between a country's chosen economic system and its political regime. A useful way of representing possible relationships is illustrated in Figure 1.2. Political systems can be characterised as ranging from democratic to authoritarian, depending on the degree of public involvement in decision-making processes. Similarly, economic systems can be seen to range from free market to planned, according to the level of state intervention in the process of resource allocation. This two-dimensional model thus provides for four major combinations of politico-economic systems, ranging from democratic–free-market on the one hand (quadrant 1) to authoritarian–planned on the other (quadrant 3).

In applying this model to specific cases, it is clear that free-market approaches to resource allocation are predominantly associated with democratic states. Such a link is not surprising. Democracy, after all, includes the notion of individuals being able to express their preferences through the ballot box and having the opportunity to replace one government with another at periodic intervals. In free markets similar processes are at work, with individuals effectively 'voting' for goods and services through the price system and their expressed preferences being reflected in the pattern of resource allocation.

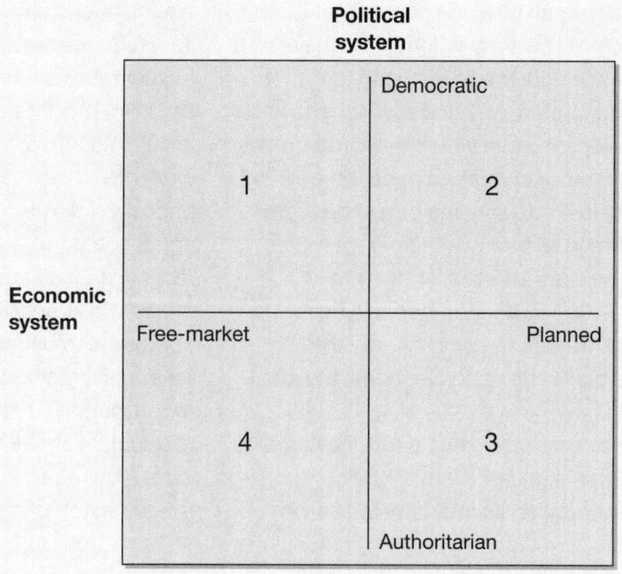

Figure 1.2   Politico-economic systems

A link between authoritarian regimes and planned economic systems can equally be rationalised, in that government control over the political system is considerably facilitated if it also directs the economy through the ownership and/or control of the means of production, distribution and exchange. In effect, the relative absence of democratic mechanisms, such as free elections and choice between alternative forms of government, is echoed in the economic sphere by the inability of individuals to exercise any real influence over resource allocation. At the extreme, this could involve a government ban on any forms of free enterprise and total government control of the pattern of output and consumption in an economy which is devoid of effective consumer sovereignty.

In practice, of course, the picture is much more complicated than suggested by this simple dichotomy. Some authoritarian states, for instance, have predominantly capitalist economic systems (quadrant 4), while some democratic countries have a substantial degree of government intervention (i.e. moving them towards quadrant 2), either by choice or from necessity (e.g. wartime). Added to this, even in states where the political or economic system appears to be the same, considerable differences can occur at an operational and/or institutional level and this gives each country a degree of uniqueness not adequately portrayed by the model. That said, it is still the case that the basic congruity between democracy and free-market systems represents a powerful and pervasive influence in the business environment of the world's principal democratic states. The process of economic reform – as in eastern Europe – accordingly tends to be accompanied by corresponding pressures for political change and these are often resisted by regimes not prepared to give up their political and economic powers and their élite status.

The macroeconomy

Levels of analysis

As indicated above, economics is concerned with the study of how society deals with the problem of scarcity and the resultant problems of what to produce, how to produce and how to distribute. Within this broad framework the economist typically distinguishes between two types of analysis:

1 **Microeconomic analysis**, which is concerned with the study of economic decision taking by both individuals and firms.
2 **Macroeconomic analysis**, which is concerned with interactions in the economy as a whole (i.e. with economic aggregates).

The microeconomic approach is exemplified by the analysis of markets and prices undertaken later in the chapter (see 'The market system') which shows, for example, how individual consumers in the market for beer might be affected by a price change. This analysis could be extended to an investigation of how the total market might respond to a movement in the price, or how a firm's (or market's) decisions on supply are affected by changes in wage rates or production techniques or some other factor. Note that in these examples, the focus of attention is on decision-taking by individuals and firms in a single industry, while interactions between this industry and the rest of the economy are ignored: in short, this is what economists call a 'partial analysis'.

In reality, of course, all sectors of the economy are interrelated to some degree. A pay award, for example, in the beer industry (or in a single firm) may set a new pay norm that workers in other industries take up and these pay increases may subsequently influence employment, production and consumer demand in the economy as a whole, which could also have repercussions on the demand for beer. Sometimes such repercussions may be relatively minor and so effectively can be ignored. In such situations the basic microeconomic approach remains valid.

In contrast, macroeconomics recognises the interdependent nature of markets and studies the interaction in the economy as a whole, dealing with such questions as the overall level of employment, the rate of inflation, the percentage growth of output in the economy and many other economy-wide aggregates – exemplified, for instance, by the analysis of international trade later in the chapter (see 'International markets and trade') and by the macroeconomic model discussed below. It should be pointed out, however, that while the distinction between the micro and macro approaches remains useful for analytical purposes, in many instances the two become intertwined. UK Chancellor Nigel Lawson's decision (in 1988) to cut the top rate of income tax from 60 per cent to 40 per cent was presented at the time as a means of boosting the economy by providing incentives for entrepreneurs – clearly a macroeconomic proposition. However, to investigate the validity of the Chancellor's view, it is necessary to lean heavily on microeconomic analysis to see how lower taxation might influence, say, an individual's preference for work over leisure. Given that macroeconomic phenomena are the result of aggregating the behaviour of individual firms and consumers, this is obviously a common situation and one which is useful to bear in mind in any study of either the firm or the economy as a whole.

The 'flows' of economic activity

Economic activity can be portrayed as a flow of economic resources into firms (i.e. productive organisations), which are used to produce output for consumption, and a corresponding flow of payments from firms to the providers of those resources, who use them primarily to purchase the goods and services produced. These flows of resources, production, income and expenditure accordingly represent the fundamental activities of an economy at work. Figure 1.3 illustrates the flow of resources and of goods and services in the economy – what economists describe as **real flows**.

In effect, firms use economic resources to produce goods and services, which are consumed by private individuals (private domestic consumption) or government (government consumption) or by overseas purchasers (foreign consumption) or by other firms (capital formation). This consumption gives rise to a flow of expenditures that represents an income for firms, which they use to purchase further resources in order to produce further output for consumption. This flow of income and expenditures is shown in Figure 1.4.

The CFI model is also discussed at
www.bized.ac.uk/learn/economics/macro/notes/income.htm

The interrelationship between **income flows** and real flows can be seen by combining the two diagrams into one, which for the sake of simplification assumes

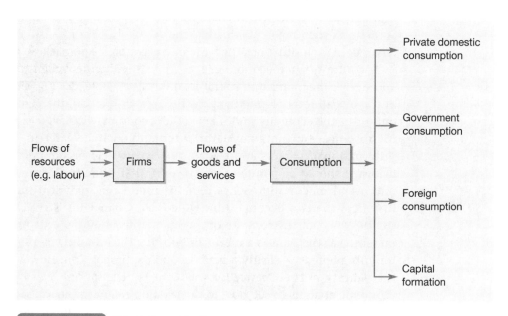

Figure 1.3 'Real flows' in the economy

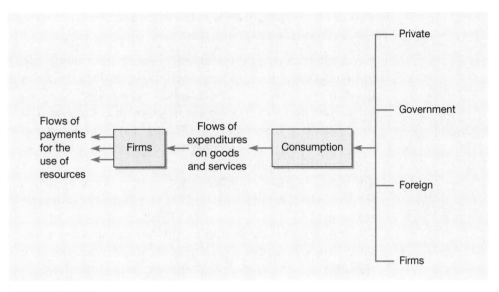

Figure 1.4 Income flows in the economy

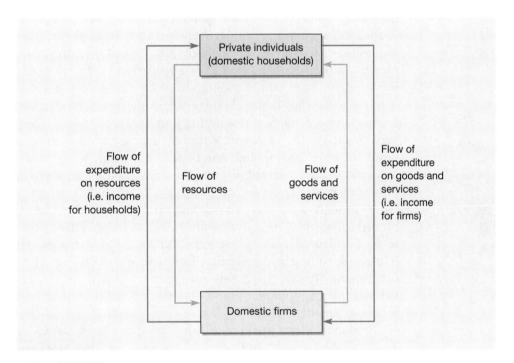

Figure 1.5 A simplified model of real flows and income flows

only two groups operate in the economy: firms as producers and users of resources, and private individuals as consumers and providers of those resources (see Figure 1.5). Real flows are shown by the arrows moving in an anti-clockwise direction, income flows by the arrows flowing in a clockwise direction.

Despite a degree of over-simplification, the model of the economy illustrated in Figure 1.5 is a useful analytical tool which highlights some vitally important aspects of economic activity which are of direct relevance to the study of business. The model shows, for example, that:

1 Income flows around the economy, passing from households to firms and back to households and on to firms, and so on, and these income flows have corresponding real flows of resources, goods and services.
2 What constitutes an income to one group (e.g. firms) represents an expenditure to another (e.g. households), indicating that income generation in the economy is related to spending on consumption of goods and services and on resources (e.g. the use of labour).
3 The output of firms must be related to expenditure by households on goods and services, which in turn is related to the income the latter receive from supplying resources.
4 The use of resources (including the number of jobs created in the economy) must also be related to expenditure by households on consumption, given that resources are used to produce output for sale to households.
5 Levels of income, output, expenditure and employment in the economy are, in effect, interrelated.

From the point of view of firms, it is clear from the model that their fortunes are intimately connected with the spending decisions of households and any changes in the level of spending can have repercussions for business activity at the micro as well as the macro level. In the late 1980s, for instance, the British economy went into recession, largely as a result of a reduction in the level of consumption that was brought about by a combination of high interest rates, a growing burden of debt from previous bouts of consumer spending, and a decline in demand from some overseas markets also suffering from recession. While many businesses managed to survive the recession, either by drawing from their reserves or slimming down their operations, large numbers of firms went out of business, as orders fell and costs began to exceed revenue. As a result, output in the economy fell, unemployment grew, investment by firms declined, and house prices fell to a point where some houseowners owed more on their mortgage than the value of their property (known as 'negative equity'). The combined effect of these outcomes was to further depress demand, as individuals became either unwilling or unable to increase spending and as firms continued to shed labour and to hold back on investment. By late 1992, few real signs of growth in the economy could be detected, unemployment stood at almost 3 million, and business confidence remained persistently low.

The gradual recovery of the British economy from mid-1993 – brought about by a return in consumer confidence in the wake of a cut in interest rates – further emphasises the key link between consumption and entrepreneurial activity highlighted in the model. Equally, it shows, as did the discussion on the recession, that a variety of factors can affect spending (e.g. government policy on interest rates) and that spending by households is only one type of consumption in the real economy. In order to gain a clearer view of how the economy works and why changes occur over time, it is necessary to refine the basic model by incorporating a number of other key variables influencing economic activity. These variables – which include savings, investment spending, government spending, taxation and overseas trade – are discussed below.

Changes in economic activity

The level of spending by consumers on goods and services produced by indigenous firms is influenced by a variety of factors. For a start, most households pay tax on income earned, which has the effect of reducing the level of income available for consumption. Added to this, some consumers prefer to save (i.e. not spend) a proportion of their income or to spend it on imported products, both of which mean that the income of domestic firms is less than it would have been had the income been spent with them. Circumstances such as these represent what economists call a **leakage** (or **withdrawal**) from the **circular flow of income** and help to explain why the revenue of businesses can fluctuate over time (see Figure 1.6).

At the same time as such 'leakages' are occurring, additional forms of spending in the economy are helping to boost the potential income of domestic firms. Savings by some consumers are often borrowed by firms to spend on investment in capital equipment or plant or premises (known as investment spending) and this generates income for firms producing capital goods. Similarly, governments use taxation to spend on the provision of public goods and services (public or government expenditure) and overseas buyers purchase products produced by indigenous firms (export spending). Together, these additional forms of spending represent an **injection** of income into the circular flow (see Figure 1.7).

While the revised model of the economy illustrated in Figure 1.7 is still highly simplified (e.g. consumers also borrow savings to spend on consumption or imports; firms also save and buy imports; governments also invest in capital projects), it demonstrates quite clearly that fluctuations in the level of economic

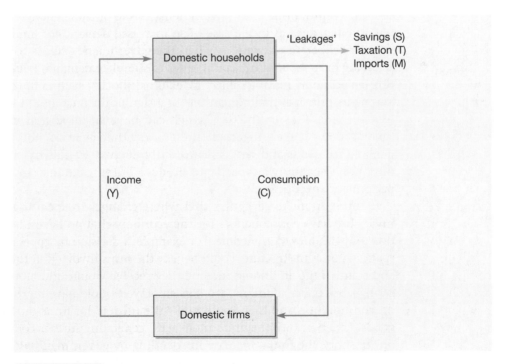

Figure 1.6   The circular flow of income with 'leakages'

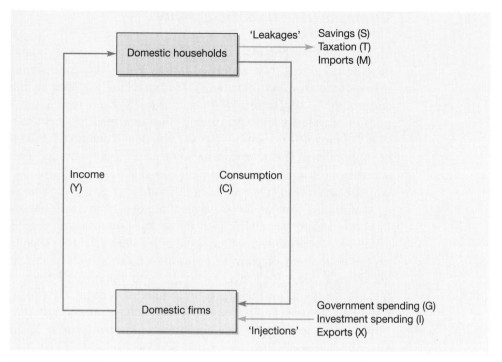

Figure 1.7   The circular flow of income with 'injections' added

activity are the result of changes in a number of variables, many of which are outside the control of firms or governments. Some of these changes are autonomous (i.e. spontaneous), as in the case of an increased demand for imports, while others may be deliberate or overt, as when the government decides to increase its own spending or to reduce taxation in order to stimulate demand. Equally, from time to time an economy may be subject to 'external shocks', such as the onset of recession among its principal trading partners or a significant price rise in a key commodity (e.g. oil price rises in 2007/8), which can have an important effect on internal income flows. Taken together, these and other changes help to explain why demand for goods and services constantly fluctuates and why changes occur not only in an economy's capacity to produce output, but also in its structure and performance over time.

It is important to recognise that where changes in spending do occur, these invariably have consequences for the economy that go beyond the initial 'injection' or 'withdrawal' of income. For example, a decision by government to increase spending on infrastructure would benefit the firms involved in the various projects and some of the additional income they receive would undoubtedly be spent on hiring labour. The additional workers employed would have more income to spend on consumption and this would boost the income for firms producing consumer goods, which in turn may hire more staff, generating further consumption and so on. In short, the initial increase in spending by government will have additional effects on income and spending in the economy, as the extra spending circulates from households to firms and back again. Economists refer to this as the **multiplier**

mini case   A change in economic fortunes

Macroeconomic analysis helps to explain how fluctuations can occur in the level of economic activity and how this impacts on employment, outcome, income and consumption. In the real world, actual changes in a country's economic fortunes can occur over differing periods of time and can be triggered by a variety of factors, as illustrated by the experiences of Japan and Brazil.

After a decade or more of stagnation and deflation in its economy, Japan has shown signs in recent years of a sustained recovery with industrial production, consumer spending and economic growth positive, while inflation appears to be under control. At least part of the explanation for the recovery of the Japanese economy has been the shift in emphasis towards trading with the booming economies in Asia and away from its traditional markets in the US. According to Japanese officials, the economy has become far more stable as Japanese businesses have shifted their attention towards trade with countries such as China, where annual rates of economic growth are on average around 10 per cent.

Brazil, too, has shown that, over time, even apparently intractable economic difficulties can be overcome. In the late 1980s and early 1990s the country was plagued with an inflation problem, with average price rises reaching 490 per cent by 1993. By mid-2008, Brazil's inflation rate was under 5 per cent and its economy was booming, thanks largely to the global demand for commodities such as iron ore, biofuels and food products. Recent oil finds off the Brazilian coast have boosted the economy's future prospects considerably, as foreign investment continues to flow into the country. One measure of the country's rising international economic status was the award of 'investment grade' by the financial rating agency Standard & Poor which helped to push the country's stock market to an all-time high.

While global economic conditions (e.g. the global downturn in 2008) and unsolved economic problems (e.g. Japan's government debt) appear to be impacting upon the recovery process, what these two examples illustrate is that improvements in an economy's performance often take a considerable time. This fact is not always captured well in economists' models of how the macroeconomy operates.

effect to emphasise the reverberative consequences of any increase or decrease in spending by consumers, firms, governments or overseas buyers.

Multiple increases in income and consumption can also give rise to an **accelerator effect**, which is the term used to describe a change in investment spending by firms as a result of a change in consumer spending. In the example above it is possible that the increase in consumption caused by the increase in government spending may persuade some firms to invest in more stock and capital equipment to meet increased consumer demands. Demand for capital goods will therefore rise, and this could cause further increases in the demand for industrial products (e.g. components, machinery) and also for consumer goods, as firms seek to increase their output to meet the changing market conditions. Should consumer spending fall, a reverse accelerator may occur and the same would apply to the multiplier as the reduction in consumption reverberates through the economy and causes further cuts in both consumption and investment. As Peter Donaldson has suggested, everything in the economy affects everything else; the economy is dynamic, interactive and mobile and is far more complex than implied by the model used in the analysis above.[5]

Government and the macroeconomy: objectives

Notwithstanding the complexities of the real economy, the link between business activity and spending is clear to see. This spending, as indicated above, comes from consumers, firms, governments and external sources and collectively can be said to represent total demand in the economy for goods and services. Economists frequently indicate this with the following notation:

Aggregate Monetary Demand = Consumer spending + Investment spending
+ Government spending + Export spending
– Import spending

or   AMD = C + I + G + X – M

Within this equation, consumer spending (C) is regarded as by far the most important factor in determining the level of total demand.

While economists might disagree about what are the most significant influences on the component elements of AMD, it is widely accepted that governments have a crucial role to play in shaping demand, not only in their own sector but also on the market side of the economy. Government policies on spending and taxation, or on interest rates, clearly have both direct and indirect influences on the behaviour of individuals and firms, which can affect both the demand and supply side of the economy in a variety of ways. Underlying these policies are a number of key objectives which are pursued by government as a prerequisite to a healthy economy and which help to guide the choice of policy options. Understanding the broad choice of policies available to government, and the objectives associated with them, is of prime importance to students of the business environment.

Most governments appear to have a number of key economic objectives, the most important of which are normally the control of inflation, the pursuit of economic growth, a reduction in unemployment, the achievement of an acceptable balance of payments situation, controlling public (i.e. government) borrowing, and a relatively stable exchange rate.

Controlling inflation

Inflation is usually defined as an upward and persistent movement in the general level of prices over a given period of time; it can also be characterised as a fall in the value of money. For governments of all political complexions reducing such movements to a minimum is seen as a primary economic objective (e.g. the current UK government's target for 'underlying inflation' was 2.5 per cent. Under the new Consumer Prices Index the target is now 2 per cent).

Monitoring trends in periodic price movements tends to take a number of forms; in the UK these have included:

1 The use of a Retail Price Index (RPI), which measures how an average family's spending on goods and services is affected by price changes. The RPI has traditionally been the measure used for headline inflation in the UK and includes mortgage interest payments.

2 An examination of the **underlying rate of inflation**, which excludes the effects of mortgage payments (known as RPIX in the UK).

3 Measuring **factory gate prices**, to indicate likely future changes in consumer prices.

4 Comparing domestic inflation rates with those of the United Kingdom's chief overseas competitors, as an indication of the international competitiveness of UK firms.

With regard to the latter, the UK now uses a new measure of inflation known as the **Consumer Prices Index (CPI)** to allow for a more direct comparison of the inflation rate in the UK with that of the rest of Europe. The CPI excludes a number of items that have historically been part of the RPIX, especially items relating to housing costs (e.g. mortgage interest payments and council tax).

In addition, changes in **monetary aggregates**, which measure the amount of money (and therefore potential spending power) in circulation in the economy, and movements of exchange rates (especially a depreciating currency) are also seen as a guide to possible future price increases, as their effects work through the economy.

Explanations as to why prices tend to rise over time vary considerably, but broadly speaking fall into two main categories. First, supply-siders tend to focus on rising production costs – particularly wages, energy and imported materials – as a major reason for inflation, with firms passing on increased costs to the consumer in the form of higher wholesale and/or retail prices. Second, demand-siders, in contrast, tend to emphasise the importance of excessive demand in the economy, brought about, for example, by tax cuts, cheaper borrowing or excessive government spending, which encourages firms to take advantage of the consumer's willingness to spend money by increasing their prices. Where indigenous firms are unable to satisfy all the additional demand, the tendency is for imports to increase. This may not only cause further price rises, particularly if imported goods are more expensive or if exchange rate movements become unfavourable, but also can herald a deteriorating balance of payments situation and difficult trading conditions for domestic businesses.

Government concern with inflation – which crosses both party and state boundaries – reflects the fact that rising price levels can have serious consequences for the economy in general and for businesses in particular, especially if a country's domestic inflation rates are significantly higher than those of its main competitors. In markets where price is an important determinant of demand, rising prices may result in some businesses losing sales, and this can affect turnover and may ultimately affect employment if firms reduce their labour force in order to reduce their costs. Added to this, the uncertainty caused by a difficult trading environment may make some businesses unwilling to invest in new plant and equipment, particularly if interest rates are high and if inflation looks unlikely to fall for some time. Such a response, while understandable, is unlikely to improve a firm's future competitiveness or its ability to exploit any possible increases in demand as market conditions change.

Rising prices may also affect businesses by encouraging employees to seek higher wages in order to maintain or increase their living standards. Where firms agree to such wage increases, the temptation, of course, is to pass this on to the consumer in the form of a price rise, especially if demand looks unlikely to be affected to any great extent. Should this process occur generally in the economy, the result may be a **wages/prices inflationary spiral**, in which wage increases push up prices which push up wage increases which further push up prices and so on. From an international competitive point of view, such an occurrence, if allowed to continue unchecked, could be disastrous for both firms and the economy. Thankfully, such an occurence tends to be relatively uncommon in most economies but, as the problems in Zimbabwe illustrate, hyperinflation can have disastrous consequences for a country's economy and its population (in mid-2008, for example, annual inflation in Zimbabwe was estimated at around 40 million per cent!).

Economic growth

Growth is an objective shared by governments and organisations alike. For governments, the aim is usually to achieve steady and sustained levels of non-inflationary growth, preferably led by exports (i.e. export-led growth). Such growth is normally indicated by annual increases in **real national income** or **gross domestic product** (where 'real' = allowing for inflation, and 'gross domestic product (GDP)' = the economy's annual output of goods and services measured in monetary terms).[6] To compensate for changes in the size of the population, growth rates tend to be expressed in terms of real national income per capita (i.e. real GDP divided by population).

Exactly what constitutes desirable levels of growth is difficult to say, except in very broad terms. If given a choice, governments would basically prefer:

- steady levels of real growth (e.g. 3–4 per cent p.a.), rather than annual increases in output which vary widely over the business cycle;
- growth rates higher than those of one's chief competitors; and
- growth based on investment in technology and on increased export sales, rather than on excessive government spending or current consumption.

It is worth remembering that, when measured on a monthly or quarterly basis, increases in output can occur at a declining rate and GDP growth can become negative. In the United Kingdom, for example, a **recession** is said to exist following two consecutive quarters of negative GDP.

From a business point of view, the fact that increases in output are related to increases in consumption suggests that economic growth is good for business prospects and hence for investment and employment, and by and large this is the case. The rising living standards normally associated with such growth may, however, encourage increased consumption of imported goods and services at the expense of indigenous producers, to a point where some domestic firms are forced out of business and the economy's manufacturing base becomes significantly reduced (often called **deindustrialisation**). Equally, if increased consumption is based largely on excessive state spending, the potential gains for businesses may be offset by the need to increase interest rates to fund that spending (where government borrowing is involved) and by the tendency of government demands for funding to **crowd out** the private sector's search for investment capital. In such cases, the short-term benefits from government-induced consumption may be more than offset by the medium- and long-term problems for the economy that are likely to arise.

Where growth prospects for the economy look good, business confidence tends to increase, and this is often reflected in increased levels of investment and stock holding and ultimately in levels of employment. In Britain, for example, the monthly and quarterly surveys by the Confederation of British Industry (CBI) provide a good indication of how output, investment and stock levels change at different points of the business cycle and these are generally seen as a good indication of future business trends, as interpreted by entrepreneurs. Other indicators – including the state of the housing market and construction generally – help to provide a guide to the current and future state of the economy, including its prospects for growth in the short and medium term.

web link   The CBI's website address is *www.cbi.org.uk*

Reducing unemployment

In most democratic states the goal of **full employment** is no longer part of the political agenda; instead government pronouncements on employment tend to focus on job creation and maintenance and on developing the skills appropriate to future demands. The consensus seems to be that in technologically advanced market-based economies some unemployment is inevitable and that the basic aim should be to reduce unemployment to a level which is both politically and socially acceptable.

As with growth and inflation, unemployment levels tend to be measured at regular intervals (e.g. monthly, quarterly, annually) and the figures are often adjusted to take into account seasonal influences (e.g. school-leavers entering the job market). In addition, the statistics usually provide information on trends in long-term unemployment, areas of skill shortage and on international comparisons, as well as sectoral changes within the economy. All of these indicators provide clues to the current state of the economy and to the prospects for businesses in the coming months and years, but need to be used with care. Unemployment, for example, tends to continue rising for a time even when a recession is over; equally, it is not uncommon for government definitions of unemployment to change or for international unemployment data to be based on different criteria.

The broader social and economic consequences of high levels of unemployment are well documented: it is a waste of resources, it puts pressure on the public services and on the Exchequer (e.g. by reducing tax yields and increasing public expenditure on welfare provision), and it is frequently linked with growing social and health problems. Its implication for businesses, however, tends to be less clear-cut. On the one hand, a high level of unemployment implies a pool of labour available for firms seeking workers (though not necessarily with the right skills), generally at wage levels lower than when a shortage of labour occurs. On the other hand, it can also give rise to a fall in overall demand for goods and services which could exacerbate any existing deflationary forces in the economy, causing further unemployment and with it further reductions in demand. Where this occurs, economists tend to describe it as **cyclical unemployment** (i.e. caused by a general deficiency in demand) in order to differentiate it from unemployment caused by a deficiency in demand for the goods produced by a particular industry (**structural unemployment**) or by the introduction of new technology which replaces labour (**technological unemployment**).

A favourable balance of payments

A country's **balance of payments** is essentially the net balance of credits (earnings) and debits (payments) arising from its international trade over a given period of time. Where credits exceed debits a balance of payments surplus exists; the opposite is described as a deficit. Understandably governments tend to prefer either equilibrium in the balance of payments or surpluses, rather than deficits. However, it would be fair to say that for some governments facing persistent balance of payments deficits, a sustained reduction in the size of the deficit may be regarded as signifying a 'favourable' balance of payments situation.

Like other economic indicators, the balance of payments statistics come in a variety of forms and at different levels of disaggregation, allowing useful comparisons to be made not only on a country's comparative trading performance, but also on the international competitiveness of particular industries and commodity groups or on the development or decline of specific external markets. Particular emphasis tends to be given to the balance of payments on current account, which measures imports and exports of goods and services and is thus seen as an indicator of the competitiveness of an economy's firms and industries. Sustained current account surpluses tend to suggest favourable trading conditions, which can help to boost growth, increase employment and investment and create a general feeling of confidence amongst the business community. They may also give rise to surpluses which domestic firms can use to finance overseas lending and investment, thus helping to generate higher levels of corporate foreign earnings in future years.

While it does not follow that a sustained current account deficit is inevitably bad for the country concerned, it often implies structural problems in particular sectors of its economy or possibly an exchange rate which favours importers rather than exporters. Many observers believe, for instance, that the progressive decline of Britain's visible trading position after 1983 was an indication of the growing uncompetitiveness of its firms, particularly those producing finished manufactured goods for consumer markets at home and abroad. By the same token, Japan's current account trade surplus of around $120 billion in late 1995 was portrayed as a sign of the cut-throat competition of Japanese firms, particularly those involved in producing cars, electrical and electronic products, and photographic equipment.

Controlling public borrowing

Governments raise large amounts of revenue annually, mainly through taxation, and use this income to spend on a wide variety of public goods and services (see below). Where annual revenue exceeds government spending, a budget surplus occurs and the excess is often used to repay past debt (formerly known in the United Kingdom as the 'public sector debt repayment' or PSDR). The accumulated debt of past and present governments represents a country's **National Debt**. In the UK this stood at over £500 billion in 2007 which was approximately 38 per cent of GDP.

In practice, most governments often face annual budget deficits rather than budget surpluses and hence have a 'public sector borrowing requirement' or PSBR (now known in the UK as **public sector net borrowing** or **PSNB**). While such deficits are not inevitably a problem, in the same way that a small personal overdraft is not necessarily critical for an individual, large scale and persistent deficits are generally seen as a sign of an economy facing current and future difficulties which require urgent government action. The overriding concern over high levels of public borrowing tends to be focused on:

1 Its impact on interest rates, given that higher interest rates tend to be needed to attract funds from private sector uses to public sector uses.
2 The impact of high interest rates on consumption and investment and hence on the prospects of businesses.
3 The danger of the public sector 'crowding out' the private sector's search for funds for investment.
4 The opportunity cost of debt interest, especially in terms of other forms of public spending.
5 The general lack of confidence in the markets about the government's ability to control the economy and the likely effect this might have on inflation, growth and the balance of payments.
6 The need to meet the 'convergence criteria' laid down at Maastricht for entry to the single currency (e.g. central government debt no higher than 3 per cent of GDP).

The consensus seems to be that controlling public borrowing is best tackled by restraining the rate of growth of public spending rather than by increasing revenue through changes in taxation, since the latter could depress demand.

A stable exchange rate

A country's currency has two values: an internal value and an external value. Internally, its value is expressed in terms of the goods and services it can buy and hence it is affected by changes in domestic prices. Externally, its value is expressed as an **exchange rate** which governs how much of another country's currency it can purchase (e.g. £1 = $2 or £1 = €1.20). Since foreign trade normally involves an exchange of currencies, fluctuations in the external value of a currency will influence the price of imports and exports and hence can affect the trading prospects for business, as well as a country's balance of payments and its rate of inflation.

On the whole, governments and businesses involved in international trade tend to prefer exchange rates to remain relatively stable, because of the greater degree of certainty this brings to the trading environment; it also tends to make overseas investors more confident that their funds are likely to hold their value. To this extent, schemes which seek to fix exchange rates within predetermined levels (e.g. the ERM), or which encourage the use of a common currency (e.g. the euro), tend to have the support of the business community, which prefers predictability to uncertainty where trading conditions are concerned.

mini case   Digging in for the long term

For firms engaged in international trade, the strength of the currency (i.e. the exchange rate) is an important consideration. As the value of one currency changes against other currencies, this usually alters the price of imported/exported products and this can make them more/less attractive to potential customers. To mitigate the impact of exchange rate changes, some firms engage in a process known as hedging, which basically involves trying to reduce or eliminate exchange rate risks, for example by buying a proportion of a currency forward (i.e. before it is needed) at an agreed price. An alternative strategy is to consider producing the product in different locations (e.g. setting up manufacturing facilities in other countries) which can offset some of the impact of currency fluctuations, as well as providing other potential benefits to a business.

A good example of the latter approach is provided by JCB, the UK-owned private company famous for its yellow construction equipment (e.g. diggers). In the 1990s, the company's business was mainly based in the UK and parts of western Europe, but faced with a limited market and a strengthening pound which made exporting difficult, the firm decided to seek a global presence by investing in manufacturing abroad. Focusing first on the US, JCB built a plant in Georgia in the late 1990s to exploit the US market; this was followed by further plants in Sao Paulo in Brazil and new plants in India near Mumbai. It also acquired a German construction firm in 2005 and opened a further factory near Shanghai in 2006, thereby adding to its global reach.

In addition to the potential currency benefits of operating in different countries, JCB has also gained a number of other advantages, including establishing a global brand name, access to low-cost suppliers and to developing markets, and reducing freight costs and tariff barriers. Globalisation, in short, can offer businesses many 'opportunities', but we must not forget that it can also give rise to substantial 'threats' at the corporate level, not least the danger of low-cost competitors invading one's own markets.

Government and the macroeconomy: policies

Governments throughout Europe and beyond play various key roles in their respective economies. These include the following functions:

- consumer of resources (e.g. employer, landowner);
- supplier of resources (e.g. infrastructure, information);
- consumer of goods and services (e.g. government spending);
- supplier of goods and services (e.g. nationalised industries);
- regulator of business activity (e.g. employment laws, consumer laws);
- regulator of the economy (e.g. fiscal and monetary policies); and
- redistributor of income and wealth (e.g. taxation system).

The extent of these roles, and their impact on the economy in general and on business in particular, varies from country to country as well as over time.

Despite the economic significance of these roles, in most market-based economies democratically elected governments prefer levels and patterns of production and consumption to be determined largely by market forces, with a minimum of government interference. This approach is exemplified by the philosophical stance of the UK and US governments in the 1980s, that became colloquially known as

'Thatcherism' (UK) and 'Reaganomics' (USA). At the same time, the recognition that market forces alone are unable to guarantee that an economy will automatically achieve the objectives established by governments has meant that state intervention – to curb inflation, encourage growth, reduce unemployment, correct a balance of payments or budgetary problem or restore currency stability – invariably occurs to some degree in all countries. In broad terms, this intervention usually takes three main forms, described as fiscal policy, monetary policy and direct controls. These policy instruments – or 'instrumental variables' – and their effects on the business community are discussed below.

Fiscal policy

As indicated above, each year governments raise and spend huge amounts of money. The UK government's estimates for 2008, for example, suggest that **government spending** will be about £618 billion and is to be allocated in the manner illustrated in Figure 1.8. This spending will be funded mainly from **taxation (direct and**

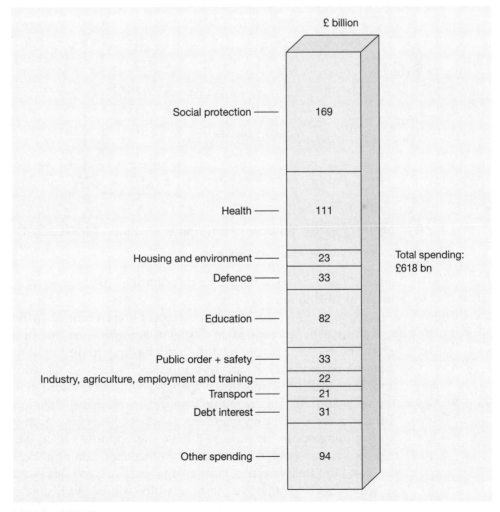

£ billion

Social protection	169
Health	111
Housing and environment	23
Defence	33
Education	82
Public order + safety	33
Industry, agriculture, employment and training	22
Transport	21
Debt interest	31
Other spending	94

Total spending: £618 bn

Figure 1.8   The allocation of UK government spending, 2008 budget

Source: Adapted from Budget Statement, 2008.

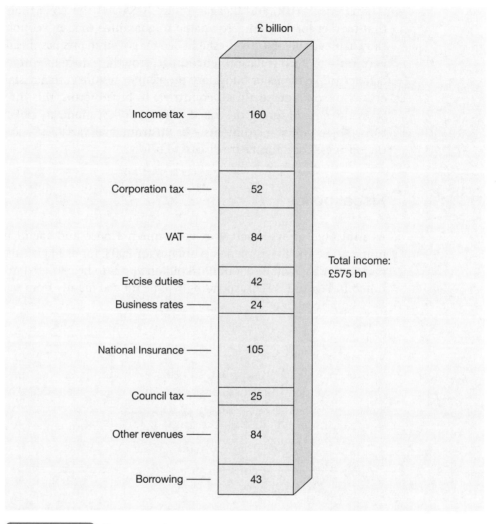

£ billion

Income tax	160
Corporation tax	52
VAT	84
Excise duties	42
Business rates	24
National Insurance	105
Council tax	25
Other revenues	84
Borrowing	43

Total income: £575 bn

Figure 1.9   Sources of government revenue, 2008 budget

Source: Adapted from Budget Statement, 2008.

indirect), and national insurance contributions (see Figure 1.9). The PSNB is estimated at £43 billion.

Fiscal policy involves the use of changes in government spending and taxation to influence the level and composition of aggregrate demand in the economy and, given the amounts involved, this clearly has important implications for business. Elementary circular flow analysis suggests, for instance, that reductions in taxation and/or increases in government spending will inject additional income into the economy and will, via the multiplier effect, increase the demand for goods and services, with favourable consequences for business. Reductions in government spending and/or increases in taxation will have the opposite effect, depressing business prospects and probably discouraging investment and causing a rise in unemployment.

Apart from their overall impact on aggregate demand, fiscal changes can be used to achieve specific objectives, some of which will be of direct or indirect benefit to the business community. Reductions in taxes on company profits and/or increases in tax allowances for investment in capital equipment can be used to encourage business to increase investment spending, hence boosting the income of firms producing industrial products and causing some additional spending on consumption. Similarly, increased government spending targeted at firms involved in exporting, or at the creation of new business, will encourage increased business activity and additionally may lead to more output and employment in the economy.

In considering the use of fiscal policy to achieve their objectives, governments tend to be faced with a large number of practical problems that generally limit their room for manoeuvre. Boosting the economy through increases in spending or reductions in taxation could cause inflationary pressures, as well as encouraging an inflow of imports and increasing the public sector deficit, none of which would be particularly welcomed by entrepreneurs or by the financial markets. By the same token, fiscal attempts to restrain demand in order to reduce inflation will generally depress the economy, causing a fall in output and employment and encouraging firms to abandon or defer investment projects until business prospects improve.

Added to this, it should not be forgotten that government decision-makers are politicians who need to consider the political as well as the economic implications of their chosen courses of action. Thus while cuts in taxation may receive public approval, increases may not, and, if implemented, the latter may encourage higher wage demands. Similarly, the redistribution of government spending from one programme area to another is likely to give rise to widespread protests from those on the receiving end of any cuts; so much so that governments tend to be restricted for the most part to changes at the margin, rather than undertaking a radical reallocation of resources and they may be tempted to fix budgetary allocations for a number of years ahead (e.g. the Comprehensive Spending Review in the UK).

Other factors too – including changes in economic thinking, self-imposed fiscal rules, external constraints on borrowing and international agreements – can also play their part in restraining the use of fiscal policy as an instrument of demand management, whatever a government's preferred course of action may be. Simple prescriptions to boost the economy through large-scale cuts in taxation or increases in government spending often fail to take into account the political and economic realities of the situation faced by most governments.

Monetary policy

Monetary policy seeks to influence monetary variables such as the money supply or rates of interest in order to regulate the economy. While the supply of money and interest rates (i.e. the cost of borrowing) are interrelated, it is convenient to consider them separately.

As far as changes in interest rates are concerned, these clearly have implications for business activity, as circular flow analysis demonstrates. Lower interest rates not only encourage firms to invest as the cost of borrowing falls, but also encourage consumption as disposable incomes rise (predominantly through the mortgage effect) and as the cost of loans and overdrafts decreases. Such increased consumption tends to be an added spur to investment, particularly if inflation rates (and, therefore 'real' interest rates) are low and this can help to boost the economy in the short term, as well as improving the supply side in the longer term.[7]

Raising interest rates tends to have the opposite effect – causing a fall in consumption as mortgages and other prices rise, and deferring investment because of the additional cost of borrowing and the decline in business confidence as consumer spending falls. If interest rates remain persistently high, the encouragement given to savers and the discouragement given to borrowers and spenders may help to generate a recession, characterised by falling output, income, spending and employment and by increasing business failure.

Changes in the **money stock** (especially credit) affect the capacity of individuals and firms to borrow and, therefore, to spend. Increases in money supply are generally related to increases in spending and this tends to be good for business prospects, particularly if interest rates are falling as the money supply rises. Restrictions on monetary growth normally work in the opposite direction, especially if such restrictions help to generate increases in interest rates which feed through to both consumption and investment, both of which will tend to decline.

As in the case of fiscal policy, government is usually able to manipulate monetary variables in a variety of ways, including taking action in the money markets to influence interest rates and controlling its own spending to influence monetary growth. Once again, however, circumstances tend to dictate how far and in what way government is free to operate. Attempting to boost the economy by allowing the money supply to grow substantially, for instance, threatens to cause inflationary pressures and to increase spending on imports, both of which run counter to government objectives and do little to assist domestic firms. Similarly, policies to boost consumption and investment through lower interest rates, while welcomed generally by industry, offer no guarantee that any additional spending will be on domestically produced goods and services, and also tend to make the financial markets nervous about government commitments to control inflation in the longer term (see below, 'The role of the central bank').

This nervousness among market dealers reflects the fact that in modern market economies a government's policies on interest rates and monetary growth cannot be taken in isolation from those of its major trading partners and this operates as an important constraint on government action. The fact is that a reduction in interest rates to boost output and growth in an economy also tends to be reflected in the exchange rate; this usually falls as foreign exchange dealers move funds into those currencies which yield a better return and which also appear a safer investment if the market believes a government is abandoning its counterinflationary policy. As the UK government found in the early 1990s, persistently high rates of interest in Germany severely restricted its room for manoeuvre on interest rates for fear of the consequences for sterling if relative interest rates got too far out of line.

Direct controls

Fiscal and monetary policies currently represent the chief policy instruments used in modern market economies and hence they have been discussed in some detail. Governments, however, also use a number of other weapons from time to time in their attempts to achieve their macroeconomic objectives. Such weapons, which are designed essentially to achieve a specific objective – such as limiting imports or controlling wage increases – tend to be known as **direct controls**. Examples of such policies include:

- *Incomes policies*, which seek to control inflationary pressures by influencing the rate at which wages and salaries rise.
- *Import controls*, which attempt to improve a country's balance of payments situation, by reducing either the supply of, or the demand for, imported goods and services.
- *Regional and urban policies*, which are aimed at alleviating urban and regional problems, particularly differences in income, output, employment, and local and regional decline.

The role of financial institutions

Interactions in the macroeconomy between governments, businesses and consumers take place within an institutional environment that includes a large number of financial intermediaries. These range from banks and building societies to pension funds, insurance companies, investment trusts and issuing houses, all of which provide a number of services of both direct and indirect benefit to businesses. As part of the financial system within a market-based economy, these institutions fulfil a vital role in channelling funds from those able and willing to lend, to those individuals and organisations wishing to borrow in order to consume or invest. It is appropriate to consider briefly this role of financial intermediation and the supervision exercised over the financial system by the central bank.

Elements of the financial system

A financial system tends to have three main elements:

1 *Lenders and borrowers* – these may be individuals, organisations or governments.
2 *Financial institutions*, of various kinds, which act as intermediaries between lenders and borrowers and which manage their own asset portfolios in the interest of their shareholders and/or depositors.
3 *Financial markets*, in which lending and borrowing takes place through the transfer of money and/or other types of asset, including paper assets such as shares and stock.

Financial institutions, as indicated above, comprise a wide variety of organisations, many of which are public companies with shareholders. Markets include the markets for short-term funds of various types (usually termed **money markets**) and those for long-term finance for both the private and public sectors (usually called the **capital market**). **Stock exchanges** normally lie at the centre of the latter, and constitute an important market for existing securities issued by both companies and government.

The vital role played by **financial intermediaries** in the operation of the financial system is illustrated in Figure 1.10 and reflects the various benefits which derive from using an intermediary rather than lending direct to a borrower (e.g. creating a large pool of savings; spreading risk; transferring short-term lending into longer-term

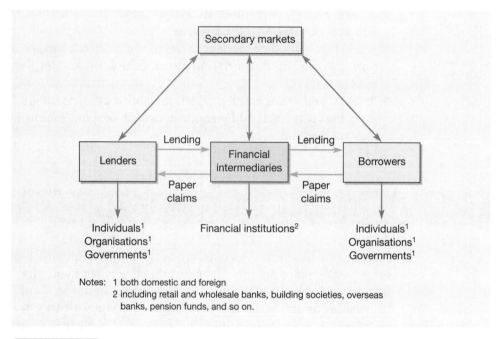

Figure 1.10 The role of financial intermediaries

borrowing; providing various types of funds transfer services). Lenders on the whole prefer low risk, high returns, flexibility and liquidity, while borrowers prefer to minimise the cost of borrowing and to use the funds in a way that is best suited to their needs. Companies, for example, may borrow to finance stock or work-in-progress or to meet short-term debts and such borrowing may need to be as flexible as possible. Alternatively, they may wish to borrow in order to replace plant and equipment or to buy new premises – borrowing which needs to be over a much longer term and which hopefully will yield a rate of return which makes the use of the funds and the cost of borrowing worthwhile.

The process of channelling funds from lenders to borrowers often gives rise to paper claims, which are generated either by the financial intermediary issuing a claim to the lender (e.g. when a bank borrows by issuing a certificate of deposit) or by the borrower issuing a claim to the financial intermediary (e.g. when government sells stock to a financial institution). These paper claims represent a liability to the issuer and an asset to the holder and can be traded on a secondary market (i.e. a market for existing securities), according to the needs of the individual or organisation holding the paper claim. At any point, financial intermediaries tend to hold a wide range of such assets (claims on borrowers), which they buy or sell ('manage') in order to yield a profit and/or improve their liquidity position. Decisions of this kind, taken on a daily basis, invariably affect the position of investors (e.g. shareholders) and customers (e.g. depositors) and can, under certain circumstances, have serious consequences for the financial intermediary and its stakeholders (e.g. the bad debts faced by western banks in the late 1980s and early 1990s).

Given the element of risk, it is perhaps not surprising that some financial institutions tend to be conservative in their attitude towards lending on funds deposited with them, especially in view of their responsibilities to their various stakeholders. UK retail banks, for instance, have a long-standing preference for financing industry's working capital rather than investment spending, and hence the latter has tended to be financed largely by internally generated funds (e.g. retained profits) or by share issues. In comparison, banks in Germany, France, the United States and Japan tend to be more ready to meet industry's medium- and longer-term needs and are often directly involved in regular discussions with their clients concerning corporate strategy, in contrast to the arm's length approach favoured by many of their UK counterparts.[8]

The role of the central bank

A critical element in a country's financial system is its **central** or **state bank**; in the United Kingdom this is the Bank of England. Like most of its overseas counterparts, the Bank of England exercises overall supervision over the banking sector with the aim of maintaining a stable and efficient financial framework as part of its contribution to a healthy economy. Its activities have a significant influence in the financial markets (especially the foreign exchange market, the gilts market and the sterling money market). These activities include the following roles:

- banker to the government;
- banker to the clearing banks;
- manager of the country's foreign reserves;
- manager of the national debt;
- manager of the issue of notes and coins;
- supervisor of the monetary sector; and
- implementer of the government's monetary policy.

In the last case, the Bank's powers were significantly enhanced following the decision by the incoming Labour government (1997) to grant it 'operational independence' to set interest rates and to conduct other aspects of monetary policy free from Treasury interference. This historic decision has given the Bank the kind of independence experienced by the US Federal Reserve and the Deutsche Bundesbank and has been designed to ensure that monetary policy is conducted according to the needs of the economy overall, particularly the need to control inflation.

For further information on the Bank of England you should consult
www.bankofengland.co.uk

Market structure

Introduction

In economics the behaviour and the performance of firms in an industry are thought to depend upon some basic structural characteristics. This view is exemplified by the **structure–conduct–performance model**, where structure determines conduct, which in turn determines performance. The basic elements included under these headings are given in Table 1.2.

The structure–conduct–performance model provides a good framework for classifying and analysing an industry. A simple example of the process can be seen in the soap powder industry. Here the market is dominated by two large producers, Unilever and Procter & Gamble. This apparent lack of competition gives rise to certain behavioural characteristics like the massive amount of advertising, the existence of many brand names and fairly uniform prices. This process will be considered in more detail later in the chapter, but the example serves to indicate the relationship between the structure of the market and the behaviour and ultimately the performance of firms in an industry.

For more information on these companies see *www.unilever.com* and *www.procterandgamble.com*

'**Market structure**' refers to the amount of competition that exists in a market between producers. The degree of competition can be thought of as lying along a continuum with very competitive markets at one end and markets in which no competition exists at all at the other end. This chapter looks at the two extremes (perfect competition and monopoly), and the market structures which exist between. The theory predicts the effects of market structure on behaviour and performance in those markets. However, as with the working of the market mechanism, the real world is often different from the theory and therefore this chapter will look at real markets and the relevance of the theory to the real world. The structure–conduct–performance model is open to criticism[9] since it says little about what determines structure in the first place. It also tends to view the firm as passive in the face of market structure, accepting the implications for conduct and performance, rather than actively trying to change and mould market structure. Michael Porter's 'five-forces model'[10] will be used to broaden out the analysis.

Table 1.2 Structure–conduct–performance model

Structural factors
- Amount of actual competition: (a) seller concentration; and (b) buyer concentration.
- Existence of potential competition.
- Cost conditions.
- Demand conditions.
- Existence of barriers to entry.

Conduct factors
- Pricing policy.
- Amount of advertising.
- Merger behaviour.
- Product differentiation.

Performance factors
- Profitability.
- Technological innovation.

Market structure is important not only because of the implications it has for conduct and performance but also because it has an impact upon the strategic possibilities which face the organisation, its ability to act strategically and the likely effects of such strategic behaviour.

In addition, this section will examine how the level of competition is measured in a market, how the level of competition varies between industries and countries, and how and why this has changed over time.

Market structures – in theory and practice

As mentioned above, market structures can be thought of as lying along a continuum with perfect competition at one end and monopoly at the other (see Figure 1.11). Both of these market structures are unrealistic representations of the real world, but are useful as benchmarks in assessing the degree of competition in a market. Between these two extremes lie other market structures, which are more realistic. Two will be described, oligopoly and monopolistic competition.

Perfect competition

This is the most competitive market structure. A number of conditions need to be fulfilled before **perfect competition** is said to exist. These conditions are as follows:

1 There are so many buyers and sellers in the market that no *one* of them can influence price through its activities.
2 The good being sold in the market is **homogeneous** (i.e. all units of the good are identical).
3 **Perfect knowledge** exists in the market. This means that producers have perfect knowledge of prices and costs of other producers and that consumers know the prices charged by all firms.
4 There exists **perfect mobility** of both the factors of production and consumers. This means that people, machines and land can be used for any purpose, and that consumers are free to purchase the good from any of the producers.
5 There are no **barriers to entry or exit** in the industry. There is nothing to prevent a new firm setting up production in the industry.

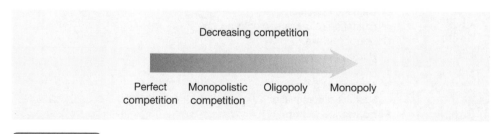

Figure 1.11   Market structures

Naturally, this is a highly theoretical model and these conditions are unlikely to be all met in reality, but if they did, and the theory is followed through, the conclusion is that there will only be one price in the market for the good being sold. For example, if one firm is charging a higher price for the good than other firms, everyone in the market will know (because of perfect knowledge), and because the good is homogeneous and because of perfect mobility on the part of consumers, consumers will simply purchase the good from another firm. The firm that was charging a higher price will be forced to reduce the price of the good in order to sell it, or face mounting stocks of the good. There is therefore only one price for the good and this will be determined by *market* demand and supply – that is, total demand and total supply, no one consumer or producer having enough market power to influence the price. Accordingly, the firm is said to be a price taker.

Price determination in perfect competition

Firms need to cover costs of production and to earn a certain level of profits in order to stay in business. This minimum level of profits is called normal profit, and profits over and above this level are called abnormal profits. If the firm is trying to maximise its profits it will decide what level of output to produce by setting the cost of producing the last unit of the good equal to the revenue gained from selling the last unit: in economic terminology, where marginal cost equals marginal revenue. Included in cost would be elements of wages, rent, rates, interest, raw materials *and* normal profits. If these costs are not being covered the firm will be making a loss.

As there is only one price in perfect competition, the revenue derived from selling the last unit must be equal to its price. Therefore, the price of the good depends on the level of marginal cost.

In the short run, individual firms can earn abnormal profits, but these are not sustainable in the longer term. If one firm is earning abnormal profits, given the assumption of perfect knowledge, everyone will know and, since freedom of entry exists, other firms will enter the market in order to earn abnormal profits. This means that there is an increase in market supply and price will fall back to a level where abnormal profits have been competed away. Similarly when losses are being made, freedom of exit means that supply will be reduced and price will rise again until normal profits have been regained.

The implications of perfect competition for market behaviour and performance are summarised in Table 1.3. Perfect competition involves very restrictive assumptions,

Table 1.3 Implications of perfect competition for conduct and performance of firms in an industry

Extent of market power	The firm has no market power at all.
Price	There will only be one price for the good. The firm will be a 'price taker'.
Advertising	There will be no advertising, as all units of the good are the same and everyone knows this.
Profitability	There can be no abnormal profits, except possibly in the very short run if a producer reduces price and captures a larger share of the market.

which will rarely be fulfilled in the real world. The usefulness of the model lies in its role as an *ideal market* in which competition is at a maximum, rather than in its applicability to the real world.

An example of perfect competition?

The nearest example to perfect competition is probably the fruit and vegetable market in the centre of a large town. The goods will be fairly homogeneous, with perhaps slight variation in the quality. Knowledge will be almost perfect with respect to prices charged, as consumers could quickly walk around the market and ascertain the price of tomatoes, for example. Mobility of consumers is also high because the sellers are located in the same place. Thus the conditions for perfect competition nearly hold. The prediction is that there will be only one price for a particular good. Again this prediction is nearly fulfilled; the price of tomatoes tends to be rather similar across such a market, and when one trader reduces the price towards the end of the day, others tend to follow suit. Another market which is said to be close to perfect competition is the stock exchange, although with the increasing use of computers this is less likely to be true in the future.

Monopoly

Monopoly lies at the opposite end of the spectrum to competition. In its purest form a monopolistic market is one in which there is no competition at all; there is a single producer supplying the whole market. The monopolist has considerable market power and can determine price or quantity sold, but not both because he or she cannot control demand. The power of the monopolist depends on the availability of substitutes, and on the existence and height of barriers to entry. If there are no close substitutes for the good being produced, or if there are high barriers to entry, the power of the monopolist will be high and abnormal profits can be earned in the long run.

A monopolist could also be a group of producers acting together to control supply to the market: for example, a **cartel** such as OPEC (Organisation of Petroleum Exporting Countries).

For information on OPEC see *www.opec.org*

In monopolistic markets the producer might be able to charge different prices for the same good: for example, on an aeroplane it is quite likely that there will be passengers sitting in the same class of seat having paid very different prices, depending upon where and when the tickets were bought. Essentially they are paying different prices for the same service, and the producer is said to be exercising **price discrimination**. Why is this possible? There are certain conditions that must hold for this type of price discrimination to occur. First, the market must be monopolistic and the producer must be able to control supply. Second, there must be groups of consumers with different demand conditions. For example, the demand for train travel by the commuter who works in London will be more inelastic than the demand of a student going to London for the day, who could use alternative forms of transport or even not go. This means that the willingness to pay among consumers will vary. The final condition necessary is that it must be possible to separate these groups in some way. For example, telephone companies are able to separate markets by time so that it is cheaper to phone after a certain time; British Rail used to separate groups by age for certain of its railcards.

The monopolist will maximise its profits by charging different prices in different markets. Price discrimination is often thought of as a bad thing as the monopolist is exploiting the consumer by charging different prices for the same good. But there are some advantages, in that it makes for better use of resources if cheap airline tickets are offered to fill an aeroplane which would otherwise have flown half-full. It can also lead to a more equitable solution in that higher-income users pay a higher price than lower-income users. The main problems with the notion of price discrimination is not that it is always a bad thing, but that it is the monopolist who has the power to decide who is charged what price.

Again the effects of monopoly on the behaviour and performance of the firm can be predicted (see Table 1.4). Like perfect competition, this is a highly theoretical model and is mainly used as a comparison with perfect competition to show the effects of the lack of competition.

Table 1.4 Implications of monopoly for conduct and performance of firms in an industry

Extent of market power	The firm has absolute market power.
Price	There will only be one price for the good, except in the case of price discrimination. The firm is a 'price maker'.
Advertising	There will be no need for advertising, as there is only one firm producing the good.
Profitability	Abnormal profits can exist in the long run as there is no competition which might erode them away.

A comparison of perfect competition and monopoly

- It would be expected that price would be higher under monopoly than under perfect competition because of the absence of competition in the monopolistic market. It is argued, for example, that the large telephone companies (including BT) are overcharging the consumer. The benefits of the considerable technological advances that have been made in this area have not been passed on fully to the consumer. This can only be sustained by virtue of the monopolistic power of the companies. *But*, to counter this it could be argued that a monopolist is in a better position to reap the benefits of economies of scale, therefore it is possible that price might be lower.
- There might be less choice under monopoly since firms do not have to continually update their products in order to stay in business. *But*, it is also possible to think of examples where monopolies provide greater choice (e.g. in the case of radio stations), where under perfect competition all radio stations would cater for the biggest market, which would be for pop music. A monopolist, however, would be able to cover all tastes with a variety of stations.
- There is less incentive to innovate under monopoly, since the monopolist is subject to less competition. *But*, equally, a monopolist might have more incentive to

innovate as it can reap the benefits in terms of higher profits. It may also have more resources to devote to innovation.

As can be seen there is not a clear set of arguments that imply that perfect competition is better than monopoly, and this is taken into account in UK competition policy.

An example of monopoly?

Although it is easy to think of examples of industries where the dominant firm has a great deal of monopoly power, there is no such thing as a pure monopoly, as substitutes exist for most goods. For example, British Rail used to have monopoly power in the market for rail travel, but there are many alternative forms of travel. The nearest examples of monopolies are the old public utilities, like gas, electricity, water and so on, many of which have been privatised.

The government, in determining whether monopoly power exists in a market, has a working definition of what constitutes a monopoly. It is when 25 per cent of the market is accounted for by one firm or firms acting together. This would form grounds for investigation by the Competition Commission. The sources of monopoly power are the existence of barriers to entry and exit and the availability of substitutes.

For information on the operation of the Competition Commission see www.competition-commission.org.uk

Oligopoly

In both perfect competition and monopoly firms make independent decisions. In the case of monopoly there are no other firms in the industry to consider; in the case of perfect competition the firm has no power to affect the market at all. So for different reasons they act as though they have no rivals. This is not true in the case of oligopoly. **Oligopoly** is where a small number of producers supply a market in which the product is differentiated in some way. The characteristics of oligopoly are:

- A great deal of **interdependence** between the firms; each firm has to consider the likely actions of other firms when making its decisions.
- A lack of **price competition** in the market; firms are reluctant to increase their prices in case their competitors do not and they might lose market share. Firms are also reluctant to reduce their prices, in case other firms do the same and a price war results which reduces prices but leaves market share unchanged and so everyone is left worse off.[11]
- The lack of price competition means that different forms of **non-price competition** take place, such as branding or advertising. Oligopolists will sell their products not by reducing the price but through heavy advertising, brand names or special offers. The Premier points scheme was a good example of such non-price competition. The purchase of petrol from certain outlets gave the customer

points which were accumulated on their Premier points card and then redeemed for money-off vouchers to be spent at Argos. Table 1.5 shows the implications of oligopoly for conduct and performance of firms in an industry.

The way in which price is determined in an oligopolistic market is through either **price leadership** or some sort of **collusion**. Price leadership is where one firm takes the lead in setting prices and the others follow suit. The price leader is not necessarily the firm with the lowest cost, as it depends upon the power of the firm. So price could be set at a higher level than in a competitive market. Collusion is an explicit or implicit agreement between firms on price, which serves to reduce the amount of competition between firms. Collusion is illegal in most countries as it is seen as a form of restrictive practice, but this does not mean that collusion does not take place. A cartel is a form of collusion where firms come together to exercise joint market power. Cartels are now illegal in most countries, but the most famous of all is OPEC which has had a dramatic effect on the oil industry over the last 30 years. Collusive agreements, as well as possibly being harmful to the consumer, tend to be unstable as there is great temptation on the part of individual firms/countries to cheat. What is clear in the case of oligopoly is that once price is set there is a reluctance to change it. Therefore price competition is replaced by non-price competition of the sort mentioned above.

Table 1.5 Implications of oligopoly for conduct and performance of firms in an industry

Extent of market power	A great deal of market power.
Price	A stable price level. Prices set by price leadership or collusion.
Advertising	Much advertising and branding. Non-price competition is common.
Profitability	Abnormal profits can exist, their extent depends on the strength of competitors.

The most often quoted examples of oligopoly are the market for tobacco and the market for soap powder. Both of these markets are dominated by a very small number of producers and both exhibit the predicted characteristics. There is little price competition and price is fairly uniform in both markets. There is a high degree of non-price competition in both markets – high advertising, strong brand names and images, and the use of special offers or gifts at times in order to sell the goods.

Compared with monopoly and perfect competition, oligopoly is a much more realistic market structure, with many markets exhibiting the characteristics stated above. Table 1.6 gives a few examples.

Table 1.6 The top firms' share of the market in the UK (percentages)

Industry	Percentages
Cigarettes[a]	91*
Brewing[b]	89**
Sugar and artificial sweeteners[c]	79*
Ice cream[c]	68*
Jeans[c]	13*

Note: * Top three firms in the industry; ** Top five firms.
Source: [a] Keynote Report, 2007; [b] Keynote Report, 2008; [c] Mintel Report, 2008.

It is interesting to note that the market shares of the top firms in all of these industries have decreased since the publication of the last edition of this text. For three of these products, this has mainly been down to an increase in the market's share of own-brand products. For sugar there has been an increase of 20 per cent in the market's share of own brands between 2002 and 2006 and the corresponding figures are 22 per cent for jeans and 3 per cent for ice creams.

For information and reports on specific industries see *www.mintel.co.uk* and *www.keynote.co.uk*

Monopolistic competition

A market structure of monopolistic competition exists when all of the conditions for perfect competition are met except for the existence of a homogeneous good, so that each firm has a monopoly over its own good but there is a great deal of competition in the market from other suppliers producing very similar products. In monopolistic competition the good is slightly differentiated in some way, either by advertising and branding or by local production. There does not have to be a technical difference between the two goods, which could be identical in composition, but there must be an 'economic difference' – that is, a difference in the way the goods are perceived by consumers. There is also some degree of consumer loyalty, so that if one firm reduces price, consumers might not necessarily move to that firm if they believe that the difference between the brands justifies the higher price. Abnormal profits can exist in the short run but cannot persist since new firms are free to enter the industry and compete away abnormal profit (see Table 1.7).

Table 1.7 Implications of monopolistic competition for conduct and performance of firms in an industry

Extent of market power	The firm has little market power.
Price	There will be small differences in price.
Advertising	There will be heavy advertising and branding.
Profitability	Small abnormal profits can exist in the short run but will be competed away in the longer run.

An example of monopolistic competition?

There are many examples of this type of industry: for example, the paint industry where ICI is the only producer of Dulux but there are many other types of paint on the market.

How accurate is the theory?

The implications of the theory of market structures for the behaviour and performance of firms are summarised in Table 1.8.

As argued above, both perfect competition and pure monopoly tend to be based on assumptions that are somewhat unrealistic and should be regarded as 'ideal

Table 1.8 Implications of theory for behaviour of firms

	Market power	Price	Advertising	Profitability
Perfect competition	None	One price	None	Only normal profits
Monopoly	Absolute	Price discrimination possible	None	Abnormal profits
Oligopoly	High	One price	High	Abnormal profits
Monopolistic competition	Little	Small differences in price	High	Only normal profits in long run

types' of market structure, in the sense that they establish the boundaries within which true markets exist and operate, and against which they can be analysed. In contrast, oligopoly and monopolistic competition are much nearer to the types of market structure which can be found in the real world, and economic theory does appear to explain and predict behaviour in these markets to a certain extent. In oligopolistic markets, for example, price tends to be **sticky** and much of the competition between firms occurs in non-price ways, particularly branding, advertising and sales promotion (see Table 1.9). Occasionally, however, **price wars** do occur – as in the petrol market in the 1980s and more recently between the four biggest supermarkets.

Table 1.9 shows the top advertisers in the United Kingdom ranked for 2006; their ranks in 1994 are also given. The names in the list are familiar and largely expected from the predictions: for example, Procter & Gamble is one of the two companies which together with Unilever account for around 90 per cent of the market for washing powder. A less familiar name is Reckitt Benckiser which subsequently acquired Boots in 2007.

Table 1.9 Top advertisers in the UK, 2006

Rank			
2006	1994	Advertiser	Total adspend (£000)
1	1	Procter & Gamble	181 023
2	3	Unilever	177 167
3	–	Central Office of Information Communication	140 758
4	36	L'Oréal Golden	120 121
5	48	British Sky Broadcasting	118 306
6	–	DFS Furniture	107 286
7	2	British Telecom	92 241
8	–	Orange	88 982
9	32	Reckitt Benckiser	83 790
10	19	Tesco	76 101

Source: Adapted from *Advertising Statistics Yearbook*, 1995 and 2007, Advertising Association, WARC.

For information on advertising see *www.adassoc.org.uk*

It is much more difficult to judge how accurate the behavioural implications are. Lack of data is one problem, as is the fact that only one structural characteristic has been considered here – the level of competition between producers. The other structural factors listed in Table 1.2 will also have an effect, like the level of demand, the degree of competition between the buyers and the degree of potential competition. Profitability, price and advertising, for instance, will be affected by the level of demand in the market.

The market system

Introduction

The market system is an economy in which all of the basic economic choices are made through the market. The **market** is a place where buyers and sellers of a product are brought together. The nature and location of the market depends on the product. For example, within your local town there is likely to be a vegetable market where you would go to buy vegetables. Here, buyers and sellers meet face to face in the same location, but this is not always the case. The market for used cars might be the local newspaper classified section; the sale of stocks and shares passes through a broker so that the buyer never meets the seller. There are many different types of market, involving different buyers and sellers. Firms sell the goods and services they produce to households on the **product markets**, while in the **factor markets** firms are buying resources such as labour and raw materials. The discussion in this chapter will concentrate on the product markets but much of the analysis could also be applied to the factor markets.

A **free market** system is one in which the basic economic choices are made through the market, without any intervention by the government. In reality, markets are not completely free; governments intervene in markets for many reasons and in many different ways, but in this chapter such intervention will be ignored.

The market mechanism

In every market there will be a buyer and a seller, and somehow they have to be brought together so that a sale can take place. The market mechanism is the way in which this takes place in a market economy. In the product market, the buyer is the household and the seller is the firm. In economic language the household **demands** the good or service and the firm **supplies** the good or service. Each of these will be considered separately first and then brought together.

Demand

The quantity demanded refers to the quantity of a good or service that households are willing and able to purchase at a particular price. This definition shows that it is **effective demand** that is important; although many people would like to own a Rolls-Royce they could not afford it and so their demand is not effective on the market. The demand for a good or service depends on a number of factors, the most important of which are:

- the price of the good;
- the prices of other goods;
- disposable income; and
- tastes.

Table 1.10 The demand for 'Real Brew' draught beer

Price (£ per pint)	Quantity demanded (000s of pints/week)
0.90	83
1.00	70
1.10	58
1.20	48
1.30	40
1.40	35
1.50	32

To begin with, the relationship between quantity demanded and price will be looked at, assuming that the other factors above remain the same. This assumption will be relaxed in the subsequent analysis.

Table 1.10 shows what happens to the quantity demanded of beer as the price per pint goes up. Note that demand is measured over some period of time. The information is then presented in a graphical form in Figure 1.12; the line joining the various combinations of price and quantity demanded is called a **demand curve**. The demand curve shows that if all of the other factors which influence demand are constant then as price goes up, quantity demanded goes down. This is commonly referred to as **the law of demand**. What happens when price rises is that some individuals will cut down their consumption of beer and others may switch to other types of beer. There are some goods where this relationship might not hold:[12] for example, in the stock market where a rise in share prices might lead to the expectation of further price rises and therefore an increase in demand on the part of those wishing to make a capital gain. However, these exceptions are rare and it is therefore safe to assume that the law of demand holds.

If the price of beer changes, there is a movement along the demand curve. For example, if the price of beer goes up from 90p a pint to £1.00 a pint, the quantity demanded goes down from 83 000 pints per week to 70 000 pints per week. In drawing the demand curve the assumption was made that other factors affecting demand are constant. If this assumption is relaxed, what happens to the demand curve?

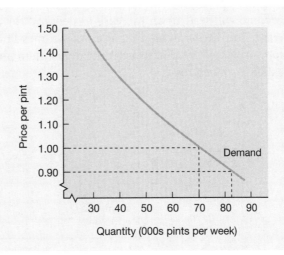

Figure 1.12   A demand curve for 'Real Brew' draught beer

Price of other goods

The quantity of beer consumed will be affected by the prices of other goods. These other goods are likely to be **substitutes** or **complements**. A substitute for beer may be lager, and if the price of lager goes down, some individuals may switch from beer to lager; thus the demand for beer goes down. What happens to the demand curve is that at all price levels, the demand for beer is now lower. Thus the demand curve shifts to the left, indicating that at £1.00 per pint only 60 000 pints of beer are demanded per week. If the price of a substitute goes up, there will be an increase in the demand for beer. The demand curve moves to the right. These movements are shown in Figure 1.13. The closer the goods are as substitutes and the greater the change in the price of the substitute, the greater will be the shift in the demand curve.

A complementary good is one which tends to be consumed with another good. For beer, it is possible that individuals eat crisps or smoke cigarettes at the same time as drinking beer. The relationship is the opposite of that for substitutes. If the price of a complement goes up, individuals might be less likely to drink beer, and demand will fall. The demand curve moves to the left. If the price of a complement goes down, the demand for beer will rise. Again the closer the goods are as complements, and the greater the price change of that complement, the greater will be the shift in the demand curve.

Disposable income

Changes in disposable income will clearly affect demand. If the economy moves into recession, then retail sales and the housing market might suffer. As incomes increase once the economy recovers, then such sectors will pick up again. Higher incomes will lead to increased consumption of most goods. If your income is boosted, how will this affect your consumption? You might buy more textbooks, and probably spend more money on leisure activities and clothes. Most students might also drink an extra pint of beer per week. Thus an increase in disposable income will lead to an increase in demand for these goods, indicated by a rightward shift in the demand curve. As incomes fall the demand for these goods will fall, indicated by a leftward shift in the demand curve. These types of goods are called **normal goods**.

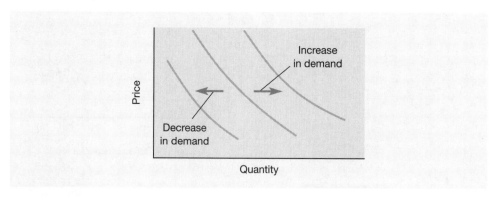

Figure 1.13   Shifting demand curves

There are goods, however, that experience a fall in demand as a result of income increases. These goods are called **inferior goods**. A good example is hard toilet paper; as individuals become richer, they are likely to substitute more expensive soft toilet paper, and thus the demand for hard toilet paper will fall.

Tastes

Taste includes attitudes and preferences of consumers, and will be affected by such things as fashion, and advertising campaigns by producers or by governments. For example, a successful advertising campaign by the government pointing out the effects of smoking would cause tastes to change and demand for cigarettes to fall.

The demand curve, then, is downward sloping, indicating that as the price of the good rises the quantity demanded by households falls, shown by a *movement along the demand curve*. Changes in the other determining factors lead to *movements of the demand curve*.

Supply

The other side of the market is the supply side. In the market for goods and services it is the firm that is the supplier. The quantity supplied of a good is defined as the quantity that firms are willing and able to supply to the market at a particular price. Again notice the wording of the definition is such that it only includes **effective supply** and, as with demand, it is measured over a specific time period.

The quantity supplied to the market depends on a number of factors, the most important of which are:

- the price of the good;
- the prices of other goods;
- the prices of the resources used to produce the good;
- technology;
- expectations; and
- number of suppliers.

In the same way as for demand, all factors other than price will be assumed to be constant and the relationship between quantity supplied and price will be considered first.

Table 1.11 provides some information on price and quantity supplied of beer. The same information is represented graphically in Figure 1.14; the line joining the points together is called the **supply curve**. The upwards-sloping curve illustrates **the law of supply**. This states that, as the price of a good rises, the quantity that firms are willing to supply also rises. This is because if costs are constant as we have assumed, then higher prices must mean higher profits to the firm.

Note that there is no supply at a price below 90p per pint; this is the minimum price required by the producer to produce the beer. If the price per pint changes there is a movement along the supply curve in the same way as for demand. If any of the other factors listed above change there will be a movement of the supply curve.

Table 1.11 The supply of 'Real Brew' draught beer

Price (£ per pint)	Quantity supplied (000s of units/week)
0.90	0
1.00	35
1.10	43
1.20	48
1.30	55
1.40	60
1.50	68

Other prices

The supply of one good can be influenced by the price of another. For example, if the brewery in which Real Brew beer is brewed is also producing lager, then an increase in the price of lager (with the price of beer remaining the same) will encourage the firm to produce less beer and more lager, as lager is now more profitable to produce. The supply curve for beer would shift to the left, indicating that at every possible price, less is now supplied than before. If the price of lager fell, the supply of beer would increase. This is shown by a rightward shift of the supply curve. The size of the shift would depend upon the degree to which the goods could be substituted for each other in production, and the size of the price change. These shifts are illustrated in Figure 1.15.

Goods can also be complements in their production process; for example, beef and leather hides. An increase in the price of beef would increase not only the supply of beef but also the supply of hides. There would be a corresponding shift in the supply curve for hides.

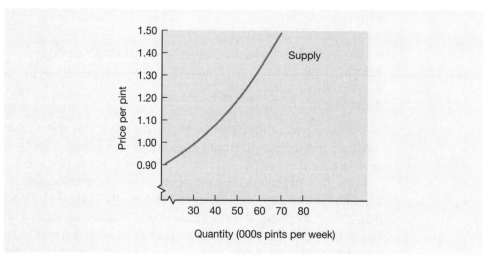

Figure 1.14   The supply of 'Real Brew' draught beer

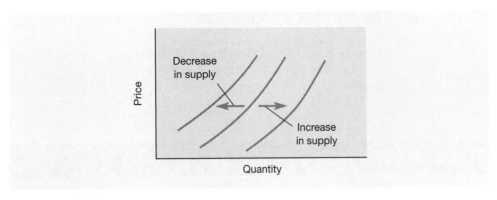

Figure 1.15   Shifting supply curves

The prices of the resources used in the production of the good

If any of the costs of production (wages, rent, rate of interest, and so on) increased, then the profitability of that good at each price would fall and there would be a tendency for supply to be reduced. The supply curve would move to the left. If costs of production fell there would be an increase in supply and a rightward movement of the supply curve. The extent of the shift depends upon the size of the price change, the significance of that factor in production, and the degree to which the factor could be substituted for another factor.

Technology

Technical development in all aspects of production has led to great improvements in output per worker. Such improvements generally result in either more being produced with the same resources, or the same being produced with fewer. In most cases it would also lead to a substitution of one factor of production for another. For example, car production becomes less labour intensive as robotic techniques take over. Even such a product as traditional British beer has benefited from significant technical improvements in production. The effect of such advances would result in increased supply at each price level and hence a movement of the supply curve to the right.

Business expectations

Expectations play a crucial role in the decision making of firms. Good expectations of the future would encourage firms to invest in new plant and machinery, which would increase their productive potential. Chancellors of the Exchequer are occasionally accused of trying to 'talk the economy up': that is, they may paint a rosy picture of the current and future state of the economy in the hope that this will enhance business expectations, and help pull the economy out of recession. If business does become increasingly confident, or perhaps more inclined to take risks, then this would shift the supply curve to the right. The reverse would shift it to the left.

The number of suppliers

As the number of suppliers in a market increases the supply will rise; the supply curve shifts to the right. If suppliers leave the market, supply will fall and the supply curve moves to the left.

Price determination

The market is the place where buyers and sellers meet and where demand and supply are brought together. The information on demand and supply is combined in Table 1.12 and presented graphically in Figure 1.16.

Table 1.12 The supply and demand for 'Real Brew' draught beer

Price (£ per pint)	Quantity demanded (000s/wk)	Quantity supplied (000s/wk)
0.90	83	0
1.00	70	35
1.10	58	43
1.20	48	48
1.30	40	55
1.40	35	60
1.50	32	68

The equilibrium price

At a price of £1.20, the quantity demanded is the same as the quantity supplied at 48 000 pints per week. At this price the amount that consumers wish to buy is the

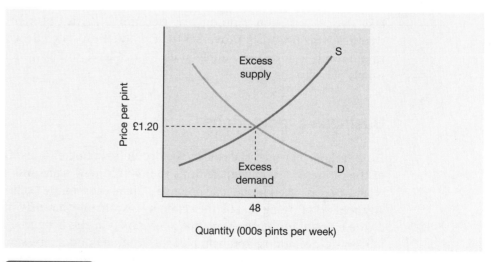

Figure 1.16 The market for 'Real Brew' draught beer

same as the amount that producers wish to sell. This price is called the **equilibrium price** and the quantity being bought and sold is called the **equilibrium quantity**. The point of equilibrium can be seen on the diagram at the point where the demand and supply curves cross.

At price levels above £1.20 the quantity that producers wish to supply is greater than the quantity consumers wish to buy. There is **excess supply** and the market is a 'buyers' market'. At prices less than £1.20 consumers wish to buy more than producers wish to supply. There is **excess demand** and the market is a **sellers' market**.

In competitive markets, situations of excess demand or supply should not exist for long as forces are put into motion to move the market towards equilibrium. For example, if the price level is £1.30 per pint, there is excess supply and producers will be forced to reduce the price in order to sell their beer. Consumers may be aware that they are in a **buyers' market** and offer lower prices, which firms might accept. For one or both of these reasons, there will be a tendency for prices to be pushed back towards the equilibrium price. The opposite occurs at prices below equilibrium and price is pushed upwards towards equilibrium.

Shifts in demand and supply

So long as the demand and supply curves in any market remain stationary, the equilibrium price should be maintained. However, there are numerous factors that could shift either or both of these curves. If this were to happen, then the old equilibrium would be destroyed and the market should work to a new equilibrium. How does this happen?

In Figure 1.17 the original equilibrium price for Real Brew draught beer is P_1. Assume that the demand curve moves from D_1 to D_2. This increase in demand could be due to a variety of factors already mentioned. For example, the price of a rival drink may have increased; disposable income could have risen; or sales may have benefited from a successful advertising campaign. In any event, at the old

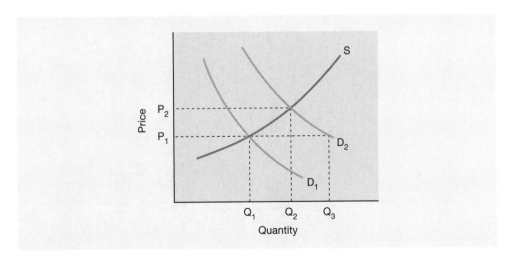

Figure 1.17 A shift in the demand curve

equilibrium price there now exists an excess of demand over supply of Q_1Q_3. It is likely that price will be bid upwards in order to ration the shortage in supply. As price rises, demand is choked off and supply exhausted. Eventually, there is a movement to a new equilibrium of P_2. At this new price both supply and demand at Q_2 are higher than they were at the previous equilibrium. If, alternatively, the demand curve had shifted to the left, then the process would have been reversed and the new equilibrium would have been at a level of demand and supply less than Q_1, with a price below P_1. Illustrate this process diagrammatically for yourself.

In Figure 1.18 there is a shift in the supply curve from S_1 to S_2. Refer back in this chapter to envisage specific reasons for such a shift. At the original equilibrium price of P_1 there would now be an excess supply over demand of Q_1Q_3. Price would therefore fall in a free market. As it does, demand will be encouraged and supply diminished. Eventually there will be a new equilibrium at P_2 with a higher quantity demanded and supplied than at the previous equilibrium. If the supply curve had instead shifted to the left, then market forces would have resulted in a lower quantity supplied and demanded than before. Once again, illustrate this diagrammatically for yourself.

The analysis so far has been relatively straightforward; it has been assumed that either the demand or the supply curve moves alone. However, it is likely that in any given time period both curves could move in any direction and perhaps even more than once.

Given the many factors that may shift both the demand and the supply curves, it is easy to imagine that markets can be in a constant state of flux. Just as the market is moving towards a new equilibrium, some other factor may change, necessitating an adjustment in an opposite direction. Given that such adjustment is not immediate, and that market conditions are constantly changing, it may be the case that equilibrium is never actually attained. It is even possible that the very process of market adjustment can be destabilising.[13] The constant movement of price implied by the analysis may also be detrimental to business. The firm might prefer to keep price constant in the face of minor changes in demand and supply.

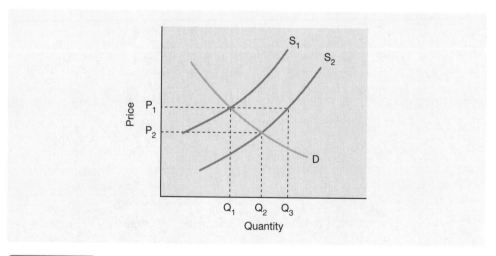

Figure 1.18   A shift in the supply curve

mini case   The price of gold

Gold as a commodity has always had a particular historical economic importance and its price is very volatile. Over 84 per cent of the gold mined each year goes into the production of jewellery, but it is the role of gold as a store of wealth that gives it such volatility. Until the 1970s the US, the UK and many other countries pegged their currencies to the value of gold – 'the gold standard'. As a result, central banks kept stocks of gold, as well as other currencies, which gives gold increased importance as a commodity.

The price of gold has been increasing since 2001 to hit $1000 per ounce in March 2008. By June the price had fallen to $880 per ounce. Explanations for these movements in gold prices can be found in the theory of demand and supply.

Supply factors

First, as a natural resource, the supply of gold is inelastic; it is mined in over 60 countries but the amount mined is small and getting smaller each year. This means that the supply curve will be inelastic (see below) – SS in Figure 1.19. Any changes in demand will have a bigger impact upon price than if the supply curve was elastic. Draw a more elastic supply curve in Figure 1.19 and see what impact that has on price.

Once the gold standard had been rejected by countries, their central banks started to sell off some of their stocks of gold; this led to increases in market supply and therefore falls in the price of gold. You should be able to draw this on a demand and supply diagram.

Demand factors

The increase in the price of gold that took place between 2001 and 2008 has mainly been down to demand factors:

● there has been higher demand for gold from oil-producing countries such as Russia and Qatar, which do not wish to hold the surpluses they have accumulated in dollars

(from exporting oil), which by 2008 was a weakened currency;
● an increasingly wealthy Chinese population has been buying gold as a store of wealth;
● western pension funds have also been very active in the closed exchanges where they can buy 'shares' in gold bars.

The effect of increasing demand is shown in Figure 1.19. Increases in demand from D_1 to D_2 to D_3 cause price to increase fairly sharply.

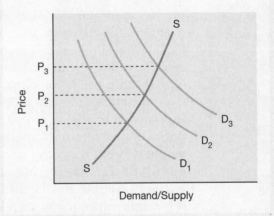

Figure 1.19   **The market for gold**

At the time of writing, the price of gold had already fallen from its peak of $1000 per ounce and the main reason for this was the stabilising of the US$. It is clear that the forces of demand and supply are very evident in the market for gold and the supply characteristics make its price more susceptible to changes in demand. This may change in the future as deep-sea mining equipment should go into action in 2010, and if gold is found in significant quantities, the supply of gold will become more elastic. Shocks to the global financial system (e.g. the global financial crisis in 2007/8) also affect the price of gold as investors look for 'safe havens' for their money. Historically, gold has been seen as one such safe haven.

Price controls

Governments occasionally take the view that a particular equilibrium price is politically, socially or economically unacceptable. In such circumstances, one course of action is the imposition of **price controls**. This involves the institutional setting of prices at either above or below the true market equilibrium. For example, if it was felt that the equilibrium price of a good was too high, then the government might try to impose a lower price on the market. This would now be the maximum acceptable price or **price ceiling**. Price may not rise above this ceiling. Alternatively, the equilibrium price could be seen as too low. In this case, a higher price, or **price floor** is imposed, below which price should not fall.

Figure 1.20 illustrates the market for a basic foodstuff. Imagine that it is wartime and the disruption has shifted the supply curve to the left. This could be largely due to a movement of resources away from the production of this good and towards munitions. The free market price at P_1 is seen to be unacceptably high relative to the pre-war price, and the decision is made to impose a price ceiling of P_2. It is hoped that such a ceiling will alleviate the problems of consumers who could not afford the free market price. The problem now is that at the price ceiling only Q_3 units will be supplied, whereas demand is for Q_2. The volume of output Q_3Q_2 therefore represents an excess of demand over supply. Many customers are frustrated in their desire to purchase that good. To help bring order to the situation, a system of rationing might be introduced. This could allocate the limited output between the many customers in a more orderly fashion than 'first come, first served'. For example, one unit could be allocated per person and priority could be given to the old and the sick. This does not solve the problem of excess demand. It is commonly found in such situations that illegal trading starts to emerge at a price above the ceiling. To obtain the good many would be willing to pay a higher price. This is commonly referred to as black market trading.

Figure 1.21 illustrates the market for a specific type of labour. The downward-sloping demand curve indicates that, at lower wages, employers will wish to take on additional workers. The supply curve shows how more people will offer

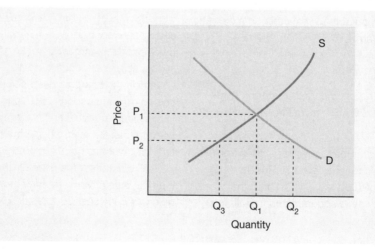

Figure 1.20   Imposition of a price ceiling

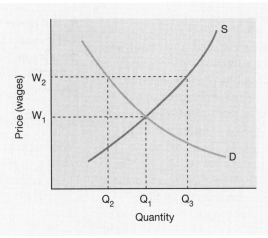

Figure 1.21   Imposition of a price floor

themselves for work as wage rates increase. At the intersection of the curves, the market is in equilibrium. Imagine that this equilibrium wage is seen to be too low, and the authorities seek to impose a minimum wage of W_2. Employers are not permitted to pay any less than this amount. It is hoped that the policy will improve the welfare of workers by raising their living standards to some acceptable level.

At this minimum wage, employment becomes more attractive, and Q_3 persons seek employment. On the other hand, employers only wish to take on Q_2 workers. There is now a situation of excess supply. Only Q_2 find work, the remainder Q_2Q_3 are unsuccessful. The policy has actually reduced the level of employment from Q_1 to Q_2. In such a situation, there will be a temptation to flout the legislation. For example, unscrupulous employers observing the ranks of unemployed would realise that many would willingly work at less than the minimum wage.

The above examples illustrate the problems that arise once price is imposed away from its equilibrium. Further examples of such price controls would include the guaranteed minimum prices to farmers within the Common Agricultural Policy (CAP) of the European Union, and various post-war attempts to control the cost of rented accommodation at a price affordable to the low paid. The former has been associated with overproduction and the need to control the mountains of excess supply, while the latter tended to result in landlords taking their properties off the rental market in order to seek more profitable returns. The success of such policies requires careful control and monitoring. In many circumstances, it might be better to consider alternative ways of achieving the policy goals.

mini case   What can be done about rising food prices?

Rising world food prices have implications for the whole world, but especially for poorer countries where incomes are low and the demand for food is high; 2008 has seen food riots in countries from Mexico to Pakistan to Burkina Faso. Even consumers in the USA have seen the rationing of rice in supermarkets. What can governments do? Demand and supply diagrams can be used to analyse some of the possibilities.

1 Price controls

One possibility is the introduction of a maximum price ceiling below the equilibrium price – at P in Figure 1.22. This has been done in India for a number of years on a range of goods and several Far Eastern countries on petrol. In 2008 the Chinese government has frozen the price of certain essential goods. There are two main problems with the use of price ceilings. First, as described in the text, there is now excess demand at the enforced price level and no incentive for more to be produced so this may lead to greater food shortages.

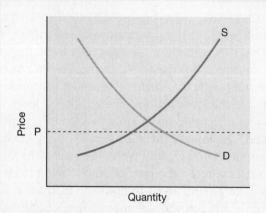

Figure 1.22   **Price ceiling**

Second, this type of price control is expensive and cannot be maintained in the long run. For example, it is estimated that the cost of the price ceiling on petrol in Malaysia is 10 per cent of government spending.

2 Rationing

In the face of food shortages, one possibility is that rationing will take place so that individuals will only be allowed a certain quantity of the product in question. This would be more equitable than a first-come, first-served basis for distribution or black market trading where the rich have more market power than the poor. The problem with food markets is that they are not free markets; there are trading blocs and trading rules which prevent an equitable distribution of food worldwide.

3 Subsidies

Farmers could be paid subsidies to increase their production of foodstuffs. These are shown in Figure 1.23.

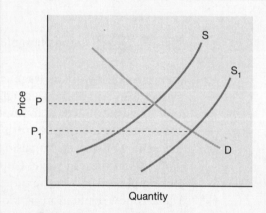

Figure 1.23   **Payment of subsidies**

The payment of a subsidy to a producer is like the opposite of a tax – it means that the costs of production are lower so that supply can be increased. The supply curve moves from S to S_1 and price falls. This overcomes the first problem with price controls – the lack of incentive to increase production. The use of demand and supply diagrams show how problems with the market mechanism can be addressed in theory. The problem is that we live in the real world and the solutions to the food crisis are more likely to be political rather than economic. For example, will the west turn away from the use of biofuels? Will trade policies be changed so that the worldwide distribution of food can be more equitable?

Elasticity of demand

It has been shown that as long as other factors affecting demand remain constant, a decrease in price would be expected to increase the quantity demanded by consumers. This knowledge is obviously of importance to business, in that it implies that sales will expand as the good becomes more price competitive. It does not, however, say anything about the degree to which sales might increase. As prices change, will demand change by a large or a small amount? At the end of the day, will the extra sales bring in more or less total revenue? In short, a measure is needed of the responsiveness of demand to price changes. In the same way the responsiveness of quantity demanded to other factors like income or other prices can also be measured. It is also important to be aware of the responsiveness of supply to changes in prices. All of these are measured by the concept of **elasticity**.

Price elasticity of demand

Figure 1.24 illustrates two different-shaped demand curves and shows the effect of a price increase from 40p to 60p in each case. On the left-hand diagram, the increase in price causes demand to fall from 25 to 20 units. Total revenue received by the producer (i.e. price multiplied by the number of units sold) changes from £10.00 (40p × 25 units) to £12.00 (60p × 20 units). As illustrated, the area A represents the gain in revenue as a result of the price change, while B shows the loss of revenue. In this case there is a clear net gain. The reason for this is that the significance of the price rise is greater than the fall in demand. Compare this with the right-hand diagram. The same price rise now causes total revenue to fall from £20.00 (40p × 50 units) to £6.00 (60p × 10 units). The loss of revenue, area B^1, is clearly greater than the gain in revenue, area A^1. There is a net loss of revenue. This is a situation where the decrease in demand is of greater significance than the increase in price.

The traditional way of measuring the responsiveness of demand to a change in price is via the concept of **price elasticity**, the formula being:

$$\text{Price elasticity of demand (Ep)} = \frac{\text{Percentage change in quantity demanded}}{\text{Percentage change in price}}$$

$$\text{Ep} = \frac{\%\ \text{change QD}}{\%\ \text{change P}}$$

The significance of this formula lies in whether the value of price elasticity is greater or less than 1. If it is greater, then the percentage change in quantity demanded is greater than the percentage change in price. Demand is referred to as being relatively **elastic**, or responsive to price changes. If, on the other hand, the percentage change in quantity demanded is less than the percentage change in price, then price elasticity will be less than 1. Demand is now referred to as being relatively **inelastic**, and demand is not very responsive to price changes.

The higher or lower the value of price elasticity, the greater or lesser the responsiveness of demand to the price change. Table 1.13 demonstrates the connection

Table 1.13 Elasticity and total revenue

Elasticity	Price change	Change in total revenue
Elastic	Upward	Downward
	Downward	Upward
Inelastic	Upward	Upward
	Downward	Downward

between price elasticity and total revenue. It will be observed that if price elasticity is greater than 1, then there is a negative relationship between price changes and total revenue. For example, an increase in price results in a decrease in total revenue. Whereas, if elasticity is less than 1, then there is a positive relationship.

Calculating elasticity

From the information portrayed in Figure 1.24, in the left-hand diagram price rose from 40p to 60p and demand fell from 25 to 20 units; thus:

$$Ep = \frac{\% \text{ change QD}}{\% \text{ change P}} = \frac{5/25 \times 100}{20/40 \times 100} = \frac{20\%}{50\%} = 0.4$$

This shows that demand is inelastic. One problem with this measurement is that if you measured elasticity when price fell from 60p to 40p the answer would be different:

$$Ep = \frac{\% \text{ change in QD}}{\% \text{ change in P}} = \frac{5/20 \times 100}{20/60 \times 100} = \frac{25\%}{33.3\%} = 0.75$$

The reason for this variation is that the percentage change in each case is being measured from a different base. When price rises from 20p to 40p, this is a 50 per

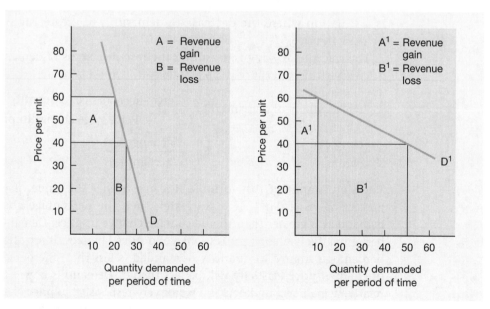

Figure 1.24 Responsiveness of demand to a price change

cent rise. Yet when it falls from 60p to 40p this is only a 33.3 per cent fall. The value of elasticity therefore varies. To avoid this ambiguity, elasticity is measured as the percentage change from the average value of price and quantity before and after the change, that is:

$$\% \text{ change} = \frac{\text{Change in value} \times 100}{\text{Average value}}$$

The value of elasticity for the price increase and decrease must now be identical:

$$Ep = \frac{\% \text{ change QD}}{\% \text{ change P}} = \frac{5/22.5 \times 100}{20/50 \times 100} = \frac{22.2\%}{40\%} = 0.55$$

The determinants of elasticity

There are a number of factors which determine how responsive quantity demanded is to price changes. First, the nature of the good and how it is viewed by consumers. A good which is a necessity will have a low value of elasticity, as an increase in price will not have a very big impact on the quantity consumed. Goods like cigarettes will have inelastic demand because they are habit forming. The tastes of consumers will be important: whether they view a television, for example, as a necessity or a luxury will determine the value of elasticity. Another factor is whether substitutes are available for the good or not. If there is no substitute for a particular good and the household wishes to continue to consume it, an increase in price will have little effect on the level of demand. Other factors include the importance of the good in the household's total expenditure. The smaller the proportion of the household's budget which is spent on a particular good, the smaller will be the effect on demand of any change in price.

Income elasticity of demand

Income elasticity of demand is a measure of the responsiveness of quantity demanded to changes in income. It can be negative in the case of inferior goods, where an increase in income leads to a fall in the demand for a good, or positive in the case of a normal good, where an increase in income leads to an increase in demand. There is also a difference between luxuries and necessities. Luxuries will have positive income elasticities with values over 1. This means that an increase in income will cause an increase in demand for that good and that a 1 per cent increase in income will cause a more than 1 per cent increase in demand. A necessity on the other hand will also have a positive income elasticity but its value will lie somewhere between 0 and 1, showing that an increase in income of 1 per cent causes an increase in demand by less than 1 per cent.

Income elasticity is calculated in a similar way to price elasticity except that it is income which is changing rather than the price of the good:

$$\text{Income elasticity} = \frac{\% \text{ change in quantity demanded}}{\% \text{ change in income}}$$

Table 1.14 Income elasticity and total expenditure

Type of good	Income elasticity	Change in total expenditure brought about by an increase in income of 1%
Inferior	Negative	Downward
Normal	Positive	Upward
Luxury	Positive and above 1	Upward by more than 1%
Necessity	Positive between 0 and 1	Upward by less than 1%

The effect of changes in income on the overall level of expenditure depends upon the type of the good being considered, as Table 1.14 shows.

Cross-price elasticity of demand

Cross-price elasticity of demand is a measure of how the demand for one good is affected by changes in the prices of other goods. It is calculated with the formula:

$$\text{Cross-price elasticity} = \frac{\%\text{ change in quantity demanded of good X}}{\%\text{ change in the price of good Y}}$$

Like income elasticity it can be positive or negative depending this time upon the nature of the relationship between the goods. If the goods are substitutes for one another, as the price of Y goes up, the quantity demanded of X will also rise, as consumers substitute the relatively cheaper good (e.g. margarine for butter). Therefore cross-price elasticity will be positive. If the goods are complements, as the price of Y rises the demand for X will fall and cross-price elasticity will be a negative value. The size will depend upon how closely the goods are related, either as substitutes or complements.

Elasticity of supply

The concept of elasticity can be applied to supply as well as demand, and is a measurement of how responsive quantity supplied is to changes in the price of a good. Figure 1.25 illustrates two differently shaped supply curves and the effect of the same price change in each case.

Elasticity of supply is measured with the following formula:

$$\text{Elasticity of supply} = \frac{\%\text{ change in quantity supplied}}{\%\text{ change in price}}$$

The higher the numerical value, the more responsive is supply to changes in price.

The main determinants of the elasticity of supply for a good are the nature of the production process and the time-scale in question. It may well be easier to increase the supply of manufactured goods than agricultural goods, given the nature of the production processes involved. Even agricultural goods can be increased in supply,

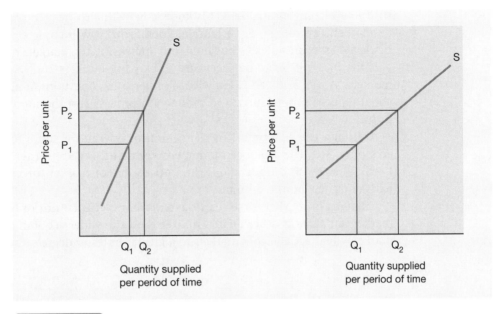

Figure 1.25 Responsiveness of supply to a price change

given time to replant stock, so supply is more responsive to price changes in the longer time period.

The importance of the market to business

All firms operate in markets, whether they are localised, national or international. Although firms might be able to influence the market conditions that face them, they need a knowledge of their own markets and how markets fit together in the market economy. Firms often have a range of products and they need to be aware of the differing conditions in each of their markets. They need a knowledge of the shape and position of the demand curve they face, including knowledge of the following aspects:

- The nature of the good they produce.
- The way in which it is viewed by consumers.
- The factors which affect the demand for their good.
- Any changes likely in the future which will affect the market.
- Any likely government intervention in the market.

Only through this information can the firm hope to retain markets, expand existing markets and move into new ones.

An understanding is also needed of the concept of elasticity of demand. Knowing how the demand for its product responds to changes in its price will help the firm in its pricing policy. Measures of income elasticity help the firm in forecasting the effects of changes in income on the demand for its products. Economic growth will affect markets with high income elasticities much more than markets with low income elasticities. This knowledge will also help the firm in developing its marketing strategy. For example, goods with low income elasticities could be marketed as 'economical', thus hopefully increasing the market share.

If the firm wishes to be successful in existing markets and to expand into new markets, as well as detailed knowledge of demand conditions, it also needs to know about its own supply curve and production process and the supply curves of other firms.

Although the economy in which the firm operates is not a totally free market economy (see 'The macroeconomic environment' earlier in the chapter), the firm needs to know and understand the importance of market forces which form the basis of our economic system.

Changes in market forces can have dramatic effects, not only on the affected market but also on other related markets and the wider economy. Changes in one market will affect all other markets to a greater or lesser degree.

The resource context

Introduction

The main aim of business is to produce goods and services that people want. This production cannot take place without people, technology and natural resources. In economics these three are called the factors of production and are categorised under the headings of labour, capital and land. This section will consider each of these in turn. Resources can be renewable or non-renewable. **Renewable resources** would include labour, water, fishing stocks, soil, air and solar power even though many of these might not be renewable for a long period of time. **Non-renewable resources** would be most minerals including oil, iron ore and coal, agricultural land, forests and electricity (in so far as most electricity is derived from minerals).

People

People are important in the economy as both producers and consumers of goods and services. For most products that are produced people are the most important input into the production process. Therefore the quantity and quality of the people available in an economy will have a considerable impact upon the economy's ability to produce.

The quantity of people available for work depends upon a variety of factors:

● the size of the total population;
● the age structure of the population;
● the working population;
● the length of the working week; and
● the wage level.

As well as the quantity of labour, productivity will be affected by its quality. This in turn depends upon:

● education and training;
● working conditions;
● welfare services (e.g. national insurance schemes which cover sickness pay, the NHS which maintains the health of workers; also many firms provide their own welfare services like private pension plans, and so on);
● motivation; and
● the quality of the other factors of production.

In this section we concentrate on the idea of the 'workforce' and associated issues, before considering the question of labour quality.

The workforce

The **workforce** is the number of people who are eligible and available to work and offer themselves up as such. The size of the workforce will be determined by the age at which people can enter employment, which in the United Kingdom is 16 years, and the age at which they leave employment. In the United Kingdom the retirement age for men is 65 years and for women will be 65 by 2020. Those included in the definition of the workforce are:

- those working in paid employment, even if they are over retirement age;
- part-time workers;
- the claimant unemployed;
- members of the armed forces; and
- the self-employed.

The workforce in 2008 was 31.7 million, which is about 51 per cent of the total population. The importance of the workforce is twofold: it produces the goods and services needed in the economy; and through the payment of taxes it supports the dependent population (i.e. the very old and the very young).

An important determinant of the size of the workforce is the participation rate (i.e. the proportion of the population who actually work).

Table 1.15 shows that the participation rate for women in the UK was 74.2 per cent in the summer of 2008; somewhat lower than the male figure of 83.8 per cent. The figures have, however, been converging over the years. Activity rates were higher for married than unmarried women.

Table 1.15 Economic activity by gender (% men 16–64 and women 16–59), June 2008

	Men	Women
Economically active	83.8	74.2
In employment	80.0	72.5
Unemployed	3.8	1.7
Economically inactive	16.2	25.8

Source: Adapted from various tables, *www.statistics.gov.uk*.

The trend has been for increased participation rates for women over time as families have become smaller and because of the changing role of women in society as a whole, labour-saving devices in the home, and government legislation to promote equal pay and treatment. Also important in this process are the changes in industrial structure which have led to more part-time service jobs.

The participation rates for both married and unmarried women have moved in a cyclical way, both dipping during the recession of the early 1980s. The general trend, however, is quite different. The participation rate of unmarried women fell between 1973 and 1998 (74 per cent to 66 per cent of the 16–59/64 age group). The participation rate for married women increased dramatically over the same period, from 55 per cent in 1973 to 74 per cent in 1998.

Table 1.16 gives some comparisons with other EU countries. The United Kingdom has the second-highest activity rates for men and women after Denmark. There are marked differences in the activity rates for women across the EU, but in every country they were lower than the male activity rate.

web link

For more information on albour markets see *www.dti.gov.uk*, *http://europa.eu.int/comn/eurostat* and *www.oecd.org*

Table 1.16 Economic activity rates* by sex for selected EU countries (%), 2006

	Males	*Females*	*All*
UK	77.3	65.8	71.5
France	68.5	57.7	63.0
Germany	72.8	62.2	67.5
Belgium	67.9	54.0	61.0
Italy	70.5	46.3	58.4
Denmark	81.2	73.4	77.4
EU-27 average	71.6	57.2	64.4

Note: * As a percentage of the working-age population.
Source: Adapted from Table 4.7, *Social Trends*, 2007, ONS, UK.

The length of the working week

The average length of time for which people work is also a significant determinant of the quantity of labour that is available in an economy. Generally, the shorter the working week, the less labour there is available. There has been, over the last hundred years, a gradual reduction in the length of the working week; 40 hours is now roughly the norm, with a gradual increase in the number of holidays that people take. More recently this trend has been reversed: the average working week in the UK was 43 hours in 2007. Table 1.17 shows the length of the average working week in selected EU countries.

Table 1.17 Average hours worked per week* for selected EU countries, 2007

	All
UK	43.0
France	41.0
Germany	41.7
Belgium	41.2
Italy	41.1
Denmark	40.4
Netherlands	40.9
EU 15 average	41.8
EU 25 average	41.8

Note: * Full-time employees.
Source: Eurostat, 2008.

Both men and women in the UK work a longer week than men and women in all other EU countries.

Innovation and technology

There are two types of innovation that can occur as a result of technological change: product innovation and process innovation. Product innovation is the development of new products, like the microprocessor, which will have far-reaching effects on business. New products impact upon the industrial structure of a country, as new industries grow and old industries disappear. This in turn will lead to changes in the occupational structure of the workforce, as we have seen. It has even had the effect of reducing the benefits large firms derive from economies of scale in cases where the technological change can be exploited by small firms as well as it can by large firms. Another example of product innovation which has affected the level of competition in the market is the development of quartz watches, which allowed Japan to enter the market and compete with Switzerland. Process innovation, on the other hand, refers to changes that take place in the production process, like the introduction of assembly-line production in the manufacture of cars. The two types of innovation are related, as the above examples show. The microprocessor (product innovation), which is a new product, has led to massive changes in the way that production and offices operate (process innovation).

Not all innovation is technological in nature; for example, changes in fashion in clothing are not technological. Innovative activity is important for all industry whether manufacturing or non-manufacturing. In some industries (e.g. pharmaceuticals, computers), innovation is essential if firms wish to remain competitive. A CBI survey of 408 companies in the UK found that the innovation activities of 84 per cent of the sample had been adversely affected by the economic slowdown post-September 11.[14]

For further information on research by the CBI see
www.cbi.org.uk (Confederation of British Industry)

Research and development

Most, but not all, technological changes have occurred through the process of **research and development** (R&D). 'Research' can be theoretical or applied, and 'development' refers to the using of the research in the production process. Most research and development carried out by private companies is directed towards applied research and development. It is designed to develop new products and production processes which will render production more profitable. It is also aimed at improving existing products and processes. Most basic theoretical research carried out in the United Kingdom is financed from public sources and is undertaken in places like the universities.

Table 1.18 shows that the level of research and development expenditure in the UK in 2006 was £14 306 million, which represents around 2 per cent of GDP. It can be seen that there are wide differences in expenditure between industries, with manufacturing involved in a great deal more research and development spending than non-manufacturing. Even within the broad category of manufacturing there are wide differences, with chemicals accounting for more than a quarter of the expenditure. Table 1.19 shows the sources from which R&D is financed. As can be seen the majority of R&D is financed by companies themselves. If R&D is split into civil and defence spending, it is clear that the government finances the majority of defence R&D, as would be expected.

For information on R&D see *www.oecd.org* or *http://europa.eu.int/comm.eurostat*

Table 1.18 Spending on R&D (£ million) in 2006 (2006 prices)

Product group	£ million	% of total
All product groups	14 306	100
All products of manufacturing industry	10 796	77
Chemical industries	4 624	33
Mechanical engineering	874	6
Electrical machinery	1 216	9
Aerospace	1 836	13
Transport	913	7
Other manufactured products	1 333	9
Non-manufactured products	3 322	24

Source: Adapted from Table 20.4, *Annual Abstract of Statistics*, ONS, UK, 2007.

Table 1.19 Sources of funds for R&D within industry in the UK for selected years

	1985	1989	1990	1993	1996	1999	2000	2001	2002	2003	2004	2005	2006
Total (£ million)	5 122	7 650	8 082	9 069	9 362	10 231	10 417	11 164	11 865	12 163	12 668	13 310	14 306
Government funds (%)	23	17	17	12	10	10	9	9	7	9	10	8	8
Overseas funds (%)	11	13	15	15	22	23	21	24	27	24	23	27	27
Mainly own funds (%)	66	69	68	72	69	67	70	67	66	67	66	65	65

Source: Adapted from *Annual Abstract of Statistics*, various years, ONS, UK.

Figure 1.26 shows that the UK tends to fare badly in international comparisons of research and development spending.

In an attempt to increase the level of R&D spending, the UK government introduced R&D tax credits for small companies in the 2000 budget. This scheme was extended to all companies in 2002. By 2006 the number of successful claims had reached 22 000.

Limits to technological change

Technological change has many effects on the economy and the environment and if uncontrolled can lead to problems, like high levels of unemployment or the exhaustion of natural resources. One area of concern is energy. The world's stock of energy is finite and we are still heavily dependent upon fuel which was formed millions of years ago. The development of nuclear power again represents a finite source of energy, and also carries with it other problems like the disposal of nuclear waste and the possibility of accidents. For these and other reasons the scale of technological change needs to be controlled.

It is also the case that technological change can lead to high levels of unemployment in industries that are in decline. This type of unemployment often takes on a regional bias as the older traditional industries tend to be located in particular parts of the country. Technological unemployment is in some respects inevitable as in a

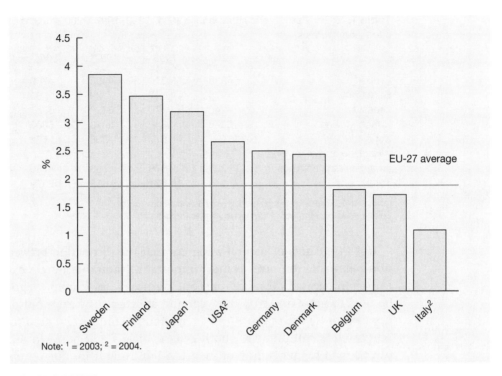

Note: [1] = 2003; [2] = 2004.

Figure 1.26 R&D spending as a percentage of GDP, all sectors, selected countries, 2005 unless otherwise indicated

Source: Chapter 5, *Eurostat Yearbook*, 2007.

changing world it would be expected that new industries would emerge and old industries die. The problem can be tackled by the government and industry through retraining, but what is also needed is a new and more flexible view of work where less time is spent working and more on leisure. Technological change can also give rise to the opposite problem of skill shortage in new industries, where particular skills are required. Technological change has not led to the massive increase in unemployment predicted by many in the 1970s and 1980s.

Natural resources

In economics, **natural resources** are put under the heading of **land** as a factor of production. It would include all natural resources like the soil, minerals, oil, forests, fish, water, the sun, and so on. The uneven distribution of natural resources throughout the world means that they can be used as economic and political weapons.

Although the area of land in a country is fixed, land as a factor of production is not completely fixed in supply as more land can be made available through land reclamation schemes and better irrigation. The productivity of agricultural land can be increased by the use of fertilisers. It is true, however, that our natural resources are in finite supply. And often their true extent is not known with certainty.

Table 1.20 The use of agricultural land in 1971, 1993, 1997, 2000, 2003 and 2007 in the UK (thousand hectares)

	1971	1993	1997	2000	2003	2007
Crops	4838	4519	4990	4709	4478	4350
Bare fallow	74	47	29	33	29	165
Grasses	7240	6770	6687	6767	6884	7141
Rough grazing*	6678	5840	5878	5803	5565	5552
Set aside	–	677	306	572	689	440
Woodland and other land on agricultural holdings	285	678	763	789	792	954
Total	19 115	18 531	18 653	18 579	18 438	18 602

Note: * Includes sole-right rough grazing and common rough grazing.
Source: Adapted from Table 21.3, *Annual Abstract of Statistics*, ONS, UK, 2008.

It is in the area of natural resources that the distinction between renewable and non-renewable resources is most important. Natural resources can be either. Land can often be used for more than one purpose – for example, agricultural land can be used to grow one crop one year and another the next – but oil, once it is used up, cannot be used again. And even though land can be used for more than one purpose it is still immobile both geographically and between different uses. Land can be used for agriculture or industry, but using it for one purpose makes it more difficult to use it for another. If a factory is built on a piece of land, it would be both expensive and time consuming to clear the land for farming.

Table 1.20 shows the changing usage of agricultural land in the UK between 1971 and 2007. There are slight differences between the years, most notably the inclusion of 'set aside' land in the 1993, 1997, 2000, 2003 and 2007 columns. This was part of EU Common Agricultural Policy where farmers were paid not to use land in an attempt to reduce the overproduction of agricultural goods.

Protection of the environment

Increased knowledge of the effects of depletion of natural resources has led to increased environmental awareness among the population. There has been an increased interest in conservation and recycling and the search for alternative forms of energy. A survey by the Department of the Environment found that 90 per cent of the adult population in the UK were either 'fairly concerned' or 'very concerned' about the environment. The issues which caused concern included traffic congestion, global warming, air and water pollution and depletion of the ozone layer. This change in public opinion has already had a major impact on the way in which business operates and is likely to have even bigger effects.

Governments in the UK and elsewhere have a variety of targets for environmental protection relating to issues such as greenhouse gas emissions, biodiversity, renewable energy, recycling, packaging and so on. Some of these targets are set through negotiations with other countries at both international (e.g. Kyoto Protocol) and supranational (e.g. EU) levels and hence are influenced by political, economic, social and technological considerations and by a variety of state and non-state actors. Given the growing importance of environmental issues in business, a separate chapter on ethics and the natural environment has been added below.

Pressure groups concerned with the environment include
www.foe.co.uk (Friends of the Earth) and *www.greenpeace.org*

mini case   Oil prices

The Organisation of Petroleum Exporting Countries (OPEC) was formed in 1960 as a cartel of the major producers and exporters of crude petroleum. It did not have much impact upon the market until the 1970s when it enforced massive increases in the price of oil. It did this through cutting back on the supply of oil, as shown in Figure 1.27. The demand curve (DD) for oil is drawn as highly inelastic in shape. The supply curve for oil prior to 1973 is shown as SS, and the equilibrium price of oil was $2.50 per barrel. In 1973 OPEC exercised its market power by restricting the output of oil to Q_2. As a result of this the price of oil rose to $12.00 per barrel.

In 2008 it is difficult to believe that the price of oil was ever $2.50 per barrel. Up to 2003 the price of oil remained below $25 per barrel but volatility in the market and rapid price rises after 9/11 and the invasion of Iraq saw a peak of $140 per barrel in June 2008. Why have prices been so volatile and why have they risen so rapidly? There are two main reasons:

1 Supply factors

No one knows the true extent of oil reserves in the world but they are finite; in the UK, for example, North Sea oil production has halved since 1999. In addition, OPEC does not want to see the price of oil fall to too low a level and will manipulate supply to achieve this. The power of OPEC to raise price in such a way depends upon its ability to restrict the supply of oil to Q_2. There are two provisos to this:

● Inherent in the operation of cartels is the incentive to cheat since if one country exceeds its quota its profitability will be increased at the expense of other countries. Such cheating was commonplace in OPEC from the late 1970s onwards. In addition to this, OPEC does not control as much of the world supply of oil as it did – it accounts for only 40 per cent of world oil production (down from 70 per cent in 1973). Both of these mean that OPEC has less power to restrict supply.

● OPEC does not want the price of oil to be too high as it encourages the search for alternative sources of energy. In the 1970s higher prices encouraged energy saving and the search for alternative sources and forms of energy.

OPEC has stated that it would like to see the price of oil remain around $100 per barrel.

2 Demand factors

The demand for oil is high and rising, especially in the developing countries. It is estimated that Russia, India and China consume 20.7 million barrels of oil per day – taking up the reduction in demand from the US where oil consumption fell in the first half of 2008. In addition, speculation on the future price of oil has also had a big impact upon demand. When growth rates slow down

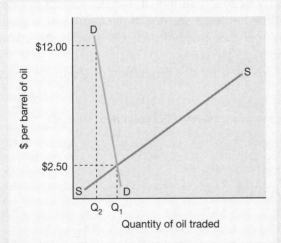

Figure 1.27   The operation of OPEC in the market for oil

investors tend to move into commodities like oil. Predictions that the price of oil could reach $200 per barrel have not helped. Speculation has two effects – it makes the price more volatile, but also means that price responds to factors which are based on perceptions rather than real forces. For example, the seemingly unrelated testing of rockets in North Korea had an impact on oil prices.

The weakening of the US$ has impacted upon the price of oil as oil is traded in dollars – it takes more dollars to buy the same amount of oil. The strengthening of the US$ and the acceptance of a rescue package for the US financial markets in October 2008 led to a fall in the price of oil to $93 dollars per barrel, but it is difficult to predict what will happen in the future. In the short term at least the anticipated worldwide recession in the wake of the global financial crisis is likely to result in a reduction in oil prices and seems destined to trigger a response from OPEC in the form of a reduction in supply in order to stop oil prices falling.

Table 1.21 Primary usage of energy in the UK (heat supplied basis); percentage of total

	1950	1970	2000	2001	2002	2003	2004	2005	2006
Solid fuel	78.6	30.7	6.8	7.2	6.9	6.8	6.5	5.9	5.9
Gas	5.9	10.7	37.6	38.2	40.0	39.6	40.4	40.8	40.7
Oil	12.2	47.2	47.9	46.1	46.5	44.7	43.8	42.9	42.7
Electricity	3.3	11.4	7.0	7.6	7.6	7.8	7.8	8.8	9.0
Renewable energy	–	–	0.9	0.9	1.0	1.2	1.3	1.7	1.8

Source: Adapted from Table 22.4, *Annual Abstract of Statistics*, ONS, 2008.

One important resource in business whose exploitation and use has a significant impact on the natural environment is energy. The UK is not well endowed with high-grade minerals; the main natural resource is energy. There is a good deposit of coal and the discovery of North Sea oil and gas has made the UK self-sufficient in energy supplies. The usage of energy has doubled since 1970 but as Table 1.21 shows there has been a change in the relative importance of the different sources of energy.

Coal has lost its place to oil and gas as the most important sources of energy. The increase in the usage of both oil and gas is due to the discovery of North Sea oil and gas in the UK. The biggest single user of energy in the UK is transport (33 per cent of energy produced), followed by the domestic sector (28 per cent) and industry (20 per cent). A small but growing source of energy in the UK is renewables, with the government's target by 2020 being 15 per cent.

There is great variation in the fuels used for the generation of electricity across Europe as Table 1.22 shows.

Table 1.22 Fuel used for electricity generation, selected EU countries (%), 2004

	Nuclear	Coal and ignite	Oil	Gas	Renewable energy	Other
France	78.3	4.5	1.0	3.7	11.5	0.9
Belgium	55.4	10.7	2.0	27.9	2.3	1.8
Sweden	51.1	0.7	1.3	1.0	45.4	0.5
Spain	22.7	28.3	8.5	20.2	18.0	2.3
Germany	27.5	48.3	1.7	11.6	9.6	1.3
UK	20.2	33.3	1.2	39.9	3.7	1.6
Netherlands	3.8	23.3	2.8	63.3	6.6	0.2
EU-15	32.3	25.4	4.7	21.4	14.8	1.5
EU-25	31.0	29.5	4.5	19.9	13.7	1.4

Source: Adapted from Figure 3, *Electricity Production by Fuel*, European Environment Agency, 2008.

There has been a dramatic rise in the amount of electricity generated by nuclear power and several EU countries use it as their primary generator of electricity. While its use produces lower emissions of greenhouse gases, there is an increased risk of accidental leakage of radioactivity as well as the problem of the disposal of radioactive waste. Electricity generation from oil and gas has tended to fall and an EU Directive now requires 20 per cent of electricity (for the EU-15 countries) to come from renewable sources by 2020. There is clearly a growing demand for alternative sources of energy. The alternatives of hydro, wind and solar energy sources will also grow in importance. In the UK the government has tried to promote the search for renewable energy sources through projects like the Non-Fossil Fuel Obligation which requires regional electricity boards to obtain a certain percentage of their electricity from clean sources. It also funds experimental work in the search for new sources of energy.

As well as recycling and searching for new sources of energy there is the concept of 'negademand' where the use of less produces negative demand for those commodities. This concept can be applied to energy and water saving, driving, shopping, etc.

For information on the natural environment in the UK see
www.environment-agency.gov.uk or *www.the-environment-council.org.uk* or
www.business-in-the-environment.org.uk
In the EU see *www.eea.eu.int* (The European Environment Agency) or
www.europa.eu.int/comm/environment/index
In the world see *www.oecd.org*

The global context of business

Introduction

Businesses operate in a global context: even if they do not trade directly with other countries, they might be affected by a domestic shortage of skilled labour or may be subject to developments on the global financial markets. There is a difference between globalisation and internationalisation in the business literature but both result in increased exposure to global forces. This means that businesses need an understanding of the process of globalisation. The nature of globalisation is changing; it used to mean the westernisation of the developing world but the newly emerging economies such as Brazil, China and India are redefining processes and institutions. In 1980 the share of the developing countries in world trade was 22 per cent, by 2005 it was 32 per cent and the World Bank predicts that their share will be 45 per cent by 2030. Globalisation is here to stay, despite apparent retreat into nationalism in light of economic conditions in 2008, so all businesses need to be aware of their global context.

Globalisation versus internationalisation

These terms are often used interchangeably but they refer to different processes. Although there is not a single accepted definition of globalisation, it is a term used to describe the process of integration on a worldwide scale of markets and production. The world is moving away from a system of national markets that are isolated from one another by trade barriers, distance or culture. Advances in technology and mass communications have made it possible for people in one part of the world to watch happenings in far off places on television or via the Internet. So, for globalisation, national boundaries are not important economically; free trade and movement of labour and other resources result in the breakdown of these boundaries and one big global marketplace. Internationalisation, on the other hand, refers to the increased links between nation states with respect to trade and the movement of resources. The important thing here is that the nation state is still important; it is participating and co-operating with other nation states to a common end.

Regionalism and regional trade agreements are important in this process – the EU is an example. The main difference is that with internationalisation, the nation state remains important whereas the process of globalisation breaks down the barriers between nation states. An extreme view of this process is called 'hyperglobalisation', where the world market is seen as a borderless global marketplace consisting of powerless nation states and powerful multinational corporations.[15] The more generally accepted view is called 'transformationalism', which sees the process of globalisation as bringing about *changes* in both the power of countries and companies and in national characteristics and culture.[16] Any differences do not disappear but are maintained, albeit in changed forms. The population in India might drink Coca-Cola and listen to western music, but this does not mean that they hold the same views and values as the west. Similarly, even within the EU national differences remain important (especially in times of crisis).

Although these definitions are important theoretically, they are difficult to apply in practice, so here the term globalisation is used to mean the process of integration of markets, however that happens. Until recently globalisation meant the westernisation (or Americanisation) of markets but the world has started to change. Companies from **emerging economies** have started to compete with the older **multinational enterprises (MNEs)** and the nature of the MNE is being redefined. Globalisation has taken place because of closer economic ties between countries and because of developments in mass communications, in transportation, electronics and the greater mobility of labour. A heated debate has taken place over the past decade between the pro- and the anti-globalisation lobbies.

The arguments put forward by the proponents of globalisation stem from the benefits brought about by increased international trade and specialisation (see 'International markets and trade' later in the chapter for a discussion). They argue that all countries open to international trade have benefited – only those that are closed to international trade (some African countries, for example) have become poorer. In the case of China, the opening up to world trade in 1978 has led to increases in GDP per capita, up from $1460 per head in 1980 to $5400 per head in 2007. The pro-globalisation arguments can be summarised as follows:

- increased globalisation leads to greater specialisation so that all countries involved benefit from the increased international trade;
- countries that are open to international trade have experienced much faster growth than countries that are not;
- barriers to trade encourage industries to be inefficient and uncompetitive;
- it is not just the large multinationals that benefit from globalisation – small and medium-sized companies are also engaged in global production and marketing.

The arguments against globalisation are just as strong. It is claimed that the benefits of higher world output and growth brought about through globalisation have not been shared equally by all countries. The main beneficiaries have been the large multinationals rather than individual countries or people. It is suggested that the international organisations that promote free trade should pay more attention to the issues of equity, human rights and environment rather than focusing simply on trade. It is also argued that increased globalisation leads to economic instability. The anti-globalisation arguments can be summarised thus:

- the benefits of globalisation have not been shared equitably throughout the world;
- globalisation undermines the power of nation states – it empowers the large multinationals at the expense of governments – many multinationals are financially bigger than nation states;
- the large organisations that promote free trade (such as the WTO and the IMF) are not democratically elected and their decisions are not made in the public eye;
- the policies of these organisations are only aimed at trade – human rights and environmental concerns are often ignored.

The main international organisations concerned with globalisation are the World Trade Organisation (WTO), the International Monetary Fund (IMF), the World Bank and the OECD. In addition to these there is the United Nations Conference on Trade and Development (UNCTAD), which is a permanent intergovernmental body of the United Nations that aims to maximise investment to the developing nations and to help them in their integration into the world economy.

There are several key elements of economic globalisation: international trade; foreign direct investment; and capital market flows. The OECD categorises members into three bands – high income countries, which includes the EU, North America and Australasia; middle income countries, which includes East Asia and the Pacific Rim; and low income countries, which includes South Asia and Africa.

International trade

The share of international trade in goods as a percentage of GDP increased between 1990 and 2005 for all income groups and particularly for the middle income group (see Table 1.23). The same is true for services. Thus there is evidence of increased globalisation. Note that there are differences within each group; in the low income group, for example, although the share has increased overall, there are countries that have experienced negative growth (Botswana and Paraguay for instance – both of which are open to international trade). Although the share of developing countries has increased over time, world markets are still dominated by the developed world, especially in high-value, high-tech products. It is also true that increased trade does not automatically lead to increased development as in parts of sub-Saharan Africa where the products sold are basic primary products.

Table 1.23 Elements of economic globalisation

	Trade in goods as a % of GDP		Gross private capital flows as a % of GDP		Gross FDI as a % of GDP	
	1990	2005	1990	2005	1990	2005
Low income	23.6	41.1	2.4	6.7	0.4	1.5
Middle income	32.5	62.1	6.6	13.3	0.9	3.1
High income	32.3	43.9	11.0	37.2	1.0	2.1

Source: Adapted from Table 6.1, *World Development Indicators*, 2007, World Bank, *www.worldbank.org/data/wdi2007.index.html*.

Capital market flows

This refers to the flows of money from private savers wishing to include foreign assets in their portfolios. This has also increased in all income bands between 1990 and 2005 (Table 1.23). The overall figures hide a greater volatility than in international trade or foreign direct investment and the fact that the flows have been largely restricted to emerging economies in East Asia. Capital market flows occur because investors want to diversify their portfolios to include foreign assets; it is therefore aimed at bringing about short-term capital gains. Unlike foreign direct investment, there is no long-term involvement on the part of the investor.

Foreign direct investment (FDI)

This refers to the establishment of production facilities in overseas countries and therefore represents a more direct involvement in the local economy (than capital market flows) and a longer-term relationship. Between 1990 and 2000, the value of **FDI** worldwide more than doubled – the two biggest recipients and donors were the UK and the USA. Since 2000 FDI has fallen in line with world economic recession but it recovered slightly by 2004 (Table 1.23). FDI represents the largest form of private capital inflow into the developing countries. The importance of FDI is considered in the case study at the end of the chapter.

Each of the three elements of economic globalisation has a different effect and carries different consequences for countries. Capital market flows are much more volatile and therefore carry higher risk – these flows introduce the possibility of 'boom and bust' for countries where capital market flows are important. The financial crises in the emerging Asian countries in the late 1990s had a lot to do with these capital flows. Openness to trade and FDI are less volatile and it is these that are favoured by the international organisations such as the World Bank and the WTO. It is also true that the benefits of globalisation have not been shared equally between those taking part – the developed nations have reaped more benefit than the poorer nations.

The role of multinational enterprises

Substantial amounts of foreign trade and hence movements of currency result from the activities of very large multinational companies or enterprises. Multinational enterprises/companies (MNEs/MNCs), strictly defined, are enterprises operating in a number of countries and having production or service facilities outside the country of their origin. These multinationals usually have their headquarters in a developed country but this is beginning to change. At one time globalisation meant that businesses were expanding from developed to developing economies. The world is a different place now – business flows in the opposite direction and often between developing countries. One indication of this is the number of companies from the emerging nations that appear in the Fortune 500 list of the world's biggest companies. Between 2003 and 2007 it had doubled from 31 to 62. Most of these come from Brazil, Russia, India and China (the BRIC countries) and include Infosys, an Indian multinational IT services company, and Lenovo, a Chinese computer manufacturer which bought IBM's personal computer business in 2005. These companies offer a different model of an MNE from the traditional one. Lenovo, for example, does not regard itself as a Chinese company; it does not have headquarters in a particular country although its marketing department is located in Bangalore – meetings of managers rotate between countries where the company has a presence.

Multinationals can diversify their operations across different countries and many are well-known household names (see Table 1.24). The footloose nature of such companies brings with it certain benefits.

Table 1.24 The world's ten largest non-financial MNEs, ranked by foreign assets, 2006

Rank	Company	Home economy	Transnationality index %*
1	General Electric	United States	53
2	British Petroleum Company plc	UK	80
3	Toyota Motor Corporation	Japan	45
4	Royal Dutch/Shell group	UK/Netherlands	70
5	Exxon Mobil Corporation	United States	68
6	Ford Motor Company	United States	50
7	Vodafone Group plc	United Kingdom	85
8	Total	France	74
9	Electicite De France	France	35
10	Wal-Mart Stores	United States	41

Note: * Measured as the average of three ratios: foreign assets to total assets, foreign sales to total sales, and foreign employment to total employment.
Source: Adapted from Annex Table A1.15, *World Develpment Report*, UNCTAD, 2008.

1 MNEs can locate their activities in the countries which are best suited for them. For example, production planning can be carried out in the parent country, the production itself can be carried out in one of the newly industrialised countries where labour is relatively cheap and marketing can be done in the parent country where such activities are well developed. The relocation of production may go some way to explaining the decline in the manufacturing sector in the developed nations.

2 An MNE can cross-subsidise its operations. Profits from one market can be used to support operations in another one. The **cross-subsidisation** could take the form of price cutting, increasing productive capacity or heavy advertising.

3 The risk involved in production is spread, not just over different markets but also over different countries.

4 MNEs can avoid tax by negotiating special tax arrangements in one of their host countries (tax holidays) or through careful use of **transfer pricing**. Transfer prices are the prices at which internal transactions take place. These can be altered so that high profits can be shown in countries where the tax rate is lower. For example, in the USA in 1999 two-thirds of foreign-based multinationals paid no federal income tax. The loss to US taxpayers from this has been estimated as in excess of $40 billion per year in unpaid taxes.

5 MNEs can take advantage of subsidies and tax exemptions offered by governments to encourage start-ups in their country.

The very size of MNEs gives rise to concern as their operations can have a substantial impact upon the economy. For example, the activities of MNEs will affect the labour market of host countries and the balance of payments. If a subsidiary is started in one country there will be an inflow of capital to that country. Once it is up and running, however, there will be outflows of dividends and profits which will affect the invisible balance. Also, there will be flows of goods within the company, and therefore between countries, in the form of semi-finished goods and raw materials. These movements will affect the exchange rate as well as the balance of payments and it is likely that the effects will be greater for developing countries than for developed countries.

There is also the possibility of exploitation of less developed countries, and it is debatable whether such footloose industries form a viable basis for economic development. Added to this, MNEs take their decisions in terms of their overall operations rather than with any consideration of their effects on the host economy. There is therefore a loss of economic sovereignty for national governments.

The main problem with multinationals is the lack of control that can be exerted by national governments. In June 2005 the OECD updated its *Guidelines for Multinational Enterprises*, which are not legally binding but are promoted by OECD member governments. These seek to provide a balanced framework for international investment that clarifies both the rights and responsibilities of the business community. It contains guidelines on business ethics, employment relations, information disclosure and taxation, among other things. In 2008 the International Accounting Standards Board is considering a proposal which would force the world's giant oil and mining companies to reveal the amount of tax paid in each country in which they have a presence. If successful, this could be in place by 2010 but there is already high-level lobbying taking place to water down the proposal. Against all this is the fact that without the presence of MNEs, output in host countries would be lower, and there is evidence that on labour market issues the multinationals do not perform badly.

Transnationality

The transnationality index gives a measure of an MNE's involvement abroad by looking at three ratios – foreign asset/total asset, foreign sales/total sales and foreign employment/total employment. As such it captures the importance of foreign activities in its overall activities. In Table 1.24 Vodafone Group plc has the highest index – this is because in all three ratios it has a high proportion of foreign involvement. Since 1990 the average index of transnationality for the top 100 MNEs has increased from 51 per cent to 55 per cent.

These multinationals are huge organisations and their market values often exceed the GNP of many of the countries in which they operate. There are over 60 000 MNEs around the world and they are estimated to account for a quarter of the world's output. The growth in MNEs is due to relaxation of exchange controls, making it easier to move money between countries, and the improvements in communication, which makes it possible to run a worldwide business from one country. The importance of multinationals varies from country to country, as Table 1.25 shows.

As can be seen, foreign affiliates are very important for some countries and not so important for others; in the case of Japan there is hardly any foreign presence at all. For all of the countries, except Finland, foreign affiliates have a bigger impact on production than employment.

Table 1.25 Share of foreign affiliates in manufacturing production and employment, 2004

Country	% share of foreign affiliates in manufacturing production	% share of foreign affiliates in manufacturing employment
Ireland	80	48
Hungary	63	42
Czech Republic	52	37
UK	41	26
Netherlands	41	25
Luxembourg	34	25
Germany	27	16
USA	21	11
Finland	16	17
Italy	15	7
Japan	3	1

Source: Adapted from OECD Science, Technology and Industry Scoreboard 2007.

Globalisation and business

Businesses of all sizes need to have an awareness of their international context. As noted above, even if they are not directly involved in international trade, firms will be affected by international forces that lie largely outside their control. Globalisation has meant that the financial crisis of 2008, for instance, has affected virtually the whole world. Some of the issues facing businesses are discussed below in brief; many of them are discussed later in the book in more detail.

Markets

Globalisation means that firms are faced with bigger markets for their products. Many of these markets are covered by **regional trade agreements (RTAs)**, which are groupings of countries set up to facilitate world trade. All such agreements have to be notified to the World Trade Organisation and they can take a variety of forms. The most basic relationship and the most common is a **free trade area**, where trade barriers between members are abolished but where each member maintains its own national barriers with non-members. An example of this is the North American Free Trade Agreement (NAFTA). Agreements can also take the form of a **customs union** or common market, where members abolish trade barriers between themselves and adopt a common external tariff which is applied to non-members. An example of this is the EU. All of these agreements increase the size of the marketplace for producers in the member countries and the enlargement of these agreements (the EU for example) means that markets are increasing all of the time.

In addition to these trade agreements, the opening up of the emerging economies (e.g. China and India) to international trade, their high growth rates and the corresponding increase in per capita income mean that there has been a massive increase in the demand for goods and services. The population in India is 1147 million, income per head has doubled since 2000 and GDP growth rate was over 9 per cent per annum between 2005 and 2008. The Chinese population stood at 1330 million in 2007, income per head has almost doubled since 2000 and the average growth rate over the 4 years up to 2008 was 11 per cent.[17] Many believe that China's high growth rate has been fuelled by exports, but recent research shows that demand is more consumption driven than previously thought.[18] It also shows that consumer demand has changed in favour of products that have a higher imported content. This is good news for the rest of the world.

Labour markets

It has been estimated that the global integration of emerging markets has doubled the supply of labour for the global production of goods. The OECD estimates that the percentage of the world population living outside their country of birth doubled between 1985 and 2005. About half of this is between the developed countries, the other half from developing to developed countries.

International labour mobility can be used by businesses for hard to fill vacancies. Typically these are at the low-skill, high-risk and low-paid end of the spectrum and at the high-skill, high-paid end. Legal labour migration can be permanent (where migrants settle permanently) or temporary (where migrants eventually return home). The regulations pertaining to these will differ. In addition to international labour migration there are three other alternatives: outsourcing (for example, the location of US call centres in India involve the movement of jobs rather than people); cross-border commuting (for example, the commuting of Poles into western Europe); or the use of Internet trade (where the work could take place anywhere).

For businesses wishing to recruit internationally, there are practical problems including locating the necessary people and dealing with the rules and regulations involved in employing migrants, such as work permits and visas. These requirements will vary from one country to another.

Other resources

As well as labour, businesses have to source and purchase other resources such as raw materials and energy. Natural resources are differentially distributed around the world and therefore they require international trade to take place if firms are to acquire these inputs. The market for energy, for example, is a global market, with attendant concerns about the environmental impact of the methods used for its generation (see the mini case study, below). The issue of resources was discussed earlier in the chapter (see 'The resource context').

mini case   UK nuclear power industry

The market for energy is global. The European Commission adopted a policy at the end of 2007 designed to promote more competition within the EU energy market. These measures include breaking the link between production and supply of energy and the establishment of an Agency for the co-operation of National Energy Regulators to facilitate cross-border energy trade. In the UK four of the main electricity suppliers are foreign owned: EDF (French), RWE (German owners of npower),

E.ON (German) and Iberdrola (Spanish owners of Scottish Power).

Because of the calls for cleaner forms of energy and the targets set for carbon emissions worldwide, there has been a search for cleaner sources of energy. One possibility is nuclear energy. The use of nuclear power in the generation of electricity in the UK is smaller than many other European countries (France, for example, generates nearly all of its electricity through nuclear power) and the UK government aims to increase this contribution and therefore reduce its reliance on fossil fuels. Of course there are arguments against this that revolve around the safety issues of nuclear power stations.

At the beginning of 2008 British Energy – which owned most of the aged British nuclear plants – was put up for sale. In September 2008 EDF, the French power giant, agreed to buy British Energy. EDF is the biggest nuclear energy producer in the world and one of the largest power suppliers. It already holds 6 per cent of the electricity industry in the UK through direct sales of electricity.

There are arguments for and against the foreign ownership of industries like energy. The main argument against is that energy is a strategic good and it is unwise to allow foreign ownership of such goods. This has been seen recently in the strategic withdrawal of gas supplies to the Ukraine by Russia. Current global economic conditions also highlight a possible problem – when times are bad, foreign-owned companies might ensure that their own consumers are supplied over those of other countries. In addition, in this case it might result in a lack of competition as British Energy owns all but two of Britain's nuclear plants and these are due to close in 2010. Of course, against this there are advantages – it is possible that a country does not have the expertise or, as in the case of building nuclear power stations, companies with the necessary capital to build them. Economies of scale mean that costs of building and maintenance can be kept low.

The proposed takeover has to be cleared by shareholders and regulators in the UK and the EU (although given EU policy it should not be a problem). EDF has plans to expand further worldwide – it already has a bid in for the US energy company Constellation Energy.

Financial markets

Businesses need to raise capital to be able to produce, trade and invest. Although much of this takes place domestically, banks operate internationally and so businesses are exposed to global forces. Never has this been seen more vividly than in the events of 2008 (see mini case study, below).

mini case   Financial markets

The speed with which the global financial crisis spread in 2008 illustrates well how interrelated financial markets are. It started in October 2007 in the USA when Citigroup announced a $6.5 billion write-off of sub-prime mortgage losses. The credit crunch worsened in the US and spread to other parts of the world but came to a head in September 2008. On 15 September Lehman Brothers was declared bankrupt – the largest in US history. That record was broken on 25 September when Washington Mutual was closed. On 29 September the House of Representatives rejected a $700 billion rescue plan for banks saddled with bad mortgage debt (although the plan was subsequently agreed). On 29 September Ireland was the first EU country to be declared officially in recession and the Irish government intervened in the financial markets to protect savers. In the UK, Bradford and Bingley was nationalised and reassurances given to savers. Similar things have been seen in other EU countries but this is not confined to the USA and Europe. In Iceland the three biggest banks have all failed. In Russia several banks have been rescued by the government and trading on the stock market temporarily suspended. The Chinese stock market values fell by 60 per cent in 2008 and the rate of interest was cut in September of that year.

At the time of writing, it is not clear where this will end. Most governments and international organisations have intervened in the markets to reassure the general public and to attempt to maintain confidence in the financial system. It is clear by the speed of all this that countries are not immune to what happens in other countries – financial markets are truly global. It is also clear that this crisis might lead to increased nationalism on the part of individual countries as they try to protect their own populations and businesses.

Globalisation and the small and medium-sized firm

There are problems for small and medium-sized enterprises (SMEs) wishing to trade internationally. They will not have the same access to resources, finance or markets as the large multinationals or even the large national companies which could either trade directly or expand internationally through mergers and takeovers. SMEs, however, have a number of options:

- **Strategic alliances** are collaborative agreements between firms to achieve a common aim, in this context a presence in other markets. These agreements can take many forms.
- **Franchising** is an arrangement where one party (the franchiser) sells the rights to another party (the franchisee) to market its product or service. There are different types of franchise relationship and this is a possibility for international expansion. It is an attractive option for companies seeking international expansion without having to undertake substantial direct investments.
- **Licensing** is where a company (the licensor) authorises a company in another country (the licensee) to use its intellectual property in return for certain considerations, usually royalties. Licensors are usually multinationals located in developed countries.
- **Joint ventures** are usually a jointly owned and independently incorporated business venture involving two or more organisations. This is a popular method of expanding abroad as each party can diversify, with the benefit of the experience of the others involved in the venture and a reduction in the level of risk. Where a large number of members is involved in such an arrangement, this is called a **consortium**.

International markets and trade

Introduction

International markets are important to most firms; even if they do not produce for the export market they may well be dependent upon raw materials which are imported and they will almost definitely be affected by movements in the exchange rate. Britain, like all other advanced industrial countries, is highly dependent upon international markets and that dependence has grown over the years. What makes international trade different from trade within a country is that the trade is taking place across national borders. Thus a system for international payments is needed. It is essential for students of business to have an understanding of international markets, exchange rates and the balance of payments.

International trade – why it takes place

Trade between countries takes place because resources are unevenly distributed through the world and the mobility of the factors of production is limited, consequently some countries are better at producing certain goods than others. Some countries could not actually produce a particular good: for example, Britain cannot produce minerals that are not indigenous or fruit that can only be grown in tropical weather conditions. If there is a demand for these goods in Britain, there are a number of possibilities: either the British could do without these goods; or an attempt could be made to grow them (in the case of the fruit) despite the climatic conditions; or Britain could buy the goods from other countries that can produce them. In other words it can trade for them.

It is easy to see that if country A can produce video cameras more cheaply than country B and B can produce wheat more cheaply than A, **specialisation** should occur and A should produce video cameras and B should produce wheat and they should trade with one another. Complete specialisation is, however, unlikely, for strategic reasons. It is also true that even if country A can produce both goods more cheaply than country B there is scope for benefits from trade. As this may not be so easy to imagine, Table 1.26 gives a numerical example. Country A can produce 100 video cameras or 100 units of wheat using 100 workers. Country B can produce 20 video cameras or 40 units of wheat with the same number of workers. Country A can therefore produce both goods at lower cost than country B. To show that even in this situation trade will benefit the world, assume that both countries produce both goods and that they each devote half of their workforce to each good.

The total output of video cameras is 60 units and of wheat is 70 units. Country A is 5 times more efficient at producing video cameras than country B, but only

Table 1.26 Production of video cameras and wheat

	Number of units that 100 workers can produce	
	Video cameras	Wheat
Country A	100	100
Country B	20	40

Table 1.27 Production of video cameras and wheat

	Video cameras	Wheat
Country A	50	50
Country B	10	20
	–	–
	60	70

Table 1.28 Production of video cameras and wheat

	Video cameras	Wheat
Country A	65	35
Country B	0	40
	–	–
	65	75

2.5 times more efficient than B in producing wheat (see Table 1.27). It would therefore benefit both countries if production was rearranged. If B specialised completely in wheat and A produced 35 units of wheat and 65 video cameras, world output would be as indicated in Table 1.28.

In short, world output has been increased and everyone is better off provided that trade takes place. This simplified example illustrates the basic argument for free trade. Free trade brings the advantages of higher world output and higher standards of living. Countries will produce the goods in which they have a cost advantage and trade with other countries for other goods. So countries can buy goods at lower prices than they could be produced for at home. Where economies of scale are present, the savings as a result of specialisation can be immense.

Theoretically, free trade brings most benefit; however, there are often restrictions to such trade and it is unlikely that complete specialisation will take place. Most countries would regard being totally dependent on another country for a particular good as a risky proposition.

Restrictions to international trade

There are a number of things that governments do to restrict international trade. These restrictions include:

- **Quotas** A physical limitation on the import of certain goods into a country, sometimes by mutual agreement (e.g. voluntary export restraints).
- **Tariffs** A tax placed on imported goods.
- **Exchange controls** A limit to the amount of a currency that can be bought, which will limit the import of goods.
- **Subsidies** Payments made to domestic producers to reduce their costs and therefore make them more competitive on world markets.
- **Qualitative controls** Controls on the quality of goods rather than on quantity or price.

All of these serve to restrict international trade, and therefore reduce specialisation on a world level. They invite retaliation and could lead to inefficiencies. **Import controls** have a wide effect on industry. The 200 per cent tariffs that the Americans threatened to impose on French cheeses and wines at the end of 1992 if the GATT talks were not successful, would have impacted on many other industries like the bottle-making industry or the insurance industry. But there are powerful arguments used in support of import controls. For example, they can be used to protect industries, whether these industries are 'infant' industries or strategic industries. In the 1999 debate within the EU on bananas, it was argued by the African, Caribbean and Pacific countries which receive preferential treatment in the EU for their bananas that the relaxation of these preferential terms might lead to the complete devastation of their economies. Import controls can also be used to improve the balance of payments position in the case where a deficit exists.

The United Kingdom is a member of a number of international organisations that serve to promote free trade and control the restrictions to free trade, like the World Trade Organisation (see the Mini case below).

mini case   The World Trade talks

The 'Doha round' of trade talks was aimed at reducing world trade barriers with the specific aim of helping the developing countries. The talks started in 2001 and were due to end in 2004 but collapsed in 2003 as poorer countries refused to continue until concessions had been promised by the richer countries. Talks restarted in 2004 but stalled again in 2006 and then restarted in July 2008. This time the talks only lasted nine days before they collapsed. There are 149 countries involved in the WTO talks, which makes agreement difficult to achieve. However, there are calls for negotiations to start again as the issues are important. The World Bank estimates that the abolition of agricultural subsidies would increase global trade by $300 billion per year by 2015. Agricultural tariffs and subsidies have disastrous effects on developing countries which are highly dependent on agriculture – in Africa, for example, 70 per cent of the population is involved in agricultural production.

The WTO wants the EU to open up its markets more readily to foreign producers. For example, the EU produces sugar at three times the world price but keeps imports of sugar out of the EU with high tariffs. The EU has offered to cut tariffs on some goods (in exchange for concessions) but wants to maintain them on 'sensitive' food products. The WTO also wants the USA to reduce the subsidies it pays to its farmers. The US has offered to reduce agricultural subsidies by up to 50 per cent, again in return for concessions. Both the EU and US want increased access to non-agricultural markets in newly developing countries like India and Brazil. These countries are reluctant to do this as the reduction of trade barriers may lead to an influx of cheap manufactured goods from China.

Complete failure of the Doha talks could see the end of multilateral trade agreements and an increased reliance on bilateral trade agreements negotiated between countries. This is problematic for businesses where bilateral agreements overlap, causing difficult regulatory requirements. The real losers in this will be the developing nations; anti-poverty groups argue very strongly that increased trade is better for these countries than increased aid. If developing countries do not become self-sufficient in trade they will continue to need aid in the future.

 For information on the work of the World Trade Organisation see *www.wto.org*

The European Union (EU)

The EU was established in 1958 by the Treaty of Rome. The six original members, France, West Germany, Italy, Holland, Belgium and Luxembourg, were joined in 1972 by the United Kingdom, Ireland and Denmark. Greece joined in 1981, followed by Spain and Portugal in 1986 and Austria, Finland and Sweden on 1 January 1995. In 2004 ten further countries joined the EU, mainly from eastern Europe: Czech Republic, Cyprus, Estonia, Hungary, Latvia, Lithuania, Malta, Poland, Slovakia and Slovenia. In January 2007 Romania and Bulgaria were admitted. These countries, along with the former East Germany, currently constitute the 27 member states of the Union, a number which is likely to grow further by the end of the decade. Other countries which are waiting to join are Croatia and Turkey.

As a result of the enlargement of the EU, a new constitution was put forward which included changes in voting rights, the size of the EU commission and maintaining national sovereignty. The new constitution had to be ratified by all member states of the EU. The new constitution was shelved in 2005 after 'no' votes in referenda held in France and the Netherlands. In 2007 a new reform treaty was agreed by EU leaders – the Lisbon Treaty – again needing to be ratified by all 27 members of the EU. Many members ratified it through their parliaments but in Ireland, the only country to hold a public vote, the vote was against ratification of the treaty. This has caused turmoil within the EU. Some have argued that the treaty is dead (Poland has decided not to put the treaty forward for ratification because of the Irish 'no' vote) while some argue that the treaty should never have been put to a public vote at all so that the 'no' vote can be ignored. The President of the EU has vowed to solve this problem by the end of 2008 so that the treaty can be put in place in 2009.

> **web link**
> For information on the European commission see *http://europa.eu.int/comm/index_en.htm*
> For European statistics see *http://europa.eu.int/comm/eurostat*

The primary aim of the Treaty of Rome was to create a '**common market**' in which member states were encouraged to trade freely and to bring their economies closer together, ultimately culminating in the creation of a '**single market**' within the Union. To bring this about, a protected free trade area or '**customs union**' was established, which involved the removal of tariff barriers between member states and the institution of a **common external tariff (CET)** on goods from outside the Union. Institutional structures and Union policies – most notably the **common agricultural policy (CAP)** – also contributed to this end and to the creation of a trading bloc of immense proportions. Within this bloc, member states were expected to gain numerous advantages, including increased trade and investment, huge economies of scale and improvements in productivity and cost reductions. To support the goal of increased trade and co-operation between community members, a **European monetary system** was established in 1979 in which a majority of member states undertook to fix their exchange rates within agreed limits.

A significant step towards the creation of a single market – capable of competing effectively with the United States and Japan – was taken in 1986 when the then 12 community members signed the Single European Act. This Act established

31 December 1992 as the target date for the creation of a Single European market: an area (comprising the 12 EU countries) without internal frontiers, in which the free movement of goods, services, people and capital was to be ensured within the provisions contained in the Treaty. Among the measures for making the single market a reality were agreements on the following issues:

- the removal or reduction in obstacles to cross-border travel and trade (e.g. customs checks);
- the harmonisation or approximation of technical and safety standards on a large number of products;
- closer approximation of excise duties and other fiscal barriers (e.g. VAT);
- the removal of legal obstacles to trade (e.g. discriminatory purchasing policies);
- the mutual recognition of qualifications.

Further steps in the development of the EU came with the decision to establish a **European Economic Area (EEA)** – which permits members of the European Free Trade Area (EFTA) to benefit from many of the single market measures – and, in particular, from the Treaty on European Union, agreed by the 12 member states in December 1991 at Maastricht. The Maastricht Treaty contained provisions for:

- increased economic and monetary union between member states;
- a single currency;
- a social charter to protect workers' rights;
- a common foreign and security policy;
- community citizenship.

These various measures were scheduled to be introduced over a number of years, although in some cases – most notably the United Kingdom – specially negotiated 'opt-out' clauses meant that some provisions were not implemented simultaneously by all member states (e.g. the single currency; the social charter).

European monetary union was finally achieved on 1 January 1999 with the creation of the Eurozone. Eleven members of the EU were included – the UK, Denmark and Sweden chose not to participate, while Greece failed the convergence criteria for membership but has since joined in 2001. In 2007, Slovenia joined the Eurozone and in 2008 Malta and Cyprus joined, taking the total up to 15 (EU-15). The Eurozone is effectively a single economic zone since it operates with a single currency – the euro – and members have given up sovereignty over monetary policy, which is now determined by the European Central Bank. National sovereignty over fiscal policy has been retained, so there can be some differences in tax rates and government spending, but this is to operate in a framework of 'harmonisation'. The creation of the Eurozone enables increased specialisation across the whole of Europe and bigger economies of scale. It embraces more than 300 million people and is responsible for one-fifth of the world's output and as such comes a close second to the USA as an economic superpower.

The UK has chosen not to join the Eurozone and the single currency until a referendum has been held. In 1997 the Chancellor of the Exchequer set out five economic tests of whether the UK should join or not. These were:

1 Are business cycles and economic structures of the UK and the Eurozone compatible and *sustainable*?

2 If problems emerge, is there sufficient flexibility to deal with them?

3 Would joining EMU encourage long-term investment in the UK?

4 What impact would it have on the competitive position of the UK's financial services industry?

5 Will joining EMU promote higher growth, stability and employment?

By 2008, the debate over membership of the euro in the UK has receded from the political agenda (at least for the time being) in view of the more pressing problems encountered by the EU during the year over the new constitution and the global financial crisis.

Notes

1 Liability may be extended where a company continues trading after insolvency.

2 It is also possible to have unlimited companies.

3 Under regulations issued in 1992 it is possible to have single member private companies with limited liability status, but these are the exception rather than the general rule.

4 A similar growth occurred in the number of 'community businesses' in Scotland during this period. Though not strictly 'co-operatives', they are also part of the so-called third sector of business.

5 Donaldson, P. and Farquhar, J., *Understanding the British Economy*, Penguin, 1988, p. 84.

6 See also the concept of Gross Value Added (GVA) which is an important measure in the estimation of GDP. National Statistics Online has a good explanation of GVA.

7 Real interest rates allow for inflation.

8 See, for example, Neale, A. and Haslam, C., *Economics in a Business Context*, Chapman & Hall, 1991, p. 141.

9 See Hay, D. A. and Morris, D. J., *Industrial Economics: Theory and Evidence*, Oxford University Press 1979, for a summary of the criticisms which are beyond the scope of this book.

10 Porter, M., *Competitive Strategy: Techniques for Analyzing Industries and Competitors*, The Free Press, New York, 1980.

11 For a full discussion of this, see Begg, D., Fischer, S. and Dornbusch, R., *Economics*, 7th edition, McGraw-Hill, 2003.

12 In such cases the demand curve would be upward sloping, indicating that as price rises demand rises. Other examples include 'snob goods', which are consumed because of their price.

13 In the markets described in this chapter there is an automatic tendency for the market to move back towards equilibrium once it is disturbed. However, it is possible for the demand and supply curves to be so shaped that once the market is disturbed it tends to move away from equilibrium rather than towards it. This is called the cobweb model. The interested reader should look at R. Lipsey, *An Introduction to Positive Economics*, Weidenfeld & Nicolson, 1989.

14 *Economic Downturn Hits Vital Innovation*, CBI survey, May 2002.

15 See Gray, J., *False Dawn: The Delusions of Global Capitalism*, Granta Books, London, 1998.

16 See Held, D., McGrew, A., Goldblatt, D. and Perraton, J., *Global Transformations: Politics, Economics and Culture*, Polity Press, Cambridge, 1999.

17 World Bank, 2008.

18 Capital Economics, 2007.

CHAPTER 2

Managing Financial Resources and Decisions

Unit 2: Managing Financial Resources and Decisions

Unit code: H/601/0548

QCF level: 4

Credit value: 15 credits

Aim

The unit aim is to provide learners with an understanding of where and how to access sources of finance for a business, and the skills to use financial information for decision making.

Unit abstract

This unit is designed to give learners a broad understanding of the sources and availability of finance for a business organisation. Learners will learn how to evaluate these different sources and compare how they are used.

They will learn how financial information is recorded and how to use this information to make decisions for example in planning and budgeting.

Decisions relating to pricing and investment appraisal are also considered within the unit. Finally, learners will learn and apply techniques used to evaluate financial performance.

Learning outcomes

On successful completion of this unit a learner will:

1 Understand the sources of finance available to a business
2 Understand the implications of finance as a resource within a business
3 Be able to make financial decisions based on financial information
4 Be able to evaluate the financial performance of a business.

Unit content

1 Understand the sources of finance available to a business

Range of sources: sources for different businesses; long term such as share capital; retained earnings; loans; third-party investment; short/medium term such as hire purchase and leasing; working capital stock control; cash management; debtor factoring

Implications of choices: legal, financial and dilution of control implications; bankruptcy

Choosing a source: advantages and disadvantages of different sources; suitability for purpose eg matching of term of finance to term of project

2 Understand the implications of finance as a resource within a business

Finance costs: tangible costs eg interest, dividends; opportunity costs eg loss of alternative projects when using retained earnings; tax effects

Financial planning: the need to identify shortages and surpluses eg cash budgeting; implications of failure to finance adequately; overtrading

Decision making: information needs of different decision makers

Accounting for finance: how different types of finance and their costs appear in the financial statements of a business; the interaction of assets and liabilities on the balance sheet and on international equivalents under the International Accounting Standards (IAS)

3 Be able to make financial decisions based on financial information

Budgeting decisions: analysis and monitoring of cash and other budgets

Costing and pricing decisions: calculation of unit costs, use within pricing decisions; sensitivity analysis

Investment appraisal: payback period; accounting rate of return; discounted cash flow techniques ie net present value; internal rate of return

Nature of long-term decisions: nature of investment; importance of true value of money; cash flow; assumptions in capital investment decisions; advantages and disadvantages of each method

4 Be able to evaluate the financial performance of a business

Terminology: introduction to debit, credit, books of prime entry, accounts and ledgers, trial balance, final accounts and international equivalents under the International Accounting Standards (IAS)

Financial statements: basic form, structure and purpose of main financial statements ie balance sheet, profit and loss account, cash flow statement, notes, preparation not required; changes to reporting requirements under the International Accounting Standards (IAS) eg statement of comprehensive income, statement of financial position; distinctions between different types of business ie limited company, partnership, sole trader

Interpretation: use of key accounting ratios for profitability, liquidity, efficiency and investment; comparison both external ie other companies, industry standards and internal ie previous periods, budgets

Learning outcomes and assessment criteria

Learning outcomes On successful completion of this unit a learner will:	Assessment criteria for pass The learner can:
LO1 Understand the sources of finance available to a business	1.1 identify the sources of finance available to a business 1.2 assess the implications of the different sources 1.3 evaluate appropriate sources of finance for a business project
LO2 Understand the implications of finance as a resource within a business	2.1 analyse the costs of different sources of finance 2.2 explain the importance of financial planning 2.3 assess the information needs of different decision makers 2.4 explain the impact of finance on the financial statements
LO3 Be able to make financial decisions based on financial information	3.1 analyse budgets and make appropriate decisions 3.2 explain the calculation of unit costs and make pricing decisions using relevant information 3.3 assess the viability of a project using investment appraisal techniques
LO4 Be able to evaluate the financial performance of a business	4.1 discuss the main financial statements 4.2 compare appropriate formats of financial statements for different types of business 4.3 interpret financial statements using appropriate ratios and comparisons, both internal and external

Guidance

Links

This unit links with the following units within this specification *Unit 6: Business Decision Making, Unit 9: Management Accounting: Costing and Budgeting, Unit 10: Financial Accounting and Reporting, Unit 11: Financial Systems and Auditing* and *Unit 12: Taxation.*

This unit also covers some of the underpinning knowledge and understanding for the NVQ in Accounting as set out in *Annexe B.*

The unit covers financial topics essential for learners who would like a career in this field and wish to gain membership of a professional accounting body.

Essential requirements

Learners will require access to financial and company reports.

Employer engagement and vocational contexts

Centres should develop links with local businesses. Many businesses and chambers of commerce want to promote local business and are often willing to provide work placements, visit opportunities, information about businesses and the local business context and guest speakers.

www.businessbritainuk.co.uk	provides information about business in Britain and has extensive links to other business and business news sites.
www.fsb.org.uk	The Federation of Small Businesses provides information, support and guidance about small businesses in the UK.

Capital markets, market efficiency and ratio analysis

Introduction

Capital markets are places where companies which need long-term finance can meet investors who have finance to offer. This finance may be equity finance, involving the issue of new ordinary shares, or debt finance, in which case companies can choose from a wide range of loans and debt securities. Capital markets are also places where investors buy and sell company and government securities. Their trading decisions reflect information on company performance provided by financial statements and financial analysis, dividend announcements by companies, market expectations on the future levels of interest rates and inflation, and investment decisions made by companies.

Both companies and investors want capital markets to assign fair prices to the securities being traded. In the language of corporate finance, companies and investors want the capital markets to be *efficient*. It is possible to describe the characteristics of an efficient capital market by considering the relationship between market prices and the information available to the market. Whether capital markets are in fact efficient is a question which has been studied extensively for many years and, in the first part of this chapter, we focus on the key topic of the efficient market hypothesis.

Shareholders make decisions on which shares to add or remove from their portfolios. Investors such as banks and other financial institutions make decisions about whether, and at what price, to offer finance to companies. Financial managers make decisions in the key areas of investment, financing and dividends. Shareholders, investors and financial managers can inform their decisions by evaluating the financial performance of companies using information from financial statements, financial databases, the financial press and the Internet. Ratio analysis of financial statements can provide useful historical information on the profitability, solvency, efficiency and risk of individual companies. By using performance measures such as economic profit and economic value added (EVA®), company performance can be linked more closely with shareholder value and shareholder wealth, and attention can be directed to ways in which companies can create more value for shareholders.

Sources of business finance

One of the key decision areas for corporate finance is the question of how a company finances its operations. If finance is not raised efficiently, the ability of a company to accept desirable projects will be adversely affected and the profitability of its existing operations may suffer. The aims of an efficient financing policy will be to raise the appropriate level of funds, at the time they are needed, at the lowest possible cost. There is clearly a link between the financing decisions made by a company's managers and the wealth of the company's shareholders. For a financing policy to be efficient, however, companies need to be aware of the sources of finance available to them.

Internal finance

Sources of finance can be divided into *external* finance and *internal* finance. By internal finance we mean cash generated by a company which is not needed to meet operating costs, interest payments, tax liabilities, cash dividends or replacement of non-current assets. This surplus cash is commonly called *retained earnings* in corporate finance. The income statement shows the profit generated by a company rather than the cash available for investment, which is perhaps best indicated by the cash flow statement. Retained earnings in the financial position statement also do not represent funds that can be invested. Only *cash* can be invested. A company with substantial retained earnings in its financial position statement, no cash in the bank and a large overdraft will clearly be unable to finance investment from retained earnings.

Another internal source of finance that is often overlooked is the savings generated by the more efficient management of working capital. This is the capital associated with short-term assets and liabilities. The more efficient management of trade receivables, inventories, cash and trade payables can reduce investment in working capital, thereby reducing a bank overdraft and its associated interest charges, or increasing the level of cash reserves.

External finance

There are many different kinds of external finance available which can be split broadly into debt and equity finance. External finance can also be classified according to whether it is short term (less than one year), medium term (between one year and five years), or long term (more than five years), and according to whether it is traded (e.g. ordinary shares and bonds) or untraded (e.g. bank loans). An indication of the range of financial instruments associated with external finance and their inter-relationships is given in Figure 2.1. You will find it useful to refer back to this exhibit as you study this chapter.

The balance between internal and external finance

Retained earnings, the major source of internal finance, may be preferred to external finance by companies for several reasons:

- retained earnings are seen as a ready source of cash;
- the decision on the amount to pay shareholders (and hence on the amount of retained earnings) is an internal decision and so does not require a company to present a case for funding to a third party;
- retained earnings have no issue costs;
- there is no dilution of control as would occur with issuing new equity shares;
- there are no restrictions on business operations as might arise with a new issue of debt.

The amount of retained earnings available will be limited by the cash flow from business operations. Most companies will therefore need at some stage to consider external sources of finance if they need to raise funds for investment projects or to

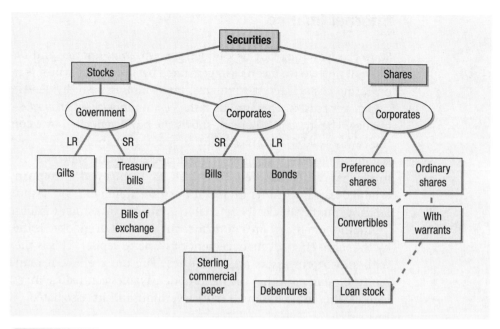

Figure 2.1 The variety of financial instruments that can be used by a company to raise finance

expand operating activities. The decision concerning the relative proportions of internal and external finance to be used for a capital investment project will depend on a number of factors.

The level of finance required

It may be possible for a company to finance small investments from retained earnings, for example replacing existing non-current assets or undertaking minor new investment projects. Larger projects are likely to require funds from outside the company.

The cash flow from existing operations

If the cash flow from existing operations is strong, a higher proportion of the finance needed for investment projects can be met internally. If the cash flow from existing operations is weak, a company will be more dependent on external financing.

The opportunity cost of retained earnings

Retained earnings are cash funds that belong to shareholders (as the owners of the company) and hence can be classed as equity financing. This means they have a required rate of return which is equal to the best return that shareholders could obtain on their funds elsewhere in the financial markets. The best alternative return open to shareholders is called the *opportunity cost* of retained earnings and the required return on equity (the cost of equity) is greater than the required return on debt (the cost of debt).

The costs associated with raising external finance

By using retained earnings, companies can avoid incurring the issue costs associated with raising external finance and will not make commitments to servicing fixed interest debt.

The availability of external sources of finance

The external sources of finance available to a company depend on its circumstances. A company which is not listed on a recognised stock exchange, for example, will find it difficult to raise large amounts of equity finance, and a company which already has a large proportion of debt finance, and is therefore seen as risky, will find it difficult to raise further debt.

Dividend policy

The dividend policy of a company will have a direct impact on the amount of retained earnings available for investment. A company which consistently pays out a high proportion of distributable profits as dividends will not have much by way of retained earnings and so is likely to use a higher proportion of external finance when funding investment projects.

Capital markets

Capital markets are markets for trading long-term financial securities. These securities were illustrated in Figure 2.1, but the most important ones for companies are ordinary shares, long-term debt securities such as secured bonds (debentures), unsecured bonds and convertible bonds, and, to a much lesser extent, preference shares. Eurobonds and public sector securities, such as Treasury bills and gilts (gilt-edged bonds), also trade on capital markets.

Capital markets have two main functions. First, they are a place where long-term funds can be raised by companies from those with funds to invest, such as financial institutions and private investors. In fulfilling this function, they are *primary markets* for new issues of equity and debt. Second, capital markets allow investors to sell their shares and bonds, or buy new ones to increase their portfolios. Here, capital markets act as *secondary markets* for dealing in existing securities. The secondary market plays a key role in corporate finance, because by facilitating the buying and selling of securities it increases their liquidity and hence their value. Investors would pay less for a security that would be difficult to sell at a later date. The secondary market is also a source of pricing information for the primary market and so helps to increase the efficiency with which the primary market allocates new funds to their best use.

The London Stock Exchange (LSE) is the main UK market for equity and bonds. Table 2.1 indicates that the number of UK-listed companies on the London Stock Exchange has declined since 1998, while the number of international-listed companies, apart from in 2007, has declined since 2000. The total market value of

Table 2.1 Companies listed on the UK stock market and the value of their equity

Year	UK-listed companies	Equity market value (£bn)	International-listed companies	Equity market value (£bn)	All listed companies	Equity market value (£bn)
1998	2087	1423	522	2804	2609	4227
1999	1945	1820	499	3578	2444	5398
2000	1904	1797	501	2526	2405	4322
2001	1809	1524	453	2580	2262	4104
2002	1701	1148	419	1902	2120	3050
2003	1557	1356	381	1975	1938	3331
2004	1465	1461	351	1972	1816	3433
2005	1358	1781	334	2254	1692	4035
2006	1276	1932	330	2374	1606	4306
2007	1239	1933	341	2293	1580	4226
2008	1174	1288	327	1609	1501	2897

Source: London Stock Exchange Market Fact Sheets, 2009.

equity peaked in 1999 at £5398bn, before falling by 43 per cent up to 2002. From 2003 the total market value of equity rose by 41 per cent to peak again in 2006, even though the number of companies continued to fall, before losing 2 per cent of value in 2007. The sharp decrease in value of 31 per cent in 2008 to £2897bn reflected the start of the 'credit crunch' and the beginning of a global economic recession.

Smaller companies which are unable to seek a listing on the main market of the LSE can apply for a listing on the Alternative Investment Market (AIM), which has been operated by the LSE since 1995. Market capitalisations on the AIM are typically between £2m and £100m. The AIM is both a primary and a secondary market for the shares of small and growing companies and has been quite successful to date. Unlike the LSE's main market, the AIM does not have any qualifying restrictions on market capitalisation, length of trading record or percentage of shares required to be held in public hands. The increasing importance of the AIM can be seen in Table 2.2, which shows that the number of companies listed on the market has

Table 2.2 The growth of the Alternative Investment Market

Year	Number of companies	Market value of equity (£m)
1995	121	2 382
1996	252	5 298
1997	308	5 655
1998	312	4 438
1999	347	13 468
2000	524	14 935
2001	629	11 607
2002	704	10 252
2003	754	18 358
2004	1021	31 753
2005	1399	56 619
2006	1634	90 666
2007	1694	67 561
2008	1233	37 732

Source: London Stock Exchange AIM Market Statistics, 2009.

increased every year since its inception up to a peak of 1694 companies in 2007. One reason for this is companies transferring to the AIM from the main market. The total market value of equity peaked in 2000, declined by 31 per cent to 2002, and then increased by an average of 72 per cent per year to a record value of £90.7bn in 2006. Market value of equity declined by 25 per cent in 2007 and 44 per cent in 2008 as the global economy moved into recession.

Capital market efficiency

What are the desirable features of capital markets such as the LSE's main market and the AIM? Dixon and Holmes (1992) suggest that transaction costs should be as low as possible, so that barriers to trading on capital markets are reduced and *operational efficiency* is promoted. Primary markets should direct funds to their most productive uses so that capital markets have *allocational efficiency*. This calls for fair prices to be provided by the secondary market, so activity on the primary market should have only a minimal effect on secondary market prices. This points to the need for *pricing efficiency*, which means that the prices of securities should reflect all relevant available information. Relevant information must be cheap to obtain and freely available to all, highlighting the need for *informational efficiency*.

Perfect markets and efficient markets

The are many references in corporate finance theory to perfect markets and efficient markets. According to Megginson (1997), a perfect market has the following characteristics:

● the absence of factors inhibiting buying and selling, such as taxes or transaction costs;
● all participants have the same expectations regarding asset prices, interest rates and other economic factors;
● entry to and exit from the market is free;
● information has no cost and is freely available to all market participants;
● a large number of buyers and sellers, none of whom dominates the market.

Clearly, no stock market anywhere in the world is a perfect market. However, companies and investors do not need capital markets to be perfect; rather, they need capital markets to be efficient and to offer fair prices so they can make reasoned investment and financing decisions. From our earlier discussion, we therefore expect an efficient capital market to have the following features:

● *Operational efficiency*: Transaction costs in the market should be as low as possible and required trading should be quickly effected.
● *Pricing efficiency*: The prices of capital market securities fully and fairly reflect all information concerning past events and all events that the market expects to occur in the future. The prices of securities are therefore fair prices.

● *Allocational efficiency*: The capital market, through the medium of pricing efficiency, allocates funds to where they can best be used.

The efficient market hypothesis is concerned with establishing the prices of capital market securities and states that the prices of securities fully and fairly reflect all relevant available information (Fama 1970). Market efficiency therefore refers to both the speed *and* the quality (i.e. direction and magnitude) of the price adjustment to new information. The testing of markets for efficiency has led to the recognition of three different levels or forms of market efficiency.

Different forms of market efficiency

Empirical tests of the efficiency of capital markets have investigated the extent to which share prices (security prices) reflect relevant information (i.e. pricing efficiency) because of a lack of data for testing allocational efficiency and operational efficiency. Many studies have investigated the extent to which it is possible for investors to make abnormal returns, which are returns in excess of expected returns, or returns in excess of those predicted by valuation methods such as the dividend growth model and the capital asset pricing model.

Weak form efficiency

Capital markets are weak form efficient if current share prices reflect all historical information, such as past share price movements. This means it is not possible to make abnormal returns in such a market by using technical analysis to study past share price movements (see section 'Technical and fundamental analysis', p. 129). Empirical evidence strongly supports the view that capital markets are weak form efficient.

Semi-strong form efficiency

Capital markets are semi-strong form efficient if current share prices reflect all historical information and all publicly available information, and if share prices react quickly and accurately to incorporate any new information as it becomes available. This means abnormal returns cannot be made in a semi-strong form efficient market by studying publicly available company information or by using fundamental analysis (see section 'Technical and fundamental analysis', p. 129). Empirical studies support the proposition that capital markets are semi-strong form efficient.

Strong form efficiency

Capital markets are said to be strong form efficient if share prices reflect *all* information, whether it is publicly available or not. If markets are strong form efficient, *no one* can make abnormal returns from share dealing, not even investors who act on 'insider information'. Capital markets clearly do not meet all the conditions for strong form efficiency, since some investors do make abnormal returns by insider dealing, as shown by occasional prosecutions in several countries for this offence. However, these cases are few in number compared to the volume of transactions in the capital market as a whole.

Testing for market efficiency

Weak form tests

If a capital market is weak form efficient, so that share prices reflect completely all past information, it will not be possible for investors to predict future share prices by studying past share price movements. Share prices will change as new information arrives on the market and, since new information arrives at random, share price movements will also appear to be random (Samuelson 1965). Many empirical studies have supported the proposition that the movement of share prices over time represents a random walk. This *random walk hypothesis* suggests that, if we know the share price at the end of one time period, we cannot predict accurately the share price at the end of the next period. Empirical evidence strongly supports the view that the relationship between share prices in different periods on well-developed capital markets is random, in which case we can say that research shows that well-developed capital markets are weak form efficient.

Empirical studies of weak form efficiency have used serial correlation tests, run tests and filter tests. One of the earliest studies testing for *serial correlation* looked for any correlation between security price changes at different points in time (Kendall 1953). The evidence from this and other studies tends to support the random walk hypothesis. Studies using *run tests* (e.g. Fama 1965) examine whether any significance can be attached to the direction of price changes by examining the length of the runs of successive price changes of the same sign. The empirical evidence indicated that the direction of price changes on any one day was independent of the direction of price changes on any other day. The distribution of directions was found to be based on pure chance, adding further support to the view that capital markets are weak form efficient. *Filter tests* try to identify any significant long-term relationships in security price movements by filtering out short-term price changes. One early study found that while filter tests could provide abnormal returns compared with a simple *buy and hold* strategy, gains were cancelled out when transaction costs were taken into account (Alexander 1961).

More recent studies have found weak evidence that a period of above-average returns may follow a long period of below-average returns (mean reversion), but the weak form of the efficient market hypothesis is still *broadly* supported (Megginson 1997; Beechey *et al.* 2000). It has also been argued from an insider perspective that trading strategies based on anomalies do not generate abnormal returns (Roll 1994).

Recent research has indicated that emerging capital markets may be weak form inefficient (Worthington and Higgs 2006; Gupta and Basu 2007; Magnus 2008), with the lower levels of liquidity and turnover associated with such markets suggested as contributory factors.

Semi-strong form tests

Tests for semi-strong form efficiency look at the speed and accuracy of share price responses to new information (event studies). In general, event studies support the view that capital markets are semi-strong form efficient.

An examination of the adjustment of share prices to the release of information about share splits found it was not possible to profit from the information because the market seemed to incorporate it efficiently and effectively (Fama *et al.* 1969). Similar findings were reached regarding earnings announcements (Ball and Brown 1968) and merger announcements (Keown and Pinkerton 1981). In fact, possible benefits arising from mergers were found to be anticipated by the capital market up to three months prior to any announcements (Franks *et al.* 1977). While event studies support the semi-strong form of the efficient market hypothesis, they also offer evidence of anomalies, such as the observation that share prices continue to rise (or fall) for a substantial period following the release of positive (or negative) information (Beechey *et al.* 2000). It has also been found that the more frequently a share is traded, the shorter the time required for its price to return to equilibrium having absorbed new information (Manganelli 2002).

Strong form tests

Because some people have access to information before other investors and so can make abnormal gains, it can be argued that capital markets are not strong form efficient. It is not possible to test for strong form efficiency *directly* by investigating the market's *use* of insider information, since by definition this information is unknown. Tests for strong form efficiency are therefore *indirect* in approach: they examine how *expert users* of information perform when compared against a yardstick such as the average return on the capital market.

Fund managers with resources to invest in discovering and analysing information may be in a better position than most to make abnormal gains. If their funds achieved above-average performances on a regular basis, this would be evidence that capital markets are not strong form efficient. A classic study of 115 mutual funds found that the majority did not make above-average returns when management costs were taken into account: in fact, their performance was inferior to a passive *buy-and-hold* strategy (Jensen 1968). Research continues to show that actively managed funds underperform the market after accounting for management costs, and in many cases before accounting for management costs as well (Megginson 1997; Beechey *et al.* 2000).

It has also been shown that investors could not benefit from the investment advice of financial tipsters (insider information becoming public information) due to the speed with which the market factored new information into share prices (Firth 1972).

Implications of the efficient market hypothesis

What are the implications for investors if the stock market is efficient?

- Paying for investment research will not produce above-average returns.
- Studying published accounts and investment tips will not produce above-average returns.
- There are no bargains (underpriced shares) to be found on the stock market.

For a company and its managers, the implications of stock market efficiency are:

- The share price of a company fairly reflects its value and market expectations about its future performance and returns. The financial manager should therefore focus on making 'good' financial decisions which increase shareholder wealth as the market will interpret these decisions correctly and the share price will adjust accordingly.

- Cosmetic manipulation of accounting information, whether through window dressing of financial statements or by massaging earnings per share, will not mislead the market.
- The timing of new issues of shares is not important since shares are never underpriced.

Technical and fundamental analysis

The efficient market hypothesis suggests that future share prices cannot be predicted by studying past prices and, as we have seen, there is extensive evidence to support this view. Despite the evidence, investment strategies based on the study of past share prices, or on the analysis of published information such as annual accounts, are common, and the view held by many financial analysts seems to be therefore that capital markets are inefficient.

Technical analysis involves the use of charts (chartism) and other methods to predict future share prices and share price trends, clearly implying that a relationship exists between past and future prices. For technical analysis to lead to abnormal returns on a regular basis, capital markets cannot even be weak form efficient. *Fundamental analysis* uses public information to calculate a fundamental value for a share and then offers investment advice by comparing the fundamental value with the current market price. It is not possible to make abnormal gains from fundamental analysis if capital markets are semi-strong form efficient, since all publicly available information will already be reflected in share prices.

Note that both technical analysis and fundamental analysis, by seeking abnormal returns, increase the speed with which share prices absorb new information and reach equilibrium, thereby preventing abnormal returns from being achieved.

Anomalies in the behaviour of share prices

Even though there is widespread acceptance that share prices respond quickly and accurately to new information, we have noted that research into market efficiency has produced evidence of anomalies in share price behaviour. Many such anomalies have been reported and investigated in the quest to understand the behaviour of share prices (Fama 1998), of which the following are examples.

Calendar effects

It has been reported that trading at particular times of the day can lead to negative or positive returns. For example, it appears that trading during the first 45 minutes on Monday mornings produces negative returns (the 'weekend effect'), whereas share prices tend to rise during the last 15 minutes of trading. While these effects have been reported, no satisfactory explanation has been offered. One suggestion is that investors evaluate their portfolios at weekends and sell on Monday mornings, whereas brokers initiate buy decisions regularly during the week. However, a 'reverse' weekend effect has been reported in a study (Brusa *et al.* 2005) that concluded that the weekend effect was related to both firm size and the nature of Friday trading.

High returns have also been noted in particular months, for example April in the UK and January in the USA. It is possible that these high returns are due to selling strategies designed to crystallise capital losses for tax purposes (known as *bed and breakfasting*) as the start of April is the end of the UK tax year. Share prices will be depressed at the start of April by such selling, but will recover as the new tax year begins. A trading strategy of buying at the start of the month and selling at the end may produce high returns in the UK in April.

Size anomalies

The returns from investing in smaller companies have been shown, in the long run, to be greater than the average return from all companies: one study, for example, found that small firms outperformed large firms by 6 per cent per year (Dimson and Marsh 1986). It has been suggested that above-average returns from small companies may compensate for the greater risk associated with them, such as the risk of financial distress (Beechey *et al.* 2000). It is possible that the growth prospects of smaller companies are better because they start from a lower base. However, it has been recognised that small companies account for only a small proportion of the equity trading on major stock exchanges and so studies of small-firm effects have little macro-economic significance (Fama 1991).

Value effects

Above-average returns can apparently be gained by investing in *value stocks*, which are shares with high earnings, cash flows or tangible assets relative to current share price: i.e. by investing in shares with low price/earnings ratios, as summarised by Beechey *et al.* (2000). It has also been shown that abnormal returns can be gained by investing in a portfolio of shares with poor past returns (De Bondt and Thaler 1985).

Behavioural finance

Behavioural finance suggests that investors do not appear *in practice* to be consistently able to make decisions that have as their objective the maximisation of their own wealth. This may be because they fail to update their information correctly (Small and Smith 2007) or because they do not make utility-maximising choices. Behavioural finance seeks to understand the market implications of the psychological factors underlying investor decisions and offers an alternative view of financial market activity to the efficient market hypothesis. It suggests that irrational investor behaviour can have significant and long-lasting effects on share price movements. While behavioural finance has not yet provided a unified theory of investor behaviour, it has had some success in explaining some anomalies in share price behaviour such as over-reaction to past price changes. A detailed discussion of behavioural finance is beyond the scope of this text; interested readers are referred to the excellent books by Shleifer (2000) and Haugen (2009), and to the survey by Barberis and Thaler (2002).

Summary

The existence of anomalies in share price behaviour suggests there are times when some share prices are not fair. Support for the efficient market hypothesis was almost universal before 1980. Since then, the theory has been regarded as an *incomplete* explanation of share price behaviour, with behavioural finance offering a growing challenge to the efficient marker hypothesis.

Research suggests that the UK and US stock markets, as well as a large number of other world-class stock markets, respond quickly and accurately to new information, and that only through insider dealing can investors make abnormal gains. Since such cases are small in number compared with the total volume of trading activity, and since legislation makes insider dealing illegal, it is likely that such well-developed capital markets are *at least* semi-strong form efficient. There is, however, evidence that emerging capital markets are weak-form inefficient. The continuing existence of anomalies in share price behaviour cannot be ignored, even though it has been suggested that some anomalies disappear when reasonable changes in research methodology are made (Fama 1998).

Assessing financial performance

In the introduction to this section, we mentioned that shareholders, investors and financial managers obtain a great deal of information about companies from their financial statements, financial databases, the financial press and the Internet. In this section we look at ratio analysis, which can be applied to financial statements and similar data in order to assess the financial performance of a company. In the section 'Economic profit and economic value added (EVA®)', p. 147 we look at ways of assessing financial performance which have closer links to shareholder wealth maximisation.

Analysis of financial performance can provide useful financial information for a wide range of user groups or stakeholders.

Shareholders

Shareholders can use analysis of financial performance to assist them in making buy and sell decisions, comparing the performance of their investments with that of similar companies, and assessing whether managers as their agents have been increasing shareholder wealth.

Investors

Investors such as banks and other financial institutions can use analysis of financial performance to inform decisions about whether to agree to requests for debt finance from companies and the terms and conditions to be attached to such finance.

Company managers

Managers can use analysis of financial performance to assess and compare the performance of different divisions and the performance of the company as a whole. They can compare their company's current performance with its performance in previous years, and against the performance of competitors.

Information sources for analysis of financial performance

Information for analysis of financial performance is initially derived from company financial statements (company accounts), but is now readily available through a variety of media. Financial databases are commonly used as a source of financial information on companies, for example, Datastream, Fame, Amadeus and LexisNexis. One advantage of using such databases is that ratio analysis can be performed by the software, although users must take care to ensure they are familiar with the definitions of the ratios provided. Useful company information can also be found on company websites on the Internet. Free company accounts can be obtained from the FT World Investor Link for many companies listed on the London Stock Exchange.

Financial statements

Figure 2.2 shows two of the financial statements of Boater plc: an income statement and a financial position statement. The ability to calculate and understand accounting ratios rests on an understanding of financial statements such as these and what they represent.

The income statement reports *financial performance* for an accounting period, which is usually one calendar year ending on the date given in the financial position statement. The income statement begins with turnover (sales) and subtracts costs incurred in producing the goods sold or the services delivered (cost of sales) to give gross profit. Costs incurred by supporting activities such as administration and distribution are then subtracted to give operating profit, also known as *profit before interest and tax*. This is the profit left after all operating costs have been deducted, hence the term operating profit.

The financial cost of meeting interest payments is subtracted to give profit before tax and the annual tax liability is subtracted to give profit after taxation (PAT). *Earnings* is the term given to profit that can be distributed to ordinary shareholders (distributable profit): in the absence of preference shares, earnings are equal to PAT; if preference shares have been issued, as in this case, earnings are equal to profit after tax and after preference dividends.

While the income statement shows the financial performance of a company during an accounting period, the financial position statement shows the financial position

Income statements for the year ended 31 December

	2009		2008	
	£000	£000	£000	£000
Turnover		5700		5300
Cost of sales		4330		4000
Gross profit		1370		1300
Administration cost		735		620
Operating profit		635		680
Interest		220		190
Profit before taxation		415		490
Taxation		125		147
Profit after taxation		290		343
Preference dividends	90		90	
Ordinary dividends	140	230	140	230
Retained profits		60		113

Financial position statements as at 31 December

	2009			2008		
	£000	£000	£000	£000	£000	£000
Non-current assets			5405			4880
Current assets:						
Inventory		900			880	
Trade receivables		460			460	
Cash		55			60	
		1415			1400	
Current liabilities:						
Trade creditors	425			190		
Bank	nil			800		
Taxation	155			110		
Dividends	230			230		
		810			1330	
Net current assets			605			70
Total assets less current liabilities			6010			4950
Long-term liabilities						
Bonds		1100			1100	
Bank loan		1000			0	
			2100			1100
			3910			3850
Capital and reserves:						
Ordinary shares, par value 100 pence			1500			1500
Preference shares, par value 100 pence			1000			1000
Share premium			500			500
Reserves			910			850
			3910			3850

Annual depreciation: £410 000 (2009) and £380 000 (2008)
Bond market price: £102 (2009) and £98 (2008)
Ordinary share price: 135 pence (2009) and 220 pence (2008)

Figure 2.2   Financial statements of Boater

of the company at the end of the accounting period. The financial position statement records the assets and liabilities of the company. Assets are divided into *non-current assets*, which are expected to be a source of economic benefit to the company over several accounting periods, and *current assets*, which are consumed or sold within an accounting period. These assets are balanced by current (short-term) liabilities, such as trade payables and overdrafts, and long-term liabilities, such as debt, shareholders' funds and preference shares. Ordinary shareholders' funds are divided into the *ordinary share account* (ordinary shares), where the nominal or face value of issued shares is recorded; the *share premium account*, which records the difference between the nominal value of shares issued and the finance raised by selling shares; and reserves, the most common of which is the cumulative *retained earnings reserve*, which increases each year by the retained profit from the income statement. If land and buildings are revalued, any gain or loss in value is recorded in a *revaluation reserve*.

Another financial statement produced by companies, which is not illustrated in Figure 2.2, is the *cash flow statement*, which shows in a formal way the sources of and uses of cash during the accounting period. Financial statements are published at least once each year as part of company accounts. The mini case below (p. 135) discusses the importance of consistency in terms of the content of company accounts and the information they provide.

Profit, EBITDA and cash

In assessing financial performance, it is important to consider the quality of the returns generated by companies. While useful information is provided by the level of profit reported in the financial statements of a company, whether before or after tax, corporate finance tends to focus on cash flows. There is a fundamental difference between accounting profit and cash flows because accounting profit is prepared by applying *accruals accounting* and *accounting policies*. An example of the significance of accruals accounting here is that reported profit includes credit sales, which become cash flows only when trade receivables settle their accounts. The significance of accounting policies is that companies with similar cash flows can report different accounting profits if their accounting policies are different.

In order to remedy some of the deficiencies of accounting profit, it has become increasingly common for companies and analysts to consider earnings before interest, tax, depreciation and amortisation (EBITDA). Since EBITDA is in essence operating profit excluding non-cash expenses such as depreciation and amortisation (a regular provision writing down intangible assets such as goodwill), it is similar to cash flow from operating activities, ignoring the effect of changes in working capital. As a measure of financial performance, EBITDA eliminates the effects of financing and capital expenditure, and hence can indicate trends in sustainable profitability. EBITDA can be compared with capital employed, as well as indicating the cash flow available to meet interest payments. It has also been suggested that EBITDA can be compared with the market value of equity plus debt, less working capital (Rutterford 1998).

There is currently intense debate over proposed new rules to implement international harmonisation of annual accounting, management and audit reporting. But take the trouble to look at leading international and national companies, in all sectors, and you will see there are still significant reporting differences and shortcomings for both interim and annual reports that have generated scant discussion.

Differences in reporting standards and procedures are ever more important because of the internationalisation of capital markets. It is increasingly unacceptable that investors in continental Western Europe, the UK and the US are not similarly well informed.

US-quoted companies publish informative quarterly reports that are by and large better than those of Europe-listed companies. The American quarterly reports show gross margins, trade receivables and trade payables; such information is unusual in interim reports of UK companies and patchy among those of continental Europeans.

When quarterly or half-yearly detailed working capital figures are published, users can assess much more effectively the company's ongoing performance and can make better judgments about any year-end 'window dressing' of figures. Such analysis, in turn, permits easier assessment of asset leverage and annual operating cash flows, which can influence performance bonuses.

In Europe, lack of interim information about costs of goods for big companies such as Cadbury-Schweppes, Nestlé and Unilever becomes particularly unfortunate for investors, analysts, bankers and those interested in macroeconomic performance. This is especially so when costs of raw materials, packaging or transport are volatile.

Cost-of-goods figures are key to assessing inflationary pressures. Their absence allows companies to disguise changes in their operating profit by temporarily reducing spending on marketing and other variable costs.

More frequent cost-of-sales information would be helpful for central banks, governments and equity and bond investors.

Hooray for the US – except that North American corporate performance reporting falls short of European practice in some important respects. While there is a wealth of information on the cost of capital and the effectiveness of management, there is no information on the cost of labour. This lack prevents effective comparisons of labour productivity trends among companies with similar activities. The travails of the US motor and air transport industries might have been identified earlier had adequate labour information been publicly available earlier.

The sparsity of employment statistics for Wal-Mart, by far the world's biggest retailer, is a telling example. The group reports that it has 1.8m employees, of whom 500 000 are abroad, but gives no information on full-time equivalents. Nor are employment costs published – although Asda, its UK subsidiary, provides full-time equivalent numbers and their costs. Leading European retailers, such as Metro of Germany and UK-based Tesco, publish comprehensive information.

Another difference in reporting is that UK-quoted companies publish detailed information on management rewards. In the US, such information is shown only in the proxy statement, a separate report.

There has been an exponential increase in US chief executives' pay, which rose 30 per cent in 2004, according to Corporate Library, a governance watchdog. Such rises have led the US Securities and Exchange Commission to press for pay to be covered in annual reports. There is even pressure in the US to have shareholder advisory votes on pay, which is now UK practice.

Success for the SEC would raise US practice to levels in the UK, which is well ahead of reporting in most of Western Europe.

Just as important as the inadequacy of some of the information published by quoted companies is the near total absence of financial information for huge private US and Canadian companies, including subsidiaries of quoted companies. It is surely unacceptable that there is such a big information lacuna regarding the performance of huge swaths of private manufacturing and financial groups, which play leading roles in the North American economy. They have sales of many billions and employ tens of thousands. Similar companies in France, Germany and the UK are required by law to file comprehensive financial statements in the public domain. Such information about US private companies would enhance competition at home and abroad.

Comparable key figures in reports are crucial for the proper allocation of resources.

Source: Martin Simons, FT.com, 13 April 2006. Reprinted with permission.

EBITDA can be criticised as a measure of cash flow since it ignores the fact that earnings and revenue are not cash flows. Simply adding back interest, depreciation and amortisation will not turn earnings back into cash. EBITDA also ignores the contribution to cash flow made by changes in working capital.

The need for benchmarks

When analysing financial performance, it is important to recognise that performance measures and financial ratios in isolation have little significance. In order to interpret the meaning of performance measures and ratios, they must be compared against appropriate benchmarks, of which the following are examples:

● financial targets set by a company's strategic plan, e.g. a target return on capital employed or economic profit;
● performance measures and ratios of companies engaged in similar business activities;
● average performance measures and ratios for the company's operations, i.e. sector averages;
● performance measures and ratios for the company from previous years, adjusted for inflation if necessary.

The benchmarks selected will depend on the purpose of the analysis. Comparing the calculated performance measures or ratios against appropriate benchmarks is not an end in itself – there is still the difficult task of interpreting or explaining any differences found.

Categories of ratios

When using ratios for analysing financial performance, calculation and interpretation is assisted by using some sort of analytical framework. We have divided ratios into groups or categories which are linked to particular areas of concern. There is widespread agreement on the main ratios included in each category, even though the same category may be given different names by different authors.

● *Profitability ratios*: return on capital employed, net profit margin, net asset turnover, gross profit margin, etc.
● *Activity ratios*: trade receivables days, trade payables days, inventory days, sales/net current assets, etc. These ratios are important in the management of working capital.
● *Liquidity ratios*: current ratio, quick ratio, etc.
● *Gearing ratios*: capital gearing ratio, debt/equity ratio, interest cover, etc. These ratios are measures of financial risk (*see* Section 9.8).

● *Investor ratios*: return on equity, dividend per share, earnings per share, dividend cover, price/earnings ratio, payout ratio, dividend yield, earnings yield, etc.

A detailed introduction to ratio analysis can be found in Elliott and Elliott (2007). Because some ratios can be defined in different ways, it is important when comparing ratios to make sure that they have been calculated on a similar basis. The golden rule is *always* to compare like with like.

The ratios discussed in the following sections are illustrated by calculations based on the accounts of Boater in Figure 2.2.

Profitability ratios

Profitability ratios indicate how successful the managers of a company have been in generating profit. Return on capital employed is often referred to as the *primary ratio*.

Return on capital employed (ROCE)

$$\frac{\text{Profit before interest and tax} \times 100}{\text{Capital employed}}$$

This ratio relates the overall profitability of a company to the finance used to generate it. It is also the product of net profit margin and asset turnover:

ROCE = Net profit margin × Asset turnover

Profit before interest and tax is often called *operating profit*, as in Figure 2.2. The meaning of *capital employed* can cause confusion, but it is simply *total assets less current liabilities* (or shareholders' funds plus long-term debt, which has a similar meaning). Another definition of capital employed with the same meaning is *non-current assets plus net working capital*. This ratio is clearly sensitive to investment in non-current assets, to the age of non-current assets (since older assets will have depreciated more than young ones) and to when assets were last revalued. There is a close link between ROCE and accounting rate of return (see 'The return on capital employed', p. 162). For Boater:

ROCE (2008) = 100 × (680/4950) = 13.7%
ROCE (2009) = 100 × (635/6010) = 10.6%

Net profit margin

$$\frac{\text{Profit before interest and tax} \times 100}{\text{Sales or turnover}}$$

This ratio, also called *operating profit margin*, indicates the efficiency with which costs have been controlled in generating profit from sales. It does not distinguish between operating costs, administrative costs and distribution costs. A fall in ROCE may be due to a fall in net profit margin, in which case further investigation may determine whether an increased cost or a fall in profit margin is the cause. For Boater:

Net profit margin (2008) = 100 × (680/5300) = 12.8%
Net profit margin (2009) = 100 × (635/5700) = 11.1%

Net asset turnover

$$\frac{\text{Sales or turnover}}{\text{Capital employed}}$$

Capital employed is defined here in the same way as for ROCE, i.e. *total assets less current liabilities*, and so the asset turnover ratio is also sensitive to non-current asset values. This ratio gives a guide to productive efficiency, i.e. how well assets have been used in generating sales. A fall in ROCE may be due to a fall in asset turnover rather than a fall in net profit margin. For Boater:

Asset turnover (2008) = 5300/4950 = 1.07 times
Asset turnover (2009) = 5700/6010 = 0.95 times

Gross profit margin

$$\frac{\text{Gross profit} \times 100}{\text{Sales or turnover}}$$

This ratio shows how well costs of production have been controlled, as opposed to distribution costs and administration costs. For Boater:

Gross profit margin (2008) = 100 × (1300/5300) = 24.5%
Gross profit margin (2009) = 100 × (1370/5700) = 24.0%

EBITDA/capital employed

$$\frac{\text{EBITDA} \times 100}{\text{Capital employed}}$$

This ratio relates earnings before interest, tax, depreciation and amortisation to the equity and debt finance used to generate it. The meaning of *capital employed* is as for ROCE, i.e. *total assets less current liabilities*. For Boater:

EBITDA (2008) = (680 + 380) = £1 060 000
EBITDA (2009) = (635 + 410) = £1 045 000
EBITDA/capital employed (2008) = 100 × (1060/4950) = 21.4%
EBITDA/capital employed (2009) = 100 × (1045/6010) = 17.4%

Activity ratios

Activity ratios show how efficiently a company has managed short-term assets and liabilities, i.e. working capital, and they are closely linked to the liquidity ratios. With each ratio, the average value for the year should be used (e.g. average level of trade receivables should be used in calculating the trade receivables' ratio), but it is common for the year-end value to be used in order to obtain figures for comparative purposes. As ratios must be calculated on a consistent basis, either year-end values or average values must be used throughout your analysis.

Trade receivables days or trade receivables' ratio

$$\frac{\text{Debtors} \times 365}{\text{Credit sales}}$$

The value of credit sales is usually not available and it is common for sales or turnover to be used as a substitute. The trade receivables days ratio gives the average period of credit being taken by customers. If it is compared with a company's allowed credit period, it can give an indication of the efficiency of trade receivables administration. For Boater:

Trade receivables days (2008) = 365 × (460/5300) = 32 days
Trade receivables days (2009) = 365 × (460/5700) = 29 days

Trade payables days or trade payables' ratio

$$\frac{\text{Trade creditors} \times 365}{\text{Cost of sales}}$$

Trade payables should be compared with credit purchases, but as this information is not always available, cost of sales is often used instead. The trade payables days ratio gives the average time taken for suppliers of goods and services to receive payment. For Boater:

Trade payables days (2008) = 365 × (190/4000) = 17 days
Trade payables days (2009) = 365 × (425/4330) = 36 days

Inventory days or inventory turnover

$$\frac{\text{Stock or inventory} \times 365}{\text{Cost of sales}}$$

This ratio shows how long it takes for a company to turn its inventories into sales. Several other ratios can be calculated by separating the total inventory figure into its component parts, i.e. raw materials, work-in-progress and finished goods. The shorter the inventory days ratio, the lower the cost to the company of holding inventory. The value of this ratio is very dependent on the need for inventory and so will vary significantly depending on the nature of a company's business. For Boater:

Inventory days (2008) = 365 × (880/4000) = 80 days
Inventory days (2009) = 365 × (900/4330) = 76 days

Cash conversion cycle

The cash conversion cycle (also called the operating cycle or working capital cycle) is found by adding inventory days and trade receivables days and then subtracting trade payables days. It indicates the period of time for which working capital financing is needed. The longer the cash conversion cycle, the higher the investment in working capital. For Boater:

Cash conversion cycle (2008) = 32 days + 80 days – 17 days = 95 days
Cash conversion cycle (2009) = 29 days + 76 days – 36 days = 69 days

Non-current asset turnover

Net asset turnover (see above) is based on capital employed, but an alternative view of asset use can be found by separating non-current assets from capital employed.

$$\frac{\text{Sales or turnover}}{\text{Non-current assets}}$$

Non-current asset turnover indicates the sales being generated by the non-current asset base of a company. Like ROCE, it is sensitive to the acquisition, age and valuation of non-current assets. For Boater:

Non-current asset turnover (2008) = 5300/4880 = 1.09 times
Non-current asset turnover (2009) = 5700/5405 = 1.05 times

Sales/net working capital

The companion ratio to non-current asset turnover compares sales to net working capital (net current assets).

$$\frac{\text{Sales or turnover}}{\text{Net current assets}}$$

This ratio shows the level of working capital supporting sales. Working capital must increase in line with sales if undercapitalisation (overtrading) is to be avoided and so this ratio can be used to forecast the level of working capital needed for a given level of sales when projecting financial statements. For Boater:

Sales/net working capital (2008) = 5300/(880 + 460 − 190) = 4.6 times
Sales/net working capital (2009) = 5700/(900 + 460 − 425) = 6.1 times

Liquidity ratios

Current ratio

$$\frac{\text{Current assets}}{\text{Current liabilities}}$$

This ratio measures a company's ability to meet its financial obligations as they fall due. It is often said that the current ratio should be around two, but what is normal will in fact vary from industry to industry: sector averages are a better guide than a rule of thumb. For Boater:

Current ratio (2008) = 1400/1330 = 1.1 times
Current ratio (2009) = 1415/810 = 1.8 times

Quick ratio

$$\frac{\text{Current assets less inventory}}{\text{Current liabilities}}$$

It is argued that the current ratio may overstate the ability to meet financial obligations because it includes inventory in the numerator. This argument has merit if it takes more than a short time to convert inventory into sales, i.e. if the inventory days ratio is not small. It is not true, however, where inventory is turned over quickly and where sales are mainly on a cash or near-cash basis, for example in the retail food trade. The quick ratio compares liquid current assets with short-term liabilities. While a common rule of thumb is that it should be close to one, in practice the sector average value should be used as a guide. For Boater:

Quick ratio (2008) = (1400 − 880)/1330 = 0.4 times
Quick ratio (2009) = (1415 − 900)/810 = 0.6 times

Gearing ratios

Gearing ratios or leverage ratios relate to how a company is financed with respect to debt and equity and can be used to assess the financial risk that arises with increasing debt.

Capital gearing ratio

$$\frac{\text{Long-term debt} \times 100}{\text{Capital employed}}$$

The purpose of this ratio is to show the proportion of debt finance used by a company. When comparing calculated values to benchmarks it is essential to confirm that the same method of calculation is used because other definitions of this ratio are found. One alternative replaces long-term debt capital with *prior charge capital*, which includes preference shares as well as debt.

A company may be thought *highly geared* if capital gearing is greater than 50 per cent using book values for debt and equity, but this is only a rule of thumb. For Boater:

Capital gearing (2008) = 100 × (1100/4950) = 22.2%
Capital gearing (2009) = 100 × (2100/6010) = 35.0%

It is usual in corporate finance to calculate gearing using market values for debt and equity. Reserves are not included in the calculation of the market value of equity. Note also that the 2009 market value of debt is the sum of the market value of the bonds and the book value of the bank loan because bank loans have no market value. For Boater plc:

Market value of equity (2008) = 1 500 000 × 2.2 = £3 300 000
Market value of equity (2009) = 1 500 000 × 1.35 = £2 025 000
Market value of bonds (2008) = 1 100 000 × 98/100 = £1 078 000
Market value of bonds (2009) = 1 100 000 × 102/100 = £1 122 000
Market value of debt (2009) = 1 122 000 + 1 000 000 = £2 122 000
Capital gearing (2008) = 100 × (1078/(1078 + 3300)) = 24.6%
Capital gearing (2009) = 100 × (2122/(2122 + 2025)) = 51.2%

Debt/equity ratio

$$\frac{\text{Long-term debt} \times 100}{\text{Share capital and reserves}}$$

This ratio serves a similar purpose to capital gearing. A company could be said to be highly geared if its debt/equity ratio were greater than 100 per cent using book values, but again this is only a rule of thumb. For Boater:

Debt/equity ratio (2008) = $100 \times (1100/3850) = 28.6\%$
Debt/equity ratio (2009) = $100 \times (2100/3910) = 53.7\%$

Using market values:

Debt/equity ratio (2008) = $100 \times (1078/3300) = 32.7\%$
Debt/equity ratio (2009) = $100 \times (2122/2025) = 104.8\%$

Interest coverage ratio and interest gearing

$$\frac{\text{Profit before interest and tax}}{\text{Interest charges}}$$

The interest coverage ratio shows how many times a company can cover its current interest payments (finance charges) out of current profits and indicates whether servicing debt may be a problem. An interest coverage ratio of more than seven times is usually regarded as safe, and an interest coverage ratio of more than three times as acceptable. These are only rules of thumb, however, and during periods of low and stable interest rates, lower levels of interest cover may be deemed acceptable. The interest coverage ratio is a clearer indication of financial distress than either capital gearing or the debt/equity ratio, since inability to meet interest payments will lead to corporate failure no matter what the level of gearing may be. For Boater:

Interest coverage ratio (2008) = $680/190 = 3.6$ times
Interest coverage ratio (2009) = $635/220 = 2.9$ times

The inverse of the interest coverage ratio is known as interest gearing or income gearing and is preferred to the interest coverage ratio by some analysts. For Boater:

Interest gearing (2008) = $100 \times (190/680) = 27.9\%$
Interest gearing (2009) = $100 \times (220/635) = 34.7\%$

Investor ratios

Investor ratios are used in corporate finance for a variety of purposes, including valuing a target company in a takeover (e.g. using the price/earnings ratio); analysing dividend policy (e.g. using the payout ratio); predicting the effect of a rights issue (e.g. using earnings yield); and assessing the effects of proposed financing (e.g. on earnings per share).

Return on equity

$$\frac{\text{Earnings after tax and preference dividends}}{\text{Shareholders' funds}}$$

Whereas ROCE looks at overall return to all providers of finance, return on equity compares the earnings attributable to ordinary shareholders with the book value of their investment in the business. *Shareholders' funds* are equal to ordinary share capital plus reserves, but exclude preference share capital. For Boater:

Return on equity (2008) = $100 \times ((343 - 90)/(3850 - 1000)) = 8.9\%$
Return on equity (2009) = $100 \times ((290 - 90)/(3910 - 1000)) = 6.9\%$

Dividend per share

$$\frac{\text{Total dividend paid to ordinary shareholders}}{\text{Number of issued ordinary shares}}$$

While the total dividend paid may change from year to year, individual shareholders will expect that dividend per share will not decrease. For Boater:

Dividend per share (2008) = $100 \times (140/1500) = 9.3$ pence
Dividend per share (2009) = $100 \times (140/1500) = 9.3$ pence

Earnings per share

$$\frac{\text{Earnings after tax and preference dividends}}{\text{Number of issued ordinary shares}}$$

Earnings per share is regarded as a key ratio by stock market investors. Take care when looking at this ratio in company accounts as there are several ways it can be calculated.

These complications are beyond the scope of this book: for further discussion, see for example Elliott and Elliott (2007). We shall calculate earnings per share by simply using earnings attributable to ordinary shareholders, so for Boater:

Earnings per share (2008) = $100 \times ((343 - 90)/1500)) = 16.9$ pence
Earnings per share (2009) = $100 \times ((290 - 90)/1500)) = 13.3$ pence

Dividend cover

$$\frac{\text{Earnings per share}}{\text{Dividend per share}}$$

Dividend cover indicates how safe a company's dividend payment is by calculating how many times the total dividend is covered by current earnings. The higher the dividend cover, the more likely it is that a company can maintain or increase future dividends. For Boater:

Dividend cover (2008) = $16.9/9.3 = 1.8$ times
Dividend cover (2009) = $13.3/9.3 = 1.4$ times

Price/earnings ratio

$$\frac{\text{Market price per share}}{\text{Earnings per share}}$$

Like earnings per share, the price/earnings ratio (P/E ratio) is seen as a key ratio by stock market investors. It shows how much an investor is prepared to pay for a company's shares, given its current earnings per share (EPS). The ratio can therefore indicate the confidence of investors in the expected future performance of a company: the higher the P/E ratio relative to other companies, the more confident the market is that future earnings will increase. A word of caution, though: a high P/E ratio could also be due to a low EPS, perhaps due to a one-off cost in the income statement. The P/E ratio can also be used to determine the value of a company. For Boater:

Price/earnings ratio (2008) = 220/16.9 = 13.0
Price/earnings ratio (2009) = 135/13.3 = 10.2

Payout ratio

$$\frac{\text{Total dividend paid to ordinary shareholders} \times 100}{\text{Earnings after tax and preference dividends}}$$

The payout ratio is often used in the analysis of dividend policy. For example, some companies may choose to pay out a fixed percentage of earnings every year and finance any investment needs not covered by retained earnings from external sources. For Boater:

Payout ratio (2008) = 100 × (140/(343 − 90)) = 55.3%
Payout ratio (2009) = 100 × (140/(290 − 90)) = 70.0%

Dividend yield

$$\frac{\text{Dividend per share} \times 100}{\text{Market price of share}}$$

Dividend yield gives a measure of how much an investor expects to gain in exchange for buying a given share, ignoring any capital gains that may arise. It is commonly quoted on a gross (before tax) basis in the financial press. For Boater, on a net (after tax) basis:

Net dividend yield (2008) = 100 × (9.3/220) = 4.2%
Net dividend yield (2009) = 100 × (9.3/135) = 6.9%

Gross dividend yield is found by 'grossing up' net dividend yield at the basic rate of income tax. Assuming a tax rate of 20 per cent, for Boater, on a gross (before tax) basis:

Gross dividend yield (2008) = 4.2 × (100/80) = 5.3%
Gross dividend yield (2009) = 6.9 × (100/80) = 8.6%

Earnings yield

$$\frac{\text{Earnings per share} \times 100}{\text{Market price of share}}$$

Earnings yield gives a measure of the potential return shareholders expect to receive in exchange for purchasing a given share; it is the reciprocal of the price/earnings ratio. The return is a potential one since few companies pay out all of their earnings as dividends. Earnings yield can be used as a discount rate to capitalise future earnings in order to determine the value of a company. For Boater:

Earnings yield (2008) = $100 \times (16.9/220) = 7.7\%$

Earnings yield (2009) = $100 \times (13.3/135) = 9.8\%$

Interpreting the financial ratios of Boater

The ratios calculated for Boater are summarised in Table 2.3. If there had been a particular focus to this analysis, only a selection of ratios would have been calculated. For example, if the focus had been on the efficiency of working capital management, no purpose would have been served by calculating the investor ratios. What

Table 2.3 Comparative financial ratios for Boater

	2009	2008
Return on capital employed	10.6%	13.7%
Net profit margin	11.1%	12.8%
Asset turnover	0.95 times	1.07 times
Gross profit margin	24.0%	24.5%
EBITDA/capital employed	17.4%	21.4%
Trade receivables days	29 days	32 days
Trade payables days	36 days	17 days
Inventory days	76 days	80 days
Cash conversion cycle	69 days	95 days
Non-current asset turnover	1.05 times	1.09 times
Sales/net working capital	6.1 times	4.6 times
Current ratio	1.8 times	1.1 times
Quick ratio	0.6 times	0.4 times
Capital gearing (book value)	35.0%	22.2%
Capital gearing (market value)	51.2%	24.6%
Debt/equity ratio (book value)	53.7%	28.6%
Debt/equity ratio (market value)	104.8%	32.7%
Interest coverage ratio	2.9 times	3.6 times
Interest gearing	34.7%	27.9%
Return on equity	6.9%	8.9%
Dividend per share	9.3 pence	9.3 pence
Earnings per share	13.3 pence	16.9 pence
Dividend cover	1.4 times	1.8 times
Price/earnings ratio	10.2	13.0
Payout ratio	70.0%	55.3%
Net dividend yield	6.9%	4.2%
Gross dividend yield	8.6%	5.3%
Earnings yield	9.8%	7.7%

is the overall assessment of financial performance indicated by Boater's ratios? The following comments are offered as a guide to some of the issues raised in each of the ratio categories, and should be studied in conjunction with Table 2.3.

Profitability

Boater's overall profitability has declined, and this is due both to a decline in turnover in relation to capital employed and to a decline in profit margins. This decline has occurred despite an increase in turnover and seems to be partly due to a substantial increase in administration costs. The decline in ROCE and EBITDA/capital employed can also be linked to replacement of the overdraft with a bank loan and substantial investment in non-current assets.

Activity and liquidity

The exchange of the overdraft for a long-term bank loan has improved both the current ratio and the quick ratio, but cash reserves have fallen. There has been little change in trade receivables days or inventory days, but trade payables days have more than doubled. Although Boater is no longer heavily reliant on an overdraft for working capital finance, the company has increased its dependence on trade payables as a source of short-term finance.

Gearing and risk

The new loan has increased gearing substantially. Although gearing does not seem to be risky using book values, the change in gearing using market values is quite large. Interest coverage now looks to be low and income gearing is increasing owing to the fall in operating profit and the increase in interest payments.

Investor interest

Even though earnings have fallen, the dividend has been maintained and, since the share price has fallen, dividend yield has increased as a result. The decrease in price/earnings ratio may indicate that investors feel that the company is unlikely to improve in the future.

Problems with ratio analysis

When using ratio analysis to evaluate financial performance, you must treat the results with caution for a number of reasons. One problem is that the financial position statement relates to a company's position on one day of the year. If the financial position statement had been prepared three months earlier, a different picture might have been presented and key financial ratios might have had different values. Tax payable and dividends due might not have been included in current liabilities, for example, and the current ratio could have looked much healthier. Should we exclude such temporary items when calculating working capital ratios?

It can be difficult to find a similar company as a basis for intercompany comparisons. No two companies are identical in every respect and so differences in commercial activity must be allowed for. As a minimum, differences in accounting policies should be considered.

The reliability of ratio analysis in the analysis of financial performance naturally depends on the reliability of the accounting information on which it is based. Financial statements have become increasingly complex and it is not easy to determine if *creative accounting* has taken place. Company accounting has been described as 'a jungle with many species of animal – some benign, some carnivorous – and its own rules' (Smith 1996). Care must be taken to identify *off-balance-sheet financing* or any complex financial instruments which may distort a company's true financial position. As shown by occasional high-profile corporate failures, identifying the financial position of a company can be difficult, even for experts.

Ratio analysis, in conclusion, must be regarded as only the beginning of the analysis of financial performance, serving mainly to raise questions which require deeper investigation before understanding begins to appear. Shareholders, investors and company managers use ratio analysis as only one of many sources of information to assist them in making decisions.

Economic profit and economic value added (EVA®)

It has long been recognised that reported earnings are an incomplete measure of company performance, since positive earnings do not guarantee that a company is increasing shareholder wealth. What is missing is an opportunity cost for the capital employed in the business, since a company must earn at least the average required rate of return on its capital employed if it is going to create an increase in value for its shareholders. A performance measure which addresses this deficiency in reported earnings is economic profit, which can be defined as operating profit after tax less a cost of capital charge on capital employed.

$$\text{Economic profit} = (\text{Operating profit} \times (1 - t)) - (K_0 \times \text{CE})$$

where: t = company taxation rate
K_0 = average rate of return required by investors
CE = book value of capital employed

An almost identical concept which is familiar to management accountants is residual income, defined as controllable contribution less a cost of capital charge on controllable investment (Drury 2008), although contribution here is before taxation.

Economic profit as defined above corrects the deficiency in earnings of failing to allow for a charge on capital employed, but it still relies on accounting data, which is open to subjective adjustment and manipulation in its preparation. There is also the problem that the book value of capital employed fails to capture accurately the capital invested in a company. For example, research and development costs produce benefits for a company over several years, but are treated as an annual expense rather than a financial position statement asset. We cannot rely on a published financial position statement to give us an accurate measure of the tangible and intangible capital invested in a company. The difficulty of extracting a fair value for invested capital from financial statements is addressed by the topical performance measure known as EVA.

EVA was trademarked and introduced by the Stern Stewart company in the 1990s with the objective of providing an overall measure of company performance that would focus managers' attention on the drivers that lead to the creation of shareholder wealth. It refined and amended the information used in the calculation of economic profit so that the two terms have become largely synonymous (Hawawini and Viallet 2002). In fact, EVA can be seen as an attempt to measure a company's economic profit rather than its accounting profit (Keown *et al.* 2003). EVA calculates an adjusted value for invested capital by making rule-based changes to the book value of capital employed. For example, it capitalises expenditure on marketing and research and development, thereby treating these expenses as assets and spreading their costs over the periods benefiting from them. EVA also calculates an adjusted value for operating profit by making complementary changes to those it makes to the value of invested capital. For example, research and development expenses included in accounting profit must be reduced in order to balance the amount included in invested capital. By making these changes to invested capital and operating profit after tax, EVA corrects the effect of financial accounting rules that ignore the ways a company creates value for shareholders. EVA can be defined as:

$$EVA = (AOP \times (1 - t)) - (WACC \times AVIC)$$

where: AOP = adjusted operating profit
t = company taxation rate
WACC = weighted average cost of capital
AVIC = adjusted value of invested capital

Alternatively:

$$EVA = (RAVIC - WACC) \times AVIC$$

where: RAVIC = required after-tax return on adjusted value of invested capital
WACC = weighted average cost of capital
AVIC = adjusted value of invested capital

While open to criticism on the basis of the subjectivity of some of the adjustments it makes to accounting information, many large organisations have adopted EVA and some positive results have been claimed from its use as a performance measure (Leahy 2000). However, it has been suggested that there is a very low empirical correlation between increases in market value and EVA (Fernandez 2003), and that EVA could be used as one of a range of performance measures, including traditional accounting-based performance measures (Kumar and Low 2002).

The usefulness of EVA lies in the attention it directs towards the *drivers* of shareholder value creation. Reflecting on the definition of EVA points to several ways in which company managers can seek to generate increased value for shareholders. This leads on to the extensive topic of value management, which is beyond the scope of this book. Briefly, the value drivers that managers may be able to influence can be seen in the following value-creating strategies:

● look for ways to increase net operating profit after tax without increasing the amount of capital invested in the company;

- undertake investment projects which are expected to generate returns in excess of the company's cost of capital;
- take steps to reduce the opportunity cost of the capital invested in the company, either by reducing the company's cost of capital or by reducing the amount of invested capital.

You will find it useful to think of examples of how these value-creating strategies can be applied in practice. For example, net operating profit after tax can be increased by eliminating unnecessary costs. Undertaking projects which generate returns in excess of the company's cost of capital can be achieved by using net present value (NPV) and internal rate of return (IRR) as investment appraisal methods (see the next section of this chapter). A company's cost of capital can be reduced by the sensible use of debt. The amount of invested capital can be reduced by disposing of unwanted assets and by returning unwanted cash to shareholders via a share repurchase scheme.

Conclusion

In this section, we have looked at some key aspects of the financing decision in corporate finance – the balance between internal and external finance, the different sources of finance available to a company, the importance of the capital markets – and have also discussed at some length the key topic of capital market efficiency. The debate about market efficiency is a continuing one and you should consider carefully the implications of market efficiency for corporate finance theory as you continue your studies.

The analysis of financial performance is a key activity providing financial information for a wide range of user groups, and we considered both ratio analysis and a currently topical performance measure, economic value added (EVA). Later chapters will discuss particular ratios in more detail, especially those concerned with working capital and gearing.

Key points

1 An efficient financing policy raises necessary funds at the required time and at the lowest cost.
2 Internal finance or retained earnings must not be confused with retained profit as only cash can be invested. Retained earnings are a major source of funds for investment.
3 The mix of internal and external finance depends on the amount of finance needed: the cash flow from existing operations; the opportunity cost of retained earnings; the cost and availability of external finance; and the company's dividend policy.
4 There are many kinds of external finance available to a company, including ordinary shares, preference shares, bonds (debentures, loan stock and convertibles) and bank loans.

5 New issues of equity and debt are made in the primary market, while securities already in issue are traded in the secondary market, which is a source of pricing information.

6 Smaller companies not ready for the full market can obtain a listing on the Alternative Investment Market (AIM).

7 An efficient market needs operational efficiency, allocational efficiency and pricing efficiency: a perfect market requires the absence of factors inhibiting buying and selling; identical expectations of participants; free entry and exit; free and readily available information; and a large number of buyers and sellers, none of whom dominates.

8 Operational efficiency means that transaction costs should be low and sales executed quickly. Pricing efficiency means that share prices fully and fairly reflect all relevant information, and so are fair prices. Allocational efficiency means that capital markets allocate funds to their most productive use.

9 Markets are weak form efficient if share prices reflect all past price movements. In such a market, abnormal returns cannot be made by studying past share price movements. Research suggests well-developed capital markets are weak form efficient.

10 The random walk hypothesis suggests there is no connection between movements in share price in successive periods. A substantial amount of research supports this view. Weak form tests include serial correlation tests, run tests and filter tests.

11 Markets are semi-strong form efficient if share prices reflect all past information and all publicly available information. In such a market, abnormal returns cannot be made by studying available company information. Research suggests well-developed capital markets are to a large extent semi-strong form efficient.

12 Tests for semi-strong form efficiency look at the speed and accuracy of share price movements to new information (event studies).

13 Markets are strong form efficient if share prices reflect *all* information. In such a market, no one can make abnormal returns. While well-developed capital markets are not totally strong form efficient, the inefficiency is perhaps limited and research suggests the UK and US stock markets have a high degree of efficiency.

14 Strong form efficiency can only be tested indirectly, for example by investigating whether fund managers can regularly make above-average returns.

15 The implications of capital market efficiency for investors are that research is pointless and no bargains exist.

16 The implications of capital market efficiency for companies are that share prices correctly value a company, the timing of new issues is irrelevant and manipulating accounts is pointless.

17 Technical analysts try to predict share prices by studying their historical movements, while fundamental analysts look for the fundamental value of a share. Neither activity is worthwhile (theoretically) in a semi-strong form efficient market.

18 A significant body of research has examined anomalies in share price behaviour, such as calendar effects, size anomalies and value effects.

19 Behavioural finance seeks to understand the market implications of the psychological factors underlying investor decisions and has had some success explaining anomalies.

20 Shareholders, investors and financial managers can use analysis of financial performance to assist them in their decisions.

21 To remedy perceived deficiencies in accounting profit, reporting earnings before interest, tax, depreciation and amortisation, (EBITDA) has become more common.

22 Performance measures and ratios mean little in isolation, but must be compared with benchmarks such as financial targets; performance measures and ratios of similar companies; sector averages; or performance measures and ratios from previous years.

23 A systematic approach to ratio analysis could look at ratios relating to profitability, activity, liquidity, gearing and investment.

24 Problems with ratio analysis include the following: financial position statement figures are *single-point* values; similar companies for comparison are hard to find; accounting policies may differ between companies; creative accounting may distort financial statements; and complex financing methods can make accounts difficult to interpret.

25 The terms 'economic profit' and 'economic value added' (EVA) have a similar meaning. EVA is the difference between operating profit after tax and a cost of capital charge on invested capital. Many large companies use EVA.

26 EVA focuses attention on the drivers of shareholder value creation. Financial managers should seek to increase net operating profit, undertake projects with a return greater than the cost of capital, and reduce the opportunity cost and amount of invested capital.

Self-test questions

Answers to these questions can be found on pages 157–158.

1 Describe the factors that influence the relative proportions of internal and external finance used in capital investment.

2 What is the relevance of the efficient market hypothesis for the financial manager?

3 Which of the following statements about the efficient market hypothesis is *not* correct?
    (a) If a stock market is weak form efficient, chartists cannot make abnormal returns.
    (b) If a stock market is strong form efficient, only people with insider information can make abnormal returns.
    (c) In a semi-strong form efficient market, fundamental analysis will not bring abnormal returns.
    (d) If a stock market is semi-strong form efficient, all past and current publicly available information is reflected in share prices.
    (e) If a stock market is weak form efficient, all historical information about a share is reflected in its current market price.

4 Explain the meaning of the following terms: allocational efficiency, pricing efficiency and operational efficiency.

5 Why is it difficult to test for strong form efficiency?

6 Describe three anomalies in share price behaviour.

7 Describe benchmarks that can be used when assessing financial performance.

8 Describe the five categories of ratios, list and define the ratios in each category and, without referring to the calculations in the text, calculate each ratio for Boater.

9 What are the potential problems associated with using ratio analysis to analyse the financial health and performance of companies?

10 Explain the meaning of economic value added (EVA). How can EVA help financial managers to create value for shareholders?

Questions for review

Questions with an asterisk (*) are at an intermediate level.

1 Distinguish between a primary and a secondary capital market and discuss the role played by these markets in corporate finance. What are the desirable features of primary and secondary capital markets?

2* Recent research into the efficient market hypothesis has explored anomalies in share price behaviour. Briefly describe some of these anomalies and suggest possible explanations.

3 The following financial statements are extracts from the accounts of Hoult Ltd:

Income statements for years ending 31 December

	Year 1	Year 2	Year 3
	€000	€000	€000
Sales	960	1080	1220
Cost of sales	670	780	885
Gross profit	290	300	335
Administration expenses	260	270	302
Operating profit	30	30	33
Interest	13	14	18
Profit before taxation	17	16	15
Taxation	2	1	1
Profit after taxation	15	15	14
Dividends	0	0	4
Retained profit	15	15	10

Financial position statements for years to 31 December

	Year 1		Year 2		Year 3	
	€000	€000	€000	€000	€000	€000
Non-current assets		160		120		100
Current assets:						
Inventory	200		210		225	
Trade receivables	160		180		250	
Cash	0		0		0	
	360		390		475	

Financial position statements for years to 31 December

	Year 1		Year 2		Year 3	
	€000	€000	€000	€000	€000	€000
Current liabilities:						
Trade payables	75		80		145	
Overdraft	70		80		110	
	145		160		255	
Net current assets		215		230		220
Total assets less current liabilities		375		350		320
8% Bonds		120		80		40
		255		270		280
Capital and reserves:						
Ordinary shares		160		160		160
Profit and loss		95		110		120
		255		270		280

Annual depreciation was €18 000 in year 1, €13 000 in year 2 and €11 000 in year 3.

The 8 per cent bonds are redeemable in instalments and the final instalment is due in year 4.

The finance director is concerned about rising short-term interest rates and the poor liquidity of Hoult Ltd. After calculating appropriate ratios, prepare a report that comments on the recent performance and financial health of Hoult Ltd.

4 Comment on the following statement:
'It is not possible to test whether a stock market is strong form efficient. In fact, the existence of insider trading proves otherwise.'

5* Comment on the following statement:
'Ratio analysis using financial statements is pointless. Only economic value added (EVA) gives a true measure of the financial performance of a company.'

Questions for discussion

Questions with an asterisk (*) are at an advanced level.

1* Dayton has asked you for advice about his investment portfolio. He is considering buying shares in companies listed on the Alternative Investment Market. Green, a friend of Dayton, has told him he should invest only in shares that are listed on an efficient capital market as otherwise he cannot be sure he is paying a fair price. Dayton has said to you that he is not sure what an 'efficient' capital market is.

(a) Explain to Dayton what characteristics are usually required to be present for a market to be described as efficient.

(b) Discuss whether the Alternative Investment Market is considered to be an efficient market.

(c) Discuss the extent to which research has shown capital markets to be efficient.

2 Critically discuss the following statements about stock market efficiency:

(a) The weak form of the efficient market hypothesis implies that it is possible for investors to generate abnormal returns by analysing changes in past share prices.

(b) The semi-strong form of the efficient market hypothesis implies that it is possible for an investor to earn superior returns by studying company accounts, newspapers and investment journals, or by purchasing reports from market analysts.

(c) The strong form of the efficient market hypothesis implies that, as share prices reflect all available information, there is no way that investors can gain abnormal returns.

3 Discuss the importance of the efficient market hypothesis to the following parties:

(a) shareholders concerned about maximising their wealth;

(b) corporate financial managers making capital investment decisions;

(c) investors analysing the annual reports of listed companies.

4* Tor plc is a large company listed on the main market of the London Stock Exchange. The objectives of the company, in the current year and in recent years, are stated by its Annual Report to be as follows:

(1) To maximise the wealth of our shareholders

(2) To give shareholders an annual return of 15% per year

(3) To increase real dividends by 4% per year

The shares of Tor plc are owned as follows:

	%
Chief executive officer	17
Managing director	6
Other directors	4
UK institutional investors	44
Foreign institutional investors	10
Small shareholders	19
	100

The following information relates to the recent performance of Tor plc.

Year	2005	2006	2007	2008	2009
Turnover (£m)	144	147	175	183	218
Earnings per share (pence)	46.8	50.7	53.3	53.7	63.7
Dividend per share (pence)	18.7	20.0	21.4	22.9	24.5
Annual inflation (%)		2.5	2.7	3.1	2.9
Price/earnings ratio (times)	8	8	10	13	15

Average values for 2009 for Tor plc's business sector are:

Dividend yield:	4.2%
Total shareholder return:	35%
Price/earnings ratio:	14 times

(a) Using the information provided, evaluate the recent performance of Tor plc and discuss the extent to which the company has achieved its declared financial objectives.

(b) Critically discuss how the problem of agency may be reduced in a company listed on the London Stock Exchange, illustrating your answer by referring to the information provided about Tor plc.

References

Alexander, S. (1961) 'Price movements in speculative markets: trends or random walks', *Industrial Management Review*, May, pp. 7–26.

Ball, R. and Brown, P. (1968) 'An empirical evaluation of accounting income numbers', *Journal of Accounting Research*, Autumn, pp. 159–78.

Barberis, N. and Thaler, R. (2002) 'A survey of behavioral finance', *Social Science Research Network Economic Library*, available at http://ssrn.com.

Beechey, M., Gruen, D. and Vickery, J. (2000) 'The efficient market hypothesis: a survey', Research Discussion Paper, Economic Research Department, Reserve Bank of Australia.

Brusa, J., Liu, P. and Schulman, C. (2005) 'Weekend effect, "reverse" weekend effect, and investor trading activities', *Journal of Business Finance and Accounting*, Vol. 32, Nos. 7 and 8, pp. 1495–517.

De Bondt, W. and Thaler, R. (1985) 'Does the stock market overreact?', *Journal of Finance*, Vol. 40, pp. 793–805.

Dimson, E. and Marsh, P. (1986) 'Event study methodologies and the size effect: the case of UK press recommendations', *Journal of Financial Economics*, Vol. 17, No. 1, pp. 113–42.

Dixon, R. and Holmes, P. (1992) *Financial Markets: An Introduction*, London: Chapman & Hall.

Drury, C. (2008) *Management and Cost Accounting*, 7th edn, London: Thomson Learning Business Press.

Elliott, B. and Elliott, J. (2007) *Financial Accounting and Reporting*, 11th edn, Harlow: FT Prentice Hall.

Fama, E. (1965) 'The behaviour of stock market prices', *Journal of Business*, January, pp. 34–106.

Fama, E. (1970) 'Efficient capital markets: a review of theory and empirical work', *Journal of Finance*, Vol. 25, pp. 383–417.

Fama, E. (1991) 'Efficient capital markets: II', *Journal of Finance*, Vol. 46, pp. 1575–617.

Fama, E. (1998) 'Market efficiency, long-term returns and behavioural finance', *Journal of Financial Economics*, Vol. 49, pp. 283–306.

Fama, E., Fisher, L., Jensen, M. and Roll, R. (1969) 'The adjustment of stock prices to new information', *International Economic Review*, Vol. 10, February, pp. 1–21.

Fernandez, P. (2003) 'EVA, Economic profit and cash value added do not measure shareholder value creation', *Journal of Applied Finance*, Vol. 9, No. 3, pp. 74–94.

Firth, M. (1972) 'The performance of share recommendations made by investment analysts and the effects on market efficiency', *Journal of Business Finance*, Summer, pp. 58–67.

Franks, J., Broyles, J. and Hecht, M. (1977) 'An industry study of the profitability of mergers in the United Kingdom', *Journal of Finance*, Vol. 32, pp. 1513–25.

Gupta, R. and Basu, P.K. (2007) 'Weak form efficiency in Indian stock markets', *International Journal of Business and Economics Research*, Vol. 6, No. 3, pp. 57–64.

Haugen, R. (2009) *The New Finance: Overreaction, Complexity and Other Consequences*, 4th edn, Upper Saddle River, NJ: Prentice-Hall.

Hawawini, G. and Viallet, C. (2002) *Finance for Executives: Managing for Value Creation*, Cincinnati, OH: South-Western/Thomson Learning.

Jensen, M. (1968) 'The performance of mutual funds in the period 1945–64', *Journal of Finance*, May, pp. 389–416.

Kendall, R. (1953) 'The analysis of economic time series, part 1: prices', *Journal of the Royal Statistical Society*, Vol. 69, pp. 11–25.

Keown, A. and Pinkerton, J. (1981) 'Merger announcements and insider trading activity', *Journal of Finance*, Vol. 36, September, pp. 855–70.

Keown, A., Martin, J., Petty, J. and Scott, D. (2003) *Foundations of Finance: The Logic and Practice of Financial Management*, Upper Saddle River, NJ: Prentice-Hall.

Kumar, S. and Low, W.L. (2002) 'Economic value added versus traditional accounting measures of performance of the companies listed on the Singapore stock exchange', *Working Paper No. 2002–5*, Strathclyde: Graduate School of Business, University of Strathclyde.

Leahy, T. (2000) 'Capitalizing on economic value added', *Business Finance*, July.

Manganelli, S. (2002) 'Duration, volume and volatility impact of trades', European Central Bank Working Paper 125.

Magnus, F.J. (2008) 'Capital market efficiency: an analysis of weak form efficiency on the Ghana stock exchange', *Journal of Money, Investment and Banking*, Issue 5, pp. 5–12.

Megginson, W.L. (1997) *Corporate Finance Theory*, Reading, MA: Addison-Wesley.

Roll, R. (1994) 'What every CEO should know about scientific progress in economics: what is known and what remains to be resolved', *Financial Management*, Vol. 23, pp. 69–75.

Rutterford, J. (ed.) (1998) *Financial Strategy*, Chichester: Wiley.

Samuelson, P. (1965) 'Proof that properly anticipated prices fluctuate randomly', *Industrial Management Review*, Vol. 6, pp. 41–9.

Shleifer, A.S. (2000) *Inefficient Markets: An Introduction to Behavioural Finance*, Oxford: Oxford University Press.

Small, K. and Smith, J. (2007) 'The hot stock tip from Debbie: implications for market efficiency', *The Journal of Behavioral Finance*, Vol. 8, No. 4, pp. 191–7.

Smith, T. (1996) *Accounting for Growth: Stripping the Camouflage from Company Accounts*, 2nd edn, London: Century Business.

Worthington, A. and Higgs, H. (2006) 'Weak form efficiency in Asian emerging and developed capital markets: comparative tests of random walk behaviour', *Accounting Research Journal*, Vol. 19, No. 1, pp. 54–63.

Recommended reading

A lucid treatment of efficient markets is found in:

Arnold, G. (2008) *Corporate Financial Management*, 4th edn, Harlow: FT Prentice Hall.

A practical and lucid discussion of ratio analysis can be found in:

Walsh, C. (2008) *Key Management Ratios*, 4th edn, Harlow: FT Prentice Hall.

Useful journal articles and other material include the following:

Fama, E. (1970) 'Efficient capital markets: a review of theory and empirical work', *Journal of Finance*, Vol. 25, pp. 383–417.

Fama, E. (1991) 'Efficient capital markets II', *Journal of Finance*, Vol. 46, pp. 1575–617.

Free company annual reports and a wealth of other business information can be obtained from the FT.com homepage: http://news.ft.com/home/uk

Another useful website is LexisNexis: http://www.lexisnexis.co.uk

Answers to self-test questions

1 This topic is discussed in 'The balance between internal and external finance', p. 121. The main factors influencing the split between internal and external finance are as follows:
   - the level of finance required;
   - the cash flow from existing operations;
   - the opportunity cost of retained earnings;
   - the costs associated with raising external finance;
   - the availability of external sources of finance;
   - dividend policy.

2 The relevance of the efficient market hypothesis for financial management is that, if the hypothesis holds true, the company's 'real' financial position will be reflected in the share price. If the company makes a 'good' financial decision, this will be reflected in an increase in the share price. Similarly, a 'bad' financial decision will cause the share price to fall. In order to maximise shareholder wealth, the financial manager need only concentrate on maximising the NPV of investment projects, and need not consider matters such as the way in which the future position of the company will be reflected in the company's financial statements. The financial manager, then, may use rational decision rules and have confidence that the market will rapidly reflect the effects of those decisions in the company's share price.

3 The incorrect statement is (b) since, if capital markets are strong form efficient, then nobody, not even people with insider information, will be able to make abnormal returns.

4 These terms are discussed in 'Perfect markets and efficient markets', p. 125.

5 It is hard to test for strong form efficiency directly, i.e. by studying the market's *use* of information, because it can always be objected that investors with access to inside information can make abnormal gains. Tests for strong form efficiency are therefore *indirect*, examining the performance of *users* of information who may have access to inside information or who have special training for share dealing, such as fund managers.

6 Anomalies in share price behaviour are discussed in 'Anomalies in the behaviour of share prices', p. 129. You could discuss calendar effects, size anomalies and value effects.

7 Financial performance measures and financial ratios mean little in isolation. In order to assess financial performance, we need to compare with benchmarks such as:
   - target performance measures set by managers;
   - sector or industry norms;
   - performance measures and ratios of similar companies;
   - performance measures and ratios of the same company from previous years.
All such comparisons should be made with caution due to the problems in analysing financial performance arising from differing accounting policies and creative accounting.

8 The answer to this question is given in 'Categories of ratios', p. 136 and following sections. You should be able to define *all* the ratios. If you cannot, study these sections further until you can. Compare your calculations to the illustrative calculations given.

9 The problems that may be encountered in using ratio analysis to assess the health and performance of companies include:
   ● all ratios are imperfect and imprecise and should be treated as guidelines;
   ● ratios are only as reliable as the accounting figures they are based on;
   ● no two companies are identical so inter-company comparisons need care;
   ● ratios mean little in isolation and need other information to explain them;
   ● ratio analysis tends to be performed on historical data and so may not be an accurate guide to either current position or future activity.

10 Economic value added (EVA) is the difference between adjusted operating profit after tax and a cost of capital charge on the adjusted value of invested capital. It can help managers to increase shareholder wealth by directing their attention to the drivers that create value for shareholders, such as increasing net operating profit after tax, investing in projects with a return greater than the company's cost of capital or reducing the cost of capital or the value of invested capital.

An overview of investment appraisal methods

Introduction

Companies need to invest in wealth-creating assets in order to renew, extend or replace the means by which they carry on their business. Capital investment allows companies to continue to generate cash flows in the future or to maintain the profitability of existing business activities. Typically, capital investment projects will require significant cash outflows at the beginning and will then produce cash inflows over several years. Capital investment projects require careful evaluation because they need very large amounts of cash to be raised and invested, and because they will determine whether the company is profitable in the future.

A company seeks to select the best or most profitable investment projects so that it can maximise the return to its shareholders. It also seeks to avoid the negative strategic and financial consequences which could follow from poor investment decisions.

Since capital investment decisions affect a company over a long period of time, it is possible to view a company and its financial position statement as the sum of the previous investment and financing decisions taken by its directors and managers.

The payback method

While research has shown that payback is the most popular investment appraisal method, it suffers from such serious shortcomings that it should only really be regarded as a first screening method. The *payback period* is the number of years it is expected to take to recover the original investment from the net cash flows resulting from a capital investment project. The decision rule when using the *payback method* to appraise investments is to accept a project if its payback period is equal to or less than a predetermined target value. It is possible to obtain an estimate of the payback period to several decimal places if cash flows are assumed to occur evenly throughout each year, but a high degree of accuracy in estimating the payback period is not desirable since it does not offer information which is especially useful. A figure to the nearest half-year or month is usually sufficient.

Example of the payback method

Consider an investment project with the cash flows given in Table 2.4.

The cash flows of this project are called *conventional* cash flows and the project is called a *conventional* project. A conventional project can be defined as one which requires a cash investment at the start of the project, followed by a series of cash

Table 2.4 Simple investment project, showing a significant initial investment followed by a series of cash inflows over the life of the project

Year	0	1	2	3	4	5
Cash flow (£)	(450)	100	200	100	100	80

Table 2.5 Cumulative cash flows for the conventional project of the previous exhibit, showing that the payback period is between three and four years

Year	Cash flow (£)	Cumulative cash flow (£)
0	(450)	(450)
1	100	(350)
2	200	(150)
3	100	(50)
4	100	50
5	80	130

inflows over the life of the project. We can see from Table 2.4 that, after three years, the project has generated total cash inflows of £400 000. During the fourth year, the remaining £50 000 of the initial investment will be recovered. As the cash inflow in this year is £100 000, and assuming that it occurs evenly during the year, it will take a further six months or 0.5 years for the final £50 000 to be recovered. The payback period is therefore 3.5 years.

It can be helpful to draw up a table of cumulative project cash flows in order to determine the payback period, as shown in Table 2.5.

The advantages of the payback method

The advantages of the payback method are that it is simple and easy to apply and, as a concept, it is straightforward to understand. The payback period is calculated using cash flows, not accounting profits, and so should not be open to manipulation by managerial preferences for particular accounting policies. If we accept that more distant cash flows are more uncertain and that increasing uncertainty is the same as increasing risk, it is possible to argue that a further advantage of the payback method is that it takes account of risk, in that it implicitly assumes that a shorter payback period is superior to a longer one.

It has been argued that payback period is a useful investment appraisal method when a company is restricted in the amount of finance it has available for investment, since the sooner cash is returned by a project, the sooner it can be reinvested into other projects. While there is some truth in this claim, it ignores the fact that there are better investment appraisal methods available to deal with capital rationing, as explained later in the section (see 'The profitability index and capital rationing', p. 176).

The disadvantages of the payback method

There are a number of difficulties in using the payback method to assess capital investment projects and these are sufficiently serious for it to be generally rejected by corporate finance theory as a credible method of investment appraisal. One of the major disadvantages is that the payback method ignores the *time value of money*, so that it gives equal weight to cash flows whenever they occur within the payback period. We can illustrate this point by referring back to the example in

Table 2.4. You can see that the payback period remains 3.5 years even if the project generates no cash inflows in the first and second years, but then a cash inflow of £400 000 occurs in the third year. In fact, any combination of cash inflows in the first three years which totals £400 000 would give the same payback period.

The problem of ignoring the time value of money is partly remedied by using the *discounted payback method* discussed later in the section (see 'The discounted payback method', p. 180).

Another serious disadvantage of the payback method is that it ignores all cash flows outside the payback period and so does not consider the project as a whole. If a company rejected all projects with payback periods greater than three years, it would reject the project given in Table 2.4. Suppose this project had been expected to have a cash inflow of £1 million in year 4. This expected cash inflow would have been ignored if the sole investment appraisal method being applied was the payback method and the project would still have been rejected. Would this have been a wealth-maximising decision for the company concerned? Hardly! In fact, the choice of the maximum payback period acceptable to a company is an arbitrary one, since it is not possible to say why one payback period is preferable to any other. Why should a project with a payback period of three years be accepted while a project with a payback period of three-and-a-half years is rejected?

In fairness, we should recognise that in practice when the payback method is used, cash flows outside of the payback period are not ignored, but are taken into consideration as part of the exercise of managerial judgement. However, this only serves to reinforce the inadequacy of the payback method as the *sole* measure of project acceptability.

The general conclusion that can be drawn from this discussion is that the payback method does not give any real indication of whether an investment project increases the value of a company. For this reason it has been argued that, despite its well-documented popularity, the payback method is not really an investment appraisal method at all, but rather a means of assessing the effect of accepting an investment project on a company's liquidity position.

The return on capital employed method

There are several different definitions of return on capital employed (ROCE), which is also called return on investment (ROI) and accounting rate of return (ARR). All definitions relate accounting profit to some measure of the capital employed in a capital investment project. One definition that is widely used is:

$$ROCE = \frac{\text{Average annual accounting profit}}{\text{Average investment}} \times 100$$

The average investment must take account of any scrap value. Assuming straight-line depreciation from the initial investment to the terminal scrap value, we have:

$$\text{Average investment} = \frac{\text{Initial investment} + \text{Scrap value}}{2}$$

Another common definition of return on capital employed (see 'Profitability ratios', p. 137) uses the initial or final investment rather than the average investment, for example:

$$\text{ROCE} = \frac{\text{Average annual accounting profit}}{\text{Initial (or final) investment}} \times 100$$

It is important to remember that return on capital employed is calculated using accounting profits, which are before-tax operating cash flows adjusted to take account of depreciation. *Accounting profits are not cash flows*, since depreciation is an accounting adjustment which does not correspond to an annual movement of cash. The *decision rule* here is to accept an investment project if its return on capital employed is greater than a target or hurdle rate of return set by the investing company. If only one of two investment projects can be undertaken (i.e. if the projects are *mutually exclusive*), the project with the higher return on capital employed should be accepted.

Example

Calculation of the return on capital employed

Carbon plc is planning to buy a new machine and has found two which meet its needs. Each machine has an expected life of five years. Machine 1 would generate annual cash flows (receipts less payments) of £210 000 and would cost £570 000. Its scrap value at the end of five years would be £70 000. Machine 2 would generate annual cash flows of £510 000 and would cost £1 616 000. The scrap value of this machine at the end of five years would be £301 000. Carbon plc uses the straight-line method of depreciation and has a target return on capital employed of 20 per cent.

Calculate the return on capital employed for both Machine 1 and Machine 2 on an average investment basis and state which machine you would recommend, giving reasons.

Suggested answer

	£
For Machine 1:	
Total cash profit = 210 000 × 5 =	1 050 000
Total depreciation = 570 000 – 70 000 =	500 000
Total accounting profit	500 000
Average annual accounting profit = 550 000/5 =	£110 000 per year
Average investment = (570 000 + 70 000)/2 =	£320 000
Return on capital employed = 100 × (110 000/320 000) =	34.4%
For Machine 2:	£
Total cash profit = 510 000 × 5 =	2 550 000
Total depreciation = 1 616 000 – 301 000 =	1 315 000
Total accounting profit	1 235 000
Average annual accounting profit = 1 235 000/5 =	£247 000 per year
Average investment = (1 616 000 + 301 000)/2 =	£958 500
Return on capital employed = 100 × (247 000/958 000) =	25.8%

Both machines have a return on capital employed greater than the target rate and so are financially acceptable, but as only one machine is to be purchased, the recommendation is that Machine 1 should be chosen, as it has a higher return on capital employed than Machine 2.

Advantages of the return on capital employed method

There are a number of reasons for the popularity of the return on capital employed method, even though it has little theoretical credibility as a method of making investment decisions. For example, it gives a value in percentage terms, a familiar measure of return, which can be compared with the existing ROCE of a company, the primary accounting ratio used by financial analysts in assessing company performance (see 'Profitability ratios', p. 137). It is also a reasonably simple method to apply and can be used to compare mutually exclusive projects. Unlike the payback method, it considers all cash flows arising during the life of an investment project and it can indicate whether a project is acceptable by comparing the ROCE of the project with a target rate, for example a company's current ROCE or the ROCE of a division.

Disadvantages of the return on capital employed method

While it can be argued that the return on capital employed method provides us with useful information about a project, as an investment appraisal method it has significant drawbacks. For example, it is not based on cash, but uses accounting profit, which is open to manipulation and is not linked to the fundamental objective of maximising shareholder wealth.

Because the method uses *average* profits, it also ignores the *timing* of profits. Consider the two projects A and B in Table 2.6. Both projects have the same initial investment and zero scrap value and hence the same average investment:

£45 000/2 = £22 500

Both projects have the same average annual accounting profit:

Project A: (−250 + 1000 + 1000 + 20 750)/4 = £5625
Project B: (6000 + 6000 + 5500 + 5000)/4 = £5625

So their return on capital employed values are identical too:

ROCE = (100 × 5625)/22 500 = 25%

Table 2.6 Illustration of how return on capital employed, which uses average accounting profit, ignores the timing of project cash flows

Year	0 £000	1 £000	2 £000	3 £000	4 £000
Project A					
cash flows	(45 000)	11 000	12 250	12 250	32 000
depreciation		11 250	11 250	11 250	11 250
accounting profit		(250)	1 000	1 000	20 750
Project B					
cash flows	(45 000)	17 250	17 250	16 750	16 250
depreciation		11 250	11 250	11 250	11 250
accounting profit		6 000	6 000	5 500	5 000

But Project B has a smooth pattern of returns, whereas Project A offers little in the first three years and a large return in the final year. We can see that, even though they both have the same ROCE, Project B is preferable to Project A by virtue of the pattern of its profits.

A more serious drawback is that the return on capital employed method does not consider the time value of money and so gives equal weight to profits whenever they occur. It also fails to take into account the length of the project life and, since it is expressed in percentage terms and is therefore a relative measure, it ignores the size of the investment made. For these reasons, the return on capital employed method cannot be seen as offering sensible advice about whether a project creates wealth or not. In order to obtain such advice, we need to use discounted cash flow methods, the most widely accepted of which is net present value.

The net present value method

The net present value (NPV) method of investment appraisal uses *discounted cash flows* to evaluate capital investment projects and is based on the sound theoretical foundation of the investment-consumption model developed by Hirshleifer (1958). It uses a *cost of capital* or target rate of return to discount all cash inflows and outflows to their *present values*, and then compares the present value of all cash inflows with the present value of all cash outflows. A *positive* net present value indicates that an investment project is expected to give a return in excess of the cost of capital and will therefore lead to an increase in shareholder wealth. We can represent the calculation of NPV algebraically as follows:

$$NPV = -I_0 + \frac{C_1}{(1+r)} + \frac{C_2}{(1+r)^2} + \frac{C_3}{(1+r)^3} + \ldots + \frac{C_n}{(1+r)^n}$$

where: I_0 is the initial investment
$C_1, C_2, \ldots, C_n$ are the project cash flows occurring in years $1, 2, \ldots, n$
r is the cost of capital or required rate of return

By convention, in order to avoid the mathematics of continuous discounting, cash flows occurring *during* a time period are assumed to occur at the *end* of that time period. The initial investment occurs at the start of the first time period. The NPV *decision rule* is to accept all independent projects with a positive net present value. If two capital investment projects are not independent but mutually exclusive, so that of the two projects available only one project can be undertaken, the project with the higher net present value should be selected.

Example

Calculation of the net present value

Carter plc is evaluating three investment projects, whose expected cash flows are given in Table 2.7. Calculate the net present value for each project if Carter's cost of capital is 10 per cent. Which project should be selected?

Project A

The cash inflows of this project are identical and so do not need to be discounted separately. Instead, we can use the cumulative present value factor (CPVF) or annuity factor for seven years at 10 per cent ($CPVF_{10,7}$), which is found from CPVF tables (see page 190) to have a value of 4.868. We have:

	£000
Initial investment	(5000)
Present value of cash inflows = £1100 × 4.868 =	5355
Net present value	355

Project A has a positive net present value of £355 000.

Project B

Because the cash inflows of this project are all different, it is necessary to discount each one separately. The easiest way to organise this calculation is by using a table, as in Table 2.8.

Using a table to organise net present value calculations is especially useful when dealing with the more complex cash flows which arise when account is taken of taxation, inflation and a range of costs or project variables. A tabular approach also aids clear thinking and methodical working in examinations. From Table 2.8, we can see that Project B has a positive net present value of £618 000.

Project C

The cash flows for the first three years are identical and can be discounted using the cumulative present value factor for three years at 10 per cent ($CPVF_{10,3}$), which is found from cumulative present value factor (CPVF) tables to be 2.487. The cash flows for years 4 to 7 are also identical and can be discounted using a cumulative present value factor.

Table 2.7 Three investment projects with different cash flow profiles to illustrate the calculation of net present value

Carter Ltd: cash flows of proposed investment projects			
Period	Project A (£000)	Project B (£000)	Project C (£000)
0	(5000)	(5000)	(5000)
1	1100	800	2000
2	1100	900	2000
3	1100	1200	2000
4	1100	1400	100
5	1100	1600	100
6	1100	1300	100
7	1100	1100	100

To find this, we subtract the cumulative present value factor for three years at 10 per cent from the cumulative present value factor for seven years at 10 per cent. From the CPVF tables, we have:

$$CPVF_{10,7} - CPVF_{10,3} = 4.868 - 2.487 = 2.381$$

	£000
Initial investment	(5000)
Present value of cash inflows, years 1 to 3 = £2000 × 2.487 =	4974
Present value of cash inflows, years 4 to 7 = £100 × 2.381 =	238
Net present value	212

Project C has a positive net present value of £212 000. If the annual cash flows are discounted separately, the NPV is £209 000, the difference being due to rounding.

The decision on project selection

We can now rank the projects in order of decreasing net present value:

Project B	NPV of £618 000
Project A	NPV of £355 000
Project C	NPV of £212 000

Which project should be selected? If the projects are mutually exclusive, then Project B should be undertaken since it has the highest NPV and will lead to the largest increase in shareholder wealth. If the projects are not mutually exclusive and there is no restriction on capital available for investment, all three projects should be undertaken since all three have a positive NPV and will increase shareholder wealth. However, the cash flows in years 4 to 7 of Project C should be investigated; they are not very large and they are critical to the project, since without them it would have a negative NPV and would therefore lead to a decrease in shareholder wealth.

Table 2.8 Calculation of net present value of Project B using a tabular approach. This approach organises the calculation and information used in a clear, easily understood format which helps to avoid errors during the calculation process

Year	Cash flow (£000)	10% present value factors	Present value (£000)
0	(5000)	1.000	(5000)
1	800	0.909	727
2	900	0.826	743
3	1200	0.751	901
4	1400	0.683	956
5	1600	0.621	994
6	1300	0.564	733
7	1100	0.513	564
		Net present value	618

Advantages of the net present value method

The net present value method of investment appraisal, being based on discounted cash flows, takes account of the *time value of money*, which is one of the key concepts in corporate finance. Net present value uses cash flows rather than accounting profit, takes account of both the amount and the timing of project cash flows, and takes account of all relevant cash flows over the life of an investment project. For all these reasons, net present value is the *academically preferred method* of investment appraisal. In all cases where there are no constraints on capital, the net present value decision rule offers sound investment advice.

Disadvantages of the net present value method

It has been argued that net present value is conceptually difficult to understand, but this is hardly a realistic criticism. It has also been pointed out that it is difficult to estimate the values of the cash inflows and outflows over the life of a project which are needed in order to calculate its net present value, but this difficulty of forecasting future cash flows is a problem of investment appraisal in general and not one that is specific to any particular investment appraisal technique. A more serious criticism is that it is only possible to accept all projects with a positive NPV in a perfect capital market, since only in such a market is there no restriction on the amount of finance available. In reality, capital is restricted or rationed (see 'The profitability index and capital rationing', p. 000) and this can limit the applicability of the NPV decision rule.

When calculating the NPV of an investment project, we tend to assume not only that the company's cost of capital is known, but also that it remains constant over the life of the project. In practice, the cost of capital of a company may be difficult to estimate and selecting an appropriate discount rate to use in investment appraisal is also not straightforward. The cost of capital is also likely to change over the life of the project, since it is influenced by the dynamic economic environment within which companies operate. However, if changes in the cost of capital can be forecast the net present value method can accommodate them without difficulty (see 'Changes in the discount rate', p. 000).

The internal rate of return method

If the cost of capital used to discount future cash flows is increased, the net present value of an investment project with conventional cash flows will fall. Eventually, as the cost of capital continues to increase, the NPV will become zero, and then negative. This is illustrated in Figure 2.3.

The *internal rate of return* (IRR) of an investment project is the cost of capital or required rate of return which, when used to discount the cash flows of a project, produces a net present value of zero. The internal rate of return method of investment appraisal involves calculating the IRR of a project, usually by linear interpolation, and then comparing it with a target rate of return or hurdle rate. The

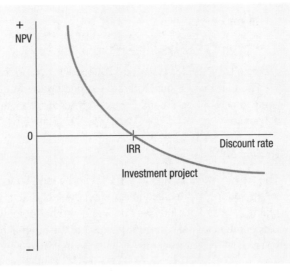

0

IRR

Discount rate

Investment project

Figure 2.3 The relationship between the net present values of a conventional project and the discount rate. The internal rate of return produces a net present value of zero

internal rate of return decision rule is to accept all independent investment projects with an IRR greater than the company's cost of capital or target rate of return.

We can restate the expression for net present value in terms of the internal rate of return as follows:

$$\frac{C_1}{(1 + r^*)} + \frac{C_2}{(1 + r^*)^2} + \frac{C_3}{(1 + r^*)^3} + \ldots + \frac{C_n}{(1 + r^*)^n} - I_0 = 0$$

where: $C_1, C_2, \ldots, C_n$ are the project cash flows occurring in years $1, 2, \ldots, n$
r^* is the internal rate of return
I_0 is the initial investment

Example

Calculation of internal rates of return

Carter plc is evaluating three investment projects, whose expected cash flows are given in Table 2.7. Calculate the internal rate of return for each project. If Carter's cost of capital is 10 per cent, which project should be selected?

Project A

In the previous example we found that (all values in £000):

$(£1100 \times CPVF_{10,7}) - £5000 = (1100 \times 4.868) - 5000 = £355$

Where project cash inflows are identical, we can determine the cumulative present value factor for a period corresponding to the life of the project and a discount rate equal to the internal rate of return. If we represent this by $(CPVF_{r,7})$, then from our above expression:

$(£1100 \times CPVF_{r^*,7}) - £5000 = 0$

Rearranging:

$$CPVF_{r^*,7} = 5000/1100 = 4.545$$

From CPVF tables (see page 190), looking along the row corresponding to seven years, we find that the discount rate corresponding to this cumulative present value factor is approximately 12 per cent. Project A therefore has an internal rate of return of 12 per cent.

Project B

The cash flows of Project B are all different and so to find its IRR we need to use linear interpolation. This technique relies on the fact that, if we know the location of any two points on a straight line, we can find any other point which also lies on that line. The procedure is to make an estimate (R_1) of the internal rate of return, giving a net present value of NPV_1. We then make a second estimate (R_2) of the internal rate of return: if NPV_1 was positive, R_2 should be higher than R_1; if NPV_1 was negative, R_2 should be lower than R_1. We then calculate a second net present value, NPV_2, from R_2. The values of R_1, R_2, NPV_1 and NPV_2 can then be put into the following expression.

$$IRR = R_1 + \frac{(R_2 - R_1) \times NPV_1}{(NPV_1 - NPV_2)}$$

We calculated earlier that the NPV of Project B was £618 000 at a discount rate of 10 per cent. If we now increase the discount rate to 20 per cent, since 10 per cent was less than the internal rate or return, we can recalculate the NPV, as shown in Table 2.9. The earlier NPV calculation is included for comparison.

Interpolating, using the method discussed earlier:

$$IRR = 10 + \frac{(20 - 10) \times 618}{618 - (-953)} = 10 + 3.9 = 13.9\%$$

So the internal rate of return of Project B is approximately 13.9 per cent.

We say 'approximately' since in using linear interpolation we have drawn a straight line between two points on a project NPV line that is in fact a curve. As shown in Figure 2.4, the straight line will not cut the x-axis at the same place as the project NPV curve, so the value we have obtained by interpolation is not the actual value of the IRR, but only an estimated value (and, for conventional projects, an underestimate). We would have

Table 2.9 Calculation of the NPV of Project B at discount rates of 10 per cent and 20 per cent as preparation for determining its IRR by linear interpolation

Year	Cash flow (£)	10% PV factors	Present value (£)	20% PV factors	Present value (£)
0	(5000)	1.000	(5000)	1.000	(5000)
1	800	0.909	727	0.833	666
2	900	0.826	743	0.694	625
3	1200	0.751	901	0.579	695
4	1400	0.683	956	0.482	675
5	1600	0.621	994	0.402	643
6	1300	0.564	733	0.335	436
7	1100	0.513	564	0.279	307
			618		(953)

obtained a different value if we had used a different estimate for R_2; for example, if we had used $R_1 = 10$ per cent and $R_2 = 15$ per cent, we would have obtained a value for the IRR of 13.5 per cent. To determine the actual IRR the interpolation calculation must be repeated, feeding successive approximations back into the calculation until the value produced no longer changes significantly. A financial calculator or a computer spreadsheet can easily do this task.

Project C

The calculation of the NPV of Project C at Carter's cost of capital of 10 per cent and a first estimate of the project IRR of 15 per cent is given in Table 2.10.

Interpolating:

$$IRR = 10 + \frac{(15 - 10) \times 209}{209 - (-244)} = 10 + 2.3 = 12.3 \text{ per cent}$$

The internal rate of return of Project C is approximately 12.3 per cent.

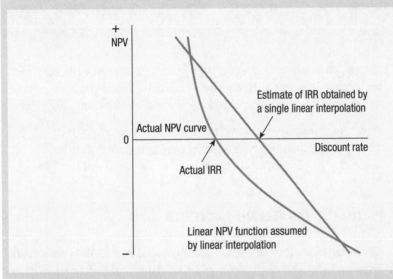

Figure 2.4 Why the IRR estimated by a single linear interpolation is only an approximation of the actual IRR of an investment project

Table 2.10 Calculation of the NPV of Project C at discount rates of 10 per cent and 15 per cent as preparation for determining its IRR by linear interpolation

Year	Cash flow (£)	10% PV factors	Present value (£)	15% PV factors	Present value (£)
0	(5000)	1.000	(5000)	1.000	(5000)
1	2000	0.909	1818	0.870	1740
2	2000	0.826	1652	0.756	1512
3	2000	0.751	1502	0.658	1316
4	100	0.683	68	0.572	57
5	100	0.621	62	0.497	50
6	100	0.564	56	0.432	43
7	100	0.513	51	0.376	38
			209		(244)

The decision on project selection

We can now summarise our calculations on the three projects:

Project A	IRR of 12.0 per cent	NPV of £355 000
Project B	IRR of 13.9 per cent	NPV of £618 000
Project C	IRR of 12.3 per cent	NPV of £209 000

All three projects have an IRR greater than Carter's cost of capital of 10 per cent, so all are acceptable if there is no restriction on available capital. If the projects are mutually exclusive, however, it is not possible to choose the best project by using the internal rate of return method. Notice that, although the IRR of Project C is higher than that of Project A, its NPV is lower. This means that the projects are ranked differently using IRR than they are using NPV. The problem of mutually exclusive investment projects is discussed below.

A comparison of the NPV and IRR methods

There is no conflict between these two discounted cash flow methods when a *single* investment project with *conventional* cash flows is being evaluated. In the following situations, however, the net present value method may be preferred:

● where mutually exclusive projects are being compared;
● where the cash flows of a project are not conventional;
● where the discount rate changes during the life of the project.

Mutually exclusive projects

Consider two mutually exclusive projects, A and B, whose cash flows are given in Table 2.11. The net present value decision rule recommends accepting Project B, since it has the higher NPV at a cost of capital of 14 per cent. However, if the projects are compared using internal rate of return, Project A is preferred as it has the higher IRR. If the projects were independent so that both could be undertaken, this conflict of preferences would not be relevant. Since the projects are mutually exclusive, however, which should be accepted?

Table 2.11 Table showing the cash flows, net present values at a cost of capital of 14 per cent and internal rates of return of two mutually exclusive projects

	Project A	Project B
Initial investment (£)	13 000	33 000
Year 1 net cash flow (£)	7 000	15 000
Year 2 net cash flow (£)	6 000	15 000
Year 3 net cash flow (£)	5 000	15 000
Net present value (£)	+1 128	+1 830
Internal rate of return (%)	19.5	17

Table 2.12 The net present values of two mutually exclusive projects at different discount rates

Discount rate (%)	12	14	16	18	20	22
Project A (£)	1593	1128	697	282	(113)	(473)
Project B (£)	3030	1830	690	(390)	(1410)	(2370)

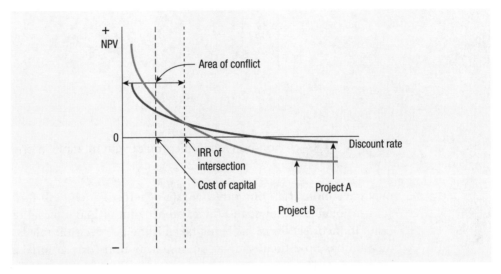

Figure 2.5   The calculated NPV of two mutually exclusive projects and the region of conflict

In all cases where this conflict occurs, the correct decision is to choose the project with the higher NPV. This decision supports the primary corporate finance objective of maximising shareholder wealth since selecting the project with the highest NPV leads to the greatest increase in the value of the company. Although Project A has the highest IRR, this is only a *relative* measure of return. NPV measures the *absolute* increase in value of the company.

In order to illustrate the conflict between the two investment appraisal methods in more detail, Table 2.12 shows the NPV of the two projects at different discount rates and Figure 2.5 displays the same information in the form of a graph.

From Figure 2.5, it can be seen that the two projects, A and B, have project lines with different slopes. For costs of capital *greater* than the IRR of the intersection of the two project lines, which occurs at approximately 16 per cent, the two methods give the same advice, which is to accept Project A. For costs of capital *less* than the IRR of the intersection, the advice offered by the two methods is in conflict and the net present value method is preferred.

Non-conventional cash flows

If an investment project has cash flows of different signs in successive periods (e.g. a cash inflow followed by a cash outflow, followed by a further cash inflow), it

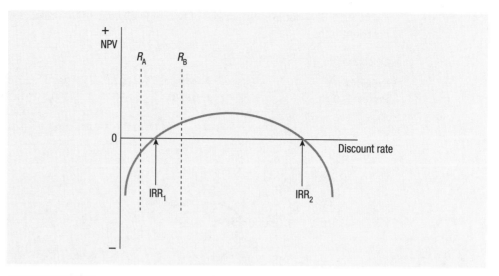

Figure 2.6   A non-conventional project with multiple internal rates of return

may have more than one internal rate of return. Such cash flows are called non-conventional cash flows, and the existence of multiple internal rates of return may result in incorrect decisions being taken if the IRR decision rule is applied. The NPV method has no difficulty in accommodating non-conventional cash flows, as can be seen from Figure 2.6.

The non-conventional project in Figure 2.6 has two internal rates of return, at IRR_1 and IRR_2. This kind of project is not unusual: for example, a mineral extraction project, with heavy initial investment in land, plant and machinery and significant environmental costs towards the end of the project life, might have this kind of NPV profile. Using the internal rate of return method, which IRR should be used to assess the project?

If the cost of capital is R_A, the project would be accepted using the internal rate of return method, since both IRR_1 and IRR_2 are greater than R_A. If the net present value method is used, however, it will be rejected, because at this discount rate it has a negative NPV and would decrease shareholder wealth.

However, if the cost of capital used to assess the project is R_B, it will be accepted using the net present value method because at this discount rate it has a positive NPV. The internal rate of return method cannot offer any clear advice since R_B is between IRR_1 and IRR_2.

In each case, the net present value method gives the correct investment advice.

Changes in the discount rate

If there are changes in the cost of capital over the life of an investment project, the net present value method can easily accommodate them. Consider the net present value expression described earlier, with the symbols having the same meaning:

$$NPV = -I_0 + \frac{C_1}{(1+r)} + \frac{C_2}{(1+r)^2} + \frac{C_3}{(1+r)^3} + \ldots + \frac{C_n}{(1+r)^n}$$

Table 2.13 Investment project in which the discount rate changes during the project life

Year	0	1	2	3
Discount rate (%)		10	10	15
Cash flow (£)	(13 000)	7000	5000	6000
PV factors	1.000	0.909	0.826	0.719
Present value (£)	(13 000)	6363	4130	4314

If the discount rates in successive years are r_1, r_2, etc., we have:

$$NPV = -I_0 + \frac{C_1}{(1 + r_1)} + \frac{C_2}{(1 + r_1)(1 + r_2)} + \dots$$

Consider the investment project in Table 2.13, where the discount rate increases in year 3 from 10 per cent to 15 per cent. The present value factor for year 3 is the present value factor for two years at 10 per cent multiplied by the present value factor for one year at 15 per cent. Using present value tables (see page 189), we have:

$$PVF_{10,2} \times PVF_{15,1} = 0.826 \times 0.870 = 0.719$$

The NPV of the project is £1807 while the IRR is approximately 18.8 per cent. The IRR, however, cannot take into account the fact that the discount rate in year 3 is different from that in years 1 and 2.

Reinvestment assumptions

The net present value method assumes that cash flows generated during the life of the project can be reinvested elsewhere at a rate equal to the cost of capital. This seems to be a sensible reinvestment assumption since the cost of capital represents an opportunity cost, i.e. the best return that could have been obtained on an alternative investment. The internal rate of return method, however, assumes that cash flows generated during the life of the project can be reinvested elsewhere at the internal rate of return. The more the IRR exceeds the cost of capital, the less likely it is that such alternative returns could be realised, and so the reinvestment assumption underlying the internal rate of return method is a doubtful one. The reinvestment assumption underlying the NPV method seems realistic.

The superiority of the net present value method

We can now summarise the arguments in favour of the net present value method of investment appraisal:

1 The NPV method gives correct advice about mutually exclusive projects.
2 The NPV method can accommodate non-conventional cash flows, when the internal rate of return method may offer multiple solutions.
3 The reinvestment assumption underlying the NPV method is realistic, but the reinvestment assumption underlying the internal rate of return method is not.

4 The NPV method can easily incorporate changes in the discount rate, whereas the internal rate of return method does not take these changes into account.

For these reasons, the net present value method is held to be technically superior to the internal rate of return method.

The internal rate of return method, however, enjoys comparable popularity. It is obviously to be preferred to both payback period and accounting rate of return as an investment appraisal method since it takes account of the time value of money, is based on cash flows and considers the whole of the project. The IRR or *yield* of an investment project is also a concept widely understood by financial analysts, investors and managers, and indicates the extent to which a project offers returns in excess of a minimum required level, i.e. it indicates a margin of safety.

This chapter has argued that discounted cash flow investment appraisal methods (i.e. NPV and IRR) are superior to simplistic investment appraisal methods (i.e. payback and return on capital employed) and this is widely accepted. Companies using discounted cash flow (DCF) investment appraisal methods should therefore perform better than those using simplistic methods. Empirical research on this question has produced mixed results, however, and Haka *et al.* (1985) found evidence that adoption of sophisticated investment appraisal methods may not necessarily, in itself, lead to improved performance. Since most companies now use more than one investment appraisal method, it is in practice difficult to isolate any beneficial effects that may be solely due to using DCF methods. This does not invalidate the academic superiority of NPV and IRR.

The profitability index and capital rationing

If a company does not have sufficient funds to undertake all projects that have a positive net present value, it is in a *capital rationing* situation. It will need to find a way of choosing between investment opportunities which maximise the return on the funds invested, i.e. it needs to *rank* investment projects in terms of desirability. The NPV method, which requires a company to invest in *all* projects with a positive NPV in order to maximise shareholder wealth, calls for the existence of a perfect market to provide any investment funds that may be required. The NPV method cannot be used to rank investment projects if capital is rationed, however, since ranking by NPV may lead to incorrect investment decisions. This is because a *combination* of smaller projects may collectively offer a higher NPV than a single project in return for the available capital, even if, when ranked by NPV, the smaller projects are ranked below the larger one.

Hard and soft capital rationing

We can distinguish between hard and soft capital rationing. Hard capital rationing occurs when the limitation on investment funds is imposed externally by the capital market. Soft capital rationing occurs when the limitation on investment funds is imposed internally by a company's managers.

Hard capital rationing

A company may be unable to raise investment finance because capital markets are depressed or because investors consider the company to be too risky. If only a small amount of finance is needed, for example to meet a marginal funding requirement, issue costs might make raising this finance unacceptably expensive. Most capital rationing is self-imposed and therefore soft in nature. While it has been unusual historically for hard capital rationing to occur, the onset of the 'credit crunch' in 2008 meant that it became more difficult to obtain suitable finance for capital investment, as illustrated by the Mini case below, where capital rationing is mentioned as a key factor shaping the mergers and acquisitions market.

Soft capital rationing

Investment funds may be restricted internally by managers for a number of reasons. They may decide against issuing more equity finance, for example, because

---

mini case   M&A surge on horizon for Europe

The corporate landscape in Europe looks set to be radically altered next year as chief executives of some of the continent's biggest public companies embark on a series of transformational deals, according to a wide-ranging study released on Friday.

A combination of the need for consolidation within some industries, attractive prices of assets and struggling players needing new ownership will spur a series of deals, echoing the experience of previous crises in the 1930s, 1970s and late 1980s. The findings come in a report by UBS and the Boston Consulting Group, based on interviews with more than 160 chief executives and senior managers of publicly listed companies in Europe. It was conducted just six weeks after the collapse of Lehman Brothers.

The impact of the credit crisis and the increased cost of short-term refinancing rates has seen several companies in Europe abandon their deals in recent weeks, including BHP Billiton's $62bn bid for Rio Tinto, which was the largest ever withdrawn deal in corporate history. Volumes for European mergers and acquisitions in the year to date are down by 20 per cent on last year.

Daniel Stillit, head of special situations research at UBS, said 2009 would see increased polarisation among companies in terms of operating performance and as consequences of selective capital rationing by banks and equity investors.

'Transformational M&A and deal-based restructuring will eventually be a big by-product,' he said.

Almost half of those companies surveyed that have a market capitalisation of $5bn–$20bn expect transformational deals in their sectors next year. UBS identified several possible deals that could take place next year, including a merger between France's Peugeot and the auto business of Italy's Fiat; France's Areva and Alstom; the UK's AstraZeneca acquiring its smaller rival Shire; and a takeover of Germany's Hochtief by ACS of Spain. BHP could also revisit its bid for Rio late next year, while Xstrata could try again for Lonmin, having acquired a blocking stake of 25 per cent to prevent other bidders from gaining control.

But the survey also revealed that some chief executives believe deal-making in the short term could be risky in the current environment. About 37 per cent cited balance sheet or financing constraints as the main reason for not doing M&A, followed by concerns that valuations of assets are still too high.

Source: *Financial Times*, 11 December 2008. Reprinted with permission.

they wish to avoid dilution (reduction) of control, or because they wish to avoid any potential dilution (reduction) of earnings per share (EPS). They may decide against raising additional debt finance through a desire to avoid increased interest payment commitments, perhaps because they are concerned about their company's existing level of gearing or financial risk. If a company is small or family-owned, its managers may limit the investment funds available as part of a policy of seeking steady growth through retained earnings, as opposed to a policy of rapid expansion.

It is possible that self-imposed capital rationing, by fostering a competitive *internal market* for available investment funds, will weed out marginal or borderline investment projects and encourage the generation of better, more robust, investment proposals.

Single-period capital rationing

In single period capital rationing the available funds are only restricted initially, i.e. in year 0. A company needs to choose the combination of projects which maximises the total NPV. Depending on the circumstances, this can be done either by ranking projects using the profitability index or by finding the NPV of possible combinations of projects.

Divisible, non-deferrable investment projects

To assist in clarifying the circumstances in which the profitability index can be used, we can define three kinds of investment project. A *divisible project* is one where any portion of the project may be undertaken; a *non-deferrable project* is one which, if it is not undertaken at the present time, cannot be undertaken later; a *non-repeatable project* is one that may be undertaken only once.

If the available investment projects are divisible, non-deferrable and non-repeatable and if capital is rationed in the initial period only, ranking projects by their absolute NPV will not lead to the correct decision since, as pointed out earlier, a project with a large NPV will be preferred over a combination of several smaller projects with a larger collective NPV. The correct approach here is to calculate a *profitability index* or benefit to cost ratio for each project and then to rank them using this measure. The profitability index tells us how much we can expect to receive, in present value terms, for each unit of currency invested in the project:

$$\text{Profitability index} = \frac{\text{Present value of future cash flows}}{\text{Value of initial capital invested}}$$

If there is no restriction on investment capital, all projects with a profitability index greater than one should be accepted. This corresponds to the NPV decision rule of accepting all projects with a positive NPV. If investment capital is restricted, the project with the highest profitability index should be undertaken, then funds should be allocated to the project with the next highest profitability index, and so on until there is no longer a whole project that can be undertaken. As the projects

Table 2.14 Example of ranking of divisible projects by profitability index in order to derive the optimum investment schedule under single-period capital rationing. Note that the ranking by absolute NPV is quite different from the ranking by profitability index

Project	A	B	C	D
Initial investment (£000)	500	650	800	850
Net present value (£000)	650	715	800	765
PV of future cash flows (£000)	1150	1365	1600	1615
Profitability index	2.3	2.1	2.0	1.9
Ranking by NPV	4	3	1	2
Ranking by profitability index	1	2	3	4

Capital available = £1 650 000

Optimum investment schedule:	NPV (£000)	Cumulative investment (£000)
£500 000 invested in Project A	650	500
£650 000 invested in Project B	715	1150
£500 000 invested in Project C	500	1650
Total NPV for £1 650 000 invested:	1865	

are divisible, the remaining funds are invested pro rata in the next best project. The total NPV arising from this investment schedule is the sum of the NPV of the complete projects, added to the pro rata share of the NPV of the partly undertaken project. This procedure is illustrated in Table 2.14.

From Table 2.14 we can see that, if we have £1 650 000 available to invest in the divisible Projects A, B, C and D, then the optimum investment is to undertake all of Projects A and B and 62.5 per cent of Project C, giving a total NPV of £1 865 000. This is preferable to investing £1 650 000 in Projects C and D, even though these have the highest NPV, since their total NPV is only £1 565 000. If Project A had been repeatable, the optimum investment schedule would have been to repeat Project A 3.3 times, giving a total NPV of £2 145 000.

The profitability index can also be defined as the ratio of net present value to initial capital invested: the optimum investment schedule decision process is the same regardless of the definition of profitability index used.

Indivisible, non-deferrable investment projects

If investment projects are not divisible, profitability indices still provide useful information, but the selection of projects can only be achieved by examining the total NPV of all possible combinations of projects. The combination with the highest NPV which does not exceed the available investment capital is optimal. Assuming that the projects in Table 2.14 are now indivisible, the optimum investment schedule is a combination of Projects C and D.

Projects A and B	Total NPV = £1 365 000
Projects A and C	Total NPV = £1 450 000
Projects A and D	Total NPV = £1 415 000
Projects B and C	Total NPV = £1 515 000
Projects B and D	Total NPV = £1 480 000
Projects C and D	Total NPV = £1 565 000

Multiple-period capital rationing

If investment funds are expected to be restricted in more than one period, the decision about which projects to choose cannot be based on ranking projects by profitability index or by trying different combinations of projects since neither of these methods takes into account the restriction on finance in future periods. The complexity of this problem means that linear programming is needed for its solution. With only two variables, the linear programming problem can be solved graphically, but, if there are more than two variables, the simplex method or a computer must be used. The solution of multiple-period capital rationing problems is not considered in this text (but see, for example, Drury 2008).

The discounted payback method

The payback method discussed earlier in the section (see 'The payback method', p. 160) can be modified by discounting the project cash flows by the company's cost of capital in order to take account of the time value of money. Consider the example given in Table 2.15, where a company with a cost of capital of 15 per cent is evaluating an investment project.

Table 2.15 Showing how cumulative NPV can be used to determine the discounted payback period for a project

Year	Cash flow (£)	15% PV factor	Present value (£)	Cumulative NPV (£)
0	(5000)	1.000	(5000)	(5000)
1	2300	0.870	2001	(2999)
2	2500	0.756	1890	(1109)
3	1200	0.658	790	(319)
4	1000	0.572	572	253
5	1000	0.497	497	750

The discounted payback period is approximately 3.5 years, compared with an undiscounted payback period of approximately 2.2 years. The discounted payback method has the same advantages and disadvantages as before except that the short-coming of failing to account for the time value of money has been overcome.

Conclusion

In this section, we have considered at an introductory level the methods used by corporate finance to evaluate investment projects. While there are a wide range of tech-niques that can be used, the net present value method enjoys the support of academics and is regarded as superior to the other investment appraisal methods discussed.

Key points

1 Payback period is the number of years it takes to recover the original investment from the cash flows resulting from a capital investment project.

2 Payback takes account of risk (if by risk we mean the uncertainty that increases as cash flows become more distant), and is a simple method to apply and understand. However, it ignores the time value of money, the timing of cash flows within the payback period and any cash flows after the payback period. It does not say whether a project is a 'good' one.

3 Return on capital employed is the ratio of average annual profit to capital invested. It is simple to apply, looks at the whole of an investment project and can be used to compare mutually exclusive projects. A project is acceptable if the ROCE exceeds a target value.

4 Return on capital employed ignores the time value of money, fails to take account of the size and timing of cash flows and uses accounting profits rather than cash flows.

5 Net present value is the difference between the present value of future benefits and the present value of capital invested, discounted at a company's cost of capital. The NPV decision rule is to accept all projects with a positive net present value.

6 The NPV method takes account of the time value of money and the amount and timing of all relevant cash flows over the life of the project.

7 The NPV method can take account of both conventional and non-conventional cash flows, can accommodate changes in the discount rate during the life of a project and gives an absolute rather than a relative measure of project desirability.

8 Difficulties with using the NPV method are: it is difficult to estimate cash flows over the project life; the cost of capital for a company may be difficult to estimate; and the cost of capital may change over the project life.

9 The internal rate of return method involves the calculation of the discount rate which gives an NPV of zero. The IRR decision rule is to accept all projects with an IRR greater than the company's target rate of return.

10 The NPV method gives correct investment advice when comparing mutually exclusive projects; IRR might not.

11 The NPV method assumes that cash flows can be reinvested at the cost of capital, while the IRR method assumes that cash flows are reinvested at the internal rate of return. Only the reinvestment assumption underlying the NPV method is realistic.

12 Capital rationing can be either hard (externally imposed) or soft (internally imposed).

13 Hard capital rationing might occur because capital markets are depressed or because a company is thought to be too risky.

14 Soft capital rationing might occur because a company wishes to avoid dilution of control, dilution of EPS or further fixed interest commitments. The company may wish to pursue a policy of steady growth or believe that restricting funds will encourage better projects.

15 In single-period capital rationing, divisible, non-deferrable and non-repeatable investment projects can be ranked using the profitability index in order to find the optimal investment schedule. The profitability index is the ratio of the present value of future cash flows divided by the initial capital invested.

16 Multiple-period capital rationing requires the use of linear programming.

Self-test questions

Answers to these questions can be found on pages 186–188.

1 Explain why the payback method cannot be recommended as the main method used by a company to assess potential investment projects.

2 Calculate the return on capital employed (average investment basis) for the following projects, and show which would be chosen if the target ROCE is 12 per cent. Assume straight-line depreciation (equal annual amounts) over the life of the project, with zero scrap value.

	Project A (£)	Project B (£)	Project C (£)
Initial investment	10 000	15 000	20 000
Net cash inflows:			
Year 1	5 000	5 000	10 000
Year 2	5 000	5 000	8 000
Year 3	2 000	5 000	4 000
Year 4	1 000	10 000	2 000
Year 5		5 000	

3 Explain the shortcomings of return on capital employed as an investment appraisal method and suggest reasons why it may be used by managers.

4 Three investment projects have the following net cash flows. Decide which of them should be accepted using the NPV decision rule if the discount rate to be applied is 12 per cent.

Year	Project A (£)	Project B (£)	Project C (£)
0	(10 000)	(15 000)	(20 000)
1	5 000	5 000	10 000
2	5 000	5 000	10 000
3	2 000	5 000	4 000
4	1 000	10 000	2 000
5		5 000	

5 List the advantages of the net present value investment appraisal method.

6 Explain how NPV and IRR deal with non-conventional cash flows.

7 Discuss the problem of choosing between mutually exclusive projects with respect to their net present values and internal rates of return.

8 Show with the aid of a numerical example how linear interpolation can be used to determine the internal rate of return of a project.

9 Explain the distinction between hard and soft capital rationing, and outline the reasons why these conditions might occur.

10 What techniques can be used to determine the optimum investment schedule for a company under conditions of capital rationing?

Questions for review

Questions with an asterisk (*) are at an intermediate level.

1* The expected cash flows of two projects are given below. The cost of capital is 10 per cent.

Period	Project A (£)	Project B (£)
0	(5000)	(5000)
1	1000	2000
2	2500	2000
3	2500	2000
4	1500	1000

(a) Calculate the payback period, net present value, internal rate of return and return on capital employed of each project.

(b) Show the rankings of the projects by each of the four methods and comment on your findings.

2 LJH plc is planning to buy a machine which will cost £900 000 and which is expected to generate new cash sales of £600 000 per year. The expected useful life of the machine will be eight years, at the end of which it will have a scrap value of £100 000. Annual costs are expected to be £400 000 per year. LJH plc has a cost of capital of 11 per cent.

(a) Calculate the payback period, return on capital employed, net present value and internal rate of return of the proposed investment.

(b) Discuss the reasons why net present value is preferred by academics to other methods of evaluating investment projects.

3* Brown Ltd is considering buying a new machine which would have a useful economic life of five years, a cost of £125 000 and a scrap value of £30 000, with 80 per cent of the cost being payable at the start of the project and 20 per cent after one year. The machine would produce 50 000 units per year of a new product with an estimated selling price of £3 per unit. Direct costs would be £1.75 per unit and annual fixed costs, including depreciation calculated on a straight-line basis (equal annual amounts), would be £40 000 per annum.

In years 1 and 2, special sales promotion expenditure, not included in the above costs, would be incurred, amounting to £10 000 and £15 000, respectively.

Evaluate the project using the NPV method of investment appraisal, assuming the company's cost of capital is 10 per cent.

4* Better plc is comparing two mutually exclusive projects, whose details are given below. The company's cost of capital is 12 per cent.

	Project A (£m)	Project B (£m)
Year 0	(150)	(152)
Year 1	40	80
Year 2	50	60
Year 3	60	50
Year 4	60	40
Year 5	80	30

(a) Using the net present value method, which project should be accepted?

(b) Using the internal rate of return method, which project should be accepted?

(c) If the cost of capital increases to 20 per cent in year 5, would your advice change?

5   The finance director of Park plc is preparing financial plans and different departments have submitted a number of capital investment applications. The managing director has said that no more than £1 million is available for new investment projects. Cash flow forecasts from the capital investment applications are as follows.

	Project A (£000)	Project B (£000)	Project C (£000)	Project D (£000)
Year 0	(340)	(225)	(350)	(275)
Year 1	105	75	90	115
Year 2	110	75	90	115
Year 3	115	75	140	115
Year 4	110	75	140	115
Year 5	105	90	140	nil

The cost of capital of Park plc is 15 per cent per year.

(a) Determine the optimum investment schedule and the net present value of the optimum investment schedule, if investment projects are divisible but not repeatable.

(b) Determine the optimum investment schedule and the net present value of the optimum investment schedule, if investment projects are not divisible and not repeatable.

(c) Discuss the reasons why the managing director of Park plc may have limited the funds available for new investment projects at the start of the next financial year, even if this results in the rejection of projects which may increase the value of the company.

Questions for discussion

Questions with an asterisk (*) are at an advanced level.

1   The finance manager of Willow plc is evaluating two mutually exclusive projects with the following cash flows.

Year	Project A (£)	Project B (£)
0	(110 000)	(200 000)
1	45 000	50 000
2	45 000	50 000
3	30 000	50 000
4	30 000	100 000
5	20 000	55 000

Willow's cost of capital is 10 per cent and both investment projects have zero scrap value. The company's current return on capital employed is 12 per cent (average investment basis) and the company uses straight-line depreciation over the life of projects.

(a) Advise the company which project should be undertaken in the following circumstances if:
  (i)   the net present value method of investment appraisal is used;
  (ii) the internal rate of return method of investment appraisal is used;
  (iii) the return on capital employed method of investment appraisal is used.

(b) Discuss the problems that arise for the net present value method of investment appraisal when capital is limited, and explain how such problems may be resolved in practice.

2   The finance director of RM plc is considering several investment projects and has collected the following information about them.

Project	Estimated initial outlay (£)	Cash inflow Year 1 (£)	Cash inflow Year 2 (£)	Cash inflow Year 3 (£)
A	200 000	150 000	150 000	150 000
B	450 000	357 000	357 000	357 000
C	550 000	863 000	853 000	853 000
D	170 000	278 000	278 000	nil
E	200 000	250 000	250 000	250 000
F	330 000	332 000	332 000	nil

Projects D and E are mutually exclusive. The capital available for investment is limited to £1m in the first year. All projects are divisible and none may be postponed or repeated. The cost of capital of RM plc is 15 per cent.

(a) Discuss the possible reasons why RM plc may be limited as to the amount of capital available for investment in its projects.

(b) Determine which investment projects the finance director of RM plc should choose in order to maximise the return on the capital available for investment. If the projects were not divisible, would you change your advice to the finance director?

(c) Critically discuss the reasons why net present value is the method of investment appraisal preferred by academics. Has the internal rate of return method now been made redundant?

3   The finance manager of Wide plc is evaluating two capital investment projects which may assist the company in achieving its business objectives. Both projects will require an initial investment of £500 000 in plant and machinery but it is not expected that any additional investment in working capital will be needed. The expected cash flows of the two projects are as follows.

Period	Broad Project (£)	Keeling Project (£)
1	60 000	220 000
2	90 000	220 000
3	140 000	50 000
4	210 000	50 000
5	300 000	50 000
6	140 000	50 000
7	100 000	200 000

The cost of capital of Wide plc is 10 per cent.

(a) For both the Broad and Keeling projects, calculate the return on capital employed, based on the average investment, the net present value and the internal rate of return.

(b) If the Broad and Keeling projects are mutually exclusive, advise Wide plc which project should be undertaken.

(c) Critically discuss the advantages and disadvantages of return on capital employed as an investment appraisal method.

References

Drury, C. (2008) *Management and Cost Accounting*, 7th edn, London: Cengage Learning, pp. 641–53.

Haka, S., Gordon, L. and Pinches, G. (1985) 'Sophisticated capital budgeting selection techniques and firm performance', *The Accounting Review*, Vol. 60, No. 4, pp. 651–69.

Hirshleifer, J. (1958) 'On the theory of optimal investment decisions', *Journal of Political Economy*, Vol. 66, pp. 329–52.

Recommended reading

Many textbooks offer the opportunity to read further on the topic of investment appraisal techniques. A useful text is:

Arnold, G. (2008) *Corporate Financial Management*, 4th edn, Harlow: FT Prentice Hall.

Answers to self-test questions

1 The payback method cannot be recommended as the main method used by a company to assess potential investment projects because it has serious disadvantages. These include the following:

- payback ignores the time value of money;
- payback ignores the timing of cash flows within the payback period;
- payback ignores post-payback cash flows;
- the choice of payback period is arbitrary;
- payback does not measure profitability.

2 *Project A*

Average annual accounting profit = (13 000 − 10 000)/4 = £750

Average annual investment = 10 000/2 = £5000

Return on capital employed = (750 × 100)/5000 = 15%

Project B

Average annual accounting profit = (30 000 × 15 000)/5 = £3000

Average annual investment = 15 000/2 = £7500

Return on capital employed = (3000 × 100)/7500 = 40%

Project C

Average annual accounting profit = (24 000 − 20 000)/4 = £1000

Average annual investment = 20 000/2 = £10 000

Return on capital employed = (1000 × 100)/10 000 = 10%

Project	ROCE (%)	Ranking
A	15	2
B	40	1
C	10	3

If the target ROCE is 12 per cent, projects A and B will be accepted.

3 The shortcomings of return on capital employed (ROCE) as an investment appraisal method are: it ignores the time value of money; it ignores the timing of cash flows; it uses accounting profits rather than cash flows; and it does not take account of the size of the initial investment. However, ROCE gives an answer as a percentage return, which is a familiar measure of return, and is a simple method to apply. It can be used to compare mutually exclusive projects, and can also indicate whether a project is a 'good' one compared to a target ROCE. For these reasons, it is used quite widely in industry.

4 *Project A*

Year	Cash flow (£)	12% discount factor	Present value (£)
0	(10 000)	1.000	(10 000)
1	5 000	0.893	4 465
2	5 000	0.797	3 985
3	2 000	0.712	1 424
4	1 000	0.636	636
		Net present value	510

Project B

Year	Cash flow (£)	12% discount factor	Present value (£)
0	(15 000)	1.000	(15 000)
1	5 000	0.893	4 465
2	5 000	0.797	3 985
3	5 000	0.712	3 560
4	10 000	0.636	6 360
5	5 000	0.567	2 835
		Net present value	6 205

Project C

Year	Cash flow (£)	12% discount factor	Present value (£)
0	(20 000)	1.000	(20 000)
1	10 000	0.893	8 930
2	10 000	0.797	7 970
3	4 000	0.712	2 848
4	2 000	0.636	1 272
		Net present value	1 020

Summary

Project	NPV (£)	Ranking
A	510	3
B	6 205	1
C	1 020	2

Since all three projects have a positive NPV, they are all acceptable.

5 The advantages of the net present value method of investment appraisal are that it:
  - takes account of the time value of money;
  - takes account of the amount and timing of cash flows;
  - uses cash flows rather than accounting profit;
  - takes account of all relevant cash flows over the life of the project;
  - can take account of both conventional and non-conventional cash flows;
  - can take account of changes in discount rate during the life of the project;
  - gives an absolute rather than a relative measure of the desirability of the project;
  - can be used to compare all investment projects.

6 If an investment project has positive and negative cash flows in successive periods (non-conventional cash flows), it may have more than one internal rate of return. This may result in incorrect decisions being taken if the IRR decision rule is applied. The NPV method has no difficulty in accommodating non-conventional cash flows.

7 There is no conflict between the NPV and IRR methods when they are applied to a single investment project with conventional cash flows. In other situations, the two methods may give conflicting results. In all cases where this conflict occurs, the project with the highest NPV should be chosen. This can be proven by examining the incremental cash flows of the projects concerned. The reason for the conflict between the two methods can also be viewed graphically.

8 The answer to this question is contained in 'The internal rate of return method', p. 168.

9 If a company is restricted in the capital available for investment, it will not be able to undertake all projects with a positive NPV and is in a capital rationing situation. Capital rationing may be either soft (owing to internal factors) or hard (owing to external factors). Soft capital rationing may arise if management adopts a policy of stable growth, is reluctant to issue new equity or wishes to avoid raising new debt capital. It may also arise if management wants to encourage competition for funds. Hard capital rationing may arise because the capital markets are depressed or because investors consider the company to be too risky.

10 If projects are divisible and independent, they can be ranked by using the profitability index or cost–benefit ratio. If projects are not divisible, then combinations of projects must be examined to find the investment schedule giving the highest NPV.

Table of present value factors

Present values of $1/(1 + r)^n$

				Discount rates (r)						
Periods (n)	**1%**	**2%**	**3%**	**4%**	**5%**	**6%**	**7%**	**8%**	**9%**	**10%**
1	0.990	0.980	0.971	0.962	0.952	0.943	0.935	0.926	0.917	0.909
2	0.980	0.961	0.943	0.925	0.907	0.890	0.873	0.857	0.842	0.826
3	0.971	0.942	0.915	0.889	0.864	0.840	0.816	0.794	0.772	0.751
4	0.961	0.924	0.888	0.855	0.823	0.792	0.763	0.735	0.708	0.683
5	0.951	0.906	0.863	0.822	0.784	0.747	0.713	0.681	0.650	0.621
6	0.942	0.888	0.837	0.790	0.746	0.705	0.666	0.630	0.596	0.564
7	0.933	0.871	0.813	0.760	0.711	0.665	0.623	0.583	0.547	0.513
8	0.923	0.853	0.789	0.731	0.677	0.627	0.582	0.540	0.502	0.467
9	0.914	0.837	0.766	0.703	0.645	0.592	0.544	0.500	0.460	0.424
10	0.905	0.820	0.744	0.676	0.614	0.558	0.508	0.463	0.422	0.386
11	0.896	0.804	0.722	0.650	0.585	0.527	0.475	0.429	0.388	0.350
12	0.887	0.788	0.701	0.625	0.557	0.497	0.444	0.397	0.356	0.319
13	0.879	0.773	0.681	0.601	0.530	0.469	0.415	0.368	0.326	0.290
14	0.870	0.758	0.661	0.577	0.505	0.442	0.388	0.340	0.299	0.263
15	0.861	0.743	0.642	0.555	0.481	0.417	0.362	0.315	0.275	0.239
16	0.853	0.728	0.623	0.534	0.458	0.394	0.339	0.292	0.252	0.218
17	0.844	0.714	0.605	0.513	0.436	0.371	0.317	0.270	0.231	0.198
18	0.836	0.700	0.587	0.494	0.416	0.350	0.296	0.250	0.212	0.180
19	0.828	0.686	0.570	0.475	0.396	0.331	0.277	0.232	0.194	0.164
20	0.820	0.673	0.554	0.456	0.377	0.312	0.258	0.215	0.178	0.149

				Discount rates (r)						
Periods (n)	**11%**	**12%**	**13%**	**14%**	**15%**	**16%**	**17%**	**18%**	**19%**	**20%**
1	0.901	0.893	0.885	0.877	0.870	0.862	0.855	0.847	0.840	0.833
2	0.812	0.797	0.783	0.769	0.756	0.743	0.731	0.718	0.706	0.694
3	0.731	0.712	0.693	0.675	0.658	0.641	0.624	0.609	0.593	0.579
4	0.659	0.636	0.613	0.592	0.572	0.552	0.534	0.516	0.499	0.482
5	0.593	0.567	0.543	0.519	0.497	0.476	0.456	0.437	0.419	0.402
6	0.535	0.507	0.480	0.456	0.432	0.410	0.390	0.370	0.352	0.335
7	0.482	0.452	0.425	0.400	0.376	0.354	0.333	0.314	0.296	0.279
8	0.434	0.404	0.376	0.351	0.327	0.305	0.285	0.266	0.249	0.233
9	0.391	0.361	0.333	0.308	0.284	0.263	0.243	0.225	0.209	0.194
10	0.352	0.322	0.295	0.270	0.247	0.227	0.208	0.191	0.176	0.162
11	0.317	0.287	0.261	0.237	0.215	0.195	0.178	0.162	0.148	0.135
12	0.286	0.257	0.231	0.208	0.187	0.168	0.152	0.137	0.124	0.112
13	0.258	0.229	0.204	0.182	0.163	0.145	0.130	0.116	0.104	0.093
14	0.232	0.205	0.181	0.160	0.141	0.125	0.111	0.099	0.088	0.078
15	0.209	0.183	0.160	0.140	0.123	0.108	0.095	0.084	0.074	0.065
16	0.188	0.163	0.141	0.123	0.107	0.093	0.081	0.071	0.062	0.054
17	0.167	0.146	0.125	0.108	0.093	0.080	0.069	0.060	0.052	0.045
18	0.153	0.130	0.111	0.095	0.081	0.069	0.059	0.051	0.044	0.038
19	0.138	0.116	0.098	0.083	0.070	0.060	0.051	0.043	0.037	0.031
20	0.124	0.104	0.087	0.073	0.061	0.051	0.043	0.037	0.031	0.026

Table of cumulative present value factors

Present values of $[1 - (1 + r)^{-n}]/r$

Discount rates (r)

Periods (n)	1%	2%	3%	4%	5%	6%	7%	8%	9%	10%
1	0.990	0.980	0.971	0.962	0.952	0.943	0.935	0.926	0.917	0.909
2	1.970	1.942	1.913	1.886	1.859	1.833	1.808	1.783	1.759	1.736
3	2.941	2.884	2.829	2.775	2.723	2.673	2.624	2.577	2.531	2.487
4	3.902	3.808	3.717	3.630	3.546	3.465	3.387	3.312	3.240	3.170
5	4.853	4.713	4.580	4.452	4.329	4.212	4.100	3.993	3.890	3.791
6	5.795	5.601	5.417	5.242	5.076	4.917	4.767	4.623	4.486	4.355
7	6.728	6.472	6.230	6.002	5.786	5.582	5.389	5.206	5.033	4.868
8	7.652	7.325	7.020	6.733	6.463	6.210	5.971	5.747	5.535	5.335
9	8.566	8.162	7.786	7.435	7.108	6.802	6.515	6.247	5.995	5.759
10	9.471	8.983	8.530	8.111	7.722	7.360	7.024	6.710	6.418	6.145
11	10.368	9.787	9.253	8.760	8.306	7.887	7.499	7.139	6.805	6.495
12	11.255	10.575	9.954	9.385	8.863	8.384	7.943	7.536	7.161	6.814
13	12.134	11.348	10.635	9.986	9.394	8.853	8.358	7.904	7.487	7.103
14	13.004	12.106	11.296	10.563	9.899	9.295	8.745	8.244	7.786	7.367
15	13.865	12.849	11.938	11.118	10.380	9.712	9.108	8.559	8.061	7.606
16	14.718	13.578	12.561	11.652	10.838	10.106	9.447	8.851	8.313	7.824
17	15.562	14.292	13.166	12.166	11.274	10.477	9.763	9.122	8.544	8.022
18	16.398	14.992	13.754	12.659	11.690	10.828	10.059	9.372	8.756	8.201
19	17.226	15.678	14.324	13.134	12.085	11.158	10.336	9.604	8.950	8.365
20	18.046	16.351	14.877	13.590	12.462	11.470	10.594	9.818	9.129	8.514

Discount rates (r)

Periods (n)	11%	12%	13%	14%	15%	16%	17%	18%	19%	20%
1	0.901	0.893	0.885	0.877	0.870	0.862	0.855	0.847	0.840	0.833
2	1.713	1.690	1.668	1.647	1.626	1.605	1.585	1.566	1.547	1.528
3	2.444	2.402	2.361	2.322	2.283	2.246	2.210	2.174	2.140	2.106
4	3.102	3.037	2.974	2.914	2.855	2.798	2.743	2.690	2.639	2.589
5	3.696	3.605	3.517	3.433	3.352	3.274	3.199	3.127	3.058	2.991
6	4.231	4.111	3.998	3.889	3.784	3.685	3.589	3.498	3.410	3.326
7	4.712	4.564	4.423	4.288	4.160	4.039	3.922	3.812	3.706	3.605
8	5.146	4.968	4.799	4.639	4.487	4.344	4.207	4.078	3.954	3.837
9	5.537	5.328	5.132	4.946	4.772	4.607	4.451	4.303	4.163	4.031
10	5.889	5.650	5.426	5.216	5.019	4.833	4.659	4.494	4.339	4.192
11	6.207	5.938	5.687	5.453	5.234	5.029	4.836	4.656	4.486	4.327
12	6.492	6.194	5.918	5.660	5.421	5.197	4.988	4.793	4.611	4.439
13	6.750	6.424	6.122	5.842	5.583	5.342	5.118	4.910	4.715	4.533
14	6.982	6.628	6.302	6.002	5.724	5.468	5.229	5.008	4.802	4.611
15	7.191	6.811	6.462	6.142	5.847	5.575	5.324	5.092	4.876	4.675
16	7.379	6.974	6.604	6.265	5.954	5.668	5.405	5.162	4.938	4.730
17	7.549	7.120	6.729	6.373	6.047	5.749	5.475	5.222	4.990	4.775
18	7.702	7.250	6.840	6.467	6.128	5.818	5.534	5.273	5.033	4.812
19	7.839	7.366	6.938	6.550	6.198	5.877	5.584	5.316	5.070	4.843
20	7.963	7.469	7.025	6.623	6.259	5.929	5.628	5.353	5.101	4.870

Making capital investment decisions

Introduction

This section looks at how proposed investments in new plant, machinery, buildings and other long-term assets should be evaluated. This is a very important area for businesses; expensive and far-reaching consequences can flow from bad investment decisions.

We shall also consider the problem of risk and how this may be taken into account when evaluating investment proposals. Finally, we shall discuss the ways that managers can oversee capital investment projects and how control may be exercised throughout the life of a project.

The nature of investment decisions

The essential feature of investment decisions is *time*. Investment involves making an outlay of something of economic value, usually cash, at one point in time, which is expected to yield economic benefits to the investor at some other point in time. Usually, the outlay precedes the benefits. Also, the outlay is typically one large amount and the benefits arrive as a series of smaller amounts over a fairly protracted period.

Investment decisions tend to be of profound importance to the business because

- *Large amounts of resources are often involved.* Many investments made by businesses involve laying out a significant proportion of their total resources (see the second Mini case on p. 193). If mistakes are made with the decision, the effects on the businesses could be significant, if not catastrophic.
- *It is often difficult and/or expensive to bail out of an investment once it has been undertaken.* It is often the case that investments made by a business are specific to its needs. For example, a hotel business may invest in a new, custom-designed hotel complex. The specialist nature of this complex will probably lead to its having a rather limited second-hand value to another potential user with different needs. If the business found, after having made the investment, that room occupancy rates were not as buoyant as was planned, the only possible course of action might be to close down and sell the complex. This would probably mean that much less could be recouped from the investment than it had originally cost, particularly if the costs of design are included as part of the cost, as they logically should be.

The mini case below gives an illustration of a major investment by a well-known business operating in the UK.

mini case   Brittany Ferries launches an investment

Brittany Ferries, the cross-Channel ferry operator, recently had a new ship built, to be named *Armorique*. The ship cost the business about €81m and is used on the Plymouth to Roscoff route as from Spring 2009. Although Brittany Ferries is a substantial business, this level of expenditure was significant. Clearly, the business believed that acquisition of the new ship would be profitable for it, but how would it have reached this conclusion?

Presumably the anticipated future cash flows from passengers and freight operators will have been major inputs to the decision. The ship was specifically designed for Brittany Ferries, so it would be difficult for the business to recoup a large proportion of its €81m should these projected cash flows not materialise.

Source: 'New €81m passenger cruise-ferry to be named "Armorique"', www.brittany-ferries.co.uk.

The issues raised by Brittany Ferries' investment will be the main subject of this section.

The next Mini case indicates the level of annual net investment for a number of randomly selected, well-known UK businesses. It can be seen that the scale of investment varies from one business to another. (It also tends to vary from one year to the next for a particular business.) In nearly all of these businesses the scale of investment is very significant.

mini case   The scale of investment by UK businesses

	Expenditure on additional non-current assets as a percentage of:	
	Annual sales revenue	End-of-year non-current assets
BT plc (telecommunications)	15.9	17.5
Babcock International Group plc (support services)	6.8	20.6
Tesco plc (supermarkets)	5.5	11.6
J D Wetherspoon plc (pub operator)	12.5	9.0
Marks and Spencer plc (stores)	7.6	14.4
National Grid plc (utilities)	48.0	19.8
J. Sainsbury plc (supermarkets)	4.0	8.9
First Group plc (passenger transport)	5.7	13.1

Source: Annual reports of the businesses concerned for the financial year ending in 2007.

This Mini case is limited to considering the non-current asset investment, but most non-current asset investment also requires a level of current asset investment to support it (additional inventories, for example), meaning that the real scale of investment is even greater, typically considerably so, than indicated above.

Activity 2.1

When managers are making decisions involving capital investments, what should the decisions seek to achieve?

Investment decisions must be consistent with the objectives of the particular business. For a private sector business, maximising the wealth of the owners (shareholders) is usually assumed to be the key financial objective.

Investment appraisal methods

Given the importance of investment decisions, it is essential that there is proper screening of investment proposals. An important part of this screening process is to ensure that the business uses appropriate methods of evaluation.

Research shows that there are basically four methods used in practice by businesses throughout the world to evaluate investment opportunities. They are:

- accounting rate of return (ARR)
- payback period (PP)
- net present value (NPV)
- internal rate of return (IRR).

It is possible to find businesses that use variants of these four methods. It is also possible to find businesses, particularly smaller ones, that do not use any formal appraisal method but rely instead on the 'gut feeling' of their managers. Most businesses, however, seem to use one (or more) of these four methods.

We are going to assess the effectiveness of each of these methods and we shall see that only one of them (NPV) is a wholly logical approach. The other three all have flaws. We shall also see how popular these four methods seem to be in practice.

To help us to examine each of the methods, it might be useful to consider how each of them would cope with a particular investment opportunity. Let us consider the following example.

Example

Billingsgate Battery Company has carried out some research that shows that the business could provide a standard service that it has recently developed.

Provision of the service would require investment in a machine that would cost £100,000, payable immediately. Sales of the service would take place throughout the next five years. At the end of that time, it is estimated that the machine could be sold for £20,000.

Inflows and outflows from sales of the service would be expected to be as follows:

Time		£000
Immediately	Cost of machine	(100)
1 year's time	Operating profit before depreciation	20
2 years' time	Operating profit before depreciation	40
3 years' time	Operating profit before depreciation	60
4 years' time	Operating profit before depreciation	60
5 years' time	Operating profit before depreciation	20
5 years' time	Disposal proceeds from the machine	20

Note that, broadly speaking, the operating profit before deducting depreciation (that is, before non-cash items) equals the net amount of cash flowing into the business. Apart from depreciation, all of this business's expenses cause cash to flow out of the business. Sales revenues lead to cash flowing in. If, for the time being, we assume that inventories, trade receivables and trade payables remain constant, operating profit before depreciation will equal the cash inflow.

To simplify matters, we shall assume that the cash from sales and for the expenses of providing the service are received and paid, respectively, at the end of each year. This is clearly unlikely to be true in real life. Money will have to be paid to employees (for salaries and wages) on a weekly or a monthly basis. Customers will pay within a month or two of buying the service. On the other hand, making the assumption probably does not lead to a serious distortion. It is a simplifying assumption that is often made in real life, and it will make things more straightforward for us now. We should be clear, however, that there is nothing about any of the four methods that *demands* that this assumption is made.

Having set up the example, we shall now go on to consider how each of the appraisal methods works.

Accounting rate of return (ARR)

The accounting rate of return (ARR) method takes the average accounting operating profit that the investment will generate and expresses it as a percentage of the average investment made over the life of the project. Thus:

$$\text{ARR} = \frac{\text{Average annual operating profit}}{\text{Average investment to earn that profit}} \times 100\%$$

We can see from the equation that, to calculate the ARR, we need to deduce two pieces of information about the particular project:

- the annual average operating profit; and
- the average investment.

In our example, the average annual operating profit *before depreciation* over the five years is £40,000 (that is, £000(20 + 40 + 60 + 60 + 20)/5). Assuming 'straight-line' depreciation (that is, equal annual amounts), the annual depreciation charge will be £16,000 (that is, £(100,000 − 20,000)/5). Thus the average annual operating profit *after depreciation* is £24,000 (that is, £40,000 − £16,000).

The average investment over the five years can be calculated as follows:

$$\text{Average investment} = \frac{\text{Cost of machine} + \text{Disposal value}}{2}$$

$$= \frac{£100,000 + £20,000}{2}$$

$$= £60,000$$

Thus, the ARR of the investment is

$$ARR = \frac{£24{,}000}{£60{,}000} \times 100\% = 40\%$$

Users of ARR should apply the following decision rules:

- For any project to be acceptable it must achieve a target ARR as a minimum.
- Where there are competing projects that all seem capable of exceeding this minimum rate (that is, where the business must choose between more than one project), the one with the higher (or highest) ARR would normally be selected.

To decide whether the 40 per cent return is acceptable, we need to compare this percentage return with the minimum rate required by the business.

Activity 2.2

Chaotic Industries is considering an investment in a fleet of ten delivery vans to take its products to customers. The vans will cost £15,000 each to buy, payable immediately. The annual running costs are expected to total £20,000 for each van (including the driver's salary). The vans are expected to operate successfully for six years, at the end of which period they will all have to be sold, with disposal proceeds expected to be about £3,000 a van. At present, the business uses a commercial carrier for all of its deliveries. It is expected that this carrier will charge a total of £230,000 each year for the next six years to undertake the deliveries.

What is the ARR of buying the vans? (Note that cost savings are as relevant a benefit from an investment as are net cash inflows.)

The vans will save the business £30,000 a year (that is, £230,000 – (£20,000 × 10)), before depreciation, in total. Thus, the inflows and outflows will be:

Time		£000
Immediately	Cost of vans (10 × £15,000)	(150)
1 year's time	Net saving before depreciation	30
2 years' time	Net saving before depreciation	30
3 years' time	Net saving before depreciation	30
4 years' time	Net saving before depreciation	30
5 years' time	Net saving before depreciation	30
6 years' time	Net saving before depreciation	30
6 years' time	Disposal proceeds from the vans (10 × £3,000)	30

The total annual depreciation expense (assuming a straight-line method) will be £20,000 (that is, (£150,000 – £30,000)/6). Thus, the average annual saving, after depreciation, is £10,000 (that is, £30,000 – £20,000).

The average investment will be

$$\text{Average investment} = \frac{£150{,}000 + £30{,}000}{2} = £90{,}000$$

and the ARR of the investment is

$$ARR = \frac{£10{,}000}{£90{,}000} \times 100\% = 11.1\%$$

ARR and ROCE

We should note that ARR and the return on capital employed (ROCE) ratio take the same approach to performance measurement, in that they both relate accounting profit to the cost of the assets invested to generate that profit. ROCE is a popular means of assessing the performance of a business, as a whole, *after* it has performed. ARR is an approach that assesses the potential performance of a particular investment, taking the same approach as ROCE, but *before* it has performed.

As we have just seen, managers using ARR will require that any investment undertaken should achieve a target ARR as a minimum. Perhaps the minimum target ROCE would be based on the rate that previous investments had actually achieved (as measured by ROCE). Perhaps it would be the industry-average ROCE.

Since private sector businesses are normally seeking to increase the wealth of their owners, ARR may seem to be a sound method of appraising investment opportunities. Operating profit can be seen as a net increase in wealth over a period, and relating it to the size of investment made to achieve it seems a logical approach.

ARR is said to have a number of advantages as a method of investment appraisal. It was mentioned earlier that ROCE seems to be a widely used measure of business performance. Shareholders seem to use this ratio to evaluate management performance, and sometimes the financial objective of a business will be expressed in terms of a target ROCE. It therefore seems sensible to use a method of investment appraisal that is consistent with this overall approach to measuring business performance. It also gives the result expressed as a percentage. It seems that many managers feel comfortable using measures expressed in percentage terms.

Problems with ARR

Activity 2.3

ARR suffers from a very major defect as a means of assessing investment opportunities. Can you reason out what this is? Consider the three competing projects whose profits are shown below. All three involve investment in a machine that is expected to have no residual value at the end of the five years. Note that all of the projects have the same total operating profits over the five years.

Time		Project A £000	Project B £000	Project C £000
Immediately	Cost of machine	(160)	(160)	(160)
1 year's time	Operating profit after depreciation	20	10	160
2 years' time	Operating profit after depreciation	40	10	10
3 years' time	Operating profit after depreciation	60	10	10
4 years' time	Operating profit after depreciation	60	10	10
5 years' time	Operating profit after depreciation	20	160	10

(*Hint*: The defect is not concerned with the ability of the decision maker to forecast future events, although this too can be a problem. Try to remember the essential feature of investment decisions, which we identified at the beginning of this section.)

The problem with ARR is that it almost completely ignores the time factor. In this example, exactly the same ARR would have been computed for each of the three projects.

Since the same total operating profit over the five years (£200,000) arises in all three of these projects, and the average investment in each project is £80,000 (that is, £160,000/2), this means that each case will give rise to the same ARR of 50 per cent (that is, £40,000/£80,000).

Given a financial objective of maximising the wealth of the owners of the business, any rational decision maker faced with a choice between the three projects set out in Activity 2.3 would strongly prefer Project C. This is because most of the benefits from the investment arise within twelve months of investing the £160,000 to establish the project. Project A would rank second and Project B would come a poor third. Any appraisal technique that is not capable of distinguishing between these three situations is seriously flawed. We shall look at why timing is so important later in the section.

There are further problems associated with the use of ARR. One of these problems concerns the approach taken to derive the average investment in a project.

The example below illustrates the daft result that ARR can produce.

Example

George put forward an investment proposal to his boss. The business uses ARR to assess investment proposals using a minimum 'hurdle' rate of 27 per cent. Details of the proposal were as follows:

Cost of equipment	£200,000
Estimated residual value of equipment	£40,000
Average annual operating profit	
before depreciation	£48,000
Estimated life of project	10 years
Annual straight-line depreciation charge	£16,000 (that is, (£200,000 – £40,000)/10)

The ARR of the project will be:

$$ARR = \frac{48{,}000 - 16{,}000}{(200{,}000 + 40{,}000)/2} \times 100\% = 26.7\%$$

The boss rejected George's proposal because it failed to achieve an ARR of at least 27 per cent. Although George was disappointed, he realised that there was still hope. In fact, all that the business had to do was to give away the piece of equipment at the end of its useful life rather than to sell it. The residual value of the equipment then became zero and the annual depreciation charge became ([£200,000 – £0]/10) = £20,000 a year. The revised ARR calculation was then as follows:

$$ARR = \frac{48{,}000 - 20{,}000}{(200{,}000 + 0)/2} \times 100\% = 28\%$$

ARR is based on the use of accounting profit. When measuring performance over the whole life of a project, however, it is cash flows rather than accounting profits that are important. Cash is the ultimate measure of the economic wealth generated by an investment. This is because it is cash that is used to acquire resources and for distribution to owners. Accounting profit, on the other hand is more appropriate for reporting achievement on a periodic basis. It is a useful measure of productive effort for a relatively short period, such as a year or half year. It is really a question of 'horses for courses'. Accounting profit is fine for measuring performance over short periods, but cash is the appropriate measure when considering the performance over the life of a project.

The ARR method can also create problems when considering competing investments of different size.

Activity 2.4

Sinclair Wholesalers plc is currently considering opening a new sales outlet in Coventry. Two possible sites have been identified for the new outlet. Site A has an area of 30,000 sq m. It will require an average investment of £6m, and will produce an average operating profit of £600,000 a year. Site B has an area of 20,000 sq m. It will require an average investment of £4m, and will produce an average operating profit of £500,000 a year.

What is the ARR of each investment opportunity? Which site would you select, and why?

The ARR of Site A is £600,000/£6m = 10 per cent. The ARR of Site B is £500,000/£4m = 12.5 per cent. Thus, Site B has the higher ARR. However, in terms of the absolute operating profit generated, Site A is the more attractive. If the ultimate objective is to increase the wealth of the shareholders of Sinclair Wholesalers plc, it might be better to choose Site A even though the percentage return is lower. It is the absolute size of the return rather than the relative (percentage) size that is important. This is a general problem of using comparative measures, such as percentages, when the objective is measured in absolute ones, like an amount of money. If businesses were seeking through their investments to generate a percentage rate of return on investment, ARR would be more helpful. The problem is that most businesses seek to achieve increases in their absolute wealth (measured in pounds, euros, dollars and so on) through their investment decisions.

The mini case below illustrates how using percentage measures can lead to confusion.

mini case Increasing road capacity by sleight of hand

During the 1970s, the Mexican government wanted to increase the capacity of a major four-lane road. It came up with the idea of repainting the lane markings so that there were six narrower lanes occupying the same space as four wider ones had previously done. This increased the capacity of the road by 50 per cent (that is, $^2/_4 \times 100$). A tragic outcome of the narrower lanes was an increase in deaths from road accidents. A year later the Mexican government had the six narrower lanes changed back to the original four wider ones.

This reduced the capacity of the road by 33 per cent (that is, $^2/_6 \times 100$). The Mexican government reported that, overall, it had increased the capacity of the road by 17 per cent (that is, 50% − 33%), despite the fact that its real capacity was identical to that which it had been originally. The confusion arose because each of the two percentages (50 per cent and 33 per cent) is based on different bases (four and six).

Source: Gigerenzer, G., *Reckoning with Risk*, Penguin, 2002.

Payback period (PP)

The payback period (PP) is the length of time it takes for an initial investment to be repaid out of the net cash inflows from a project. Since it takes time into account, the PP method seems to go some way towards overcoming the timing problem of ARR – or at first glance it does.

It might be useful to consider PP in the context of the Billingsgate Battery example. We should recall that essentially the project's cash flows are:

Time		£000
Immediately	Cost of machine	(100)
1 year's time	Operating profit before depreciation	20
2 years' time	Operating profit before depreciation	40
3 years' time	Operating profit before depreciation	60
4 years' time	Operating profit before depreciation	60
5 years' time	Operating profit before depreciation	20
5 years' time	Disposal proceeds	20

Note that all of these figures are amounts of cash to be paid or received (we saw earlier that operating profit before depreciation is a rough measure of the cash flows from the project).

As the payback period is the length of time it takes for the initial investment to be repaid out of the net cash inflows, it will be three years before the £100,000 outlay is covered by the inflows. This is still assuming that the cash flows occur at year ends. The payback period can be derived by calculating the cumulative cash flows as follows:

Time		Net cash flows £000	Cumulative cash flows £000	
Immediately	Cost of machine	(100)	(100)	
1 year's time	Operating profit before depreciation	20	(80)	(−100 + 20)
2 years' time	Operating profit before depreciation	40	(40)	(−80 + 40)
3 years' time	Operating profit before depreciation	60	20	(−40 + 60)
4 years' time	Operating profit before depreciation	60	80	(20 + 60)
5 years' time	Operating profit before depreciation	20	100	(80 + 20)
5 years' time	Disposal proceeds	20	120	(100 + 20)

We can see that the cumulative cash flows become positive at the end of the third year. Had we assumed that the cash flows arise evenly over the year, the precise payback period would be

$$2 \text{ years} + (^{40}/_{60}) \text{ years} = 2^2/_3 \text{ years}$$

where 40 represents the cash flow still required at the beginning of the third year to repay the initial outlay, and 60 is the projected cash flow during the third year.

We must now ask how to decide whether three years is an acceptable payback period.

The decision rule for using PP is:

- For a project to be acceptable it would need to have a payback period shorter than a maximum payback period set by the business.
- If there were two (or more) competing projects whose payback periods were all shorter than the maximum payback period requirement, the project with the shorter (or shortest) payback period should be selected.

If, for example, Billingsgate Battery had a maximum acceptable payback period of four years, the project would be undertaken. A project with a longer payback period than four years would not be acceptable.

Activity 2.5

What is the payback period of the Chaotic Industries project from Activity 2.2?

The inflows and outflows are expected to be:

Time		Net cash flows £000	Cumulative net cash flows £000	
Immediately	Cost of vans	(150)	(150)	
1 year's time	Net saving before depreciation	30	(120)	(−150 + 30)
2 years' time	Net saving before depreciation	30	(90)	(−120 + 30)
3 years' time	Net saving before depreciation	30	(60)	(−90 + 30)
4 years' time	Net saving before depreciation	30	(30)	(−60 + 30)
5 years' time	Net saving before depreciation	30	0	(−30 + 30)
6 years' time	Net saving before depreciation	30	30	(0 + 30)
6 years' time	Disposal proceeds from the vans	30	60	(30 + 30)

The payback period here is five years; that is, it is not until the end of the fifth year that the vans will pay for themselves out of the savings that they are expected to generate.

The PP method has certain advantages. It is quick and easy to calculate, and can be easily understood by managers. The logic of using PP is that projects that can recoup their cost quickly are economically more attractive than those with longer payback periods, that is, it emphasises liquidity. PP is probably an improvement on ARR in respect of the timing of the cash flows. PP is not, however, the whole answer to the problem.

Problems with PP

Activity 2.6

In what respect is PP not the whole answer as a means of assessing investment opportunities? Consider the cash flows arising from three competing projects:

Time		Project 1 £000	Project 2 £000	Project 3 £000
Immediately	Cost of machine	(200)	(200)	(200)
1 year's time	Operating profit before depreciation	70	20	70
2 years' time	Operating profit before depreciation	60	20	100
3 years' time	Operating profit before depreciation	70	160	30
4 years' time	Operating profit before depreciation	80	30	200
5 years' time	Operating profit before depreciation	50	20	440
5 years' time	Disposal proceeds	40	10	20

(*Hint*: Again, the defect is not concerned with the ability of the manager to forecast future events. This is a problem, but it is a problem whatever approach we take.)

The PP for each project is three years and so the PP method would regard the projects as being equally acceptable. It cannot distinguish between those projects that pay back a significant amount early in the three-year payback period and those that do not.

In addition, this method ignores cash flows after the payback period. A decision maker concerned with increasing owners' wealth would prefer Project 3 because the cash flows come in earlier (most of the initial cost of making the investment has been repaid by the end of the second year) and they are greater in total.

The cumulative cash flows of each project in Activity 2.6 are set out in Figure 2.7.

We can see that the PP method is not concerned with the profitability of projects; it is concerned simply with their payback period. Thus cash flows arising beyond the payback period are ignored. While this neatly avoids the practical problems of forecasting cash flows over a long period, it means that relevant information could be ignored.

We may feel that, by favouring projects with a short payback period, the PP method does at least provide a means of dealing with the problems of risk and uncertainty. However, this is a fairly crude approach to the problem. It looks only at the risk that the project will end earlier than expected. However, this is only one of many risk areas. What, for example, about the risk that the demand for the product may be less than expected? There are more systematic approaches to dealing with risk that can be used and we shall look at these later in the chapter.

PP takes some note of the timing of the costs and benefits from the project. Its key deficiency, however, is that it is not linked to promoting increases in the wealth of the business and its owners. PP will tend to recommend undertaking projects that pay for themselves quickly.

The PP method requires the managers of a business to select a maximum acceptable payback period. This maximum period, in practice, will vary from one business

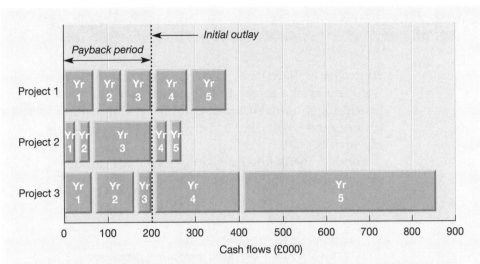

The payback method of investment appraisal would view Projects 1, 2 and 3 as being equally attractive. In doing so, the method completely ignores the fact that Project 3 provides most of the payback cash earlier in the three-year period and goes on to generate large benefits in later years.

Figure 2.7   The cumulative cash flows of each project in Activity 2.6

to the next. The mini case below provides some evidence of the length of payback period required by small to medium-sized businesses when investing in new forms of energy generation.

mini case   Payback time

When it comes to self-generation of renewable energy, UK SMEs (small and medium size enterprises) want an unrealistically quick return on investment according to research carried out by energy consultancy energyTEAM. Nearly three quarters would need payback within three years in order to justify introducing such measures. Only four per cent are prepared for this process to take over five years despite growing concern over commercial energy usage. EnergyTEAM's study revealed that 40 per cent of enterprises with 50 to 500 employees would have to be convinced of a return on investment in just one year before they would proceed down the route of self-generation.

When asked which method of self-generation they would be most inclined to choose, over half of respondents highlighted solar power as the preferred method. This is despite the fact that solar has one of the largest payback times, at around ten years.

Brian Rickerby, joint Managing Director of energyTEAM, said 'I can understand that seeking a quick return is a pragmatic, business-like approach, but unfortunately this is not realistic when it comes to energy issues. Self-generation technologies must be viewed as a long-term strategy that will have a significant positive impact for many years to come.'

Source: 'SMEs' unrealistic demands on renewables', *Sustain*, Vol. 8, Issue 5, 2007, p. 74.

Net present value (NPV)

From what we have seen so far, it seems that to make sensible investment decisions, we need a method of appraisal that both considers *all* of the costs and benefits of each investment opportunity, and makes a logical allowance for the *timing* of those costs and benefits. The net present value (NPV) method provides us with this.

Consider the Billingsgate Battery example's cash flows, which we should recall can be summarised as follows:

Time		£000
Immediately	Cost of machine	(100)
1 year's time	Operating profit before depreciation	20
2 years' time	Operating profit before depreciation	40
3 years' time	Operating profit before depreciation	60
4 years' time	Operating profit before depreciation	60
5 years' time	Operating profit before depreciation	20
5 years' time	Disposal proceeds	20

Given that the principal financial objective of the business is to increase owners' wealth, it would be very easy to assess this investment if all of the cash inflows and outflows were to occur now (all at the same time). All that we should need to do would be to add up the cash inflows (total £220,000) and compare them with the cash outflows (£100,000). This would lead us to the conclusion that the project should go ahead because the business, and its owners, would be better off by £120,000. Of course, it is not as easy as this because time is involved. The cash outflow (payment) will occur immediately if the project is undertaken. The inflows (receipts) will arise at a range of later times.

The time factor is an important issue because people do not normally see £100 paid out now as equivalent in value to £100 receivable in a year's time. If we were to be offered £100 in 12 months' time in exchange for paying out £100 now, we should not be prepared to accept the offer unless we wished to do someone a favour.

Activity 2.7

Why would you see £100 to be received in a year's time as not equal in value to £100 to be paid immediately? (There are basically three reasons.)

The reasons are:

- interest lost
- risk
- effects of inflation.

We shall now take a closer look at these three reasons in turn.

Interest lost

If we are to be deprived of the opportunity to spend our money for a year, we could equally well be deprived of its use by placing it on deposit in a bank or building society. In this case, at the end of the year we could have our money back and have interest as well. Thus, by investing the funds in some other way, we shall be incurring an *opportunity cost*. We should remember from an earlier section (see 'The opportunity cost of retained earnings', p. 122) that an opportunity cost occurs where one course of action, for example making an investment, deprives us of the opportunity to derive some benefit from an alternative action, for example putting the money in the bank and earning interest.

From this we can see that any investment opportunity must, if it is to make us wealthier, do better than the returns that are available from the next best opportunity. Thus, if Billingsgate Battery Company sees putting the money in the bank on deposit as the alternative to investment in the machine, the return from investing in the machine must be better than that from investing in the bank. If the bank offered a better return, the business, and its owners, would become wealthier by putting the money on deposit.

Risk

All investments expose their investors to risk. For example, buying a machine to manufacture a product, or to provide a service, to be sold in the market, on the strength of various estimates made in advance of buying the machine, exposes the business to risk. Things may not turn out as expected.

Activity 2.8

Can you suggest some areas where things could go other than according to plan in the Billingsgate Battery Company example?

We have come up with the following:

- The machine might not work as well as expected; it might break down, leading to loss of the business's ability to provide the service.
- Sales of the service may not be as buoyant as expected.
- Labour costs may prove to be higher than expected.
- The sale proceeds of the machine could prove to be less than were estimated.

It is important to remember that the decision whether to invest in the machine must be taken *before* any of these things are known. For example, it is only after the machine has been purchased that we could discover that the level of sales which had been estimated before the event is not going to be achieved. It is not possible to wait until we know for certain whether the market will behave as we expected before we buy the machine. We can study reports and analyses of the market. We can commission sophisticated market surveys, and these may give us more confidence in the likely outcome. We can advertise widely and try to promote sales. Ultimately, however, we have to decide whether to jump off into the dark and accept the risk if we want the opportunity to make profitable investments.

The mini case below gives some some impression of the extent to which businesses believe that investment outcomes turn out as expected.

mini case   Size matters

Ninety-nine manufacturing businesses in the Cambridge area of the UK were asked the extent to which past investments performed in line with earlier expectations. The results, broken down according to business size, are set out below.

	Large %	Size of business Medium %	Small %	All %
Underperformed	8	14	32	14
Performed as expected	82	72	68	77
Overperformed	10	14	0	9

It seems that smaller businesses are much more likely to get it wrong than mediumsized or larger businesses. This may be because small businesses are often younger and, therefore, less experienced both in the techniques of forecasting and in managing investment projects. They are also likely to have less financial expertise. It also seems that small businesses have a distinct bias towards overoptimism and do not take full account of the possibility that things will turn out worse than expected.

Source: Baddeley, M., 'Unpacking the black box: an econometric analysis of investment strategies in real world firms', CEPP Working Paper No. 08/05, University of Cambridge, p. 14.

Normally, people expect to receive greater returns where they perceive risk to be a factor. Examples of this in real life are not difficult to find. One such example is that banks tend to charge higher rates of interest to borrowers whom the bank perceives as more risky. Those who can offer good security for a loan, and who can point to a regular source of income, tend to be charged lower rates of interest.

Going back to Billingsgate Battery Company's investment opportunity, it is not enough to say that we should not advise making the investment unless the returns from it are as high as those from investing in a bank deposit. Clearly we should want returns above the level of bank deposit interest rates, because the logical equivalent of investing in the machine is not putting the money on deposit but making an alternative investment that is risky.

We have just seen that investors tend to expect a higher rate of return from investment projects where the risk is perceived as being higher. How risky a particular project is, and therefore how large this risk premium should be, are, however, matters that are difficult to handle. It is usually necessary to make some judgement on these questions. We shall come back to the size of the risk premium later in the chapter when we consider how the level of risk can be assessed.

Inflation

If we are to be deprived of £100 for a year, when we come to spend that money it will not buy as much as it would have done a year earlier. Generally, we shall not be able to buy as many tins of baked beans or loaves of bread or bus tickets as we could have done a year earlier. This is because of the loss in the purchasing power of money, or inflation, which occurs over time. Clearly, the investor needs compensating for this loss of purchasing power if the investment is to be made. This compensation is on top of a return that takes account of what could have been gained from an alternative investment of similar risk.

In practice, interest rates observable in the market tend to take inflation into account. Rates that are offered to potential building society and bank depositors include an allowance for the rate of inflation that is expected in the future.

What will a logical investor do?

As we have seen, logical investors who are seeking to increase their wealth will only be prepared to make investments that will compensate for the loss of interest and purchasing power of the money invested and for the fact that the returns expected may not materialise (risk). This is usually assessed by seeing whether the proposed investment will yield a return that is greater than the basic rate of interest (which would include an allowance for inflation) plus a risk premium.

These three factors (interest lost, risk and inflation) are set out in Figure 2.8.

Naturally, investors need at least the minimum returns before they are prepared to invest. However, it is in terms of the effect on their wealth that they should logically assess an investment project. Usually it is the investment with the highest percentage return that will make the investor most wealthy, but we shall see later in this section that this is not always the case. For the time being, therefore, we shall concentrate on wealth.

Let us now return to the Billingsgate Battery Company example. We should recall that the cash flows expected from this investment are:

Time		£000
Immediately	Cost of machine	(100)
1 year's time	Operating profit before depreciation	20
2 years' time	Operating profit before depreciation	40
3 years' time	Operating profit before depreciation	60
4 years' time	Operating profit before depreciation	60
5 years' time	Operating profit before depreciation	20
5 years' time	Disposal proceeds	20

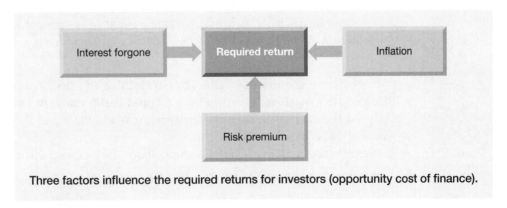

Three factors influence the required returns for investors (opportunity cost of finance).

Figure 2.8 The factors influencing the returns required by investors from a project

We have already seen that it is not sufficient just to compare the basic cash inflows and outflows for the investment. It would be useful if we could express each of these cash flows in similar terms, so that we could make a direct comparison between the sum of the inflows over time and the immediate £100,000 investment. Fortunately, we can do this.

Let us assume that, instead of making this investment, the business could make an alternative investment with similar risk and obtain a return of 20 per cent a year.

Activity 2.9

We know that Billingsgate Battery Company could alternatively invest its money at a rate of 20 per cent a year. How much do you judge the present (immediate) value of the expected first year receipt of £20,000 to be? In other words, if instead of having to wait a year for the £20,000, and being deprived of the opportunity to invest it at 20 per cent, you could have some money now, what sum to be received now would you regard as exactly equivalent to getting £20,000 but having to wait a year for it?

We should obviously be happy to accept a lower amount if we could get it immediately than if we had to wait a year. This is because we could invest it at 20 per cent (in the alternative project). Logically, we should be prepared to accept the amount that, with a year's income, will grow to £20,000. If we call this amount PV (for present value) we can say

$$PV + (PV \times 20\%) = £20,000$$

– that is, the amount plus income from investing the amount for the year equals the £20,000.

If we rearrange this equation we find

$$PV \times (1 + 0.2) = £20,000$$

(Note that 0.2 is the same as 20 per cent, but expressed as a decimal.) Further rearranging gives

$$PV = £20,000/(1 + 0.2) = £16,667$$

Thus, rational investors who have the opportunity to invest at 20 per cent a year would not mind whether they have £16,667 now or £20,000 in a year's time. In this sense we can say that, given a 20 per cent alternative investment opportunity, the present value of £20,000 to be received in one year's time is £16,667.

If we derive the present value (PV) of each of the cash flows associated with Billingsgate's machine investment, we could easily make the direct comparison between the cost of making the investment (£100,000) and the various benefits that will derive from it in years 1 to 5.

We can make a more general statement about the PV of a particular cash flow. It is:

PV of the cash flow of year n = actual cash flow of year n divided by $(1 + r)^n$

where n is the year of the cash flow (that is, how many years into the future) and r is the opportunity investing rate expressed as a decimal (instead of as a percentage).

We have already seen how this works for the £20,000 inflow for year 1 for the Billingsgate project. For year 2 the calculation would be:

$$\text{PV of year 2 cash flow (that is, £40,000)} = £40,000/(1 + 0.2)^2 = £40,000/(1.2)^2$$
$$= £40,000/1.44 = £27,778$$

Thus the present value of the £40,000 to be received in two years' time is £27,778.

Activity 2.10

See if you can show that an investor would find £27,778, receivable now, as equally acceptable to receiving £40,000 in two years' time, assuming that there is a 20 per cent investment opportunity.

The reasoning goes like this:

	£
Amount available for immediate investment	27,778
Add Income for year 1 (20% × 27,778)	5,556
	33,334
Add Income for year 2 (20% × 33,334)	6,667
	40,001

(The extra £1 is only a rounding error.)
   This is to say that since the investor can turn £27,778 into £40,000 in two years, these amounts are equivalent. We can say that £27,778 is the present value of £40,000 receivable after two years (given a 20 per cent rate of return).

Now let us calculate the present values of all of the cash flows associated with the Billingsgate machine project and from them the *net present value (NPV)* of the project as a whole.
   The relevant cash flows and calculations are as follows:

Time	Cash flow £000	Calculation of PV	PV £000
Immediately (time 0)	(100)	$(100)/(1 + 0.2)^0$	(100.00)
1 year's time	20	$20/(1 + 0.2)^1$	16.67
2 years' time	40	$40/(1 + 0.2)^2$	27.78
3 years' time	60	$60/(1 + 0.2)^3$	34.72
4 years' time	60	$60/(1 + 0.2)^4$	28.94
5 years' time	20	$20/(1 + 0.2)^5$	8.04
5 years' time	20	$20/(1 + 0.2)^5$	8.04
Net present value (NPV)			24.19

Note that $(1 + 0.2)^0 = 1$.

Once again, we must ask how we can decide whether the machine project is acceptable to the business. In fact, the decision rule for NPV is simple:

● If the NPV is positive the project should be accepted; if it is negative the project should be rejected.
● If there are two (or more) competing projects that have positive NPVs, the project with the higher (or highest) NPV should be selected.

In this case, the NPV is positive, so we should accept the project and buy the machine. The reasoning behind this decision rule is quite straightforward. Investing in the machine will make the business, and its owners, £24,190 better off than they would be by taking up the next best opportunity available to it. The gross benefits from investing in this machine are worth a total of £124,190 today, and since the business can 'buy' these benefits for just £100,000 today, the investment should be made. If, however, the present value of the gross benefits were below £100,000, it would be less than the cost of 'buying' those benefits and the opportunity should, therefore, be rejected.

Activity 2.11

What is the *maximum* the Billingsgate Battery Company should be prepared to pay for the machine, given the potential benefits of owning it?

The business would logically be prepared to pay up to £124,190 since the wealth of the owners of the business would be increased up to this price – although the business would prefer to pay as little as possible.

Using discount tables

Deducing the present values of the various cash flows is a little laborious using the approach that we have just taken. To deduce each PV we took the relevant cash flow and multiplied it by $1/(1 + r)^n$. There is a slightly different way to do this. Tables exist that show values of this discount factor for a range of values of r and n. Such a table appears at the end of the previous section, on p. 189. Take a look at it.

Look at the column for 20 per cent and the row for one year. We find that the factor is 0.833. This means that the PV of a cash flow of £1 receivable in one year is £0.833. So the present value of a cash flow of £20,000 receivable in one year's time is £16,660 (that is, 0.833 × £20,000), the same result as we found doing it manually.

Activity 2.12

What is the NPV of the Chaotic Industries project from Activity 2.2, assuming a 15 per cent opportunity cost of finance (discount rate)? You should use the discount table on p. 189.

Remember that the inflows and outflow are expected to be:

Time		£000
Immediately	Cost of vans	(150)
1 year's time	Net saving before depreciation	30
2 years' time	Net saving before depreciation	30
3 years' time	Net saving before depreciation	30
4 years' time	Net saving before depreciation	30
5 years' time	Net saving before depreciation	30
6 years' time	Net saving before depreciation	30
6 years' time	Disposal proceeds from the vans	30

The calculation of the NPV of the project is as follows:

Time	Cash flows £000	Discount factor (15% – from the table)	Present value £000
Immediately	(150)	1.000	(150.00)
1 year's time	30	0.870	26.10
2 years' time	30	0.756	22.68
3 years' time	30	0.658	19.74
4 years' time	30	0.572	17.16
5 years' time	30	0.497	14.91
6 years' time	30	0.432	12.96
6 years' time	30	0.432	12.96
		NPV	(23.49)

Activity 2.13

How would you interpret this result?

The fact that the project has a negative NPV means that the present values of the benefits from the investment are worth less than the cost of entering into it.
Any cost up to £126,510 (the present value of the benefits) would be worth paying, but not £150,000.

The discount table shows how the value of £1 diminishes as its receipt goes further into the future. Assuming an opportunity cost of finance of 20 per cent a year, £1 to be received immediately, obviously, has a present value of £1. However, as the time before it is to be received increases, the present value diminishes significantly, as is shown in Figure 2.9.

The discount rate and the cost of capital

We have seen that the appropriate discount rate to use in NPV assessments is the opportunity cost of finance. This is, in effect, the cost to the business of the finance needed to fund the investment. It will normally be the cost of a mixture of funds (shareholders' funds and borrowings) employed by the business and is often referred to as the cost of capital.

Why NPV is better

From what we have seen, NPV seems to be a better method of appraising investment opportunities than either ARR or PP. This is because it fully takes account of each of the following:

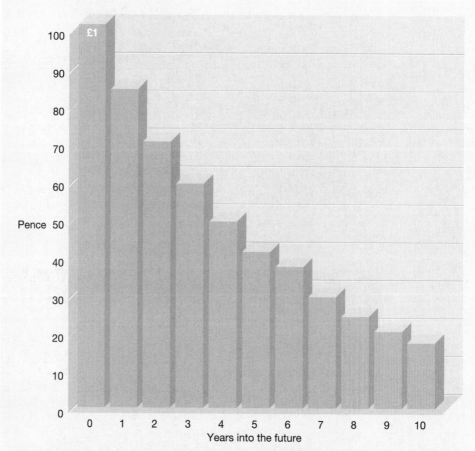

The present value of a future receipt (or payment) of £1 depends on how far in the future it will occur. Those that will occur in the near future will have a larger present value than those whose occurrence is more distant in time.

Figure 2.9 Present value of £1 receivable at various times in the future, assuming an annual financing cost of 20 per cent

- *The timing of the cash flows.* By discounting the various cash flows associated with each project according to when each one is expected to arise, NPV takes account of the time value of money. Associated with this is the fact that by discounting, using the opportunity cost of finance (that is, the return that the next best alternative opportunity would generate), the net benefit *after* financing costs have been met is identified (as the NPV of the project).
- *The whole of the relevant cash flows.* NPV includes *all* of the relevant cash flows irrespective of when they are expected to occur. It treats them differently according to their date of occurrence, but they are all taken into account in the NPV, and they all have an influence on the decision.
- *The objectives of the business.* NPV is the only method of appraisal in which the output of the analysis has a direct bearing on the wealth of the owners of the business (with a limited company, the shareholders). Positive NPVs enhance

wealth; negative ones reduce it. Since we assume that private sector businesses seek to increase owners' wealth, NPV is superior to the other two methods (ARR and PP) that we have already discussed.

We saw earlier that a business should take on all projects with positive NPVs, when their cash flows are discounted at the opportunity cost of finance. Where a choice has to be made between projects, the business should normally select the one with the higher or highest NPV.

NPV's wider application

NPV is considered the most logical approach to making business decisions about investments in productive assets. The same logic makes NPV equally valid as the best approach to take when trying to place a value on any economic asset, that is, an asset that seems capable of yielding financial benefits. This would include a share in a limited company and a loan. In fact, when we talk of *economic value*, we mean a value that has been derived by adding together the discounted (present) values of all future cash flows from the asset concerned.

The mini case below provides an estimate of the NPV that is expected from one interesting project.

mini case   A real diamond geezer

Alan Bond, the disgraced Australian businessman and America's Cup winner, is looking at ways to raise money in London for an African diamond mining project. Lesotho Diamond Corporation (LDC) is a private company in which Mr Bond has a large interest. LDC's main asset is a 93 per cent stake in the Kao diamond project in the southern African kingdom of Lesotho.

Mr Bond says, on his personal website, that the Kao project is forecast to yield 5m carats of diamonds over the next 10 years and could become Lesotho's biggest foreign currency earner.

SRK, the mining consultants, has estimated the net present value of the project at £129m.

It is understood that Mr Bond and his family own about 40 per cent of LDC. Mr Bond has described himself as 'spearheading' the Kao project.

Source: Adapated from *Bond seeks funds in London to mine African diamonds*, by Rebacca Bream, ft.com, © The Financial Times Limited, 23 April 2007.

Internal rate of return (IRR)

This is the last of the four major methods of investment appraisal that are found in practice. It is quite closely related to the NPV method in that, like NPV, it also involves discounting future cash flows. The internal rate of return (IRR) of a particular investment is the discount rate that, when applied to its future cash flows, will produce an NPV of precisely zero. In essence, it represents the yield from an investment opportunity.

Activity 2.14

We should recall that, when we discounted the cash flows of the Billingsgate Battery Company machine investment opportunity at 20 per cent, we found that the NPV was a positive figure of £24,190 (see p. 275). What does the NPV of the machine project tell us about the rate of return that the investment will yield for the business (that is, the project's IRR)?

The fact that the NPV is positive when discounting at 20 per cent implies that the rate of return that the project generates is more than 20 per cent. The fact that the NPV is a pretty large figure implies that the actual rate of return is quite a lot above 20 per cent. We should expect increasing the size of the discount rate to reduce NPV, because a higher discount rate gives a lower discounted figure.

It is somewhat laborious to deduce the IRR by hand, since it cannot usually be calculated directly. Iteration (trial and error) is the approach that must usually be adopted. Fortunately, computer spreadsheet packages can deduce the IRR with ease. The package will also use a trial and error approach, but at high speed.

Despite it being laborious, we shall now go on and derive the IRR for the Billingsgate project by hand.

Let us try a higher rate, say 30 per cent, and see what happens.

Time	Cash flow £000	Discount factor (30% – from the table)	PV £000
Immediately (time 0)	(100)	1.000	(100.00)
1 year's time	20	0.769	15.38
2 years' time	40	0.592	23.68
3 years' time	60	0.455	27.30
4 years' time	60	0.350	21.00
5 years' time	20	0.269	5.38
5 years' time	20	0.269	5.38
		NPV	(1.88)

In increasing the discount rate from 20 per cent to 30 per cent, we have reduced the NPV from £24,190 (positive) to £1,880 (negative). Since the IRR is the discount rate that will give us an NPV of exactly zero, we can conclude that the IRR of Billingsgate Battery Company's machine project is very slightly below 30 per cent. Further trials could lead us to the exact rate, but there is probably not much point, given the likely inaccuracy of the cash flow estimates. It is probably good enough, for practical purposes, to say that the IRR is about 30 per cent.

The relationship between the NPV method discussed earlier and the IRR is shown graphically in Figure 2.10 using the information relating to the Billingsgate Battery Company.

We can see that, where the discount rate is zero, the NPV will be the sum of the net cash flows. In other words, no account is taken of the time value of money. However, as the discount rate increases there is a corresponding decrease in the NPV of the project. When the NPV line crosses the horizontal axis there will be a zero NPV, and that represents the IRR.

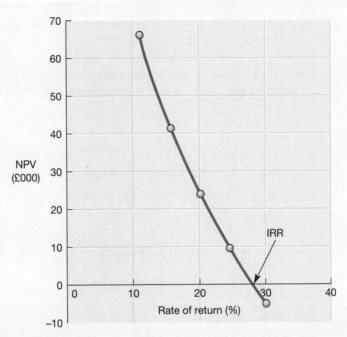

If the discount rate were zero, the NPV would be the sum of the net cash flows. In other words, no account would be taken of the time value of money. However, if we assume increasing discount rates, there is a corresponding decrease in the NPV of the project. When the NPV line crosses the horizontal axis there will be a zero NPV, and the point where it crosses is the IRR.

Figure 2.10   The relationship between the NPV and IRR methods

Activity 2.15

What is the internal rate of return of the Chaotic Industries project from Activity 2.2? You should use the discount table on p. 189. (*Hint*: Remember that you already know the NPV of this project at 15 per cent (from Activity 2.12).)

Since we know that, at a 15 per cent discount rate, the NPV is a relatively large negative figure, our next trial is using a lower discount rate, say 10 per cent:

Time	Cash flows £000	Discount factor (10% – from the table)	Present value £000
Immediately	(150)	1.000	(150.00)
1 year's time	30	0.909	27.27
2 years' time	30	0.826	24.78
3 years' time	30	0.751	22.53
4 years' time	30	0.683	20.49
5 years' time	30	0.621	18.63
6 years' time	30	0.564	16.92
6 years' time	30	0.564	16.92
		NPV	(2.46)

This figure is close to zero NPV. However, the NPV is still negative and so the precise IRR will be a little below 10 per cent.

We could undertake further trials in order to derive the precise IRR. If, however, we have to calculate the IRR manually, further iterations can be time-consuming.

We can get an acceptable approximation to the answer fairly quickly by first calculating the change in NPV arising from a 1 per cent change in the discount rate. This can be done by taking the difference between the two trials (that is, 15 per cent and 10 per cent) that we have already carried out (in Activities 2.12 and 2.15):

Trial	Discount factor	Net present value
	%	£000
1	15	(23.49)
2	10	(2.46)
Difference	5	21.03

The change in NPV for every 1 per cent change in the discount rate will be

$$(21.03/5) = 4.21$$

The reduction in the 10% discount rate required to achieve a zero NPV would therefore be

$$(2.46)/4.21 \times 1\% = 0.58\%$$

The IRR is therefore

$$(10.00 - 0.58)\% = 9.42\%$$

However, to say that the IRR is about 9 or 10 per cent is near enough for most purposes.

Note that this approach assumes a straight-line relationship between the discount rate and NPV. We can see from Figure 2.10 that this assumption is not strictly correct. Over a relatively short range, however, this simplifying assumption is not usually a problem and so we can still arrive at a reasonable approximation using the approach that we took in deriving the 9.42 per cent IRR.

In practice, most businesses have computer software packages that will derive a project's IRR very quickly. Thus, in practice it is not usually necessary either to make a series of trial discount rates or to make the approximation that we have just considered.

Users of the IRR method should apply the following decision rules:

● For any project to be acceptable, it must meet a minimum IRR requirement. This is often referred to as the *hurdle rate* and, logically, this should be the opportunity cost of finance.
● Where there are competing projects (that is, the business can choose only one of two or more viable projects), the one with the higher (or highest) IRR should be selected.

IRR has certain attributes in common with NPV. All cash flows are taken into account, and their timing is logically handled.

The mini case below provides some idea of the IRR for one form of renewable energy.

mini case   The answer is blowin' in the wind

'Wind farms are practically guaranteed to make returns once you have a licence to operate,' says Bernard Lambilliotte, chief investment officer at Ecofin, a financial group that runs Ecofin Water and Power Opportunities, an investment trust.

'The risk is when you have bought the land and are seeking a licence,' says Lambilliotte. 'But once it is built and you are plugged into the grid it is risk-free. It will give an internal rate of return in the low to mid-teens.' Ecofin's largest investment is in Sechilienne, a French company that operates wind farms in northern France and generates capacity in the French overseas territories powered by sugar cane waste.

Source: Batchelor, C., 'A hot topic, but poor returns', ft.com, 27 August 2005.

The next mini case gives some examples of IRRs sought in practice.

mini case   Rates of return

IRR rates for investment projects can vary considerably. Here are a few examples of the expected or target returns from investment projects of large businesses.

- Forth Ports plc, a port operator, concentrates on projects that generate an IRR of at least 15 per cent.
- Rok plc, the builder, aims for a minimum IRR of 15% from new investments.
- Hutchison Whampoa, a large telecommunications business, requires an IRR of at least 25 per cent from its telecom projects.

- Airbus, the plane maker, expects an IRR of 13 per cent from the sale of its A380 superjumbo aircraft.
- Signet Group plc, the jewellery retailer, requires an IRR of 20 per cent over five years when appraising new stores.

Sources: 'FAQs, Forth Ports plc', www.forthports.co.uk; Numis Broker Research Report www.rokgroup.com, 17 August 2006, p. 31; 'Hutchison Whampoa', Lex column, ft.com, 31 March 2004; 'Airbus hikes A380 break-even target', ft.com, 20 October 2006, 'Risk and other factors', Signet Group plc, www.signetgroupplc.com, 2006.

Problems with IRR

The main disadvantage of IRR, relative to NPV, is the fact that it does not directly address the question of wealth generation. It could therefore lead to the wrong decision being made. This is because IRR will always rank a project with an IRR of 25 per cent above one with an IRR of 20 per cent, assuming an opportunity cost of finance of, say, 15 per cent. Although accepting the project with the higher percentage return will often generate more wealth, this may not always be the case. This is because IRR completely ignores the *scale of investment*.

With a 15 per cent cost of finance, £15 million invested at 20 per cent for one year will make us wealthier by £0.75 million (that is, $15 \times (20 - 15)\% = 0.75$). With the same cost of finance, £5 million invested at 25 per cent for one year will make us only £0.5 million (that is, $5 \times (25 - 15)\% = 0.50$). IRR does not recognise this. It should be acknowledged that it is not usual for projects to be competing where there is such a large difference in scale. Even though the problem may be rare and so, typically, IRR will give the same signal as NPV, a method that is always reliable (NPV) must be better to use than IRR. This problem with percentages is another example of the one illustrated by the Mexican road discussed in the mini case on p. 199.

A further problem with the IRR method is that it has difficulty handling projects with unconventional cash flows. In the examples studied so far, each project has a negative cash flow arising at the start of its life and then positive cash flows thereafter. However, in some cases, a project may have both positive and negative cash flows at future points in its life. Such a pattern of cash flows can result in there being more than one IRR, or even no IRR at all. This would make the IRR method difficult to use, although it should be said that this is quite rare in practice. This is never a problem for NPV, however.

Some practical points

When undertaking an investment appraisal, there are several practical points that we should bear in mind:

- *Past costs*. As with all decisions, we should take account only of relevant costs in our analysis. This means that only costs that vary with the decision should be considered. Thus, all past costs should be ignored as they cannot vary with the decision. In some cases, a business may incur costs (such as development costs and market research costs) *before* the evaluation of an opportunity to launch a new product. As those costs have already been incurred, they should be disregarded, even though the amounts may be substantial. Costs that have already been committed but not yet paid should also be disregarded. Where a business has entered into a binding contract to incur a particular cost, it becomes in effect a past cost even though payment may not be due until some point in the future.
- *Common future costs*. It is not only past costs that do not vary with the decision; some future costs may also be the same. For example, the cost of raw materials may not vary with the decision whether to invest in a new piece of manufacturing plant or to continue to use existing plant.
- *Opportunity costs*. Opportunity costs arising from benefits forgone must be taken into account. Thus, for example, when considering a decision concerning whether or not to continue to use a machine already owned by the business, the realisable value of the machine might be an important opportunity cost.
- *Taxation*. Owners will be interested in the after-tax returns generated from the business, and so taxation will usually be an important consideration when making an investment decision. The profits from the project will be taxed, the capital investment may attract tax relief and so on. Tax is levied at significant rates. This means that, in real life, unless tax is formally taken into account, the wrong decision could easily be made. The timing of the tax outflow should also be taken into account when preparing the cash flows for the project.
- *Cash flows not profit flows*. We have seen that for the NPV, IRR and PP methods, it is cash flows rather than profit flows that are relevant to the assessment of investment projects. In an investment appraisal requiring the application of any

of these methods we may be given details of the profits for the investment period. These need to be adjusted in order to derive the cash flows. We should remember that the operating profit *before* non-cash items (such as depreciation) is an approximation to the cash flows for the period, and so we should work back to this figure.

When the data are expressed in profit rather than cash flow terms, an adjustment in respect of working capital may also be necessary. Some adjustment should be made to take account of changes in working capital. For example, launching a new product may give rise to an increase in the net investment made in trade receivables and inventories less trade payables, requiring an immediate outlay of cash. This outlay for additional working capital should be shown in the NPV calculations as part of the initial cost. However, at the end of the life of the project, the additional working capital will be released. This divestment results in an effective inflow of cash at the end of the project; it should also be taken into account at the point at which it is received.

- *Year-end assumption.* In the examples and activities that we have considered so far in this chapter, we have assumed that cash flows arise at the end of the relevant year. This is a simplifying assumption that is used to make the calculations easier. (However, it is perfectly possible to deal more precisely with the cash flows.) As we saw earlier, this assumption is clearly unrealistic, as money will have to be paid to employees on a weekly or monthly basis and credit customers will pay within a month or two of buying the product or service. Nevertheless, it is probably not a serious distortion. We should be clear, however, that there is nothing about any of the four appraisal methods that demands that this assumption be made.
- *Interest payments.* When using discounted cash flow techniques (NPV and IRR), interest payments should not be taken into account in deriving the cash flows for the period. The discount factor already takes account of the costs of financing, and so to take account of interest charges in deriving cash flows for the period would be double counting.
- *Other factors.* Investment decision making must not be viewed as simply a mechanical exercise. The results derived from a particular investment appraisal method will be only one input to the decision-making process. There may be broader issues connected to the decision that have to be taken into account but which may be difficult or impossible to quantify.

The reliability of the forecasts and the validity of the assumptions used in the evaluation will also have a bearing on the final decision.

Activity 2.16

The directors of Manuff (Steel) Ltd are considering closing one of the business's factories. There has been a reduction in the demand for the products made at the factory in recent years, and the directors are not optimistic about the long-term prospects for these products. The factory is situated in the north of England, in an area where unemployment is high.

The factory is leased, and there are still four years of the lease remaining. The directors are uncertain whether the factory should be closed immediately or at the end of the period of the lease. Another business has offered to sub-lease the premises from Manuff at a rental of £40,000 a year for the remainder of the lease period.

The machinery and equipment at the factory cost £1,500,000, and have a statement of financial position (balance sheet) value of £400,000. In the event of immediate closure, the machinery and equipment could be sold for £220,000. The working capital at the factory is £420,000, and could be liquidated for that amount immediately, if required. Alternatively, the working capital can be liquidated in full at the end of the lease period. Immediate closure would result in redundancy payments to employees of £180,000.

If the factory continues in operation until the end of the lease period, the following operating profits (losses) are expected:

	Year 1	Year 2	Year 3	Year 4
	£000	£000	£000	£000
Operating profit/(loss)	160	(40)	30	20

The above figures include a charge of £90,000 a year for depreciation of machinery and equipment. The residual value of the machinery and equipment at the end of the lease period is estimated at £40,000.

Redundancy payments are expected to be £150,000 at the end of the lease period if the factory continues in operation. The business has an annual cost of capital of 12 per cent. Ignore taxation.

(a) Determine the relevant cash flows arising from a decision to continue operations until the end of the lease period rather than to close immediately.
(b) Calculate the net present value of continuing operations until the end of the lease period, rather than closing immediately.
(c) What other factors might the directors take into account before making a final decision on the timing of the factory closure?
(d) State, with reasons, whether or not the business should continue to operate the factory until the end of the lease period.

Your answer should be as follows:
(a) Relevant cash flows

		Years			
	0	1	2	3	4
	£000	£000	£000	£000	£000
Operating cash flows (Note 1)		250	50	120	110
Sale of machinery (Note 2)	(220)				40
Redundancy costs (Note 3)	180				(150)
Sub-lease rentals (Note 4)		(40)	(40)	(40)	(40)
Working capital invested (Note 5)	(420)				420
	(460)	210	10	80	380

Notes:
1 Each year's operating cash flows are calculated by adding back the depreciation charge for the year to the operating profit for the year. In the case of the operating loss, the depreciation charge is deducted.

2　In the event of closure, machinery could be sold immediately. Thus an opportunity cost of £220,000 is incurred if operations continue.

3　If operations are continued, there will be a saving in immediate redundancy costs of £180,000. However, redundancy costs of £150,000 will be paid in four years' time.

4　If operations are continued, the opportunity to sub-lease the factory will be forgone.

5　Immediate closure would mean that working capital could be liquidated. If operations continue, this opportunity is foregone. However, working capital can be liquidated in four years' time.

(b)

Discount rate 12 per cent	1.000	0.893	0.797	0.712	0.636
Present value	(460)	187.5	8.0	57.0	241.7
Net present value	34.2				

(c)　Other factors that may influence the decision include:

● *The overall strategy of the business*. The business may need to set the decision within a broader context. It may be necessary to manufacture the products at the factory because they are an integral part of the business's product range. The business may wish to avoid redundancies in an area of high unemployment for as long as possible.

● *Flexibility*. A decision to close the factory is probably irreversible. If the factory continues, however, there may be a chance that the prospects for the factory will brighten in the future.

● *Creditworthiness of sub-lessee*. The business should investigate the creditworthiness of the sub-lessee. Failure to receive the expected sub-lease payments would make the closure option far less attractive.

● *Accuracy of forecasts*. The forecasts made by the business should be examined carefully. Inaccuracies in the forecasts or any underlying assumptions may change the expected outcomes.

(d)　The NPV of the decision to continue operations rather than close immediately is positive. Hence, shareholders would be better off if the directors took this course of action. The factory should therefore continue in operation rather than close down. This decision is likely to be welcomed by employees and would allow the business to maintain its flexibility.

Investment appraisal in practice

Many surveys have been conducted in the UK into the methods of investment appraisal used by businesses. They have shown the following features:

● Businesses tend to use more than one method to assess each investment decision.
● The discounting methods (NPV and IRR) have become increasingly popular over time, with these two becoming the most popular in recent years.
● The continued popularity of PP, and to a lesser extent ARR, despite their theoretical shortcomings.

● A tendency for larger businesses to rely more heavily on discounting methods than smaller businesses.

The mini case below shows the results of a recent survey of UK manufacturing businesses regarding their use of investment appraisal methods.

mini case   A survey of UK business practice

A survey of 83 of the UK's largest manufacturing businesses examined the investment appraisal methods used to evaluate both strategic and non-strategic projects. Strategic projects usually aim to increase or change the competitive capabilities of a business, for example by introducing a new manufacturing process. Although a definition was provided, survey respondents were able to decide for themselves what constituted a strategic project. The results of the survey are set out below.

Method	Non-strategic projects Mean score	Strategic projects Mean score
Net present value	3.6829	3.9759
Payback	3.4268	3.6098
Internal rate of return	3.3293	3.7073
Accounting rate of return	1.9867	2.2667

Response scale: 1 = never, 2 = rarely, 3 = often, 4 = mostly, 5 = always.

We can see that, for both non-strategic and strategic investments, the NPV method is the most popular. As the sample consists of large businesses (nearly all with total sales revenue in excess of £100 million), a fairly sophisticated approach to evaluation might be expected. Nevertheless, for non-strategic investments, the payback method comes second in popularity. It drops to third place for strategic projects.

The survey also found that 98 per cent of respondents used more than one method and 88 per cent used more than three methods of investment appraisal.

Source: Based on information in Alkaraan, F. and Northcott, D., 'Strategic capital investment decision-making: a role for emergent analysis tools? A study of practice in large UK manufacturing companies', *The British Accounting Review*, No. 38, 2006, p. 159.

A survey of US businesses also shows considerable support for the NPV and IRR methods. There is less support, however, for the payback method and ARR. The next mini case sets out some of the main findings.

mini case   A survey of US practice

A survey of the chief financial officers (CFOs) of 392 US businesses examined the popularity of various methods of investment appraisal.

Figure 2.11 shows the percentage of businesses surveyed that always, or almost always, used the four methods discussed in this chapter.

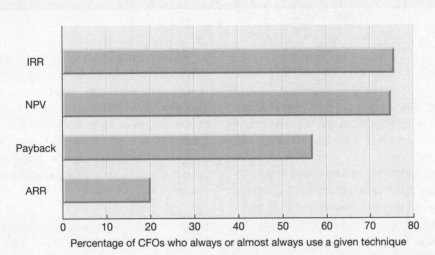

The IRR and NPV methods are both widely used and are much more popular than the payback and accounting rate of return methods. Nevertheless, the payback method is still used always, or almost always, by a majority of US businesses.

Figure 2.11   The use of investment appraisal methods among US businesses

Source: Based on information in Graham, R. and Harvey, C., 'How do CFOs make capital budgeting and capital structure decisions?', *Journal of Applied Corporate Finance*, Vol. 15, No. 1, 2002.

Activity 2.17

Earlier in the chapter we discussed the theoretical limitations of the PP method. Can you explain the fact that it still seems to be a popular method of investment appraisal among businesses?

A number of possible reasons may explain this finding:

- PP is easy to understand and use.
- It can avoid the problems of forecasting far into the future.
- It gives emphasis to the early cash flows when there is greater certainty concerning the accuracy of their predicted value.
- It emphasises the importance of liquidity. Where a business has liquidity problems, a short payback period for a project is likely to appear attractive.

PP can provide a convenient, though rough and ready, assessment of the profitability of a project, in the way that it is used in the following mini case.

mini case · An investment lifts off

SES Global is the world's largest commercial satellite operator. This means that it rents satellite capacity to broadcasters, governments, telecommunications groups and internet service providers. It is a risky venture that few are prepared to undertake. As a result, a handful of businesses dominates the market.

Launching a satellite requires a huge initial outlay of capital, but relatively small cash outflows following the launch. Revenues only start to flow once the satellite is in orbit. A satellite launch costs around €250m. The main elements of this cost are the satellite (€120m), the launch vehicle (€80m), insurance (€40m) and ground equipment (€10m).

According to Romain Bausch, president and chief executive of SES Global, it takes three years to build and launch a satellite. However, the average lifetime of a satellite is fifteen years during which time it is generating revenues. The revenues generated are such that the payback period is around four to five years.

Source: Satellites need space to earn, ft.com (Burt, T.), © The Financial Times Limited, 14 July 2003.

The popularity of PP may suggest a lack of sophistication by managers, concerning investment appraisal. This criticism is most often made against managers of smaller businesses. This point is borne out by both of the surveys discussed above, which have found that smaller businesses are much less likely to use discounted cash flow methods (NPV and IRR) than are larger ones. Other surveys have tended to reach a similar conclusion.

IRR may be popular because it expresses outcomes in percentage terms rather than in absolute terms. This form of expression appears to be more acceptable to managers, despite the problems of percentage measures that we discussed earler. This may be because managers are used to using percentage figures as targets (for example, return on capital employed).

The next mini case shows extracts from the 2006 annual report of a well-known business: Rolls-Royce plc, the builder of engines for aircraft and other purposes.

mini case · The use of NPV at Rolls-Royce

In its 2007 annual report and accounts, Rolls-Royce plc stated:

The Group continues to subject all investments to rigorous examination of risks and future cash flows to ensure that they create shareholder value. All major investments require Board approval.

The Group has a portfolio of projects at different stages of their life cycles. Discounted cash flow analysis of the remaining life of projects is performed on a regular basis.

Source: Rolls-Royce plc Annual Report 2007.

Rolls-Royce makes clear that it uses NPV (the report refers to creating shareholder value and to discounted cash flow, which strongly imply NPV). It is interesting to note that Rolls-Royce not only assesses new projects but also reassesses existing ones. This must be a sensible commercial approach. Businesses should not continue with existing projects unless those projects have a positive NPV based on future cash flows. Just because a project seemed to have a positive NPV before it started does not mean that this will persist in the light of changing circumstances. Activity 2.16 (pp. 219–221) considered a decision on whether to close down a project.

Self-assessment question 2.1

Beacon Chemicals plc is considering buying some equipment to produce a chemical named X14. The new equipment's capital cost is estimated at £100,000. If its purchase is approved now, the equipment can be bought and production can commence by the end of this year. £50,000 has already been spent on research and development work. Estimates of revenues and costs arising from the operation of the new equipment appear below.

	Year 1	Year 2	Year 3	Year 4	Year 5
Sales price (£/litre)	100	120	120	100	80
Sales volume (litres)	800	1,000	1,200	1,000	800
Variable cost (£/litre)	50	50	40	30	40
Fixed cost (£000)	30	30	30	30	30

If the equipment is bought, sales of some existing products will be lost, and this will result in a loss of contribution of £15,000 a year over its life.

The accountant has informed you that the fixed cost includes depreciation of £20,000 a year on the new equipment. It also includes an allocation of £10,000 for fixed overheads. A separate study has indicated that if the new equipment were bought, additional overheads, excluding depreciation, arising from producing the chemical would be £8,000 a year. Production would require additional working capital of £30,000.

For the purposes of your initial calculations ignore taxation.

Required:
(a) Deduce the relevant annual cash flows associated with buying the equipment.
(b) Deduce the payback period.
(c) Calculate the net present value using a discount rate of 8 per cent.

(*Hint*: You should deal with the investment in working capital by treating it as a cash outflow at the start of the project and an inflow at the end.)

The answer to this question can be found at the end of this section.

Investment appraisal and strategic planning

So far, we have tended to view investment opportunities as if they are uncon-nected, independent entities. In practice, however, successful businesses are those that set out a clear framework for the selection of investment projects. Unless this framework is in place, it may be difficult to identify those projects that are likely to generate a positive NPV. The best investment projects are usually those that match the business's internal strengths (for example, skills, experience, access to finance) with the opportunities available. In areas where this match does not exist, other businesses, for which the match does exist, are likely to have a distinct competitive advantage. This advantage means that they are likely to be able to provide the product or service at a better price and/or quality.

Establishing what is the best area or areas of activity and style of approach for the business is popularly known as *strategic planning*. Strategic planning tries to identify the direction in which the business needs to go, in terms of products, markets, financing and so on, to best place it to generate profitable investment opportunities. In practice, strategic plans seem to have a timespan of around five years and generally tend to ask the question: where do we want our business to be in five years' time and how can we get there?

The following mini case shows how easyJet made an investment that fitted its strategic objectives.

mini case   easyFit   FT

easyJet, the UK budget airline, bought a small rival airline, GB Airways Ltd (GB) in late 2007 for £103m. According to an article in the *Financial Times*:

GB is a good strategic fit for easyJet. It operates under a British Airways franchise from Gatwick, which happens to be easyJet's biggest base. The deal makes easyJet the single largest passenger carrier at the UK airport. There is plenty of scope for scale economies in purchasing and back office functions. Moreover, easyJet should be able to boost GB's profitability by switching the carrier to its low-cost business model . . . easyJet makes an estimated £4 a passenger, against GB's £1. Assuming easyJet can drag up GB to its own levels of profitability, the company's value to the low-cost carrier is roughly four times its standalone worth.

The article makes the point that this looks like a good investment for easyJet, because of the strategic fit. For a business other than easyJet, the lack of strategic fit might well have meant that buying GB for exactly the same price of £103 million would not have been a good investment.

Source: Easy ride, ft.com (Hughes, C.), © The Financial Times Limited, 26 October 2007.

Dealing with risk

As we discussed earlier, all investments are risky. This means that consideration of risk is an important aspect of financial decision making. Risk, in this context, is the extent and likelihood that what is projected to occur will not actually happen. It is a particularly important issue in the context of investment decisions, because of

1 The relatively long timescales involved. There is more time for things to go wrong between the decision being made and the end of the project.
2 The size of the investment. If things go wrong, the impact can be both significant and lasting.

Various approaches to dealing with risk have been proposed. These fall into two categories: assessing the level of risk and reacting to the level of risk. We now consider formal methods of dealing with risk that fall within each category.

Assessing the level of risk

Sensitivity analysis

One popular way of attempting to assess the level of risk is to carry out a sensitivity analysis on the proposed project. This involves an examination of the key input values affecting the project to see how changes in each input might influence the viability of the project.

First, the investment is appraised, using the best estimates for each of the input factors (for example, labour cost, material cost, discount rate and so on). Assuming that the NPV is positive, each input value is then examined to see how far the estimated figure could be changed before the project becomes unviable for that reason alone. Let us suppose that the NPV for an investment in a machine to provide a particular service is a positive value. If we were to carry out a sensitivity analysis on this project, we should consider in turn each of the key input factors:

- initial outlay for the machine;
- sales volume and selling price;
- relevant operating costs;
- life of the project; and
- financing costs (to be used as the discount rate).

We should seek to find the value that each of them could have before the NPV figure would become negative (that is, the value for the factor at which NPV would be zero). The difference between the value for that factor at which the NPV would equal zero and the estimated value represents the margin of safety for that particular input. The process is set out in Figure 2.12.

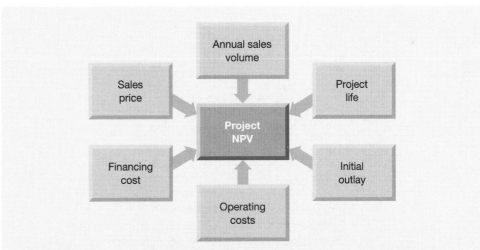

Sensitivity analysis involves identifying the key factors that affect the project. In the figure, six factors have been identified for the particular project. (In practice, the key factors are likely to vary between projects.) Once identified, each factor will be examined in turn to find the value it should have for the project to have a zero NPV.

Figure 2.12   Factors affecting the sensitivity of NPV calculations

A computer spreadsheet model of the project can be extremely valuable for this exercise because it then becomes a very simple matter to try various values for the input data and to see the effect of each. As a result of carrying out a sensitivity analysis, the decision maker is able to get a 'feel' for the project, which otherwise might not be possible. The example below, which illustrates a sensitivity analysis is, however, straightforward and can be undertaken without recourse to a spreadsheet.

Example

S. Saluja (Property Developers) Ltd intends to bid at an auction, to be held today, for a manor house that has fallen into disrepair. The auctioneer believes that the house will be sold for about £450,000. The business wishes to renovate the property and to divide it into flats, to be sold for £150,000 each. The renovation will be in two stages and will cover a two-year period. Stage 1 will cover the first year of the project. It will cost £500,000 and the six flats completed during this stage are expected to be sold for a total of £900,000 at the end of the first year. Stage 2 will cover the second year of the project. It will cost £300,000 and the three remaining flats are expected to be sold at the end of the second year for a total of £450,000. The cost of renovation will be the subject of a binding contract with local builders if the property is bought. There is, however, some uncertainty over the remaining input values. The business estimates its cost of capital at 12 per cent a year.

(a) What is the NPV of the proposed project?
(b) Assuming none of the other inputs deviates from the best estimates provided,
    (1) What auction price would have to be paid for the manor house to cause the project to have a zero NPV?
    (2) What cost of capital would cause the project to have a zero NPV?
    (3) What is the sale price of each of the flats that would cause the project to have a zero NPV? (Each flat is projected to be sold for the same price: £150,000.)
(c) Is the level of risk associated with the project high or low? Discuss your findings.

Solution

(a) The NPV of the proposed project is as follows:

	Cash flows £	Discount factor 12%	Present value £
Year 1 (£900,000 – £500,000)	400,000	0.893	357,200
Year 2 (£450,000 – £300,000)	150,000	0.797	119,550
Less initial outlay			(450,000)
Net present value			26,750

(b) (1) To obtain a zero NPV, the auction price would have to be £26,750 higher than the current estimate – that is, a total price of £476,750. This is about 6 per cent above the current estimated price.
    (2) As there is a positive NPV, the cost of capital that would cause the project to have a zero NPV must be higher than 12 per cent. Let us try 20 per cent.

	Cash flows £	Discount factor 20%	Present value £
Year 1 (£900,000 – £500,000)	400,000	0.833	333,200
Year 2 (£450,000 – £300,000)	150,000	0.694	104,100
Less initial outlay			(450,000)
Net present value			(12,700)

As the NPV using a 20 per cent discount rate is negative, the 'break-even' cost of capital lies somewhere between 12 per cent and 20 per cent. A reasonable approximation is obtained as follows:

	Discount rate	Net present value
	%	£
	12	26,750
	20	(12,700)
Difference	8	39,450

The change in NPV for every 1 per cent change in the discount rate will be

39,450/8 = £4,931

The reduction in the 20 per cent discount rate required to achieve a zero NPV would therefore be

12,700/4,931 = 2.6%

The cost of capital (that is, the discount rate) would, therefore, have to be 17.4 per cent (20.0 − 2.6) for the project to have a zero NPV.

This calculation is, of course, the same as that used earlier in the chapter, when calculating the IRR of a project. In other words, 17.4 per cent is the IRR of the project.

(3) To obtain a zero NPV, the sale price of each flat must be reduced so that the NPV is reduced by £26,750. In year 1, six flats are sold, and in year 2, three flats are sold. The discount factor at the 12 per cent rate is 0.893 for year 1 and 0.797 for year 2. We can derive the fall in value per flat (Y) to give a zero NPV by using the equation

$$(6Y \times 0.893) + (3Y \times 0.797) = £26,750$$
$$Y = £3,452$$

The sale price of each flat necessary to obtain a zero NPV is therefore

£150,000 − £3,452 = £146,548

This represents a fall in the estimated price of 2.3 per cent.

(c) These calculations indicate that the auction price would have to be about 6 per cent above the estimated price before a zero NPV is obtained. The margin of safety is, therefore, not very high for this factor. In practice this should not represent a real risk because the business could withdraw from the bidding if the price rises to an unacceptable level.

The other two factors represent serious risks, because only after the project is at a very late stage can the business be sure as to what actual cost of capital and price per flat will prevail. The calculations reveal that the price of the flats would only have to fall by 2.3 per cent from the estimated price before the NPV is reduced to zero. Hence, the margin of safety for this factor is even smaller. However, the cost of capital is less sensitive to changes and there would have to be an increase from 12 per cent to 17.4 per cent before the project produced a zero NPV. It seems from the calculations that the sale price of the flats is the most sensitive factor to consider. A careful re-examination of the market value of the flats seems appropriate before a final decision is made.

There are two major drawbacks with the use of sensitivity analysis:

- It does not give managers clear decision rules concerning acceptance or rejection of the project and so they must rely on their own judgement.
- It is a static form of analysis. Only one input is considered at a time, while the rest are held constant. In practice, however, it is likely that more than one input value will differ from the best estimates provided. Even so, it would be possible to deal with changes in various inputs simultaneously, were the project data put onto a spreadsheet model. This approach, where more than one variable is altered at a time, is known as scenario building.

The mini case below describes an evaluation of a mining project that incorporated sensitivity analysis to test the robustness of the findings.

mini case   Golden opportunity

In 2006, Eureka Mining plc undertook an evaluation of the opportunity to mine copper and gold deposits at Miheevskoye, which is located in the Southern Urals region of the Russian Federation. Using three investment appraisal methods, the business came up with the following results:

IRR %	Pre-tax NPV US$m	Payback period Years
20.4	178.8	3.8

Sensitivity analysis was carried out on four key variables – the price of copper, the price of gold, operating costs and capital outlay costs – to help assess the riskiness of the project. This was done by assessing the IRR, NPV and PP, making various assumptions regarding the prices of copper and gold and about the percentage change in both the operating and the capital costs. The following table sets out the findings.

Copper price

	IRR %	Pre-tax NPV US$m	Payback period Years
Average spot* copper price US$/lb			
1.10	8.8	(18.4)	8.1
1.20	14.8	80.2	5.0
1.40	25.7	277.3	3.0
1.50	30.8	375.9	2.7

Gold price

	IRR %	Pre-tax NPV US$m	Payback period Years
Average spot* gold price US$/oz			
450	18.9	152.0	4.0
500	19.6	165.4	3.9
600	21.2	192.2	3.6
650	21.9	205.6	3.5

Operating costs

Percentage change	Average total costs (lb copper equivalent)			
–20	$0.66	26.68	298.5	3.0
–10	$0.72	23.7	238.6	3.3
+10	$0.83	17.1	118.9	4.4
+20	$0.88	13.6	59.0	5.3

Capital costs

	Initial capital (US$m)			
–20	360	28.6	261.8	2.8
–10	405	24.1	220.3	3.2
+10	495	17.3	137.2	4.4
+20	540	14.7	95.7	5.1

* The spot price is the price for immediate delivery of the mineral.

In its report, the business stated:

> This project is most sensitive to percentage changes in the copper price which have the largest impact, whereas movements in the gold price have the least. The impact of changes in operating costs is more significant than capital costs.

Source: Adapted from 'Eureka Mining PLC – drilling report', www.citywire.co.uk, 26 July 2006.

Expected net present value

Another means of assessing risk is through the use of statistical probabilities. It may be possible to identify a range of feasible values for each of the items of input data and to assign a probability of occurrence to each of these values. Using this information, we can derive an expected net present value (ENPV), which is, in effect, a weighted average of the possible outcomes where the probabilities are used as weights. To illustrate this method, let us consider the following example.

Example

C. Piperis (Properties) Ltd has the opportunity to acquire a lease on a block of flats that has only two years remaining before it expires. The cost of the lease would be £100,000. The occupancy rate of the block of flats is currently around 70 per cent and the flats are let almost exclusively to naval personnel. There is a large naval base located nearby, and there is little other demand for the flats. The occupancy rate of the flats will change in the remaining two years of the lease, depending on the outcome of a defence review. The navy is currently considering three options for the naval base. These are:

- *Option 1.* Increase the size of the base by closing down a base in another region and transferring the personnel to the one located near the flats.
- *Option 2.* Close down the naval base near to the flats and leave only a skeleton staff there for maintenance purposes. The personnel would be moved to a base in another region.
- *Option 3.* Leave the base open but reduce staffing levels by 20 per cent.

The directors of Piperis have estimated the following net cash flows for each of the two years under each option and the probability of their occurrence:

	£	Probability
Option 1	80,000	0.6
Option 2	12,000	0.1
Option 3	40,000	0.3
		1.0

Note that the sum of the probabilities is 1.0 (in other words it is certain that one of the possible options will arise). The business has a cost of capital of 10 per cent.

Should the business purchase the lease on the block of flats?

Solution

To calculate the expected NPV of the proposed investment, we must first calculate the weighted average of the expected outcomes for each year, using the probabilities as weights, by multiplying each cash flow by its probability of occurrence. Thus, the expected annual net cash flows will be:

	Cash flows	Probability	Expected cash flows
	£		£
	(a)	(b)	(a × b)
Option 1	80,000	0.6	48,000
Option 2	12,000	0.1	1,200
Option 3	40,000	0.3	12,000
Expected cash flows in each year			61,200

Having derived the expected annual cash flows, we can now discount these using a rate of 10 per cent to reflect the cost of capital:

Year	Expected cash flows	Discount rate	Expected present value
	£	10%	£
1	61,200	0.909	55,631
2	61,200	0.826	50,551
			106,182
Initial investment			(100,000)
Expected NPV			6,182

We can see that the expected NPV is positive. Hence, the wealth of shareholders is expected to increase by purchasing the lease.

The expected NPV approach has the advantage of producing a single numerical outcome and of having a clear decision rule to apply. If the expected NPV is positive, we should invest; if it is negative, we should not.

However, the approach produces an average figure, and it may not be possible for this figure actually to result. This point was illustrated in the previous example where the expected annual cash flow (£61,200) does not correspond to any of the stated options.

Perhaps more importantly, using an average figure can obscure the underlying risk associated with the project. Simply deriving the ENPV, as in the example, can be misleading. Without some idea of the individual possible outcomes and their probability of occurring, the decision maker is in the dark. In the example, were either of Options 2 or 3 to occur, the investment would be adverse (wealth-destroying). It is 40 per cent probable that one of these two options will occur, so this is a significant risk. Only should Option 1 arise (60 per cent probable) would investing in the flats represent a good decision. Of course, in advance of making the investment, which option will actually occur is not known. None of this should be taken to mean that the investment in the flats should not be made, simply that the decision maker is better placed to make a judgement where information on the possible outcomes is available. Activity 2.18 further illustrates this point.

Activity 2.18

Qingdao Manufacturing Ltd is considering two competing projects. Details are as follows:

- Project A has a 0.9 probability of producing a negative NPV of £200,000 and a 0.1 probability of producing a positive NPV of £3.8m.
- Project B has a 0.6 probability of producing a positive NPV of £100,000 and a 0.4 probability of producing a positive NPV of £350,000.

What is the expected net present value of each project?

The expected NPV of Project A is

$$[(0.1 \times £3.8m) - (0.9 \times £200,000)] = £200,000$$

The expected NPV of Project B is

$$[(0.6 \times £100,000) + (0.4 \times £350,000)] = £200,000$$

Although the expected NPV of each project in Activity 2.18 is identical, this does not mean that the business will be indifferent about which project to undertake. We can see from the information provided that Project A has a high probability of making a loss whereas Project B is not expected to make a loss under either possible outcome. If we assume that the shareholders dislike risk – which is usually the case – they will prefer the directors to take on Project B as this provides the same level of expected return as Project A but for a lower level of risk.

It can be argued that the problem identified above may not be significant where the business is engaged in several similar projects. This is because a worse than expected outcome on one project may well be balanced by a better than expected outcome on another project. However, in practice, investment projects may be unique events and this argument will not then apply. Also, where the project is large in relation to other projects undertaken, the argument loses its force. There is also the problem that a factor that might cause one project to have an adverse outcome could also have adverse effects on other projects. For example, a large, unexpected increase in the price of oil may have a simultaneous adverse effect on all of the investment projects of a particular business.

Where the expected NPV approach is being used, it is probably a good idea to make known to managers the different possible outcomes and the probability attached to each outcome. By so doing, the managers will be able to gain an insight to the *downside risk* attached to the project. The information relating to each outcome can be presented in the form of a diagram if required. The construction of such a diagram is illustrated in the following example.

Example

Zeta Computing Services Ltd has recently produced some software for a client organisation. The software has a life of two years and will then become obsolete. The cost of producing the software was £10,000. The client has agreed to pay a licence fee of £8,000 a year for the software if it is used in only one of its two divisions, and £12,000 a year if it is used in both of its divisions. The client may use the software for either one or two years in either division but will definitely use it in at least one division in each of the two years.

Zeta believes there is a 0.6 chance that the licence fee received in any one year will be £8,000 and a 0.4 chance that it will be £12,000. There are, therefore, four possible outcomes attached to this project (where p denotes probability):

- *Outcome 1.* Year 1 cash flow £8,000 ($p = 0.6$) and Year 2 cash flow £8,000 ($p = 0.6$). The probability of both years having cash flows of £8,000 will be

  $0.6 \times 0.6 = 0.36$

- *Outcome 2.* Year 1 cash flow £12,000 ($p = 0.4$) and Year 2 cash flow £12,000 ($p = 0.4$). The probability of both years having cash flows of £12,000 will be

  $0.4 \times 0.4 = 0.16$

- *Outcome 3.* Year 1 cash flow £12,000 ($p = 0.4$) and Year 2 cash flow £8,000 ($p = 0.6$). The probability of this sequence of cash flows occurring will be

  $0.4 \times 0.6 = 0.24$

- *Outcome 4.* Year 1 cash flow £8,000 ($p = 0.6$) and Year 2 cash flow £12,000 ($p = 0.4$). The probability of this sequence of cash flows occurring will be

  $0.6 \times 0.4 = 0.24$

The information in the above example can be displayed in the form of a diagram, as in Figure 2.13.

The source of probabilities

As we might expect, assigning probabilities to possible outcomes can often be a problem. There may be many possible outcomes arising from a particular investment project, and to identify each outcome and then assign a probability to it may prove to be an impossible task. When assigning probabilities to possible outcomes, an objective or a subjective approach may be used. Objective probabilities are based on information gathered from past experience. Thus, for example, the transport manager of a business operating a fleet of vans may be able to provide information concerning the possible life of a new van based on the record of similar vans

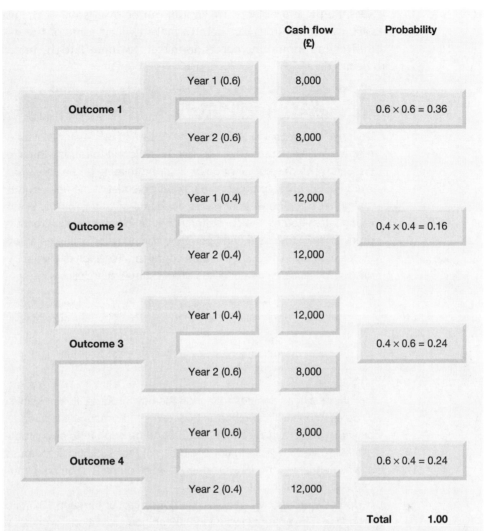

There are four different possible outcomes associated with the project, each with its own probability of occurrence. The sum of the probabilities attached to each outcome must equal 1.00, in other words it is certain that one of the possible outcomes will occur. For example, Outcome 1 would occur where only one division uses the software in each year.

Figure 2.13 The different possible project outcomes for the Zeta project

acquired in the past. From the information available, probabilities may be developed for different possible lifespans. However, the past may not always be a reliable guide to the future, particularly during a period of rapid change. In the case of the vans, for example, changes in design and technology or changes in the purpose for which the vans are being used may undermine the validity of past data.

Subjective probabilities are based on opinion and will be used where past data are either inappropriate or unavailable. The opinions of independent experts may provide a useful basis for developing subjective probabilities, though even these may contain bias, which will affect the reliability of the judgements made.

Despite these problems, we should not be dismissive of the use of probabilities. Assigning probabilities can help to make explicit some of the risks associated with a project and should help decision makers to appreciate the uncertainties that have to be faced.

Activity 2.19

Devonia (Laboratories) Ltd has recently carried out successful clinical trials on a new type of skin cream that has been developed to reduce the effects of ageing. Research and development costs incurred relating to the new product amounted to £160,000. In order to gauge the market potential of the new product, independent market research consultants were hired at a cost of £15,000. The market research report submitted by the consultants indicates that the skin cream is likely to have a product life of four years and could be sold to retail chemists and large department stores at a price of £20 per 100 ml container. For each of the four years of the new product's life, sales demand has been estimated as follows:

Number of 100 ml containers sold	Probability of occurrence
11,000	0.3
14,000	0.6
16,000	0.1

If the business decides to launch the new product, it is possible for production to begin at once. The equipment necessary to produce it is already owned by the business and originally cost £150,000. At the end of the new product's life, it is estimated that the equipment could be sold for £35,000. If the business decides against launching the new product, the equipment will be sold immediately for £85,000, as it will be of no further use.

The new product will require one hour's labour for each 100 ml container produced. The cost of labour is £8.00 an hour. Additional workers will have to be recruited to produce the new product. At the end of the product's life, the workers are unlikely to be offered further work with the business and redundancy costs of £10,000 are expected. The cost of the ingredients for each 100 ml container is £6.00. Additional overheads arising from production of the new product are expected to be £15,000 a year.

The new skin cream has attracted the interest of the business's competitors. If the business decides not to produce and sell the skin cream, it can sell the patent rights to a major competitor immediately for £125,000.

Devonia has a cost of capital of 12 per cent.

(a) Calculate the expected net present value (ENPV) of the new product.
(b) State, with reasons, whether or not Devonia should launch the new product.

Ignore taxation.

Your answer should be as follows:

(a) Expected sales volume per year = (11,000 × 0.3) + (14,000 × 0.6) + (16,000 × 0.1)
= 13,300 units

Expected annual sales revenue = 13,300 × £20
                              = £266,000
Annual labour   = 13,300 × £8
                              = £106,400
Annual ingredient costs   = 13,300 × £6
                              = £79,800

Incremental cash flows:

	Years				
	0	1	2	3	4
	£	£	£	£	£
Sale of patent rights	(125.0)				
Sale of equipment	(85.0)				35.0
Sales revenue		266.0	266.0	266.0	266.0
Cost of ingredients		(79.8)	(79.8)	(79.8)	(79.8)
Labour costs		(106.4)	(106.4)	(106.4)	(106.4)
Redundancy					(10.0)
Additional overheads		(15.0)	(15.0)	(15.0)	(15.0)
	(210.0)	64.8	64.8	64.8	89.8
Discount factor (12%)	1.000	0.893	0.797	0.712	0.636
	(210.0)	57.9	51.6	46.1	57.1
ENPV	2.7				

(b) As the ENPV of the project is positive, accepting the project would increase the wealth of shareholders. However, the ENPV is very low in relation to the size of the project and careful checking of the key estimates and assumptions would be advisable. A relatively small downward revision of sales (volume and/or price) or upward revision of costs could make the project ENPV negative.

It would be helpful to derive the NPV for each of the three possible outcomes regarding sales levels. This would enable the decision maker to have a clearer view of the risk involved with the investment.

Reacting to the level of risk

The logical reaction to a risky project is to demand a higher rate of return. Clear observable evidence shows that there is a relationship between risk and the return required by investors. It was mentioned earlier, for example, that a bank would normally ask for a higher rate of interest on a loan where it perceives the borrower to be less likely to be able to repay the amount borrowed.

When assessing investment projects, it is normal to increase the NPV discount rate in the face of increased risk – that is, to demand a risk premium: the higher the level of risk, the higher the risk premium that will be demanded. The risk premium is added to the 'risk-free' rate of return to derive the total return required (the risk-adjusted discount rate). The risk-free rate is normally taken to be equivalent to the rate of return from government loan notes. In practice, a business may divide projects into low-, medium- and high-risk categories and then assign a risk premium to each category. The cash flows from a particular project will then be discounted using a rate based on the risk-free rate plus the appropriate risk premium. Since all investments are risky to some extent, all projects will have a risk premium linked to them.

The relationship between risk and return is illustrated in Figure 2.14.

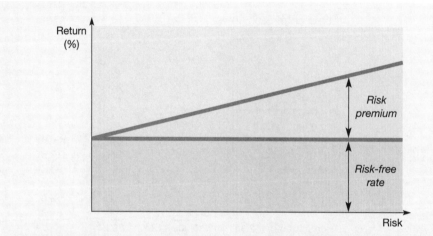

It is logical to take account of the riskiness of projects by changing the discount rate. A risk premium is added to the risk-free rate to derive the appropriate discount rate. A higher return will normally be expected from projects where the risks are higher; thus, the riskier the project, the higher the risk premium.

Figure 2.14 Relationship between risk and return

Activity 2.20

Can you think of any practical problems with estimating an appropriate value for the risk premium for a particular project?

Subjective judgement tends to be required when assigning an investment project to a particular risk category and then in assigning a risk premium to each category. The choices made will reflect the personal views of the managers responsible and these may differ from the views of the shareholders they represent. The choices made can, nevertheless, make the difference between accepting and rejecting a particular project.

Managing investment projects

So far, we have been concerned with the process of carrying out the necessary calculations that enable managers to select among already identified investment opportunities. This topic is given a great deal of emphasis in the literature on investment appraisal. Though the assessment of projects is undoubtedly important, we must bear in mind that it is only *part* of the process of investment decision making. There are other important aspects that managers must also consider.

It is possible to see the investment process as a sequence of five stages, each of which managers must consider. The five stages are set out in Figure 2.15 and described below.

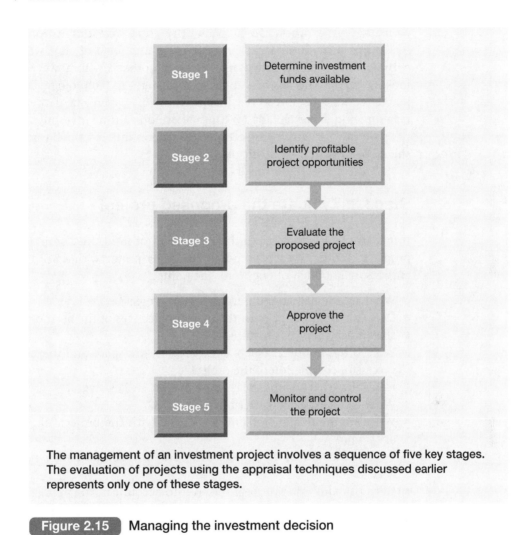

The management of an investment project involves a sequence of five key stages. The evaluation of projects using the appraisal techniques discussed earlier represents only one of these stages.

Figure 2.15   Managing the investment decision

Stage 1: Determine investment funds available

The amount of funds available for investment may be determined by the external market for funds or by internal management. In practice, it is often the latter that has the greater influence on the amount available. In either case, it may be that the funds will not be sufficient to finance the profitable investment opportunities available. This shortage of investment funds is known as *capital rationing*. When it arises managers are faced with the task of deciding on the most profitable use of those funds available.

Stage 2: Identify profitable project opportunities

A vital part of the investment process is the search for profitable investment opportunities. The business should carry out methodical routines for identifying feasible projects. This may be done through a research and development department or by some other means. Failure to do so will inevitably lead to the business losing its competitive position with respect to product development, production methods or market penetration. To help identify good investment opportunities, some businesses provide financial incentives to members of staff who come forward with good investment proposals. The search process will, however, usually involve looking outside the business to identify changes in technology, customer demand, market conditions and so on. Information will have to be gathered and this may take some time, particularly for unusual or non-routine investment opportunities.

As we saw earlier in this section, it is important that the business's investments should fit in with its strategic plans.

Stage 3: Evaluate the proposed project

If management is to agree to the investment of funds in a project, there must be a proper screening of each proposal. For larger projects, this will involve providing answers to a number of questions, including:

- What are the nature and purpose of the project?
- Does the project align with the overall objectives of the business?
- How much finance is required?
- What other resources (such as expertise, work space and so on) are required for successful completion of the project?
- How long will the project last and what are its key stages?
- What is the expected pattern of cash flows?
- What are the major problems associated with the project and how can they be overcome?
- What is the NPV of the project? How does this compare with other opportunities available?
- Have risk and inflation been taken into account in the appraisal process and, if so, what are the results?

The ability and commitment of those responsible for proposing and managing the project will be vital to its success. This means that, when evaluating a new project, one consideration will be the quality of those proposing it. In some cases, senior managers may decide not to support a project that appears profitable on paper if they lack confidence in the ability of key managers to see it through to completion.

Stage 4: Approve the project

Once the managers responsible for investment decision making are satisfied that the project should be undertaken, formal approval can be given. However, a decision on a project may be postponed if senior managers need more information from those proposing the project, or if revisions to the proposal are required. In some cases, the proposal may be rejected if the project is considered unprofitable or likely to fail. Before rejecting a proposal, however, the implications of not pursuing the project for such areas as market share, staff morale and existing business operations must be carefully considered.

Stage 5: Monitor and control the project

Making a decision to invest in, say, the plant needed to provide a new service does not automatically cause the investment to be made and provision of the service to go smoothly ahead. Managers will need to manage the project actively through to completion. This, in turn, will require further information-gathering exercises.

Management should receive progress reports at regular intervals concerning the project. These reports should provide information relating to the actual cash flows for each stage of the project, which can then be compared against the forecast figures provided when the proposal was submitted for approval. The reasons for significant variations should be ascertained and corrective action taken where possible. Any changes in the expected completion date of the project or any expected variations from budget in future cash flows should be reported immediately; in extreme cases, managers may even abandon the project if circumstances appear to have changed dramatically for the worse. We saw in the second mini case on p. 224 that Rolls-Royce undertakes this kind of reassessment of existing projects. No doubt most other well-managed businesses do this too.

Project management techniques (for example, critical path analysis) should be employed wherever possible and their effectiveness reported to senior management.

An important part of the control process is a post-completion audit of the project. This is, in essence, a review of the project's performance to see if it lived up to expectations and whether any lessons can be learned from the way that the investment process was carried out. In addition to an evaluation of financial costs and benefits, non-financial measures of performance such as the ability to meet deadlines and levels of quality achieved should also be reported.

The fact that a post-completion audit is an integral part of the management of the project should also encourage those who submit projects to use realistic estimates. The next mini case provides some evidence of a need for greater realism.

---

mini case   Looking on the bright side

McKinsey and Co, the management consultants, surveyed 2,500 senior managers worldwide during the spring of 2007. The managers were asked their opinions on investments made by their businesses in the previous three years. The general opinion is that estimates for the investment decision inputs had been too optimistic. For example, sales levels had been overestimated in about 50 per cent of cases, but underestimated in less than 20 per cent of cases. It is not clear whether the estimates were sufficiently inaccurate to call into question the decision that had been made.

The survey went on to ask about the extent to which investments made seemed, in the light of the actual outcomes, to have been mistakes. Managers felt that 19 per cent of investments that had been made should not have gone ahead. On the other hand, they felt that 31 per cent of rejected projects should have been taken up.

Managers also felt that 'good money was thrown after bad' in that existing investments that were not performing well were continuing to be supported in a significant number of cases.

Source: 'How companies spend their money: a McKinsey global survey', www.theglobalmarketer.com, 2007.

Other studies confirm a tendency among managers to use overoptimistic estimates when preparing investment proposals. (See note 1 at the end of the section.) It seems that sometimes this is done deliberately in an attempt to secure project approval. Where overoptimistic estimates are used, the managers responsible may well find themselves accountable at the post-completion audit stage. Such audits, however, can be difficult and time-consuming to carry out, and so the likely benefits must be weighed against the costs involved. Senior management may feel, therefore, that only projects above a certain size should be subject to a post-completion audit.

The mini case below describes how two large retailers, Tesco plc and Kingfisher plc, use post-completion audit approaches to evaluating past investment projects.

mini case   Looking back

In its 2008 corporate governance report, Tesco plc, the supermarket chain, stated:

All major initiatives require business cases to be prepared, normally covering a minimum period of five years. Post-investment appraisals, carried out by management, determine the reasons for any significant variance from expected performance.

In its 2007/8 financial review, Kingfisher plc, the home improvement retailer, stated:

An annual post-investment review process will continue to review the performance of all projects above £0.75 million which were completed in the prior year. The findings of this exercise will be considered by both the new Retail Board and the main Board and directly influence the assumptions for similar project proposals going forward.

Sources: The websites of Tesco plc (www.tescocorporate.com) and Kingfisher plc (www.kingfisher co.uk).

As a footnote to our discussion of business investment decision making, the next mini case looks at one of the world's biggest investment projects, which has proved to be a commercial disaster, despite being a technological success.

mini case   Wealth lost in the chunnel

The tunnel, which runs for 31 miles between Folkestone in the UK and Sangatte in Northern France, was started in 1986 and opened for public use in 1994. From a technological and social

perspective it has been a success, but from a financial point of view it has been a disaster. The tunnel was purely a private sector venture for which a new business, Eurotunnel plc, was created. Relatively little public money was involved. To be a commercial success the tunnel needed to cover all of its costs, including interest charges, and leave sufficient to enhance the shareholders' wealth. In fact the providers of long-term finance (lenders and shareholders) have lost virtually all of their investment. Though the main losers were banks and institutional investors, many individuals, particularly in France, bought shares in Eurotunnel.

Key inputs to the pre-1986 assessment of the project were the cost of construction and creating the infrastructure, the length of time required to complete construction and the level of revenue that the tunnel would generate when it became operational.

In the event

● Construction cost was £10 billion – it was originally planned to cost £5.6 billion.
● Construction time was seven years – it was planned to be six years.
● Revenues from passengers and freight have been well below those projected – for example, 21 million annual passenger journeys on Eurostar trains were projected; the numbers have consistently remained at around 7 million.

The failure to generate revenues at the projected levels has probably been the biggest contributor to the problem. When preparing the projection, planners failed to take adequate account of two crucial factors:

1 Fierce competition from the ferry operators. At the time (pre-1986), many thought that the ferries would roll over and die.
2 The rise of no-frills, cheap air travel between the UK and the continent.

The commercial failure of the tunnel means that it will be very difficult in future for projects of this nature to be funded by private funds.

Sources: Annual reports of Eurotunnel plc; Randall, J., 'How Eurotunnel went wrong', BBC news, 13 June 2005, www.newsvote.bbc.co.uk.

Summary

The main points of this section may be summarised as follows:

Accounting rate of return (ARR) is the average accounting profit from the project expressed as a percentage of the average investment.
● Decision rule – projects with an ARR above a defined minimum are acceptable; the greater the ARR, the more attractive the project becomes.
● Conclusion on ARR:
  – Does not relate directly to shareholders' wealth – can lead to illogical conclusions.
  – Takes almost no account of the timing of cash flows.
  – Ignores some relevant information and may take account of some that is irrelevant.
  – Relatively simple to use.
  – Much inferior to NPV.

Payback period (PP) is the length of time that it takes for the cash outflow for the initial investment to be repaid out of resulting cash inflows.
● Decision rule – projects with a PP up to a defined maximum period are acceptable; the shorter the PP, the more attractive the project.
● Conclusion on PP:

- Does not relate to shareholders' wealth.
- Ignores inflows after the payback date.
- Takes little account of the timing of cash flows.
- Ignores much relevant information.
- Does not always provide clear signals and can be impractical to use.
- Much inferior to NPV, but it is easy to understand and can offer a liquidity insight, which might be the reason for its widespread use.

Net present value (NPV) is the sum of the discounted values of the net cash flows from the investment.

- Money has a time value.
- Decision rule – all positive NPV investments enhance shareholders' wealth; the greater the NPV, the greater the enhancement and the greater the attractiveness of the project.
- PV of a cash flow = cash flow $\times 1/(1 + r)^n$, assuming a constant discount rate.
- Discounting brings cash flows at different points in time to a common valuation basis (their present value), which enables them to be directly compared.
- Conclusion on NPV:
  - Relates directly to shareholders' wealth objective.
  - Takes account of the timing of cash flows.
  - Takes all relevant information into account.
  - Provides clear signals and is practical to use.

Internal rate of return (IRR) is the discount rate that, when applied to the cash flows of a project, causes it to have a zero NPV.

- Represents the average percentage return on the investment, taking account of the fact that cash may be flowing in and out of the project at various points in its life.
- Decision rule – projects that have an IRR greater than the cost of capital are acceptable; the greater the IRR, the more attractive the project.
- Cannot normally be calculated directly; a trial and error approach is often necessary.
- Conclusion on IRR:
  - Does not relate directly to shareholders' wealth. Usually gives the same signals as NPV but can mislead where there are competing projects of different size.
  - Takes account of the timing of cash flows.
  - Takes all relevant information into account.
  - Problems of multiple IRRs when there are unconventional cash flows.
  - Inferior to NPV.

Use of appraisal methods in practice:

- All four methods identified are widely used.
- The discounting methods (NPV and IRR) show a steady increase in usage over time.
- Many businesses use more than one method.
- Larger businesses seem to be more sophisticated in their choice and use of appraisal methods than smaller ones.

Investment appraisal and strategic planning

It is important that businesses invest in a strategic way so as to play to their strengths.

Dealing with risk

- Sensitivity analysis (SA) is an assessment, taking each input factor in turn, of how much each one can vary from estimate before a project is not viable.
  - Provides useful insights to projects.
  - Does not give a clear decision rule, but provides an impression.
  - It can be rather static, but scenario building solves this problem.
- Expected net present value (ENPV) is the weighted average of the possible outcomes for a project, based on probabilities for each of the inputs:
  - Provides a single value and a clear decision rule.
  - The single ENPV figure can hide the real risk.
  - Useful for the ENPV figure to be supported by information on the range and dispersion of possible outcomes.
  - Probabilities may be subjective (based on opinion) or objective (based on evidence).
- Reacting to the level of risk:
  - Logically, high risk should lead to high returns.
  - Using a risk-adjusted discount rate, where a risk premium is added to the risk-free rate, is a logical response to risk.

Managing investment projects

- Determine investment funds available – dealing, if necessary, with capital rationing problems.
- Identify profitable project opportunities.
- Evaluate the proposed project.
- Approve the project.
- Monitor and control the project – using a post-completion audit approach.

Note

1 Linder, S., 'Fifty years of research on accuracy of capital expenditure project estimates: a review of findings and their validity', Otto Beisham Graduate School of Management, April 2005.

Further reading

If you would like to explore the topics covered in this section in more depth, we recommend the following books:

McLaney, E., *Business Finance: Theory and Practice*, 8th edn, Financial Times Prentice Hall, 2009, chapters 4, 5 and 6.

Pike, R. and Neale, B., *Corporate Finance and Investment*, 5th edn, Prentice Hall, 2006, chapters 5, 6 and 7.

Arnold, G., *Corporate Financial Management*, 3rd edn, Financial Times Prentice Hall, 2005, chapters 2, 3 and 4.

Drury, C., *Management and Cost Accounting*, 8th edn, Thomson Learning, 2009, chapters 13 and 14.

Review questions

Answers to these questions can be found at the end of this section.

1 Why is the net present value (NPV) method of investment appraisal considered to be theoretically superior to other methods that are found in practice?
2 The payback method has been criticised for not taking the time value of money into account. Could this limitation be overcome? If so, would this method then be preferable to the NPV method?
3 Research indicates that the IRR method is extremely popular even though it has shortcomings when compared to the NPV method. Why might managers prefer to use IRR rather than NPV when carrying out discounted cash flow evaluations?
4 Why are cash flows rather than profit flows used in the IRR, NPV and PP methods of investment appraisal?

Exercises

Exercises 3 to 8 are more advanced than 1 and 2. Questions 1, 5, 6, 7 and 8 have answers at the end of this section.

1 The directors of Mylo Ltd are currently considering two mutually exclusive investment projects. Both projects are concerned with the purchase of new plant. The following data are available for each project:

	Project 1 £000	Project 2 £000
Cost (immediate outlay)	100	60
Expected annual operating profit (loss):		
Year 1	29	18
2	(1)	(2)
3	2	4
Estimated residual value of the plant	7	6

The business has an estimated cost of capital of 10 per cent, and uses the straight-line method of depreciation for all non-current (fixed) assets when calculating operating profit. Neither project would increase the working capital of the business. The business has sufficient funds to meet all capital expenditure requirements.

Required:
(a) Calculate for each project:
    (1) The net present value.
    (2) The approximate internal rate of return.
    (3) The payback period.
(b) State which, if either, of the two investment projects the directors of Mylo Ltd should accept, and why.

2 C. George (Controls) Ltd manufactures a thermostat that can be used in a range of kitchen appliances. The manufacturing process is, at present, semi-automated. The equipment used cost £540,000, and has a written-down (balance sheet)

value of £300,000. Demand for the product has been fairly stable, and output has been maintained at 50,000 units a year in recent years.

The following data, based on the current level of output, have been prepared in respect of the product:

	Per unit	
	£	£
Selling price		12.40
Labour	(3.30)	
Materials	(3.65)	
Overheads: Variable	(1.58)	
Fixed	(1.60)	
		(10.13)
Operating profit		2.27

Although the existing equipment is expected to last for a further four years before it is sold for an estimated £40,000, the business has recently been considering purchasing new equipment that would completely automate much of the production process. The new equipment would cost £670,000 and would have an expected life of four years, at the end of which it would be sold for an estimated £70,000. If the new equipment is purchased, the old equipment could be sold for £150,000 immediately.

The assistant to the business's accountant has prepared a report to help assess the viability of the proposed change, which includes the following data:

	Per unit	
	£	£
Selling price		12.40
Labour	(1.20)	
Materials	(3.20)	
Overheads: Variable	(1.40)	
Fixed	(3.30)	
		(9.10)
Operating profit		3.30

Depreciation charges will increase by £85,000 a year as a result of purchasing the new machinery; however, other fixed costs are not expected to change.

In the report the assistant wrote:

> The figures shown above that relate to the proposed change are based on the current level of output and take account of a depreciation charge of £150,000 a year in respect of the new equipment. The effect of purchasing the new equipment will be to increase the operating profit to sales revenue ratio from 18.3% to 26.6%. In addition, the purchase of the new equipment will enable us to reduce our inventories level immediately by £130,000.
>
> In view of these facts, I recommend purchase of the new equipment.

The business has a cost of capital of 12 per cent.

Required:

(a) Prepare a statement of the incremental cash flows arising from the purchase of the new equipment.

(b) Calculate the net present value of the proposed purchase of new equipment.

(c) State, with reasons, whether the business should purchase the new equipment.

(d) Explain why cash flow forecasts are used rather than profit forecasts to assess the viability of proposed capital expenditure projects.

Ignore taxation.

3 The accountant of your business has recently been taken ill through overwork. In his absence his assistant has prepared some calculations of the profitability of a project, which are to be discussed soon at the board meeting of your business. His workings, which are set out below, include some errors of principle. You can assume that the statement below includes no arithmetical errors.

	Year 1 £000	Year 2 £000	Year 3 £000	Year 4 £000	Year 5 £000	Year 6 £000
Sales revenue		450	470	470	470	470
Less Costs						
Materials		126	132	132	132	132
Labour		90	94	94	94	94
Overheads		45	47	47	47	47
Depreciation		120	120	120	120	120
Working capital	180					
Interest on working capital		27	27	27	27	27
Write-off of development costs		30	30	30		
Total costs	180	438	450	450	420	420
Operating profit/(loss)	(180)	12	20	20	50	50

$$\frac{\text{Total profit (loss)}}{\text{Cost of equipment}} = \frac{(£28,000)}{£600,000} = \text{Return on investment (4.7\%)}$$

You ascertain the following additional information:

● The cost of equipment contains £100,000, being the carrying (balance sheet) value of an old machine. If it were not used for this project it would be scrapped with a zero net realisable value. New equipment costing £500,000 will be purchased on 31 December Year 0. You should assume that all other cash flows occur at the end of the year to which they relate.

● The development costs of £90,000 have already been spent.

● Overheads have been costed at 50 per cent of direct labour, which is the business's normal practice. An independent assessment has suggested that incremental overheads are likely to amount to £30,000 a year.

● The business's cost of capital is 12 per cent.

Required:

(a) Prepare a corrected statement of the incremental cash flows arising from the project. Where you have altered the assistant's figures you should attach a brief note explaining your alterations.

(b) Calculate:

(1) The project's payback period.

(2) The project's net present value as at 31 December Year 0.

(c) Write a memo to the board advising on the acceptance or rejection of the project.

Ignore taxation in your answer.

4 Arkwright Mills plc is considering expanding its production of a new yarn, code name X15. The plant is expected to cost £1 million and have a life of five years and a nil residual value. It will be bought, paid for and ready for operation on 31 December Year 0. £500,000 has already been spent on development costs of the product, and this has been charged in the income statement in the year it was incurred.

The following results are projected for the new yarn:

	Year 1 £m	Year 2 £m	Year 3 £m	Year 4 £m	Year 5 £m
Sales revenue	1.2	1.4	1.4	1.4	1.4
Costs, including depreciation	1.0	1.1	1.1	1.1	1.1
Profit before tax	0.2	0.3	0.3	0.3	0.3

Tax is charged at 50 per cent on annual profits (before tax and after depreciation) and paid one year in arrears. Depreciation of the plant has been calculated on a straight-line basis. Additional working capital of £0.6m will be required at the beginning of the project and released at the end of Year 5. You should assume that all cash flows occur at the end of the year in which they arise.

Required:
(a) Prepare a statement showing the incremental cash flows of the project relevant to a decision concerning whether or not to proceed with the construction of the new plant.
(b) Compute the net present value of the project using a 10 per cent discount rate.
(c) Compute the payback period to the nearest year. Explain the meaning of this term.

5 Newton Electronics Ltd has incurred expenditure of £5 million over the past three years researching and developing a miniature hearing aid. The hearing aid is now fully developed, and the directors are considering which of three mutually exclusive options should be taken to exploit the potential of the new product. The options are as follows:

1 The business could manufacture the hearing aid itself. This would be a new departure, since the business has so far concentrated on research and development projects. However, the business has manufacturing space available that it currently rents to another business for £100,000 a year. The business would have to purchase plant and equipment costing £9 million and invest £3 million in working capital immediately for production to begin.

A market research report, for which the business paid £50,000, indicates that the new product has an expected life of five years. Sales of the product during this period are predicted as follows:

	Predicted sales for the year ended 30 November				
	Year 1	Year 2	Year 3	Year 4	Year 5
Number of units (000s)	800	1,400	1,800	1,200	500

The selling price per unit will be £30 in the first year but will fall to £22 in the following three years. In the final year of the product's life, the selling price will fall to £20. Variable production costs are predicted to be £14 a unit, and fixed production costs (including depreciation) will be £2.4 million a year. Marketing costs will be £2 million a year.

The business intends to depreciate the plant and equipment using the straight-line method and based on an estimated residual value at the end of the five years of £1 million. The business has a cost of capital of 10 per cent a year.

2   Newton Electronics Ltd could agree to another business manufacturing and marketing the product under licence. A multinational business, Faraday Electricals plc, has offered to undertake the manufacture and marketing of the product, and in return will make a royalty payment to Newton Electronics Ltd of £5 per unit. It has been estimated that the annual number of sales of the hearing aid will be 10 per cent higher if the multinational business, rather than Newton Electronics Ltd, manufactures and markets the product.

3   Newton Electronics Ltd could sell the patent rights to Faraday Electricals plc for £24 million, payable in two equal instalments. The first instalment would be payable immediately and the second at the end of two years. This option would give Faraday Electricals the exclusive right to manufacture and market the new product.

Required:
(a) Calculate the net present value (as at 1 January Year 1) of each of the options available to Newton Electronics Ltd.
(b) Identify and discuss any other factors that Newton Electronics Ltd should consider before arriving at a decision.
(c) State what you consider to be the most suitable option, and why.

Ignore taxation.

6   Chesterfield Wanderers is a professional football club that has enjoyed considerable success in both national and European competitions in recent years. As a result, the club has accumulated £10 million to spend on its further development. The board of directors is currently considering two mutually exclusive options for spending the funds available.

The first option is to acquire another player. The team manager has expressed a keen interest in acquiring Basil ('Bazza') Ramsey, a central defender, who currently plays for a rival club. The rival club has agreed to release the player immediately for £10 million if required. A decision to acquire 'Bazza' Ramsey would mean that the existing central defender, Vinnie Smith, could be sold to another club. Chesterfield Wanderers has recently received an offer of £2.2 million for this player. This offer is still open but will only be accepted if 'Bazza' Ramsey joins Chesterfield Wanderers. If this does not happen, Vinnie Smith will be expected to stay on with the club until the end of his playing career in five years' time. During this period, Vinnie will receive an annual salary of £400,000 and a loyalty bonus of £200,000 at the end of his five-year period with the club.

Assuming 'Bazza' Ramsey is acquired, the team manager estimates that gate receipts will increase by £2.5 million in the first year and £1.3 million in each of the four following years. There will also be an increase in advertising and sponsorship revenues of £1.2 million for each of the next five years if the player is acquired. At the end of five years, the player can be sold to a club in a lower division and Chesterfield Wanderers will expect to receive £1 million as a transfer fee. During his period at the club, 'Bazza' will receive an annual salary of £800,000 and a loyalty bonus of £400,000 after five years.

The second option is for the club to improve its ground facilities. The west stand could be extended and executive boxes could be built for businesses wishing to offer corporate hospitality to clients. These improvements would also cost £10 million and would take one year to complete. During this period, the west stand would be closed, resulting in a reduction of gate receipts of £1.8 million. However, gate receipts for each of the following four years would be £4.4 million higher than current receipts. In five years' time, the club has plans to sell the existing grounds and to move to a new stadium nearby. Improving the ground facilities is not expected to affect the ground's value when it comes to be sold. Payment for the improvements will be made when the work has been completed at the end of the first year. Whichever option is chosen, the board of directors has decided to take on additional ground staff. The additional wages bill is expected to be £350,000 a year over the next five years.

The club has a cost of capital of 10 per cent. Ignore taxation.

Required:
(a) Calculate the incremental cash flows arising from each of the options available to the club.
(b) Calculate the net present value of each of the options.
(c) On the basis of the calculations made in (b) above, which of the two options would you choose and why?
(d) Discuss the validity of using the net present value method in making investment decisions for a professional football club.

7 Simtex Ltd has invested £120,000 to date in developing a new type of shaving foam. The shaving foam is now ready for production and it has been estimated that the new product will sell 160,000 cans a year over the next four years. At the end of four years, the product will be discontinued and replaced by a new product.

The shaving foam is expected to sell at £6 a can and the variable cost is estimated at £4 per can. Fixed cost (excluding depreciation) is expected to be £300,000 a year. (This figure includes £130,000 in fixed cost incurred by the existing business that will be apportioned to this new product.)

To manufacture and package the new product, equipment costing £480,000 must be acquired immediately. The estimated value of this equipment in four years' time is £100,000. The business calculates depreciation using the straight-line method, and has an estimated cost of capital of 12 per cent.

Required:
(a) Deduce the net present value of the new product.
(b) Calculate by how much each of the following must change before the new product is no longer profitable:
    (i)   the discount rate;
    (ii) the initial outlay on new equipment;
    (iii) the net operating cash flows;
    (iv) the residual value of the equipment.
(c) Should the business produce the new product?

8 Kernow Cleaning Services Ltd provides street-cleaning services for local councils in the far south west of England. The work is currently labour-intensive and few machines are used. However, the business has recently been considering the purchase of a fleet of street-cleaning vehicles at a total cost of £540,000. The vehicles have a life of four years and are likely to result in a considerable saving of labour costs. Estimates of the likely labour savings and their probability of occurrence are set out below.

	Estimated savings £	Probability of occurrence
Year 1	80,000	0.3
	160,000	0.5
	200,000	0.2
Year 2	140,000	0.4
	220,000	0.4
	250,000	0.2
Year 3	140,000	0.4
	200,000	0.3
	230,000	0.3
Year 4	100,000	0.3
	170,000	0.6
	200,000	0.1

Estimates for each year are independent of other years. The business has a cost of capital of 10 per cent.

Required:

(a) Calculate the expected net present value (ENPV) of the street-cleaning machines.

(b) Calculate the net present value (NPV) of the worst possible outcome and the probability of its occurrence.

Solution to self-assessment question

1 Beacon Chemicals plc

(a) Relevant cash flows are as follows:

	Year 0 £000	Year 1 £000	Year 2 £000	Year 3 £000	Year 4 £000	Year 5 £000
Sales revenue		80	120	144	100	64
Loss of contribution		(15)	(15)	(15)	(15)	(15)
Variable costs		(40)	(50)	(48)	(30)	(32)
Fixed costs (Note 1)		(8)	(8)	(8)	(8)	(8)
Operating cash flows		17	47	73	47	9
Working capital	(30)					30
Capital cost	(100)					
Net relevant cash flows	(130)	17	47	73	47	39

Notes:

1. Only the fixed costs that are incremental to the project (only existing because of the project) are relevant. Depreciation is irrelevant because it is not a cash flow.

2. The research and development cost is irrelevant since it has been spent irrespective of the decision on X14 production.

(b)

	Year 0 £000	Year 1 £000	Year 2 £000	Year 3 £000
Cumulative cash flows	(130)	(113)	(66)	7

Thus the equipment will have repaid the initial investment by the end of the third year of operations, that is, the payback period is three years.

(c)

	Year 0 £000	Year 1 £000	Year 2 £000	Year 3 £000	Year 4 £000	Year 5 £000
Discount factor	1.00	0.926	0.857	0.794	0.735	0.681
Present value	(130)	15.74	40.28	57.96	34.55	26.56
Net present value	45.09	(That is, the sum of the present values for years 0 to 5.)				

Solutions to review questions

1 NPV is usually considered the best method of assessing investment opportunities because it takes account of:

- *The timing of the cash flows.* By *discounting* the various cash flows associated with each project according to when it is expected to arise, it recognises the fact that cash flows do not all occur simultaneously. Associated with this is the fact that, by discounting using the opportunity cost of finance (that is, the return which the next best alternative opportunity would generate), it is possible to identify the net benefit after financing costs have been met (as the NPV).
- *The whole of the relevant cash flows.* NPV includes all of the relevant cash flows irrespective of when they are expected to occur. It treats them differently according to their date of occurrence, but they are all taken account of in the NPV and they all have, or can have, an influence on the decision.
- *The objectives of the business.* NPV is the only method of appraisal where the output of the analysis has a direct bearing on the wealth of the business. (Positive NPVs enhance wealth; negative ones reduce it). Since most private sector businesses seek to increase their value and wealth, NPV clearly is the best approach to use, at least out of the methods we have considered so far.

NPV provides clear decision rules concerning acceptance/rejection of projects and the ranking of projects. It is fairly simple to use, particularly with the availability of modern computer software that takes away the need for routine calculations to be done manually.

2 The payback method, in its original form, does not take account of the time value of money. However, it would be possible to modify the payback method to accommodate this requirement. Cash flows arising from a project could be discounted, using the cost of finance as the appropriate discount rate, in the same way as with the NPV and IRR methods. The discounted payback approach is used by some businesses and represents an improvement on the original approach described in the chapter. However, it still retains the other flaws of the original payback approach that were discussed: for example, it ignores relevant data after the payback period. Thus, even in its modified form, the PP method cannot be regarded as superior to NPV.

3 The IRR method does appear to be preferred to the NPV method among many
practising managers. The main reasons for this seem to be as follows:
  ● A preference for a percentage return ratio rather than an absolute figure as a
    means of expressing the outcome of a project. This preference for a ratio may
    reflect the fact that other financial goals of the business are often set in terms
    of ratios (for example, return on capital employed).
  ● A preference for ranking projects in terms of their percentage return. Managers
    feel it is easier to rank projects on the basis of percentage returns (though NPV
    outcomes should be just as easy for them). We saw in the chapter that the IRR
    method could provide misleading advice on the ranking of projects, and the
    NPV method was preferable for this purpose.

4 Cash flows are preferred to profit flows because cash is the ultimate measure of
economic wealth. Cash is used to acquire resources and for distribution to shareholders. When cash is invested in an investment project an opportunity cost is
incurred, as the cash cannot be used in other investment projects. Similarly,
when positive cash flows are generated by the project it can be used to reinvest
in other investment projects.

Profit, on the other hand, is relevant to reporting the productive effort for a
period. This measure of effort may have only a tenuous relationship to cash
flows for a period. The conventions of accounting may lead to the recognition of
gains and losses in one period and the relevant cash inflows and outflows occurring in another period.

Solutions to selected exercises

1 Mylo Ltd

(a) The annual depreciation of the two projects is:

$$\text{Project 1: } \frac{(£100,000 - £7,000)}{3} = £31,000$$

$$\text{Project 2: } \frac{(£60,000 - £6,000)}{3} = £18,000$$

Project 1

(1)

	Year 0 £000	Year 1 £000	Year 2 £000	Year 3 £000
Operating profit/(loss)		29	(1)	2
Depreciation		31	31	31
Capital cost	(100)			
Residual value				7
Net cash flows	(100)	60	30	40
10% discount factor	1.000	0.909	0.826	0.751
Present value	(100.00)	54.54	24.78	30.04
Net present value	9.36			

(2) Clearly the IRR lies above 10%; try 15%:

15% discount factor	1.000	0.870	0.756	0.658
Present value	(100.00)	52.20	22.68	26.32
Net present value	1.20			

Thus the IRR lies a little above 15%, perhaps around 16%.

(3) To find the payback period, the cumulative cash flows are calculated:

Cumulative cash flows	(100)	(40)	(10)	30

Thus the payback will occur after 3 years if we assume year-end cash flows.

Project 2

(1)

	Year 0 £000	Year 1 £000	Year 2 £000	Year 3 £000
Operating profit/(loss)		18	(2)	4
Depreciation		18	18	18
Capital cost	(60)			
Residual value		—	—	6
Net cash flows	(60)	36	16	28
10% discount factor	1.000	0.909	0.826	0.751
Present value	(60.00)	32.72	13.22	21.03
Net present value	6.97			

(2) Clearly the IRR lies above 10%; try 15%:

15% discount factor	1.000	0.870	0.756	0.658
Present value	(60.00)	31.32	12.10	18.42
Net present value	1.84			

Thus the IRR lies a little above 15%; perhaps around 17%.

(3) The cumulative cash flows are:

Cumulative cash flows	(60)	(24)	(8)	20

Thus the payback will occur after 3 years (assuming year-end cash flows).

(b) Presuming that Mylo Ltd is pursuing a wealth-enhancement objective, Project 1 is preferable since it has the higher NPV. The difference between the two NPVs is not significant, however.

5 Newton Electronics Ltd

(a)

Option 1

	Year 0 £m	Year 1 £m	Year 2 £m	Year 3 £m	Year 4 £m	Year 5 £m
Plant and equipment	(9.0)					
Sales revenue		24.0	30.8	39.6	26.4	10.0
Variable costs		(11.2)	(19.6)	(25.2)	(16.8)	(7.0)
Fixed costs (ex. dep'n)		(0.8)	(0.8)	(0.8)	(0.8)	(0.8)
Working capital	(3.0)					3.0
Marketing costs		(2.0)	(2.0)	(2.0)	(2.0)	(2.0)
Opportunity costs		(0.1)	(0.1)	(0.1)	(0.1)	(0.1)
	(12.0)	9.9	8.3	11.5	6.7	4.1
Discount factor 10%	1.000	0.909	0.826	0.751	0.683	0.621
Present value	(12.0)	9.0	6.9	8.6	4.6	2.5
NPV	19.6					

Option 2

	Year 0 £m	Year 1 £m	Year 2 £m	Year 3 £m	Year 4 £m	Year 5 £m
Royalties	–	4.4	7.7	9.9	6.6	2.8
Discount factor 10%	1.000	0.909	0.826	0.751	0.683	0.621
Present value	–	4.0	6.4	7.4	4.5	1.7
NPV	24.0					

Option 3

	Year 0	Year 2
Instalments	12.0	12.0
Discount factor 10%	1.000	0.826
Present value	12.0	9.9
NPV	21.9	

(b) Before making a final decision, the board should consider the following factors:

  (1) The long-term competitiveness of the business may be affected by the sale of the patents.

  (2) At present, the business is not involved in manufacturing and marketing products. Would a change in direction be desirable?

  (3) The business will probably have to buy in the skills necessary to produce the product itself. This will involve costs, and problems could arise. Has this been taken into account?

  (4) How accurate are the forecasts made and how valid are the assumptions on which they are based?

(c) Option 2 has the highest NPV and is therefore the most attractive to share-holders. However, the accuracy of the forecasts should be checked before a final decision is made.

6 Chesterfield Wanderers

(a) and (b)

Player option

	Year 0 £000	Year 1 £000	Year 2 £000	Year 3 £000	Year 4 £000	Year 5 £000
Sale of player	2,200					1,000
Purchase of Bazza	(10,000)					
Sponsorship, and so on		1,200	1,200	1,200	1,200	1,200
Gate receipts		2,500	1,300	1,300	1,300	1,300
Salaries paid		(800)	(800)	(800)	(800)	(1,200)
Salaries saved		400	400	400	400	600
	(7,800)	3,300	2,100	2,100	2,100	2,900
Discount factor 10%	1.000	0.909	0.826	0.751	0.683	0.621
Present values	(7,800)	3,000	1,735	1,577	1,434	1,801
NPV	1,747					

Ground improvement option

	Year 1 £000	Year 2 £000	Year 3 £000	Year 4 £000	Year 5 £000
Ground improvements	(10,000)				
Increased gate receipts	(1,800)	4,400	4,400	4,400	4,400
	(11,800)	4,400	4,400	4,400	4,400
Discount factor 10%	0.909	0.826	0.751	0.683	0.621
Present values	(10,726)	3,634	3,304	3,005	2,732
NPV	1,949				

(c) The ground improvement option provides the higher NPV and is therefore the preferable option, based on the objective of shareholder wealth maximisation.

(d) A professional football club may not wish to pursue an objective of shareholder wealth enhancement. It may prefer to invest in quality players in an attempt to enjoy future sporting success. If this is the case, the NPV approach will be less appropriate because the club is not pursuing a strict wealth-related objective.

7 Simtex Ltd

(a) Net operating cash flows each year will be:

	£000	£000
Sales revenue (160 × £6)		960
Less		
Variable costs (160 × £4)	640	
Relevant fixed costs	170	810
		150

The estimated NPV of the new product can then be calculated:

	£000
Annual cash flows (150 × 3.038*)	456
Residual value of equipment (100 × 0.636)	64
	520
Less Initial outlay	480
Net present value	40

* This is the sum of the 12 per cent discount factors over four years. Where the cash flows are constant, it is a quicker procedure than working out the present value of cash flows for each year and then adding them together.

(b) (i) Assume the discount rate is 18%. The net present value of the project would be:

	£000
Annual cash flows (150 × 2.690)	404
Residual value of equipment (100 × 0.516)	52
	456
Less Initial outlay	480
NPV	(24)

Thus an increase of 6%, from 12% to 18%, in the discount rate causes a fall from +40 to −24 in the NPV, a fall of 64 or 10.67 (that is, 64/6) for each 1% rise in the discount rate. So a zero NPV will occur with a discount rate approximately equal to 12 + (40/11.67) = 15.4%. (This is, of course, the IRR.)

This higher discount rate represents an increase of about 28% on the existing cost of capital figure.

(ii) The initial outlay on equipment is already expressed in present-value terms and so, to make the project no longer viable, the outlay will have to increase by an amount equal to the NPV of the project (that is, £40,000) – an increase of 8.3% on the stated initial outlay.

(iii) The change necessary in the annual net cash flows to make the project no longer profitable can be calculated as follows:

Let Y = change in the annual operating cash flows. Then

$$(Y \times \text{cumulative discount rates for a four-year period}) - NPV = 0$$

This can be rearranged as

$$Y \times \text{cumulative discount factors for a four-year period} = NPV$$
$$Y \times 3.038 = £40,000$$
$$Y = £40,000/3.038$$
$$Y = \underline{£13,167}$$

In percentage terms, this is a decrease of 8.8% on the estimated cash flows.

(iv) The change in the residual value required to make the new product no longer profitable can be calculated as follows:

Let V = change in the residual value:

$$(V \times \text{discount factor at end of four years}) - NPV \text{ of product} = 0$$

This can be rearranged as follows:

$$V \times \text{discount factor at end of four years} = NPV \text{ of product}$$
$$V \times 0.636 = £40,000$$
$$V = £40,000/0.636$$
$$V = \underline{£62,893}$$

This is a decrease of 63.9% in the residual value of the equipment.

(c) The NPV of the product is positive and so it will increase shareholder wealth. Thus, it should be produced. The sensitivity analysis suggests that the initial outlay and the annual cash flows are the most sensitive variables for managers to consider.

8 Kernow Cleaning Services Ltd

(a) The first step is to calculate the expected annual cash flows:

Year 1	£
£80,000 × 0.3	24,000
£160,000 × 0.5	80,000
£200,000 × 0.2	40,000
	144,000

Year 2	£
£140,000 × 0.4	56,000
£220,000 × 0.4	88,000
£250,000 × 0.2	50,000
	194,000

Year 3	£
£140,000 × 0.4	56,000
£200,000 × 0.3	60,000
£230,000 × 0.3	69,000
	185,000

Year 4	£
£100,000 × 0.3	30,000
£170,000 × 0.6	102,000
£200,000 × 0.1	20,000
	152,000

The expected net present value (ENPV) can now be calculated as follows:

Period	Expected cash flow £	Discount rate 10%	Expected PV £
0	(540,000)	1.000	(540,000)
1	144,000	0.909	130,896
2	194,000	0.826	160,244
3	185,000	0.751	138,935
4	152,000	0.683	103,816
ENPV			(6,109)

(b) The worst possible outcome can be calculated by taking the lowest values of savings each year, as follows:

Period	Cash flow £	Discount rate 10%	PV £
0	(540,000)	1.000	(540,000)
1	80,000	0.909	72,720
2	140,000	0.826	115,640
3	140,000	0.751	105,140
4	100,000	0.683	68,300
NPV			(178,200)

The probability of occurrence can be obtained by multiplying together the probability of *each* of the worst outcomes above, that is $0.3 \times 0.4 \times 0.4 \times 0.3 = 0.014$.

Thus, the probability of occurrence is 1.4%, which is very low.

Accounting rules and regulations

A principled approach

FSA should avoid 'lengthy rule book' says ICAEW

Paul Grant

The Financial Services Authority needs to avoid drawing up a 'lengthy rule book' in response to the financial crisis and instead adopt a principles-based approach in its reform of banking regulation.

In its submitted response to the Turner Review, the ICAEW said the City regulator should instead address operational fallings as well as weaknesses in system design and regulatory policy. It should also strive to avoid losing the positive aspects of the work it had previously undertaken from the pressure to change.

'The arguments that the FSA should move towards a more principles-based approach remain valid not least in that such an approach deals better with changing financial markets than a lengthy rule book,' said PwC partner and chair of the ICAEW Financial Service Faculty's Risk and Regulation Committee, John Tattersall.

Iain Coke, head of Financial Services Faculty, added: 'Communication, cooperation and coordination between the tripartite authorities can, and should, be improved. It is vital, however the system is structured, that it is made to work effectively at both policy and operational levels. Part of the solution here is for there to be closer dialogue between the FSA and the audit profession on systematic risks.'

Accountancy Age, 17 June 2009.

Source: Reproduced with permission from Incisive Media Ltd.

Questions relating to this news story can be found on page 281

Introduction

In this section we outline the conventional accounting rules that are commonly adopted in practice and the legislation that governs accounting. We then examine the role of the UK's Accounting Standards Board along with the International Accounting Standards Board in the preparation of financial statements. The section closes with a review of the attempts made to develop a framework of accounting based on generally accepted principles.

Why this section is important

This chapter is important for non-accountants for the following reasons.

1 It underpins almost the entire contents of this book. So if you are to understand what accountants do and why they do it, you must be familiar with the rules and regulations that they adopt.

2 You need to have some familiarity with the legal requirements governing accounting in the UK.

3 Similarly it is necessary to have some knowledge of the quasi-legal role that the Accounting Standards Board and the International Accounting Standards Board play in UK financial reporting.

4 You must have a grasp of the attempts made to base accounting practice on generally accepted accounting principles (GAAP).

The need for rules

Most games have an agreed set of rules. Rules define the game and they provide a structure that every player is expected to follow. If you are a footballer, for example, you are expected to follow the rules that apply to football. Without them football (as we know it) would just become a totally uncoordinated and chaotic kick-about.

Unlike football or any other game, no one actually sat down and devised a set of accounting rules. What happened was that over a long period of time entities (mainly sole traders) gradually adopted similar procedures for recording their transactions and assessing how the business had performed at a regular and fixed interval. In other words, such procedures eventually became generally accepted and they became the rules that virtually everyone adopted. The development of accounting rules over the centuries to where we are today is shown in Figure 2.16.

There was nothing indisputable about such rules, of course, in the sense that if you drop an apple it falls to the ground. The accounting rules that evolved were man-made and you could argue against them. You were also free to choose whether to adopt them or follow your own rules. If you did, of course, you might cause a great deal of confusion (just as you would in football if you adopted your own rules) but that would be up to you.

Many accountants these days do not like to describe conventional accounting procedures as 'rules' because that gives the impression that they are prescriptive. So you will come across a bewildering number of different terms such as assumptions, axioms, concepts, objectives, policies, postulates, principles and procedures. It is quite easy to have an argument about each of these descriptions. For example, if you are told that 'this procedure is a *principle* of accounting' it sounds as though there is a moral code underpinning how that procedure should be dealt with, like being told that 'murder is wrong' and 'hanging is the answer'. Whereas in accounting all we are really saying is that 'this is the way that we usually do it', i.e. it is a convention.

We do not believe that it is necessary to get bogged down in such arguments so, in this book, for convenience and to avoid repetition we will generally refer to conventional accounting practices as 'accounting rules'. But why do we need some rules? Surely there is nothing more to accounting than the equivalent of adding 2 and 2 together and making sure that the answer is 4? Well, not quite.

In order to explain why, we need to re-examine what we mean by 'accounting'. Consider the following definition:

Accounting is a service provided for those who need information about an entity's financial performance, its assets and it liabilities.

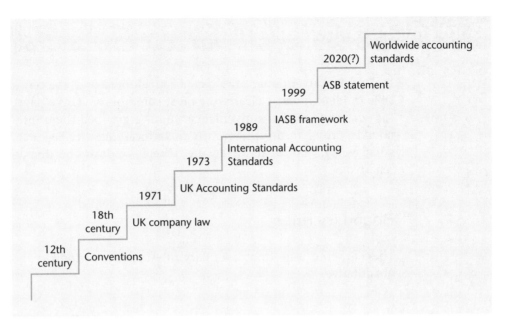

Figure 2.16 **The development of accounting rules**

Now even with perhaps such a broad definition it is possible to spot fairly quickly some of the difficulties involved in carrying out that brief. Some of the questions we might ask are as follows.

1 Why is the type of information? Qualitative, quantitative or both?
2 Who wants it? Owners? Workers? Customers? Are their wants the same?
3 What is meant by an entity? Where do you draw the line?
4 How do you report the information that you are going to provide? On the basis of numbers, e.g. six cows and a hundred sheep? Or do you use a common measure such as translating everything into monetary values?
5 Do you report on a regular basis? And over what period? Every week or every five years?

It is in response to such questions that over the centuries common procedures have evolved. Unfortunately, they are no longer necessarily suitable for a fast-moving highly technological age. The questions may remain the same but we need to come up with different answers. The search is on.

However, before we set off on that journey we need to review the answers that used to be acceptable. We do so in the next section.

Activity 2.21

Consult the most comprehensive dictionary you can find in your college/university library. Write down the meaning of the following words. They may have several meanings so extract the one that relates more to fact or truth.

(1) assumptions; (2) axioms; (3) concepts; (4) conventions; (5) postulates; (6) principles; and (7) procedures.

Consider carefully the definitions that you have extracted. Do they all have a similar meaning?

Conventional accounting rules

Dozens of conventional rules have been adopted over the centuries but it is possible to identify fairly clearly the most common ones. We have selected fourteen for our purposes. For convenience we have grouped them into three categories: boundary rules, measurement rules and ethical rules (see Figure 2.17). We start with what we call 'boundary' rules, i.e. where we draw the line at what should be reported.

Boundary rules

There are four important boundary rules: entity, periodicity, going concern and quantitative.

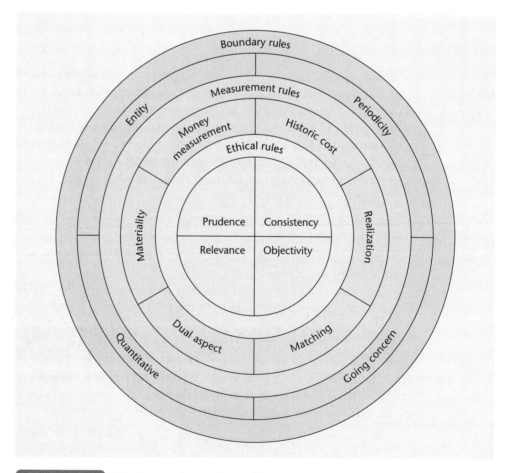

Figure 2.17   The basic accounting rules

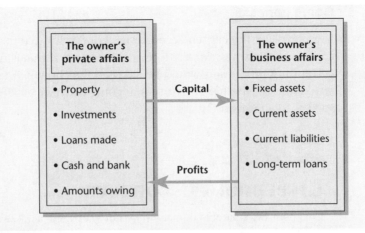

Figure 2.18   The entity rule: separation of business and private affairs

Entity

It is customary to keep strictly separate the affairs of a business from the private affairs of its owners. In practice, it is not always easy to distinguish precisely between what is 'business' and what is 'private', especially in the cases of sole trader and partnership entities. The close interrelationship between what are effectively two separate entities is shown in Figure 2.18.

Periodicity

The main accounting period is usually considered to be twelve months. This is an arbitrary period of time especially in the case of entities that have an unlimited life. In the western agrarian world it does reflect the four seasons of the year although this is now of little relevance to manufacturing and service entities. Indeed, in the fashion industry, for example, a much shorter accounting period might by more appropriate since fashions and tastes change quite quickly. A year is, however, a practical period of time because most people can relate to what happened last year, whereas it is much more difficult over (say) a five-year period.

Activity 2.22

List three advantages and disadvantages of preparing financial accounts only once a year.

Advantages	Disadvantages
1	1
2	2
3	3

Going concern

Irrespective of the chosen accounting period it is usual to assume that an entity will continue in business for the foreseeable future. If this is not the case then different accounting procedures would be adopted. But how is it possible to determine with any certainty whether an entity is a 'going concern' especially when business is bad such as in a recession?

News clip

Liverpool FC concern

Liverpool FC's parent company may not be able to continue trading as a going concern. KPMG auditors warned that it needs to refinance its £350m debt. The parent company, Kop Football Holding, suffered a £42.6m loss last year with interest payments accounting for £36.5m of that loss. The Club itself had a turnover of £159.1m and a net profit of £10.2m.

Source: Adapted from www.accountancyage.com, 5 June 2009.

Quantitative

Accounting information is usually restricted to that which can be easily quantified. Value considerations, such as how long the business has been in existence or the length of service of the staff are usually ignored. And yet surely these factors are worth something to a long-established entity compared with a newly created business?

Measurement rules

Measurement rules determine how data should be recorded. There are six important ones. They are: money measurement, historic cost, realization, matching, dual aspect and materiality. First, the money measurement rule.

Money measurement

Such information that can be easily quantified is given a monetary value. But the value of money changes over a period of time. During inflationary periods its value goes down, i.e. the same quantity of money buys fewer goods and services than the year before. Deflationary periods can also occur but they are quite rare and they are usually quite short. In inflationary and deflationary circumstances it is misleading to compare one year's results with that of another without allowing for the effect of the value of money either going up or going down.

Historic cost

Assets (such as cars) and liabilities (such as amounts owed to a creditor) are usually valued at their historic cost, i.e. at the price paid for them when they were originally purchased or sold. However, apart from the impact of inflation or deflation, assets and liabilities may change their value owing to such factors as wear and tear and obsolescence.

Realization

When goods are sold or purchased or sold on credit terms it is customary practice to treat them as being exchanged at the point when the legal title to the goods is transferred, i.e. when they are realized. In modern manufacturing and trading conditions that point is not necessarily obvious and it remains a major issue that the accountancy profession is still trying to sort out.

Activity 2.23

A contracting company divides each of its sales into five stages: (1) on order; (2) on despatch; (3) on installation; (4) on commissioning; and (5) on completion of a 12-month warranty period.

Assume that an order for Contract A for £100,000 was signed on 1 January 2011. The contract is expected to be completed on 31 December 2013 and the warranty period will end on 31 December 2014. In which year would you consider that the £100,000 has been 'realized'?

Matching

The matching rule is illustrated in Figure 2.19.

This rule is closely related to the realization rule. Accounts are not usually prepared on the basis of cash received and cash paid during (say) a 12-month period because there is often a delay between the receipt and the payment of cash depending

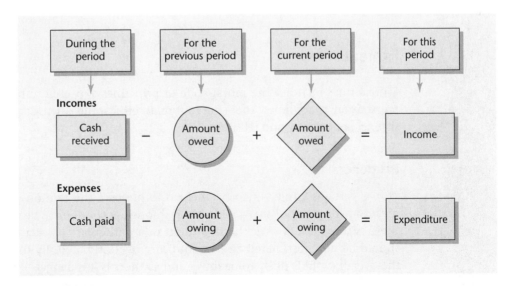

Figure 2.19   The matching rule

on the credit period given. This means that a comparison based on cash received/ cash paid may be misleading when one year is compared with another. When preparing the accounts at the end of a year, therefore, it is necessary to allow for what was *owed to* the entity and *owing* by it at both the beginning and the end of the year, i.e. opening and closing debtors and creditors. This procedure often involves making an estimate of the amounts due to be received and sometimes the amounts due to be paid. Any estimate, of course, can be wrong because it is likely that some debts will not be settled. If this proves to be the case then the accounts for that year will be incorrect.

Dual aspect

Any transaction involves someone giving something and someone else receiving it. So the basic rule is: *record **every** transaction twice* even if it is an internal transaction. As a result a recording system known as *double-entry book-keeping* evolved. This system has many practical advantages and most entities (apart from perhaps very small ones) now adopt it.

Materiality

The adoption of many of the conventional accounting procedures can result in a tremendous amount of work, e.g. in estimating the amount of bad debts. However, if the eventual results of that extra work are likely to be immaterial or insignificant, i.e. they do not have any meaningful effect on the overall results, then there does not appear to be much point in sticking strictly to the 'rules'. It would not be customary, for example, to estimate the value of small amounts of stationery at the year end and include them in 'stocks' or 'inventories'. But what does 'small' mean in this context? Stationery worth £200 may be material to a one-woman business but mean nothing to a multinational company. So materiality is a matter of context; it requires judgement and different people will come to a difference conclusion.

Ethical rules

Ethical rules relate to the moral code or principles expected to be adopted in the preparation of accounts. There are four main ethical rules. They are: prudence, consistency, objectivity and relevance.

Prudence

This is perhaps a rule which has helped to preserve the cautious, careful and pernickety perception of the typical old-fashioned accountant. The rule states that if there is some doubt over the treatment of a particular transaction, then income should be underestimated and expenditure overestimated. By following this rule the overall profit is likely to be lower and so there is less danger of it being paid out to the owners and hence not being recoverable.

Consistency

The same accounting policies and rules should be followed in successive accounting periods unless there is a fundamental change in circumstances that makes such a change justifiable. It is not usually acceptable, for example, to adopt a different accounting method simply because the profit for a particular accounting period is low.

Objectivity

This rule requires you to avoid personal bias and prejudice when selecting and applying the accounting rules. This is not always easy, of course, but an important part of your college or university education is to train you to argue both sides of a case irrespective of just how you feel. This training helps you to deal with problems objectively without letting your own personal feelings overwhelm a particular decision.

Relevance

Financial statements should not include matters that prevent users from gaining what they need to know. The overall picture may be obscured if too much information or too much detail is given. So, in short, the information provided must be *relevant*. In the jargon of the accountancy profession this means that financial statements should give a true and fair view of the financial affairs of the entity.

You are going to come across all the rules that we have discussed in this section in one form or another throughout the rest of the book but we now need to examine which professional and statutory requirements cover accounting. We turn to this topic in the next section.

Activity 2.24

Review the 14 conventional rules we have outlined in this section. Then on the table below score each one according to whether you think that in practice it is easy to apply. Use the following scale: (1) very easy; (2) easy; (3) neither easy nor difficult; (4) difficult; and (5) very difficult.

Boundary rules	Score	Measurement rules	Score	Ethical rules
Entity		Money measurement		Prudence
Periodicity		Historic cost		Consistency
Going concern		Realization		Objectivity
Quantitative		Matching		Relevance
		Dual aspect		
		Materiality		

Sources of authority

The application of the rules summarized in the previous section in an increasingly sophisticated banking, commercial, industrial, political, technological and social society began to cause problems for accountants and the users of financial statements as the twentieth century progressed. A number of fire-fighting solutions were then put forward in all attempt to deal with the numerous problems that began to erupt. During the 1960s it became obvious that the system had begun to break down and that something needed to be done.

What did happen was that the UK accountancy profession began to develop what are called *accounting standards*. It was not long before *international accounting standards* also began to be developed. Such standards now play a very important part in the UK regulatory framework. We shall be examining them in detail later in this section.

Parliament also played its part in an attempt to come up with some solutions to the financial reporting problem. It takes time to get legislation through Parliament but even so it managed to pass seven Companies Acts in 22 years (between 1967 and 1989). It then took another 17 years before another Companies Act was passed in 2006 (a massive one as it turned out). We will have a look at it a little later in the section.

There is also another source of authority: the London Stock Exchange (LSE). The LSE is regulated by the Financial Services Agency (FSA). The FSA is an independent non-governmental body set up by the Financial Service and Market Act 2000. It is responsible for the UK financial services industry and its powers are wide-ranging. They include rule-making, investigatory powers and enforcement powers.

The LSE plays a very important part in financial reporting but much of it is irrelevant for our purposes. This means that there are three main sources of authority governing accounting regulation in the UK that we need to examine: (1) the Companies Act 2006; (2) UK Accounting Standards; and (3) International Accounting Standards (IASs). These three sources are examined in some detail in the following sections. The relationship between these sources is shown in Figure 2.20.

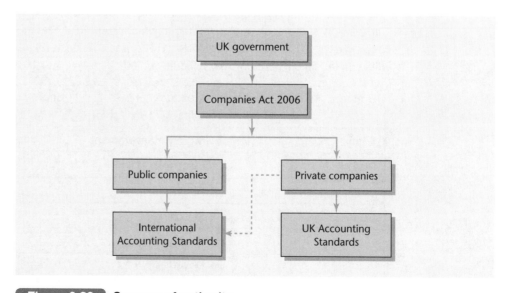

Figure 2.20   Sources of authority

Activity 2.25

Do you think that by law shareholders should have complete freedom of information, i.e. the right to be given all the information that they want about a company in which they hold shares? What practical problems might arise if this were the case?

Companies Act 2006

There are no specific legal or statutory requirements dealing with sole trader and partnership accounts in the Companies Act or elsewhere. This means that the owners and managers of such entities may keep what accounting records that suit them (if any) and prepare periodic accounts when and in what form they wish. However, if they are registered for Value Added Tax they will need to keep adequate records that satisfy the somewhat severe requirements of Her Majesty's Revenue and Customs. Similarly, as the owners of a business they will need to include any profit due to them on their own personal income tax return. As a result of such considerations most entities have to keep some basic accounting records and to compile a rudimentary profit and loss account once a year. The precise form and content of such records and accounts is up to them.

A new form of partnership, limited liability partnerships, was introduced in 2001. The 2006 Companies Act also covers some aspects of this type of entity but as we are not covering LLPs in this section we do not need to go into the details.

In this section we are mainly concerned with the limited liability company type of entity. The legislation dealing with the formation, management, operation (including the accounting requirements) and reporting of such entities is now contained in the new Act of 2006 although it only became fully operable in October 2009. The Act is extremely detailed and complex. It is the largest Act ever passed by Parliament. No doubt you will be relieved to know that for your purposes (at least at this stage of your career) most of it is way beyond this book. And that includes the accounting bits!

Right, so what *do* you need to know for now? We will try to give you the answer to this question as plainly and as simply as we can. The following is an extremely brief summary of what you need to know.

1 The Act deals with the entire operation and management of companies so it encompasses much more than simply 'the accounts'. The 'Accounts and Records' are covered in Part 15. This part forms a relatively small section of the entire Act and much of it is based on earlier legislation.

2 It classifies companies into 'small', 'medium' and 'large. This classification is based on a requirement to satisfy two out of three criteria: turnover, balance sheet totals and number of employees. The respective quantitative amounts are given in the Act but they are subject to amendment from time to time by Statutory Instrument (SI), which we come back to later.

3 A company has a duty to keep what are referred to as 'adequate accounting records'. This means that (a) the company's transactions can be shown and

explained; (b) the financial position of the company can be disclosed at any time; (c) its accounts comply with either the Act or with European Union (EU) requirements.

4   A company must keep a daily record of money received and paid and a record of its assets and liabilities.

5   Companies dealing in stocks (apart from retail traders) have to keep a record of their purchases and sales during a financial year, details of their suppliers and customers, and their year end stocks.

6   The Act makes a distinction between (a) publicly traded companies and (b) non-publicly traded companies. A publicly traded company is basically a company that is permitted to offer its shares to the public on a regulated market, i.e. a Stock Exchange. In the United Kingdom you should be able to recognize such companies fairly easily because they have to put PLC, plc or public limited company after their name. Similarly, non-publicly traded companies must put LTD, ltd or limited after their name.

7   PLCs in member states of the EU must use what are called *International Accounting Standards* (IASs) when preparing *consolidated* accounts, i.e. when all the accounts forming part of a family of closely connected companies are combined. The accounts are then known as the *group* accounts. This requirement applies to every one of the 27 member countries of the EU.

8   In preparing their accounts non-publicly traded companies in the UK have a choice. They can use either (a) the accounting requirements of the Companies Act 2006 plus UK Accounting Standards; or (b) just IASs.

The 'Annual Accounts' section of the Act (in Part 15) is much broader in scope than was the case in earlier Companies Acts, the precise detail being left to the Secretary of State to determine. The form, content and terminology of accounts, for example, are not set out in the legislation (as they were in the 1985 and 1989 Companies Acts). This does not mean that companies are free to decide these things for themselves. Instead the details are decided by the Secretary of State and he (it's usually a 'he') issues his instructions in the form of an SI This is known as *secondary legislation*.

SIs enable the Secretary of State to make changes to *primary* legislation without needing to put another Bill before Parliament. Such a procedure is perfectly legitimate because Parliamentary time is short and the government's legislative programme is usually very full. The SI procedure enables changes to be made to non-controversial matters contained in legislation when circumstances change, e.g. the definition of 'small', 'medium' and 'large' companies. Turnover and balance sheet totals (in sterling) can get out of date very quickly, so it makes sense if they are kept up to date on a regular basis without having to introduce even more legislation.

An SI dealing with the form and content of accounts was issued about 18 months after the Companies Act 2006 received the Royal Assent. As it turned out the requirements were almost identical to those detailed in the 1985 and 1989 Companies Acts. This is a good example of the Act, despite its size, not having a major impact on conventional accounting practices – at least for those companies that did not have to switch to IASs.

We now turn to examine the second main source of accounting authority: UK Accounting Standards'. We do so below.

Activity 2.26

How confusing do you think it is in the UK to have two options in preparing a company's financial statements: (1) UK company law + UK Accounting Standards; and (2) IASs? Mark your score on the following scale: 1 = totally confusing; 5 = no confusion.

Totally confusing   no confusion

1	2	3	4	5

UK Accounting Standards

News clip

John Varley

John Varley, the Chief Executive Officer of Barclays Bank, has called for global consistency of accounting standards if another financial crisis is to be avoided in future.

Source: Adapted from www.accountancyage.com/articles, 23 April 2009.

It would be helpful if we first define what is meant by an 'accounting standard'. The Companies Act 2006 gives us a definition although it is not a particularly clear one. According to the Act, accounting standards are:

> . . . statements of standard accounting practice issued by such body as may be prescribed by regulations. (CA 2006, S464(1))

In less legalistic language this means that: statements of standard accounting practice (SSAPs) are authorative pronouncements that explain how to deal with specific accounting problems such as the valuation of closing stocks or the treatment of research expenditure. The regulations referred to above usually come in the form of SIs. In the UK there is currently one such prescribed body called the Accounting Standards Board (ASB). Many other countries have a similar body. A brief history of the ASB now follows.

During the 1960s a number of contentious company mergers and takeovers took place. These events received a great deal of publicity and they both annoyed and puzzled the general public in equal measure. What was particularly puzzling to the public was that at the beginning of the week one set of accountants could decide that a company had made a profit and then by the end of that week another set of accountants would decide that it had actually made a loss. 'How was it possible,' many people asked, 'for different accountants to arrive at such conflicting results when they both used the same information?' It then began to dawn on the public that there was much more to accounting than simply adding up a lot of figures. And when reality struck home there was outrage. The figures could be fiddled: accountants were not saints after all!

The Institute of Chartered Accountants in England and Wales (ICAEW) was the first professional body to act. In 1970 it founded what was initially called the Accounting Standards Steering Committee (ASSC). It was renamed as the Accounting Standards Committee (ASC) in 1976 but in 1990 it was replaced by the Accounting Standards Board (ASB). By 1996 all the other five major professional accountancy bodies had become ASB members. Throughout this entire period the basic role of the ASSC/ASC/ASB remained unchanged, i.e. to develop definitive standards for financial reporting.

The ASB's main aim is to establish and to improve standards of financial accounting and reporting for the benefit of users, preparers and auditors of financial information. It aims to do so by achieving a number of objectives. In summary they are as follows:

1 To develop accounting principles.
2 To provide a framework to resolve accounting issues.
3 To issue accounting standards.
4 To amend existing accounting standards.
5 To address promptly any urgent accounting issues.
6 To work with other accounting standard setting bodies and institutions.

The ASB operates under the umbrella of the *Financial Reporting Council* (FRC). The FRC is a private limited company. Its main objectives are (i) to provide support for the ASB and the Financial Reporting Panel; and (ii) to encourage good financial reporting. Its funds come from a number of sources such as the accounting profession, the banking and insurance companies, the London Stock Exchange and the government.

Most of the ASB's funds come from the FRC. This arrangement might suggest that the FRC has ultimate control over the formulation and issue of accounting standards. This is not the case. The ASB has complete autonomy over them.

ASB standards are called *Financial Reporting Standards* (FRSs). By the spring of 2010, 30 FRSs had been issued. In addition, 12 ASB standards, known as *Statements of Standard Accounting Practice* (or SSAPs) were still mandatory although they will eventually be phased out. The accounting problems covered in FRSs include acquisitions and mergers (FRS 6), goodwill and intangible assets (FRS 10), and life assurance (FRS 27). SSAPs that have not yet been withdrawn cover topics such as stocks and long-term contracts (SSAP 9) and accounting for pension costs (SSAP 24). The SSAPs still in existence give you some indication that they deal with issues that are either less controversial or more difficult to deal with.

We now turn to have a look at the third main source of accounting regulation in the UK: International Accounting Standards.

Activity 2.27

From what you know so far about the ASB what are your views?

1 Do you think that there is a need for such a body? [Yes] [No]
2 If yes, (a) it should it be (i) state owned [ ] or (ii) privately owned [ ]? and
   (b) should it lay down (i) detailed rules [ ] or (ii) give just general guidance [ ]?
   (tick your responses).
3 If no, why not? Give your reasons.

International Accounting Standards

News clip

ACCA backs International Accounting Standards

Accountancy Age has reported that the Association of Chartered Certified Accountants has called on world leaders at a forthcoming G20 summit to throw their weight behind international financial reporting standards. The Association regards it 'a major failing that IFRS are not already the global accounting language for all financial professionals'.

Source: Adapted from www.accountancyage.com/articles, 10 March 2009.

International Accounting Standards are issued by what is now called the International Accounting Standards Board (IASB). The IASB was originally created in 1973 as the International Accounting Standards Committee (IASC) but it changed its name in 2001. The main aim of the IASC was to make financial statements much more comparable on an international basis. It was hoped to achieve this aim by issuing International Accounting Standards (IASs).

The IASB's aim is similar. It is as follows:

> Our mission is to develop, in the public interest, a single set of high quality, understandable and international financial reporting standards (IFRSs) for general purpose financial statements.

The IASB operates through a body called the International Accounting Standards Committee Foundation (IASCF). The IASCF is an independent, private, not-for-profit sector organization governed by 22 trustees from a number of different countries and professional backgrounds. It is funded by a voluntary system of donors from international accounting firms, business associations and organizations and central banks. The IASC Foundation appoints the IASB's board of 14 members who are recruited from many wide-ranging backgrounds. It also finances, governs and oversees the IASB.

The IASB works closely with national standard setting bodies (such as the ASB in the UK) to ensure that accounting standards throughout the world are as comparable as possible. The number of countries either permitting or requiring the use of its standards continued to grow to 120 by the beginning of 2010. The big breakthrough came in 2002 when the EU decided that as from 2005 publicly traded companies should adopt its standards. The next big hurdle facing the IASB is to encourage the USA to adopt its standards. Discussions have been taking place for some years. The indications are that the USA is 'mindful' to do so (using diplomatic language) but up to date the discussions have not been successful. We return to this point later in the chapter.

The IASB's standards are called *International Financial Reporting Standards* (IFRSs). Between 2001 and the spring of 2010, eight IFRSs had been issued and were still effective. This may not seem very many but the work programme had been deliberately slowed down between 2005 and 2009 to allow more time for new IFRSs to be implemented. The topics that they deal with include such matters as insurance contracts (IFRS 4) and operating segments (IFRS 8). The slow-down meant that 29 of the original *International Accounting Standards* (IASs) were still in use in the spring of 2010. The problems that they deal with range from the presentation of financial statements (IAS 1) to one coping with agriculture activity (IAS 41). Many of these accounting standards are highly technical and are certainly way beyond what you need to know until you become a very senior manager.

Now that we have given you some idea of the importance and status of both the ASB and the IASB in accounting regulation we are in a position to examine what these two bodies have done to improve their performance. We do so in the next part of this section.

Activity 2.28

Log on to the IASB website.   Insert the current date:

Answer the following questions:

1 How many countries have now adopted IFRSs?
2 How many IFRSs have now been issued.
3 How many IASs are still in use?

An accounting framework

News clip

A principled approach to standards

In a recently issued policy paper on the international accounting standard setting process, the International Federation of Accountants has argued that the key to successful standard setting is the identification of 'the underlying principles'.

Source: Adapted from *Financial Management*, February 2009, p. 7.

Until 2005 IASs and IFRSs were not a significant feature of UK financial reporting and SSAPs and FRSs took priority in the preparation of financial statements. The ASB certainly did not ignore the work of the IASB and the two bodies had a close working relationship but the ASB had a legal and professional status in the UK which the IASB did not have. That all changed in 2005 once the EU decided to adopt International Accounting Standards. As a member of the EU the UK was bound to accept the decision.

There were two basic differences between UK Accounting Standards and International Accounting Standards:

1 They did not always deal with the same accounting problems. This was perhaps because what was a contentious issue in the UK was not necessarily so in the rest of the world (and vice versa).
2 If the ASB and the IASB did issue an accounting standard dealing with the same problem, the IASB's solution tended to be more generalized (possibly because it had to be acceptable in so many different and disparate countries). This was an advantage for the UK because it meant that compliance with a UK standard almost automatically meant compliance with the equivalent IAS one.

The ASB and the IASB did have one thing in common when framing their respective accounting standards: they were largely fire-fighting exercises dealing with what happened to be a problem at that particular time. This meant that there was often little consistency in the way that the various issues were tackled. It eventually became apparent that accounting standards should be built on a basic framework or foundation. This would then enable solutions to different problems to be based on the same basic principles or rules. As a result, accounting standards would have a common theme running through them.

Academic accountants had argued for years that there was a need for such a framework. They referred to it as a *conceptual* framework which no doubt frightened the more practically trained accountants to death. Nevertheless, both the ASB and the IASB and similar standard setting bodies in many other countries were working on such a project. The IASB was the first to publish its ideas in a document called *Framework for the Preparation and Presentation of Financial Statements* (note that it did not include the word 'concept' in its title). The ideas in it relied very heavily on work done on the same subject in the USA as well as in Australia and Canada. We shall refer to it as the *Framework* from now on.

The ASB took a great deal longer to produce its own framework. It was not until 1999 that it published what it called *Statement of principles for financial reporting*. It is very similar to the Framework. As it is, in effect, a more up-to-date version of it, we will use the Statement to summarize what we need for this section. The relevant points are as follows.

1 The *objective* of financial statements is: to provide information about the reporting entity's financial performance and financial position that is useful to a wide range of users for assessing the stewardship of the entity's management and for making economic decisions.
2 The *users* of financial statements are: (i) investors; (ii) lenders; (iii) suppliers and other trade creditors; (iv) employees; (v) customers; (vi) governments and their agencies; and (vii) the public. These users are depicted in Figure 2.21.

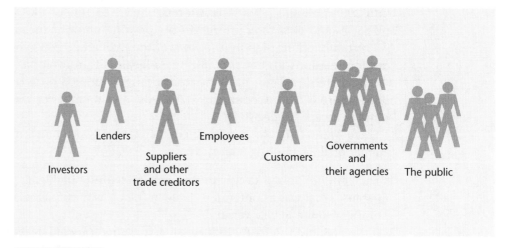

Figure 2.21   The main users of financial statements

Source: Statement of Principles for Financial Reporting, ASB 1999.

3 The *reporting entity* is a cohesive economic unit, its boundary being determined by what it can control both directly and indirectly.

4 The *qualitative characteristics* of financial information are summarized below. Note how they relate very closely to the four ethical accounting rules we discussed earlier in the section, i.e. prudence, consistency, objectivity and relevance.

(a) *Relevance*. Financial statements should meet the needs of users and be *timely*, i.e. not to be so out of date that they have become irrelevant for decision making purposes. This characteristic, in effect, presupposes the incorporation of the *materiality* concept because information that is not helpful for decision making is irrelevant.

(b) *Reliability*. Users should be able to rely on the information contained within the financial statements. It should be free from material error, represent faithfully what it is supposed to represent, be free from bias (i.e. it should be **neutral**), and be compatible with the substance of transactions and not simply just because it is lawful. It should also be complete provided that it is material, and a *prudent* approach should be adopted when it is unclear how a particular transaction should be accounted for. So materiality, prudence and also objectivity are all inherent in this characteristic.

(c) *Comparability*. Financial statements containing the results for comparative periods should be prepared on a consistent basis. In other words, they should be prepared on the same basis each year. Comparability is almost the same concept as our consistency rule.

(d) *Understandability*. Financial statements should be capable of being understood by those users who have some knowledge of accounting, business activities and economic affairs and who are willing to study the financial statements diligently. The financial statements themselves should not, however, to be so simple that the information becomes meaningless.

5 The *elements* of financial information are the 'building blocks' used in the construction of the financial statements. They include what assets and liabilities the

entity owns, what interest the owners have in the entity, what contributions and distributions the owners have made, and what has been paid out to them.

6 The Statement recognises that assets and liabilities need to be *measured* so that they can be included in the financial statements. They can be included at either their historical cost or at their current value. Historical cost is the more usual. Current cost is a method that relates to the loss an entity would suffer if the entity was deprived of an asset. So it is sometimes called 'deprival value' or 'loss to the business'. We shall not be dealing with current value accounting in this section.

7 Financial statements should be presented clearly, effectively, simply and straightforwardly.

You might also think that despite the fuss that we have made in this section about the need to develop a workable framework, the outcome so far has not been very impressive. Both the Framework and the Statement are quite vague in their requirements and perhaps they lack a more prescriptive approach.

You would be right but if the profession went down that road we would be moving to what is called a *rules-based* approach to accounting. The main problems with this approach are that (i) it is difficult to formulate rules that accommodate every eventuality and (ii) ways will always be found of getting round whatever rules are formulated. So a culture develops and creates a climate whereby the attitude becomes '*if it's not in the rules you can do what you like*'. As we indicated earlier in the chapter, the USA has adopted a *rules-based* approach while EU countries all use a *principles-based* approach. This approach allows for individual circumstances to be taken into account but it can result in apparent inconsistencies in the accounts of different entities. This fundamental difference between the EU's and the USA's methods of accounting is the main reason why the USA has been reluctant to adopt IASs but political considerations have, no doubt, also played a part.

Activity 2.29

UK Accounting Standards are based on generally accepted *principles*. Some other countries prefer a *rules-based system*. Which approach do you favour?

1 (a) principles   [ ] (b) rules-based   [ ] (tick which).
2 Give three reasons for your choice.

Questions you should ask

This is an important sections; it outlines a number of accounting issues that will face you when you become a manager in the real world. We suggest that among the long list of questions that you might well ask are the following.

● Are we subject to the Companies Act 2006?
● Do we adopt International Accounting Standards or UK (or own country's) standards?

- What accounting rules do we follow in the preparation of our financial statements?
- Are we without doubt a going concern?
- How do we determine what is an immaterial item?
- To what extent does neutrality override the need to be prudent?

Conclusion

In this section we have identified 14 conventional accounting rules and introduced you to the accounting provisions of Companies Act 2006 along with the additional semi-statutory requirements specified by the Accounting Standards Board and the International Accounting Standards Board.

The section enables you to grasp the fundamentals of what accountants do, why they do it and what the law requires them to do. Other sections in this chapter show you how to prepare financial statements based on what is required. By knowing why and how they are prepared you will find that they will be of much greater benefit to you in making and taking the types of decision that your job requires.

Key points

1 In preparing financial statements, accountants use a number of conventional accounting rules (sometimes called principles); these rules have evolved over many centuries.

2 Such rules may be classified into boundary rules (entity, periodicity, going concern and quantitative); measurement rules (money measurement, historic cost, realization, matching, dual aspect and materiality); and ethical rules (prudence, consistency, objectivity and relevance).

3 The main source of legislation affecting accounting matters in the UK is the Companies Act 2006; the Act is primarily concerned with companies and limited liability partnerships.

4 The Act delegates much of the detail involving the preparation and reporting of financial statements to the International Accounting Standards Board (for publicly quoted group companies) and the UK Accounting Standards Board (for other companies).

5 The IASB issues International Financial Reporting Standards (IFRSs) and the ASB Financial Reporting Standards (FRSs) to help companies deal with contentious and difficult accounting matters. Other countries have their own accounting standards boards but many of them also use IASs.

6 Financial statements in the UK have always been prepared on a custom and practice basis but both the IASB and the ASB have issued a framework outlining the principles that entities are expected to follow in preparing such statements. Both frameworks are similar and they incorporate in one form or another all the 14 rules detailed in the first part of this chapter.

Check your learning

1 In an accounting context name three other terms that are similar in meaning to 'rules'.

2 Identify three categories of accounting rules.

3 What accounting rule is used to describe a defined period of time?

4 What is a going concern?

5 What is matching?

6 What does dual aspect mean?

7 When is a transaction not material?

8 What criteria are used to determine whether items are relevant?

9 Name three important sources of authority governing accounting matters affecting UK companies?

10 What do the following initials stand for: (a) CA; (b) SI; (c) ASB; (d) IASB; (e) SSAP; (f) IAS; (g) FRS; (h) IFRS?

11 What is an accounting standard?

12 What is a conceptual framework?

13 What is the objective of financial statements?

14 List seven user groups of accounting information.

15 What is a reporting entity?

16 List the qualitative characteristics of financial information.

News story quiz

Remember the news story at the beginning of the section? Go back to that story and reread it before answering the following questions.

This article relates back to the financial crisis that in 2007 struck the banking system in Britain and in many other countries. However, the points raised in the article are also relevant today as well as for other economic sectors.

Questions

1 What is the difference between a rule book and a principles approach to accounting matters?

2 Why does a principles approach necessarily deal better with changing financial markets and by implication with financial statements?

3 Closer dialogue is seen to be partly the answer for dealing with problems of systematic risk in auditing, but what else might be needed?

Presentation of financial statements

Introduction

The main purpose of this chapter is to explain the requirements of international standard IAS1 *Presentation of Financial Statements*. The current version of this standard was issued in September 2007 and has effect for accounting periods beginning on or after 1 January 2009 (though earlier application is permitted).

The objective of IAS1 is to specify the overall structure and content of general-purpose financial statements and so ensure that an entity's financial statements are comparable with those of previous periods and with those of other entities. The standard sets out:

(a) the general features of financial statements
(b) guidelines with regard to their structure, and
(c) minimum requirements for their content.

IAS1 is of general application and does not deal with specific transactions or events. These are dealt with in other international standards.

This chapter also outlines the main requirements of international standard IAS34 *Interim Financial Reporting*.

Objective of financial statements

The requirements of IAS1 apply to all general-purpose financial statements prepared and presented in accordance with international standards. General-purpose financial statements are those intended for users who are not in a position to demand reports that are tailored for their own particular information needs.

According to IAS1, the objective of such financial statements is *"to provide information about the financial position, financial performance and cash flows of an entity that is useful to a wide range of users in making economic decisions"*. Apart from a slight difference in wording, this definition is of course the same as the one given in the IASB *Framework*. In order to meet this objective, general-purpose financial statements should provide information about an entity's:

(a) assets, liabilities and equity
(b) income and expenses, including gains and losses
(c) contributions by and distributions to owners in their capacity as owners
(d) cash flows.

This information is given in four primary financial statements. Further information is given in the notes which accompany these statements.

Components of financial statements

IAS1 states that a complete set of financial statements comprises:

(a) a statement of financial position as at the end of the accounting period
(b) a statement of comprehensive income for the period
(c) a statement of changes in equity for the period
(d) a statement of cash flows for the period
(e) a set of notes, which provide a summary of the entity's significant accounting policies together with other explanatory information
(f) a statement of financial position as at the beginning of the earliest comparative period presented, if the entity has applied an accounting policy retrospectively or has made a retrospective restatement of items in its financial statements.

These titles have replaced the more traditional titles used in the previous version of IAS1 (e.g. "balance sheet", "cash flow statement") and are thought by the IASB to reflect more closely the function of each statement. However, entities are allowed to use titles for the financial statements other than those used in the standard if they so wish.

The structure and content of most of the statements is specified in IAS1. But the statement of cash flows is dealt with by IAS7 *Statement of Cash Flows*. It is important to appreciate that the notes which accompany the four primary statements are an integral part of the financial statements and so fall within the scope of IAS1 and all of the other international standards.

In addition to the items listed above, IAS1 recognises that an entity's annual report might contain other statements such as an environmental report or value added statement. These other statements are not part of the financial statements and are therefore outside the scope of international standards.

General features

Under the heading "general features", IAS1 sets out a number of general rules which relate to the presentation of financial statements. Some of these are very obviously based upon principles established in the IASB *Framework*. The main areas dealt with in this part of IAS1 are:

(a) fair presentation and compliance with international standards
(b) going concern basis and accrual basis
(c) materiality and aggregation
(d) offsetting
(e) frequency of reporting
(f) comparative information
(g) consistency of presentation.

Each of these is considered below.

Fair presentation and compliance with international standards

Financial statements must present fairly the financial position, financial performance and cash flows of the entity concerned. This requires that the effects of transactions and other events should be faithfully represented in accordance with the definitions and recognition criteria for assets, liabilities, income and expenses set out in the IASB *Framework*. It may be assumed that the application of international standards will result in financial statements that achieve a fair presentation. An entity which produces financial statements that comply with international standards must make an explicit and unreserved statement to that effect in the notes. A fair presentation also requires the entity to:

(a) select and apply appropriate accounting policies in accordance with the requirements of international standard IAS8
(b) provide information that is relevant, reliable, comparable and understandable
(c) provide further disclosures if compliance with international standards is insufficient to enable users to understand the impact of transactions and other events.

On very rare occasions, compliance with a requirement in an international standard may produce misleading information and so conflict with the objective of financial statements.

In these circumstances, the entity should depart from that requirement and the notes should disclose that the entity has complied with international standards except that it has departed from a particular requirement in order to achieve a fair presentation. The notes should identify the title of the standard concerned, the nature of the departure, the reason for the departure, the accounting treatment that the standard would have required, the accounting treatment actually adopted and the financial impact of the departure.

Going concern basis and accrual basis

Financial statements should be prepared on the going concern basis unless the entity intends to cease trading or has no realistic alternative but to do so. If there are significant doubts concerning the entity's ability to continue as a going concern, the uncertainties which give rise to these doubts should be disclosed. If financial statements are *not* prepared on a going concern basis, that fact should be disclosed, together with the basis on which the financial statements are prepared and the reasons for which the entity is not regarded as a going concern.

Financial statements other than the statement of cash flows should also be prepared using the accrual basis of accounting. The statement of cash flows is an obvious exception to this rule since, by definition, it is prepared on a cash basis.

Materiality and aggregation

IAS1 defines materiality by stating that *"omissions or mis-statements of items are material if they could, individually or collectively, influence the economic decisions that users make on the basis of the financial statements"*. IAS1 further states that materiality should be judged in context and that either the size or nature of an item, or a combination of both, could determine whether or not the item is material.

In general, financial statements are prepared by analysing transactions and other events into classes and then aggregating (i.e. totalling) each of these classes to produce line items which appear in the statements. For instance, all sales transactions are aggregated into a single revenue figure shown in the statement of comprehensive income. IAS1 requires that each material class of similar items should be presented separately in the financial statements. If an item is not individually material, it may be aggregated with other line items.

IAS1 explicitly states that there is no need to satisfy the disclosure requirements of an international standard if the information disclosed would not be material. This means that compliance with the standards can be achieved without having to disclose immaterial items, whether in the primary financial statements or in the accompanying notes.

Offsetting

In general, assets and liabilities should be reported separately in the statement of financial position and should not be offset against one another. Similarly, income and expenses should be reported separately in the statement of comprehensive income. IAS1 takes the view that offsetting should not be allowed, since this would normally detract from users' ability to understand transactions and other events.

However, this general rule does not apply in a specific instance if another international standard permits or requires offsetting in that instance.

Frequency of reporting

Financial statements should normally be presented at least annually. If an entity changes its accounting date and so presents a set of financial statements for a period which is longer or shorter than one year, the entity should disclose:

(a) the reason for using a period that is longer or shorter than one year
(b) the fact that the comparative amounts given for the previous period are not directly comparable with those given for the current period.

Comparative information

Unless another international standard permits or requires otherwise, IAS1 requires that entities should present (as a minimum) comparative information in respect of the previous period for all amounts reported in the financial statements.

Comparatives should also be given for narrative information if this would be relevant to an understanding of the current period's financial statements.

Consistency of presentation

In order to maintain comparability, the way in which items are presented and classified in the financial statements should generally be consistent from one accounting period to the next. However, this rule does not apply if:

(a) it is apparent that a different presentation or classification would be more appropriate, following either a significant change in the nature of the entity's operations or a review of its financial statements
(b) a different presentation or classification is required by an international standard.

Structure and content of financial statements

The majority of IAS1 is concerned with the structure and content of an entity's financial statements. The standard requires that certain items should be shown in the statement of financial position, the statement of comprehensive income and the statement of changes in equity. Other items should be shown either in these statements or in the notes. IAS1 does not deal with the statement of cash flows, since this is the subject of IAS7 *Statement of Cash Flows*. The main headings in this part of IAS1 are:

(a) identification of the financial statements
(b) the statement of financial position
(c) the statement of comprehensive income
(d) the statement of changes in equity
(e) the notes.

Each of these is considered below.

Identification of the financial statements

The first point made in this part of IAS1 is that the financial statements should be clearly identified as such and distinguished from any other information which may be given in the same published document (e.g. a management review). Since international standards apply only to the financial statements, it is important that users can distinguish information that has been prepared in accordance with standards from information that has not.

Furthermore, each component of the financial statements should be clearly identified and the following information should be displayed prominently and repeated where necessary for a proper understanding of the information presented:

(a) the name of the reporting entity
(b) whether the financial statements are for a single entity or a group

(c) the date of the end of the reporting period or the period covered by the set of financial statements or notes

(d) the presentation currency used

(e) the level of rounding used (e.g. £000 or £m).

The statement of financial position

An important requirement of IAS1 with regard to the statement of financial position (formerly known as the balance sheet) is that current and non-current assets should be presented separately and that current and non-current liabilities should also be presented separately. For an entity which supplies goods or services within a clearly identifiable operating cycle, this separation provides useful information by:

(a) distinguishing the net assets that are continuously circulating as working capital from those used in the long-term, and

(b) highlighting the assets that are expected to be realised within the current operating cycle and the liabilities that are due for settlement within the same period.

IAS1 establishes a set of criteria which should be used to distinguish between current and non-current assets and another set of criteria which should be used to distinguish between current and non-current liabilities.

Current and non-current assets

An asset is classified as a current asset if it satisfies *any* of the following criteria:

(a) it is expected to be realised, or is intended for sale or consumption, within the entity's normal operating cycle

(b) it is held primarily for the purpose of being traded

(c) it is expected to be realised within 12 months after the reporting period

(d) it is cash or a cash equivalent as defined by international standard IAS7 unless it is restricted from being used to settle a liability for at least 12 months after the reporting period.

An asset that satisfies none of these criteria is a non-current asset. The operating cycle of an entity is defined as *"the time between the acquisition of assets for processing and their realisation in cash and cash equivalents"*. If an entity's normal operating cycle cannot be clearly identified, it is assumed to be 12 months. Note that current assets include items such as inventories and trade receivables that are expected to be realised during the normal operating cycle, even if they are not expected to be realised within 12 months.

IAS1 does not require the use of the terms "current" and "non-current" and other descriptions could be used so long as their meaning is clear. However, these terms are used extensively in practice.

Current and non-current liabilities

A liability is classified as a current liability if it satisfies *any* of the following criteria:

(a) it is expected to be settled in the entity's normal operating cycle
(b) it is held primarily for the purpose of being traded
(c) it is due to be settled within 12 months after the reporting period
(d) the entity does not have an unconditional right to defer settlement of the liability for at least 12 months after the reporting period.

A liability that satisfies none of these criteria is a non-current liability. Current liabilities include items such as trade payables and accrued expenses that are expected to be settled during the normal operating cycle, even if they are not expected to be settled within 12 months. Current liabilities also include items such as bank overdrafts, dividends payable and taxes which are not settled as part of the normal operating cycle but which are due to be settled within 12 months.

Information to be presented in the statement of financial position

IAS1 does not require any particular format for the statement of financial position. Nor does it prescribe the order in which items should be shown. But the standard does provide a minimum list of line items that should be presented separately in the statement if their size or nature is such that separate presentation is relevant to an understanding of the entity's financial position. Additional line items, headings and subtotals should also be presented where relevant. The main line items listed by IAS1 are as follows:

(a) property, plant and equipment
(b) investment property
(c) intangible assets
(d) financial assets
(e) investments accounted for by the equity method
(f) inventories
(g) trade and other receivables
(h) cash and cash equivalents
(i) assets classified as "held for sale"
(j) trade and other payables
(k) provisions
(l) financial liabilities
(m) current tax assets and liabilities
(n) deferred tax assets and liabilities
(o) liabilities included in disposal groups held for sale
(p) non-controlling interests
(q) issued equity capital and reserves

The order of the items and the descriptions used may be amended in accordance with the nature of the entity and its transactions, so as to provide relevant information. Item (p) will arise only if the entity is a member of a group.

Format of the statement of financial position

Although IAS1 does not prescribe a format for the statement of financial position, the implementation guidance that accompanies the standard includes an illustration which shows one way in which the statement may be presented. A slightly simplified version of this illustration is shown in Figure 2.22 below. This illustrative format is not prescriptive and other formats may be used if appropriate.

XYZ plc – Statement of financial position as at 31 December 2009

	2009 £000	2008 £000
ASSETS		
Non-current assets		
Property, plant and equipment	xxx	xxx
Intangible assets	xxx	xxx
Investments	xxx	xxx
	xxx	xxx
Current assets		
Inventories	xxx	xxx
Trade receivables	xxx	xxx
Cash and cash equivalents	xxx	xxx
	xxx	xxx
Total assets	xxx	xxx
EQUITY AND LIABILITIES		
Equity		
Share capital	xxx	xxx
Retained earnings	xxx	xxx
Other reserves	xxx	xxx
Total equity	xxx	xxx
Non-current liabilities		
Long-term borrowings	xxx	xxx
Deferred tax	xxx	xxx
Long-term provisions	xxx	xxx
Total non-current liabilities	xxx	xxx
Current liabilities		
Trade and other payables	xxx	xxx
Short-term borrowings	xxx	xxx
Current tax payable	xxx	xxx
Short-term provisions	xxx	xxx
Total current liabilities	xxx	xxx
Total liabilities	xxx	xxx
Total equity and liabilities	xxx	xxx

Figure 2.22   Illustrative format of the statement of financial position

Information in the statement of financial position or in the notes

IAS1 requires that the line items presented in the statement of financial position should be sub-classified, either in the statement itself or in the notes. These sub-classifications should be appropriate to the entity's operations but also depend to some extent on the requirements of other international standards. Examples given in IAS1 include the following:

(a) property, plant and equipment is sub-classified in accordance with IAS16 *Property, Plant and Equipment*
(b) receivables are analysed into trade receivables, prepayments, other receivables etc.
(c) inventories are sub-classified in accordance with IAS2 *Inventories*
(d) provisions are analysed into those relating to employee benefits and other provisions
(e) share capital and reserves are analysed into their various classes.

IAS1 also requires further disclosures with regard to share capital and reserves. These disclosures may be given in the statement of financial position or the statement of changes in equity, or in the notes. The disclosures include:

(f) for each class of share capital:
   (i) the number of shares authorised
   (ii) the number of shares issued and fully paid, and issued but not fully paid
   (iii) the par value per share
   (iv) a reconciliation of the number of shares outstanding at the beginning and end of the accounting period
   (v) the rights, preferences and restrictions attaching to that class of shares
(g) a description of the nature and purpose of each reserve.

The statement of comprehensive income

IAS1 requires that all items of income or expense that are recognised in an accounting period should be presented either:

(a) in a single statement of comprehensive income, or
(b) in two separate statements, comprising:
   (i) an income statement which shows components of the entity's profit or loss, and
   (ii) a statement of comprehensive income which begins with the profit or loss for the period and shows components of the entity's "other comprehensive income".

International standards which require certain items of income or expense to be shown in other comprehensive income (and so excluded from profit or loss) include:

(a) IAS16 *Property, Plant and Equipment*, with regard to surpluses arising on revaluation of tangible non-current assets

(b) IAS38 *Intangible Assets*, with regard to surpluses arising on revaluation of intangible assets

(c) IAS39 *Financial Instruments: Recognition and Measurement*, with regard to gains or losses on the re-measurement of available-for-sale investments.

Information presented in the statement of comprehensive income

As with the statement of financial position, IAS1 does not require any specific format for the statement of comprehensive income. Instead, the standard provides a minimum list of line items that should be presented separately in this statement. Additional line items, headings and subtotals should be presented where relevant. The main items listed by IAS1 are as follows:

(a) revenue

(b) finance costs

(c) profits or losses accounted for by the equity method

(d) tax expense

(e) profit or loss after tax relating to discontinued operations

(f) profit or loss for the period

(g) each component of other comprehensive income

(h) total comprehensive income for the period

Items (a) to (f) may be presented in a separate income statement (see above). The order of the items and the descriptions used may be amended where this is necessary to explain the entity's financial performance.

An important further requirement of IAS1 is that an entity should *not* present any items of income or expense as "extraordinary" items, either in the statement of comprehensive income or in a separate income statement (if presented) or in the notes.

Groups of companies

If the financial statements are for a group of companies, the statement of comprehensive income must also disclose:

(a) the amount of the profit or loss for the period which is attributable to non-controlling interests and the amount which is attributable to the owners of the parent company

(b) the amount of the total comprehensive income for the period which is attributable to non-controlling interests and the amount which is attributable to the owners of the parent company.

Information in the statement of comprehensive income or in the notes

In addition to the items which must be presented in the statement of comprehensive income, further items of income and expense should be disclosed separately (either in the statement itself or in the notes) if material. The entity must also present an analysis of expenses using a classification based on either:

(a) the nature of the expenses, or
(b) the function of the expenses within the entity.

Entities are encouraged to present this analysis in the statement of comprehensive income but it may be presented instead in the notes which accompany the financial statements. An analysis which is based on the nature of the expenses might include headings such as depreciation, employee benefits, motor expenses etc. An analysis based on function would normally classify expenses into cost of sales, distribution costs and administrative expenses. An entity which analyses expenses by function must also provide additional information on the nature of expenses, including depreciation and employee benefits.

Format of the statement of comprehensive income

The implementation guidance which accompanies IAS1 provides two illustrations of the statement of comprehensive income. One of these shows a single statement with expenses analysed by function and the other shows two separate statements with expenses analysed by nature. Simplified versions of these illustrations are shown in Figures 2.23a, 2.23b and 2.23c below. As with the statement of financial position, IAS1 makes it clear that these formats are only illustrations and that other formats may be used if appropriate.

XYZ plc – Statement of comprehensive income for year to 31 December 2009	2009 £000	2008 £000
Revenue	xxx	xxx
Cost of sales	(xxx)	(xxx)
Gross profit	xxx	xxx
Other income	xxx	xxx
Distribution costs	(xxx)	(xxx)
Administrative expenses	(xxx)	(xxx)
Other expenses	(xxx)	(xxx)
Finance costs	(xxx)	(xxx)
Profit before tax	xxx	xxx
Tax expense	(xxx)	(xxx)
Profit for the year	xxx	xxx
Other comprehensive income for the year		
Gains on property revaluation	xxx	xxx
Available-for-sale financial assets	xxx	xxx
Tax relating to other comprehensive income	(xxx)	(xxx)
Other comprehensive income for the year net of tax	xxx	xxx
TOTAL COMPREHENSIVE INCOME FOR THE YEAR	xxx	xxx

Figure 2.23a Single statement of comprehensive income (expenses analysed by function)

XYZ plc – Income statement for year to 31 December 2009

	2009 £000	2008 £000
Revenue	xxx	xxx
Other income	xxx	xxx
Changes in inventories of finished goods and WIP	(xxx)	(xxx)
Raw material and consumables used	(xxx)	(xxx)
Employee benefits expense	(xxx)	(xxx)
Depreciation and amortisation expense	(xxx)	(xxx)
Impairment of property, plant and equipment	(xxx)	(xxx)
Other expenses	(xxx)	(xxx)
Finance costs	(xxx)	(xxx)
Profit before tax	xxx	xxx
Tax expense	(xxx)	(xxx)
Profit for the year	xxx	xxx

Figure 2.23b Separate income statement (expenses analysed by nature)

XYZ plc – Statement of comprehensive income for year to 31 December 2009

	2009 £000	2008 £000
Profit for the year	xxx	xxx
Other comprehensive income for the year		
Gains on property revaluation	xxx	xxx
Available-for-sale financial assets	xxx	xxx
Tax relating to other comprehensive income	(xxx)	(xxx)
Other comprehensive income for the year net of tax	xxx	xxx
TOTAL COMPREHENSIVE INCOME FOR THE YEAR	xxx	xxx

Figure 2.23c Separate statement of comprehensive income

The statement of changes in equity

A statement of changes in equity shows how each component of equity has changed during an accounting period. In the case of a company, the components of equity will be share capital and each of the company's reserves. IAS1 requires that the following items are presented in the statement of changes in equity:

(a) total comprehensive income for the period
(b) for each component of equity, the effects of any retrospective application of an accounting policy or retrospective restatement of items, in accordance with international standard IAS8

(c) for each component of equity, a reconciliation of the opening and closing balance of that component, separately disclosing changes resulting from:

  (i)   profit or loss

  (ii) each item of other comprehensive income

  (iii) transactions with the owners of the entity, separately showing distributions to owners (e.g. dividends) and contributions by owners (e.g. share issues).

The amount of dividends per share must also be shown either in the statement of changes in equity or in the notes.

The implementation guidance to IAS1 provides an illustration of the statement of changes in equity and a simplified version of this illustration is shown in Figure 2.24.

XYZ plc – Statement of changes in equity for the year to 31 December 2009

	Share capital £000	Retained earnings £000	Revaluation surplus £000	Total equity £000
Balance at 1 January 2008	XXX	XXX	XXX	XXX
Changes in accounting policy	—	XXX	—	XXX
Restated balance	XXX	XXX	XXX	XXX
Changes in equity for 2008				
Dividends		(XXX)		(XXX)
Total comprehensive income	—	XXX	XXX	XXX
Balance at 31 December 2008	XXX	XXX	XXX	XXX
Changes in equity for 2009				
Issue of share capital	XXX			XXX
Dividends		(XXX)		(XXX)
Total comprehensive income	—	XXX	XXX	XXX
Balance at 31 December 2009	XXX	XXX	XXX	XXX

Figure 2.24   Statement of changes in equity

The notes to the financial statements

As mentioned earlier in this section, the notes which accompany the statement of financial position, the statement of comprehensive income, the statement of cash flows and the statement of changes in equity are an integral part of the financial statements and so fall within the scope of international standards. IAS1 states that the notes should:

(a) present information about the basis of preparation of the financial statements and the accounting policies which have been used, including:

  – the measurement bases used in preparing the financial statements

  – other accounting policies relevant to an understanding of the financial statements

(b) disclose information required by international standards, to the extent that this is not presented elsewhere in the financial statements

(c) provide any additional information which is relevant to an understanding of any of the financial statements.

The notes should be presented in a systematic manner and should be cross-referenced to the four primary financial statements. The notes normally begin with a statement of compliance with international standards. There should then be a summary of significant accounting policies, followed by supporting information for line items presented in the four primary statements and further disclosures as necessary.

Sources of estimation uncertainty

When determining the amount at which assets or liabilities should be shown or "carried" in the financial statements, it may be necessary to estimate the effects of uncertain future events (such as technological change) and make assumptions. If there is a significant risk that these uncertain future events may cause a material adjustment to the carrying amount of assets or liabilities within the next financial year, IAS1 requires that the notes to the financial statements should explain the key sources of estimation uncertainty and disclose the assumptions that have been made.

Other disclosures

Other disclosures required in the notes include:

(a) the amount of any dividends declared before the financial statements were authorised for issue but not recognised during the period
(b) the amount of any unrecognised cumulative preference dividends
(c) unless disclosed elsewhere, the entity's domicile and legal form, its country of incorporation, the address of its registered office and the nature of its operations.

If an entity is a subsidiary it should disclose the name of its parent and the name of the ultimate parent of the group.

Interim financial reporting

IAS34 *Interim Financial Reporting* applies if an entity publishes an interim financial report that is stated to comply with international standards. An interim financial report is defined by IAS34 as "*a financial report containing either a complete set of financial statements . . . or a set of condensed financial statements . . . for an interim period*". An interim period is a period which is less than a full financial year.

The standards do not actually require entities to publish interim financial reports. But some entities whose shares are publicly traded might be required to do so by governments or stock exchanges. Other entities might do so voluntarily. In these cases, interim financial reports might be presented half-yearly or quarterly in addition to the main annual report. Interim financial reports that are stated to comply with international standards must satisfy the requirements of IAS34. A brief summary of these requirements is as follows:

(a) An interim financial report may consist of a complete set of financial statements as prescribed by IAS1. Alternatively, an entity may provide a condensed set of financial statements consisting of:
   - a condensed statement of financial position
   - a condensed statement of comprehensive income, presented as either:
     - a single statement, or
     - a separate income statement and statement of comprehensive income
   - a condensed statement of changes in equity
   - a condensed statement of cash flows
   - selected explanatory notes.

   These condensed financial statements should include, at a minimum, each of the headings and subtotals that were included in the entity's most recent annual financial statements. Additional items should be presented if their omission would make the condensed statements misleading. Unfortunately, the term "headings and subtotals" is not defined in IAS34 and so is open to interpretation. In practice, condensed financial statements tend to follow the same format as complete financial statements, so that the "condensed" nature of the statements is confined largely to the notes.

(b) Basic and diluted earnings per share figures should be presented in the statement of comprehensive income or the separate income statement, whether complete or condensed.

(c) The main explanatory notes which should be provided (if the information concerned is material and is not disclosed elsewhere in the interim report) include:
   - a statement that the same accounting policies have been used in the interim financial statements as in the most recent annual statements, or a description of the nature and effect of any changes in policy
   - explanatory comments about the seasonality of the entity's operations
   - the nature and amount of any unusual items
   - the nature and amount of any changes made to estimates from previous periods, if these have a material effect on the interim financial statements
   - issues and repayments of debt securities (e.g. loan stock) or shares
   - dividends paid
   - certain segment information
   - any material events that have occurred subsequent to the end of the interim period
   - any changes to the composition of the entity during the interim period, including business combinations
   - any changes in contingent assets or contingent liabilities since the end of the last annual reporting period.

   The entity should also disclose any further transactions or events that are material to an understanding of the interim period.

(d) The same accounting policies should be applied in the interim financial statements as in the annual financial statements, except for changes in accounting policy which are made after the most recent annual statements and which will be reflected in the next annual statements.

Summary

- IAS1 defines a complete set of financial statements as consisting of a statement of financial position, a statement of comprehensive income, a statement of changes in equity, a statement of cash flows and a set of notes.

- The effects of transactions and other items should be faithfully represented in the financial statements. The application of international standards will normally ensure that this is the case.

- Financial statements should be prepared on the going concern basis (unless this does not apply) and on the accruals basis.

- The way in which items are presented and classified in the financial statements should generally be consistent from one accounting period to the next. Comparative information should normally be disclosed in respect of the previous period for all amounts reported in the financial statements.

- Financial statements should be clearly identified as such and each statement should be clearly labelled. Financial statements should normally be presented at least annually.

- In general, current and non-current assets and current and non-current liabilities should be shown separately in the statement of financial position. IAS1 defines the term "current" and "non-current" in each case.

- IAS1 lists the main line items that should be presented in the statement of financial position. The standard also lists further disclosures that should be made in the statement of financial position or in the notes.

- IAS1 also lists the main line items that should be presented in the statement of comprehensive income and requires an analysis of expenses (by nature or by function) to be shown in the statement itself or in the notes.

- The statement of changes in equity shows the changes in each component of equity during an accounting period. The statement shows total comprehensive income for the period and discloses transactions between the entity and its owners.

- IAS1 does not require any particular format for the financial statements but does provide some illustrative examples.

- The notes to the financial statements are within the scope of international standards. They provide information about measurement bases and accounting policies, together with supporting information for line items in the main financial statements and further information which is required by international standards or which is relevant to an understanding of the financial statements.

- The current version of IAS1 takes effect for accounting periods beginning on or after 1 January 2009. Earlier application is permitted.

- International standard IAS34 prescribes the minimum content of an interim financial report (if one is published) but does not require entities to publish such a report.

Exercises

1 International standard IAS1 lists seven "general features" relating to the presentation of financial statements. These are:
  (a) fair presentation and compliance with international standards
  (b) going concern basis and accrual basis
  (c) materiality and aggregation
  (d) offsetting
  (e) frequency of reporting
  (f) comparative information
  (g) consistency of presentation.

  Explain the main requirements of IAS1 in relation to each of these considerations.

2 (a) Distinguish between current assets and non-current assets.
  (b) Distinguish between current liabilities and non-current liabilities.
  (c) Explain why these distinctions are useful.

3 Explain the purpose of a statement of changes in equity and list the main items that should be shown in this statement.

4 You have been asked to help prepare the financial statements of Tanhosier Ltd for the year ended 31 March 2010. A trial balance as at 31 March 2010 is shown below.

	£000	£000
Sales		50,332
Purchases	29,778	
Property, plant and equipment – cost	59,088	
Property, plant and equipment – accumulated depreciation		25,486
Inventories as at 1 April 2009	7,865	
Interest	200	
Accruals		426
Distribution costs	8,985	
Administrative expenses	7,039	
Retained earnings		23,457
Trade receivables	9,045	
Cash at bank	182	
8% bank loan repayable 2013		5,000
Share capital		10,000
Share premium		5,000
Trade payables		2,481
	122,182	122,182

The following further information is available:

(i)   The share capital of the company consists of ordinary shares with a nominal value of £1 each.
(ii) No dividends are to be paid for the current year.
(iii) The sales figure in the trial balance includes the sales made on credit for April 2010 amounting to £3,147,000.
(iv) The inventories at the close of business on 31 March 2010 cost £8,407,000. Included in this figure are inventories that cost £480,000, but which can be sold for only £180,000.
(v)   Transport costs of £157,000 relating to March 2010 are not included in the trial balance as the invoice was received after the year end.

(vi) Interest on the bank loan for the last six months of the year has not been included in the trial balance.

(vii) The corporation tax charge for the year has been calculated as £235,000.

Draft the statement of comprehensive income of Tanhosier Ltd for the year to 31 March 2010 and a statement of financial position at that date. *(Amended from AAT)*

5 List the main types of information which should be provided in the notes which accompany and form an integral part of the financial statements.

6 The following trial balance has been extracted from the books of Walrus plc as at 31 March 2010:

	£000	£000
Land, at cost	120	
Buildings, at cost	250	
Equipment, at cost	196	
Vehicles, at cost	284	
Goodwill, at cost	300	
Accumulated depreciation at 1 April 2009:		
Buildings		90
Equipment		76
Vehicles		132
Inventory at 1 April 2009	107	
Trade receivables and payables	183	117
Allowance for receivables		8
Bank balance		57
Corporation tax		6
Ordinary shares of £1 each		200
Retained earnings at 1 April 2009		503
Sales		1,432
Purchases	488	
Directors' fees	150	
Wages and salaries	276	
General distribution costs	101	
General administrative expenses	186	
Dividend paid	20	
Rents received		30
Disposal of vehicle		10
	2,661	2,661

The following information is also available:

1 The company's non-depreciable land was valued at £300,000 on 31 March 2010 and this valuation is to be incorporated into the accounts for the year to 31 March 2010.

2 The company's depreciation policy is as follows:

Buildings 4% p.a. straight line
Equipment 40% p.a. reducing balance
Vehicles 25% p.a. straight line

In all cases, a full year's depreciation is charged in the year of acquisition and no depreciation is charged in the year of disposal. None of the assets had been fully depreciated by 31 March 2009.

On 1 February 2010, a vehicle used entirely for administrative purposes was sold for £10,000. The sale proceeds were banked and credited to a disposal account but no other entries were made in relation to this disposal. The vehicle had cost £44,000 in August 2006. This was the only disposal of a non-current asset made during the year to 31 March 2010.

3 Depreciation is apportioned as follows:

	Distribution costs	Administrative expenses
Buildings	50%	50%
Equipment	25%	75%
Vehicles	70%	30%

4 The company's inventory at 31 March 2010 is valued at £119,000.

5 Trade receivables include a debt of £8,000 which is to be written off. The allowance for receivables is to be adjusted to 4% of the receivables which remain after this debt has been written off.

6 Corporation tax for the year to 31 March 2009 was over-estimated by £6,000. The corporation tax liability for the year to 31 March 2010 is estimated to be £30,000.

7 One-quarter of wages and salaries were paid to distribution staff and the remaining three-quarters were paid to administrative staff.

8 General administrative expenses include bank overdraft interest of £9,000.

9 A dividend of 10p per ordinary share was paid on 31 December 2009. No further dividends are proposed for the year to 31 March 2010.

Required:

Prepare the following financial statements for Walrus plc in accordance with the requirements of international standards:

(a) a statement of comprehensive income for the year to 31 March 2010

(b) a statement of financial position as at 31 March 2010

(c) a statement of changes in equity for the year to 31 March 2010.   *(CIPFA)*

7 Chilwell Ltd prepares financial statements to 31 October each year. The company's trial balance at 31 October 2010 is as follows:

	£	£
Land at valuation	250,000	
Buildings at cost	300,000	
Equipment and motor vehicles at cost	197,400	
Allowances for depreciation at 1 November 2009:		
Buildings		60,000
Equipment and motor vehicles		105,750
Disposal of vehicle		18,000
Inventory at 1 November 2009	87,520	
Trade receivables and payables	71,500	103,290
Allowance for doubtful receivables at 1 November 2009		1,520
Bank balance		10,390
Taxation	8,400	
9% Loan stock (repayable 2014)		120,000
Purchases and sales	483,230	1,025,420
Returns inwards and outwards	27,110	12,570
Directors' fees	50,000	
Wages and salaries	102,400	
General administrative expenses	143,440	
General distribution costs	107,050	
Royalties received		10,270
Interest paid	6,220	
Dividends paid	35,000	
Ordinary shares of £1		80,000
Revaluation reserve		75,000
Retained earnings at 1 November 2009		247,060
	1,869,270	1,869,270

The following information is also available:

1 Land is non-depreciable and is to be revalued at £280,000 on 31 October 2010.

2 The buildings were acquired on 1 November 1999. At that time, their useful life was estimated to be 50 years and it was decided to adopt the straight-line method of depreciation, assuming no residual value. On 1 November 2009, it was determined that the useful life of the buildings would end on 31 October 2039. The estimate of residual value remains unchanged.

3 Equipment and vehicles are depreciated at 25% per annum on the reducing balance basis. A full year's depreciation is charged in the year of acquisition. No depreciation is charged in the year of disposal. In June 2010, a distribution vehicle which had cost £64,000 in February 2006 was sold for £18,000. This amount was debited to the bank account and credited to a disposal account, but no further entries have yet been made with regard to this disposal.

4 Depreciation of buildings should be split 70:30 between administrative expenses and distribution costs. Depreciation of equipment and vehicles should be split 40:60 between administrative expenses and distribution costs.

5 The cost of inventory at 31 October 2010 is £92,280.

6 Trade receivables include bad debts of £2,000 which should be written off. The allowance for doubtful receivables should then be adjusted to 2% of the remaining trade receivables.

7 The company's tax liability for the year to 31 October 2009 was underestimated by £8,400. The liability for the year to 31 October 2010 is estimated to be £20,000 and falls due on 1 August 2011.

8 The loan stock was issued on 1 January 2010. Interest is payable half-yearly on 30 June and 31 December. The interest due on 30 June 2010 was paid on the due date. Accrued interest at 31 October 2010 has not yet been accounted for.

9 Directors' fees are to be treated as administrative expenses. Wages and salaries should be split 50:50 between administrative expenses and distribution costs.

10 A 1 for 2 bonus issue of ordinary shares was made on 1 July 2010, financed out of retained earnings. No entries have yet been made in relation to this issue.

Required:

Prepare the following financial statements for Chilwell Ltd in accordance with the requirements of international standards:

(a) a statement of comprehensive income for the year to 31 October 2010

(b) a statement of changes in equity for the year to 31 October 2010

(c) a statement of financial position as at 31 October 2010.

Formal notes to the accounts are not required, but all workings should be shown.

(CIPFA)

Interpretation of accounts

Two years too old

'Insolvencies are not our fault,' says Euler chief

David Jetuah

The CEO of Britain's biggest credit insurer has dismissed accusations that companies have been driven into administration by the withdrawal of cover from suppliers, and warned that businesses can no longer rely on statutory accounts for their credit ratings.

Fabrice Desnos, CEO of Euler Hermes UK, said: 'it's got nothing to do with us. If anything, it proves how difficult it is to analyse credit risk based on statutory accounts, because some statements in the public domain are not as strong as they first look.

'Historical accounts are getting too old to be meaningful. In a time of crisis, you can't rely on performance figures on a period two years in the past.'

Desnos's remarks follow claims that companies would be forced out of business because insurers were beginning to withdraw trade credit insurance if management accounts were not made available instead of statutory accounts lodged with Companies House.

Desnos said he was not unsympathetic to the plight of companies in the current climate, and the most timely set of figures could only help companies secure cover,

'Not disclosing information to the credit insurer means you don't think your suppliers need to know uptodate information about the company.'

He added: 'Companies have to realise that when they are sharing this information with the credit insurer they are sharing it confidentially.'

Source: *Accountancy Age*, 7 May 2009.

Source: Reproduced with permission from Incisive Media Ltd.

Introduction

In this section we cover what accountants call the 'interpretation of accounts'. In essence, all that this means is that you dig behind the figures shown in the financial statements in order to make more sense of them and to put them into context. You will often see, for example, a newspaper screaming in large headlines that Company X has made a profit of (say) £50 million. In absolute terms £50 million is certainly a lot of money but what does it mean? Is it a lot compared with what it took to make it? Is it a lot compared with other similar companies? How does it compare with previous years? And is it up to expectations?

These questions cannot always be answered directly from the financial statements themselves. The figures may have to be reworked and then compared with other similar data. So interpreting accounts is a type of detective work: you look for the evidence, you analyse it and then you give your verdict.

This section explains how you do the detective work. There are various ways of going about it but we will be concentrating on *ratio analysis*. This is one of the most common methods used in interpreting accounts and we shall be spending a lot of time on it.

Why this section is important

For non-accountants this section is one of the most important in the book. In your professional life you could rely entirely on your accountants to present you with any financial information that *they* think you might find useful. In time and with some experience you might understand most of it. The danger is that you might take the figures at their face value, just as you might when you read an eye-catching newspaper headline.

You could be misled by such headlines and then take what might turn out to be a most unwise decision, e.g. buying or selling shares or perhaps even making a takeover bid for a company! For example, an alleged £15 billion profit might be a record but how can we be certain that it is significant? The short answer is that we can't unless we relate it to something else, such as what sum of money it took to earn that profit or what profit other similar companies have made.

Accountants refer to the explanation process as the *interpretation of accounts*. After working your way through the section you too will be able to interpret a set of accounts so that when you read a story in the newspaper or you come across some financial statements you can make much more sense of the information and you can put it into context, i.e. compare it with something meaningful. This is sometimes referred to as 'reading between the lines of the balance sheet'. We hope that by the end of the section you too can read between these lines, and for that matter between the lines of all the other financial statements as well. Such a skill is vital if you are to become a *really* effective manager.

Nature and purpose

News clip

Distortion fear

The recession has increased pressure to distort earnings figures. According to a survey of 1000 internal auditors from 25 countries, 86% of them believe that there is now a greater risk of 'inappropriate earnings management and other misconduct'.

Source: Adapted from www.accountancyage.com/news, 9 July 2009.

In the following part of this section we explain what accountants mean when they talk about interpreting a set of accounts, why such an exercise is necessary and who might have need of it.

Definition

The verb 'to interpret' has several different meanings. Perhaps the most common is 'to convert' or 'to translate' the spoken word of one language into another, but it also has other meanings such as 'to construe', 'to define' or 'to explain'. We will use the latter meaning. Our definition of what we mean by the *interpretation of accounts* may then be expressed as follows:

> A detailed explanation of the financial performance of an entity incorporating data and other quantitative and qualitative information extracted from both internal and external sources.

Limited information

By this stage of your accounting studies you will no doubt have realized that the amount of information contained in a set of accounts prepared for *internal* purposes is considerable. Even published accounts can be quite detailed. The 2008 annual report and accounts of Cairn Energy plc, for example, an oil and gas exploration and production company, covers 136 pages. You would think that accounts of this length would provide you with all the information that you would ever want to know about the company but unfortunately this is not necessarily the case. There are three main reasons why this may not be so.

- *Structural*. Financial accounts are prepared on the basis of a series of accounting rules. Even financial accounts prepared for internal purposes contain a restricted amount of information and this is especially the case with published accounts. Only information that can be translated easily into quantitative financial terms is usually included, and also some highly arbitrary assessments have to be made about the treatment of certain matters such as stock valuation, depreciation and bad debts. Furthermore financial accounts are also usually prepared on a historical basis so they may be out-of-date by the time that they become available, the details may relate at best to one or two accounting periods and probably no allowance will have been made for inflation.
- *Absolute*. The monetary figures are presented almost solely in absolute terms. For example, Cairn's revenue for 2008 was $299.3 million and its profit before tax was $440.9 million. So how, you might ask, can the profit be higher than the sales revenue? Exactly. This is a good example of why we need to dig behind the figures; it's why we need to *interpret* them.
- *Contextual*. Even if you could grasp the size and significance of what sales of $300 million and profits of $440 million meant, in isolation they do not tell us very much. In order to make them more meaningful they need to be put in context perhaps by comparing them with previous years' results or with companies in the same industry.

Users

Company law concentrates almost exclusively on shareholders but there are many other user groups. We reproduce the seven main user groups in Table 2.16.

Table 2.16 Users of financial accounts and their questions

User group	Questions asked
Customers	How do its prices compare with its competitors?
Employees	Has it enough money to pay my wages?
Governments and their agencies	Can the company pay its taxes?
Investors	What's the dividend like?
Lenders	Will I get my interest paid?
Public	Is the company likely to stay in business?
Suppliers and other creditors	Will we get paid what we are owed?

Beside each group we have posed a question that a user in each particular group may well ask.

The questions in Table 2.16 cannot always be answered directly from the financial statements. For example, investors asking the question 'What's the dividend like?' will find that the annual report and accounts gives them the dividend per share for the current and the previous year in *absolute* amounts. Somewhere within the annual report and accounts the percentage increase may be given but that still does not really answer the question. Investors will probably want to know how their dividend relates to what they have invested in the company (what accountants call the 'yield'). As most investors probably paid different amounts for their shares it would be impossible to show each individual shareholder's yield in the annual account, so investors have to calculate it for themselves.

Activity 2.30

Taking the seven user groups listed in Table 2.16, what other questions do you think that each user group would ask? List each user group and all the questions that you think each would ask. Then insert:

(a) where the basic information could be found in the annual report and accounts to answer each question; and

(b) what additional information would be required to answer each question fully.

Procedure

In this next part of the section we outline the basic procedure involved in interpreting a set of accounts. The scale and nature of your investigation will clearly depend on its purpose so we can only point you in the right direction. For example, if you were working for a large international company proposing to take over a foreign company, you would need a vast amount of information and it might take months before you had completed your investigation. By contrast, if you were a private individual proposing to invest £1000 in Tesco plc, you might just spend part of Saturday morning reading what the city editor of your favourite newspaper had to say about the company (although we would recommend you to do much more than that).

In essence an exercise involving the interpretation of accounts involves four main stages:

- collecting the information;
- analysing it;
- interpreting it;
- reporting the findings.

Collecting the information

This stage involves you first conducting a fairly general review of the international economic, financial, political and social climate and a more specific one of the *country* in which the entity operates. In broad terms, you are looking to see whether it is politically and socially stable with excellent prospects for sound and continuing economic growth. Then you should look at the particular *industry* in which it operates. Ask yourself the following questions.

- Is the government supportive of the industry?
- Is there an expanding market for its products?
- Is there sufficient land and space available for development?
- Is there a reliable infrastructure, e.g. utility supplies and a transport network?
- Are there grants and loans available for developing enterprises?
- Is there an available and trained labour force near by?

Once you have got all this macro and micro information you will need to obtain as much information about the *entity* as you can get. This will involve finding out about its history, structure, management, operations, products, markets, labour record and financial performance. These days you should be able to obtain much of this information from the Internet but don't forget about old-fashioned sources such as the company's interim and annual reports and accounts, press releases, trade circulars and analysts' reviews.

By the end of this early stage of your investigation you will probably already have a 'feel' or a strong impression about the entity but your work is not yet over. Indeed, there is still a great deal more work to do.

Analysing the information

Analysing the information involves putting together all the information you have collected and making sense of it. In this chapter as we are primarily concerned with the accounting aspects of business so we will concentrate on how you can begin to make sense of the *financial* information that you have collected.

The main source of such information will normally be the entity's annual report and accounts. In order to make our explanation easier to follow we will assume that we are dealing primarily with public limited liability companies (although you will find that much of what we have to say is relevant when dealing with other types of entities).

There are four main techniques that you can use in interpreting a set of financial statements: horizontal analysis, trend analysis, vertical analysis and ratio analysis.

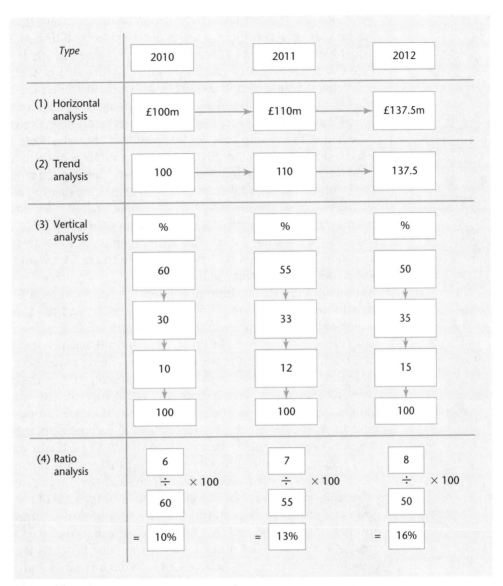

Figure 2.25 Interpreting accounts: main analytical techniques

Figure 2.25 depicts a diagrammatic representation of these different types of analyses. A brief description of each one is outlined below.

1 *Horizontal analysis.* This technique involves making a line-by-line comparison of the company's accounts for each accounting period chosen for the investigation. You may have noted, for example, that the sales for the year 2010 were £100m, £110m in 2011 and £137.5m in 2012 and so on. This type of comparison across a row of figures is something that we do naturally but such a casual observation is not very effective when we are faced with a great many detailed figures. In order to grasp what they mean, at the very least we would need to calculate the changes from one year to the next. Even then their significance might still be hard to take in. So we would probably have to calculate the *percentage* increases year-by-year (10% for 2011 and 25% in 2012 in the above example) and this could involve an awful lot of work with a pen, paper and a calculator, or preferably a spreadsheet.

2 *Trend analysis.* This is similar to horizontal analysis except that all the figures in the first set of accounts in a series are given a base line of 100 and the subsequent sets of accounts are converted to that base line. So if the sales for 2010 were £50m, £70 for 2011 and £85m for 2012, the sales of £50m for 2010 would be given a base line of 100; the 2011 sales would then become 140 (70 × 100/50) and the 2012 sales 170 (85 × 100/50). This method enables us to grasp much more easily the changes in the absolute costs and values shown in the financial statements. For example, if we told you that the sales were £202,956,000 for 2011 and £210,161,000 in 2012 it is not too difficult to calculate that they have gone up by about £7m but the figures are still too big for most of us to absorb. The changes that have taken place would be much easier to take in if they are all related to a base line of 100. In this example, the sales for 2011 would then be given a value of 100, with 103 (210,161 × 100/202,956) for 2012, an increase of about 3% (it's actually 3.6%). The figures then begin to mean something because by converting in this way they relate more to our experience of money terms and values in our everyday life.

3 *Vertical analysis.* This technique requires the figures in each financial statement (usually restricted to the profit and loss account and the balance sheet) to be expressed as a percentage of the total amount. For example, assume that a company's trade debtors were £10m in 2011 and the balance sheet total was £50m; in 2012 the trade debtors were £12m and the balance sheet total was £46m. Trade debtors would then be shown as representing 20% of the balance sheet total (10 × 100/50) in 2011 and 26% in 2012 (12 × 100/46). This would be considered quite a large increase so the reasons for it would need to be investigated. The modern practice of using lots of sectionalized accounts and subtotals means that it is not always easy to decide what *is* the total of a particular financial statement. If you come across this difficulty we suggest that you use the sales revenue figure for the total of the profit and loss account and the total of net assets (or shareholders' funds, it should be the same figure!) for the total of the balance sheet.

4 *Ratio analysis.* A ratio is simply the division of one arithmetical amount by another arithmetical amount expressed as a percentage or as a factor. Ratio analysis is a most useful means of comparing one figure with another because it expresses the relationship between lots of amounts easily and simply. If the cost of sales for 2011 was £12m, for example, and the sales revenue was £20m, we would express the relationship as 60% (12 × 100/20) sales or 0.6 to 1 (12/20). Ratio analysis is such an important technique in the interpretation of accounts that we will be dealing with it in some detail a little later in the section.

Activity 2.31

State whether the following assertions are true or false:

(a) Ratio analysis is only one form of analysis that can be used in interpreting accounts. *True/false*

(b) Ratio analysis aims to put the financial results of an entity into perspective. *True/false*

(c) Ratio analysis helps to establish whether or not an entity is a going concern. *True/false*

Interpreting the information

This is the third stage in a broad interpretative exercise. By this stage of your investigation you would have collected a great deal of information about the company you are investigating and you would have put that information into context by subjecting it to a whole battery of analyses. Now you have to use all the information that you have before you to interpret or to *explain* what has happened. Some of the questions you might ask yourself include the following.

- What does it tell me about the company's performance?
- Has the company done well compared with other financial periods?
- How does it compare with other companies in the same sector of the economy?
- Are the world economic, political and social circumstances favourable to trade generally?
- What are they like for this company's industry?
- What are the prospects for the region in which this company does its business?

Asking and answering such questions might seem a formidable task but like anything else, the more practice you get, the easier it becomes. In any case, by this time your initial research and your various analyses will have given you a strong indication about the company's progress and its future prospects. You will have realized that there are a number of obvious strengths and weaknesses and a variety of positive and negative factors and trends.

When you have come to a conclusion based on the evidence and the analysis that you have framed, you have one further task: report it to whoever asked you to do the study in the first place.

Reporting the findings

In most interpretive exercises of the type described in this section you will probably have to write a written report. Many people are fearful of having to commit themselves to paper and they find this part of the exercise very difficult. However, having to write something down helps you to think more clearly and logically. It may also throw up gaps in your argument, so regard this part of the exercise as more of an opportunity than a threat.

The format of your report will depend on its purpose but basically it should be broken down into three main sections. Your first section should be an *introduction* in which you outline the nature and purpose of your report including a brief outline of its structure. The second part should contain your *discussion* section in which you present your evidence and your assessment of what the evidence means. In the third *concluding* section summarize briefly the entire study, list your conclusions and state your recommendations.

In the next part of this section we consider in much more detail one of the analytical techniques mentioned earlier in the chapter: *ratio analysis*.

Ratio analysis

We are now going to spend the rest of this section dealing with ratio analysis in some detail. Before we begin you should note the following points.

- There are literally hundreds of ratios that we could produce but most accountants have just a few favourites.
- Always check the definition of a particular ratio you come across because while the name may be familiar to you, the definition could be different from the one that you use.
- There is no standard system for grouping ratios into representative categories.
- Strictly limit the number of ratios you adopt. If you use 20 different types of ratio, for example, and you are covering a five-year period, you have 100 ratios to calculate *and* to incorporate in your analysis. That's a lot to handle!

In this section we are going to limit the number of accounting ratios that we cover to just 15. In order to simplify our discussion, we will also group them into four broad categories (although there is some overlap between them):

- liquidity ratios;
- profitability ratios;
- efficiency ratios;
- investment ratios.

A diagrammatic representation of this classification and the names of the ratios included in each grouping are shown in Figure 2.26.

We start our detailed study with what we call *liquidity* ratios.

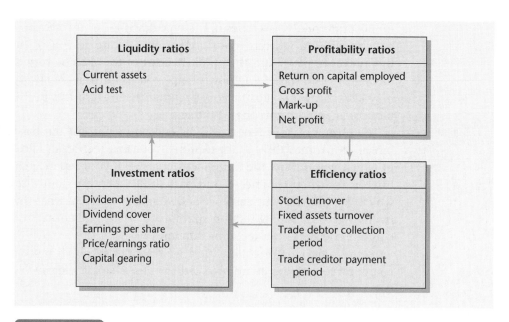

Figure 2.26   Accounting ratios: classification

Liquidity ratios

Insolvencies soar

Liquidations went up by 56% in the first quarter of 2009 compared with the same period in 2008. The recession is blamed as backers of companies do not want to throw more good money after bad. As a result companies are experiencing some severe liquidity problems.

Source: Adapted from www.accountancyage.com/articles/print/2241538, 1 May 2009.

Liquidity ratios measure the extent to which assets can be turned into cash quickly. In other words, they try to assess how much cash the entity has available in the short term (this usually means within the next twelve months). For example, it is easy to extract the total amount of trade debtors and trade creditors from the balance sheet, but are they too high? We cannot really tell until we put them into context. We can do this by calculating two liquidity ratios known as the *current assets ratio* and the *acid test ratio*.

Current assets ratio

The *current assets ratio* is calculated as follows:

$$\frac{\textbf{current assets}}{\textbf{current liabilities}}$$

It is usually expressed as a factor, e.g. 3 to 1, or 3 : 1 although you will sometimes see it expressed as a percentage (300% in our example, i.e. $\frac{3}{1} \times 100$).

The term 'current' means receivable or payable within the next twelve months. The entity may not always have to settle all of its current liabilities within the next week or even the next month. Be careful before you assume that a factor of (say) 1 : 2 suggests that the company will be going into immediate liquidation. Some creditors, such as tax and dividends, may not have to be paid for several weeks. In the meantime, the company may receive regular receipts of cash from its debtors and it may be able to balance these against what it has to pay to its creditors. In other instances, some entities (such as supermarkets) may have a lot of cash trade, and it is possible that they then may have a current assets ratio of less than 2 : 1. This is not likely to be a problem for them because they are probably collecting sufficient amounts of cash daily through the checkouts. In some cases, however, a current assets ratio of less than 2 : 1 may signify a serious financial position, especially if the current assets consist of a very high proportion of stocks. This leads us on to the second liquidity ratio, the *acid test ratio*.

Acid test ratio

It may not be easy to dispose of stocks in the short term as they cannot always be quickly turned into cash. In any case, the entity would then be depriving itself of those very assets that enable it to make a trading profit. It seems sensible, therefore, to see what would happen to the current ratio if stocks were not included in the definition of current assets. This ratio is called the acid test (or quick) ratio. It is calculated as follows:

$$\frac{\text{current assets} - \text{stocks}}{\text{current liabilities}}$$

Like the current ratio, the acid test ratio is usually expressed as a factor (or occasionally as a percentage). It is probably a better measure of an entity's immediate liquidity position than the current assets ratio because it may be difficult to dispose of the stocks in the short term. Do not assume, however, that if current assets less stocks are less than current liabilities, the entity's cash position is vulnerable. As we explained above, some of the current liabilities may not be due for payment for some months. Some textbooks suggest that the acid test ratio must be at least 1 : 1, but again there is no evidence to support this assertion so use it only as a guide.

Activity 2.32

Fill in the blanks in the following equations.

(a) $\dfrac{\text{Current assets}}{\text{Current liabilities}} = \dfrac{£65\,500}{\underline{\quad\quad}} = 1.60$

(b) $\dfrac{\text{Current assets} - \underline{\qquad\qquad}}{\text{Current liabilities}}$

Profitability ratios

News clip

Spotting trouble

A number of UK firms are running summer schools in order to help junior auditors spot companies facing financial difficulties. They will be trained to look for unrealistic cash flow forecasts and other forecasts as well as covenant and financing arrangements that might cause problems.

Source: Adapted from www.accountancyage.com/2223899, 14 August 2008.

Users of accounts will want to know how much profit a business has made, and then to compare it with previous periods or with other entities. The absolute level of accounting profit will not be of much help, because it needs to be related to the size of the entity and how much capital it has invested in it. There are four main profitability ratios. We examine each of them below.

Return on capital employed ratio

The best way of assessing profitability is to calculate a ratio known as the *return on capital employed* (ROCE) ratio. It can be expressed quite simply as

$$\frac{\text{profit}}{\text{capital}} \times 100$$

This ratio is usually expressed as a percentage and it is one of the most important. Even so, there is no common agreement about how it should be calculated. The problem is that both 'profit' and 'capital' can be defined in several different ways. As a result, a variety of ROCE ratios can be produced merely by changing the definitions of either profit or capital. For our purposes you need to be aware of only four definitions of ROCE. They are as follows.

(1) $$\frac{\text{net profit before taxation}}{\text{shareholders' funds}} \times 100$$

This definition measures the pre-tax profit against what the shareholders have invested in the entity. Use it if you want to know how profitable the entity has been as a whole.

(2) $$\frac{\text{net profit after taxation}}{\text{shareholders' funds}} \times 100$$

This definition is similar to the previous one except that it measures post-tax profit against the shareholders' investment in the company. Taxation is normally regarded as an *appropriation* of profit and not as an expense. The tax payable will be based on the profit for the year and a company has no option other than to pay it. The distinction between tax as an appropriation and tax as a profit is blurred, and some accountants prefer to use this definition as a measure of overall profitability. However, bear in mind that the taxation charge in the accounts can be subject to various accounting adjustments so you would have to be careful using this definition in comparing one company with another company.

(3) $$\frac{\text{net profit after taxation and preference dividends}}{\text{shareholders' funds – preference dividends}} \times 100$$

This definition should be used if you want to assess how profitable the company has been from an *ordinary* shareholder's point of view. It measures how much profit could be distributed to ordinary shareholders as a proportion of what they have invested in the business.

(4) $$\frac{\text{profit before taxation and interest}}{\text{shareholders' funds + long-terms loans}} \times 100$$

This definition measures what profit has been earned in relation to what has been used to *finance* the entity in total. Interest is a cost of borrowing money so it is added back to the profit made. Similarly long-term loans are added to the shareholders' funds because that gives us the *total* financial investment in the entity. Use this definition if you want to know how profitable the entity has been in relation to what it has taken to finance it.

The above definitions use the closing shareholders' funds but sometimes a simple average, is adoped, e.g. (opening + closing shareholders funds) ÷ 2.

Activity 2.33

There are many other ways of calculating ROCE other than the four listed above. Divide a page into two broad columns. In the left-hand column list all the various levels of profit that you would find in a published profit and loss account (e.g. operating profit). In the right-hand column list all the various levels or types of capital shown in a published balance sheet (e.g. total assets). Then try to relate each definition of profit to a compatible definition of capital.

Remember that what you are trying to do is to find how much profit (however defined) has been earned for the particular level or type of capital invested. So the numerator (profit) has got to be compatible with the denominator (the capital employed).

Gross profit ratio

The *gross profit ratio* enables us to judge how successful the entity has been at trading. It is calculated as follows:

$$\frac{\text{gross profit}}{\text{sales}} \times 100$$

The gross profit ratio measures how much profit the entity has earned in relation to the amount of sales that it has made. The definition of gross profit does not usually cause any problems. Most entities adopt the definition we have used in this book, namely sales less the cost of goods sold [the cost of sales being (opening stock + purchase) − closing stock] and so meaningful comparisons can usually be made between different entities. However, if you are using published accounts, sales may be described as 'turnover' and the cost of sales may well include production costs (which are not usually disclosed). Be wary, therefore, if you are using publishing accounts to make comparisons between different companies.

Mark-up ratio

The gross profit ratio complements another main trading ratio, which we will refer to, for convenience, as the *mark-up ratio*. This is calculated as follows:

$$\frac{\text{gross profit}}{\text{cost of goods sold}} \times 100$$

Mark-up ratios measure the amount of profit added to the cost of goods sold. The cost of goods sold plus profit equals the sales revenue. The mark-up may be reduced to stimulate extra sales activity, but this will have the effect of reducing the gross profit. However, if extra goods are sold there may be a greater volume of sales and this will help to compensate for the reduction in the mark-up on each unit.

Net profit ratio

Owners sometimes like to compare their net profit with the sales revenue. This can be expressed in the form of the *net profit ratio*. It is calculated as follows:

$$\frac{\text{net profit before taxation}}{\text{sales}} \times 100$$

It is difficult to compare the net profit ratio for different entities fairly. Individual operating and financing arrangements vary so much that entities are bound to have different levels of expenditure no matter how efficient one entity is compared with another. So it may only be realistic to use the net profit ratio in making *internal* comparisons. Over a period of time a pattern may emerge and it might then be possible to establish a trend. If you use the net profit ratio to make intercompany comparisons, make sure you allow for different circumstances.

In published accounts you might also want to substitute 'operating profit' or 'profit on ordinary activities before tax' for net profit.

Efficiency ratios

News clip

Late payment problems

Three in five businesses are being affected by late payments according to a survey done by Tenon Recovery. Its national head said that cash flow is fundamental to business survival and late payments are part of it. He argued that businesses must adopt a responsible attitude to avoid the domino effect of businesses collapsing. They should also have clear payment terms, credit control procedures, chase slow-paying customers and make their own payments on time.

Source: Adapted from www.accountancyage.com/articles/print2240410, 15 April 2009.

Traditional accounting statements do not tell us how *efficiently* an entity has been managed, i.e. how well its resources have been looked after. Accounting profit may, to some extent, be used as a measure of efficiency. However, it is subject to a great many arbitrary adjustments and in this context it can be misleading. What we need to do is to make comparisons between different periods and with other similar companies.

There are very many different types of ratios that we can use to measure the efficiency of a company, but here we will cover only the more common ones.

Stock turnover ratio

The stock turnover ratio may be calculated as follows:

$$\frac{\text{cost of goods sold}}{\text{closing stock}}$$

The stock turnover ratio is normally expressed as a number (e.g. 5 or 10 times) and not as a percentage.

Instead of using the cost of goods sold, sometimes it is necessary to substitute sales revenue. This should be avoided if at all possible as the sales revenue will include a profit loading. As this may be subject to change, the stock turnover will become distorted so making it difficult to make meaningful comparisons.

As far as the closing stock is concerned some accountants prefer to use an average, often a simple average, i.e. opening stock + closing stock/2, especially if trade is seasonal or the year end falls during a quiet period.

The greater the turnover of stock, the more efficient the entity would appear to be in purchasing and selling goods. A stock turnover of 2 times, for example, would suggest that the entity has about six months of sales in stock. In most circumstances this would appear to be a high relative volume, whereas a stock turnover of (say) 12 times would mean that the entity had only a month's normal sales in stock.

Fixed assets turnover ratio

Another important area to examine, from the point of view of efficiency, relates to fixed assets. Fixed assets (such as plant and machinery) enable the business to function more efficiently, and so a high level of fixed assets ought to generate more sales. We can check this by calculating a ratio known as the fixed asset turnover ratio. This may be done as follows:

$$\frac{\text{sales}}{\text{fixed assets at net book value}}$$

The more times that the fixed assets are covered by the sales revenue, the greater the recovery of the investment in fixed assets. The fixed assets turnover ratio may also be expressed as a percentage.

This ratio is really only useful if it is compared with previous periods or with other companies. In isolation it does not mean very much. For example, is a turnover of 5 good and one of 4 poor? All we can suggest is that if the trend is upwards, then the investment in fixed assets is beginning to pay off, at least in terms of increased sales. Note also that the ratio can be strongly affected by the company's depreciation policies. There is a strong argument, therefore, for taking the *gross* book value of the fixed assets and not the *net* book value.

Activity 2.34

A company has a turnover of £4,000,000 for the year to 31 December 2012. At that date the gross book value of its fixed assets was £22,000 and the net book value £12,000. When measuring the efficiency with which its uses its fixed assets, is it more meaningful to use the gross book value in relation to turnover or the net book value? Give your reasons.

Gross book value ☐   Net book value ☐

Reason: _____

Trade debtor collection period ratio

Investing in fixed assets is all very well but there is not much point in generating extra sales if the customers do not pay for them. Customers might be encouraged to buy more by a combination of lower selling prices and generous credit terms. If the debtors are slow at paying, the entity might find that it has run into cash flow problems. So it is important for it to watch the trade debtor position very carefully. We can check how successful it has been by calculating the *trade debtor collection period*. The ratio may be calculated as follows:

$$\frac{\textbf{closing trade debtors}}{\textbf{credit sales}} \times \textbf{365}$$

The average trade debtors term is sometimes used instead of the closing trade debtors, i.e. $\frac{1}{2}$ (opening trade debtors + closing trade debtors).

It is important to relate trade debtors to *credit* sales if at all possible and so cash sales should be excluded from the calculation. The method shown above for calculating the ratio would relate the closing trade debtors to *x* days' sales, but it would be possible to substitute weeks or months for days. It is not customary to express the ratio as a percentage.

An acceptable debtor collection period cannot be suggested as much depends on the type of trade in which the entity is engaged. Some entities expect settlement within 28 days of delivery of the goods or on immediate receipt of the invoice. Other entities might expect settlement within 28 days following the end of the month in which the goods were delivered. On average this adds another 14 days (half a month) to the overall period of 28 days. If this is the case, a company would appear to be highly efficient in collecting its debts if the average debtor collection period was about 42 days. The United Kingdom experience is that the *median* debtor collection period is about 50 days.

Like most of the other ratios, it is important to establish a trend. If the trend is upwards, then it might suggest that the company's credit control procedures have begun to weaken.

Activity 2.35

A company's sales for 2012 were £4452 million and its trade debtors for that year were £394 million. Assuming that all the sales were made on credit terms, do you think that its debtor collection was efficient?

Yes ☐   No ☐

Reason: _____

Trade creditor payment period

A similar ratio can be calculated for the trade creditor payment period. The formula is as follows:

$$\frac{\text{closing trade creditors}}{\text{total credit purchases}} \times 365$$

Average trade creditors may be substituted for the closing trade creditors like the trade debtor collection period ratio and this may be a simple average (opening trade debtors + closing trade debtors/2) or a more complex one. The trade creditors should be related to credit purchases (although this information will often not be available), and weeks or months may be substituted for the number of days. Again, like the trade debtor collection period, it is not usual to express this ratio as a percentage.

In published accounts you might have to calculate the purchases figure for yourself. The accounts should disclose the opening and closing stock figures and the cost of sales. By substituting them in the equation [(opening stock + purchases) – closing stock = cost of sales] you can calculate the purchases. Other expenses may have been included in the cost of sales but unless these have been disclosed you will just have to accept the cost of sales figure shown in the accounts.

An upward trend in the average level of trade creditors would suggest that the entity is having some difficulty in finding the cash to pay its creditors. Indeed, it might be a sign that it is running into financial difficulties.

Investment ratios

News clip

Football clubs face financial meltdown

According to *The Observer* British football clubs face financial meltdown as a result of excessive debt and massive wages paid to players. The paper reports that there will be some insolvencies since in the summer clubs do not earn much income while they have the same overhead expenditure. Those clubs that are highly geared both financially and operationally face particular difficulties as season ticket sales, sponsorship earnings and corporate box deals all begin to drop.

Source: Adapted from *The Observer*, 5 April 2009, p. 6 Business.

The various ratios examined previously are probably of interest to all users of accounts, such as creditors, employees and managers, as well as to shareholders. There are some other ratios that are primarily (although not exclusively) of interest to prospective investors. These are known as *investment ratios*.

Dividend yield

The first investment ratio that you might find useful is the *dividend yield*. It usually applies to ordinary shareholders and it may be calculated as follows:

$$\frac{\text{dividend per share}}{\text{market price per share}} \times 100$$

The dividend yield measures the rate of return that an investor gets by comparing the cost of his shares with the dividend receivable (or paid). For example, if an investor buys 100 £1 ordinary shares at a market rate of 200p per share, and the dividend was 10p per share, the yield would be 5 per cent (10/200 × 100). While he may have invested £200 (100 × £2 per share), as far as the company is concerned he will be registered as holding 100 shares at a nominal value of £1 each (100 shares × £1). He would be entitled to a dividend of £10 (10p × 100 shares) but from his point of view he will only be getting a return of 5 per cent, i.e. £10 for his £200 invested.

Dividend cover

Another useful investment ratio is called *dividend cover*. It is calculated as follows:

$$\frac{\text{net profit} - \text{taxation} - \text{preference dividend}}{\text{ordinary dividends}}$$

This ratio shows the number of times that the ordinary dividend could be paid out of current earnings. The dividend is usually described as being *x* times covered by the earnings. So if the dividend is covered twice, the company would be paying out half of its earnings as an ordinary dividend.

Earnings per share

Another important investment ratio is that known as *earnings per share* (EPS). This ratio enables us to put the profit into context and to avoid looking at it in simple absolute terms. It is usually looked at from the ordinary shareholder's point of view. The following formula is used to calculate what is called the *basic* earnings per share:

$$\frac{\text{net profit} - \text{preference shares}}{\text{number of ordinary shares}}$$

In published accounts you will sometimes see other definitions of the EPS. The calculations involved in obtaining them are often highly complex. We recommend you to stick to the above definition, i.e. basically, net profit less preference dividends divided by the number of ordinary shares.

EPS enables a fair comparison to be made between one year's earnings and another by relating the earnings to something tangible, i.e. the number of shares in issue.

Price to earnings ratio

Another common investment ratio is the *price to earnings ratio* (P/E). It is calculated as follows:

$$\frac{\text{market price per share}}{\text{earnings per share}}$$

The P/E ratio enables a comparison to be made between the earnings per share (as defined above) and the market price. It tells us that the market price is x times the earnings. It means that it would take x years before we recovered the market price paid for the shares out of the earnings (assuming that they remained at that level and that they were all distributed). So the P/E ratio is a multiple of earnings. A high or low ratio can only be judged in relation to other companies in the same sector of the market.

A high P/E ratio means that the market thinks that the company's future is a good one. The shares are in demand, so the price of the shares will be high. Of course it would take you a long time to get your 'earnings' back (even if the company paid them all out as dividends) but the expectation is that the company will be able to increase its earnings and that sometime in the future it will be able to pay out a higher dividend. As a result the shares are a good buy from that point of view.

Activity 2.36

At 5 October 2009 Dawson's P/E ratio was 88.2 while Experian's was 2.4. Both are grouped in the 'support services' sector of the economy. What do these P/E ratios tell you about the market's perception of these two companies?

Capital gearing ratio

The last ratio that we are going to consider is the *capital gearing ratio*. Companies are financed out of a mixture of share capital, retained profits and loans. Loans may be long-term (such as debentures) or short-term (such as credit given by trade creditors). In addition, the company may have set aside all sorts of provisions (e.g. for taxation) which it expects to meet sometime in the future. These may also be regarded as a type of loan. From an ordinary shareholder's point of view, even preference share capital can be classed as a loan because the preference share-holders may have priority over ordinary shareholders both in respect of dividends and upon liquidation. So if a company finances itself from a high level of loans, there is obviously a higher risk in investing in it. This arises for two main reasons:

- the higher the loans, the more interest the company will have to pay; that may affect the company's ability to pay an ordinary dividend;
- if the company cannot find the cash to repay its loans then the ordinary shareholders may not get any money back if the company goes into liquidation.

There are many different ways of calculating capital gearing but we prefer the following formula.

$$\frac{\text{preference shares} + \text{long-term loans}}{\text{shareholders' funds} + \text{long-term loans}} \times 100$$

A company that has financed itself out of a high proportion of loans (e.g. in the form of a combination of preference shares and long-term loans) is known as a highly-geared company. Conversely, a company with a low level of loans is regarded as being low-geared. Note that 'high' and 'low' in this context are relative terms. A highly-geared company is potentially a higher risk investment as it has to earn sufficient profit to cover the interest payments and the preference dividend before it can pay out any ordinary dividend. This should not be a problem when profits are rising but if they are falling then they may not be sufficient to cover even the preference dividend.

We have now reviewed 15 common accounting ratios. There are many others that could have been included. However, the 15 selected are enough for you to be able to interpret a set of accounts. Many of the ratios are not particularly helpful if they are used in isolation but as part of a detailed analysis they can be invaluable.

Activity 2.37

Company A has a capital gearing of 10%, Company B 40%, and Company C 60%. What effect will such gearing ratios have on each company's reported profits when they are (a) rising steeply; (b) or falling sharply?

Company	Effect on profits	
	Rising	Falling
A		
B		
C		

We will now show how the 15 ratios can be used to interpret the accounts of a small company.

An illustrative example

We will now bring together much of the material that we have covered so far in this section in the form of a practical example. The example is meant to provide you with a framework for interpreting accounts. We have tried to make it as simple as possible and to reduce the arithmetic involved.

When you are faced with having to interpret a set of accounts in your work or in your private life you will probably be faced with a huge amount of additional information. And yet some information that you will probably need will be missing. For example, published accounts almost certainly only give you the 'cost of sales' and not the 'cost of goods sold' as defined in this book. This means that you will not be able to calculate the gross profit using the conventional formula. Besides some missing information much of what is available will be highly complex and technical and you will have to sort it out for yourself using the notes attached to the accounts.

All of this may seem that you will face an almost impossible task. This is not so. With the guidance provided in this section and more generally throughout the rest of the chapter, you should soon be able to interpret a set of accounts. Here goes.

Example

Interpreting company accounts

You are presented with the following information relating to Gill Limited.

Gill Limited
Profit and loss account for the year to 31 March 2012

	2011	2012
	£000	£000
Sales	160	200
Cost of goods sold	(96)	(114)
Gross profit	64	86
Operating expenses	(30)	(34)
Debenture interest	(5)	(5)
Net profit before tax	29	47
Tax	(9)	(12)
Net profit after tax	20	35
Dividends paid		
Preference shares	(2)	(2)
Ordinary shares	(8)	(10)
	(10)	(12)
Retained profit	10	23

Balance sheet at 31 March 2012

	2011	2012
	£000	£000
Fixed assets (at net book value)	300	320
Current assets		
Stocks	15	20
Trade debtors	40	50
Cash and bank	3	1
	58	71
Current liabilities		
Trade creditors	(25)	(35)
Net current liabilities	33	36
	333	356

Capital and reserves		
Share capital (£1 ordinary shares)	200	200
Preference shares (£1 shares; 8%)	25	25
Retained earnings	58	81
	283	306
Long-term liabilities		
Debentures (10%)	50	50
	333	356

Additional information:

1 All sales and all purchases are on credit terms.
2 The opening stock at 1 April 2010 was £20,000.
3 There were no accruals or prepayments at the end of either 2011 or 2012.
4 Assume that both the tax and the dividends had been paid before the end of the year.
5 The market price of the ordinary shares at the end of both years was estimated to be 126p and 297p respectively.

Required:

(a) Calculate appropriate liquidity, profitability, efficiency and investment ratios for both 2011 and 2012.
(b) Comment briefly on the company's financial performance for the year to 31 March 2012.

Answer to Example

(a) Significant accounting ratios

Gill Limited

	2011	2012
Liquidity ratios		
Current assets:		
$\dfrac{\text{Current assets}}{\text{Current liabilities}}$	$\dfrac{58}{25}$	$\dfrac{71}{35}$
	$= 2.3$	$= 2.0$
Acid test:		
$\dfrac{\text{Current assets} - \text{stock}}{\text{Current liabilities}}$	$\dfrac{58 - 15}{25}$	$\dfrac{71 - 20}{35}$
	$= 1.7$	$= 1.5$
Profitability ratios		
Return on capital employed:		
$\dfrac{\text{Net profit before tax}}{\text{Shareholders' funds}} \times 100$	$\dfrac{29}{283} \times 100$	$\dfrac{47}{306} \times 100$
	$= 10.2\%$	$= 15.4\%$
$\dfrac{\text{Net profit before tax}}{\text{Shareholders' funds}} \times 100$	$\dfrac{20}{283} \times 100$	$\dfrac{35}{306} \times 100$
	$= 7.1\%$	$= 11.4\%$

$\dfrac{\text{Profit after tax and preference dividend}}{\text{Shareholders' funds } - \text{ preference shares}} \times 100$	$\dfrac{18}{283-25} \times 100$ $= 7.0\%$	$\dfrac{33}{306-25} \times 100$ $= 11.7\%$
$\dfrac{\text{Profit before tax and interest}}{\text{Shareholders' funds } + \text{ long-term loans}} \times 100$	$\dfrac{29+5}{333} \times 100$ $= 10.2\%$	$\dfrac{47+5}{356} \times 100$ $= 14.6\%$

Gross profit ratio:

$\dfrac{\text{Gross profit}}{\text{Sales}} \times 100$	$\dfrac{64}{160} \times 100$ $= 40\%$	$\dfrac{86}{200} \times 100$ $= 43\%$

Mark-up ratio:

$\dfrac{\text{Gross profit}}{\text{Cost of goods sold}} \times 100$	$\dfrac{64}{96} \times 100$ $= 66.7\%$	$\dfrac{86}{114} \times 100$ $= 75.4\%$

Net profit ratio:

$\dfrac{\text{Net profit before tax}}{\text{Sales}} \times 100$	$\dfrac{29}{160} \times 100$ $= 18.1\%$	$\dfrac{47}{200} \times 100$ $= 23.5\%$

Efficiency ratios

Stock turnover:

$\dfrac{\text{Cost of goods sold}}{\text{Stock}}$	$\dfrac{96}{15}$ $= 6.4$ times	$\dfrac{114}{20}$ $= 5.7$ times

Fixed assets turnover:

$\dfrac{\text{Sales}}{\text{Fixed assets (NBV)}}$	$\dfrac{160}{300}$ $= 0.5$ times	$\dfrac{200}{320}$ $= 0.6$ times

Trade debtor collection period:

$\dfrac{\text{Trade debtors}}{\text{Credit sales}} \times 365$	$\dfrac{40}{160} \times 365$ $= 92$ days	$\dfrac{50}{200} \times 365$ $= 92$ days

Trade creditor payment period:

$\dfrac{\text{Trade creditors}}{\text{Purchases}} \times 365$	$\dfrac{25}{91} \times 365$ $= 101$ days	$\dfrac{35}{119} \times 365$ $= 108$ days

Purchases:

Opening stock +	20	15
Purchases*	91	119
	111	134
− Closing stock =	15	20
Cost of goods sold	96	114

* by deduction

Investment ratios

Dividend yield:

$$\frac{\text{Dividend per share}}{\text{Market price per share}} \times 100 \qquad \frac{4^*}{126} \times 100 \qquad \frac{5^*}{297} \times 100$$

$$= 3.2\% \qquad = 1.7\%$$

*Dividend per share:

$$\frac{\text{Dividends}}{\text{Issued share capital}} \times 100 \qquad \frac{8}{200} \times 100 \qquad \frac{10}{200} \times 100$$

$$= 4\text{p} \qquad = 5\text{p}$$

Dividend cover:

$$\frac{\text{Net profit after tax and preference dividend}}{\text{Ordinary dividends}} \qquad \frac{20 - 2}{8} \qquad \frac{35 - 2}{10}$$

$$= 2.25 \text{ times} \qquad = 3.3 \text{ times}$$

Earnings per share:

$$\frac{\text{Net profit after tax and preference dividend}}{\text{Number of shares}} \qquad \frac{20 - 2}{200} \qquad \frac{35 - 2}{200}$$

$$= 9\text{p} \qquad = 16.5\text{p}$$

Price/earnings:

$$\frac{\text{Market price per share}}{\text{Earnings per share}} \qquad \frac{126}{9} \qquad \frac{297}{16.5}$$

$$= 14 \qquad = 18$$

Capital gearing:

$$\frac{\text{Preference shares + long-term loans}}{\text{Shareholders' funds + long-term loans}} \times 100 \qquad \frac{25 + 50}{333} \times 100 \qquad \frac{25 + 50}{356} \times 100$$

$$= 22.5\% \qquad = 21.1\%$$

(b) Comments on the company's financial performance for the year to 31 March 2012

In answering Part (b) of the question we will confine our comments to just a few brief points.

Liquidity

Cash flow

The company had a small cash balance at the end of each year (£3000 and £1000 respectively). We have not been provided with a cash flow statement but it is possible to prepare a simple one for 2012.

Cash flow statement for the year to 31 March 2012

	£000
Net profit before debenture interest and taxation (47 + 5)	52
Increase in stock	(5)
Increase in trade debtors	(10)
Increase in trade creditors	10
Increase in fixed assets	(20)
Interest paid	(5)
Tax paid	(12)
Dividends paid	(12)
Decrease in cash during the year	(2)
Cash at 1.4.11	3
Cash at 31.3.12	1

- Increases in stock and trade debtor balances of £15,000 were offset by a smaller increase in trade creditors of £10,000. An increase in fixed assets and tax paid was largely responsible for a decrease in the cash position at the end of 2012.

- Both the current assets and the acid test ratios were well within the generally accepted ranges.

Profitability

- All measures of profit show a healthy return on capital employed in both years with an increase in 2012.

- We do not, however, know how the ROCE ratios compare with other companies. The increases may have been partly due to a significant increase in mark-up on sales. If this is so, this would suggest that the company is selling in an elastic market and that it has been able to increase its selling prices without any great difficulty resulting in an increase in sales of 25% (from £160,000 to £200,000).

- The gross profit ratio showed a reasonable increase in 2012.

- Similarly the net profit ratio shows a healthy increase indicating that operational expenses are under control despite the company being busier.

Efficiency

- The stock turnover ratio has fallen from 6.4 times to 5.7 times. In other words the stock is not being used in production quite as quickly in 2012 as it was in 2011. This needs to be investigated. It may well be that the company has purchased more stock than was needed to meet the 25% increase in sales.

- The fixed assets turnover is very low in both years although it did increase slightly in 2012. Indeed it would appear that the company is not recovering in sales what it has invested in fixed assets. Perhaps this is because there is a long time-lag between the installation of plant and machinery and the expected upturn in sales. Again this is something that needs further investigation.

- The trade debtor position is very high (92 days in each year). This may be the industrial sector norm but it still needs investigation. The company could run into cash flow problems if its customers are slow to pay. This ratio may be related to the even higher trade creditor payment period (101 days and 108 days respectively).

If the company is not receiving cash from its debtors it will not have the cash to pay its creditors. There is, therefore, a danger that it could possibly be going to run into a severe cash flow problem.

Investment

- This is a private company so it is difficult to read too much into the investment ratios. The dividend yield has fallen by nearly half but the dividend cover shows a healthy increase.

- The increase in the earnings per share is much more than healthy: it increased by over 83% in 2012.

- The market appears to view the prospects for the company favourably as the price/earnings ratio increased from 14 to 18.

- At just over 20% the capital gearing is sufficiently low to satisfy the ordinary shareholders that if future profits increase their dividends are likely to grow without any problems arising. Similarly if profits fall, the payments to both debenture holders and preference shareholders will not swallow up a huge proportion of whatever profits are made, leaving the ordinary dividend fairly safe.

Conclusion

- There are a few caveats: (1) we don't have any information about the overall environment in which the company operates; (2) we are provided with only limited internal data; (3) we only have the accounts for a two-year period; and (4) we don't know how this company compares with other private companies in the same industry.

- The company appears to be profitable, generally efficient and not a huge investments risk. There is a peculiar relationship between the fixed assets and the sales and the underlying cash flow position is weak because the company is not chasing up its debtors fast enough. As a result it is not able to pay its creditors very quickly. This means that if they begin to demand quicker payment the company could find itself facing great financial difficulties. If it cannot obtain the necessary credit then there may even be questions about whether it is able to continue as a going concern and it might then have to go into liquidation.

Questions you should ask

As far as this section is concerned, there are two situations in which you might find yourself: either with a set of financial accounts that will have been interpreted for you or some that you might have to interpret for yourself. Irrespective of which situation you find yourself in, you might find it useful to ask (or ask yourself) the following questions.

- How reliable is the basic accounting information underpinning this information in front of me?

- Have consistent accounting policies been adopted throughout the period covered?
- If not, has each year's results been adjusted on to the same accounting basis?
- Were there any unusual items in any year that may have distorted a comparative analysis?
- Was the rate of inflation significant in any year covered by the report?
- If so, should the basic accounting data be adjusted to allow for it?
- What are the three or four most significant changes in these accounts during the period they cover?
- Are there any apparent causal links between them, such as greater efficiency resulting in a higher level of profitability or higher profits causing cash flow problems?
- What are the most important factors that this report tells me about the company's progress during the period in question and its prospects for the future?

Conclusion

This section has explained how you can examine the financial performance of a company (or other entity) over a certain period of time. If a detailed examination is required it may be necessary to examine the general business environment and economic sector in which it operates. Much information will also be collected about the company itself. One of the main sources of information will be its annual report and accounts.

While a great deal of information may be found in the annual reports and accounts that information has to be put into context as the absolute numbers disclosed are often large, do not mean much in isolation, and are often difficult to understand. This means that the accounts need to be analysed. There are four main types of analysis:

- horizontal analysis, involving a line-by-line inspection across the various time periods;
- trend analysis, in which all the data are indexed to a base of 100;
- vertical analysis, where each period's data is expressed as a percentage of a total;
- ratio analysis, which requires a comparison to be made of one item with another item expressing the relationship as either a percentage or a factor.

All of these four types of analyses rely primarily on the accounting data. Such data are subject to a number of reservations, such as the accounting policies and the methods used in preparing the accounts. These reservations must be allowed for when interpreting a set of accounts, especially when a comparison is made with other companies since accounting policies and methods are often different.

Ratio analysis is the most important of the four types of analyses. There are literally hundreds of ratios that could be calculated, plus some highly specialist ones that relate to particular industries. In this section we have selected just 15 common but important ratios and grouped them under four headings:

- liquidity ratios, which help to decide whether an entity has enough cash to continue as a going concern;
- profitability ratios, which measure the profit an entity has made;
- efficiency ratios, which ratios show how well the entity has used its resources;
- investment ratios, which help to consider the investment potential of an entity.

Irrespective of the category into which they fall, ratios should only be regarded as a signpost: in themselves they do not actually *interpret* the accounts for you. They are merely an arithmetical device that points you in the right direction and help you to assess what *has* happened and to predict what *might* happen. They provide you with the evidence, but you have to use that evidence to come to a verdict.

Key points

1 The interpretation of accounts involves examining financial accounts in some detail so as to be able to explain what has happened and to predict what is likely to happen.
2 The examination can be undertaken by using a number of techniques, such as horizontal analysis, trend analysis, vertical analysis and ratio analysis.
3 Ratio analysis is a common method of interpreting accounts. It involves comparing one item in the accounts with another closely related item. Ratios are normally expressed in the form of a percentage or a factor. There are literally hundreds of recognized accounting ratios (excluding those that relate to specific industries) but we have restricted our study to just 15.
4 Not all of the ratios covered in this chapter will be relevant for non-manufacturing, non-trading or not-for-profit entities. It is necessary to be selective in your choice of ratios.
5 When one item is related to another item in the form of a ratio, it is important to make sure that there is a close and logical correlation between the two items.
6 In the case of some ratios, different definitions can be adopted. This applies particularly to ROCE and capital gearing. In other cases annual averages are used instead of year end balances. This applies especially to ratios relating to stocks, debtors and creditors.
7 Assessing trends and calculating ratios is not the same as interpreting a set of financial accounts. Interpretation involves using a wide range of information sources as well as the incorporation of various types of analyses into a cohesive appraisal of an entity's past performance and its future prospects.

Budgeting

When budgets go wrong

Was Dickens right?

Annual income twenty pounds, annual expenditure nineteen nineteen six, result happiness. Annual income twenty pounds, annual expenditure twenty pounds ought and six, result misery. (Mr Micawber in *David Copperfield* by Charles Dickens).

Kesa, Europe's third largest electrical retailer was presumably reasonably happy because its actual sales for the year to 30 April 2009 fell by 6.2 per cent – only slightly above the budgeted loss of between 5 and 6 per cent. By contrast WPP, the world's largest marketing and communications group was perhaps feeling miserable because its actual adjusted margins (a measure of profitability) were expected to be 12.5 per cent against a budget of 14.3 per cent. The shortfall arose largely because the company had failed to reduce its staff costs in line with the expected fall in sales.

But it's not only in the private sector that there can be differences between the actual and the budgeted results. For example, the National Audit Office qualified the 2008/2009 results of five government departments – including the Treasury! The Treasury had apparently incurred £24bn more expenditure than had been authorised by Parliament.

Budgets also go wrong in other countries in both the private and public sectors. A somewhat extreme case arose in the United States. It involved a company called KV Pharmaceutical Company. Its audit committee found problems not only with the company's budgetary control procedures but it also uncovered deficiencies in managerial conduct, human resource functions, and compliance with the Food and Drug Administration. Some very severe measures had to be taken including strengthening and enhancing the internal audit, budgeting and forecasting processes.

As a result of all these events there may have been some misery among the staff at KV Pharmaceutical. The Chairman would certainly have felt miserable because he was fired. In such circumstances even Dickens might have struggled hard to find a much more explicit way of describing it.

Sources: Based on www.ft.com, 24 June 2009; www.ft.com, 27 June 2009; *The Financial Times*, 27 August 2009; www.AccountancyAge.com, 21 July 2009; *St Louis Business Journal*, 23 June 2009.

Introduction

This section explores the nature and purpose of a budget. It outlines the various types of budgets, how they all fit together and how they may be used to keep a tight control of an entity's operations. It also explains that budgets and budgetary control are not neutral techniques. They have an impact on human behaviour and this has to be taken into account when using them.

Why this section is important

The more knowledge that you have as a manager, the more influence you will be able to exert. This applies particularly to budgeting. So this section is important for the following reasons.

- Your job will probably involve you in supplying information for budgetary purposes. It is easier to supply what is needed if you know what it is for and how it will be used.
- You are likely to have to prepare a budget for your department. Obviously, it is easier to do this if you have had some training in how to do it.
- You may be supplied with various reports that show your budgeted results against actual results. You may then be asked what you are going to do to correct any variance. The impact that this will have on you will depend on a number of factors, such as how familiar you are with the way that the information has been compiled, what inherent deficiencies it may have and what reliability you can place on it.

Budgeting is not a process that is of interest only to accountants. It should involve the whole entity. As a manager you will find that if you throw yourself wholeheartedly into the process it will help you to do your job more effectively.

Budgeting and budgetary control

News clip

Line by line

When asked how costs could be cut dramatically, Dave Barger, Chief Executive Officer of JetBlue said that his team regularly went through the company's budget 'line by line' in order to find whether cost savings could be made that had the least impact on customers and crew members.

Source: Adapted from *Fortune*, 8 December 2008, p. 16.

We start our analysis by explaining what we mean by a 'budget' and 'budgetary control'.

Budget

The term *budget* is probably well understood by the layman. Many people, for example, 'budget' for their own household expenses even if it is only by making a rough comparison between next month's salary and the next month's expenditure. Such a budget may not be very detailed but it contains all the main features of what accountants mean by a budget. There are as follows:

- *Policies*: a budget is based on the policies needed to fulfil the objectives of the entity.
- *Data*: it is usually expressed in monetary terms.
- *Documentation*: it is usually written down.
- *Period*: it relates to a future period of time.

Most entities will usually prepare a considerable number of what might be called sub-budgets. A manufacturing entity, for example, might prepare sales, production and administration budgets. These budgets would then be combined into an overall budget known as a *master budget*. A master budget is made up of a budgeted profit and loss account, a budgeted balance sheet and a budgeted cash flow statement.

Once a master budget has been prepared, it will be examined closely to see whether the overall plan can be accommodated. It might be the case, for example, that the sales budget indicates a large increase in sales. This will have required the production budgets to be prepared on the basis of this extra sales demand. The cash budget, however, might show that the entity could not finance the extra sales and production activity out of its budgeted cash resources, so additional financing arrangements will have to be made because obviously no entity would normally turn down the opportunity of increasing its sales.

Budgets are useful because they encourage managers to examine what they have done in relation to what they *could* do. However, the full benefits of a budgeting system only became apparent when it is used for *control* purposes. This involves making a constant comparison between the actual results and the budgeted results, and then taking any necessary corrective action. This procedure is called 'budgetary control'.

Activity 2.38

Write down three reasons why a manufacturing company might prepare budgets.

Budgetary control

When the actual results for a period are compared with the budgeted results and it is seen that there are material (or significant) differences (called variances) then corrective action must be taken to ensure that future results will conform to the budget. This is the essence of budgetary control, as can be seen in Figure 2.27. It has several important features.

- *Responsibilities*: managerial responsibilities are clearly defined.
- *Action plan*: individual budgets lay down a detailed plan of action for a particular sphere of responsibility.
- *Adherence*: managers have a responsibility to adhere to their budgets once the budgets have been approved.
- *Monitoring*: the actual performance is monitored constantly and compared with the budgeted results.
- *Correction*: corrective action is taken if the actual results differ significantly from the budget.
- *Approval*: departures from the budget are only permitted if they have been approved by senior management.
- *Variances*: those that are unaccounted for are subject to individual investigation.

Any variance that occurs should be investigated carefully. The current actual performance will then be immediately brought back into line with the budget if this is

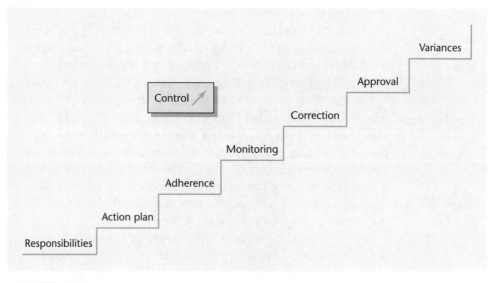

Figure 2.27 Budgetary control: features

considered necessary. Sometimes the budget itself will be changed, e.g. if there is an unexpected increase in sales. Such changes may, of course, have an effect on the other budgets and so cannot be done in isolation.

Now that we have outlined the nature and purpose of budgeting and budgetary control, we are in a position to investigate how the system works.

Procedure

News clip

Sandwiches and sausage rolls

The bakery chain Greggs is budgeting for 'marginally positive' 'like-for-like sales growth' this year. Apparently the recession has helped the company's results because more people are seeking value by purchasing its 99p sandwiches and 55p sausage rolls.

Source: Adapted from www.ft.com/cms, 11 March 2009.

In order to make it easier for you to follow the budget procedure we will break it down into four main stages: (1) who administers it; (2) what they aim to do; (3) the length of the budget period; and (4) how the master budget is made up. These four stages are shown in pictorial form in Figure 2.28. We start by first examining the administration of the budget process.

 👤👤👤	Administration	Who looks after the budgetary process?
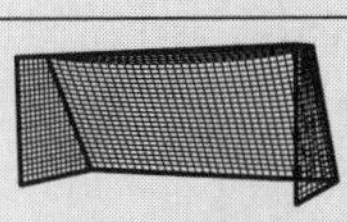 (goal)	Objectives	Where do we want to be at the end of the period?
31.12.50?	Period	How long should the budgetary period be?
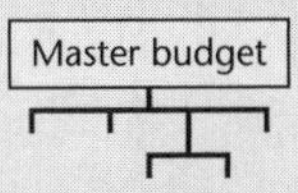 Master budget	Composition	What individual budgets should make up the master budget?

Figure 2.28   Budget procedure

Administration

The budget procedure may be administered by a special budget committee or it may be supervised by the accounting function. It will be necessary for the budget committee to lay down general guidelines in accordance with the company's objectives and to ensure that individual departments do not operate completely independently. The production department, for example, will need to know what the company is budgeting to sell so that it can prepare its own budget on the basis of those sales. However, the detailed production budget must still remain the entire responsibility of the production manager.

This procedure is in line with the concept of responsibility accounting. If the control procedure is to work properly, managers must be given responsibility for clearly defined areas of activity, such as their particular cost centre. They are then fully answerable for all that goes on there. Unless managers are given complete authority to act within clearly defined guidelines, they cannot be expected to account for something for which they are not responsible. This means that if the budgeting control system is to work, managers must help prepare, amend and approve their own cost centre's budget.

Activity 2.39

A budget can act as a measure against which actual performance can be matched. However, some experts argue that when a measure becomes a target ('you must meet your budget') it becomes meaningless. To what extent do you think that budgeting is a waste of time? Mark your response on a scale like the one below.

Waste of time   *Valuable means of control*

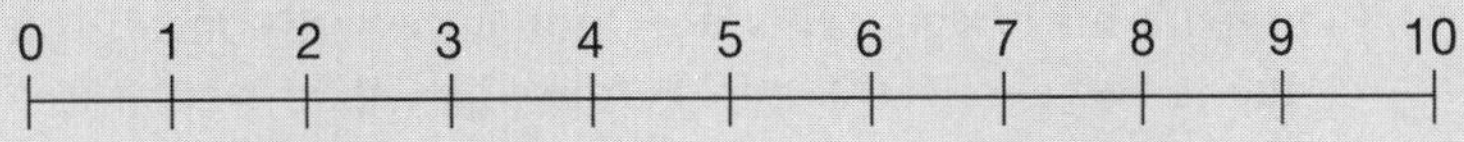

0   1   2   3   4   5   6   7   8   9   10

Objectives

The budget procedure starts with an examination of the entity's objectives. These may be very simple. They may include, for example, an overall wish to maximize profits, to foster better relations with customers, or to improve the working conditions of employees. Once an entity has decided on its overall objectives, it is in a position to formulate some detailed plans.

These will probably start with a *forecast*. There is a technical difference between a forecast and a budget. A forecast is a prediction of what is *likely* to happen, whereas a budget is a carefully prepared plan of what *should* happen.

Period

The main budget period is usually based on a calendar year. It could be shorter or longer depending on the nature of the product cycle. The fashion industry, for example, may adopt a short budget period of less than a year, while the construction industry may opt for a five-year period. Irrespective of the industry, however, a calendar year is usually a convenient period to choose as the base period because it fits in with financial accounting requirements.

Besides determining the main budget period, it is also necessary to prepare budgets for much shorter periods. These are required for budgetary control purposes in order to compare the actual results with the budgeted results on a frequent basis. The sub-budget periods for some activities may need to be very short if very tight control is to be exercised over them, e.g. the cash budget may need to be broken down into weeks, while the administration budget only into quarters.

Composition

In order to give you as wide a picture of the budgeting process as possible we will assume that we are dealing with a manufacturing company in the private sector. In practice the structure and content is likely to be extremely complex but we have stripped it down to its bare minimum. Even so, if you look at Figure 2.29 you will see that it still looks very involved. But don't worry. Later on in the section we will be using a quantitative example to illustrate the process and then it should all click into place.

In commercial organizations, the first budget to be prepared is usually the sales budget. Once the sales for the budget period (and for each sub-budget period) have been determined the next stage is to calculate the effect on production. This will then enable an agreed level of activity to be determined. The *level of activity* may be expressed in so many units or as a percentage of the theoretical productive capacity of the entity. Once the level of activity has been established then departmental managers can be instructed to prepare their budgets on that basis.

Let us assume, for example, that 1000 units can be sold for a particular budget period. The production department manager will need this information in order to prepare his budget. This does not necessarily mean that he will budget for a production level of 1000 units because he will also have to allow for the budgeted level of opening and closing stocks.

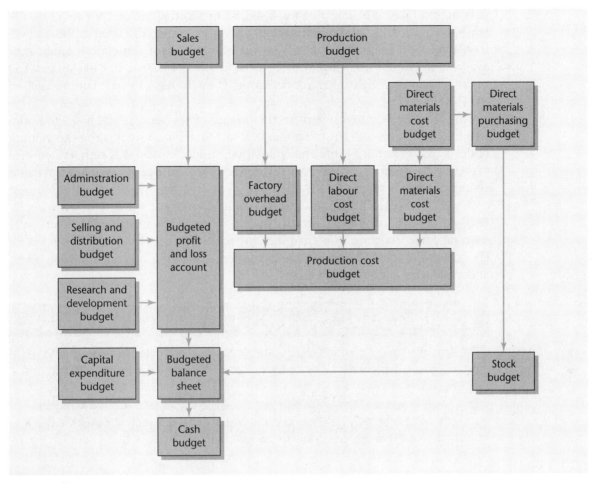

Figure 2.29   Functional budgets

Source: Adapted from Chartered Institute of Management Accountants (2005). CIMA Official Terminology, Oxford: CIMA Publishers.

The budgeted production level will then be translated into how much material and labour will be required to meet that particular level. Similarly, it will be necessary to prepare overhead budgets. Much of the general overhead expenditure of the company (such as factory administrative costs, head office costs and research and development expenditure) will be fixed and it will not be affected by the activity level. One type of overhead, however, that may be affected by the activity level is the sales and distribution overhead budget because, for example, an increase in the number of units sold may involve additional delivery costs.

Not all entities start the budget process with sales. Local authorities are a good example. They usually prepare a budget on the basis of what they are likely to spend. The total budgeted expenditure is then compared with the total amount of council tax (after allowing for grants and other income) needed to cover it. If the political cost of an increase in council tax appears to be too high then the council will require a reduction in the budgeted expenditure. Once the budget has been set, and the council tax has been levied on that basis, departments have to work within the budgets laid down. However, since the budget will have been prepared on an estimate of the actual expenditure for the last two or three months of the old financial year, account has to be taken of any a surplus or shortfall brought forward into the current year. If the estimate eventually proves excessive, the local authority will have overtaxed for that year. This means that it has got some additional funds available to cushion the current year's expenditure. Of course, if it has undertaxed for any balance brought forward, departments might have to start cutting back in the current year.

This process is quite different in the private sector because the budgeted sales effectively determine all the other budgets. In a local authority it is the expenditure budgets that determine what the council tax should be and it is only the control exercised by central government and by the local authority itself that places a ceiling on what is spent.

A budget prepared for a particular department, cost centre or any other responsibility centre is known as a *functional budget*. Once all the functional budgets have been prepared, they are combined into the *master budget*. The master budget is, in effect, a consolidated budgeted profit and loss account, a budgeted balance sheet and a budgeted cash flow statement.

Activity 2.40

(a) Assuming that a company has overestimated the budgeted level of activity, suggest ways in which it can bring its actual results back into line with the budget.

(b) If a local authority has underestimated its expenditure for the last two months of the old financial year (February and March) what can it do to cover the deficit in the new financial year (April to the next March)?

An initial draft of the master budget may not be acceptable to the senior management of the company. This may be because it cannot cope with that particular budgeted level of activity, e.g. as a result of production or cash constraints. Indeed, one of the most important budgets is the *cash budget*. The cash budget translates all the other functional budgets (including that for capital expenditure) into cash terms. It will show in detail the pattern of cash inputs and outputs for the main budget period, as well as for each sub-budget period. If it shows that the company will have difficulty in financing a particular budgeted level of activity (or if there is going to be a period when cash is exceptionally tight), the management will have an opportunity to seek out alternative sources of finance.

This latter point illustrates the importance of being aware of future commitments, so that something can be done in advance if there are likely to be constraints (irrespective of their nature). The master budget usually takes so long to prepare, however, that by the time it has been completed it will be almost impossible to make major alterations (although IT developments are now making this less of a difficulty). It is then tempting for senior management to make changes to the functional budgets without referring them back to individual cost-centre managers. It is most unwise to make changes in this way because it is then difficult to use such budgets for control purposes. If managers have not agreed to the changes, they will argue with considerable force that they can hardly take responsibility for budgets that have been imposed on them.

Activity 2.41

XYZ Limited is a manufacturing company. It prepares an annual master budget. Suggest the length of the sub-budget period for each of the following functions: (a) cash; (b) purchasing; and (c) research.

In the next section we use a comprehensive example to illustrate how all the functional budgets fit together.

A comprehensive example

Activity 2.42

List three benefits that you think the preparation of a master budget provides.

It would be very difficult to follow the basic procedures involved in the preparation of functional budgets if we used an extremely detailed example. The example that we are going to work through cuts out much of the detail and only illustrates the main procedures. Nevertheless, there are still 14 steps to take!

Example

Preparation of functional budgets

Sefton Limited manufactures one product known as EC2. The following information relates to the preparation of the budget for the year to 31 March 2012:

1 Sales budget details for product EC2:
　Expected selling price per unit: £100.
　Expected sales in units: 10,000.
　All sales are on credit terms.
2 EC2 requires 5 units of raw material E and 10 units of raw material C. E is expected to cost £3 per unit, and C £4 per unit. All goods are purchased on credit terms.
3 Two departments are involved in producing EC2: machining and assembly. The following information is relevant:

	Direct labour per unit of product (hours)	Direct labour rate per hour £
Machining	1.00	6
Assembling	0.50	8

4 The finished production overhead costs are expected to amount to £100,000.

5 At 1 April 2011, 800 units of EC2 are expected to be in stock at a value of £52,000, 4500 units of raw material E at a value of £13,500, and 12,000 units of raw materials at a value of £48,000. Stocks of both finished goods and raw materials are planned to be 10 per cent above the expected opening stock levels as at 1 April 2011.

6 Administration, selling and distribution overhead is expected to amount to £150,000.

7 Other relevant information:

(a) Opening trade debtors are expected to be £80,000. Closing trade debtors are expected to amount to 15 per cent of the total sales for the year.

(b) Opening trade creditors are expected to be £28,000. Closing trade creditors are expected to amount to 10 per cent of the purchases for the year.

(c) All other expenses will be paid in cash during the year.

(d) Other balances at 1 April 2011 are expected to be as follows:

	£	£
Share capital: ordinary shares		225 000
Retained profits		17 500
Proposed dividend		75 000
Fixed assets at cost	250 000	
Less: Accumulated depreciation	100 000	
		150 000
Cash at bank and in hand		2 000

8 Capital expenditure will amount to £50,000, payable in cash on 1 April 2011.

9 Fixed assets are depreciated on a straight-line basis at a rate of 20 per cent per annum on cost.

Required:

As far as the information permits, prepare all the relevant budgets for Sefton Limited for the year to 31 March 2012.

Answer to Example

In order to make it easier for you to become familiar with the budgeting procedure we will take you through it step by step.

Step 1: Prepare the sales budget

Units of EC2		Selling price per unit		Total sales value
		£		£
10 000	×	100	=	1 000 000

Step 2: Prepare the production budget

	Units
Sales of EC2	10 000
Less: Opening stock	800
	9 200
Add: Desired closing stock (opening stock + 10%)	880
Production required	= 10 080

Step 3: Prepare the direct materials usage budget

Direct materials:

E: 5 units × 10 080 = 50 400 units

C: 10 units × 10 080 = 100 800 units

Step 4: Prepare the direct materials purchases budget

Direct materials:	=	E (units)	C (units)
Usage (as per Step 3)		50 400	100 800
Less: Opening stock		4 500	12 000
		45 900	88 800
Add: Desired closing stock (opening stock + 10%)		4 950	13 200
		50 850	102 000
		× £3	× £4
Direct material purchases	=	£152 550	= £408 000

Step 5: Prepare the direct labour budget

	Machining	Assembling
Production units (as per Step 2)	10 080	10 080
× direct labour hours required	× 1 DLH	× 0.50 DLH
	10 080 DLH	5 040 DLH
× direct labour rate per hour	× £6	× £8
Direct labour cost	= £60 480	= £40 320

Step 6: Prepare the fixed production overhead budget

Given:	£100 000

Step 7: Calculate the value of the closing raw material stock

Raw material	Closing stock* (units)		Cost per unit £		Total value £
E	4 950	×	3	=	14 850
C	13 200	×	4	=	52 800
					67 650

* Derived from Step 4.

Step 8: Calculate the value of the closing finished stock

	£	£
Unit cost:		
Direct material E: 5 units × £3 per unit	15	
Direct material C: 10 units × £4 per unit	40	55
Direct labour for machining: 1 hour × £6 per DLH	6	
Direct labour for assembling: 0.50 hours × £8 per DLH	4	10
Total direct cost	=	65
× units in stock		× 880
Closing stock value	=	57 200

Step 9: Prepare the administration, selling and distribution budget

Given: £150 000

Step 10: Prepare the capital expenditure budget

Given: £50 000

Step 11: Calculate the cost of goods sold

	£
Opening stock (given)	52 000
Manufacturing cost:	
Production units (Step 2) × total direct cost (Step 3) = 10 080 × £65	655 200
	707 200
Less: Closing stock (Step 8: 880 units × £65)	57 200
Cost of goods sold (10 000 units) =	650 000
(or 10 000 units × total direct costs of £65 per unit)	

Step 12: Prepare the cash budget

	£	£
Receipts		
Cash from debtors:		
Opening debtors	80 000	
Sales	1 000 000	
	1 080 000	
Less: Closing debtors (15% × £1 000 000)	150 000	
Payments		
Cash payments to creditors:		
Opening creditors	28 000	
Purchases [Step 4: (£152 550 + 408 000)]	560 550	
	588 550	
Less: Closing creditors (£560 550 × 10%)	56 055	532 495
Wages (Step 5: £60 480 + 40 320)		100 800
Fixed production overhead		100 000
Administration, selling and distribution overhead		150 000
Capital expenditure		50 000
Dividend paid for 2011		75 000
		1 008 295
		£
Net receipts		(78 295)
Add: Opening cash		2 000
Budgeted closing cash balance (overdrawn)		(76 295)

Step 13: Prepare the budgeted profit and loss account

	£	£
Sales (Step 1)		1 000 000
Less: Variable cost of sales (Step 8: 10 000 × £65)		650 000
Gross margin		350 000
Less: Fixed production overhead (Step 6)	100 000	
Depreciation [(£250 000 + 50 000) × 20%]	60 000	160 000
Production margin		190 000
Less: Administration, selling and distribution		
Overhead (Step 9)		150 000
Budgeted net profit		40 000

Step 14: Prepare the budgeted balance sheet

	£	£	£
Fixed assets (at cost)			300 000
Less: Accumulated depreciation			160 000
			140 000
Current assets			
Raw materials (Step 7)		67 650	
Finished stock (Step 8)		57 200	
Trade debtors (15% × £1 000 000)		150 000	
		274 850	
Less: Current liabilities			
Trade creditors			
[Step 4: 10% × (£152 550 + 408 000)]	56 055		
Bank overdraft (Step 12)	76 295	132 350	142 500
			282 500
Financed by:			
Share capital			
Ordinary shares			225 000
Retained profits (£17 500 + 40 000)			57 500
			282 500

Fixed and flexible budgets

Budgeting for typewriters

The New York Police Department are still using old-fashioned typewriters because vouchers and property forms are still recorded on carbon paper. The outdated equipment is so cumbersome that officers are less likely to make arrests for minor offences. During the last two years the NYPD has spent more than £612,000 on buying and upkeeping new typewriters. And that means that they still have to budget for them!

Source: Adapted from www.guardian.co.uk/world/2009, 17 July 2009.

The master budget becomes the detailed plan for future action that everyone is expected to work towards. However, some entities only use the budgeting process as a *planning* exercise. Once the master budget has been agreed, there may be no attempt to use it as a control technique. So the budget may be virtually ignored and it may not be compared with the actual results. If this is the case, then the company is not getting the best out of the budgeting system.

As was suggested earlier, budgets are particularly useful if they are also used as a means of control. The control is achieved if the actual performance is compared with the budgeted performance. Significant variances should then be investigated and any necessary corrective action taken.

The constant comparison of the actual results with the budgeted results may be done either on a *fixed* or a *flexible* budget basis. A fixed budget basis means that the actual results for a particular period are compared with the original budgets. This is as you would expect because the budget is a measure and a measure has to be rigid: you would get some very misleading results if you used an elastic ruler to measure distances! Similarly, an elastic-type budget might also give some highly unreliable results. In some cases, however, a variable measure is used in budgeting in order to allow for certain circumstances that might have taken place *since* the budgets were prepared. Accountants call this *flexing* the budget. A flexible budget is an original budget that has been amended to take account of the *actual* level of activity.

This procedure might appear somewhat contradictory. Surely changing a budget once it has been agreed is similar to using an elastic ruler to measure distances? This is not necessarily the case in budgeting.

As we explained earlier, in order to prepare their budgets, some managers (especially production managers) will need to be given the budgeted level of activity. This means that such budgets will be based on a given level of activity. If the *actual* level of activity is greater (or less) than the budgeted level, however, managers will have to allow for more (or less) expenditure on materials, labour and other expenses.

Suppose, for example, that a manager has prepared his budget on the basis of an anticipated level of activity of 70 per cent of the plant capacity. The company turns out to be much busier than expected and it achieves an actual level of activity of 80 per cent. The production manager is likely to have spent more on materials, labour and other expenses than he originally thought. If the actual performance is then compared with the budget, i.e. on a fixed budget basis, it will look as though he had spent a great deal more than he had anticipated. And, of course, he has, although *some* of it, at least, must have been beyond his control because of the increased activity. It is considered only fair, therefore, to allow for those costs for which he is not responsible. So there is a need to flex the budget, i.e. revise it on

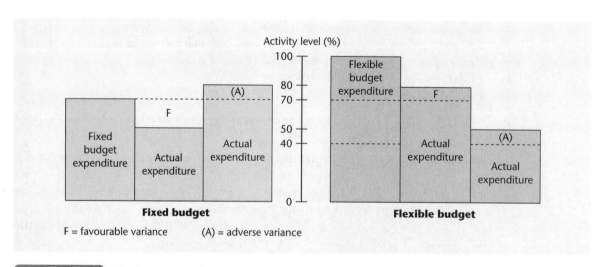

F = favourable variance   (A) = adverse variance

Figure 2.30   Flexing the budget

the basis of what it would have been if the manager had budgeted for an activity of 80 per cent instead of 70 per cent. The other assumptions and calculations made at the time the budget was prepared (such as material prices and wage rates) would not be amended. Figure 2.30 portrays this argument in pictorial form, which perhaps makes it easier for you to understand.

If a company operates a flexible budget system, the budgets may be prepared on the basis of a wide range of possible activity levels. This is a time-consuming method, and managers would be very lucky if they prepared one that happened to be identical to the *actual* level of activity. The best method is to wait until the actual level of activity is known before the budget is flexed.

The operation of a flexible budgetary system is shown in the following example.

Example

Flexible budget procedure

The following information had been prepared for Carp Limited for the year to 30 June 2012.

	Budget	Actual
Level of activity	50%	60%
	£	£
Costs:		
Direct materials	50 000	61 000
Direct labour	100 000	118 000
Variable overhead	10 000	14 000
Total variable cost	160 000	193 000
Fixed overhead	40 000	42 000
Total costs	200 000	235 000

Required:
Prepare a flexed budget operating statement for Carp Limited for the year to 30 June 2012.

Answer to Example

Carp Ltd
Flexed budget operating statement for the year 30 June 2012

	Fixed budget	Flexed budget	Actual costs	Variance (col. 2 less col. 3) favourable/
Activity level	50%	60%	60%	(adverse)
	£	£	£	£
Direct materials	50 000	60 000	61 000	(1 000)
Direct labour	100 000	120 000	118 000	2 000
Variable overhead	10 000	12 000	14 000	(2 000)
Total variable costs	160 000	192 000	193 000	(1 000)
Fixed overhead	40 000	40 000	42 000	(2 000)
Total costs	200 000	232 000	235 000	(3 000)

Tutorial notes

1 All the budgeted *variable* costs have been flexed by 20% because the actual activity was 60% compared with a budgeted level of 50%, i.e. a 20% increase

$$\left(\frac{60\% - 50\%}{50\%} \times 100\right)$$

2 The budgeted fixed costs are not flexed because, by definition, they should not change with activity.

3 Instead of using the total fixed budget cost of £200,000, the total flexed budget costs of £232,000 can be compared more fairly with the total actual cost of £235,000.

4 Note that the terms 'favourable' and 'adverse' (as applied to variances) mean favourable or adverse to profit. In other words, profit will be either greater (if a variance is favourable) or less (if it is adverse) than the budgeted profit.

5 The reasons for the variances between the actual costs and the flexed budget will need to be investigated. The flexed budget shows that even allowing for the increased activity, the actual costs were in excess of the budget allowance.

6 Similarly, it will be necessary to investigate why the actual activity was higher than the budgeted activity. It could have been caused by inefficient budgeting or by quite an unexpected increase in sales activity. While this would normally be welcome, it might place a strain on the productive and financial resources of the company. If the increase is likely to be permanent, management will need to make immediate arrangements to accommodate the new level of activity.

Activity 2.43

On a scale of 0 to 5 how far do you think that a flexible budgeting system leads to a loss of managerial control (0 being total loss and 5 being no loss whatsoever)?

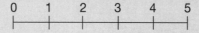

Behavioural consequences

News clip

Working together

Finance and marketing professionals have sometimes had a disjointed working relationship. Now the Chartered Institute of Management Accountants has got together with the Chartered Institute of Marketing and the Direct Marketing Association. It is felt that there is a need for a closer working relationship at a time when businesses may be tempted to slash marketing budgets in order to cut costs.

Source: Adapted from *Financial Management*, June 2009, p. 7.

Budgeting and budgetary control systems are not neutral. They have an impact on people causing them to react favourably, unfavourably or with indifference. If managers react favourably then their budgets are likely to be accurate and relevant. Similarly, any information provided for them will be welcomed and it will be taken seriously. As a result, any necessary corrective action required will be pursued with some vigour.

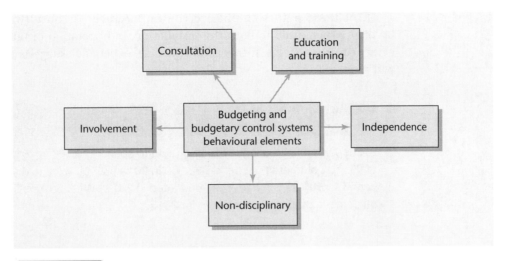

Figure 2.31   Budgeting: behavioural elements

Managers who react unfavourably or with indifference may prepare budgets that are inaccurate or irrelevant and under considerable protest. Obviously such managers are not likely to take seriously any notice or any action based on suspect data.

It follows from the above that for a budgeting and budgetary control systems to work effectively, a number of important elements must be present, as seen in Figure 2.31 and summarized below.

- *Consultation.* Managers must be consulted about any proposal to install a budgeting or a budgetary control system.
- *Education and training.* Managers must undergo some education and training so that they are fully aware of the relevance and importance of budgeting and budgetary control systems and the part that they are expected to play.
- *Involvement.* Managers must be directly involved in the installation of the system and especially so in their own responsibility centre.
- *Independence.* Managers should prepare their own budgets (subject to some general guidelines) instead of having them imposed on them. Imposed budgets (as they are called) usually mean that managers do not take them seriously and they will then disclaim responsibility for any variances that may have occurred.
- *Non-disciplinary.* Managers should not be disciplined for any variances (especially if a budget has been imposed) unless they are obviously guilty of negligence. Budgetary control is a means of finding out *why* a variance occurred. It is not supposed to be a vehicle for disciplining managers.

With regards to the last point, if managers believe that the budgeting or budgetary control system operates against them rather than for them, they are likely to undermine it. This may take the form of *dysfunctional behaviour*, i.e. behaviour that may be in their own interest but not in the best interests of the company. They may, for example, act aggressively, become uncooperative, blame other managers, build a great deal of slack (i.e. tolerance) into their budgets, make decisions on a short-term basis or avoid making them altogether, and spend money unnecessarily up to the budget level that they have been given.

All of these points emphasize the importance of consulting managers and involving them fully in both the installation and operation of budgeting and budgetary control systems. If this is not the case, experience suggests that such systems will not work.

Activity 2.44

As a departmental manager you budgeted to spend £10,000 in 2013. You spent £9000. You budgeted to spend £12,000 in 2014 but you were told you could only spend £11,000 as you had 'over-budgeted in 2013'. What are you likely to do when you come to prepare your budget for 2015?

Questions you should ask

This is a most important chapter for non-accountants because you are likely to be involved in the budgetary process no matter what junior or senior position you hold. If your employer uses an imposed budgetary control system you may not have as much freedom to ask questions but you might want to point out as diplomatically as you can that there are problems with such systems. You might also like to put the following questions to the accountants and senior managers.

- How far is the time spent on preparing budgets cost effective?
- Do you think that budgets prepared for a calendar year is too long a period?
- Should those costs (and revenues) that relate to a longer timescale be apportioned to sub-budget periods?
- Is it appropriate to compare actual events with fixed budgets or should we use flexible budgets?
- Why can't I be responsible for preparing my own department's budget?
- Why do you alter my budget after I have prepared it?
- Do you expect me to be responsible for any variances that are outside my control?
- Why punish me and my staff when we were not responsible either for the budget or for what went wrong with it?

Conclusion

The full benefits of budgeting can only be gained if it is combined with a budgetary control system. The preparation of budgets is a valuable exercise in itself because it forces management to look ahead to what *might* happen rather than to look back at what *did* happen. However, it is even more valuable if it is also used as a form of control.

Budgetary control enables actual results to be measured frequently against an agreed budget (or plan). Departures from that budget can then be quickly spotted and steps taken to correct any unwelcome trends. There is a strong case for arguing that the comparison of actual results with a fixed budget may not be particularly helpful if the actual level of activity is different from that budgeted. It is recommended, therefore, that actual results should be compared with a flexed budget.

As so many functional budgets are based on the budgeted level of activity, it is vital that it is determined as accurately as possible, since an error in estimating the level of activity could affect the whole of the company's operational and financial activities. So it is important that any difference between the actual and the budgeted level of activity is investigated carefully.

Budgeting and budgetary control systems may be resented by managers and they might then react to the systems in such a way to protect their own position. This may not be of benefit to the entity as a whole.

Key points

1 A budget is a short-term plan.
2 Budgetary control is a cost control method that enables actual results to be compared with the budget, thereby enabling any necessary corrective action to be taken.
3 The preparation of budgets will be undertaken by a budget team.
4 Managers must be responsible for producing their own functional budgets.
5 Functional budgets are combined to form a master budget.
6 A fixed budget system compares actual results with the original budgets.
7 In a flexed budget system the budget may be flexed (or amended) to bring it into line with the actual level of activity.
8 A budgeting and budgetary control system is not neutral. It may cause managers to act in a way that is not in the best interests of the entity.

Check your learning

1 What is a budget?
2 List its essential features.
3 What is meant by 'budgetary control'?
4 List its essential features.
5 What is a variance?
6 What is a forecast?
7 How long is a normal budgeting period?
8 What is a sub-budget period?
9 What administration procedures does a budgeting system require?

Decision making

Pricing decisions

News clip

Munich Re

Munich Re, the world's largest reinsurer, has coped well in the financial crisis. The second quarter results were better than the first quarter and this July's insurance treaty renewals showed a price increase of 4.4%. Mr von Bomhard, the Chief Executive, said that he was not unhappy with the pricing level but he thought that the market should shift more quickly into a 'hardening mode'.

Source: Adapted from www.ft.com/cms, 5 August 2009.

A very important decision that managers have to make in both the profit-making sector and the not-for-profit sector is that relating to pricing. Supermarkets, for example, have to price their goods, while local authorities have to decide what to charge for adult education, leisure centres and meals on wheels.

Two types of pricing decisions can be distinguished. The first relates to the prices charged to customers or clients external to the entity. We will refer to this type as *external* pricing. The second type relates to prices charged by one part of an entity to another part, such as when components are supplied by one segment to another segment. This type of pricing is known as *transfer* pricing. We will deal with each type separately.

External pricing

External selling prices may be based either on market prices or on cost (see Figure 2.32). We will deal first with market-based prices.

Market-based pricing

Many goods and services are sold in highly competitive markets. This means that there may be many suppliers offering identical or near-identical products and they will be competing fiercely in respect of price, quality, reliability and service. If the demand for a product is *elastic*, then the lower the price the more units that will be sold. The opposite also applies and higher prices will result in fewer goods being sold. The demand for most everyday items of food, for example, is elastic.

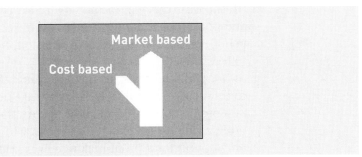

Figure 2.32   External pricing decisions

It follows that when demand is elastic it is unlikely that individual sellers can determine their own selling prices. So within narrow limits, they will have to base their selling prices on what is being charged in the market. Otherwise if they charge more than the market price their sales will be reduced. If they charge less than the market then their sales will increase but the market will quickly adjust to a lower level of selling prices.

Where market conditions largely determine a supplier's selling prices, it is particularly important to ensure that tight control is exercised over costs. Otherwise the gap between total sales revenue and total costs (i.e. the profit) will be insufficient to ensure an adequate return on capital employed.

In some cases the demand for goods is *inelastic* – i.e. price has little or no effect on the number of units sold. The demand for writing paper and stationery, for example, tends to be inelastic, probably because it is an infrequent purchase and it is not a significant element in most people's budgets. So when the demand for goods is inelastic, suppliers have much more freedom in determining their own selling prices and they may then base them on cost.

Cost-based pricing

There are a number of cost-based pricing methods. We summarize the main ones below and the circumstances in which they are most likely to be used.

- *Below variable cost.* This price would be used:
  - when an entity was trying to establish a new product on the market;
  - when an attempt was being made to drive out competitors;
  - as a loss leader, i.e. to encourage other goods to be bought.
  A price at this level could only be sustained for a very short period (unless it is used as a loss leader) since each unit sold would not be covering its variable cost.
- *At variable cost.* Variable cost prices may be used:
  - to launch a new product;
  - to drive out competition;
  - in difficult trading conditions;
  - as a loss leader; price could be held for some time but ultimately some contribution will be needed to cover the fixed costs.
- *At total production cost.* This will include the unit's direct costs and a share of the production overheads. Prices at this level could be held for some time (perhaps when demand is low) but eventually the entity would need to cover its non-production overheads and to make a profit.
- *At total cost.* This will include the direct cost and a share of both the production and non-production overheads. Again, such prices could be held for a very long period, perhaps during a long recession, but eventually some profit would need to be earned.
- *At cost plus.* The cost-plus method would either relate to total production cost or to total cost. The 'plus' element would be an addition to the cost to allow for non-production overhead and profit (in the case of total production cost) and for profit alone (in the case of total cost). In the long run, cost-plus prices are the only option for a profit-making entity. However, if prices are based entirely on cost then inefficiencies may be automatically built into the pricing system and this could lead to uncompetitiveness.

Activity 2.45

Make a list of all the factors that you think may determine the demand for a product.

Transfer pricing

News clip

Transfer pricing problems

Dixons (DGS International) has been informed that it is in breach of HM Revenue and Custom transfer pricing guidelines and it may have to pay back hundreds of millions of pounds. Transfer pricing relates to the value placed on assets or goods moved internally from one subsidiary to another – usually across international borders. HMRC pursues cases where it believes the price has been set artificially low for tax purposes.

Source: Adapted from www.accountancyage.com/articles/print/2240985, 23 April 2009.

In large entities it is quite common for one segment to trade with another segment. So what is 'revenue' to one segment will be 'expenditure' to the other. This means that when the results of all the various segments are consolidated, the revenue recorded in one segment's books of account will cancel out the expenditure in the other segment's books. Does it matter, therefore, what prices are charged for internal transfers?

The answer is 'Yes it does' because some segments (particularly if they are divisions of companies) are given a great deal of autonomy. They may have the authority, for example, to purchase goods and services from outside the entity. They almost certainly will do so if the price and service offered externally appears to be superior to any internal offer and this may cause them to suboptimize, i.e. to act in *their* own best interest although it may not be in the best interests of the entity as a whole.

Let us suppose that segment A fixes its transfer price on a cost-plus basis, say at £10 per unit. Segment B finds that it can purchase an identical unit externally at £8 per unit. Segment B is very likely to accept the external offer. But segment A's costs may be based on *absorbed costs*. The *extra cost* (i.e. the variable cost) of meeting segment B's order may be much less than the external price of £8 per unit. In these circumstances it may not be beneficial for the *entity as a whole* for segment B to purchase the units from an outside supplier.

It follows that a transfer price should to be set at a level that will encourage a supplying segment to trade internally and to discourage a receiving segment to buy its goods externally. There are various transfer-pricing methods that can be adopted (see Figure 2.33). We review the main ones below.

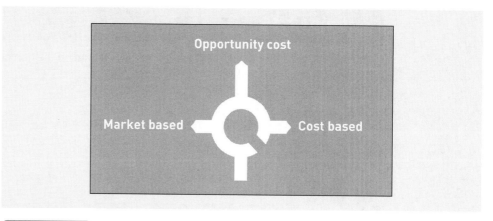

Figure 2.33 Transfer pricing decision

- *Market price.* If there are identical or similar goods and services offered externally, transfer prices based on market prices will neither encourage nor discourage supplying or receiving segments to trade externally.
- *Adjusted market price.* Market prices may be reduced in recognition of the lower costs attached to internal trading, e.g. advertising, administration and financing costs. This method encourages segments to trade with each other.
- *Total cost or total cost plus.* A transfer price based on total cost will include the direct costs plus a share of both production and non-production overhead. Total cost-plus methods allow for some profit. The main problems attached to the total-cost methods is that they build inefficiencies into the transfer price (as there is no incentive to control costs) and they therefore encourage suboptimization.
- *At variable cost or variable cost plus.* The variable cost method itself does not encourage a supplying segment to trade internally as no incentive is built into the transfer price, but a percentage addition may provide some incentive since it enables some contribution to be made towards fixed costs. However, transfer prices based on variable costs may be very attractive to *receiving* segments as the transfer price normally compares favourably with the external price. If the variable cost method is adopted it is recommended that it is based on the *standard* variable cost.
- *Negotiated price.* This method involves striking a bargain between the supplying and receiving segments based on a combination of market price and costs. As long as the discussions are mutually determined this method can be highly successful.
- *Opportunity cost.* This method may be somewhat impractical, but if the costs can be quantified it is the ideal one to adopt. A transfer price based on the opportunity cost comprises two elements: first, the standard variable cost in the supplying segment, and second the entity's opportunity cost resulting from the transaction. It is the second element that is the hardest to determine.

Activity 2.46

What is the best way out of the transfer price dilemma? Should it be based on market prices or on costs? Suppose as a manager you have the freedom to negotiate your own transfer prices with other divisional managers. Summarize the arguments that you would use in any ensuing discussions.

Special orders

On some occasions an entity may be asked to undertake an order beyond its normal trading arrangement and to quote a price for it. Such arrangements are known as *special orders*. The potential customer or client would normally expect to pay a lower price than the entity ordinarily charges, as well as possibly receiving some favourable treatment. What pricing policy should the entity adopt when asked to quote for a special order? Much will depend on whether it has some surplus capacity. If this is the case, it may be prepared to quote a price below variable cost if it wants to avoid a possible shutdown. However, the minimum price that it would *normally* be willing to accept would be equal to the incremental (or extra) cost of accepting the order.

The incremental cost involved may be the equivalent of the variable cost. Prices based at or below the variable cost would be extremely competitive, thereby helping to ensure that the customer accepted the quotation. The work gained would then absorb some of the entity's surplus capacity and help to keep its workforce occupied. There is also the possibility that the customer may place future orders at prices that would enable the entity to make a profit on them. But there is then the danger that in the meantime more profitable work has to be rejected because the entity cannot cope with both the special order and the additional work.

A price in excess of the variable cost would make a contribution towards fixed costs and this would clearly be the preferred option. The quoted price would have to be judged very finely because the higher the price the greater the risk that the customer would reject the quotation. So the decision would involve trying to determine what other suppliers are likely to charge and what terms they would offer.

An indication of the difficulties associated with determining whether a special order should be accepted is demonstrated in the example below.

Example

A special order

Amber Limited has been asked by a customer to supply a specially designed product. The customer has indicated that he would be willing to pay a maximum price of £100 per unit. The cost details are as follows.

Unit cost	£	£
Contract price		100
Less: Variable costs		
Direct materials	40	
Direct labour (2 hours)	30	
Variable overhead	10	80
Contribution		20

At a contract price of £100 per unit, each unit would make a contribution of £20. The customer is prepared to take 400 units, and so the total contribution towards fixed costs would be £8000 (400 units × £20). However, Amber has a shortage of direct labour and some of the staff would have to be switched from other orders to work on the special order. This would mean an average loss in contribution of £8 for every direct labour hour worked on the special order.

Required:
Determine whether Amber Limited should accept the special order.

Answer to Example

In order to determine whether Amber Limited should accept the special order, the extra contribution should be compared with the loss of contribution by having to switch the workforce from other orders. The calculations are as follows.

	£
Total contribution from the special order (400 units × £20 per unit)	8 000
Less: the opportunity cost of the normal contribution foregone	
[800 direct labour hours (400 units × 2 DLH) × £8 per unit]	6 400
Extra contribution	1 600

Tutorial notes

Before coming to a decision, the following points should also be considered. You will see that they range well beyond simple cost factors.
1 The costings relating to the special order should be carefully checked.
2 The customer should be asked to confirm in writing that it would be willing to pay a selling price of £100 per unit.
3 Determine whether the customer is likely to place additional orders for the product or not.
4 Check that the average contribution of £8 per direct labour hour, obtained from other orders, applies to the workforce that would be switched to the special order, i.e. is the contribution from the other orders that would be lost more or less than £8 per direct labour hour?
5 Is it possible that new staff could be recruited to work on the special order?
6 Is more profitable work likely to come along in the meantime? Would it mean that it could not be accepted during the progress of the order?

Recommendation

Assuming that the points raised in the above notes are satisfied, then the recommendation would be to accept the special order at a price of £100 per unit. This would mean that Amber's total contribution would be increased by £1600.

The management accountant's main role in dealing with special orders would be to supply historical and projected cost data of the financial consequences of particular options. The eventual decision would be taken by senior management using a wide range of quantitative and qualitative information. The type of questions asked would be similar to some of the issues covered in the tutorial notes in the solution to the example above.

Activity 2.47

The country is experiencing a deep recession. Trade is very bad. Then, rather unexpectedly, Company X is asked to supply one of its main products to a new customer, but unfortunately at a price well below the product's variable cost.

In two adjacent columns list (a) all the reasons why it should accept the order; and (b) why it should be rejected. Overall, what would be your decision?

Questions you should ask

The questions that you should put to your accountants about any specific de-cision-making problem will revolve round the robustness of the data that they have used and any non-quantitative factors they have incorporated into their recommendations. You could use the following questions as a guide.

- Where have you got the data from?
- How reliable are the basic facts?
- What assumptions have you adopted?
- Have you included only relevant costs?
- Have you tested the results on a probability basis?
- What non-quantitative factors have you been able to identify?
- Is it possible to put any monetary value on them?
- Do you think that we should go ahead with this proposal?

CHAPTER 3
Organisations and Behaviour

Unit 3: Organisations and Behaviour

Unit code: H/601/0551

QCF level: 4

Credit value: 15 credits

Aim

The aim of this unit is to give learners an understanding of individual and group behaviour in organisations and to examine current theories and their application in managing behaviour in the workplace.

Unit abstract

This unit focuses on the behaviour of individuals and groups within organisations. It explores the links between the structure and culture of organisations and how these interact and influence the behaviour of the workforce. The structure of a large multi-national company with thousands of employees worldwide will be very different from a small local business with 20 employees. The way in which an organisation structures and organises its workforce will impact on the culture that develops within the organisation. This system of shared values and beliefs will determine and shape the accepted patterns of behaviour of an organisation's workforce. The culture in organisations that differ in size, for example, or are from different sectors of the economy can be very different.

The structure and culture of an organisation are key factors which contribute to motivating the workforce at all levels of the organisation. The Japanese were instrumental in developing a culture of 'continuous improvement through teamwork' in their manufacturing industry. This culture has now been exported around the world and encapsulates the way in which structure and culture contribute to patterns of behaviour in the workplace. This unit will develop learner understanding of the behaviour of people within organisations and of the significance that organisational design has on shaping that behaviour.

Learning outcomes

On successful completion of this unit a learner will:

1 Understand the relationship between organisational structure and culture
2 Understand different approaches to management and leadership
3 Understand ways of using motivational theories in organisations
4 Understand mechanisms for developing effective teamwork in organisations

Unit content

1 **Understand the relationship between organisational structure and culture**

Types of organisation and associated structures: functional, product-based, geographically based, multi-functional and multi-divisional structures, matrix, centralisation and decentralisation; organisational charts; spans of control; internal and external network structures; flexible working

Organisational culture: classification of organisational culture – power culture, role culture, task culture, person culture; cultural norms and symbols; values and beliefs; development of organisational culture

Diagnosing behavioural problems: concepts; principles; perspectives; methodology

Perception: definition; perceptual selection; perception and work behaviour; attitude; ability and aptitude; intelligence

Significance and nature of individual differences: self and self-image; personality and work behaviour; conflict

Individual behaviour at work: personality, traits and types; its relevance in understanding self and others

2 **Understand different approaches to management and leadership**

Development of management thought: scientific management; classical administration; bureaucracy; human relations approach; systems approach; contingency approach

Functions of management: planning; organising; commanding; coordinating; controlling

Managerial roles: interpersonal; informational; decisional

Nature of managerial authority: power; authority; responsibility; delegation; conflict

Frames of reference for leadership activities: opportunist; diplomat; technician; achiever; strategist; magician; pluralistic; transformational; change

3 **Understand ways of using motivational theories in organisations**

Motivation theories: Maslow's Hierarchy of Needs; Herzberg's Motivation – Hygiene theory; McGregor's Theory X and Y; Vroom and Expectancy theories; Maccoby, McCrae and Costa – personality dimensions

Motivation and performance: rewards and incentives; motivation and managers; monetary and non-monetary rewards

Leadership: leadership in organisations; managers and leaders; leadership traits; management style; contingency approach; leadership and organisational culture

Leadership and successful change in organisations: pluralistic; transformational; communications; conflict

4 **Understand mechanisms for developing effective teamwork in organisations**

Teams and team building: groups and teams; informal and formal groups; purpose of teams; selecting team members; team roles; Belbin's theory; stages in team development; team building; team identity; team loyalty; commitment to shared beliefs; multi-disciplinary teams

Team dynamics: group norms; decision-making behaviour; dysfunctional teams; cohesiveness

Impact of technology on team functioning: technology; communication; change; networks and virtual teams; global and cross-cultural teams

Learning outcomes and assessment criteria

Learning outcomes On successful completion of this unit a learner will:	Assessment criteria for pass The learner can:
LO1 Understand the relationship between organisational structure and culture	1.1 compare and contrast different organisational structures and culture 1.2 explain how the relationship between an organisation's structure and culture can impact on the performance of the business 1.3 discuss the factors which influence individual behaviour at work
LO2 Understand different approaches to management and leadership	2.1 compare the effectiveness of different leadership styles in different organisations 2.2 explain how organisational theory underpins the practice of management 2.3 evaluate the different approaches to management used by different organisations
LO3 Understand ways of using motivational theories in organisations	3.1 discuss the impact that different leadership styles may have on motivation in organisations in periods of change 3.2 compare the application of different motivational theories within the workplace 3.3 evaluate the usefulness of a motivation theory for managers
LO4 Understand mechanisms for developing effective teamwork in organisations	4.1 explain the nature of groups and group behaviour within organisations 4.2 discuss factors that may promote or inhibit the development of effective teamwork in organisations 4.3 evaluate the impact of technology on team functioning within a given organisation

Guidance

Links

This unit links to the following units within this specification *Unit 21: Human Resource Management, Unit 22: Managing Human Resources, Unit 23: Human Resources Development* and *Unit 24: Employee Relations*.

This unit also links to the Management and Leadership NOS as mapped in *Annexe B*.

Essential requirements

There are no essential or unique resources required for the delivery of this unit.

Employer engagement and vocational contexts

Centres should develop links with local businesses. Many businesses and chambers of commerce want to promote local business and are often willing to provide guest speakers, visit opportunities and information about the operation of their businesses.

Business organisations: the internal environment

Introduction

The internal features of business organisations have received considerable attention from scholars of organisation and management, and a large number of texts have been devoted to this aspect of business studies.[1] In the discussion below, the aim is to focus on three areas of the internal organisation that relate directly to a study of the business environment: approaches to understanding organisations, organisational structures, and key functions within the enterprise. Further insight into these aspects and into management and organisational behaviour generally can be gained by consulting the many specialist books in this field.

A central theme running through any analysis of the internal environment is the idea of **management**, which has been subjected to a wide variety of definitions. As used in this context, management is seen both as a system of roles fulfilled by individuals who manage the organisation (e.g. entrepreneur, resource manager, co-ordinator, leader, motivator, organiser) and as a process which enables an organisation to achieve its objectives. The essential point is that management should be seen as a function of organisations, rather than as a controlling element, and its task is to enable the organisation to identify and achieve its objectives and to adapt to change. Managers need to integrate the various influences on the organisation – including people, technology, systems and the environment – in a manner best designed to meet the needs of the enterprise at the time in question and be prepared to institute change as and when circumstances dictate.

Approaches to organisation and management

An important insight into the principles which are felt to underlie the process of management can be gained by a brief examination of organisational theories. These theories or approaches – some of which date back to the late nineteenth century – represent the views of both practising managers and academics as to the factors that determine organisational effectiveness and the influences on individuals and groups within the work environment. Broadly speaking, these approaches can be broken down into three main categories: the classical approach, the human relations approach, and the systems approach.[2]

The classical approach

Classical theories of organisation and management mostly date from the first half of the twentieth century and are associated with the work of writers such as Taylor, Fayol, Urwick and Brech. In essence, the classicists viewed organisations as formal structures established to achieve a particular number of objectives under the direction of management. By identifying a set of principles to guide managers in the design of the organisational structure, the proponents of the classical view believed that organisations would be able to achieve their objectives more effectively. Fayol, for example, identified fourteen principles which included the division of work, the scalar chain, centralisation and the unity of command – features which also found expression in Weber's notion of 'bureaucracy'. Urwick's rules or principles similarly emphasised aspects of organisation structure and operations – such as specialisation, co-ordination, authority, responsibility and the span of control – and were presented essentially as a code of good management practice.

Within the classical approach special attention is often given to two important sub-groupings, known as **scientific management** and **bureaucracy**. The former is associated with the pioneering work of F. W. Taylor (1856–1915) who believed that scientific methods could be attached to the design of work so that productivity could be increased. For Taylor, the systematic analysis of jobs (e.g. using some form of work study technique) was seen as the key to finding the best way to perform a particular task and thereby of achieving significant productivity gains from individuals which would earn them increased financial rewards. In Taylor's view, the responsibility for the institution of a scientific approach lay with management, under whose control and direction the workers would operate to the mutual benefit of all concerned.

The second sub-group, bureaucracy, draws heavily on the work of Max Weber (1864–1920) whose studies of authority structures highlighted the importance of 'office' and 'rules' in the operation of organisations. According to Weber, bureaucracy – with its system of rules and procedures, specified spheres of competence, hierarchical organisation of offices, appointment based on merit, high level of specialisation and impersonality – possessed a degree of technical superiority over other forms of organisation, and this explained why an increasing number of enterprises were becoming bureaucratic in structure. Over 50 years after Weber's studies were first published in English, bureaucratic organisation remains a key feature of many enterprises throughout the world and is clearly linked to increasing organisational size and complexity. Notwithstanding the many valid criticisms of Weber's work, it is difficult to imagine how it could be otherwise.

The human relations approach

Whereas the classical approach focuses largely on structure and on the formal organisation, the **human relations approach** to management emphasises the importance of people in the work situation and the influence of social and psychological factors in shaping organisational behaviour. Human relations theorists have primarily been concerned with issues such as individual motivation, leadership, communications and group dynamics and have stressed the significance of the informal pattern of relationships which exist within the formal structure. The factors influencing human behaviour have accordingly been portrayed as a key to achieving greater organisational effectiveness, thus elevating the 'management of people' to a prime position in the determination of managerial strategies.

The early work in this field is associated with Elton Mayo (1880–1949) and with the famous Hawthorne Experiments, conducted at the Western Electric Company (USA) between 1924 and 1932. What these experiments basically showed was that individuals at work were members of informal (i.e. unofficial) as well as formal groups and that group influences were fundamental to explaining individual

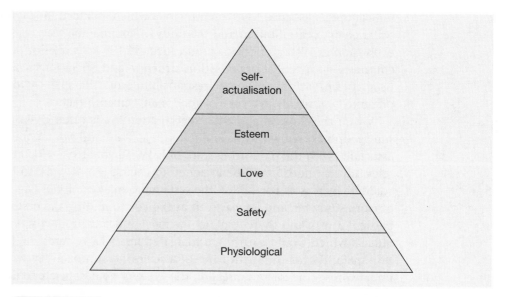

Figure 3.1   A hierachy of needs

behaviour. Later work by writers such as Maslow, McGregor, Argyris, Likert and Herzberg continued to stress the importance of the human factor in determining organisational effectiveness, but tended to adopt a more psychological orientation, as exemplified by Maslow's 'hierarchy of needs' and McGregor's 'Theory X and Theory Y'. Maslow's central proposition was that individuals seek to satisfy specific groups of needs, ranging from basic physiological requirements (e.g. food, sleep, sex), through safety, love and esteem, to self-actualisation (i.e. self-fulfilment), progressing systematically up the hierarchy as each lower-level need is satisfied (see Figure 3.1). To McGregor individuals at work were seen by management as either inherently lazy (Theory X) or committed to the organisation's objectives and often actively seeking responsibility (Theory Y). These perceptions consequently provided the basis for different styles of management, which ranged from the coercive to the supportive.

McGregor's concern with management styles is reflected in later studies, including Ouichi's notion of Theory Z.[3] According to Ouichi one of the key factors in the success of Japanese manufacturing industries was their approach to the management of people. Theory Z organisations were those which offered workers long-term (often lifetime) employment, a share in decision making, opportunities for training, development and promotion, and a number of other advantages which gave them a positive orientation towards the organisation. For Ouichi, the key to organisational effectiveness lay in the development of a Japanese-style Theory Z environment, adapted to western requirements.

The systems approach

More recent approaches to organisation and management have helped to integrate previous work on structures, people and technology, by portraying organisations as socio-technical systems interacting with their environment. Under this approach – which became popular in the 1960s – organisations were seen as complex systems of people, tasks and technologies that were part of and interacted with a larger environment, comprising a wide range of influences. This environment was frequently subject to fluctuations, which on occasions could become turbulent (i.e. involving rapid and often unpredictable change). For organisations to survive and prosper, adaptation to environmental demands was seen as a necessary requirement and one which was central to the process of management.

The essence of the **systems approach** is that organisations, including those involved in business, are open systems, interacting with their environment as they convert inputs into output. Inputs include people, finance, materials and information, provided by the environment in which the organisation exists and operates. Output comprises such items as goods and services, information, ideas and waste, discharged into the environment for consumption by 'end' or 'intermediate' users and in some cases representing inputs used by other organisations.

Systems invariably comprise a number of **sub-systems** through which the process of conversion or transformation occurs. Business organisations, for example, usually have sub-systems which deal with activities such as production, marketing, accounting and human resource management and each of these in turn may involve smaller sub-systems (e.g. sales, quality control, training) which collectively constitute the whole. Just as the organisation as a system interacts with its environment, so do the sub-systems and their component elements, which also interact with each other. In the case of the latter, the boundary between sub-systems is usually known as an 'interface'.

While the obvious complexities of the systems approach need not be discussed, it is important to emphasise that most modern views of organisations draw heavily on the work in this area, paying particular attention to the interactions between people, technology, structure and environment and to the key role of management in directing the organisation's activities towards the achievement of its goals. Broadly speaking, management is seen as a critical sub-system within the total organisation, responsible for the co-ordination of the other sub-systems and for ensuring that internal and external relationships are managed effectively. As changes occur in one part of the system these will induce changes elsewhere and this will require a management response that will have implications for the organisation and for its sub-systems. Such changes may be either the cause or effect of changes in the relationship between the organisation and its environment, and the requirement for managers is to adapt to the new conditions without reducing the organisation's effectiveness.

Given the complex nature of organisations and the environments in which they operate, a number of writers have suggested a **contingency approach** to organisational design and management (e.g. Lawrence and Lorsch, Woodward, Perrow, Burns and Stalker).[4] In essence, this approach argues that there is no single form of organisation best suited to all situations and that the most appropriate organisational structure and system of management is dependent upon the contingencies of the situation (e.g. size, technology, environment) for each organisation. In some cases a bureaucratic structure might be the best way to operate, while in others much looser and more organic methods of organisation might be more effective. In short, issues of organisational design and management depend on choosing the best combination in the light of the relevant situational variables; this might mean different structures and styles coexisting within an organisation.

Organisational structures

Apart from the very simplest form of enterprise in which one individual carries out all tasks and responsibilities, business organisations are characterised by a division of labour which allows employees to specialise in particular roles and to occupy designated positions in pursuit of the organisation's objectives. The resulting pattern of relationships between individuals and roles constitutes what is known as the organisation's structure and represents the means by which the purpose and work of the enterprise is carried out. It also provides a framework through which communications can occur and within which the processes of management can be applied.

Responsibility for establishing the formal structure of the organisation lies with management and a variety of options is available. Whatever form is chosen, the basic need is to identify a structure which will best sustain the success of the enterprise and will permit the achievement of a number of important objectives. Through its structure an organisation should be able to:

- achieve efficiency in the utilisation of resources;
- provide opportunities for monitoring organisational performance;
- ensure the accountability of individuals;
- guarantee co-ordination between the different parts of the enterprise;
- provide an efficient and effective means of organisational communication;
- create job satisfaction, including opportunities for progression; and
- adapt to changing circumstances brought about by internal or external developments.

In short, structure is not an end in itself, but a means to an end and should ideally reflect the needs of the organisation within its existing context and taking into account its future requirements.

---

mini case   'Into the Dragon's Den'

As this section illustrates, the structure of an organisation is a means by which an enterprise can achieve its objectives. As the environment in which a business operates changes, firms should be willing to adapt the structure to meet the new circumstances. This might mean moving beyond the traditional models discussed below, in an effort to improve performance.

The global pharmaceutical giant GlaxoSmithKline (GSK) illustrates this idea of an evolving organisational structure. In July 2008, GSK announced that in future its scientists would have to pitch their ideas for new drugs to a development board, based essentially on the lines of the 'Dragon's Den', a popular UK television programme where would-be entrepreneurs seek to gain backing for their ideas from a group of financiers. The board will include two venture capitalists and will be a mixture of executives from inside the company and GSK outsiders. The plan is to stimulate innovation by requiring smaller teams of scientists to pitch three-year business plans to the new drug discovery investment board in an effort to secure funding for new drug treatments.

You can access the website for GSK at *www.gsk.com*

The essence of structure is the division of work between individuals and the formal organisational relationships that are created between them. These relationships will be reflected not only in individual job descriptions, but also in the overall **organisation chart** which designates the formal pattern of role relationships, and the interactions between roles and the individuals occupying those roles. Individual authority relationships can be classified as line, staff, functional and lateral and arise from the defined pattern of responsibilities, as follows:

- *Line relationships* occur when authority flows vertically downward through the structure from superior to subordinate (e.g. managers–section leader–staff).
- *Staff relationships* are created when senior personnel appoint assistants who normally have no authority over other staff but act as an extension of their superior.
- *Functional relationships* are those between specialists (or advisers) and line managers and their subordinates (e.g. when a specialist provides a common service throughout the organisation but has no authority over the users of the service). The personnel or computing function may be one such service that creates a functional relationship. (Note that specialists have line relationships with their own subordinates.)
- *Lateral relationships* exist across the organisation, particularly between individuals occupying equivalent positions within different departments or sections (e.g. committees, heads of departments, section leaders).

With regard to the division of work and the grouping of organisational activities, this can occur in a variety of ways. These include:

- *By function or major purpose*, associated particularly with departmental structures.
- *By product or service*, where individuals responsible for a particular product or service are grouped together.
- *By location*, based on geographical criteria.
- *By common processes* (e.g. particular skills or methods of operation).
- *By client group* (e.g. children, the disabled, the elderly).

In some organisations a particular method of grouping will predominate; in others there will tend to be a variety of types and each has its own particular advantages and disadvantages. In the discussion below, attention is focused on five main methods of grouping activities in business organisations. Students should attempt to discover what types of structure exist within their own educational institution and the logic (if any) which underlies the choices made.

Functional organisation

The functional approach to organisation is depicted in Figure 3.2. As its name indicates, in this type of structure activities are clustered together by common purpose or function. All marketing activities, for example, are grouped together as a

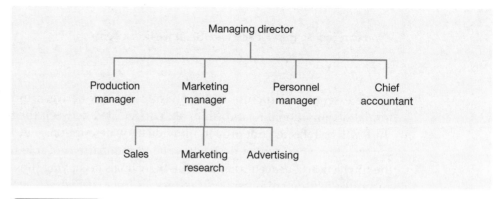

Figure 3.2   A functional organisation structure

common function, typically within a marketing department. Similarly, other areas of activity, such as production, finance, personnel and research and development, have their own specialised sections or departments, responsible for all the tasks required of that function.

Apart from its obvious simplicity, the functional organisation structure allows individuals to be grouped together on the basis of their specialisms and technical expertise, and this can facilitate the development of the function they offer as well as providing a recognised path for promotion and career development. On the downside, functional specialisation, particularly through departments, is likely to create sectional interests which may operate to the disadvantage of the organisation as a whole, particularly where inequalities in resource allocation between functions become a cause for interfunction rivalry. It could also be argued that this form of structure is most suited to single-product firms and that it becomes less appropriate as organisations diversify their products and/or markets. In such circumstances, the tendency will be for businesses to look for the benefits which can arise from specialisation by product or from the divisionalisation of the enterprise.

Organisation by product or service

In this case the division of work and the grouping of activities is dictated by the product or service provided (see Figure 3.3), such that each group responsible for a

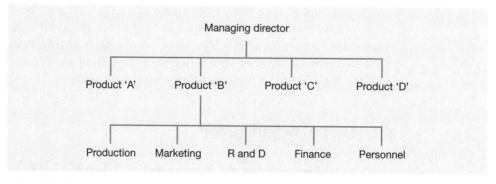

Figure 3.3   A product-based structure

particular part of the output of the organisation may have its own specialist in the different functional areas (e.g. marketing, finance, personnel). One advantage of this type of structure is that it allows an organisation to offer a diversified range of products, as exemplified by the different services available in National Health Service hospitals (e.g. maternity, orthopaedic, geriatric, and so forth). Its main disadvantage is the danger that the separate units or divisions within the enterprise may attempt to become too autonomous, even at the expense of other parts of the organisation, and this can present management with problems of co-ordination and control.

The divisional structure

As firms diversify their products and/or markets – often as a result of merger or takeover – a structure is needed to co-ordinate and control the different parts of the organisation. This structure is likely to be the divisional (or multi-divisional) company.

A **divisionalised structure** is formed when an organisation is split up into a number of self-contained business units, each of which operates as a profit centre. Such a division may occur on the basis of product or market or a combination of the two, with each unit tending to operate along functional or product lines, but with certain key functions (e.g. finance, personnel, corporate planning) provided centrally, usually at company headquarters (see Figure 3.4).

The main benefit of the multi-divisional company is that it allows each part of what can be a very diverse organisation to operate semi-independently in producing and marketing its products, thus permitting each division to design its offering to suit local market conditions – a factor of prime importance where the firm operates on a multinational basis. The dual existence of divisional **profit centres** and a central unit responsible for establishing strategy at a global level can, however, be a source of considerable tension, particularly where the needs and aims of the centre appear to conflict with operations at the local level or to impose

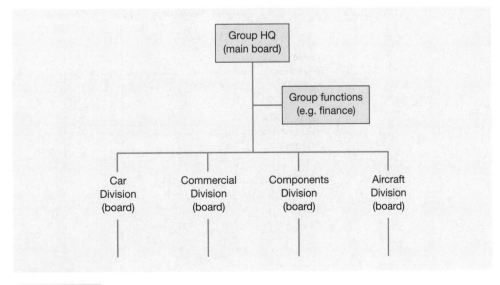

Figure 3.4   A divisional structure

burdens seen to be unreasonable by divisional managers (e.g. the allocation of central overhead costs).

Much the same kind of arguments apply to the **holding company**, though this tends to be a much looser structure for managing diverse organisations, favoured by both UK and Japanese companies. Under this arrangement, the different elements of the organisation (usually companies) are co-ordinated and controlled by a parent body, which may be just a financial entity established to maintain or gain control of other trading companies. Holding companies are associated with the growth of firms by acquisition which gives rise to a high degree of product or market diversification. They are also a popular means of operating a multinational organisation.

Matrix structures

A **matrix** is an arrangement for combining functional specialisation (e.g. through departments) with structures built around products, projects or programmes (see Figure 3.5). The resulting grid (or matrix) has a two-way flow of authority and responsibility. Within the functional elements, the flow is vertically down the line from superior to subordinate and this creates a degree of stability and certainty for the individuals located within the department or unit. Simultaneously, as a member of a project group or product team, an individual is normally answerable horizontally to the project manager whose responsibility is to oversee the successful completion of the project, which in some cases may be of very limited duration.

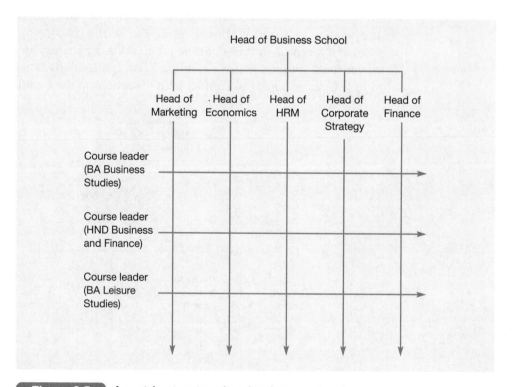

Figure 3.5   A matrix structure in a business school

Matrix structures offer various advantages, most notably flexibility, opportunities for staff development, an enhanced sense of ownership of a project or programme, customer orientation and the co-ordination of information and expertise. On the negative side, difficulties can include problems of co-ordination and control, conflicting loyalties for staff and uncertain lines of authority. It is not uncommon in an organisation designed on matrix lines for project or programme leaders to be unsure of their authority over the staff from the contributing departments. Nor is it unknown for functional managers to withdraw their co-operation and/or support for projects located outside their immediate sphere of influence.

Project teams

Despite its flexibility, the matrix often has a degree of permanence; in contrast, the project team is essentially a temporary structure established as a means of carrying out a particular task, often in a highly unstable environment. Once the task is complete, the team is disbanded and individuals return to their usual departments or are assigned to a new project.

Fashioned around technical expertise rather than managerial rank and often operating closely with clients, project teams are increasingly common in high-technology firms, construction companies and in some types of service industry, especially management consultancies and advertising. Rather than being a replacement for the existing structure, they operate alongside it and utilise in-house staff (and in some cases, outside specialists) on a project-by-project basis. While this can present logistical and scheduling problems and may involve some duplication of resources, it can assist an organisation in adapting to change and uncertainty and in providing products to the customer's specifications. Project teams tend to be at their most effective when objectives and tasks are well defined, when the client is clear as to the desired outcome and when the team is chosen with care.

---

mini case   Royal Dutch Shell

In March 1995 the multinational Anglo-Dutch oil giant, Royal Dutch Shell, announced its intention to radically change its long-admired matrix organisation (see, for example, the *Financial Times*, 30 March 1995). For historical reasons, Shell had developed a structure based on geographically defined operating companies. These operating companies had executives representing national or regional units, business sectors (or divisions) and functions such as finance. Within this three-dimensional matrix, powerful individuals were able to influence the organisation's policies at regional level and a considerable bureaucracy was required to 'police' the matrix and to co-ordinate decisions between the different elements of the structure.

Faced with growing global competition and shareholder pressure for improved performance, Shell decided to restructure the organisation by attacking problems of overstaffing and bureaucracy and by eliminating many of the regional fiefdoms through which the company had come to run its worldwide empire. Its plan involved shaping the group around five business organisations covering its main activities (e.g. exploration and production, refining and marketing, etc.), with each operating company reporting to and receiving its strategic targets from whichever of the five organisations were relevant to its activities. A new system of business committees was given responsibility for strategic and investment decisions within the different organisations, although executive authority rested with the operating companies. Through this arrangement Shell hoped to retain the sensitivity to local market needs that had traditionally been part of its organisational creed.

In a further effort to improve the company's performance, Shell indicated that more restructuring needed to take place (see, for example, the *Guardian*, 15 December 1998). Part of its blueprint for reshaping itself for the twenty-first century included additional streamlining of its management structure, away from committee-based decision making and towards a system based on American-style chief executives.

Subsequently in October 2004 the company announced the merger of its two elements – Royal Dutch and Shell Transport and Trading – into a single company, to be known as Royal Dutch Shell plc. The new entity comprises an Executive Board, a Supervisory Board, a Board of Management and a Board of Directors for Shell Transport. Members of the Executive Committee are also members of the latter two boards.

 web link   The website address for Royal Dutch Shell is *www.shell.com*

The virtual organisation

As indicated above, traditional organisations have structures which are designed to facilitate the transformation of inputs into output. Increasingly as the business environment changes, relationships both within and between organisations have needed to become more flexible and this has given rise to such developments as the growth in teleworking and the establishment of dynamic broker/agent networks involving considerable outsourcing of sub-tasks to 'agents' (e.g. manufacturing, distribution) by the core organisation (the 'broker'). It is fair to say that this demand for greater flexibility has been driven partly by the market and partly by cost considerations and the process of change has been facilitated by relatively rapid developments in information technology. One area currently exciting the interest of writers on management and organisation is the concept of the **virtual organisation**, arguably the ultimate form of organisational flexibility.

In essence a virtual organisation or firm signifies an extremely loose web of essentially freelance individuals or businesses who organise themselves to produce a specific customer product (e.g. an individual holiday package with particular features unique to the customer). Without any permanent structure or hierarchy this so-called firm can constantly change its shape and, despite existing across space and time, tends to appear edgeless, with its inputs, outputs and employees increasingly dispersed across the linked world of information systems. Given modern forms of communication, the potential exists for a totally electronic-based organisation trading in expertise and information with no real-world physical identity. This stands in stark contrast to the traditional view of the firm as an arrangement which adds value by transforming basic economic inputs (e.g. land, labour, capital) into physical outputs or services.

For a useful reading list on virtual organisations *see*
www–users.cs.york.ac.uk/~kimble/teaching/mis/Virtual_Organisations.html

Structural change

Internal change is an important feature of the modern business organisation. In order to remain competitive and meet stakeholder needs, a firm may have to find ways to restructure its organisation as the environment in which it operates changes. Solutions can range from a partial or wholesale shift in the organisation's structural form to strategies for reducing the overall size and shape of the company (e.g. **downsizing**) or a radical redesign of business processes (e.g. **re-engineering**).

Whereas business re-engineering normally connotes a root-and-branch reform of the way in which the business operates, downsizing essentially involves shrinking the organisation to make it leaner and fitter and hopefully more flexible in its response to the marketplace. For some companies this means little more than reducing the size of the workforce through natural wastage and/or redundancies, as and when opportunities arise; for others it involves delayering the organisation by removing a tier, or tiers, of management, thus effectively flattening the organisation's hierarchy and helping it to reduce its unit costs of production.

In its most systematic and long-term form, downsizing can be used as a vehicle for cultural change through which an organisation's employees are encouraged to embrace notions of continuous improvement and innovation, and to accept that structural reform is a permanent and natural state of affairs. Under such an approach, retraining and reskilling become vital tools in implementing the chosen strategy and in shaping the organisation to meet the demands of its changing environment. The danger is, however, that a firm may become too concerned with restructuring as a cure for all its problems, when the real cause of its difficulties lies in its marketplace. Cutting the number of employees, in such a situation, is unlikely to make unattractive products attractive, nor is it likely to boost morale within the organisation.

Organisation cultures and contexts

Types of culture

This section outlines three ways of describing and comparing cultures.

Competing values framework

The competing values model developed by Quinn *et al.* (2003) is based on the inherent tensions between flexibility or control and between an internal or an external focus. Figure 3.6 shows four cultural types.

Open systems

This represents an open systems view, in which people recognise that the external environment plays a significant role, and is a vital source of ideas, energy and resources. It also sees the environment as complex and turbulent, requiring entrepreneurial, visionary leadership and flexible, responsive behaviour. Key motivating factors are growth, stimulation, creativity and variety. Examples are start-up firms and new business units – organic, flexible operations.

Rational goal

Members see the organisation as a rational, efficiency-seeking unit. They define effectiveness in terms of production or economic goals that satisfy external requirements. Managers create structures to deal with the outside world. Leadership tends to be directive, goal oriented and functional. Key motivating factors include competition and the achievement of predetermined ends. Examples are large, established businesses – mechanistic.

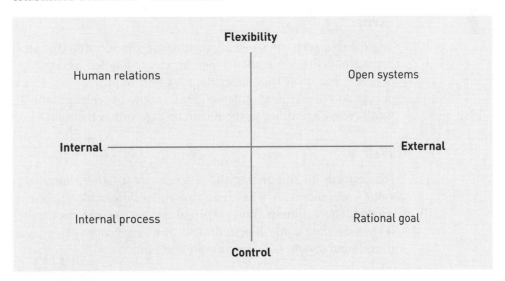

Figure 3.6 Types of organisational culture

Source: Based on Quinn et al. (2003).

Internal process

Here members pay little attention to the external world, being more focused on internal matters. Their goal is to make the unit efficient, stable and controlled. Goals are known, tasks are repetitive, and methods stress specialisation, rules and procedures. Leaders tend to be conservative and cautious, emphasising technical issues. Key motivating factors include security, stability and order. Examples include utilities and public authorities – suspicious of change.

Human relations

People emphasise the value of informal interpersonal relations rather than formal structures. They try to maintain the organisation and nurture its members, defining effectiveness in terms of their well-being and commitment. Leaders tend to be participative, considerate and supportive. Motivating factors include attachment, cohesiveness and membership. Examples are found in voluntary groups, professional service firms and some internal support functions.

Charles Handy's cultural types

Charles Handy (1993), developing an idea of Roger Harrison, distinguished four cultures, which he designated power, role, task and person culture.

Power

A dominant central figure holds power: others follow the centre's policy and interpret new situations in the way the leader would. Many entrepreneurial firms operate in this way, with few rules but with well-understood, implicit codes on how to behave and work. The firm relies on the individual rather than on seeking consensus through discussion.

Role

Typical characteristics of this culture are the job description or the procedure. Managers define what they expect in clear, detailed job descriptions. They select people for a job if they meet the specified requirements. Procedures guide how people and departments interact. If all follow the rules coordination is straightforward. People's position in the hierarchy determines their power.

Task

People focus on completing the task or project rather than their formal role. They value each other for what they can contribute and expect everyone to help as needed. The emphasis is on getting the resources and people for the job and then relying on their commitment and enthusiasm. People will typically work in teams, to combine diverse skills into a common purpose.

Person

The individual is at the centre and any structure or system is there to serve them. The form is unusual – small professional and artistic organisations are probably closest to it, and perhaps experiments in communal living. They exist to meet the needs of the professionals or the members, rather than some larger organisational goal.

Activity 3.1   Cultural examples

For each of Handy's four cultural types, identify an example from within this text that seems to correspond most closely to that form.

- What clues about the company have you used to decide that allocation?
- Why do you think that culture is suitable for that organisation?
- What evidence would you seek to decide if that culture was suitable?
- Compare the similarities and differences in the competing values and Handy models.

Multiple cultures

The third perspective introduces the idea that organisations have not one, but several cultures. Early discussions of culture (Peters and Waterman, 1982) explored the benefits to an organisation of a single, unified culture. In contrast, Martin (2002) suggested that observers could take one of three perspectives towards a culture:

1 **Integration** – a focus on identifying consistencies in the data, and using those common patterns to explain events.
2 **Differentiation** – a focus on conflict, identifying different and possibly conflicting views of members towards events.
3 **Fragmentation** – a focus on the fluid nature of organisations, and on the interplay and change of views about events.

Ogbonna and Harris (1998; 2002) provided empirical support for this view, based on interviews with staff at all levels of three retailing companies. They found that the position of a person in the hierarchy determined their perspective on the culture, and concluded that attempts to introduce cultural change based on head office values were unlikely to work. As consensus on culture was unlikely, they advised managers to recognise the range of sub-cultures within their oganisation, and only seek to reconcile those differences that were essential to policy. They also observed that culture remains a highly subjective idea, largely in the eye of the beholder 'and is radically different according to an individual's position in the hierarchy'.

Culture and performance

Schein, and most other writers on culture, see it as something that can be managed as a tool to improve organisational performance, though others question this link. Kotter and Heskett (1992) studied 207 companies and attempted to relate the strength of their culture to economic performance. Although the variables were positively correlated, the relationship was much weaker than advocates of culture as a factor in performance have predicted. Some doubt the ability of managers to change a culture. The next Key Ideas feature illustrates one of these critical views.

Table 3.1 Hierarchical position and cultural perspectives

Position in hierarchy	Cultural perspective	Description	Example
Head office managers	Integration	Cultural values should be shared across the organisation. Unified culture both desirable and attainable	'If we can get every ... part of the company doing what they should be doing, we'll beat everybody.'
Store managers	Differentiation	Reconciling conflicting views of head office and shop floor. See cultural pluralism as inevitable	'People up at head office are all pushing us in different directions. Jill in Marketing wants customer focus, June in Finance wants lower costs.'
Store employees	Fragmented	Confused by contradictory nature of the espoused values. See organisation as complex and unpredictable	'One minute it's this, the next it's that. You can't keep up with the flavour of the month.'

Source: Based on Ogbonna and Harris (1998); Ogbonna and Harris (2002).

key ideas

Martin Parker – a critical perspective on culture

Parker (2000) takes a sceptical view of the idea that a strong culture improves performance, while acknowledging that it 'begins to put forward a valuable language which can be used to represent organization and organizing' (p. 10). His book is an attempt to rescue culture from 'managerialism', and includes a valuable historical chapter, and some extended case studies.

He reviews three popular managerialist works (Ouchi, 1981; Deal and Kennedy, 1982; Peters and Waterman, 1982) and comments critically on their methods (lack of counter-examples, and companies with strong cultures that failed); the limited range of economic sectors; and the sales promotion. He suggests that one of the attractions of their work may have been that readers saw it as a counter to earlier views that stressed bureaucratic, quantitative and rational methods for controlling staff. Yet promoting culture as an organisational tool, while apparently more humane, may have the same intention: 'to intervene in the identity of the employee just as all organisational control strategies ... have done' (p. 25).

He concluded that rather than the single strong culture advocated by the managerialist writers, organisations have multiple cultures reflecting three divisions by which people distinguish themselves – space/function, generation, and occupation/profession. Even if these overlap, they illuminate the perspectives from which members view events, and that are likely to hinder attempts to develop unified, consensual cultures to control employees.

Source: Parker (2000).

Others suggest that while the link to performance may be unclear the underlying ideas may be more beneficial than harmful – including in not-for-profit settings. Watson (1994) suggested:

> people do not wander away from serving the key purposes of the organisation's founders or leaders. The tightness of control comes from people choosing to do what is required of them because they wish to serve the values which they share with those in charge. These values, typically focusing on quality of service to customers, are transmitted and manifested in the organisation's culture. This culture uses stories, myths and legends to keep these values alive and people tend to be happy to share these values and subscribe to the corporate legends because to do so is to find meaning in their lives. (p. 16)

Thompson and McHugh (2002), while also critical of much writing on the topic, observe that:

> Creating a culture resonant with the overall goals is relevant to any organisation, whether it be a trade union, voluntary group or producer co-operative. Indeed, it is more important in such consensual groupings. Co-operatives, for example, can

case study   Nokia – the case continues www.nokia.com

In May 2004 the company had surprised the market by announcing that its share of the handset market had slipped to 29 per cent, against 35 per cent the previous year. However, it also pointed out that demand was growing rapidly in China, India and Russia, and many consumers in established markets were upgrading to colour screens and camera phones. Sales of 3G infrastructure equipment were growing as operators became more confident in the success of that technology.

Since 2004 the company has had four divisions – the main handsets business; mobile infrastructure (which builds networks for operators such as Vodafone); multi-media services: and enterprise solutions. Analysts saw this as an attempt to diversify into new growth areas, and to reduce dependence on handsets. In 2006 Nokia reached a deal with Siemens to merge their network businesses, creating the world's third largest network equipment supplier. By 2007 it appeared to have regained its customary market share of 35 per cent of handset sales.

One factor in the company's sustained success appears to have been a culture that encourages cooperation within teams and across internal and external boundaries. Jorma Ollila, CEO until 2006, believed that Nokia's innovative capacity springs from multi-functional teams working together to bring new insights to products and services. Staff in the four divisions work in teams that may remain constant for many years – but which are from time to time combined with other teams to work on a common task.

The company also encourages a culture of communication by creating small groups from around the company to work on a strategic issue for four months. This helps them to build ties with many parts of the company – some of which continue during later work. The induction process for new employees also encourages team building and cooperation: the newcomer's manager must introduce them to at least 15 people within and outside the team.

Source: *Economist*, 19 June 2004; *Financial Times*, 20 June 2006.

Case question

Which of the cultural types identified by Quinn *et al.* (2003) would you expect to find within Nokia's handset business?

degenerate organisationally because they fail to develop adequate mechanisms for transmitting the original ideals from founders to new members and sustaining them through shared experiences. (pp. 208–209)

As managers work within a culture, they will also be working in an external context – and perhaps asking whether the internal culture can meet the expectations from outside. To consider that carefully, they need some tools for analysing that external world.

Individual differences and diversity

The recognition of individuality

Organisations are made up of their individual members. The individual is a central feature of organisational behaviour, whether acting in isolation or as part of a group, in response to expectations of the organisation, or as a result of the influences of the external environment. Where the needs of the individual and the demands of the organisation are incompatible, this can result in frustration and conflict. It is the task of management to integrate the individual and the organisation and to provide a working environment that permits the satisfaction of individual needs as well as the attainment of organisational goals.

Managing relationships at work has always been a key skill, but the speed at which organisations and the external environment are undergoing change places increasing pressure on individuals at work. The effective management of people requires not only an understanding of the individual employees but also recognition of the culture of the organisation. What is expected and accepted in one organisation may not be the same in another. For instance, creativity and individuality may be encouraged in one business but undermined by bureaucracy in another.

A discussion of individual behaviour in organisations is therefore riddled with complexity and contradictions. Managers are required to be competent at selecting the individuals who will be valuable to the organisation. They need to be observant about the individuals who are performing well and have the potential to develop within the organisation. They also need to be able to value individual difference and be sensitive to contrasting needs. Finally managers need to know themselves and understand their uniqueness and the impact their personality has on others.

Individual differences and change

Sensitivity to individual needs and differences, especially in terms of their resilience, becomes particularly significant when organisations embark on change initiatives. Even when the change appears to be relatively straightforward, the reality is likely to be messy and complex. When organisations are working through change and when change appears to be externally imposed, the management of people takes on a different dimension in terms of the sensitivity required. In this situation there is an implicit requirement of changes in attitudes and beliefs. Such changes may lead to new mindsets, new attitudes and new perceptions that enable people to cope and adjust to the different world. At these times effective management is vital; managers will be expected to understand the strains that their employees feel during times of change, but at the same time be able to deal with their own stress levels.

How do individuals differ?

Our sense of self is shaped by our inherited characteristics and by influences in our social environment. The process of growing up – such as the impact of our early family life and the country in which we live – has a significant part to play in our identity. Most social scientists would agree that both inherited and environmental factors are important in our development, and it is the way in which these factors interact which is the key to our adult personality. However, scientists differ with regard to the weight they place on these factors – some believing that our personality is heavily influenced by our inherited characteristics and will never change, others believing the reverse.

But first, what are the differences among individuals? These include:

- ethnic origin
- physique
- gender
- early family experiences
- social and cultural factors
- national culture
- motivation
- attitudes
- personality traits and types
- intelligence and abilities
- perception.

Some of these characteristics are shared with others, for example individuals who are from the same ethnic group or who have the same ability levels or who share similar physical attributes such as short-sightedness. But our uniqueness stems from the dynamic ways in which these inherited and environmental factors combine and interact. The ways in which it is possible to differentiate between individuals include an understanding of personality, the heart of individual differences and the importance and functions of attitudes.

Personality

Personality may be viewed as consisting of stable characteristics that explain why a person behaves in a particular way. So, for instance, independence, conscientiousness, agreeableness and self-control would be examples of these personality characteristics. However, it is only when we see/hear/observe a person that we can gain an understanding of their personality. For example, a person who is independent may show that characteristic by displaying a strong sense of self-sufficiency. We would expect him or her to take the initiative and not to depend on other people. Furthermore, if the characteristic is 'stable' we can rely on this being a consistent part of the person's behaviour. We would be surprised if the person one day demonstrated autonomy and initiative and the next withdrew and delayed any decisions. We anticipate that individuals are generally consistent in the way in which they respond to situations.

There are times when we might be surprised by somebody's behaviour and we may feel they are 'acting out of character'. Of course this would be known only if we had an understanding of their 'typical behaviour' in the first place. Individuals may exaggerate or suppress certain personality traits, for example if they are under stress or influenced by drink/drugs. It is self-evident that managers need to learn the art of 'reading' people's behaviour in order to manage relationships effectively.

Nomothetic and idiographic approaches

Broadly speaking, personality studies can be divided into two main approaches, labelled as nomothetic and idiographic.

The **nomothetic approach** is a measurable and specific perspective that looks at the identification of traits and personality as a collection of characteristics. These characteristics are ones that can be described, identified and measured and therefore can be subjected to observation and tests. This perspective is especially helpful for managers when they are involved in the selection, training and development of individuals. Nomothetic approaches tend to view environmental and social influences as minimal and view personality as consistent, largely inherited and resistant to change. Although they would not diminish the difficulties that measuring personality brings, nomothetic approaches would claim that it is possible to measure and predict the ways in which personality types would behave given certain circumstances.

Nomothetic researchers closely align themselves to studies that are 'scientific' in a positivistic sense. (The term positivism refers to the branch of science that is exclusively based on the objective collection of observable data – data that are beyond question.) Such an approach transfers methods used in natural sciences to the social world. Some psychologists are interested in describing and measuring characteristics and comparing individuals' scores. Does this person exhibit more or less than 'average' of this particular trait? Being able to predict behaviour is a major aim and outcome of this approach.

The **idiographic approach** is a holistic and dynamic perspective which insists that managers take into account a 'whole' understanding of the individual at work. This may also require going beyond the study of pure psychology to an understanding of the societal context in which the person lives. These are called idiographic approaches and are particularly pertinent in understanding motivation, career development and team relationships.

Idiographic approaches are concerned with understanding the uniqueness of individuals and the development of the self-concept. They regard personality development as a process that is open to change. They regard individuals as responding to the environment and people around them and see the dynamics of the interactions as playing a critical part in shaping personality. The measurement of traits is seen as largely inappropriate in that one person's responses may not be comparable to another's. They suggest that personality assessment is not a valid method of understanding the unique ways in which a person understands and responds to the world. The depth and richness of a person's personality cannot be revealed in superficial paper-and-pencil questionnaires. Furthermore, the categories defined by psychologists are too narrow in scope and depth.

Table 3.2 The role of early experiences – what is its impact?

Environment is significant	Inherited characteristics are significant
Approach taken by idiographic approaches	*Approach taken by nomothetic theorists*
The personalities of the two pharmacists described above are the culmination of experiences. Their personalities have been shaped by the people around them from their very earliest years. Early family life – the relationship between family members, the size of the family, the rewards and punishments exercised by parents – would have had an influence on the type of person each is now. In other words, the environment and early learning experiences have significantly contributed to their personality development.	The pharmacists inherited a genetic make-up which would remain core and would be resistant to change. Early experiences, while they may shape the person to a certain extent, do not alter the inherited make-up. Intelligence, physical appearances, physiological reactions are 'wired' in from birth – the 'core' of the individual is a 'given'.

Theory and the world of work

The application of theory to the world of work is not always easy and some find the process confusing when theory does not match with their experiences. Psychological investigations emphasise the complexity and variety of individual behaviour and insist that simple answers and explanations are generally inadequate. The study of personality provides an excellent example of some of the complexities involved in applying psychological theory in practice.

Consider two individuals who share similar characteristics. They are both 24 years old and have lived in the same area; both have a first-class honours degree in pharmacy and they have identical personality assessment profiles. However, we would still predict differences with regard to their attitude and performance in the workplace. In addition, differences would be predicted in the ways they interact with others. If one of the pharmacists was male and/or African, a further set of assumptions might be made. It is not only the features themselves which identify individuals as being different, it is also their interaction which leads to a unique pattern of behaviour. The complexities of the process pose a number of questions that interest psychologists and evoke different responses (see Table 3.2).

Ability

Individuals vary with regard to their mental abilities and the extent to which they apply them at work, and different occupations require different skills, competencies and abilities. The 'happy' scenario is one where a match occurs between the individual's abilities and their occupation, but reality suggests that this is not always the case. The extremes include employees bored rigid with a simple task who become careless and make a succession of mistakes, and the employees who have

	Sensing types		Intuitive types	
Introverts	**ISTJ** Quiet, serious, earn success by thoroughness and dependability. Practical, matter-of-fact, realistic and responsible. Decide logically what should be done and work towards it steadily, regardless of distractions. Take pleasure in making everything orderly and organised – their work, their home, their life. Value traditions and loyalty.	**ISFJ** Quiet, friendly, responsible, and conscientious. Committed and steady in meeting their obligations. Thorough, painstaking and accurate. Loyal, considerate, notice and remember specifics about people who are important to them, concerned with how others feel. Strive to create an orderly and harmonious environment at work and at home.	**INFJ** Seek meaning and connection in ideas, relationships and material possessions. Want to understand what motivates people and are insightful about others. Conscientious and committed to their firm values. Develop a clear vision about how best to serve the common good. Organised and decisive in implementing their vision.	**INTJ** Have original minds and great drive for implementing their ideas and achieving their goals. Quickly see patterns in external events and develop long-range explanatory perspectives. When committed, organise a job and carry it through. Sceptical and independent, have high standards of competence and performance – for themselves and others.
	ISTP Tolerant and flexible, quiet observers until a problem appears, then act quickly to find workable solutions. Analyse what makes things work and readily get through large amounts of data to isolate the core of practical problems. Interested in cause and effect, organise facts using logical principles, value efficiency.	**ISFP** Quiet, friendly, sensitive and kind. Enjoy the present moment, what's going on around them. Like to have their own space and to work within their own time frame. Loyal and committed to their values and to people who are important to them. Dislike disagreements and conflicts, do not force their opinions or values on others.	**INFP** Idealistic, loyal to their values and to people who are important to them. Want an external life that is congruent with their values. Curious, quick to see possibilities, can be catalysts for implementing ideas. Seek to understand people and to help them fulfil their potential. Adaptable, flexible and accepting unless a value is threatened.	**INTP** Seek to develop logical explanations for everything that interests them. Theoretical and abstract, interested more in ideas than in social interaction. Quiet, contained, flexible and adaptable. Have unusual ability to focus in depth to solve problems in their area of interest. Sceptical, sometimes critical, always analytical.
Extraverts	**ESTP** Flexible and tolerant, they take a pragmatic approach focused on immediate results. Theories and conceptual explanations bore them – they want to act energetically to solve the problem. Focus on the here-and-now, spontaneous, enjoy each moment that they can be active with others. Enjoy material comforts and style. Learn best through doing.	**ESFP** Outgoing, friendly and accepting. Exuberant lovers of life, people and material comforts. Enjoy working with others to make things happen. Bring common sense and a realistic approach to their work, and make work fun. Flexible and spontaneous, adapt readily to new people and environments. Learn best by trying a new skill with other people.	**ENFP** Warmly enthusiastic and imaginative. See life as full of possibilities. Make connections between events and information very quickly, and confidently proceed based on the patterns they see. Want a lot of affirmation from others, and readily give appreciation and support. Spontaneous and flexible, often rely on their ability to improvise and their verbal fluency.	**ENTP** Quick, ingenious, stimulating, alert and outspoken. Resourceful in solving new and challenging problems. Adept at generating conceptual possibilities and then analysing them strategically. Good at reading other people. Bored by routine, will seldom do the same thing the same way, apt to turn to one new interest after another.
	ESTJ Practical, realistic, matter-of-fact. Decisive, quickly move to implement decisions. Organise projects and people to get things done, focus on getting results in the most efficient way possible. Take care of routine details. Have a clear set of logical standards, systematically follow them and want others to also. Forceful in implementing their plans.	**ESFJ** Warm-hearted, conscientious and cooperative. Want harmony in their environment, work with determination to establish it. Like to work with others to complete tasks accurately and on time. Loyal, follow through even in small matters. Notice what others need in their day-to-day lives and try to provide it. Want to be appreciated for who they are and for what they contribute.	**ENFJ** Warm, empathetic, responsive and responsible. Highly attuned to the emotions, needs and motivations of others. Find potential in everyone, want to help others fulfil their potential. May act as catalysts for individual and group growth. Loyal, responsive to praise and criticism. Sociable, facilitate others in a group, and provide inspiring leadership.	**ENTJ** Frank, decisive, assume leadership readily. Quickly see illogical and inefficient procedures and policies, develop and implement comprehensive systems to solve organisational problems. Enjoy long-term planning and goal setting. Usually well informed, well read, enjoy expanding their knowledge and passing it on to others. Forceful in presenting their ideas.

Figure 3.7   The Myers–Briggs Type Indicator® (MBTI®) assessment tool showing characteristics frequently associated with particular personality types

Source: Modified and reproduced by special permission of the publisher, CPP, Inc., Mountain View, CA 94043 from the *Introduction to Type®, Sixth Edition* booklet by Isabel Briggs Myers, revised by Linda K. Kirby and Katharine D. Myers. Copyright © 1998 by Peter B. Myers and Katharine D. Myers, All rights reserved. Further reproduction is prohibited without the publisher's written consent. Introduction to Type® is a registered trademark of the MBTI Trust, Inc. in the United States and other countries.

been promoted beyond their capability. The result could be stress either for the individuals unable to cope or for their colleagues who are picking up the debris left behind.

In a similar vein to the studies of personality, different schools of thought have emerged with regard to the study of abilities. Similar debates to the ones that surround the study of personality have also swirled around the research on intelligence.

- Is intelligence inherited? Is it constant throughout life? Is it dependent upon our life's experiences, our culture, our education, etc.?
- What is the nature of intelligence? Can it be measured and how?

Is intelligence inherited?

The **nativists** believe that intelligence is mostly inherited (nature), while the **empiricists** believe that our environment shapes our behaviour and mental abilities (nurture). Howe[5] summarises recent convincing evidence to lend support to the empiricists. He cites evidence from early intervention programmes such as Head Start initiatives to show that intervention can have an impact on IQ. He concludes: 'The empirical findings provide no support for the pessimistic conclusion that low intelligence and the problems associated with it are inevitable and unalterable.'

The political implications of research into the nature of intelligence are striking. Some of the earliest theories influenced the educational philosophy of England and Wales, including how children were selected for different types of secondary education and the kind of help that should be given to children with special needs.

The nature of intelligence

Arguments have raged within psychologists' circles as to the nature of intelligence. Is it dependent on a general overall factor that will have an overarching effect on specific activities? Or are specific activities independent of each other? In other words, if a child shows a high level of ability at mathematics, is this dependent on an overall high general ability? General ability can be seen as a kind of powerhouse that releases some of its energy into the child's ability at mathematics. (For other children it may act as a limiting factor.) Spearman[6] proposed a two-factor theory of intelligence and suggested that every intellectual task involves a level of mental agility – a general factor (g) – plus specific abilities (s). This idea, developed by Vernon,[7] resulted in a model that placed abilities in a hierarchy (see Figure 3.8). Abilities at the lower end of the hierarchy are more likely to correlate, hence if a child has a good vocabulary, they are more likely to have abilities in reading and comprehension too.

Thurstone[8] claimed seven primary mental abilities that can be separately measured resulting in a profile of scores:

- spatial ability
- perceptual speed
- numerical reasoning
- verbal reasoning

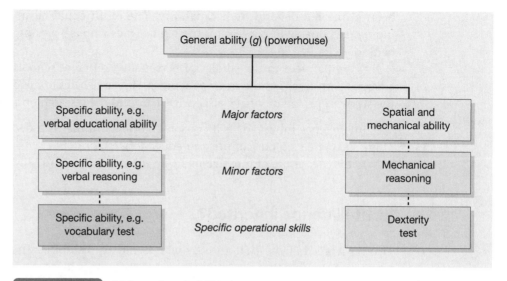

Figure 3.8 **A hierarchy of abilities**

Source: Adapted from Vernon, P. E. *The Structure of Human Abilities*, Methuen and Co. (1950). Reproduced with permission from Taylor and Francis.

- memory
- verbal fluency
- inductive reasoning.

Intelligence – one or many?

Guilford[9] criticised theories that aimed to simplify intelligence into a small number of factors. He devised a model that identified 120 different abilities (see Figure 3.9) and suggested that intellectual ability requires individuals to think in one of three dimensions:

- **Content.** What must the individual think about (for example, meaning of words or numbers)?
- **Operation.** What kind of thinking is the individual required to do (for example, recognising items, solving a problem, evaluating an outcome)?
- **Product.** What kind of outcome or answer is required (for example, classifying or reordering items)?

Guilford also expressed concern about the convergent nature of tests that required a single solution or answer. He suggested that tests should also be looking at an individual's ability to produce divergent answers.

Multiple intelligences

Gardner[10] felt that intelligent behaviour that could be observed in everyday life was excluded from these earlier studies. He believed that the simplification of intelligence in terms of an IQ measure was unrealistic and failed to take into account the

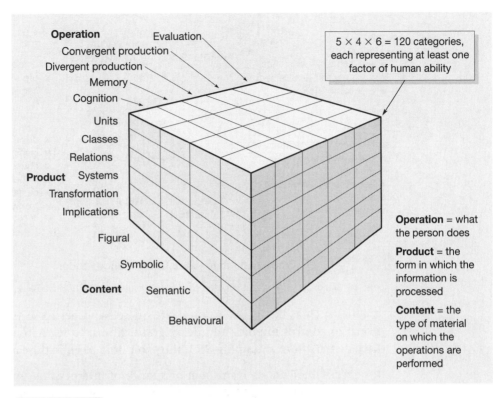

Figure 3.9   **Guilford's structure of the intellect model**

Source: From Guilford, J. P. 'Three Faces of Intellect', *American Psychologist*, vol. 14, pp. 469–79. Reproduced with permission from APA.

full range of intelligent activity. He suggested there was a multiple of intelligences and categorised them into six varieties (all of which could be further divided):

Verbal Mathematical }	Akin to the factors described in earlier theories
Spatial capacity	Ability shown by artists and architects
Kinaesthetic	Abilities of a physical nature
Musical	Abilities of musicianship
Personal intelligences }	Interpersonal – skills with other people Intrapersonal – knowing oneself

Emotional intelligence (EI)

A development of some of Gardner's ideas was made by Goleman who in 1955 published his ground-breaking work on EI (or EQ, for Emotional Quotient). Goleman agreed that the classical view of intelligence was too narrow. He felt that the emotional qualities of individuals should be considered. These, he felt, played a vital role in the application of intelligence in everyday life. He identified the key characteristics as:

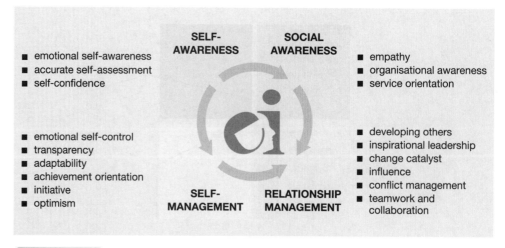

Figure 3.10   **Emotional Intelligence Competence Model**

abilities such as being able to motivate oneself and persist in the face of frustrations; to control impulse and delay gratification; to regulate one's moods and keep distress from swamping the ability to think; to empathise and to hope.[11]

Emotional intelligence is the sum of a range of interpersonal skills that form the public persona. EI has received considerable attention over the last few years as the concept has been identified as a key aspect of managing people effectively. Goleman argues for a more empathetic style of management and suggests that EI predicts top performance and accounts for more than 85 per cent of outstanding performance in top leaders.[12] The Hay Group, working with Goleman, have identified 18 specific competencies that make up the four components of emotional intelligence and have produced an inventory designed to measure emotional competence (see Figure 3.10). The Emotional Competence Inventory defines EI as 'The capacity for recognising our own feelings and those of others, for motivating ourselves and for managing emotions within ourselves and with others.'[13]

Significance of emotional intelligence

Recognising and understanding the implications of emotions and being able accurately to self-assess one's inner resources, abilities and limits are key to becoming an emotionally intelligent leader. Being able to read emotional currents is an important skill for managers to develop and employ. It requires them to know and understand the individuals within their teams and the way in which the individuals relate and interact.

Recent research from the Chartered Management Institute identifies EI as one of the key skills managers and leaders will need in the coming decade.[14] According to Landale it should really be no surprise to find EQ so much in demand.

After all, we work in structures which are much flatter than ever. We have to be much faster on our feet with both colleagues and clients and, whatever the team structure, there is increasing proximity for us to build the relationships we need – fast. In this context EQ is the glue that holds people and teams together.[15]

Developing EI

Landale refers to the importance of empathy in EI which both involves how a person self-manages and addresses how to engage with the emotions of others, and suggests a six-step process for developing EI.

- Know what you feel.
- Know why you feel it.
- Acknowledge the emotion and know how to manage it.
- Know how to motivate yourself and make yourself feel better.
- Recognise the emotions of other people and develop empathy.
- Express your feelings appropriately and manage relationships.

> There seems little doubt that managers and leaders who have trained up in EQ have far more initiative in dealing with organizational life than those who don't. Stress will always exist at work, but EQ gives people the tools and ways of thinking to manage it to their advantage.[16]

A number of steps in raising emotional intelligence are also suggested by Garrett, including ensuring staff are managing their interpersonal relationships before a problem arises, focusing first on leaders and creating an EQ culture for the organisation about itself and the companies it deals with.[17] According to Dann, becoming highly self-aware allows an individual to recognise inner and outer conflict and develop more proactive self-management. Developing greater social awareness allows the fostering of productive relations and a greater degree of engagement between employees and management. A manager with a high EQ benefits both the organisation and the individual.[18]

Approaches to organisation and management

Theory of management

A central part of the study of organisation and management is the development of management thinking and what might be termed management theory. The application of theory brings about change in actual behaviour. Managers reading the work of leading writers on the subject might see in their ideas and conclusions a message about how they should behave. This will influence their attitudes towards management practice.

The study of management theory is important for the following reasons:

- It helps to view the interrelationships between the development of theory, behaviour in organisations and management practice.
- An understanding of the development of management thinking helps in understanding principles underlying the process of management.
- Knowledge of the history helps in understanding the nature of management and organisational behaviour and reasons for the attention given to main topic areas.
- Many of the earlier ideas are of continuing importance to the manager and later ideas on management tend to incorporate earlier ideas and conclusions.
- Management theories are interpretive and evolve in line with changes in the organisational environment.

As McGregor puts it:

Every managerial act rests on assumptions, generalizations, and hypotheses – that is to say, on theory. Our assumptions are frequently implicit, sometimes quite unconscious, often conflicting; nevertheless, they determine our predictions that if we do a, b will occur. Theory and practice are inseparable.[19]

Miner makes the point that the more that is known about organisations and their methods of operation, the better the chances of dealing effectively with them. Understanding may be more advanced than prediction, but both provide the opportunity to influence or to manage the future. Theory provides a sound basis for action.[20] However, if action is to be effective, the theory must be adequate and appropriate to the task and to improved organisational performance. It must be a 'good' theory.

Developments in management and organisational behaviour

It is helpful, therefore, to trace major developments in management and organisational behaviour and what has led to the concentration of attention on such topics as motivation, groups, leadership, structure, and organisation development.[21]

Writing on organisation and management, in some form or another, can be traced back thousands of years.[22] Also, Shafritz makes an interesting observation about the contribution of William Shakespeare (1564–1616):

While William Shakespeare's contribution to literature and the development of the English language have long been acknowledged and thoroughly documented, his contribution to the theory of management and administration have been all but ignored. This is a surprising oversight when you consider that many of his plays deal with issues of personnel management and organizational behavior.[23]

However, the systematic development of management thinking is viewed, generally, as dating from the end of the nineteenth century with the emergence of large industrial organisations and the ensuing problems associated with their structure and management.[24] In order to help identify main trends in the development of organisational behaviour and management theory, it is usual to categorise the work of writers into various 'approaches', based on their views of organisations, their structure and management. Although a rather simplistic process, it does provide a framework in which to help direct study and focus attention on the progression of ideas concerned with improving organisational performance.

A framework of analysis

There are, however, many ways of categorising these various approaches. For example, Skipton attempts a classification of 11 main schools of management theory.[25] Whatever form of categorisation is adopted, it is possible to identify a number of other approaches, or at least sub-divisions of approaches, and cross-grouping among the various approaches. The choice of a particular categorisation is therefore largely at the discretion of the observer.

The following analysis will revolve around a framework based on four main approaches, shown in Figure 3.11:

- classical – including scientific management and bureaucracy;
- human relations – including neo-human relations;
- systems;
- contingency.

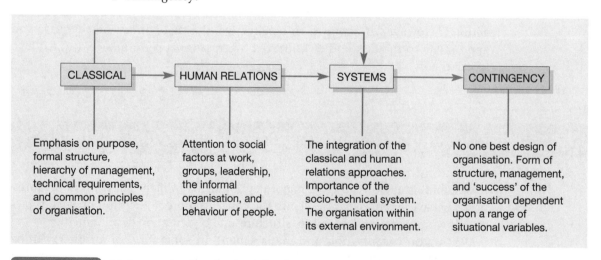

Figure 3.11   Main approaches to organisation, structure and management

Attention is also drawn to other 'approaches' or ideas, including:

- decision-making;
- social action;
- postmodernism.

The classical approach

The **classical** writers thought of the organisation in terms of its purpose and formal structure. They placed emphasis on the planning of work, the technical requirements of the organisation, principles of management, and the assumption of rational and logical behaviour. The analysis of organisation in this manner is associated with work carried out initially in the early part of the last century, by such writers as Taylor, Fayol, Urwick, Mooney and Reiley, and Brech. Such writers were laying the foundation for a comprehensive theory of management.

A clear understanding of the purpose of an organisation is seen as essential to understanding how the organisation works and how its methods of working can be improved. Identification of general objectives would lead to the clarification of purposes and responsibilities at all levels of the organisation and to the most effective structure. Attention is given to the division of work, the clear definition of duties and responsibilities, and maintaining specialisation and co-ordination. Emphasis is on a hierarchy of management and formal organisational relationships.

Sets of principles

The classical writers (also variously known as the formal or scientific management writers – although scientific management is really only a part of the classical approach) were concerned with improving the organisation structure as a means of increasing efficiency. They emphasised the importance of principles for the design of a logical structure of organisation. Their writings were in a normative style and they saw these principles as a set of 'rules' offering general solutions to common problems of organisation and management.

Most classical writers had their own set of principles but among the most publicised are those of Fayol and Urwick. Fayol recognised there was no limit to the principles of management but in his writing advocated 14.[26] Urwick originally specified eight principles, but these were revised to ten in his later writing.[27]

Mooney and Reiley set out a number of common principles which relate to all types of organisations. They place particular attention on:

- **the principle of co-ordination** – the need for people to act together with unity of action, the exercise of authority and the need for discipline;
- **the scalar principle** – the hierarchy of organisation, the grading of duties and the process of delegation; and
- **the functional principle** – specialisation and the distinction between different kinds of duties.[28]

Brech attempts to provide a practical approach to organisation structure based on tried general principles as opposed to the concentration on specific cases or complex generalisations of little value to the practising manager. He sets out the various functions in the organisation and the definition of formal organisational relationships.[29] Although clearly a strong supporter of the formal approach in some of his views such as, for example, on the principle of span of control, Brech is less definite than other classical writers and recognises a degree of flexibility according to the particular situation.

Brech does place great emphasis, however, on the need for written definition of responsibilities and the value of job descriptions as an aid to effective organisation and delegation. This work builds on the ideas of earlier writers, such as Urwick, and therefore provides a comprehensive view of the classical approach to organisation and management.

Evaluation of the classical approach

The classical writers have been criticised generally for not taking sufficient account of personality factors and for creating an organisation structure in which people can exercise only limited control over their work environment. The idea of sets of principles to guide managerial action has also been subject to much criticism. For example, Simon writes:

> Organisational design is not unlike architectural design. It involves creating large, complex systems having multiple goals. It is illusory to suppose that good designs can be created by using the so-called principles of classical organisation theory.[30]

Research studies have also expressed doubt about the effectiveness of these principles when applied in practice.[31] However, the classical approach prompted the start of a more systematic view of management and attempted to provide some common principles applicable to all organisations. These principles are still of relevance in that they offer a useful starting point in attempting to analyse the effectiveness of the design of organisation structure. The application of these principles must take full account of:

- the particular situational variables of each individual organisation; and
- the psychological and social factors relating to members of the organisation.

Major sub-groupings

Two major 'sub-groupings' of the classical approach are:

1 scientific management, and
2 bureaucracy.

Scientific management

Many of the classical writers were concerned with the improvement of management as a means of increasing productivity. At this time emphasis was on the problem of obtaining increased productivity from individual workers through the technical structuring of the work organisation and the provision of monetary incentives as the motivator for higher levels of output. A major contributor to this approach was F. W. Taylor (1856–1917), the 'father' of scientific management.[32] Taylor believed that in the same way that there is a best machine for each job, so there is a best working method by which people should undertake their jobs. He considered that all work processes could be analysed into discrete tasks and that by scientific method it was possible to find the 'one best way' to perform each task. Each job was broken down into component parts, each part timed and the parts rearranged into the most efficient method of working.

Principles to guide management

Taylor was a believer in the rational–economic needs concept of motivation. He believed that if management acted on his ideas, work would become more satisfying and profitable for all concerned. Workers would be motivated by obtaining the highest possible wages through working in the most efficient and productive way. Taylor was concerned with finding more efficient methods and procedures for co-ordination and control of work. He set out a number of principles to guide management. These principles are usually summarised as:

- the development of a true science for each person's work;
- the scientific selection, training and development of the workers;
- co-operation with the workers to ensure work is carried out in the prescribed way;
- the division of work and responsibility between management and the workers.

In his famous studies at the Bethlehem Steel Corporation, Taylor, who was appointed as a management consultant, applied his ideas on scientific management to the handling of pig iron. A group of 75 men were loading an average of $12\frac{1}{2}$ tons per man per day. Taylor selected a Dutch labourer, called Schmidt, whom he reported to be a 'high-priced' man with a reputation for placing a high value on money, and a man of limited mental ability. By following detailed instructions on when to pick up the pig iron and walk, and when to sit and rest, and with no back talk, Schmidt increased his output to $47\frac{1}{2}$ tons per day. He maintained this level of output throughout the three years of the study. In return Schmidt received a 60 per cent increase in wages compared with what was paid to the other men.

One by one other men were selected and trained to handle pig iron at the rate of $47\frac{1}{2}$ tons per day and in return they received 60 per cent more wages. Taylor drew attention to the need for the scientific selection of the workers. When the other labourers in the group were trained in the same method, only one in eight was physically capable of the effort of loading $47\frac{1}{2}$ tons per day, although there was a noticeable increase in their level of output.

Reactions against scientific management

There were strong criticisms of, and reaction against, scientific management methods from the workers who found the work boring and requiring little skill. Despite these criticisms Taylor attempted to expand the implementation of his ideas in the Bethlehem Steel Corporation. However, fears of mass redundancies persuaded the management to request Taylor to moderate his activities. Yet Taylor's belief in his methods was so strong that he would not accept management's interference and eventually they dispensed with his services.

Scientific management was applied for a time in other countries with similar criticisms and hostile reactions. The ideas of scientific management were also adopted in the American Watertown Arsenal despite the lingering doubts of the controller. He was not convinced about the benefits of paying bonuses based on methods which reduced time taken to complete a job; also the workers reacted unfavourably to time and motion studies and he was fearful of a strike. The controller eventually gave way, however, and the scientific management approach was adopted – to be followed almost immediately by a strike of moulding workers. The strike at Watertown Arsenal led to an investigation of Taylor's methods by a House of Representatives Committee which reported in 1912.

The conclusion of the committee was that scientific management did provide some useful techniques and offered valuable organisational suggestions, but gave production managers a dangerously high level of uncontrolled power. The studies at Watertown Arsenal were resumed but the unions retained an underlying hostility towards scientific management. A subsequent attitude survey among the workers revealed a broad level of resentment and hostility, by both union and non-union members, to scientific management methods. As a result of this report the Senate banned Taylor's methods of time study in defence establishments.

Taylorism as management control

There has also been considerable interest in 'Taylorism' as representing a system of management control over workers. Taylor placed emphasis on the content of a 'fair day's work' and on optimising the level of workers' productivity. A major obstacle to this objective was 'systematic soldiering' and what Taylor saw as the deliberate attempt by workers to promote their best interests and to keep employers ignorant of how fast work, especially piece-rate work, could be carried out.

According to Braverman, scientific management starts from the capitalist point of view and method of production, and the adaptation of labour to the needs of capital. Taylor's work was more concerned with the organisation of labour than with the development of technology. A distinctive feature of Taylor's thought was the concept of management control.[33] Braverman suggests Taylor's conclusion was that workers should be controlled not only by the giving of orders and maintenance of discipline but also by removing from them any decisions about the manner in which their work was to be carried out. By division of labour, and by dictating precise stages and methods for every aspect of work performance, management could gain control of the actual process of work. The rationalisation of production processes and division of labour tends to result in the de-skilling of work and this may be a main strategy of the employer.[34]

Cloke and Goldsmith also suggest that Taylor was the leading promoter of the idea that managers should design and control the work process scientifically in order to guarantee maximum efficiency. He believed in multiple layers of management to supervise the work process and in rigid, detailed control of the workforce.

Taylor's theories justified managerial control over the production process and removed decision making from employees and from owners as well. The increasingly authoritative operational role of management diminished the direct involvement of owners in day-to-day decision making. Managers saw this as an opportunity to solidify their power and adopted Taylor's ideas wholesale. In the process, they affirmed efficiency over collaboration, quantity over quality, and cost controls over customer service.[35]

critical reflection

'Despite the strong criticisms of scientic management, in the right circumstances the underlying principles still have relevance and much to offer business organisations today. It is just that many commentators appear reluctant to openly admit that this is the case.'

What are your views? Where could scientific management be applied for the best overall effect?

Relevance of scientific management

While Taylor's work is often criticised today it should be remembered that he was writing at a time of industrial reorganisation and the emergence of large, complex organisations with new forms of technology. Taylor's main concern was with the efficiency of both workers and management. He believed his methods of scientific management would lead to improved management–labour relations and contribute to improved industrial efficiency and prosperity.

Taylor adopted an instrumental view of human behaviour together with the application of standard procedures of work. Workers were regarded as rational, economic beings motivated directly by monetary incentives linked to the level of work output. Workers were viewed as isolated individuals and more as units of production to be handled almost in the same way as machines. Hence, scientific management is often referred to as a machine theory model.

Taylor's work continues to evoke much comment and extreme points of view. For example, Rose suggests:

It is difficult to discuss the 'contribution' of F. W. Taylor to the systematic study of industrial behaviour in an even-tempered way. The sheer silliness from a modern perspective of many of his ideas, and barbarities they led to when applied in industry, encourage ridicule and denunciation.[36]

The theme of inefficiency

Rose argues that Taylor's diagnosis of the industrial situation was based on the simple theme of inefficiency. Among his criticisms are that Taylor selected the best workers for his experiments and assumed that workers who were not good at one particular task would be best at some other task. There is, however, no certainty of this in practice. Taylor regarded workers from an engineering viewpoint and as machines, but the one best way of performing a task is not always the best method for every worker.

The reduction of physical movement to find the one best way is not always beneficial and some 'wasteful' movements are essential to the overall rhythm of work. Rose also argues that the concept of a fair day's pay for a fair day's work is not purely a technical matter. It is also a notion of social equity and not in keeping with a scientific approach. Drucker, however, claims:

> Frederick Winslow Taylor may prove a more useful prophet for our times than we yet recognize . . . Taylor's greatest impact may still be ahead . . . the under-developed and developing countries are now reaching the stage where they need Taylor and 'scientific management' . . . But the need to study Taylor anew and apply him may be the greatest in the developed countries.[37]

According to Drucker, the central theme of Taylor's work was not inefficiency but the need to substitute industrial warfare by industrial harmony. Taylor sought to do this through:

- higher wages from increased output;
- the removal of physical strain from doing work the wrong way;
- development of the workers and the opportunity for them to undertake tasks they were capable of doing; and
- elimination of the 'boss' and the duty of management to help workers.

Drucker also suggests that Taylor's idea of functional foremen can be related to what is now known as matrix organisation. Support for Drucker's views appears to come from Locke who asserts that much of the criticism of Taylor is based on a misunderstanding of the precepts and that many of his ideas are accepted by present-day managers.[38]

Impetus to management thinking

Whatever the opinions on scientific management, Taylor and his disciples have left to modern management the legacy of such practices as work study, organisation and methods, payment by results, management by exception and production control. The development of mass assembly line work ('Fordism'), which was invented by Henry Ford in 1913 and which dominated production methods in Western economies, can be seen to have many common links with the ideas of scientific management.[39] The concept of Six Sigma can also be related to Taylor's quest for 'systematic management'. For example, in his book on the future of management, Hamel makes the following observation:

> One can imagine Taylor looking down from his well-ordered heaven and smiling fondly at the Six Sigma acolytes who continue to spread his gospel. (His only surprise might be that 21st-century managers are still obsessing over the same problems that occupied his inventive mind a hundred years earlier.)[40]

KEY IDEAS

Hanger Insertion

- The new programme involving the process of hanging merchandise on hangers efficiently and effectively.

The purposes of this new programme:

- To assist the stores in better customer service – by having the merchandise ready to go on the floor, saving space in the stockroom, and creating customer goodwill.
- To increase the units per hour produced.
- To perform the job duties as efficiently and effectively as possible.

TECHNIQUES

- Keep the necessary items needed in your range. All supplies should be within arm's reach. For example, place the trash bin next to you, have your hanger supply near you. You should not need to take any steps.

- For ANY prepack, Unpack merchandise in the prepack or unpack enough of the prepack in the amount to be placed on the trolley, tearing the plastic off of the entire group.
  Lay the merchandise out on the unpack table, and if applies, unfold each piece, removing tissue, etc.
  Insert the hangers and hang the *entire group* of merchandise at once.

- When removing hangers from the merchandise, have the merchandise in a group on the unpack table; remove these hangers working from the front to the back.

- When inserting hangers, as a group, insert working from the back to the front of the group on the unpack table. Hang pieces as a group.

- If merchandise is bulky, Leave merchandise folded, **remove all of the plastic at once**, insert hangers for merchandise unpacked, hang all pieces on the trolley, then remove at the same time all excess plastic, clips, etc.

- When possible, it is more efficient to remove all the plastic at once after the merchandise is hung.

- When hanging pants, skirts, etc., slip the hanger over both sides of the piece of merchandise and push metal clips down at the same time. This will alleviate additional steps.

- When pants are in plastic and hangers have to be removed, hang them first, take pants off hangers, lay on table, throw away plastic, insert hangers.

- When having to button pants, skirts, etc., take the top of the button through the hole first. This makes the process flow easier and more efficient.

- Put your supply of hangers in the cover of a tote and place on the table next to you.

Figure 3.12   Hanger Insertion Programme: an example of scientific management

The principles of Taylor's scientific approach to management appear still to have relevance today. We can see examples of Taylorism alive and well, and management practices based on the philosophy of his ideas. As an example, Figure 3.12 shows a 'Hanger Insertion Programme' for a large American department store. Large hotel organisations often make use of standard recipes and performance standard manuals and it is common for housekeeping staff to have a prescribed layout for each room, with training based on detailed procedures and the one best way. Staff may be expected to clean a given number of rooms per shift with financial incentives for additional rooms. The strict routine, uniformity, clearly specified tasks, detailed checklists and close control in fast-food restaurants such as McDonald's also suggest close links with scientific management.

Whatever else Taylor did, at least he gave a major impetus to the development of management thinking and the later development of organisational behaviour. For example, Crainer and Dearlove suggest that although Taylor's theories are now largely outdated, they still had a profound impact throughout the world and his mark can be seen on much of the subsequent management literature.[41] And Stern goes a stage further:

> The 'scientific management' of Frederick Taylor . . . shaped the first coherent school of thought with application to the industrialised world. He was our first professional guru and Taylorism – with its twin goals of productivity and efficiency – still influences management thinking 100 years on.[42]

It is difficult to argue against the general line of Taylor's principles but they are subject to misuse. What is important is the context and manner in which such principles are put into effect. There is arguably one best way *technically* to perform a job, particularly, for example, with factory assembly line production. However, account needs to be taken of human behaviour. People tend to have their preferred way of working and the need for variety and more interesting or challenging tasks. Provided work is carried out safely and to a satisfactory standard and completed on time, to what extent should management *insist* on the 'one best way'?

It seems that Taylor did not so much ignore (as is often suggested) but was more *unaware* of the complexity of human behaviour in organisations and the importance of the individual's feelings and sentiments, group working, managerial behaviour and the work environment. However, we now have greater knowledge about social effects within the work organisation and about the value of money, incentives, motivation, and job satisfaction and performance.

Bureaucracy

A form of structure to be found in many large-scale organisations is **bureaucracy**. Its importance in the development of organisation theory means that it is often regarded as a subdivision under the classical heading and studied as a separate approach to management and the organisation of work. The ideas and principles of the classical writers were derived mainly from practical experience. Writers on bureaucracy, however, tend to take a more theoretical view.

Weber, a German sociologist, showed particular concern for what he called 'bureaucratic structures', although his work in this area came almost as a side issue to his main study on power and authority.[43] He suggested that 'the decisive reason for the advance of bureaucratic organization has always been its purely technical superiority over any other form of organization'. Weber pointed out that the definition of tasks and responsibilities within the structure of management gave rise to a permanent administration and standardisation of work procedures notwithstanding changes in the actual holders of office.

The term 'bureaucracy' has common connotations with criticism of red tape and rigidity, though in the study of organisations and management it is important that the term is seen not necessarily in a deprecative sense but as applying to certain structural features of formal organisations. Weber analysed bureaucracies not empirically but as an 'ideal type' derived from the most characteristic bureaucratic features of all known organisations. He saw the development of bureaucracies as a means of introducing order and rationality into social life.

Main characteristics of bureaucracies

Weber did not actually define bureaucracy but did attempt to identify the main characteristics of this type of organisation. He emphasised the importance of administration based on expertise (rules of experts) and administration based on discipline (rules of officials).

- The tasks of the organisation are allocated as official duties among the various positions.
- There is an implied clear-cut division of labour and a high level of specialisation.
- A hierarchical authority applies to the organisation of offices and positions.
- Uniformity of decisions and actions is achieved through formally established systems of rules and regulations. Together with a structure of authority, this enables the co-ordination of various activities within the organisation.
- An impersonal orientation is expected from officials in their dealings with clients and other officials. This is designed to result in rational judgements by officials in the performance of their duties.
- Employment by the organisation is based on technical qualifications and constitutes a lifelong career for the officials.[44]

The four main features of bureaucracy are summarised by Stewart as specialisation, hierarchy of authority, system of rules and impersonality.

- **Specialisation** applies more to the job than to the person undertaking the job. This makes for continuity because the job usually continues if the present job-holder leaves.

- **Hierarchy of authority** makes for a sharp distinction between administrators and the administered or between management and workers. Within the management ranks there are clearly defined levels of authority. This detailed and precise stratification is particularly marked in the armed forces and in the civil service.
- **System of rules** aims to provide for an efficient and impersonal operation. The system of rules is generally stable, although some rules may be changed or modified with time. Knowledge of the rules is a requisite of holding a job in a bureaucracy.
- **Impersonality** means that allocation of privileges and the exercise of authority should not be arbitrary, but in accordance with the laid-down system of rules. In more highly developed bureaucracies there tend to be carefully defined procedures for appealing against certain types of decisions. Stewart sees the characteristic of impersonality as the feature of bureaucracy which most distinguishes it from other types of organisations. A bureaucracy should not only be impersonal but be seen to be impersonal.[45]

Criticisms of bureaucracy

Weber's concept of bureaucracy has a number of disadvantages and has been subject to severe criticism.

- The over-emphasis on rules and procedures, record keeping and paperwork may become more important in its own right than as a means to an end.
- Officials may develop a dependence upon bureaucratic status, symbols and rules.
- Initiative may be stifled and when a situation is not covered by a complete set of rules or procedures there may be a lack of flexibility or adaptation to changing circumstances.
- Position and responsibilities in the organisation can lead to officious bureaucratic behaviour. There may also be a tendency to conceal administrative procedures from outsiders.
- Impersonal relations can lead to stereotyped behaviour and a lack of responsiveness to individual incidents or problems.

Restriction of psychological growth

One of the strongest critics of bureaucratic organisation, and the demands it makes on the worker, is Argyris.[46] He claims that bureaucracies restrict the psychological growth of the individual and cause feelings of failure, frustration and conflict. Argyris suggests that the organisational environment should provide a significant degree of individual responsibility and self-control; commitment to the goals of the organisation; productiveness and work; and an opportunity for individuals to apply their full abilities.

When these ideas are related to the main features of bureaucracy discussed above, such as specialisation, hierarchy of authority, system of rules and impersonality, it is perhaps easy to see the basis of Argyris' criticism.

A similar criticism is made by Caulkin who refers to the impersonal structure of bureaucracy as constructed round the post rather than the person and the ease with which it can be swung behind unsocial or even pathological ends.

> The overemphasis on process rather than purpose, fragmented responsibilities and hierarchical control means that it's all too easy for individuals to neglect the larger purposes to which their small effort is being put.[47]

Evaluation of bureaucracy

The growth of bureaucracy has come about through the increasing size and complexity of organisations and the associated demand for effective administration. The work of the classical writers has given emphasis to the careful design and planning of organisation structure and the definition of individual duties and responsibilities. Effective organisation is based on structure and delegation through different layers of the hierarchy. Greater specialisation and the application of expertise and technical knowledge have highlighted the need for laid-down procedures.

Bureaucracy is founded on a formal, clearly defined and hierarchical structure. However, with rapid changes in the external environment, de-layering of organisations, empowerment and greater attention to meeting the needs of customers, there is an increasing need to organise for flexibility. Peters and Waterman found that excellent American companies achieved quick action just because their organisations were fluid and had intensive networks of informal and open communications.[48] By contrast, the crisis IBM experienced in the 1980s/1990s over the market for personal computers is explained at least in part by its top-heavy corporate structure, cumbersome organisation and dinosaur-like bureaucracy.[49]

According to Cloke and Goldsmith, management and bureaucracy can be thought of as flip sides of the same coin. The elements of bureaucracy generate organisational hierarchy and management, while managers generate a need for bureaucracy.

> Bureaucracies provide a safe haven where managers can hide from responsibility and avoid being held accountable for errors of judgement or problems they created or failed to solve. In return, managers are able to use bureaucratic rules to stifle self-management and compel employees to follow their direction . . . Yet bureaucratic systems can be broken down and transformed into human-scale interactions. We have seen countless managers recreate themselves as leaders and facilitators, employees reinvent themselves as responsible self-managing team members, and bureaucracies transform into responsive, human-scale organizations. Alternatives to organizational hierarchy are both practical and possible.[50]

Organisational solutions

As organisations face increasing global competitiveness and complex demands of the information and technological age, the need arises for alternative forms of corporate structure and systems. Ridderstrale points out that in the past century the hallmark of a large company was hierarchy, which rests on principles at odds with the new strategic requirements. 'Bureaucracies allowed people with knowledge to control ignorant workers. Now, new structures are needed as knowledge spreads.' Ridderstrale suggests four specific ways in which high-performing organisations have responded to increasingly complex knowledge systems by developing organisational solutions which depart from the traditional bureaucratic model:

- more decentralised and flatter structures in order that quick decisions can be taken near to where the critical knowledge resides. Flatter structures can be achieved by increasing the span of control and reducing layers from the top or removing layers of middle management;
- the use of more than a single structure in order that knowledge may be assembled across the boundaries of a traditional organisation chart. If people

have less permanent places in the hierarchy they are more readily able to move across functional and geographical borders;

- converting companies into learning organisations and giving every employee the same level of familiarity with personnel and capabilities. Successful companies develop a detailed inventory of core competencies. In order fully to exploit current knowledge, managers need to know what the company knows;
- the broader sharing of expertise and knowledge, which may be located in the periphery where little formal authority resides. Managers need to share principles to ensure coordination and to encourage 'lowest common denominators' and the development of 'tribal' qualities through shared ownership and rewards, common norms, culture and values.[51]

Public sector organisations

In the case of public sector organisations, in particular, there is a demand for uniformity of treatment, regularity of procedures and public accountability for their operations. This leads to adherence to specified rules and procedures and to the keeping of detailed records. In their actual dealings with public sector organisations people often call for what amounts to increased bureaucracy, even though they may not use that term. The demands for equal treatment, for a standard set of regulations that apply to everyone, and that decisions should not be left to the discretion of individual managers are in effect demands for bureaucracy.

Green argues that, although bureaucracies are becoming less and less the first-choice format for organisational shape, there is still a place for bureaucracy in parts of most organisations and especially public sector organisations such as local authorities and universities. The use and implementation of tried and tested rules and procedures help to ensure essential values and ethics, and that necessary functions are run on a consistent and fair basis.[52] New forms of information technology such as electronic transactions processed from home or public access terminals are likely to change processes of government service delivery, administrative workloads and the nature of bureaucracy.[53]

Relevance today

By their very nature, bureaucracies are likely to attract criticism. For example, there appears to be a particular dilemma for management in personal service industries. The underlying characteristics of bureaucracy would seem to restrict personal service delivery which requires a flexible approach, responsiveness to individual requirements and the need for initiative and inventiveness.[54] Much of this criticism is valid, but much also appears unfair.

Stewart suggests that more organisations today contain mainly or a considerable number of professionals. Such organisations will still have bureaucratic features although there is more reliance on professional discretion and self-regulation than on control through rules and regulations.[55] However, despite new forms of organisation which have emerged, many writers suggest that bureaucracy is still relevant today as a major form of organisation structure.[56]

'Despite the frequent criticisms of bureaucratic structures, it is difficult to envisage how large-scale organisations, especially within the public sector, could function effectively without exhibiting at least some of the features of a bureaucracy. Demands for alternative forms of structure are unrealistic.'

How would you attempt to justify the benefits of bureaucratic structures?

Structuralism

Sometimes Weber's work is associated with the ideas of writers such as Karl Marx under the sub-heading of the structuralism approach, which is a synthesis of the classical (or formal) school and the human relations (or informal) school.[57] A major line of thought was that the earlier approaches were incomplete and lacked adequate theoretical assumptions and background. The structuralism approach provides a radical perspective of social and organisational behaviour.[58] Greater attention should be given to the relationship between the formal and informal aspects of the organisation, and the study of conflict between the needs of the individual and the organisation, and between workers and management. Structuralism is sometimes associated as part of a broader human relations approach, which is discussed below.

The human relations approach

The main emphasis of the classical writers was on structure and the formal organisation, but during the 1920s, the years of the Great Depression, greater attention began to be paid to the social factors at work and to the behaviour of employees within an organisation – that is, to human relations.

The Hawthorne experiments

The turning point in the development of the human relations movement ('behavioural' and 'informal' are alternative headings sometimes given to this approach) came with the famous experiments at the Hawthorne plant of the Western Electric Company near Chicago, America (1924–32) and the subsequent publication of the research findings.[59] Among the people who wrote about the Hawthorne experiments was Elton Mayo (1880–1949), who is often quoted as having been a leader of the researchers. However, there appears to be some doubt as to the extent to which Mayo was actually involved in conducting the experiments and his exact contribution to the human relations movement.[60]

There were four main phases to the Hawthorne experiments:

- the illumination experiments;
- the relay assembly test room;
- the interviewing programme;
- the bank wiring observation room.

The illumination experiments

The original investigation was conducted on the lines of the classical approach and was concerned, in typical scientific management style, with the effects of the intensity of lighting upon the workers' productivity. The workers were divided into two groups, an experimental group and a control group. The results of these tests were inconclusive as production in the experimental group varied with no apparent relationship to the level of lighting, but actually increased when conditions were made much worse. Production also increased in the control group although the lighting remained unchanged. The level of production was influenced, clearly, by factors other than changes in physical conditions of work. This prompted a series of other experiments investigating factors of worker productivity.

The relay assembly test room

In the relay assembly test room the work was boring and repetitive. It involved assembling telephone relays by putting together a number of small parts. Six women workers were transferred from their normal departments to a separate area. The researchers selected two assemblers who were friends with each other. They then chose three other assemblers and a layout operator. The experiment was divided into 13 periods during which the workers were subjected to a series of planned and controlled changes to their conditions of work, such as hours of work, rest pauses and provision of refreshments. The general environmental conditions of the test room were similar to those of the normal assembly line.

During the experiment the observer adopted a friendly manner, consulting the workers, listening to their complaints and keeping them informed of the experiment. Following all but one of the changes (when operators complained too many breaks made them lose their work rhythm) there was a continuous increase in the level of production. The researchers formed the conclusion that the extra attention given to the workers, and the apparent interest in them shown by management, were the main reasons for the higher productivity. This has become famous as the 'Hawthorne Effect'.

The interviewing programme

Another significant phase of the experiments was the interviewing programme. The lighting experiment and the relay assembly test room drew attention to the form of supervision as a contributory factor to the workers' level of production. In an attempt to find out more about the workers' feelings towards their supervisors and their general conditions of work, a large interviewing programme was introduced. More than 20,000 interviews were conducted before the work was ended because of the depression.

Initially, the interviewers approached their task with a set of prepared questions, relating mainly to how the workers felt about their jobs. However, this method produced only limited information. The workers regarded a number of the questions as irrelevant; also they wanted to talk about issues other than just supervision and immediate working conditions. As a result, the style of interviewing was changed to become more non-directive and open-ended. There was no set list of questions and the workers were free to talk about any aspect of their work. The interviewers set out to be friendly and sympathetic. They adopted an impartial, non-judgemental approach and concentrated on listening.

Using this approach, the interviewers found out far more about the workers' true feelings and attitudes. They gained information not just about supervision and working conditions but also about the company itself, management, work group relations and matters outside of work such as family life and views on society in general. Many workers appeared to welcome the opportunity to have someone to talk to about their feelings and problems and to be able to 'let off steam' in a friendly atmosphere. The interviewing programme was significant in giving an impetus to present-day human resource management and the use of counselling interviews, and highlighting the need for management to listen to workers' feelings and problems. Being a good listener is arguably even more important for managers in today's work organisations and it is a skill which needs to be encouraged and developed.[61]

The bank wiring observation room

Another experiment involved the observation of a group of 14 men working in the bank wiring room. It was noted that the men formed their own informal organisation with sub-groups or cliques, and with natural leaders emerging with the consent of the members. The group developed its own pattern of informal social relations and 'norms' of what constituted 'proper' behaviour. Despite a financial incentive scheme where the workers could receive more money the more work produced, the group decided on a level of output well below the level they were capable of producing.

Group pressures on individual workers were stronger than financial incentives offered by management. The group believed that if they increased their output, management would raise the standard level of piece rates. The importance of group 'norms' and informal social relations are discussed later in the chapter (see 'The nature of work groups and teams', p. 446).

Evaluation of the human relations approach

The human relations approach has been subjected to severe criticism. The Hawthorne experiments have been criticised, for example, on methodology and on failure of the investigators to take sufficient account of environmental factors – although much of this criticism is with the value of hindsight. The human relations writers have been criticised generally for the adoption of a management perspective, their 'unitary frame of reference' and their oversimplified theories.[62]

Other criticisms of the human relations approach are that it is insufficiently scientific and that it takes too narrow a view. It ignores the role of the organisation itself in how society operates.

Sex power differential

There are a number of interpretations of the results of the Hawthorne experiments, including the possible implications of the 'sex power differential' between the two groups. In the relay assembly room where output increased, the group was all female, while in the bank wiring room where output was restricted, the group was all male. The workers in the relay assembly test room were all young unmarried women. All except one were living at home with traditional families of immigrant background. In the work environment of the factory the women had been subjected to frequent contact with male supervisors and therefore 'the sex power hierarchies in the home and in the factory were congruent'. It is suggested, therefore, that it was only to be expected that the women agreed readily to participate with management in the relay assembly test room experiment.[63]

Importance of the Hawthorne experiments

Whatever the interpretation of the results of the Hawthorne experiments, they did generate new ideas concerning the importance of work groups and leadership, communications, output restrictions, motivation and job design. They placed emphasis on the importance of personnel management and gave impetus to the work of the human relations writers. The Hawthorne experiments undoubtedly marked a significant step forward in providing further insight into human behaviour at work and the development of management thinking. The Hawthorne experiments are regarded as one of the most important of all social science investigations and are recognised as probably the single most important foundation of the human relations approach to management and the development of organisational behaviour.

In a review of humane approaches to management, Crainer asserts: 'The Hawthorne Studies were important because they showed that views of how managers behaved were a vital aspect of motivation and improved performance. Also, the research revealed the importance of informal work groups.'[64]

Humanisation of the work organisation

Whereas supporters of the classical approach sought to increase production by rationalisation of the work organisation, the human relations movement has led to ideas on increasing production by humanising the work organisation. The classical approach adopted more of a managerial perspective, while the human relations approach strove for a greater understanding of people's psychological and social needs at work as well as improving the process of management. It is usually regarded as the first major approach to organisation and management to show concern for industrial sociology.

The human relations approach recognised the importance of the informal organisation which will always be present within the formal structure. This informal organisation will influence the motivation of employees who will view the organisation for which they work through the values and attitudes of their colleagues. Their view of the organisation determines their approach to work and the extent of their motivation to work well or otherwise.

Human relations writers demonstrated that people go to work to satisfy a complexity of needs and not simply for monetary reward. They emphasised the importance of the wider social needs of individuals and gave recognition to the work organisation as a social organisation and the importance of the group, and group values and norms, in influencing individual behaviour at work. It has been commented that the classical school was concerned about 'organisations without people' and the human relations school about 'people without organisations'.

critical reflection

'The human relations approach to organisations and management makes all the right sounds with an emphasis on humane behaviour, considerate management and recognition of the informal organisation. However, it is more about what people would like to believe and lacks credibility and substance.'

To what extent do the criticisms and shortcomings of the human relations approach detract from its potential benefits?

Neo-human relations

Certainly there were shortcomings in the human relations approach and assumptions which evolved from such studies as the Hawthorne experiments were not necessarily supported by empirical evidence. For example, the contention that a satisfied worker is a productive worker was not always found to be valid. However, the results of the Hawthorne experiments and the subsequent attention given to the social organisation and to theories of individual motivation gave rise to the work of those writers in the 1950s and 1960s who adopted a more psychological orientation. New ideas on management theory arose and a major focus of concern was the personal adjustment of the individual within the work organisation and the effects of group relationships and leadership styles. This group of writers is often (and more correctly) categorised separately under the heading of '**neo-human relations**'. The works of these writers are summarised broadly below.

The work of Maslow

A major impetus for the neo-human relations approach was the work of Maslow who, in 1943, put forward a theoretical framework of individual personality development and motivation based on a hierarchy of human needs.[65] The hierarchy ranges through five levels from, at the lowest level, physiological needs, through safety needs, love needs and esteem needs, to the need for self-actualisation at the highest level. Individuals advance up the hierarchy only as each lower-level need is satisfied. Although Maslow did not originally intend this need hierarchy to be applied necessarily to the work situation it has, nevertheless, had a significant impact on management approaches to motivation and the design of work organisation to meet individual needs. The work of Maslow provides a link with the earlier human relations approach.

Some leading contributors

Among the best-known contributors to the neo-human relations approach are Herzberg and McGregor. Herzberg isolated two different sets of factors affecting motivation and satisfaction at work. One set of factors comprises those which, if absent, cause dissatisfaction. These are 'hygiene' or 'maintenance' factors which are concerned basically with job environment. However, to motivate workers to give of their best, proper attention must be given to a different set of factors, the 'motivators' or 'growth' factors. These are concerned with job content.[66]

McGregor argued that the style of management adopted is a function of the manager's attitudes towards human nature and behaviour at work. He put forward two suppositions called Theory X and Theory Y which are based on popular assumptions about work and people.[67]

Other major contributors to the neo-human relations approach are Likert, whose work includes research into different systems of management;[68] McClelland, with ideas on achievement motivation;[69] and Argyris, who considered the effects of the formal organisation on the individual and psychological growth in the process of self-actualisation.[70] Argyris' major contributions include his work on organisational learning and on effective leadership.[71]

The neo-human relations approach has generated a large amount of writing and research not only from original propounders but also from others seeking to establish the validity, or otherwise, of their ideas. This has led to continuing attention being given to such matters as organisation structuring, group dynamics, job satisfaction, communication and participation, leadership styles and motivation. It has also led to greater attention to the importance of interpersonal interactions, the causes of conflict and recognition of 'employee relations' problems.

The systems approach

More recently, attention has been focused on the analysis of organisations as 'systems' with a number of interrelated sub-systems. The classical approach emphasised the technical requirements of the organisation and its needs – 'organisations without people'; the human relations approaches emphasised the psychological and social aspects, and the consideration of human needs – 'people without organisations'.

The **systems approach** attempts to reconcile these two earlier approaches and the work of the formal and the informal writers. Attention is focused on the total work organisation and the interrelationships of structure and behaviour, and the range of variables within the organisation. This approach can be contrasted with a view of the organisation as separate parts. The systems approach encourages managers to view the organisation both as a whole and as part of a larger environment. The idea is that any part of an organisation's activities affects all other parts.

Systems theory

Systems theory is not new and has been used in the natural and physical sciences for a number of years. One of the founders of this approach was the biologist Ludwig von Bertalanffy who used the term 'systems theory' in an article published in 1951 and who is generally credited with having developed the outline of General Systems Theory.[72] The systems approach to organisation has arisen, at least in part, therefore, from the work of biologists, and Miller and Rice have likened the commercial and industrial organisation to the biological organism.[73]

Using a General Systems Theory (GST) approach, Boulding classified nine levels of systems of increasing complexity according to the state of development and knowledge about each level.[74] Organisations are complex social systems and are more open to change than lower-level simple dynamic or cybernetic systems. Boulding felt there were large gaps in both theoretical and empirical knowledge of the human level and the social organisations level of systems, although some progress has now been made with recent theories of organisational behaviour.

The business organisation as an open system

The business organisation is an open system. There is continual interaction with the broader external environment of which it is part. The systems approach views the organisation within its total environment and emphasises the importance of multiple channels of interaction. Criticisms of earlier approaches to organisation are based in part on the attempt to study the activities and problems of the organisation solely in terms of the internal environment.

The systems approach views the organisation as a whole and involves the study of the organisation in terms of the relationship between technical and social variables within the system. Changes in one part, technical or social, will affect other parts and thus the whole system.

Longwall coal-mining study

The idea of socio-technical systems arose from the work of Trist and others, of the Tavistock Institute of Human Relations, in their study of the effects of changing technology in the coal-mining industry in the 1940s.[75] The increasing use of mechanisation and the introduction of coal-cutters and mechanical conveyors enabled coal to be extracted on a 'longwall' method.

Shift working was introduced, with each shift specialising in one stage of the operation – preparation, cutting or loading. However, the new method meant a change in the previous system of working where a small, self-selecting group of miners worked together, as an independent team, on one part of the coalface – the 'single place' or 'shortwall' method.

Technological change had brought about changes in the social groupings of the miners. It disrupted the integration of small groups and the psychological and sociological properties of the old method of working. There was a lack of co-operation between different shifts and within each shift, an increase in absenteeism, scapegoating and signs of greater social stress. The 'longwall' method was socially disruptive and did not prove as economically efficient as it could have been with the new technology.

The researchers saw the need for a socio-technical approach in which an appropriate social system could be developed in keeping with the new technical system. The result was the 'composite longwall' method with more responsibility to the team as a whole and shifts carrying out composite tasks, the reintroduction of multiskilled roles and a reduction in specialisation. The composite method was psychologically and socially more rewarding and economically more efficient than the 'longwall' method.

The socio-technical system

The concept of the organisation as a 'socio-technical' system directs attention to the transformation or conversion process itself, to the series of activities through which the organisation attempts to achieve its objectives. The **socio-technical system** is concerned with the interactions between the psychological and social factors and the needs and demands of the human part of the organisation, and its structural and technological requirements.

Recognition of the socio-technical approach is of particular importance today. People must be considered as at least an equal priority along with investment in technology. For example, Lane *et al.* point out that major technological change has brought about dramatic changes in worker behaviour and requirements. It is people who unlock the benefits and opportunities of information communication technology.[76]

Technology determinism

The concept of socio-technical systems provides a link between the systems approach and a sub-division, sometimes adopted – the **technology approach**. Writers under the technology heading attempt to restrict generalisations about organisations and management and emphasise the effects of varying technologies on organisation structure, work groups and individual performance and job satisfaction. This is in contrast with the socio-technical approach which did not regard technology, *per se*, as a determinant of behaviour.

Under the heading of the technology approach could be included the work of such writers as Walker and Guest (effects of the assembly line production method on employee behaviour);[77] Sayles (relationship between technology and the nature of work groups);[78] and Blauner (problems of 'alienation' in relation to different work technologies).[79]

The role of the manager

The meaning of management

Management is a generic term and subject to many interpretations. A number of contrasting ideas are attributed to the meaning of management and to the work of a manager.[80] There are also different ways of viewing the study and knowledge of management. For example, Shafritz observes that today's cultured managers could find answers to many business problems from the work of Shakespeare.

> For more than forty years I have been speaking prose without knowing it. It is the same with Shakespeare. Most managers have read at least some of his plays, but have yet to realize that they have been studying management.[81]

Knights and Willmott refer to managing as an everyday activity that involves interactions between people that 'are not unrelated or entirely dissimilar to other spheres of life, except perhaps in the rhetoric and hype that surround management'. They contend that most established textbooks about management and organisation provide little that enables practising managers to make sense of their particular problem or dilemma, and in order to appreciate the living of management draw on a number of contemporary novels.[82]

In certain respects everyone can be regarded as a manager, at least to some extent. We all manage our own time and everyone has some choice whether or not to do something, and some control, however slight, over the planning and organisation of their work. However, we are concerned with management as involving people looking beyond themselves and exercising formal authority over the activities and performance of other people.

Manager as a job title

Even within a work organisation you cannot identify a manager necessarily by what a person is called or by their job title. In some organisations there is a liberal use of the title 'manager' in an apparent attempt to enhance the status and morale of staff. As a result there are a number of people whose job title includes the term manager but who, in reality, are not performing the full activities of a manager. Yet there are many people whose job title does not include the term manager (for example, group accountant, head chef, chief inspector, captain, head teacher, production controller, district nursing officer, company secretary) but who, in terms of the activities they undertake and the authority and responsibility they exercise, may be very much a manager.

Management as making things happen

For our purposes, therefore, we can regard management as:

- taking place within a structured organisational setting with prescribed roles;
- directed towards the attainment of aims and objectives;
- achieved through the efforts of other people; and
- using systems and procedures.

At its most basic, management may be viewed as 'making things happen'.

Management is active, not theoretical. It is about changing behaviour and making things happen. It is about developing people, working with them, reaching objectives and achieving results. Indeed, all the research into how managers spend their time reveals that they are creatures of the moment, perpetually immersed in the nitty-gritty of making things happen.[83]

Managers born or made? Management an art or science?

There is frequent debate about whether managers are born or made or whether management is an art or a science. Briefly, the important point is that neither of these is a mutually exclusive alternative. The answer to either question is surely a combination of both. Even if there are certain innate qualities that make for a potentially good manager, these natural talents must be encouraged and developed through proper guidance, education and training, and planned experience.

Clearly, management must always be something of an art, especially in so far as it involves practice, personal judgement and dealing with people. However, it still requires knowledge of the fundamentals of management, and competence in the application of specific skills and techniques – as illustrated, for example, with developments in information technology.

> The trouble is that, for all the techniques at their disposal, managers generally act at a very intuitive level. Managers may have absorbed the latest thinking on core competencies, but are more likely to base a decision on prejudice or personal opinion rather than a neat theory.[84]

The discussion of management as an art or a science is developed by Watson who suggests that in order to make sense of the complex and highly ambiguous situations in which managers find themselves, management can be viewed not only as both art and science but also magic and politics (see Figure 3.13).[85]

The emergence of management

Peter Drucker, who is widely regarded as the guru of management gurus, has written about the significance in social history of the emergence of management:

> The emergence of management as an essential, a distinct and a leading institution is a pivotal event in social history. Rarely, if ever, has a new basic institution, a new leading group, emerged as fast as has management since the turn of this [20th] century. Rarely in human history has a new institution proven indispensable so quickly; and even less often has a new institution arrived with so little opposition, so little disturbance, so little controversy.[86]

Drucker sees management as denoting a function as well as the people who discharge it, a social position and authority, and also a discipline and field of study. 'Management is tasks. Management is a discipline. But management is also people. Every achievement of management is the achievement of a manager. Every failure is a failure of a manager.'[87] Other writers, however, take the view that management is not a separate discipline. The problem is identifying a single discipline that encompasses the work of a manager, or agreeing the disciplines that a manager

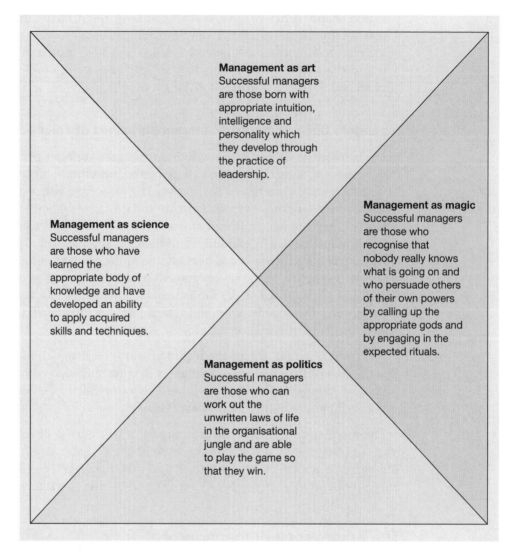

Figure 3.13 Management as art, science, magic and politics

Source: From Watson, T. J. *Management, Organisation and Employment Strategy*, Routledge and Kegan Paul (1986), p. 29. Reproduced by permission of the publishers, Routledge, a division of Taylor & Francis, Ltd.

needs in order effectively to carry out this work. Note, however, the discussion on the changing role of managers at the end of this chapter.

Significance of cultural influences

Schneider and Barsoux contend that trying to define the meaning of management shows up differences in beliefs and values. Cultural influences are a significant feature of management. Managers in some countries might have more concern for the 'spiritual' aspects of management, while in others there would be greater concern for the business sense. Developing people through work could be seen as an intrusion of privacy, and others may perceive empowerment as another name for manipulation.[88] According to Francesco and Gold, if international managers are to perform successfully in the global economy they need to understand the effects of different cultures on organisational behaviour. Reliance on theories developed in one culture is not sufficient.[89]

Management and administration

There is often confusion over different interpretations of the two terms 'management' and 'administration'. One of the main reasons for this confusion would seem to result from the translation of Fayol's book *Administration industrielle et générale* from the French into English. In the original (1929) English edition there was a direct translation of 'administration', but in the wider republication of the book in 1949 the term 'management' replaced 'administration' in the title. In the introduction to the revised edition, Urwick indicates regret at this change and also expresses concern at the possible division between management being seen to apply only to business organisations, and (public) administration as applying to the same functions in public service organisations.[90]

Dictionary definitions tend to see the two words as synonymous. Management is sometimes referred to as 'administration of business concerns' and administration as 'management of public affairs'. However, the term 'management' is now used far more widely within the public sector. There is clearly an overlap between the two terms and they tend to be used, therefore, in accordance with the convenience of individual writers. This confirms the feeling that although most people perceive a difference between the two terms, this difference is not easy to describe.

Administration part of management

There appears, therefore, to be growing acceptance of the term management as the general descriptive label and administration as relating to the more specific function of the implementation of systems and procedures instigated by management. Administration can be seen as taking place in accordance with some form of rules or procedures, whereas management implies a greater degree of discretion. For our purposes, management is viewed as applying to both private and public sector organisations; and administration is interpreted as that part of the management process concerned with the design and implementation of systems and procedures to help meet stated objectives. Systems of communication and procedures relating to information technology are particularly important today.

The process of management

The nature of management is variable. It relates to all activities of the organisation and is not a separate, discrete function. It cannot be departmentalised or centralised. With the possible exception of the board of directors, or similar, an organisation cannot have a department of management in the same way as it

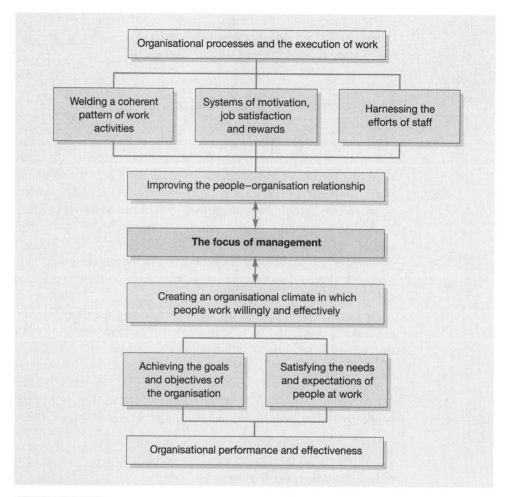

Figure 3.14   The central focus of management

can have a department for other functions, such as research and development, production, marketing, accounting, or human resources. Management is seen best, therefore, as a process common to all other functions carried out within the organisation. Through the execution of work, the central focus of management is on achieving the goals and objectives of the organisation, and satisfying the needs and expectations of its members. **Management is essentially an integrating activity.** (See Figure 3.14.)

But what does the process of management actually involve and what activities does it encompass? Management is a complex and discursive subject. Despite the widespread use of the term and the large amount written about the subject, it is not easy to find agreement on a simple yet comprehensive definition of management or of a manager. Moreover, **'management' is not homogeneous. It takes place in different ways and at different levels of the organisation.** One approach, especially favoured by classical writers, is to analyse the nature of management and to search for common activities (or functions, or elements) applicable to managers in all organisations.

Common activities of management

One of the first, and most widely quoted, analyses is that given by Henri Fayol, who divided the activities of industrial undertakings into six groups:

- technical (production, manufacture and adaptation);
- commercial (buying, selling, exchange and market information);
- financial (obtaining capital and making optimum use of available funds);
- security (safeguarding property and persons);
- accounting (information on the economic position, stocktaking, balance sheet, costs, statistics); and
- managerial. (The term 'management' is a translation of the French term 'administration'.)[91]

The managerial activity is divided into five elements of management, which are defined as: 'to forecast and plan, to organise, to command, to co-ordinate and to control'. Fayol describes these elements as:

- **Planning** (translated from the French *prévoir* = to foresee, and taken to include forecasting) – examining the future, deciding what needs to be achieved and developing a plan of action.
- **Organising** – providing the material and human resources and building the structure to carry out the activities of the organisation.
- **Command** – maintaining activity among personnel, getting the optimum return from all employees in the interests of the whole organisation.
- **Co-ordination** – unifying and harmonising all activities and effort of the organisation to facilitate its working and success.
- **Control** – verifying that everything occurs in accordance with plans, instructions, established principles and expressed command.

critical reflection

'It is difficult to think of any aspect of the functioning of the organisation or behaviour of people that does not concern, or relate back to, management in some way. For example, personality clashes could be traced back to management procedures for recruitment and selection, socialisation and training, teamwork or the level and style of supervision.'

How many examples can you think of that contradict this assertion?

Principles of management

Fayol also suggests that a set of well-established principles would help concentrate general discussion on management theory. He emphasises, however, that these principles must be flexible and adaptable to changing circumstances. Fayol recognised that there was no limit to the principles of management but in his writing advocated 14 of them.

1 **Division of work**. The object is to produce more and better work from the same effort, and the advantages of specialisation. However, there are limits to division of work which experience and a sense of proportion tell us should not be exceeded.

2 **Authority and responsibility**. Responsibility is the corollary of authority. Wherever authority is exercised responsibility arises. The application of sanctions is essential to good management, and is needed to encourage useful actions and to discourage their opposite. The best safeguard against abuse of authority is the personal integrity of the manager.

3 **Discipline** is essential for the efficient operation of the organisation. Discipline is in essence the outward mark of respect for agreements between the organisation and its members. The manager must decide on the most appropriate form of sanction in cases of offences against discipline.

4 **Unity of command**. In any action an employee should receive orders from one superior only; if not, authority is undermined and discipline, order and stability threatened. Dual command is a perpetual source of conflicts.

5 **Unity of direction**. In order to provide for unity of action, co-ordination and focusing of effort, there should be one head and one plan for any group of activities with the same objective.

6 **Subordination of individual interest to general interest**. The interest of the organisation should dominate individual or group interests.

7 **Remuneration of personnel**. Remuneration should as far as possible satisfy both employee and employer. Methods of payment can influence organisational performance and the method should be fair and should encourage keenness by rewarding well-directed effort, but not lead to overpayment.

8 **Centralisation** is always present to some extent in any organisation. The degree of centralisation is a question of proportion and will vary in particular organisations.

9 **Scalar chain**. The chain of superiors from the ultimate authority to the lowest ranks. Respect for line authority must be reconciled with activities which require urgent action, and with the need to provide for some measure of initiative at all levels of authority.

10 **Order**. This includes material order and social order. The object of material order is avoidance of loss. There should be an appointed place for each thing, and each thing in its appointed place. Social order involves an appointed place for each employee, and each employee in his or her appointed place. Social order requires good organisation and good selection.

11 **Equity**. The desire for equity and for equality of treatment are aspirations to be taken into account in dealing with employees throughout all levels of the scalar chain.

12 **Stability of tenure of personnel**. Generally, prosperous organisations have a stable managerial personnel, but changes of personnel are inevitable and stability of tenure is a question of proportion.

13 **Initiative**. This represents a source of strength for the organisation and should be encouraged and developed. Tact and integrity are required to promote initiative and to retain respect for authority and discipline.

14 **Esprit de corps** should be fostered, as harmony and unity among members of the organisation is a great strength in the organisation. The principle of unity of command should be observed. It is necessary to avoid the dangers of divide

and rule of one's own team, and the abuse of written communication. Wherever possible verbal contacts should be used.

A number of these principles relate directly to, or are influenced by, the organisation structure in which the process of management takes place. Fayol's set of principles can be compared, therefore, with those given by Urwick.

Relevance today

Inevitably there are doubts about the relevance of these activities and principles today but it is hard to argue against their continuing, underlying importance. What is perhaps debatable is the manner of their interpretation and implementation. In an article bringing together the thinking of senior members of the Institute of Administrative Management, Moorcroft suggests that Fayol's five elements of management are still recognised as relevant and appropriate for the managers of today and tomorrow. However, although some of the principles of management remain fresh and relevant, at the start of a new millennium a new set of principles is needed to guide a manager's everyday actions. These 'principles' are not offered as an exclusive or authoritative list but are proposed as a thought-provoking starting point to address the management problems awaiting us in the new millennium (see Figure 3.15).[92]

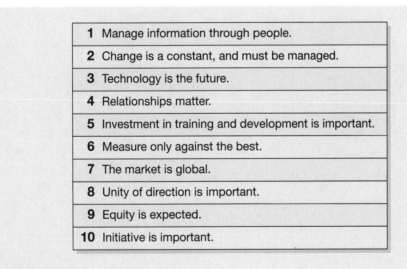

| **1** Manage information through people. |
| **2** Change is a constant, and must be managed. |
| **3** Technology is the future. |
| **4** Relationships matter. |
| **5** Investment in training and development is important. |
| **6** Measure only against the best. |
| **7** The market is global. |
| **8** Unity of direction is important. |
| **9** Equity is expected. |
| **10** Initiative is important. |

Figure 3.15   **Ten new principles for effective administrative management**

Source: From Moorcroft, R. 'Managing in the 21st Century', *Manager, The British Journal of Administrative Management*, January/February 2000, p. 10. Reproduced with permission from The Institute of Administrative Management.

Managing in organisations

Henry Mintzberg – ten management roles

Mintzberg (1973) used structured observations to gather data on how managers spent their time – though from only five chief executives. Despite this limitation others (e.g. Martinko and Gardner, 1990) have supported Mintzberg's main conclusion that managers' work was varied and fragmented. He identified ten management roles in the three categories shown – informational, interpersonal and decisional – all of which are means of influencing other people. Table 3.3 lists these roles, with the right-hand column giving contemporary examples from an account by the manager of a project to distribute funds to schools to improve nutrition.

Informational roles

Managing depends on obtaining information about external and internal events, and passing it to others. The *monitor role* involves seeking out, receiving and screening information to understand the organisation and its environment. It

Table 3.3 Mintzberg's ten management roles

Category	Role	Activity	Examples from a school nutrition project
Informational	**Monitor**	Seek and receive information, scan reports, maintain interpersonal contacts	Collect and review funding applications; set up database to monitor application process
	Disseminator	Forward information to others, send memos, make phone calls	Share content of applications with team members by e-mail
	Spokesperson	Represent the unit to outsiders in speeches and reports	Present application process at internal and external events
Interpersonal	**Figurehead**	Perform ceremonial and symbolic duties, receive visitors	Sign letters of award to successful applicants
	Leader	Direct and motivate subordinates, train, advise and influence	Design and coordinate process with team and other managers
	Liaison	Maintain information links in and beyond the organisation	Become link person for government bodies to contact for progress reports
Decisional	**Entrepreneur**	Initiate new projects, spot opportunities, identify areas of business development	Use initiative to revise application process and to introduce electronic communication
	Disturbance handler	Take corrective action during crises, resolve conflicts amongst staff, adapt to changes	Holding face-to-face meetings with applicants when the outcome was negative; handling staff grievances
	Resource allocator	Decide who gets resources, schedule, budget, set priorities	Ensure fair distribution of grants nationally
	Negotiator	Represent unit during negotiations with unions, suppliers, and generally defend interests	Working with sponsors and government to ensure consensus during decision making

Source: Based on Mintzberg (1973), and private communication from the project manager.

comes from papers and reports, and from chance conversations with customers or new contacts at conferences and exhibitions. Much of this information is oral (gossip as well as formal meetings), building on personal contacts. In the *disseminator role* the manager shares information by forwarding reports, passing on rumours or briefing staff. As a *spokesperson* the manager transmits information to people outside the organisation – speaking at a conference, briefing the media or giving the department's view at a company meeting. Michael O'Leary at Ryanair is renowned for flamboyant statements to the media about competitors or officials in the European Commission with whose policies he disagrees.

Interpersonal roles

Interpersonal roles arise directly from a manager's formal authority and status, and shape relationships with people within and beyond the organisation. In the *figurehead role* the manager is a symbol, representing the unit in legal and ceremonial duties such as greeting a visitor, signing legal documents, presenting retirement gifts or receiving a quality award. The *leader role* defines the manager's relationship with other people (not just subordinates), including motivating, communicating and developing their skills and confidence. As one manager commented:

> I am conscious that due to conflicting priorities I am unable to spend as much time interacting with staff members as I would like. I try to overcome this by leaving my door open whenever I am alone as an invitation to staff to come in and interrupt me, and to encourage the staff to come to me to discuss any problems that may arise.

The *liaison role* focuses on contacts with people outside the immediate unit. Managers maintain a network in which they trade information and favours for mutual benefit with clients, government officials, customers and suppliers. For some managers, particularly chief executives and sales managers, the liaison role takes a high proportion of their time and energy.

management
in practice

Strengthening interpersonal roles

A company restructured its regional operations, closed a sales office in Bordeaux and transferred the work to Paris. The sales manager responsible for south-west France was now geographically distant from her immediate boss and the rest of the team. This caused severe problems of communication and loss of teamwork. She concluded that the interpersonal aspects of the role were vital as a basis for the informational and decisional roles. The decision to close the office had broken these links.

She and her boss agreed to try the following solutions:

- a 'one-to-one' session of quality time to discuss key issues during monthly visits to head office;
- daily telephone contact to ensure speed of response and that respective communication needs were met;
- use of fax and e-mail at home to speed up communications.

These overcame the break in interpersonal roles caused by the location change.

Source: Private communication.

Decisional roles

In the *entrepreneurial role* managers demonstrate creativity and initiate change. They see opportunities and create projects to deal with them. Managers play this role when they introduce a new product or create a major change programme. Managers play the *disturbance-handler role* when they deal with problems and changes that are unexpected.

management in practice

Two examples of handling disturbance

In early 2004 Doreen Tobin, chief financial officer of Vivendi Universal, the French media and communications group that has owned Universal Music Group since 2000, announced that it planned to cut €400 million from its cost base by 2005. The company had just reported a loss of €1.1 billion, which she blamed on the recent contraction in the music industry. The saving will come from cuts in back-office staff, lower royalties to artists, and a reduction in the number of artists whose work it promotes.

In the same year the chief executive of Lego, the Danish toy maker, unveiled a wide-ranging restructuring programme, under which it would cut jobs, reduce costs and sell non-core businesses. He said that it had recently misjudged part of the market and lost substantial sales, but that it now wanted to deal with its serious earnings crisis by improving its competitive edge and returning the focus to basic play materials.

Source: Various published information.

The *resource-allocator role* involves choosing amongst competing demands for money, equipment, personnel and other resources. How much of her budget should a housing manager spend on different types of project? What proportion of the budget should a company spend on advertising or to improve a product? The manager of an ambulance service regularly decides between paying overtime to staff to replace an absent team member or letting service quality decline until a new shift starts. This is close to the *negotiator role*, in which managers seek agreement with other parties on whom they depend. When managers at Ryanair want to change the fees they pay to an airport they try to negotiate a new deal with the owners.

The nature of leadership

The leadership relationship

Whatever the perceived approach to leadership, the most important point is the nature of the leadership relationship and the manner in which the leader influences the behaviour and actions of other people. Leadership is a dynamic form of behaviour and there are a number of variables that affect the leadership relationship. For example, Bass reviews leadership influence in terms of persuasion, a power relation, an instrument of goal achievement, an emerging effect of interaction and the initiation of structure.[93] Four major variables are identified by McGregor as:

- the characteristics of the leader;
- the attitude, needs and other personal characteristics of the followers;
- the nature of the organisation, such as its purpose, its structure, and the tasks to be performed; and
- the social, economic and political environment.

McGregor concludes that 'leadership is not a property of the individual, but a complex relationship among these variables'.[94]

According to Kouzes and Posner, 'credibility is the foundation of leadership'. From extensive research in over 30 countries and response to the question of what people 'look for and admire in a leader, in a person whose direction they would willingly follow', people have consistently replied that they want

> leaders who exemplify four qualities: they want them to be honest, forward-looking, inspiring and competent. In our research our respondents strongly agree that they want leaders with integrity and trustworthiness, with vision and a sense of direction, with enthusiasm and passion, and with expertise and a track record for getting things done.[95]

Fullan refers to the importance of relationship building as a basic component of the change process and effective leadership: 'Leaders must be consummate relationship builders with diverse people and groups – especially with people different from themselves. Effective leaders constantly foster purposeful interaction and problem solving, and are wary of easy consensus.'[96]

Power and leadership influence

Within an organisation, leadership influence will be dependent upon the type of power that the leader can exercise over the followers. The exercise of power is a social process which helps to explain how different people can influence the behaviour/actions of others. Five main sources of power upon which the influence of the leader is based have been identified by French and Raven as reward power, coercive power, legitimate power, referent power and expert power.[97] We shall consider these in terms of the manager (as a leader) and subordinate relationship.

- **Reward power** is based on the subordinate's *perception* that the leader has the ability and resources to obtain rewards for those who comply with directives; for example, pay, promotion, praise, recognition, increased responsibilities, allocation and arrangement of work, granting of privileges.

- **Coercive power** is based on fear and the subordinate's *perception* that the leader has the ability to punish or to bring about undesirable outcomes for those who do not comply with directives; for example, withholding pay rises, promotion or privileges; allocation of undesirable duties or responsibilities; withdrawal of friendship or support; formal reprimands or possibly dismissal. This is in effect the opposite of reward power.
- **Legitimate power** is based on the subordinate's *perception* that the leader has a right to exercise influence because of the leader's role or position in the organisation. Legitimate power is based on authority, for example that of managers and supervisors within the hierarchical structure of an organisation. Legitimate power is therefore 'position' power because it is based on the role of the leader in the organisation, and not on the nature of the personal relationship with others.
- **Referent power** is based on the subordinate's *identification* with the leader. The leader exercises influence because of perceived attractiveness, personal characteristics, reputation or what is called 'charisma'. For example, a particular manager may not be in a position to reward or punish certain subordinates, but may still exercise power over the subordinates because the manager commands their respect or esteem.
- **Expert power** is based on the subordinate's *perception* of the leader as someone who is competent and who has some special knowledge or expertise in a given area. Expert power is based on credibility and clear evidence of knowledge or expertise; for example, the expert knowledge of 'functional' specialists such as the human resources manager, management accountant or systems analyst. The expert power is usually limited to narrow, well-defined areas or specialisms.

Subordinates' perception of influence

It is important to note that these sources of power are based on the subordinates' perception of the influence of the leader, whether it is real or not. For example, if a leader has the ability to control rewards and punishments but subordinates do not believe this, then in effect the leader has no reward or coercive power. Similarly, if subordinates in a line department believe a manager in a (different) staff department has executive authority over them then even if, *de facto*, that manager has no such authority there is still a perceived legitimate power.

French and Raven point out that the five sources of power are interrelated and the use of one type of power (for example, coercive) may affect the ability to use another type of power (for example, referent). Furthermore, the same person may exercise different types of power, in particular circumstances and at different times.

Other sources of power

Finlay suggests that in addition to the five sources of power identified by French and Raven can be added:

- **personal power**, supported and trusted by their colleagues and subordinates; and
- **connection power**, which results from personal and professional access to key people and information.[98]

Yukl suggests that a further relevant source of power is control over information.[99]

> You have to look at leadership through the eyes of the followers and you have to live the message. What I have learned is that people become motivated when you guide them to the source of their own power and when you make heroes out of employees who personify what you want to see in the organisation.
>
> Anita Roddick[100]

Power, responsibility and wisdom

Lloyd suggests that the way we think about leadership is a contributory factor to the leadership crisis. Leadership has traditionally been associated with those who have power and there is a need to re-examine the core relationship between power and responsibility. Rather than gaining and keeping power for ourselves, more emphasis should be given to unifying consideration of the two concepts together with greater attention to the subject of wisdom.

> The new agenda moves us from that narrow focus to a much broader concept of leadership that is more concerned with how power is used, i.e. in whose interest power is used. This explicitly recognises that the use of power is deeply values driven . . . We need to give much greater attention to the values agenda by exploring wisdom, then seeing that emphasis reflected as wise leadership.[101]

critical reflection

'Despite the vast amount of writing on the subject by both academics and practising managers, it is extremely difficult to give a precise and agreed meaning of leadership. Nor is there agreement on one best model or style of leadership, or how leadership potential can best be developed.'

Do you find this confusing and a hindrance to your studies? What do you believe are the essential and distinctive characteristics that make for an effective leader?

Approaches to leadership

Due to its complex and variable nature there are many alternative ways of analysing leadership. It is helpful, therefore, to have some framework in which to consider different approaches to study of the subject.

One way is to examine managerial leadership in terms of:

- the qualities or traits approach;
- the functional or group approach, including action-centred leadership;
- leadership as a behavioural category;
- styles of leadership;
- contingency theories;
- transitional or transformational leadership; and
- inspirational or visionary leadership. (See Figure 3.16.)

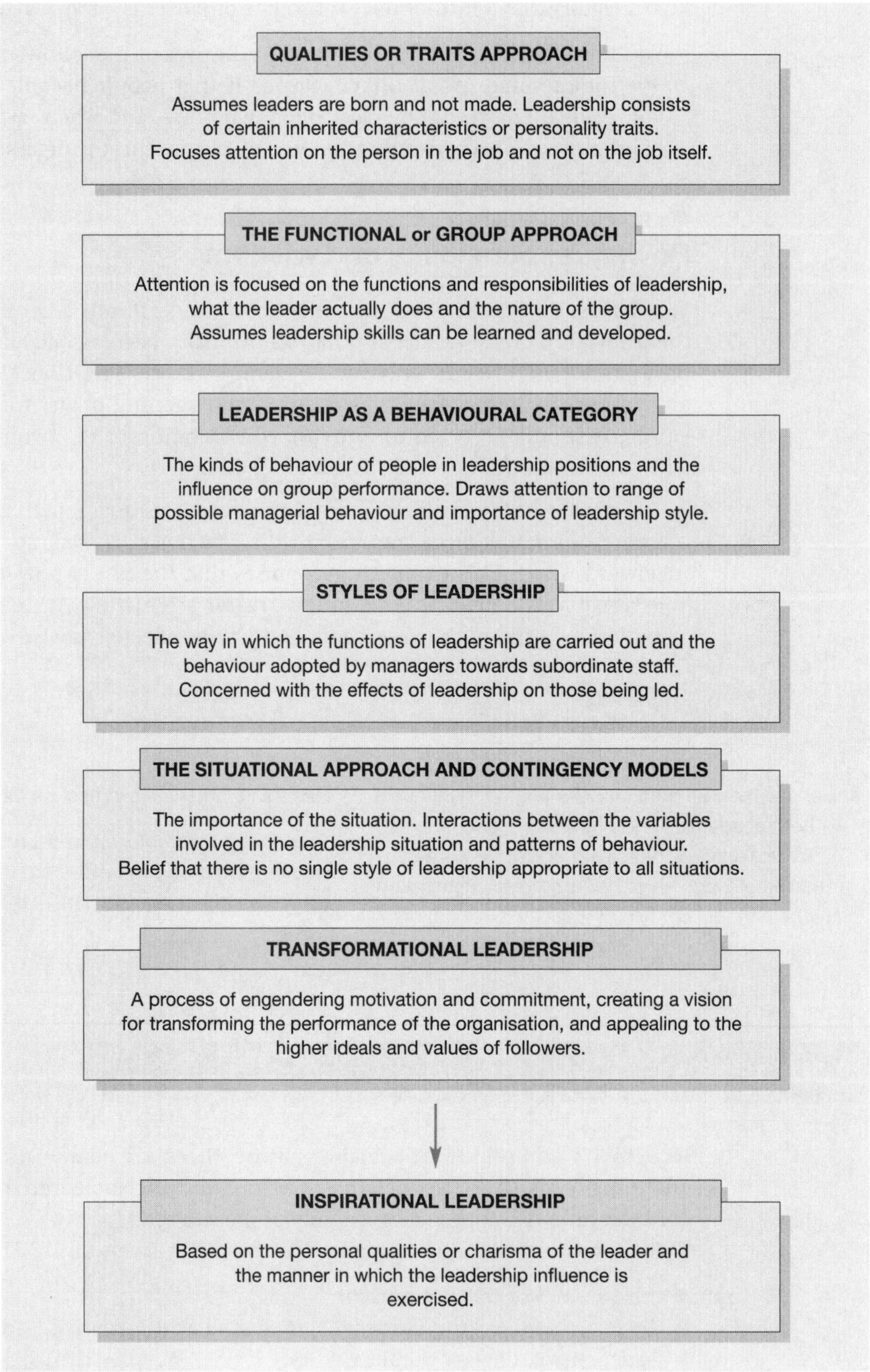

QUALITIES OR TRAITS APPROACH

Assumes leaders are born and not made. Leadership consists
of certain inherited characteristics or personality traits.
Focuses attention on the person in the job and not on the job itself.

THE FUNCTIONAL or GROUP APPROACH

Attention is focused on the functions and responsibilities of leadership,
what the leader actually does and the nature of the group.
Assumes leadership skills can be learned and developed.

LEADERSHIP AS A BEHAVIOURAL CATEGORY

The kinds of behaviour of people in leadership positions and the
influence on group performance. Draws attention to range of
possible managerial behaviour and importance of leadership style.

STYLES OF LEADERSHIP

The way in which the functions of leadership are carried out and the
behaviour adopted by managers towards subordinate staff.
Concerned with the effects of leadership on those being led.

THE SITUATIONAL APPROACH AND CONTINGENCY MODELS

The importance of the situation. Interactions between the variables
involved in the leadership situation and patterns of behaviour.
Belief that there is no single style of leadership appropriate to all situations.

TRANSFORMATIONAL LEADERSHIP

A process of engendering motivation and commitment, creating a vision
for transforming the performance of the organisation, and appealing to the
higher ideals and values of followers.

INSPIRATIONAL LEADERSHIP

Based on the personal qualities or charisma of the leader and
the manner in which the leadership influence is
exercised.

Figure 3.16   A framework for the study of managerial leadership

The qualities or traits approach

The first approach assumes that leaders are born and not made. Leadership consists of certain inherited characteristics, or personality traits, which distinguish leaders from their followers: the so-called Great Person theory of leadership. The **qualities approach** focuses attention on the man or woman in the job and not on the job itself. It suggests that attention is given to the selection of leaders rather than to training for leadership.

Drucker (writing originally in 1955) makes the point that:

> Leadership is of utmost importance. Indeed there is no substitute for it. But leadership cannot be created or promoted. It cannot be taught or learned.[102]

There have been many research studies into the common traits of leadership. For example, Bass reports on numerous studies of traits of leadership from 1904 to 1970 including those relating to personal characteristics such as chronological age, physical appearance (including a positive correlation between height and weight), speech, capacity, achievement, participation, responsibility and status. A conclusion, perhaps not surprisingly, suggests that although personality is a factor in differentiating leadership it is not a matter of the mere possession of some combination of traits. Leaders acquire status through a working relationship with members of a group.[103]

Attempts at identifying common personality, or physical and mental, characteristics of different 'good' or 'successful' leaders have met with little success.[104] Investigations have identified lists of traits that tend to be overlapping, contradictory or with little correlation for most features. It is noticeable that 'individuality' or 'originality' usually features in the list. This itself suggests that there is little in common between specific personality traits of different leaders. It is perhaps possible therefore to identify general characteristics of leadership ability, such as self-confidence, initiative, intelligence and belief in one's actions, but research into this area has revealed little more than this.

Limitations of the traits approach

There are three further limitations with this approach.

- First, there is bound to be some subjective judgement in determining who is regarded as a 'good' or 'successful' leader. (This can make for an interesting class discussion.)
- Second, the lists of possible traits tend to be very long and there is not always agreement on the most important.
- Third, it ignores the situational factors.

Even if it were possible to identify an agreed list of more specific qualities, this would provide little explanation of the nature of leadership. It would do little to help in the development and training of future leaders. Although there is still limited interest in the qualities, or traits, approach, attention has been directed more to other approaches to leadership. The qualities or traits approach gives rise to the questions of whether leaders are born or made and whether leadership is an art or a science. The important point, however, is that **these are not mutually exclusive alternatives**. Even if there are certain inborn qualities that make for a good leader, these natural talents need encouragement and development. Even if leadership is something of an art, it still requires the application of special skills and techniques.

The functional (or group) approach

This approach to leadership focuses attention not on the personality of the leader, nor on the man or woman in the job, *per se*, but on the functions of leadership. Leadership is always present in any group engaged in a task. The functional approach views leadership in terms of how the leader's behaviour affects, and is affected by, the group of followers. This approach concentrates on the nature of the group, the followers or subordinates. It focuses on the content of leadership. Greater attention can be given to the successful training of leaders and to the means of improving the leaders' performance by concentrating on the functions which will lead to effective performance by the work group.

The functional approach believes that the skills of leadership can be learned, developed and perfected. In contrast to the view of Drucker (referred to above), Kotter makes the point that successful companies do not wait for leaders to come along. 'They actively seek out people with leadership potential and expose them to career experiences designed to develop that potential. Indeed, with careful selection, nurturing and encouragement, dozens of people can play important leadership roles in a business organisation.'[105] A similar point is made by Whitehead:

> There has been a dramatic change in how management thinkers regard leadership today. Leaders are not born, they say, but made. And the good news is everyone can do it. You don't have to be promoted to a management position. You can be a leader whatever job you do. You don't have to be the boss to be a leader.[106]

Action-centred leadership

A general theory on the functional approach is associated with the work of John Adair and his ideas on action-centred leadership which focuses on what leaders actually *do*.[107] The effectiveness of the leader is dependent upon meeting three areas of need within the work group: the need to achieve the common **task**, the need for **team maintenance**, and the **individual needs** of group members. Adair symbolises these needs by three overlapping circles (see Figure 3.17).

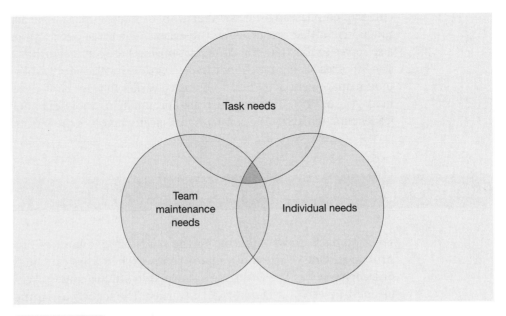

Figure 3.17   **Interaction of needs within the group**

Source: Adair, J. *Action-Centred Leadership*, Gower Press (1979), p. 10. Reproduced with permission from John Adair.

Task needs involve:

- achieving the objectives of the work group;
- defining group tasks;
- planning the work;
- allocation of resources;
- organisation of duties and responsibilities;
- controlling quality and checking performance;
- reviewing progress.

Team maintenance needs involve:

- maintaining morale and building team spirit;
- the cohesiveness of the group as a working unit;
- setting standards and maintaining discipline;
- systems of communication within the group;
- training the group;
- appointment of sub-leaders.

Individual needs involve:

- meeting the needs of the individual members of the group;
- attending to personal problems;
- giving praise and status;
- reconciling conflicts between group needs and needs of the individual;
- training the individual.

The action by the leader in any one area of need will affect one or both of the other areas of need. The ideal position is where complete integration of the three areas of need is achieved. Adair draws attention to the value of the three overlapping circles in emphasising the essential unity of leadership: a single action can be multi-functional in that it touches all three areas. The three-circle approach used by Adair also serves to illustrate the close relationship between leadership and management. The list of leadership functions can be connected with Henri Fayol's classic list of common management activities[108] (discussed earlier in this chapter – see 'The role of the manager', p. 419). Building the team and satisfying individual needs would include leadership. Achieving the common task clearly involves the process of management.

Leadership as a behavioural category

This approach draws attention to the kinds of behaviour of people in leadership situations. One of the most extensive research studies on behavioural categories of leadership was the Ohio State Leadership Studies undertaken by the Bureau of Business Research at Ohio State University. The focus was on the effects of leadership styles on group performance. Results indicated two major dimensions of leadership behaviour, labelled 'consideration' and 'initiating structure'.[109]

- **Consideration** reflects the extent to which the leader establishes trust, mutual respect and rapport with the group and shows concern, warmth, support and consideration for subordinates. This dimension is associated with two-way communication, participation and the human relations approach to leadership.
- **Initiating structure** reflects the extent to which the leader defines and structures group interactions towards attainment of formal goals and organises group activities. This dimension is associated with efforts to achieve organisational goals.

Consideration and initiating structure can be seen as the same as maintenance function (building and maintaining the group as a working unit and relationships among group members) and task function (accomplishment of specific tasks of the groups and achievement of goals). Consideration and initiating structure were found to be uncorrelated and independent dimensions. Leadership behaviour could, therefore, be shown on two separate axes. A high-consideration, high-structure style appears to be generally more effective in terms of subordinate satisfaction and group performance, but the evidence is not conclusive and much seems to depend upon situational factors. However, later findings suggest that the best leadership style entails high levels of both people-centred and task-centred dimensions.[110]

Employee or production-centred supervisors

Another major research study was carried out at the University of Michigan Institute for Social Research at the same time as the Ohio State studies. Effective supervisors (measured along dimensions of group morale, productivity and cost reduction) appeared to display four common characteristics:

- delegation of authority and avoidance of close supervision;
- an interest and concern in their subordinates as individuals;
- participative problem-solving; and
- high standards of performance.

Group interaction analysis	Task functions	Maintenance functions
Ohio State leadership study	Initiating structure	Consideration
University of Michigan study	Production-centred supervision	Employee-centred supervision
McGregor, assumptions about people and work	Theory X	Theory Y
Blake and McCanse, Leadership Grid®	Concern for production	Concern for people

Figure 3.18   Two major dimensions of managerial leadership

Likert, who has summarised the findings of the University of Michigan studies, used the terms **employee-centred** and **production-centred** supervisors.[111] These terms are similar to the dimensions of consideration and structure. The first three of these supervisory characteristics are examples of consideration. The fourth characteristic exemplifies structure. Like consideration and structure, employee-centred and production-centred supervision need to be balanced. Likert concluded that employee-centred supervisors who get best results tend to recognise that one of their main responsibilities is production. Both the Ohio State and the University of Michigan studies appear to support the idea that there is no single behavioural category of leadership that is superior. There are many types of leadership behaviour and their effectiveness depends upon the variables in any given situation.

Major dimensions of managerial leadership

Despite the many types of actual leadership behaviour, we have seen that there appears to be general agreement on two major dimensions of managerial leadership. This can be extended to include the works of McGregor and of Blake and McCanse (see Figure 3.18).

Styles of leadership

Attention to leadership as a behavioural category has drawn attention to the importance of leadership style. In the work situation it has become increasingly clear that managers can no longer rely solely on the use of their position in the hierarchical structure as a means of exercising the functions of leadership. In order to get the best results from subordinates the manager must also have regard for the need to encourage high morale, a spirit of involvement and co-operation, and a willingness to work. This gives rise to consideration of the style of leadership and provides another heading under which to analyse leadership behaviour.

Leadership style is the way in which the functions of leadership are carried out, the way in which the manager typically behaves towards members of the group.

The attention given to leadership style is based on the assumption that subordinates are more likely to work effectively for managers who adopt a certain style of leadership than for managers who adopt alternative styles. Attention to the manager's style of leadership has come about because of a greater understanding of the needs and expectations of people at work. It has also been influenced by such factors as:

- increasing business competitiveness and recognition of efficient use of human resources;
- changes in the value-system of society;
- broader standards of education and training;
- advances in scientific and technical knowledge;
- changes in the nature of work organisation;
- pressure for a greater social responsibility towards employees, for example through schemes of participation in decision-making and work/life balance; and
- government legislation, for example in the areas of employment protection, and the influence of the European Union.

All of these factors have combined to create resistance against purely autocratic styles of leadership.

Broad framework of leadership style

There are many dimensions to leadership and many possible ways of describing leadership style, such as dictatorial, unitary, bureaucratic, benevolent, charismatic, consultative, participative and abdicatorial. With so many potential descriptions of leadership styles it is useful to have a broad framework in which to focus attention and study. The style of managerial leadership towards subordinate staff and the focus of power can therefore be considered within a simplified three-fold heading.

- The authoritarian (autocratic) style is where the focus of power is with the manager and all interactions within the group move towards the manager. The manager alone exercises decision-making and authority for determining policy, procedures for achieving goals, work tasks and relationships, control of rewards or punishments.
- The democratic style is where the focus of power is more with the group as a whole and there is greater interaction within the group. The leadership functions are shared with members of the group and the manager is more part of a team. The group members have a greater say in decision-making, determination of policy, implementation of systems and procedures.
- A laissez-faire (genuine) style is where the manager observes that members of the group are working well on their own. The manager consciously makes a decision to pass the focus of power to members, to allow them freedom of action 'to do as they think best', and not to interfere; but is readily available if help is needed. There is often confusion over this style of leadership behaviour. The word 'genuine' is emphasised because this is to be contrasted with the manager

who could not care, who deliberately keeps away from the trouble spots and does not want to get involved. The manager just lets members of the group get on with the work in hand. Members are left to face decisions that rightly belong with the manager. This is more a non-style of leadership or it could perhaps be labelled as abdication.

Continuum of leadership behaviour

One of the best-known works on leadership style is that by Tannenbaum and Schmidt (see Figure 3.19).[112] Originally written in 1958 and updated in 1973, their work suggests a continuum of possible leadership behaviour available to a manager and along which various styles of leadership may be placed. The continuum presents a range of action related to the degree of authority used by the manager and to the area of freedom available to non-managers in arriving at decisions. The Tannenbaum and Schmidt continuum can be related to McGregor's supposition of Theory X and Theory Y. Boss-centred leadership is towards Theory X and subordinate-centred leadership is towards Theory Y.

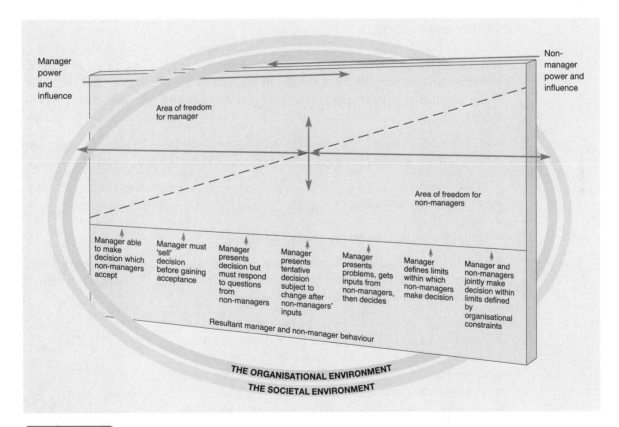

Figure 3.19   Continuum of manager–non-manager behaviour

Four main styles of leadership

Moving along the continuum, the manager may be characterised according to the degree of control that is maintained. Neither extreme of the continuum is absolute as there is always some limitation on authority and on freedom. This approach can be seen as identifying four main styles of leadership by the manager: tells, sells, consults, joins.

- **Tells**. The manager identifies a problem, makes a decision and announces this to subordinates, expecting them to implement it without an opportunity for participation.
- **Sells**. The manager still makes a decision but recognises the possibility of some resistance from those faced with the decision and attempts to persuade subordinates to accept it.
- **Consults**. The manager identifies the problem but does not make a decision until the problem is presented to the group, and the manager has listened to the advice and solutions suggested by subordinates.
- **Joins**. The manager defines the problem and the limits within which the decision must be made and then passes to the group, with the manager as a member, the right to make decisions.

Three main forces

Tannenbaum and Schmidt suggest that there are three factors, or forces, of particular importance in deciding what types of leadership are practicable and desirable. These are: forces in the manager, forces in the subordinate and forces in the situation.

Forces in the manager. The manager's behaviour will be influenced by their personality, background, knowledge and experiences. These internal forces will include:

- value-systems
- confidence in subordinates
- leadership inclinations
- feelings of security in an uncertain situation.

Forces in the subordinate. Subordinates are influenced by many personality variables and their individual set of expectations about their relationship with the manager. Characteristics of the subordinate are:

- the strength of the need for independence
- readiness to assume responsibility for decision-making
- the degree of tolerance for ambiguity
- interest in the problem and feelings as to its importance
- understanding and identification with the goals of the organisation
- necessary knowledge and experience to deal with the problem
- the extent of learning to expect to share in decision-making.

The greater the positive response to these characteristics, the greater freedom of action can be allowed by the manager.

Forces in the situation. The manager's behaviour will be influenced by the general situation and environmental pressures. Characteristics in the situation include:

- type of organisation
- group effectiveness
- nature of the problem
- pressure of time.

Tannenbaum and Schmidt conclude that successful leaders are keenly aware of those forces which are most relevant to their behaviour at a particular time. They are able to behave appropriately in terms of their understanding of themselves, the individuals and the group, the organisation, and environmental influences. Successful managers are both perceptive and flexible. Forces lying outside the organisation are also included. Tannenbaum and Schmidt suggest a new continuum of patterns of leadership behaviour in which the total area of freedom shared between managers and non-managers is redefined constantly by interactions between them and the forces in the environment.

critical reflection

'The Tannenbaum and Schmidt continuum is probably the single most important and relevant study of leadership. Successful managers clearly need to be both consistent in personality and behaviour, yet adaptable to the three forces that continually influence their leadership style and decision-making along the various points of the continuum.'

To what extent can you argue against this assertion? What do you think is the single most important study of leadership?

The nature of work groups and teams

Formal and informal groups

Groups are deliberately planned and created by management as part of the formal organisation structure. However, groups will also arise from social processes and informal organisation. The informal organisation arises from the interaction of people working within the organisation and the development of groups with their own relationships and norms of behaviour, irrespective of those defined within the formal structure. This leads to a major distinction between formal and informal groups.

Formal groups

Groups are formed as a consequence of the pattern of organisation structure and arrangements for the division of work, for example the grouping together of common activities into sections. Groups may result from the nature of technology employed and the way in which work is carried out, for example the bringing together of a number of people to carry out a sequence of operations on an assembly line. Groups may also develop when a number of people of the same level or status within the organisation see themselves as a group, for example departmental heads of an industrial organisation or chief officers of a local authority. **Formal groups** are created to achieve specific organisational objectives and are concerned with the **co-ordination of work activities**. People are brought together on the basis of defined roles within the structure of the organisation. The nature of the tasks to be undertaken is a predominant feature of the formal group. Goals are identified by management, and certain rules, relationships and norms of behaviour established.

Formal groups tend to be relatively permanent, although there may be changes in actual membership. However, temporary formal groups may also be created by management, as with for example the use of project teams in a matrix organisation. Formal work groups can be differentiated in a number of ways, for example on the basis of membership, the task to be performed, the nature of technology, or position within the organisation structure.

Virtuoso teams

Boynton and Fischer draw attention to 'virtuoso teams' that are formed specifically for big change in organisations. They are comprised of individual superstars or virtuosos with a single clear, ambitious mandate and are not intended to remain together over multiple initiatives or projects. Virtuoso teams require a special kind of leadership and to be managed in a manner that unleashes the maximum contribution from each individual superstar. Although most organisations rarely form such teams, they are required for radical change opportunities that represent a significant departure from prior practice and/or how an organisation conducts its business. Examples of big changes that required a virtuoso team are the Manhattan Project, Thomas Edison's inventory factory and Roald Amundsen's polar expedition.[113]

Informal groups

The formal structure of the organisation, and system of role relationships, rules and procedures, will always be augmented by interpretation and development at the informal level. Informal groups are based more on personal relationships and agreement of group members than on defined role relationships. They serve to satisfy psychological and social needs not related necessarily to the tasks to be undertaken. Groups may devise ways of attempting to satisfy members' affiliation and other social motivations lacking in the work situation. Membership of informal groups can cut across the formal structure. They may comprise individuals from different parts of the organisation and/or from different levels of the organisation, both vertically and diagonally, as well as from the same horizontal level. An informal group could also be the same as the formal group, or it might comprise a part only of the formal group (see Figure 3.20).

Members of an informal group may appoint their own leader who exercises authority by the consent of the members themselves. The informal leader may be chosen as the person who reflects the attitudes and values of the members, helps to resolve conflict, leads the group in satisfying its goals, or liaises with management or other people outside the group. The informal leader may often change according to the particular situation facing the group. Although not usually the case, it is possible for the informal leader to be the same person as the formal leader appointed officially by management.

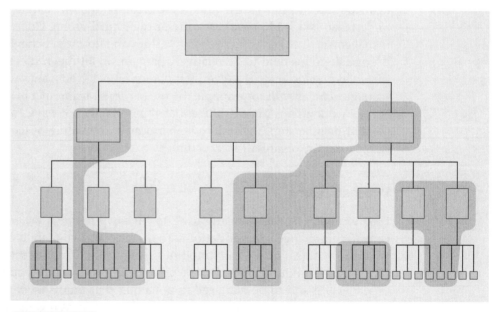

Figure 3.20 Examples of informal groups within the formal structure of an organisation

Major functions of informal groups

Lysons suggests four main reasons for informal groups:

- **The perpetuation of the informal group 'culture'.** Culture in this context means a set of values, norms and beliefs which form a guide to group acceptance and group behaviour. Unless you broadly subscribe to the group culture, you will not belong and will be an 'outsider' or 'isolate'.
- **The maintenance of a communication system.** Groups want all the information that affects their welfare, either negatively or positively. If groups are not apprised of policies and motives behind actions, they will seek to tap into formal communication channels and spread information among group members.
- **The implementation of social control.** Conformity to group culture is enforced by such techniques as ridicule, ostracism and violence.
- **The provision of interest and fun in work life.** Many jobs are monotonous and fail to hold workers' attention. Work may also offer few prospects. Workers may try to compensate by interpersonal relations provided by the group and in such activities as time wasting by talking, gambling, practical joking and drinking.[114]

We humans are a gregarious lot. We like to gather together and establish our own social networks, which are often the real key to creativity and innovation in organisations . . . But many managers are unaware that seemingly pointless social networking does in fact play a crucial part in the way people interact with each other and get work done.

Sue Law[115]

An example of informal groups

A lack of direction and clear information flow within the formal structure can give rise to uncertainty and suspicion. In the absence of specific knowledge, the grapevine takes on an important role, rumours start and the informal part of the organisation is highlighted, often with negative results. A typical example concerned an industrial organisation in a highly competitive market and experiencing a drop in sales. Two top managers had suddenly lost their jobs without any apparent explanation and there were board meetings seemingly every other day. Although there was no specific information or statements from top management, the general feeling among the staff was that whatever was about to happen was most unlikely to be good news.

At lunchtime three junior members of staff, one female and two male, each from different departments, were having a chat. With a half smile the female member said to the others that she could well be seeing a lot more of both or at least one of them before long. She said that she had heard, unofficially, from her manager that the department was about to be awarded a very profitable order. She surmised that other departments, which she had also heard had lost their parts of the same contracts and not had many orders recently, would have to integrate into the successful department with the possible loss of certain jobs. The other two members both believed this and talked about it within their own departments as if it were a fact. The result? Even more uncertainty throughout the organisation, increased gloom and distraction from the task. In fact, no such integration did take place, only a minor restructuring of the organisation with no direct loss of jobs other than through voluntary early retirement. However, it proved very difficult for top management to quash effectively the rumour and restore trust and morale.

critical reflection

'Given the obvious importance of social networks and interpersonal relationships for both the morale and job satisfaction of staff and their levels of work performance, the main focus in the study of organisational behaviour should be on the operations and management of the informal organisation.'

Can you present a counter argument to this contention?

Reasons for formation of groups or teams

Individuals will form into groups or teams, both formal and informal, for a number of reasons.

- **Certain tasks can be performed only through the combined efforts of a number of individuals working together.** The variety of experience and expertise among members provides a synergetic effect that can be applied to the increasingly complex problems of modern organisations.
- **Collusion between members** in order to modify formal working arrangements more to their liking – for example, by sharing or rotating unpopular tasks. Membership therefore provides the individual with opportunities for initiative and creativity.
- **Companionship and a source of mutual understanding and support from colleagues.** This can help in solving work problems and also to militate against stressful or demanding working conditions.
- **Membership provides the individual with a sense of belonging**. It provides a feeling of identity and the chance to acquire role recognition and status within the group or team. See the discussion on social identity theory later in this chapter.
- **Guidelines on generally acceptable behaviour**. It helps to clarify ambiguous situations such as the extent to which official rules and regulations are expected to be adhered to in practice, the rules of the game and what is seen as the correct actual behaviour. The informal organisation may put pressure on members to resist demands from management on such matters as higher output or changes in working methods. Allegiance to the group or team can serve as a means of control over individual behaviour and individuals who contravene the norms are disciplined.

- **Protection for its membership**. Group or team members collaborate to protect their interests from outside pressures or threats.

Individuals have varying expectations of the benefits from group membership, relating to both work performance and social processes. However, working in groups may mean that members spend too much time talking among themselves rather than doing. Groups may also compete against each other in a non-productive manner. It is a question of balance. It is important, therefore, that the manager understands the reasons for the formation of groups and is able to recognise likely advantageous or adverse consequences for the organisation.

Group cohesiveness and performance

Social interaction is a natural feature of human behaviour but ensuring harmonious working relationships and effective teamwork is not an easy task. The manager's main concern is that members of a work group co-operate in order to achieve the results expected of them. Co-operation among members is likely to be greater in a united, cohesive group. Membership of a cohesive group can be a rewarding experience for the individual, can contribute to the promotion of morale and can aid the release of creativity and energy. Members of a high-morale group are more likely to think of themselves as a group and work together effectively. Strong and cohesive work groups can, therefore, have beneficial effects for the organisation. There are many factors which affect group cohesiveness and performance that can be summarised under four broad headings, as shown in Figure 3.21.

Membership

Size of the group

As a group increases in size, problems arise with communications and co-ordination. Large groups are more difficult to handle and require a higher level of supervision. Absenteeism also tends to be higher in larger groups. When a group becomes too large it may split into smaller units and friction may develop between the sub-groups.

It is difficult to put a precise figure on the ideal size of a work group and there are many conflicting studies and reports. Much will depend upon other variables, but it seems to be generally accepted that cohesiveness becomes more difficult to achieve when a group exceeds 10–12 members.[116] Beyond this size the group tends to split into sub-groups. A figure of between five and seven is often quoted as an apparent optimum size for full participation within the group. Many readers will be familiar with the classic 1957 movie *Twelve Angry Men* in which one juror persuades the other 11 to change their minds over a murder verdict. This drew attention to a range of intra-group conflicts and the difficulty in groups of more than ten people attempting to reach consensus.

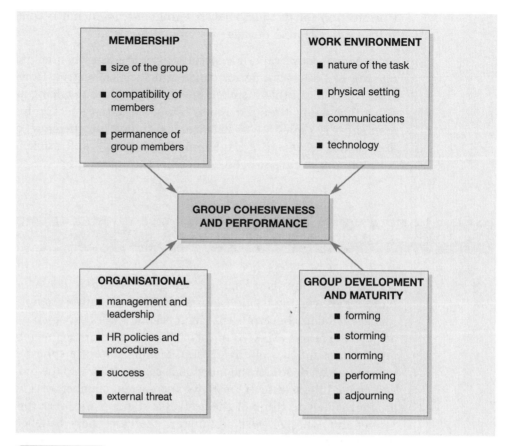

Figure 3.21 Factors contributing to group cohesiveness and performance

Cane asks the question: how many people should be in a team?

The answers from different organisations as to what is the perfect number vary from between four and fifteen depending on a whole range of variables. Fifteen is about the maximum number of people anyone can communicate with without having to raise their voice significantly and any less than four has a restriction in the amount of creativity and variety that can be produced. It is interesting to note that these figures range between the maximum and minimum numbers of sports teams – perhaps less of a coincidence than it seems.[117]

Compatibility of members

The more homogeneous the group in terms of such features as shared backgrounds, interests, attitudes and values of its members, the easier it is usually to promote cohesiveness. Variations in other individual differences, such as the personality or skills of members, may serve to complement each other and help make for a cohesive group. However, such differences may be the cause of disruption and conflict. Conflict can also arise in a homogeneous group where members are in competition with each other. Individual incentive payment schemes, for example, may be a source of conflict.

Permanence of group members

Group spirit and relationships take time to develop. Cohesiveness is more likely when members of a group are together for a reasonable length of time and changes occur only slowly. A frequent turnover of members is likely to have an adverse effect on morale and on the cohesiveness of the group.

Work environment

Nature of the task

Where workers are involved in similar work, share a common task or face the same problems, this may assist cohesiveness. The nature of the task may serve to bring people together when it is necessary for them to communicate and interact regularly with each other in the performance of their duties – for example, members of a research and development team. Even if members of a group normally work at different locations they may still experience a feeling of cohesiveness if the nature of the task requires frequent communication and interaction – for example, security guards patrolling separate areas who need to check with each other on a regular basis. However, where the task demands a series of relatively separate operations or discrete activities – for example, on a machine-paced assembly line – it is more difficult to develop cohesiveness. Individuals may have interactions with colleagues on either side of them but little opportunity to develop a common group feeling.

Physical setting

Where members of a group work in the same location or in close physical proximity to each other this will generally help cohesiveness. However, this is not always the case. For example, in large open-plan offices staff often tend to segregate themselves from colleagues and create barriers through the strategic siting of such items as filing cabinets, bookcases or indoor plants. The size of the office and the number of staff in it are, of course, important considerations in this case. Isolation from other groups of workers will also tend to build cohesiveness. This often applies to a smaller number of workers on a night shift.

Communications

The more easily members can communicate freely with each other, the greater the likelihood of group cohesiveness. Communications are affected by the work environment, by the nature of the task and by technology. For example, difficulties in communication can arise with production systems where workers are stationed continuously at a particular point with limited freedom of movement. Even when opportunities exist for interaction with colleagues, physical conditions may limit effective communication. For example, the technological layout and high level of noise with some assembly line work can limit contact between workers. Restrictions on opportunities for social interaction can hamper internal group unity. This can be a major reason why getting a team to work well is such a challenge in large organisations.

Technology

We can see that the nature of technology and the manner in which work is carried out have an important effect on cohesiveness and relate closely to the nature of the task, physical setting and communications. Where the nature of the work process involves a craft or skill-based 'technology' there is a higher likelihood of group cohesiveness. However, with machine-paced assembly line work it is more difficult to develop cohesiveness. Technology also has wider implications for the operation and behaviour of groups and therefore is considered in a separate section later in this section.

Organisational

Management and leadership

Teams tend to be a mirror image of their leaders. The form of management and style of leadership adopted will influence the relationship between the group and the organisation and are major determinants of group cohesiveness. In general terms, cohesiveness will be affected by such things as the manner in which the manager gives guidance and encouragement to the group, offers help and support, provides opportunities for participation, attempts to resolve conflicts and gives attention to both employee relations and task problems.

McKenna and Maister draw attention to the importance of the group leader establishing a level of trust among the group by helping them understand the behaviours that build trust. 'The job of the group leader is to encourage people to earn the trust of others in their group and then show them how it can translate into greater commitment, greater creativity, greater professional satisfaction, and better performance.'[118] Farrell makes the point that managers are ultimately responsible for creating a balance in the workplace and should take the lead in setting standards of behaviour in teams.[119]

HR policies and procedures

Harmony and cohesiveness within the group are more likely to be achieved if HR policies and procedures are well developed and perceived to be equitable, with fair treatment for all members. Attention should be given to the effects that appraisal systems, discipline, promotion and rewards, and opportunities for personal development have on members of the group.

Success

The more successful the group, the more cohesive it is likely to be, and cohesive groups are more likely to be successful. Success is usually a strong motivational influence on the level of work performance. Success or reward as a positive motivator can be perceived by group members in a number of ways, for example the satisfactory completion of a task through co-operative action, praise from management, a feeling of high status, achievement in competition with other groups, or benefits gained, such as high wage payments from a group bonus incentive scheme.

External threat

Cohesiveness may be enhanced by members co-operating with one another when faced with a common external threat, such as changes in their method of work or the appointment of a new manager. Even if the threat is subsequently removed, the group may continue to have a greater degree of cohesiveness than before the threat arose. Conflict between groups will also tend to increase the cohesiveness of each group and the boundaries of the group become drawn more clearly.

Group development and maturity

The degree of cohesiveness is affected also by the manner in which groups progress through the various stages of development and maturity before getting down to the real tasks in hand. This process can take time and is often traumatic for the members. Bass and Ryterband identify four distinct stages in group development:

- mutual acceptance and membership;
- communication and decision-making;
- motivation and productivity; and
- control and organisation.[120]

An alternative, and more popular, model by Tuckman identifies five main successive stages of group development and relationships: **forming**, **storming**, **norming**, **performing** and **adjourning**.[121]

- **Stage 1 – forming.** The initial formation of the group and the bringing together of a number of individuals who identify, tentatively, the purpose of the group, its composition and terms of reference. At this stage consideration is given to the hierarchical structure of the group, pattern of leadership, individual roles and responsibilities, and codes of conduct. There is likely to be considerable anxiety as members attempt to create an impression, to test each other and to establish their personal identity within the group.
- **Stage 2 – storming.** As members of the group get to know each other better they will put forward their views more openly and forcefully. Disagreements will be expressed and challenges offered on the nature of the task and arrangements made in the earlier stage of development. This may lead to conflict and hostility. The storming stage is important because, if successful, there will be discussions on reforming arrangements for the working and operation of the group, and agreement on more meaningful structures and procedures.
- **Stage 3 – norming.** As conflict and hostility start to be controlled, members of the group will establish guidelines and standards and develop their own norms

of acceptable behaviour. The norming stage is important in establishing the need for members to co-operate in order to plan, agree standards of performance and fulfil the purpose of the group.

● **Stage 4 – performing.** When the group has progressed successfully through the three earlier stages of development it will have created structure and cohesiveness to work effectively as a team. At this stage the group can concentrate on the attainment of its purpose and performance of the common task is likely to be at its most effective.

● **Stage 5 – adjourning.** This refers to the adjourning or disbanding of the group because of, for example, completion of the task, members leaving the organisation or moving on to other tasks. Some members may feel a compelling sense of loss at the end of a major or lengthy group project and their return to independence is characterised by sadness and anxiety. Managers may need to prepare for future group tasks and engendering team effort.

Another writer suggests that new groups go through the following stages:

– *the polite stage;*
– *the why are we here, what are we doing stage;*
– *the power stage, which dominant will emerge;*
– *the constructive stage when sharing begins; and*
– *the unity stage – this often takes weeks, eating together, talking together.*[122]

Creative leadership and group development

In an examination of creative leadership and team effectiveness, Rickards and Moger propose a modification to the Tuckman model and suggest a two-barrier model of group development. Creative leadership is suggested as producing new routines or protocols designed as *benign structures* which help teams progress through the first barrier at Tuckman's *storm* stage (a behavioural barrier), and beyond a second barrier at the *norm* stage (a norm-breaking barrier). From empirical studies of small groups and project teams Rickards and Moger put forward two challenges to the prevailing model of team development:

(i) Weak teams posed the question 'what is happening if a team fails to develop beyond the storm stage?'

(ii) The exceptional teams posed the question 'what happens if a team breaks out of the performance norms developed?'

The suggestion is that the teams are differentiated by two barriers to performance. The weak barrier is behavioural and defeated a minority of teams; the strong barrier was a block to creativity or innovation, and defeated the majority of those teams who passed through the weak barrier. The two-barrier model provides a starting point for exploring the impact and influence of a team leader on the performance of teams. Rickards and Moger suggest seven factors through which a leader might influence effective team development:

● building a platform of understanding;
● creating a shared vision;

- a creative climate;
- a commitment to idea ownership;
- resilience to setbacks;
- developing networking skills;
- learning from experience.[123]

critical reflection

'The most important factor influencing group cohesiveness and performance is the style of leadership. Leaders are the role models who set the culture and values for the organisation and the group. It is therefore the leaders who make a group become a team.'

What are your views? How do **you** *think a group becomes a team?*

Social identity theory

Within work organisations there will be a number of different but overlapping groups representing a variety of functions, departments, occupations, technologies, project teams, locations or hierarchical levels. Organisational effectiveness will be dependent upon the extent to which these groups co-operate together, but often the different groupings are part of a network of complex relationships resulting in competitiveness and conflict. A feature of the importance and significance of group membership is the concept of social identity theory. Tajfel and Turner originally developed the idea of social identity theory as a means of understanding the psychological basis of inter-group discrimination.[124] Individuals are perceived as having not just one 'personal self' but a number of 'selves' derived from different social contexts and membership of groups.

Because of the need for a clear sense of personal identity, the groups or social categories with which we associate are an integral part of our self-concept (social identity). A natural process of human interaction is social categorisation by which we classify both ourselves and other people through reference to our own social identity. For example, membership of high-status groups can increase a person's perceived self-esteem. According to Guirdham 'self-categorisation is the process that transforms a number of individuals into a group.'[125] See Figure 3.22.

Haslam refers to the relationship between individuals and groups in an understanding of organisational behaviour, and argues that:

> in order to understand perception and interaction in organizational contexts we must do more than just study the psychology of individuals as **individuals**. Instead, we need to understand how social interaction is bound up with individuals' **social identities** – their definition of themselves in terms of group memberships.[126]

We identify ourselves in terms of membership of certain social groupings and differentiate ourselves from other social groupings. This leads to minimising differences between members of our own groupings (in-groups) and maximising

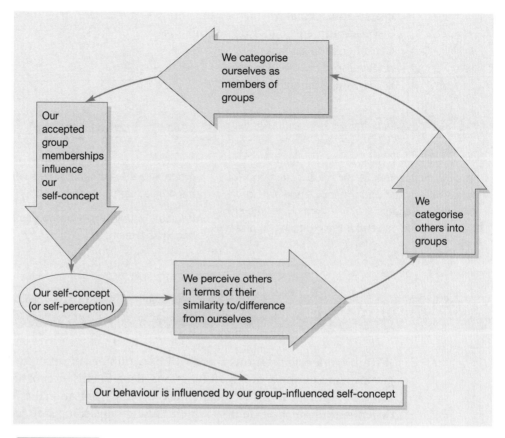

Figure 3.22   **Processes of social and self-categorisation**

Source: Guirdham, M. *Interactive Behaviour at Work*, third edition, Financial Times Prentice Hall (2002), p. 119.
Reproduced with permission of Pearson Education Ltd.

differences from other groupings (out-groups). Over time the sense of shared identity with the in-group increases a feeling of what is right and proper and highlights
differences from the out-groups.[127] As a result, this reinforces both social identity
with our own category and the projection of negative perceptions and stereotypes
towards out-groups. Stereotyping can lead to shared attitudes to out-groups and to
increased conflict amongst work groups. Tajfel and Turner suggest that the mere
act of individuals categorising themselves as group members leads them to exhibit
in-group favouritism. Hewstone *et al.* suggest that even without realising it, we tend
usually to favour the groupings we belong to more than denigrate out-groups.
Successful inter-group bias enhances self-esteem.[128]

Potential disadvantages of strong, cohesive groups

If the manager is to develop effective work groups, attention should be given
to those factors that influence the creation of group identity and cohesiveness.
This may result in greater interaction between members, mutual help and social

satisfaction, lower turnover and absenteeism, and often higher production.[129] However, strong and cohesive groups also present potential disadvantages for management. Cohesive groups do not necessarily produce a higher level of output. Performance varies with the extent to which the group accepts or rejects the goals of the organisation. Furthermore, with a very high level of cohesiveness and attention to social activities, there may even be a fall in output. The level of production is likely to conform to a standard acceptable as a norm by the group. It may be remembered that in the bank wiring room experiment of the Hawthorne studies, group norms imposed a restriction on the workers' level of output.

Once a group has become fully developed and created cohesiveness, it is more difficult for the manager successfully to change the attitudes and behaviour of the group. It is important that the manager should attempt to influence the group during the norming stage when members are establishing guidelines and standards and their own norms of acceptable behaviour. When a group has become fully developed and established its own culture it is more difficult to change the attitudes and behaviour of its members.

Inter-group conflict

Strong, cohesive groups may develop a critical or even hostile attitude towards people outside the group or members of other groups. This can be the case, for example, when group cohesiveness is based on common status, qualifications, technical expertise or professional standing. Group cohesiveness may result in lack of co-operation with, or opposition to, non-members. As a result, resentment and inter-group conflict may arise to the detriment of the organisation as a whole. (Recall the discussion on social identity theory, above.) In order to help prevent, or overcome, unconstructive inter-group conflict, the manager should attempt to stimulate a high level of communication and interaction between the groups and to maintain harmony. Rotation of members among different groups should be encouraged.

Yet, inter-group rivalry may be deliberately encouraged as a means of building stronger within-group cohesiveness. The idea is that a competitive element may help to promote unity within a group. However, inter-group rivalry and competition need to be handled carefully. The manager should attempt to avoid the development of 'win–lose' situations. Emphasis should be placed on overall objectives of the organisation and on superordinate goals. These are goals over and above the issues at conflict and which, if they are to be achieved, require the co-operation of the competing groups.

Characteristics of an effective work group

The characteristics of an effective work group are not always easy to isolate clearly. The underlying feature is a spirit of co-operation in which members work well together as a united team and with harmonious and supportive relationships. This may be evidenced when members of a group exhibit:

- a belief in shared aims and objectives;
- a sense of commitment to the group;
- acceptance of group values and norms;
- a feeling of mutual trust and dependency;
- full participation by all members and decision-making by consensus;
- a free flow of information and communications;
- the open expression of feelings and disagreements;
- the resolution of conflict by the members themselves;
- a lower level of staff turnover, absenteeism, accidents, errors and complaints.

However, as Brooks points out, as teams operate at the higher order of group dynamics this list is arguably more reflective of 'effective **work teams** rather than work groups and this is how it should be – these are teams not groups'.[130]

The effects of technology

Technology is clearly a major influence on the pattern of group operation and behaviour. The work organisation may limit the opportunities for social interaction and the extent to which individuals are able to identify themselves as members of a cohesive work group. This in turn can have possible adverse effects on attitudes to work and the level of job satisfaction. In many assembly line production systems, for example, relationships between individual workers are determined by the nature of the task, the extent to which individual jobs are specified and the time cycle of operations.

ACAS draws attention to technological advances and how new technology enables production to be tailored quickly to customer requirements, often on an individual basis.

Mass production techniques, where jobs are broken down into simple tasks, are not suitable for the new customer focused manufacturing nor the expectations of an educated workforce. Organisations need workers to be more flexible, to co-operate with other workers, supervisors and managers throughout the organisation, to operate sophisticated technology and to be more adaptable. In addition, the sheer complexity of operations in industry, commerce and the services places them beyond the expertise and control of any one individual. In these circumstances some form of teamwork becomes not just desirable but essential.[131]

Impact of information technology

The impact of information technology demands new patterns of work organisation and affects the formation and structure of groups. It will influence where and how people interact. Movement away from large-scale centralised organisations to smaller working units can help create an environment in which workers may relate more easily to each other. Improvements in telecommunications mean, on one hand, that support staff need no longer be located within the main production unit. On the other hand, modern methods of communication mean that individuals may work more on their own, from their homes, shared offices or hotels, or work more with machines than with other people.[132]

Virtual teams

The combination of increasing globalisation and widespread developments in information and communications technology has given greater emphasis to the opportunities for, and need of, **virtual teams**. Instead of involving face-to-face proximity, virtual teams are a collection of people who are geographically separated but still work together closely. The primary interaction among members is by some electronic information and communication process. This enables organisations to function away from traditional working hours and the physical availability of staff. Computer-based information systems and increased wireless connectivity further the opportunities for virtual working. By their very nature, virtual teams are likely to be largely self-managed.

According to Hall, the virtual team is a potential future compromise between fully fledged teams and well-managed groups.

> I am watching the rise of this idea with interest but am sceptical that it will actually create a 'third way'. Real teams can only be forged in the crucible of personal interaction: videoconferences and Net communications are still poor substitutes for this. Of course, once a team has formed it can use these media, as members will know each other well, but that's not the important bit. It's the forming, norming and storming that make a team.[133]

Management and communication skills

However, Parker highlights that remote working may also have an impact on the social aspects of organisational working with an increasing feeling of isolation.

> Remote teamworking is not simply a matter of ensuring staff have access to a laptop and telephone line, and assuming that they will be able to continue with their work. The management and communication skills that this new working culture requires are also key to success.[134]

A similar point is made by Norval who maintains that many remote workers can feel isolated and that the organisation is ignoring them, and this can affect their motivation. Without the visual sense and informal communications within the office, managers need to make a more conscious effort to build rapport and to rethink their management style.[135]

Symons considers that one advantage of virtual teamworking using asynchronous media is the clarity and richness of contributions when respondents are removed from the urgency of immediate interaction and that this can be particularly relevant in cross-cultural groups. However, as the leader cannot influence by their physical presence, and as hierarchies fade on-line, managing dispersed teams requires a range of subtly different leadership skills. It is important to develop mutual trust and a democratic approach of shared control and decision-making, and to adopt the role and style of a coach. 'The leader has to establish and maintain "credit" with the group, as "position power" has little or no currency in virtual working.'[136]

Garrett maintains that collaborating with other people in different cities or countries is not always a successful arrangement and lists the following suggestions for helping to organise the virtual team:

- **Say hello** – the most successful teams spend time during their formation period face-to-face getting to know each other.
- **Build trust** – to hold the team together so that you can depend on other team members and feel comfortable opening up to them.
- **Recruit with care** – people who can communicate in the right way at the right time are more likely to be successful in virtual teams.
- **Don't rely on email** – the written word is easily misunderstood so supplement its use with other forms of communication.
- **Encourage dissent** – without face-to-face meetings people become reluctant to speak out but a healthy organisation needs people to speak out and challenge leaders and each other.
- **Use technology thoughtfully** – used badly, sophisticated tools can be a disaster, and people need to be trained to use the technology, not simply have it imposed on them.
- **Measure outcomes** – focus on the outcomes rather than time management, find a personal way to appraise performance, rather than email, and hold regular chats with members.
- **Do say** 'By proactively creating virtual teams we can go where talent is, extend our reach and work more efficiently.'
- **Don't say** 'We call them a virtual team because they're not quite the real thing.'[137]

Cultural diversity

One reason for the growth in virtual teams is because of increasing globalisation and team members working and living in different countries. This gives rise to potential difficulties of cultural diversity. As Francesco and Gold point out:

> The more culturally diverse the members, the more difficult it is to manage a virtual team. Cultural diversity, which will be increasingly common, adds to the complexity of managing virtual teams because different values, customs, and traditions require more leadership under conditions that reduce the ability to use direct leadership.[138]

And according to Murray, although virtual working presents some unexpected benefits, if managing diversity in the workplace is a tough task for business leaders, the challenges of keeping executives from different backgrounds working together in various parts of the world is even more difficult. Virtual working does not eradicate the sort of cultural misunderstandings that can arise in a face-to-face situation.

Cultural or behavioural differences that can manifest themselves in face-to-face working situations can be exacerbated in virtual teamworking, particularly when the group has members from different backgrounds.[139]

'With the continual increase in globalisation and advances in new technology and communications the days of people spending most of their time working alongside the same colleagues are gone. Global virtual teams are the way forward.'

How far do you agree? What difficulties and problems do you foresee?

Remote teamworking at the Prudential[140]

Remote teamworking is not simply a matter of ensuring staff have access to a laptop and a telephone line and assuming that they will be able to continue with their work. The management and communications skills that this new working culture requires are also key to success. When one of Britain's leading financial services providers, Prudential, decided to introduce extensive remote working as part of its drive to build stronger customer relationships they called on the experience and expertise of Chameleon Training and Consulting. The Prudential were keen to ensure that their employees not only had the technology but also the skills to maximise the individual and business benefits offered by this new way of working. Chris Parker, Chameleon's Marketing Manager, explains how technology is only the starting point to developing an effective remote team.

Technology has been a constant driver for change in British business over the last decade. The myth has been that the technological changes alone have single-handedly propelled workplace culture from the age of telephone and typewriters into the broadband world of high speed networks, email and mobile communication, mobile phones and laptops. The reality is a need to adapt management techniques, working culture and employee skill levels. Working in the training and HR industry we know that these requirements cannot be ignored. In addition, many companies have attempted to introduce technology for the sake of it, or brought in 'new' gadgets without looking at the impact on the organisation, or individual workers, and have spent even less time looking at the role training can play in integrating the new technology into the processes and working culture of an organisation.

The pace of change

Prudential is one of the largest and most prestigious financial services organisations, with more than 150 years' experience building long and successful relationships with shareholders, customers and policyholders alike. The financial services industry has changed and continues to change at a faster pace than almost any other, and for this reason, technology, and the delivery of the skills required to integrate new ways of working into employees' daily processes and functions, is more important than in any other area of business.

Practice Head of Prudential's B2B division, and responsible for the development of the team, Martin Boniface says that this changing marketplace was one of the core reasons

Prudential decided to change their working culture, embracing technology, and ensuring that their employees have the skills to work effectively in this new environment. 'We realised that technology, and the effective utilisation of it through training, offered us a flexible, customer facing approach to our business, offering benefits for the company, its customers and Prudential employees.'

How to achieve this was going to be another matter entirely, and one which would prove to be far more wide-ranging than originally thought.

A question of image

According to Boniface, 'We wanted to develop a culture where we were able to be proactive, rather than reactive to the needs of our customers. One of the challenges that Prudential faced in this changeable market was to move away from the traditional view of the "man from the Pru" that policyholders know, towards a more modern image in keeping with the changing market's requirements, and this needed to be replicated throughout the business. Representatives were spending hours travelling to visit corporate customers, while still spending time at a centralised office. We realised that in order to offer a more customer focused approach to our corporate clients, we would have to fundamentally change our working culture.' Remote working was positively encouraged for staff in the B2B division at Prudential, with employees using laptops and mobile phones to allow the team to function effectively, but initially this was the exception rather than the rule.

Focus on the customer

'In the B2B division, we made some fairly radical changes,' says Boniface. 'We realised that remote working was the way forward for us, and reorganised our business to focus on our customers, rather than their geographical location – as had been the way in the past. This meant that remote working now became the rule, with the exception of members of our support team who still had a centrally based office location. The ability of our employees to work remotely allowed us to spend more time concentrating on the individual requirements of our corporate customers, and offered financial and efficiency benefits for both the company and our employees. We weren't asking our staff to travel from their homes to an office, and spend hours travelling out to customers' premises, back to the office, before heading home in the evening. This energised and invigorated the team instantly.'

Managing culture change

Having implemented this new way of working for a couple of months, it became obvious that while much of the culture change was beneficial, there were also areas which could be improved, and some that emerged which had not been expected. 'It was at this point that Prudential looked for expert help in remote team management, in order to refine and improve the new remote teamworking practices, and develop solutions designed to enable staff to manage their new working environment and the change of culture,' says Philippa Muress, Chameleon's Head of Consultancy Services. 'Having trialled remote working, Prudential carried out a number of focus groups to identify areas which needed refining. As a result, we were presented with a number of management challenges and objectives.'

Whilst the remote teamworking had been generally successful, with Prudential ensuring that staff had been supported in terms of hardware, with budgets provided for selecting computer technology, installing high speed communications access, and addressing Health and Safety issues, an overwhelming need for emotional support and remote, or virtual, team building had been identified.

The significant difference between central office-based working and remote working is that it is difficult to develop a team spirit, a sense of camaraderie, working remotely through new electronic and telecommunications methods. Morale and motivation had also been identified as areas with which Prudential's new virtual team required some assistance.

'Communication and trust are key elements of developing strong remote teamworking,' says Philippa Muress. 'There is a difference between managing a team in a traditional office environment, and managing a remote team of workers which requires new skills and new management techniques. Some of these skills can be adapted from traditional management methodology, but there are also specific techniques and skills, which are critical in the development of an effective remote team. These are exactly the areas which we help organisations to develop through our Managing Remote Teams programmes.'

'You can't control the volume of email,' adds Boniface. 'You have no way of knowing the emotional state of the recipient of an email, or how they perceive the content of the message, which means that trust has to be central to the team, and clarity is essential to avoid misunderstandings.' The ability for open discussion where things are unclear forms a central part of ensuring that the team is both effective and efficient. 'The last thing you want is for conflicts to grow from small misunderstandings because someone has not picked up the phone to say "Do I understand this correctly?".'

The delivery of the course has taken a number of different forms, with Chameleon using a blend of input sessions, assessment tools and role-play techniques during the implementation of the first phase of Prudential's Remote Teams training. Issues of management techniques, motivation and empowerment, and developing a team spirit from remote locations have all been central in the work, ensuring that staff have received a totally bespoke solution tailored to the specific needs of the organisation. Philippa Muress says, 'One of the most important parts of developing a training programme is ensuring that the development and implementation addresses the aims and objectives of both the team and the wider organisation. When developing an effective remote team it is important that you don't isolate the remote members from the rest of the organisation.'

The programme has highlighted the development needs, not only of the managers and remote workers, but also of those who provide support back in the office, and one-day workshops have been arranged for the whole team. 'We recognise the need for a strategic and co-ordinated programme of change in order to develop long-standing effective and successful remote teams,' says Boniface. 'There is a very important coaching element to the remote teams programme which Chameleon has developed for us, which offers vital support and reassurance. Working remotely can be a lonely experience if the necessary skill training is not in place, and we're delighted with the way that Chameleon has been there at every step. Our single point of contact has been one of their Remote Team experts, who understands our business, our aims and our specific business focus.'

Enjoying the benefits of managed change

The benefits of this new virtual team are already being experienced at 'the Pru'. Their vision of creating a more customer-faced commercial approach is generating more business with less cost (which has occurred, in part, as a result of the reduced requirement for desk space), and has raised customer satisfaction levels in the process.

In a market which has experienced considerable change, this has generated substantial competitive advantage for the company, and boosted morale within the CRM team. Chameleon's Philippa Muress says that the benefits experienced by the Prudential are all classic traits of effective Remote Teams training. 'Technology is only the beginning of developing a remote team environment – without the necessary tools to manage the new working practices, the new approach to managing and being managed, and the new communication and emotional skills, remote teamworking will not bring the efficiencies and financial rewards which can be achieved with a co-ordinated, structured and expertly delivered programme.'

Source: 'Remote Team Working at Prudential', *Manager, The British Journal of Administrative Management*, March/April 2002, pp. 30–1.

Working in groups and teams

Belbin's team roles

One of the most popular and widely used analyses of individual roles within a work group or team is that developed by Meredith Belbin. Following years of research and empirical study, Belbin concludes that groups composed entirely of clever people, or of people with similar personalities, display a number of negative results and lack creativity. The most consistently successful groups comprise a range of roles undertaken by various members. The constitution of the group itself is an important variable in its success.[141] Initially, Belbin identified eight useful types of contribution – or team roles.

A **team role** is described as a pattern of behaviour, characteristic of the way in which one team member interacts with another whose performance serves to facilitate the progress of the team as a whole. In a follow-up publication, Belbin discusses the continual evolution of team roles, which differ in a few respects from those originally identified, and adds a ninth role.[142] Strength of contribution in any one role is commonly associated with particular weaknesses. These are called allowable weaknesses. Members are seldom strong in all nine team roles. A description of the evolved nine team roles is given in Table 3.4.

The types of people identified are useful team members and form a comprehensive list. These are the key team roles and the primary characters for successful teams. Creative teams require a balance of all these roles and comprise members

Table 3.4 Belbin's evolved nine team roles

Roles and descriptions – team-role contribution		Allowable weaknesses
Plant	Creative, imaginative, unorthodox. Solves difficult problems.	Ignores details. Too preoccupied to communicate effectively.
Resource investigator	Extravert, enthusiastic, communicative. Explores opportunities. Develops contacts.	Over-optimistic. Loses interest once initial enthusiasm has passed.
Co-ordinator	Mature, confident, a good chairperson. Clarifies goals, promotes decision-making. Delegates well.	Can be seen as manipulative. Offloads personal work.
Shaper	Challenging, dynamic, thrives on pressure. Has the drive and courage to overcome obstacles.	Can provoke others. Hurts people's feelings.
Monitor-Evaluator	Sober, strategic and discerning. Sees all options. Judges accurately.	Lacks drive and ability to inspire others.
Teamworker	Co-operative, mild, perceptive and diplomatic. Listens, builds, averts friction.	Indecisive in crunch situations.
Implementer	Disciplined, reliable, conservative and efficient. Turns ideas into practical actions.	Somewhat inflexible. Slow to respond to new possibilities.
Completer	Painstaking, conscientious, anxious. Searches out errors and omissions. Delivers on time.	Inclined to worry unduly. Reluctant to delegate.
Specialist	Single-minded, self-sharing, dedicated. Provides knowledge and skills in rare supply.	Contributes on only a narrow front. Dwells on technicalities.

Source: Belbin, R. M. *Team Roles at Work*, Butterworth-Heinemann (a division of Reed Elsevier UK Ltd) and Belbin Associates (1993), p. 23. Reproduced with permission.

who have characteristics complementary to each other. 'No one's perfect, but a team can be.' Belbin claims that good examples of each type would prove adequate for any challenge, although not all types are necessarily needed. Other members may be welcome for their personal qualities, for example a sense of humour, but experience suggests there is no other team role that it would be useful to add.

Back-up team roles

The most consistently successful teams were 'mixed' with a balance of team roles. The role that a person undertakes in a group is not fixed and may change according to circumstances.

Individuals may have a 'back-up team role' with which they have some affinity other than their primary team role. If certain roles were missing, members would call upon their back-up roles. Team roles differ from what Belbin calls 'functional roles'. These are the roles that members of a team perform in terms of the specifically technical demands placed upon them. Team members are typically chosen for functional roles on the basis of experience and not personal characteristics or aptitudes.

Belbin has developed a Self-Perception Inventory designed to provide members of a group with a simple means of assessing their best team roles.

The value of Belbin's team-roles inventory

Despite possible doubts about the value of Belbin's Self-Perception Inventory, it remains a popular means of examining and comparing team roles. For example, in order to explore whether local government managers were distinctively different from the model of private sector management, Arroba and Wedgwood-Oppenheim compared samples of the two groups of managers and Belbin's key team roles. There were noticeable similarities between the two groups, with the noticeable exception of the marked difference between private sector managers and local government officers in the score for teamworkers and the team roles they preferred to adopt. The individual characteristics of managers in the two sectors differed. The data implied that local government officers were committed to organisational objectives and dedicated to task achievement, but the low score for teamworkers suggested the high commitment to organisational tasks was not supplemented by a concern for interpersonal processes. In local government, the drive and enthusiasm and emphasis on task were exaggerated, while attention to idea generation and productive interpersonal relationships was less marked.[143]

Team roles among UK managers

Using Belbin's model, Fisher *et al.* undertook a study of the distribution of team roles among managers. Recently, many layers of management have been removed and the gap in people to lead and motivate has increasingly been filled by the creation of multitudes of teams. The participants of the study were 1,441 male and 355 female managers, all with some management experience. All had completed a personality questionnaire and were candidates short-listed for a range of managment positions in both the private and public sectors. The study analysed data supplied by ASE/NFER Publishing Company and results were then compared with the Belbin model. The data broadly agreed with the Belbin model. The authors conclude that as much is still unknown about teams, it is reassuring that further support has been found for the popular Belbin team-role model. There are several unresolved problems with teamworking but these might lie more with practices in staff recruitment than in team theory.[144]

critical reflection

'Belbin's evolved team roles serve little practical value. Behaviour does not fit into neat categories and most people do not acknowledge allowable weaknesses. The two most important roles for effective teamwork are (i) a strong and decisive leader and (ii) the humorist to make people laugh and reduce tension.'

What are your views? How would you explain your role as a team member?

Patterns of communication

The level of interaction among members of a group or team is influenced by the structuring of channels of communication. Laboratory research by Bavelas[145] and subsequent studies by other researchers such as Leavitt[146] have resulted in the design of a series of communication networks. These networks were based on groups of five members engaged in a number of problem-solving tasks. Members were permitted to communicate with each other by written notes only and not everyone was always free to communicate with everyone else.

There are five main types of communication networks – wheel, circle, all-channel, Y and chains (see Figure 3.23).

- The **wheel**, also sometimes known as the star, is the most centralised network. This network is most efficient for simple tasks. Problems are solved more quickly with fewer mistakes and with fewer information flows. However, as the problems become more complex and demands on the link person increase, effectiveness suffers. The link person is at the centre of the network and acts as the focus of activities and information flows and the co-ordinator of group tasks. The central person is perceived as leader of the group and experiences a high level of satisfaction. However, for members on the periphery, the wheel is the least satisfying network.
- The **circle** is a more decentralised network. Overall it is less efficient. The group is unorganised, with low leadership predictability. Performance tends to be slow and erratic. However, the circle is quicker than the wheel in solving complex problems and also copes more efficiently with change or new tasks. The circle network is most satisfying for all the members. Decision-making is likely to involve some degree of participation.
- The **all-channel (or comcon)** network is a decentralised network that involves full discussion and participation. This network appears to work best where a high

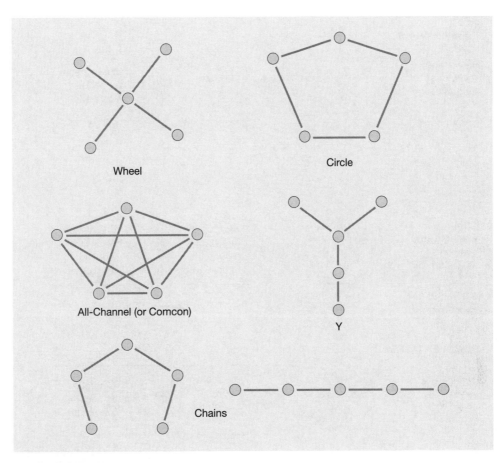

Wheel

Circle

All-Channel (or Comcon)

Y

Chains

Figure 3.23   Communication networks

level of interaction is required among all the members in order to solve complex problems. Leadership predictability is very low. There is a fairly high level of satisfaction for members. The all-channel network may not stand up well under pressure, in which case it will either disintegrate or re-form into a wheel network.

• A 'Y' or **chain** network might be appropriate for more simple problem-solving tasks, requiring little interaction among members. These networks are more centralised, with information flows along a predetermined channel. Leadership predictability is high to moderate. There is a low to moderate level of satisfaction for members.

The relationship between centralised and decentralised networks and performance of the group is outlined in Figure 3.24.

Implications for the manager

Despite the obvious artificiality and limitations of these communication network studies, they do have certain implications for the manager. Knowledge of the findings may be applied to influence the patterns of communication in meetings and committees. They also provide a reasonable representation of the situations

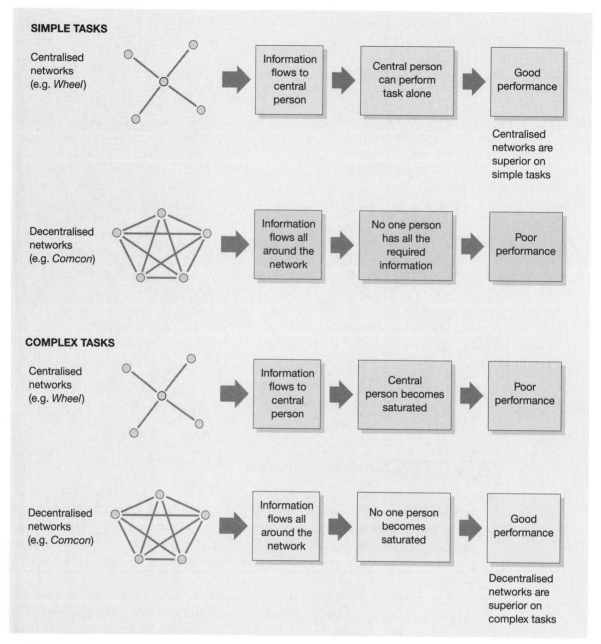

Figure 3.24 Communication networks and task complexity

Source: Greenberg, J. and Baron, R. A. *Behavior in Organizations*, sixth edition, Prentice Hall Inc. (1995), p. 306. Reproduced with permission from Pearson Education, Inc.

that might apply in large organisations. It will be interesting for the manager to observe the patterns of communication adopted by different groups in different situations. The manager can also note how communication networks change over time and how they relate to the performance of the group.

No one network is likely to be effective for a range of given problems. The studies draw attention to the part of the manager's job that is to ensure the most appropriate communication network for the performance of a given task. Problems which require a high level of interaction among members of the group may not be handled efficiently if there are inadequate channels of communication or sharing of information. The choice of a particular communication network may involve trade-offs between the performance of the work group and the satisfaction of its members.

Notes

1 See, for example, Mullins, L. J., *Management and Organisational Behaviour*, 8th edition, Financial Times/Prentice Hall, 2007; Cole, G. A., *Management: Theory and Practice*, 6th edition, Thomson, 2004.

2 For a more detailed account of the three approaches see, *inter alia*, the texts referred to in n. 1.

3 Ouichi, W. G., *Theory Z: How American Business can Meet the Japanese Challenge*, Addison-Wesley, 1981.

4 The contingency approach is discussed in Cole, *op. cit.*

5 Howe, M. J. A. 'Can IQ Change?', *The Psychologist*, February 1998, pp. 69–72.

6 Spearman, C. *The Abilities of Man*, Macmillan (1927).

7 Vernon, P. E. *The Structure of Human Abilities*, Methuen and Co. (1950).

8 Thurstone, L. L. 'Primary Mental Abilities', *Psychometric Monographs*, no. 1, 1938.

9 Guilford, J. P. 'Three Faces of Intellect', *American Psychologist*, vol. 14, pp. 469–79.

10 Gardner, H. *Frames of Mind*, second edition, Fontana (1993).

11 Goleman, D. *Emotional Intelligence*, Bloomsbury (1996), p. 34.

12 Goleman, D. *Working with Emotional Intelligence*, Bantam Books, New York (1998).

13 Boyatzis, R., Goleman, D. and Hay/McBer, *Emotional Competence Inventory Feedback Report*, Hay Group (1999).

14 'Management Futures: The World in 2018', Chartered Management Institute, March 2008.

15 Landale, A. 'Must Have EQ', *Manager: The British Journal of Administrative Management*, February/March 2007, pp. 24–5.

16 Ibid.

17 Garrett, A. 'Crash Course in Raising Emotional Intelligence', *Management Today*, August 2005, p. 16.

18 Dann, J. 'Managing Your Emotions', *Professional Manager*, vol. 17, no. 4, July 2008, pp. 32–4.

19 McGregor, D. *The Human Side of Enterprise*, Penguin (1987), p. 6.

20 Miner, J. B. *Theories of Organizational Behaviour*, Dryden Press (1980).

21 See, for example, Mullins, L. J. 'Approaches to Management', *Management Accounting*, vol. 57, no. 4, April 1979, pp. 15–18, and Mullins, L. J. 'Some Further Approaches to Management Theory', *Management Accounting*, vol. 58, no. 3, March 1980, pp. 30–3.

22 See, for example, George, C. S. *The History of Management Thought*, second edition, Prentice Hall (1972).

23 Shafritz, J. M. *Shakespeare on Management*, Carol Publishing Group (1992), p. xi.

24 For a review of management thinking see, for example, Sheldrake, J. *Management Theory: From Taylorism to Japanization*, International Thomson Business Press (1996). See also Flores, G. N. and Utley, D. R. 'Management Concepts in Use – a 12-Year Perspective', *Engineering Management Journal*, vol. 12, no. 3, September 2000, pp. 11–17.

25 Skipton, M. D. 'Management and the Organisation', *Management Research News*, vol. 5, no. 3, 1983, pp. 9–15.

26 Fayol, H. *General and Industrial Management*, Pitman (1949). See also Gray, I. *Henri Fayol's General and Industrial Management*, Pitman (1988).

27 Urwick, L. *Notes on the Theory of Organization*, American Management Association (1952).

28 Mooney, J. D. and Reiley, A. C. *The Principles of Organization*, Harper and Bros (1939); revised by Mooney, J. D., Harper & Row (1947).

29 Brech, E. F. L. *Organisation: The Framework of Management*, second edition, Longman (1965).

30 Simon, H. A. *Administrative Behaviour*, third edition, Free Press (1976), p. xxii.

31 Woodward, J. *Industrial Organization: Theory and Practice*, second edition, Oxford University Press (1980).

32 Taylor, F. W. *Scientific Management*, Harper & Row (1947). Comprises 'Shop Management' (1903), 'Principles of Scientific Management' (1911) and Taylor's testimony to the House of Representatives' Special Committee (1912).

33 Braverman, H. *Labor and Monopoly Capital*, Monthly Review Press (1974).

34 For a study of employers' labour relations policies, including comments on the work of Braverman, see Gospel, H. F. and Littler, C. R. (eds) *Managerial Strategies and Industrial Relations*, Heinemann Educational Books (1983).

35 Cloke, K. and Goldsmith, J. *The End of Management and the Rise of Organizational Democracy*, Jossey-Bass (2002), p. 27.

36 Rose, M. *Industrial Behaviour*, Penguin (1978), p. 31. See also Rose, M. *Industrial Behaviour*, second edition, Penguin (1988), ch. 2.

37 Drucker, P. F. 'The Coming Rediscovery of Scientific Management', *The Conference Board Record*, vol. 13, June 1976, pp. 23–7; reprinted in Drucker, P. F. *Towards the Next Economics and Other Essays*, Heinemann (1981).

38 Locke, E. A. 'The Ideas of Frederick W. Taylor: An Evaluation', *Academy of Management Review*, vol. 7, no. 1, January 1982, pp. 14–24.

39 For a discussion on 'Fordism', see, for example, Fincham, R. and Rhodes, P. S. *The Individual, Work and Organization*, second edition, Weidenfeld and Nicolson (1992).

40 Hamel, G. *The Future of Management*, Harvard Business School Press (2007), p. 13.

41 Crainer, S. and Dearlove, D. *Financial Times Handbook of Management*, second edition, Financial Times Prentice Hall (2001).

42 Stern, S. 'Guru Guide', *Management Today*, October 2001, pp. 83–4.

43 Weber, M. *The Theory of Social and Economic Organization*, Collier Macmillan (1964).

44 Blau, P. M. and Scott, W. R. *Formal Organizations*, Routledge and Kegan Paul (1966).

45 Stewart, R. *The Reality of Management*, third edition, Butterworth-Heinemann (1999).

46 Argyris, C. *Integrating the Individual and the Organization*, John Wiley & Sons (1964).

47 Caulkin, S. 'Faceless Corridors of Power', *Management Today*, January 1988, p. 65.

48 Peters, T. J. and Waterman, R. H. *In Search of Excellence*, Harper & Row (1982).

49 Tibballs, G. *Business Blunders*, Robinson Publishing (1999).

50 Cloke, K. and Goldsmith, J. *The End of Management and the Rise of Organizational Democracy*, Jossey-Bass (2002), pp. 92–4.

51 Ridderstrale, J. 'Business Moves Beyond Bureaucracy', in Pickford, J. (ed.) *Financial Times Mastering Management 2.0*, Financial Times Prentice Hall (2001), pp. 217–20.

52 Green, J. 'Is Bureaucracy Dead? Don't Be So Sure', *Chartered Secretary*, January 1997, pp. 18–19.

53 See, for example, Waller, P. 'Bureaucracy Takes New Form', *Professional Manager*, May 1998, p. 6.

54 See Mullins, L. J. *Hospitality Management and Organisational Behaviour*, fourth edition, Longman (2001).

55 Stewart, R. *The Reality of Management*, third edition, Butterworth-Heinemann (1999).

56 See, for example, Wilson, F. A. *Organizational Behaviour: A Critical Introduction*, Oxford University Press (1999).

57 For example, see Etzioni, A. *Modern Organizations*, Prentice Hall (1964), p. 41.

58 See, for example, Aktouf, O. 'Management and Theories of Organizations in the 1990s: Towards a Critical Radical Humanism?', *Academy of Management Review*, vol. 17, no. 3, 1992, pp. 407–31.

59 There are many versions of the Hawthorne experiments. Among the most thorough accounts is Roethlisberger, F. J. and Dickson, W. J. *Management and the Worker*, Harvard University Press (1939). See also Landsberger, H. A. *Hawthorne Revisited*, Cornell University Press, Ithaca (1958).

60 See, for example, Rose, M. *Industrial Behaviour*, second edition, Penguin (1988).

61 See, for example, Buggy, C. 'Are You Really Listening?', *Professional Manager*, July 2000, pp. 20–2.

62 Silverman, D. *The Theory of Organisations*, Heinemann (1970).

63 Stead, B. A. *Women in Management*, Prentice Hall (1978), p. 190.

64 Crainer, S. *Key Management Ideas: Thinkers That Changed the Management World*, third edition, Financial Times Prentice Hall (1998), p. 111.

65 Maslow, A. H. 'A Theory of Human Motivation', *Psychological Review*, vol. 50, no. 4, July 1943, pp. 370–96.

66 Herzberg, F. W., Mausner, B. and Snyderman, B. B. *The Motivation to Work*, second edition, Chapman and Hall (1959).

67 McGregor, D. *The Human Side of Enterprise*, Penguin (1987).

68 Likert, R. *New Patterns of Management*, McGraw-Hill (1961). See also Likert, R. *The Human Organization*, McGraw-Hill (1967); Likert, R. and Likert, J. G. *New Ways of Managing Conflict*, McGraw-Hill (1976).

69 McClelland, D. C. *Human Motivation*, Cambridge University Press (1988).

70 Argyris, C. *Understanding Organizational Behavior*, Tavistock Publications (1960) and *Integrating the Individual and the Organization*, Wiley (1964).

71 See, for example, Caulkin, S. 'Chris Argyris', *Management Today*, October 1997, pp. 58–9.

72 Bertalanffy, L. von 'Problems of General Systems Theory: A New Approach to the Unity of Science', *Human Biology*, vol. 23, no. 4, December 1951, pp. 302–12.

73 Miller, E. J. and Rice, A. K. *Systems of Organization*, Tavistock Publications (1967).

74 Boulding, K. 'General Systems Theory – The Skeleton of Science', *Management Science*, vol. 2, no. 3, April 1956, pp. 197–208.

75 Trist, E. L., Higgin, G. W., Murray, H. and Pollock, A. B. *Organizational Choice*, Tavistock Publications (1963).

76 Lane, T., Snow, D. and Labrow, P. 'Learning to Succeed with ICT', *The British Journal of Administrative Management*, May/June 2000, pp. 14–15.

77 Walker, C. R. and Guest, R. H. *The Man on the Assembly Line*, Harvard University Press (1952). See also Walker, C. R., Guest, R. H. and Turner, A. N. *The Foreman on the Assembly Line*, Harvard University Press (1956).

78 Sayles, L. R. *Behaviour of Industrial Work Groups*, Wiley (1958).

79 Blauner, R. *Alienation and Freedom*, University of Chicago Press (1964).

80 See, for example, Margretta, J. *What Management Is: How it Works and Why it's Everyone's Business*, HarperCollins (2002).

81 Shafritz, J. M. *Shakespeare on Management*, Carol Publishing Group (1992), p. xii.

82 Knights, D. and Willmott, H. *Management Lives: Power and Identity in Work Organizations*, Sage Publications (1999), pp. viii–ix.

83 Crainer, S. *Key Management Ideas: Thinkers That Changed the Management World*, third edition, Financial Times Prentice Hall (1998), p. xi.

84 Crainer, S. 'The Rise of Guru Scepticism', *Management Today*, March 1996, p. 51.

85 Watson, T. J. *Management, Organisation and Employment Strategy*, Routledge and Kegan Paul (1986).

86 Drucker, P. F. *The Practice of Management*, Heinemann Professional (1989), p. 3.

87 Drucker, P. F. *Management*, Pan Books (1979), p. 14.

88 Schneider, S. C. and Barsoux, J. *Managing Across Cultures*, second edition, Financial Times Prentice Hall (2003).

89 Francesco, A. M. and Gold, B. A. *International Organizational Behavior*, second edition, Prentice Hall (2005).

90 Fayol, H. *General and Industrial Management*, Pitman (1949). See also Gray, I. *Henri Fayol's General and Industrial Management*, Pitman Publishing (1988).

91 Fayol, H. *General and Industrial Management*, Pitman (1949).

92 Moorcroft, R. 'Managing in the 21st Century', *The British Journal of Administrative Management*, January/February 2000, pp. 8–10.

93 Bass, B. M. *Handbook of Leadership: Theory, Research and Managerial Applications*, third edition, The Free Press (1990), p. 11.

94 McGregor, D. *The Human Side of Enterprise*, Penguin (1987), p. 182.

95 Kouzes, J. M. and Posner, B. Z. 'The Janusian Leader', in Chowdhury, S. (ed.) *Management 21C*, Financial Times Prentice Hall (2000), p. 18.

96 Fullan, M. *Leading in a Culture of Change*, Jossey-Bass (2001), p. 5.

97 French, J. R. P. and Raven, B. 'The Bases of Social Power', in Cartwright, D. and Zander, A. F. (eds) *Group Dynamics: Research and Theory*, third edition, Harper and Row (1968).

98 Finlay, P. *Strategic Management: An Introduction to Business and Corporate Strategy*, Financial Times Prentice Hall (2000), p. 103.

99 Yukl, G. *Leadership in Organizations*, sixth edition, Pearson Prentice Hall (2006).

100 Roddick, A. *Body and Soul*, Ebury Press (1991), p. 214.

101 Lloyd, B. 'Balancing Power with Responsibility and Wisdom', *Professional Manager*, vol. 17, no. 3, May 2008, p. 37.

102 Drucker, P. F. *The Practice of Management*, Heinemann Professional (1989), p. 156.

103 Bass, B. M. *Handbook of Leadership: Theory, Research and Managerial Applications*, third edition, The Free Press (1990).

104 See, for example, Bryman, A. 'Leadership in Organisations', in Clegg, S. Hardy, C. and Nord, W. (eds) *Managing Organsations: Current Issues*, Sage (1999), pp. 26–62.

105 Kotter, J. P. 'What Leaders Really Do', *Harvard Business Review*, May–June 1990, p. 103.

106 Whitehead, M. 'Everyone's a Leader Now', *Supply Management*, 25 April 2002, pp. 22–4.

107 Adair, J. *Action-Centred Leadership*, Gower Press (1979). See also Adair, J. *The Skills of Leadership*, Gower Press (1984).

108 Adair, J. *Leadership and Motivation*, Kogan Page (2006).

109 Fleishman, E. A. 'Leadership Climate, Human Relations Training and Supervisory Behavior', in Fleishman, E. A. and Bass, A. R. *Studies in Personnel and Industrial Psychology*, third edition, Dorsey (1974).

110 Bryman, A. 'Leadership in Organisations', in Clegg, S. Hardy, C. and Nord, W. (eds) *Managing Organisations: Current Issues*, Sage (1999), pp. 26–62.

111 Likert, R. *New Patterns of Management*, McGraw-Hill (1961).

112 Tannenbaum, R. and Schmidt, W. H. 'How to Choose a Leadership Pattern', *Harvard Business Review*, May–June 1973, pp. 162–75, 178–80.

113 Boynton, A. and Fischer, B. *Virtuoso Teams: Lessons from Teams that Changed their Worlds*, Financial Times Prentice Hall (2005).

114 Lysons, K. 'Organisational Analysis', *Supplement to The British Journal of Administrative Management*, no. 18, March/April 1997.

115 Law, S. 'Beyond the Water Cooler', *Professional Manager,* January 2005, pp. 26–8.

116 See, for example, Jay, A. *Corporation Man*, Penguin (1975). In an amusing historical account of the development of different forms of groups, Jay suggests that ten is the basic size of human grouping.

117 Cane, S. *Kaizen Strategies for Winning Through People*, Pitman Publishing (1996), p. 131.

118 McKenna, P. J. and Maister, D. H. 'Building Team Trust', *Consulting to Management*, vol. 13, no. 4, December 2002, pp. 51–3.

119 Farrell, E. 'Take the Lead in Setting Standards of Behaviour in Your Team', *Professional Manager*, vol. 19, no. 1, January 2009, p. 14.

120 Bass, B. M. and Ryterband, E. C. *Organizational Psychology*, second edition, Allyn and Bacon (1979).

121 Tuckman, B. W. 'Development Sequence in Small Groups', *Psychological Bulletin*, vol. 63, 1965, pp. 384–99; and Tuckman, B. W. and Jensen, M. C. 'Stages of Small Group Development Revised', *Group and Organizational Studies,* vol. 2, no. 3, 1977, pp. 419–27.

122 Cited in Green, J. 'Are Your Teams and Groups at Work Successful?', *Administrator*, December 1993, p. 12.

123 Rickards, T. and Moger, S. 'Creative Leadership and Team Effectiveness: Empirical Evidence for a Two Barrier Model of Team Development', working paper presented at the Advanced Seminar Series, University of Uppsala, Sweden, 3 March 2009. See also Rickards, T. and Moger, S. 'Creative Leadership Processes in Project Team Development: An Alternative to Tuckman's Stage Model?', *British Journal of Management*, Part 4, 2000, pp. 273–83.

124 Tajfel, H. and Turner, J. C. 'The Social Identity Theory of Intergroup Behavior', in Worchel, S. and Austin, L. W. (eds) *Psychology of Intergroup Relations*, Nelson-Hall (1986), pp. 7–24.

125 Guirdham, M. *Interactive Behaviour at Work*, third edition, Financial Times Prentice Hall (2002), p. 118.

126 Haslam, S. A., *Psychology in Organizations: The Social Identity Approach*, second edition, Sage Publications (2004), p. 17.

127 See, for example, Flynn, F. J., Chatman, J. A. and Spataro, S. E. 'Getting to Know You: The Influence of Personality on Impressions and Performance of Demographically Different People in Organizations', *Administrative Science Quarterly*, vol. 46, 2001, pp. 414–42.

128 Hewstone, M., Ruibin, M. and Willis, H. 'Intergroup Bias', *Annual Review of Psychology*, vol. 53, 2002, pp. 575–604.

129 Argyle, M. *The Social Psychology of Work*, second edition, Penguin (1989).

130 Brooks, I. *Organisational Behaviour: Individuals, Groups and Organisation*, third edition, Financial Times Prentice Hall (2006), p. 99.

131 ACAS *Teamwork: Success Through People* advisory booklet, ACAS (2007), p. 8.

132 See, for example, Kinsman, F. 'The Virtual Office and the Flexible Organisation', *Administrator*, April 1994, pp. 31–2; and Chowdhury, S. *Management 21C*, Financial Times Prentice Hall (2000).

133 Hall, P. 'Team Solutions Need Not Be the Organisational Norm', *Professional Manager*, July 2001, p. 45.

134 Parker, C. 'Remote Control – a Case Study', *Manager, The British Journal of Administrative Management*, March/April 2002, p. 30.

135 Norval, D. in conversation with Law, S. 'Beyond the Water Cooler', *Professional Manager*, January 2005, pp. 26–8.

136 Symons, J. 'Taking Virtual Team Control', *Professional Manager*, vol. 12, no. 2, March 2003, p. 37.

137 Garrett, A. 'Crash Course in Managing a Virtual Team', *Management Today*, September 2007, p. 20.

138 Francesco, A. M. and Gold, B. A. *International Organizational Behavior,* second edition, Pearson Prentice Hall (2005), p. 118.

139 Murray, S. 'Virtual Teams: Global Harmony Is Their Dream', *Financial Times*, 11 May 2005.

140 Reproduced with permission from *Manager, The British Journal of Administrative Management*, March/April 2002, pp. 30–1, and with the permission of Murray Blair, Chameleon Training and Consulting, Surrey.

141 Belbin, R. M. *Management Teams: Why They Succeed or Fail*, Butterworth-Heinemann (1981).

142 Belbin, R. M. *Team Roles at Work*, Butterworth-Heinemann (1993).

143 Arroba, T. and Wedgwood-Oppenheim, F. 'Do Senior Managers Differ in the Public and Private Sector? An Examination of Team-Role Preferences', *Journal of Managerial Psychology*, vol. 9, no.1, 1994, pp. 13–16.

144 Fisher, S. G., Hunter, T. A. and Macrosson, W. D. K. 'The Distribution of Belbin Team Roles among UK Managers', *Personnel Review*, vol. 29, no. 2, 2000, pp. 124–40.

145 Bavelas, A. 'A Mathematical Model for Group Structures', *Applied Anthropology*, vol. 7, 1948, pp. 19–30, and Bavelas, A. 'Communication Patterns in Task-Oriented Groups', in Lasswell, H. N. and Lerner, D. (eds) *The Policy Sciences*, Stanford University Press (1951).

146 Leavitt, H. J. 'Some Effects of Certain Communication Patterns on Group Performance', *Journal of Abnormal and Social Psychology*, vol. 46, 1951, pp. 38–50. See also Leavitt, H. J. *Managerial Psychology*, fourth edition, University of Chicago Press (1978).

CHAPTER 4
Marketing Principles

Unit 4:   Marketing Principles

Unit code: F/601/0556

QCF level: 4

Credit value: 15 credits

Aim

This unit aims to provide learners with understanding and skills relating to the fundamental concepts and principles that underpin the marketing process.

Unit abstract

This is a broad-based unit which gives learners the opportunity to apply the key principles of marketing.

First, the unit looks at the definitions of marketing, and what is meant by a marketing orientation and the marketing process.

Next, learners consider the use of environmental analysis in marketing and carry out their own analyses at both macro and micro levels. They will also investigate the importance of market segmentation and how this leads to the identification and full specification of target groups. Learners then consider buyer behaviour and positioning.

The unit looks at the main elements of both the original and the extended marketing mix. This includes an introduction to the concept of the product life cycle, new product development, pricing strategies, distribution options and the promotion mix.

Finally, learners will develop their own marketing mixes to meet the needs of different target groups. This includes considering the differences when marketing services as opposed to goods. A range of other contexts is examined including marketing to businesses instead of consumers and the development of international markets.

Learning outcomes

On successful completion of this unit a learner will:

1 Understand the concept and process of marketing
2 Be able to use the concepts of segmentation, targeting and positioning
3 Understand the individual elements of the extended marketing mix
4 Be able to use the marketing mix in different contexts

Unit content

1 Understand the concept and process of marketing

Definitions: alternative definitions including those of the Chartered Institute of Marketing and the American Marketing Association; satisfying customer needs and wants; value and satisfaction; exchange relationships; the changing emphasis of marketing

Marketing concept: evolution of marketing; marketing orientations; societal issues and emergent philosophies; customer and competitor orientation; efficiency and effectiveness; limitations of the marketing concept

Marketing process overview: marketing audit; integrated marketing; environmental analysis; SWOT analysis; marketing objectives; constraints; options; plans to include target markets and marketing mix; scope of marketing

Costs and benefits: links between marketing orientation and building competitive advantage; benefits of building customer satisfaction; desired quality; service and customer care; relationship marketing; customer retention; customer profitability; costs of a too narrow marketing focus

2 Be able to use the concepts of segmentation, targeting and positioning

Macro environment: environmental scanning; political, legal, economic, socio-cultural, ecological and technological factors

Micro environment: stakeholders (organisation's own employees, suppliers, customers, intermediaries, owners, financiers, local residents, pressure groups and competitors); direct and indirect competitors; Porter's competitive forces

Buyer behaviour: dimensions of buyer behaviour; environmental influences; personal variables – demographic, sociological, psychological – motivation, perception and learning; social factors; physiological stimuli; attitudes; other lifestyle and life cycle variables; consumer and organisational buying

Segmentation: process of market selection; macro and micro segmentation; bases for segmenting markets (geographic, demographic, psychographic and behavioural); multi-variable segmentation and typologies; benefits of segmentation; evaluation of segments and targeting strategies; positioning; segmenting industrial markets; size; value; standards; industrial classification

Positioning: definition and meaning; influence over marketing mix factors

3 Understand the individual elements of the extended marketing mix

Product: products and brands – features, advantages and benefits; the total product concept; product mix; product life cycle and its effect on other elements of the marketing mix; product strategy; new product development; adoption process

Place: customer convenience and availability; definition of channels; types and functions of intermediaries; channel selection; integration and distribution systems; franchising; physical distribution management and logistics; ethical issues

Price: perceived value; pricing context and process; pricing strategies; demand elasticity; competition; costs, psychological, discriminatory; ethical issues

Promotion: awareness and image; effective communication; integrated communication process (SOSTT + 4Ms); promotional mix elements; push and pull strategies; advertising above and below the line including packaging; public relations and sponsorship; sales promotion; direct marketing and personal selling; branding, internet and online marketing

The shift from the 4Ps to the 7Ps: product-service continuum; concept of the extended marketing mix; the significance of the soft elements of marketing (people, physical evidence and process management)

4 Be able to use the marketing mix in different contexts

Consumer markets: fast moving consumer goods; consumer durables; coordinated marketing mix to achieve objectives

Organisational markets: differences from consumer markets; adding value through service; industrial; non-profit making; government; re-seller

Services: nature and characteristics of service products (intangibility, ownership, inseparability, perishability, variability, heterogeneity – the 7Ps); strategies; service quality; elements of physical product marketing; tangible and intangible benefits

International markets: globalisation; cultural differences; standardisation versus adaptation; the EU; benefits and risks; market attractiveness; international marketing mix strategies

Learning outcomes and assessment criteria

Learning outcomes On successful completion of this unit a learner will:	Assessment criteria for pass The learner can:
LO1 Understand the concept and process of marketing	1.1 explain the various elements of the marketing process 1.2 evaluate the benefits and costs of a marketing orientation for a selected organisation
LO2 Be able to use the concepts of segmentation, targeting and positioning	2.1 show macro and micro environmental factors which influence marketing decisions 2.2 propose segmentation criteria to be used for products in different markets 2.3 choose a targeting strategy for a selected product/service 2.4 demonstrate how buyer behaviour affects marketing activities in different buying situations 2.5 propose new positioning for a selected product/service
LO3 Understand the individual elements of the extended marketing mix	3.1 explain how products are developed to sustain competitive advantage 3.2 explain how distribution is arranged to provide customer convenience 3.3 explain how prices are set to reflect an organisation's objectives and market conditions 3.4 illustrate how promotional activity is integrated to achieve marketing objectives 3.5 analyse the additional elements of the extended marketing mix
LO4 Be able to use the marketing mix in different contexts	4.1 plan marketing mixes for two different segments in consumer markets 4.2 illustrate differences in marketing products and services to businesses rather than consumers 4.3 show how and why international marketing differs from domestic marketing

Guidance

Links

Learners who have achieved a BTEC Higher Nationals in Business have, for many years, been given entry to and exemptions from some parts of the Chartered Institute of Marketing's professional examinations. Further information can be found in the *Professional Body Recognition* booklet available from the Edexcel website.

This unit forms the basis of the Higher National marketing pathway linking with other marketing units: *Unit 17: Marketing Intelligence, Unit 18: Advertising and Promotion in Business, Unit 19: Marketing Planning* and *Unit 20: Sales Planning and Operations*. There is also a link to *Unit 1: Business Environment* in relation to the areas of stakeholders, effects of demand elasticity on pricing and external market factors. The unit also provides links to *Unit 30: Internet Marketing* and *Unit 41: Contemporary Issues in Marketing Management*.

Essential requirements

There are no essential or unique resources required for the delivery of this unit.

Employer engagement and vocational contexts

Centres should develop links with local businesses. Many businesses and chambers of commerce want to promote local business and are often willing to provide work placements, visit opportunities, information about businesses and the local business context and guest speakers.

www.businessbritainuk.co.uk	provides information about business in Britain and has extensive links to other business and business news sites.
www.fsb.org.uk	The Federation of Small Businesses provides information, support and guidance about small businesses in the UK.

Marketing dynamics

Introduction

You will have some sort of idea of what marketing is, since you are, after all, exposed to marketing in some form every day. Every time you buy or use a product, go window shopping, see an advertising hoarding, watch an advertisement, listen to friends telling you about a wonderful new product they've tried, or even when you surf the internet to research a market, company or product for an assignment, you are reaping the benefits (or being a victim) of marketing activities. When marketing's outputs are so familiar, it is easy to take it for granted and to judge and define it too narrowly by what you see of it close to home. It is a mistake, however, to dismiss marketing as 'just advertising' or 'just selling' or 'making people buy things they don't really want'.

What this chapter wants to show you is that marketing does, in fact, cover a very wide range of absolutely essential business activities that bring you the products you *do* want, when you want them, where you want them, but at prices you can afford, and with all the information you need to make informed and satisfying consumer choices. And that's only what marketing does for you! Widen your thinking to include what marketing can similarly do for organisations purchasing goods and services from other organisations, and you can begin to see why it is a mistake to be too cynical about professionally practised marketing. None of this is easy. The outputs of marketing, such as the packaging, the advertisements, the glossy brochures, the all-singing, all-dancing websites, the enticing retail outlets and the incredible bargain value prices, look slick and polished, but a great deal of management planning, analysis and decision-making has gone on behind the scenes in order to bring all this to you. By the time you have finished this chapter, you should appreciate the whole range of marketing activities, and the difficulties of managing them.

Example

The humble olive tree is the start of a marketing and distribution process that blossoms into an industry employing 2.5 million people across the EU, roughly one-third of all EU farmers. The large producers are based in Spain, Italy and Greece. Their olives are sent to pressing mills and refineries and eventually end up in brands such as Bestfood's Napolina, available on supermarket shelves.

In the UK, there has traditionally never been the same consumer interest in using olive oil for cooking compared with other European countries. An Italian consumer, for example, typically purchases around 12 litres of olive oil per year compared with the average British consumer's miserly 2 litres. That is changing, however. Recent sales growth levels of around 8.5 per cent per annum have been recorded in the UK as consumers have became aware of the health benefits and the variety of cooking uses. Typical purchasers are ABC1 housewives, aged between 35 and 64.

The UK brand manager for Napolina must make a number of important marketing decisions. There is a need to inform sometimes confused consumers about the different oils and their cooking uses, as there is no tradition of olive oil usage for them to draw on. That in itself is not enough: for Napolina it is important that consumers are aware of its brand and its advantages over its competitors, and thus develop a predisposition to pick up and buy Napolina at the point of sale. The brand must compete with its rivals, so it has to remain fresh and innovative, exploiting the potential of various product variants such as light, mild, and flavoured oils, among others. The brand's distribution network has to be developed and managed through both wholesale and retail outlets to get the product to the mass market. In particular, that can mean persuading supermarkets to stock the Napolina brand rather than, or alongside, others, including the supermarket's own label. All of this, along with decisions on labelling, packaging, pricing, and promotion combine to form the marketing offer.

These marketing decisions are all made within the context of the wider social, business and legislative environment. For example, to improve consumer confidence, the EU has laid down specific olive oil quality and labelling standards to protect and inform the consumer. There are requirements for packaging and labelling covering things such as the list of ingredients, datemarks, the name and address of the manufacturer or packer, and any special information on storage. At the heart of all the brand marketing decisions, however, there must be a clear understanding of customer needs and what it takes to encourage greater consumption across an EU that is far from standard in its acceptance and use of the product (*The Grocer*, 2004; http://www.defra.gov.uk; http://www.europa.eu.int).

Before launching further into detailed descriptions, explanations and analyses of the operational tasks that make up the marketing function, however, it is important to lay a few foundations about what marketing really is, and to give you a more detailed overview of why it is so essential and precisely what it involves in practice.

This section defines and explores marketing as a philosophy of doing business which puts the customer first, and therefore casts the marketing department in the role of 'communicator' between the organisation and the outside world. Marketers have to tackle a surprising wide range of tasks on a daily basis to fulfil that function, and these too are defined. After you read this section, marketing should mean a lot more to you than 'advertising', and you will appreciate that 'making people buy things they don't want' is the one thing that successful marketers do not do.

Marketing defined

This first part of the section is going to explore what marketing is and its evolution. First, we shall look at currently accepted definitions of marketing, then at the history behind those definitions. Linked with that history are the various business orientations outlined on pp. 494–499. These show how marketing is as much a philosophy of doing business as a business function in its own right. It is important to get this concept well established before moving on.

What marketing means

Here are two popular and widely accepted definitions of marketing. The first is the definition preferred by the UK's Chartered Institute of Marketing (CIM), while the second is that offered by the American Marketing Association (AMA):

Marketing is the management process responsible for identifying, anticipating, and satisfying customer requirements profitably. (CIM, 2001)

Marketing is the process of planning and executing the conception, pricing, promotion and distribution of ideas, goods and services to create exchange and satisfy individual and organisational objectives. (AMA, 1985)

Both definitions make a good attempt at capturing concisely what is actually a wide and complex subject. Although they have a lot in common, each says something important that the other does not emphasise. Both agree on the following points.

Marketing is a management process

Marketing has just as much legitimacy as any other business function, and involves just as much management skill. It requires planning and analysis, resource allocation, control and investment in terms of money, appropriately skilled people and physical resources. It also, of course, requires implementation, monitoring and evaluation. As with any other management activity, it can be carried out efficiently and successfully – or it can be done poorly, resulting in failure.

Marketing is about giving customers what they want

All marketing activities should be geared towards this. It implies a focus towards the customer or end consumer of the product or service. If 'customer requirements' are not satisfactorily fulfilled, or if customers do not obtain what they want and need, then marketing has failed both the customer and the organisation.

The CIM definition adds a couple of extra insights.

Marketing identifies and anticipates customer requirements

This phrase has a subtle edge to it that does not come through strongly in the AMA definition. It is saying that the marketer creates some sort of offering only after researching the market and pinpointing exactly what the customer will want. The AMA definition is ambiguous because it begins with the 'planning' process, which may or may not be done with reference to the customer.

---

marketing in action   Welcome aboard

The chances are that most of you will not yet be among the target market for cruise holidays. The general perception of cruises tends to be of formal dinners attended by well-off pensioners enjoying their moment of glory at the Captain's table. On board luxury, gluttony and an endless stream of activities appropriate for those of a typical average age of 55 are occasionally interrupted by brief, highly packaged on-shore visits with minimum interaction with the local culture. Typical passengers with Silversea Cruises, for example, which operates at the premium end of the market, are described as an affluent, sophisticated couple who enjoy the club-like atmosphere, exquisite cuisine and polished service.

Cruise ships now offer exciting experiences in locations that interest a different clientele. This ship docked in Seward, Alaska, boasts a large decktop swimming pool.

Source © Richard Cummins/Corbis

Although the cruise ship vacation market has often experienced some stormy waters associated with international events, especially terrorism, it has still seen significant growth. The number of UK cruise bookings is around one million per annum and globally it was recently forecast that the 11.2 million passengers carried in 2002 will grow to 17 million by 2010. By way of comparison, the UK alone sells conventional package holidays to around 21 million people each year. That is the challenge for the cruise operators such as Silversea Cruises and Cunard. If the appeal can be broadened to stretch the age range down to those who are 45 and over, or even 35 and over, it will help to steer cruises out of a narrow niche into a more mainstream holiday package market.

So, here's the major marketing challenge: how do you make new cruise products more appealing to younger people who might well want a little more than tuxedos and ballroom dancing? The answer may lie in the concept of a floating holiday resort with a wider appeal. Now on offer are a wider range of holiday experiences reflected in different and distinctive brands. Island Cruises has targeted the top end of the package holiday market with cruise holidays starting at £750 per person. Out goes the formality, in come flexible dining times, a choice of restaurants and no fixed table plans. It seeks to reflect the elements of a better quality package holiday within a cruise experience. Action Ashore has gone even further with its range of on-shore activities such as water rafting, jeep safaris, mountain biking and even scuba diving.

Cruise ship offerings are evolving into three main groups:

- Mainstream: First-time cruisers, repeat passengers, young and old alike. Mainstream cruise lines target singles, families, and groups – anyone who is looking for a fun and exhilarating holiday.
- Premium: First-timers and experienced passengers who enjoy a more upmarket experience in lower-key surroundings. Premium lines attract families, singles, and groups. The average age tends to be higher on trips of more than 7–10 days.
- Luxury: Well-heeled couples and singles accustomed to the best travel accommodation and service. Travelling in style to far-flung corners of the globe is the dream of luxury-minded passengers. These cruises are full of 'Enrichment Programs' with celebrity entertainers, scholarly guest speakers, and culinary classes all augmenting more traditional shipboard activities. Libraries are well stocked with books and videos. These adult-orientated luxury cruise lines are usually inappropriate for children and teens. The lack of organised activities makes them unappealing to young families.

Newer brands can position themselves to appeal to different lifestyle and demographic groups, but for established operators such as Cunard there is a need to balance the interests of its established, original target group with the demands of the younger, more active customer who needs to be tempted with more than the basic mainstream experience. Cunard has, for example, relaxed the formal dress code to two nights a week on some cruises. The communications appeal has been changed to focus on the experiences and feelings passengers can enjoy during the holiday rather than depicting just the product, the ship, on-board facilities and shore locations. Widening the target group is not without risk, if the more traditional, experienced cruisers have different expectations from the first timers who have been attracted perhaps by the novelty, lower prices and more informal activities. When passengers on the Aurora suffered from an on-board stomach virus outbreak, some cruisers were accused of poor personal hygiene standards. Some of the traditional, experienced cruisers commented that there has been a 'massive degradation' of the type of people on board cruise ships.

So the marketing offer is evolving but some doubt whether it will really be possible to change the appeal sufficiently to attract a more youthful 35-year-old to cruising. Younger cruisers may make the sector look more appealing, but it is also important to retain customers who value the more traditional offers. New cruise liners, better facilities, interesting activities and new communication strategies may all help, but will the appeal really broaden? As people remain active for longer, perhaps it will only be the late 40s and 50s age groups that will appreciate and take full advantage of the potential for self-development through cruising. In that case, the age range appeal may change only a little, but the expectations may change a lot. Either way, many of us will become prime targets in the end, as an ageing population, the desire for more challenging and fulfilling experiences, and increasing affluence put the cruise experience within the reach of many more than just the original small niche. The smart cruise operators will need to understand the needs of the different customer groups and reflect that in what they offer. And after all what is wrong with a touch of premium luxury?

Sources: Johnson (2003); http://www.cruisediva.com.

Marketing fulfils customer requirements profitably

This pragmatic phrase warns the marketer against getting too carried away with the altruism of satisfying the customer! In the real world, an organisation cannot please all of the people all of the time, and sometimes even marketers have to make compromises. The marketer has to work within the resource capabilities of the organisation, and specifically work within the agreed budgets and performance targets set for the marketing function. Nevertheless, profitability can still be questionable. Marketing practice and, in part, marketing thinking, is now accepted within many non-profit organisations, from schools and universities to hospitals, voluntary organisations and activist groups such as Greenpeace and Friends of the Earth. Each must manage its dealings with its various publics and user groups and manage them efficiently and effectively, but not for profit. That important context aside, most commercial companies exist to make profits, and thus profitability is a legitimate concern. Even so, some organisations would occasionally accept the need to make a loss on a particular product or sector of a market in order to achieve wider strategic objectives. As long as those losses are planned and controlled, and in the longer run provide some other benefit to the organisation, then they are bearable. In general terms, however, if an organisation is consistently failing to make profits, then it will not survive, and thus marketing has a responsibility to sustain and increase profits.

The AMA definition goes further.

Marketing offers and exchanges ideas, goods and services

This statement is close to the CIM's 'profitably', but a little more subtle. The idea of marketing as an exchange process is an important one, and was first proposed by

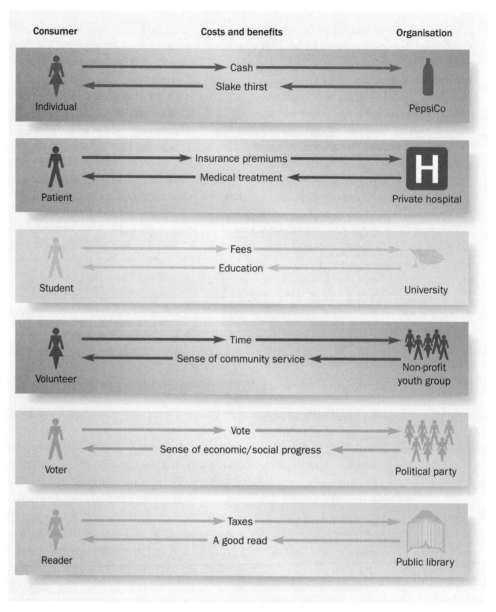

Figure 4.1   Exchange transactions

Alderson (1957). The basic idea is that I've got something you want, you've got something I want, so let's do a deal. For the most part, the exchange is a simple one. The organisation offers a product or service, and the customer offers a sum of money in return for it. Pepsi offers you a can of cola and you offer payment; you sign a contract to offer your services as an employee and the organisation pays you a salary; the hospital offers to provide healthcare and the individual, through taxes or insurance premiums, offers to fund it. A range of further examples is shown diagramatically in Figure 4.1.

What all these examples have in common is the assumption that both parties value what the other has to offer. If they didn't, they would not be obliged to enter into the bargain. It is up to the marketer to make sure that customers value what the organisation is offering so highly that they are prepared to give the organisation what it wants in return. Whether the marketer is offering a product, a service or an idea (such as the environmental causes 'sold' by Greenpeace), the essence of the exchange is mutual value. From mutual value can come satisfaction and possible repeat purchases.

Pricing, promotion and distribution of ideas, goods and services

In saying that marketing involves the conception, pricing, promotion and distribution of ideas, goods and services, the AMA definition is a little more specific in describing the ways in which marketers can stimulate exchanges. It suggests a proactive seller as well as a willing buyer. By designing products, setting sensible, acceptable and justifiable prices, creating awareness and preferences, and ensuring availability and service, the marketer can influence the volume of exchanges. Marketing can be seen, therefore, as a demand management activity on the part of the selling organisation.

Both the CIM and the AMA definitions of marketing, despite their popular usage, are increasingly being criticised as failing to reflect the role and reality of marketing for the twenty-first century. Some criticism concerns the increasing importance of the globalisation of business and the focus on customer retention, relationship building and maintenance that characterises many markets (Christopher *et al.*, 1991; Grönroos, 1997).

Relationship marketing

The traditional definitions of marketing tend to reflect a view that the transaction between buyer and seller is primarily seller-oriented, that each exchange is totally discrete, and thus lacking any of the personal and emotional overtones that emerge in a long-term relationship made up of a series of exchanges between the same buyer and seller. In B2B markets in particular, each of these exchanges could involve a complex web of interactions between the staff of both organisations, each seeking to work together for their mutual benefit against a history of previous exchanges. Dwyer *et al.* (1987), Gummesson (1987) and Turnbull and Valla (1986) particularly highlight the importance of enduring buyer–seller relationships as a major influence on decision-making in international B2B markets.

In some circumstances, however, the traditional non-relationship view is perfectly appropriate. A traveller on an unknown road passing through a foreign country may stop at a wayside café, never visited before and never to be visited again. The decision to purchase is thus going to be influenced by the ease of parking, the décor and the ambience rather than by any feeling of trust or commitment to the patron. The decision, in short, is based on the immediate and specific marketing offering. Well-lit signs, a menu in your own language and visibly high hygiene standards will all influence the decision to stop. This scenario describes an approach to marketing where the focus is on a single exchange or transaction between the buyer and the seller and that influences the seller to make the menu look good, the parking available and the décor attractive. The chances of your becoming a regular customer in this instance are, of course, unlikely unless you are a frequent traveller on that route. In contrast, a relationship-focused approach to marketing describes a network of communications and contacts between the buyer and the seller and a series of exchanges over time. Both parties have to be satisfied with the relationship and achieve their respective objectives from it. Marketing, therefore, is part of an interactive process between people, over time, of which relationship creation, building and management are vital cornerstones (Grönroos, 1997; Sheth *et al.*, 1988). Individual exchanges between buyer and seller are important and influenced by previous experiences, good and bad, but any seller that is concerned with the one-off sale and the immediate gain may find that the longer-term interests of both parties are not well served. Companies such as Volvo have supplier relationships that go back fifty years. Unlike the situation with the single exchange or transaction where profits are expected to follow from today's exchanges, in relationship marketing the time perspective can be very long indeed.

Relationship marketing is not just a B2B phenomenon, however. Internet and direct marketing are creating new opportunities for organisations in mass markets to become much closer to their customers. Consumers often stay loyal to familiar brands, retailers and suppliers for many years and with the enormous power of new technology, individual consumers can be identified and profiles developed, whether through loyalty schemes, monitoring internet shopping behaviour or other ways of capturing detailed information. It is now possible to track the purchase behaviour of individual shoppers and to create a database for directly targeted communication, and with such power it would be a foolish marketer who did not try to maintain customer loyalty and hence improve sales.

| Example |

Fitness clubs have taken relationship marketing seriously in order to hang on to their customers. Over the past ten years membership of fitness clubs has grown significantly and operators such as Holmes Place, Fitness First, LA Fitness and David Lloyd Leisure have all established a share of the market. Mintel (2003) suggests that around 3.6 million Britons were members of private health and fitness clubs at the end of 2002, over 7 per cent of the UK population. Far from being the domain of bodybuilders, fitness is now a popular pastime for under 24s, and older age groups see club membership as a 'fashion and lifestyle statement'. Recruitment is not enough, however. Clubs have to retain their members too and build relationships with them. Holmes Place revamped its website to offer members exclusive health information and it will use a monthly newsletter to keep in touch. LA Fitness went further by launching a new customer relationship management package that uses detailed customer information to target retention campaigns more appropriately. By linking marketing communications with customer profiles the company will be able to track usage behaviours and tailor messages appropriately to particular groups of members (*Precision Marketing*, 2004).

Wider definition of marketing

So, definitions of marketing are moving away from the single exchange, seller-focused perspective adopted by the CIM and AMA definitions towards more socially relevant and relationship-oriented definitions that are considered to reflect the reality of modern marketing far better. Although relationship marketing over time focuses on customers' needs and attitudes as important points of concern, it can also embrace social and ethical concerns as well as issues more directly related to the series of transactions.

A definition that includes the important elements of both the AMA and CIM definitions, but still embraces the evolving relationship orientation, is offered by Grönroos (1997):

> Marketing is to establish, maintain and enhance relationships with customers and other partners, at a profit, so that the objectives of the parties involved are met. This is achieved by mutual exchange and fulfillment of promises.

Such relationships are usually, but not necessarily always, long-term. Some could be little more than a single episode but others could be very enduring. This definition still reflects a managerial orientation towards marketing, but emphasises the mutually active role that both partners in the exchange play. It does not list the activities that marketers undertake, but instead is more concerned with the partnership idea, the concept that marketing is about doing something *with* someone, not doing something *to* them. Of course, not all transactions between buyers and sellers can be considered to be part of a relationship, especially where the purchase does not involve much risk or commitment from the purchaser and thus there is little to gain from entering a relationship (Berry, 1983). This was clearly shown in the wayside café example cited earlier. Overall, however, marketing is increasingly about relationships in both B2B and consumer markets.

The idea of fulfilling promises is also an important one, as marketing is all about making promises to potential buyers. If the buyer decides, after the event, that the seller did not live up to those promises, the chances are that they will never buy again from that seller. If, on the other hand, the buyer decides that the seller has fulfilled their promises, then the seeds of trust are sown, and the buyer may be prepared to begin a long-term relationship with the seller.

Between them, therefore, the three definitions offered say just about everything there is to say about the substance and basic philosophy of marketing. Few would argue with any of that now, but marketing has not always been so readily accepted in that form, as the next two subsections show.

The development of marketing

The basic idea of marketing as an exchange process has its roots in very ancient history, when people began to produce crops or goods surplus to their own requirements and then to barter them for other things they wanted. Elements of marketing, particularly selling and advertising, have been around as long as trade itself, but it took the industrial revolution, the development of mass production techniques and the separation of buyers and sellers to sow the seeds of what we recognise as marketing today.

In the early days, the late nineteenth and early twentieth centuries, goods were sufficiently scarce and competition sufficiently underdeveloped that producers did not really need marketing. They could easily sell whatever they produced ('the production era' in which a 'production orientation' was adopted). As markets and technology developed, competition became more serious and companies began to produce more than they could easily sell. This led to 'the sales era', lasting into the 1950s and 1960s, in which organisations developed increasingly large and increasingly pushy sales forces, and more aggressive advertising approaches (the 'selling orientation').

It was not really until the 1960s and 1970s that marketing generally moved away from a heavy emphasis on post-production selling and advertising to become a more comprehensive and integrated field, earning its place as a major influence on corporate strategy ('marketing orientation'). This meant that organisations began to move away from a 'sell what we can make' type of thinking, in which 'marketing' was at best a peripheral activity, towards a 'find out what the customer wants and then we'll make it' type of market driven philosophy. Customers took their rightful place at the centre of the organisation's universe. This finally culminated, in the 1980s, in the wide acceptance of marketing as a strategic concept, and yet there is still room for further development of the marketing concept, as new applications and contexts emerge.

Historically, marketing has not developed uniformly across all markets or products. Retailers, along with many consumer goods organisations, have been at the forefront of implementing the marketing concept. Benetton, for instance, developed a strong, unique, international product and retail store image, but within the basic formula is prepared to adapt its merchandising and pricing strategies to suit the demands of different geographic markets. The financial services industry, however, has only very recently truly embraced a marketing orientation, some ten years or more behind most consumer goods. Knights *et al.* (1994), reviewing the development of a marketing orientation within the UK financial services industry, imply that the transition from a selling to a marketing orientation was 'recent and rapid'. They cite research by Clarke *et al.* (1988) showing that the retail banks were exceptionally early, compared with the rest of the sector, in becoming completely marketing driven. The rest have since followed.

Business orientations

We discuss below the more precise definitions of the alternative approaches to doing business that were outlined above. We then describe the characteristic management thinking behind them, and show how they are used today. Table 4.1 further summarises this information.

Production orientation

The emphasis with a production orientation is on making products that are affordable and available, and thus the prime task of management is to ensure that the organisation is as efficient as possible in production and distribution techniques. The main assumption is that the market is completely price sensitive, which means that customers are only interested in price as the differentiating factor between competing products and will buy the cheapest. Customers are thus knowledgeable about relative prices, and if the organisation wants to bring prices down, then it must tightly control costs. This is the philosophy of the production era, and was

Table 4.1 Marketing history and business orientations – a summary

Orientation	Focus	Characteristics and aims	Eavesdropping	Main era (generalised)		
				USA	Western Europe	Eastern Europe
Production	Manufacturing	● Increase production ● Cost reduction and control ● Make profit through volume	'Any colour you want – as long as it's black'	Up to 1940s	Up to 1950s	Late 1980s
Product	Goods	● Quality is all that matters ● Improve quality levels ● Make profit through volume	'Just look at the quality of the paintwork'	Up to 1940s	Up to 1960s	Largely omitted
Selling	Selling what's produced – seller's needs	● Aggressive sales and promotion ● Profit through quick turnover of high volume	'You're not keen on the black? What if I throw in a free sun-roof?'	1940–1950s	1950–1960s	Early 1990s
Marketing	Defining what customers want – buyer's needs	● Integrated marketing ● Defining needs in advance of production ● Profit through customer satisfaction and loyalty	'Let's find out if they want it in black, and if they would pay a bit more for it'	1960s onwards	1970s onwards	Mid-1990s onwards
Ethical and sustainable marketing	Serving the needs of the buyer with due respect for the welfare of society and the environment	● Integrated ethical marketing ● Defining needs and designing and producing products to minimise harm/damage ● Profit through customer satisfaction and loyalty, and through societal acceptance	'Let's find out if they want it in black, and then produce it as "greenly" as possible and think about what to do when its useful life ends'	Mid-1990s onwards	Mid-1990s onwards	Late 1990s onwards

predominant in Central and Eastern Europe in the early stages of the new market economies. Apart from that, it may be a legitimate approach, in the short term, where demand outstrips supply, and companies can put all their effort into improving production and increasing supply and worry about the niceties of marketing later.

A variation on that situation happens when a product is really too expensive for the market, and therefore the means have to be found to bring costs, and thus prices, down. This decision, however, is as likely to be marketing as production driven, and may involve technologically complex, totally new products that neither the producer nor the customer is sure of. Thus DVD players, videos, camcorders and home computers were all launched on to unsuspecting markets with limited supply and high prices, but the manufacturers envisaged that with extensive marketing and the benefits gained from progressing along the production and technology learning curve, high-volume markets could be opened up for lower-priced, more reliable products.

Product orientation

The product orientation assumes that consumers are primarily interested in the product itself, and buy on the basis of quality. Since consumers want the highest level of quality for their money, the organisation must work to increase and improve its quality levels. At first glance, this may seem like a reasonable proposition, but the problem is the assumption that consumers *want this product*. Consumers do not want products, they want solutions to problems, and if the organisation's product does not solve a problem, they will not buy it, however high the quality level is. An organisation may well produce the best ever record player, but the majority of consumers would rather buy a cheap CD player. In short, customer needs rather than the product should be the focus.

Example

A modern form of production orientation can occur when an organisation becomes too focused on pursuing a low-cost strategy in order to achieve economies of scale, and loses sight of the real customer need. Tetra Pak, one of the market leaders in carton manufacture, ran into problems in the 1990s by concentrating on the interests of its direct customers rather than those of the end user. The focus was on production efficiency, i.e. how many cartons could be filled per hour, rather than on the problems of actually using a carton. Despite making nearly 90 billion cartons each year, the Swedish company did not fully address the problem that some of the cartons were difficult to open and tended to spill their contents rather easily all over the floor. It clearly had the know-how to solve the problem, but in the pursuit of a low-cost operator position, allowed its rival from Norway, Elo Pak, to develop a pack with a proper spout and a plastic cap that was more in tune with customer needs.

Tetra Pak learnt its lesson about listening to its immediate customers, the carton fillers, and those at next stage in the distribution channel, the grocery trade and ultimately the consumer. Only by understanding everyone's needs is it better able to innovate to deliver the specific solutions the carton fillers want. Thus the benefits claimed for the recently introduced Tetra Recart carton package include portability, easy opening and pouring, and convenient, space-saving stackability in kitchen cupboards. The focus has to be as much on making food safe, available and convenient to the end consumer, as on the cost effectiveness of the fillers' packaging solutions. That said, Tetra Pak still claims that the square shape of Tetra Recart offers efficiency gains throughout the distribution chain because up to 50 per cent more packages can be placed on a standard pallet and the shape also translates into superior on-shelf performance in supermarkets. So, avoiding a production orientation may not be as obvious as first imagined, as it requires close understanding of different levels of the distribution chain. For Tetra Pak it is even more of a challenge as it operates in 165 markets and produces 105 billion packages a year. In case you can't imagine that, all those packs standing end to end would cover a distance equivalent to 16 round trips to the moon (Mans, 2000; http://www.tetrapak.com).

In a review of the history of marketing thinking in China, Deng and Dart (1999) considered the market orientation of traditional state enterprises. From 1949 until economic reform began in 1979, Chinese organisations were part of a very rigid, planned economy. During that time denying marketing was a fundamental part of the political belief system and with a low GDP per capita and widespread scarcity of consumer goods, there was little, if any, incentive for the development of marketing activities (Gordon, 1991). The focus was on manufacturing output and all major marketing decisions such as product range, pricing and selection of distribution channels were controlled by government. The state set production targets for each enterprise, distributed their products, assigned personnel, allocated supplies and equipment, retained all profit and covered all losses (Zhuang and Whitehill, 1989; Gordon, 1991). The priority was production and virtually any product would do.

Since the reforms and the opening up of the economy, most enterprises, even if state-owned, have to now make marketing decisions as they are no longer allocated production inputs, nor are their outputs assigned to prearranged buyers. Price controls have been relaxed and distribution lists from the state ended. However, the transition process is not yet complete: many state-owned enterprises are being subsidised to retain employment levels and government power is still great. Most Chinese brands still have a long way to go before they can challenge European brands in consumer perception. Much of the growth has been based on Western multinationals benefiting from low-cost labour by contracting out the bulk of manufacturing while marketing is handled elsewhere. However, this may be transitory as once Chinese companies have gained experience of high-specification manufacturing, and learned some marketing and global branding skills, they may be better able to exploit the low-cost base themselves and create and establish their own seriously competitive brands (Prystay, 2003).

Sales orientation

The basis for the sales orientation way of thinking is that consumers are inherently reluctant to purchase, and need every encouragement to purchase sufficient quantities to satisfy the organisation's needs. This leads to a heavy emphasis on personal selling and other sales stimulating devices because products 'are sold, not bought', and thus the organisation puts its effort into building strong sales departments, with the focus very much on the needs of the seller, rather than on those of the buyer. Home improvement organisations, selling, for example, double glazing and cavity wall insulation, have tended to operate like this, as has the timeshare industry.

Schultz and Good (2000) proposed that a sales orientation can also emerge from commission-based reward and remuneration packages for sales people, even though the seller might actually want longer-term customer relationships to be established. When the pressure is on to make a sale and to achieve target sales volumes there is a danger that the sales person will focus on the one-off sale rather than the long-term relationship. There is a tension between the need to spend time on relationships and the urge to move on to the next sale.

Marketing orientation

The organisation that develops and performs its production and marketing activities with the needs of the buyer driving it all, and with the satisfaction of that buyer as the main aim, is marketing-oriented. The motivation is to 'find wants and fill them' rather than 'create products and sell them'. The assumption is that customers are not necessarily price driven, but are looking for the total offering that best fits their needs, and therefore the organisation has to define those needs and develop appropriate offerings. This is not just about the core product itself, but also about pricing, access to information, availability and peripheral benefits and services that add value to the product. Not all customers, however, necessarily want exactly the same things. They can be grouped according to common needs and wants, and the organisation can produce a specifically targeted marketing package that best suits the needs of one group, thus increasing the chances of satisfying that group and retaining its loyalty.

marketing in action   Crunch time for Apple?

Apple has had a tough time competing with Microsoft and its PC platform for computers. In the UK its share of the personal computer market for business and consumers slipped to just 1.7 per cent, a situation repeated in many other European markets. Although often the choice for users in the creative industries, Apple just lacked consumer acceptance among other, larger groups of computer users. Although Apple claimed to have a technically superior and easier to use product, its specialised, almost elitist branding did not make much impression on potential buyers.

All that may have been true before the launch of Apple's iPod, its digital music player. The iPod has established a 50 per cent share of the digital music player market despite competition from Microsoft, Virgin and Sony. iTunes, Apple's online music download service, covers 70 per cent of the legal download market, equating to 100 million downloads worldwide. By developing an innovative product that was well matched to a more mobile consumer demanding easy and instant gratification, Apple has become almost the Microsoft of the music download business (Stones, 2004). Not only has iPod been a major contributor to Apple's profits, its success has had a positive effect on sales of Apple's iBook and PowerBook notebook computers through greater brand awareness and loyalty.

By spotting an opportunity and getting into the market first, Apple gained an early and significant lead. It deliberately reassessed its marketing strategy for distribution by opening 101 company-owned retail stores in addition to its online store. By being able to control its own retail space it has been able to give the product appropriate in-store attention to allow high degrees of customer interactivity and to offer over 400 accessories. Apple's pricing was deliberately aligned with a premium perception, at 79p per download in the UK and 68p elsewhere in Europe.

The key question, however, is how long iPod will retain its dominant position. Mobile phone companies keen to expand beyond voice and text messaging have entered the music download market as a way of recouping their huge investments in 3G technology. History is not on the side of iPod. Palm in PDAs (personal digital assistants), Nintendo in game consoles and indeed Apple in PCs are all examples of companies with technological and marketing leads that were subsequently eroded. Often, new competitors come in offering more features at lower prices, taking advantage of further advances. Korean iRiver introduced an MP3 player with a colour screen that also allowed the downloading of photos, and Archos, from France, launched various jukebox-cum-colour photo wallets. Both manufacturers, along with others, sell small, portable devices which play music and video. However, Apple is not standing idly by. Recently it launched the iPod Shuffle, a flash player that costs $99 (with a capacity of 120 songs) or $149 (240 songs). It is the size of a pack of chewing gum, although some commentators believe that Apple must be careful not to cannibalise the higher-priced, feature-packed iPod (Burrows and Park, 2005).

As the market grows and becomes more of a mass market than a niche, Apple might also have to look for new ways to promote iTunes. Currently the focus is on owning the download rather than 'renting' a favourite song on a subscription basis. Subscription services, where a regular monthly premium enables easy and frequent access, is a very low-cost way of exploring music alternatives and discovering new sounds without the need for ownership. Meledo is considering offering subscribers to particular bands early, and semi-exclusive access to new releases at a premium price. It has already launched a service to enable customers to send songs to friends and lovers that enables a free preview.

To give flexibility in pricing and profit management, Apple needs to ensure that economies of scale can be achieved in production, and that means gaining access to a wider cross-section of the market. In part this could be achieved by licensing the technology to other hardware suppliers such as Hewlett Packard and Motorola who will resell the iPod under their own brand names. If Apple could find more alliances such as with Amazon, Cisco and Nokia, it would be in a stronger position to establish a long-term industry standard and to achieve much wider distribution (Burrows and Lowry, 2004).

So Apple will need to be one beat ahead of the rest if it wants to maintain its early lead in a market still in its infancy. This will have implications for all of its marketing activities in an environment that will become more highly competitive as technologies and customer needs evolve.

Sources: Burrows (2004); Burrows and Lowry (2004); Burrows and Park (2005); Durman (2005); *The Economist* (2005); Morrison (2004); Rigby (2004); Stones (2004).

A marketing orientation is far more, however, than simply matching products and services to customers. It has to emerge from an organisational philosophy, an approach to doing business that naturally places customers and their needs at the heart of what the organisation does. Not all organisations do this to the same extent, although many are trying to move towards it.

Henderson (1998), however, urges caution in assuming that a marketing orientation is a guarantee of success in achieving above average performance. There are many internal and external factors at work in determining success, of which effective marketing thinking is but one. If marketing dominates the rest of the organisation it can help to diminish key competencies in other areas such as manufacturing productivity or technological innovation. Furthermore, the marketing department approach to organising the marketing function can isolate marketing from design, production, deliveries, technical service, complaints handling, invoicing and other customer-related activities. As a consequence, the rest of the organisation could be alienated from marketing, making the coordination of customer and market-oriented activities across the organisation more difficult (Piercy, 1992). This underlines the importance of Narver and Slater's (1990) three key factors that help the marketing function to achieve above average performance:

- *Interfunctional orientation* enabling cooperation between the management functions to create superior value
- *Competitor orientation* to retain an edge
- *Customer orientation*.

Having established the importance of the marketing concept to an organisation, the chapter now turns to the issue of how it is developing further to meet the changing demands of society.

Emergent marketing philosophies

The marketing concept and the philosophy of a marketing orientation continue to evolve. In increasingly competitive global markets consisting of increasingly demanding customers, organisations are continually striving to find more effective ways of attracting and retaining customers, and sometimes that could mean refining further exactly what marketing means.

Corporate social responsibility: societal and ethical marketing

Corporate social responsibility suggests that organisations should not only consider their customers and their profitability, but also the good of the wider communities, local and global, within which they exist. As Smith and Higgins (2000) put it, consumers now are not only looking for environmentally sensitive and ethically considerate products, but also for businesses to demonstrate a wider set of ethical commitments to society, '[A business] must, as should we all, become a "good citizen"'. Carroll (1999) provides an excellent review of the history and evolution of the CSR concept, but it is his own 1991 paper which provides the basis for the most succinct definition of CSR which will underpin the coverage of CSR in this section:

> . . . four kinds of social responsibilities constitute total CSR: economic, legal, ethical and philanthropic . . . [B]usiness should not fulfill these in sequential fashion but . . . each is to be fulfilled at all times . . . The CSR firm should strive to make a profit, obey the law, be ethical, and be a good corporate citizen. (Carroll, 1991, pp. 40–3, as summarised by Carroll, 1999)

Marketing within a CSR context is concerned with ensuring that organisations handle marketing responsibly, and in a way that contributes to the well-being of society. Consumers have become increasingly aware of the social and ethical issues involved in marketing, such as the ethics of marketing to children, fair trade with third-world suppliers, the ecological impact of business, and the extent of good 'corporate citizenship' displayed by companies, for example. Companies looking to establish a reputable and trustworthy image as a foundation for building long-term relationships with their customers thus need to consider the philosophy of CSR seriously if they are to meet their customers' wider expectations, and create and maintain competitive advantage (Balestrini, 2001). Indeed, some companies, such as Body Shop, have adopted a very proactive approach to societal marketing and have made CSR a central pillar of their whole business philosophy (see Hartman and Beck-Dudley, 1999 for a detailed discussion of marketing ethics within Body Shop International).

The Responsible Century?, a survey published in 2000 by Burson-Marsteller and the Prince of Wales' Business Leaders' Forum, gathered opinions from 100 leading business opinion-formers and decision-makers from France, Germany and the UK. Two-thirds 'agreed strongly' that CSR will be important in the future and 89 per cent said that their future decisions would be influenced by CSR (CSR Forum, 2001). Interestingly, the survey points to a shift away from defining CSR purely in terms of hard, quantifiable issues such as environmental performance, charitable donations to an emphasis on softer issues such as treatment of employees, commitment to local communities and ethical business conduct. Internal as well as external behaviour now matters.

CSR is rapidly changing from being a 'would like' to a 'must have' feature of business. Although at the time of writing businesses are under no obligation to report on their CSR activities in the UK, many already do and it is likely that pressure for transparency on CSR will only increase. The latest buzzword in corporate accountability is '360 degree reporting' which acknowledges the need to produce annual reports that take a much more holistic view of a company's activities to meet the information needs of pressure groups, those looking for ethical investments, and the wider audience interested in CSR, rather than just shareholders and traditional bankers. Companies in potentially sensitive sectors, such as utilities and transport, have begun to produce separate reports on their CSR performance, for example utility company Kelda Group's annual *Corporate Social Responsibility Review*, water company Severn Trent's *Corporate Responsibility Report*, Network Rail's *Corporate Responsibility Report*, and British Nuclear Fuel's *Corporate Responsibility Report*. These documents may not have the most imaginative titles, but they do represent an important step in the evolution of corporate reporting.

corporate social responsibility in action   Consumers behaving badly?

While we are all so busy demanding that organisations take their CSR seriously, it is perhaps easy to forget that responsibilities and obligations of 'good citizenship' extend to us as consumers as well. Don't organisations also have the right to ask just how ethical their customers are? Babakus *et al.* (2004) undertook a survey across six different countries to explore the nature of consumer ethical beliefs and the influences on them. Eleven behavioural scenarios were presented to respondents who were then asked to indicate their degree of (dis)approval of that behaviour on a 1 to 5 scale, where 1 represented 'wrong' and 5 represented 'not wrong'. Across the whole sample, for instance, respondents tended to regard behaviours such as 'taking towels from hotels and blankets from aircraft as souvenirs' as far less wrong than 'drinking a can of soda in a supermarket and not buying it'. Age and nationality both appeared to be significant influencers. Thus in general, respondents from Brunei, Hong Kong and the USA were more disapproving of the behaviours than respondents from Austria, France and the UK. Younger consumers (aged under 35) from the USA, France and the UK tended to be more tolerant of unethical consumer behaviour than older people. Young French consumers think that there is nothing wrong with 'cutting in when there is a long line' while young Austrians found this the least acceptable of all the scenarios. Interestingly, the Austrian respondents, regardless of age, were far more tolerant of 'reporting a lost item as stolen to

an insurance company to collect the money' than any other nationality.

For marketers, it is perhaps a case of 'caveat vendor' and an indication of the need to make clear to customers what is expected of them and the consequences that will follow unethical behaviour on their part. It is a fine line for organisations to tread, however. Undoubtedly, record companies are well within their legal and ethical rights to take legal action against individuals caught with illegal music downloads, but the publicity given to what are perceived as heavy-handed tactics does not reflect well on corporate reputations. An article in *The Daily Mail* (Poulter, 2005) is a typically emotive report, in that it highlights a couple of individual cases of children as young as 12 receiving demands to pay thousands of pounds in compensation or face legal action. There is an interesting phrase in this article, 'many of those being hit by music industry bosses are ordinary families, rather than criminal gangs', implying that context makes a difference to how behaviour is perceived and judged. However, at least one of the so-called pirates has seen the error of his ways: 'When you compare that with slogging about a music store to buy an album that costs £12 and has only two or three tunes that you like, it's not hard to see why so many people do it. I know it is stealing. I am stealing from someone what they have rightfully earned' (as quoted by Poulter, 2005).

Sources: Babakus *et al.* (2004); Poulter (2005).

Example

Severn Trent plc, based in the UK Midlands, has a turnover of some £1.6 billion and employs over 14,000 people across the UK, US and Europe. With its strapline 'The Environment is Our Business', Severn Trent takes CSR very seriously. As an environmental services company, concerned with water treatment, waste disposal and utilities, it has always been focused on 'green' issues, but its commitment to CSR goes much further than that. In its *Corporate Responsibility Report: Stewardship 2004* it states 'Every business needs ideals above those of simply making money. And no business can operate in isolation from society . . . We believe that business is part of the process of achieving a sustainable future for society as a whole. Business must practice stewardship of natural resources, recognise its role as an integral part of the communities within which it operates, and be accountable for its activities . . . As a business we are both a corporate citizen, with opportunities to shape the lives of the communities where we operate, and an employer, with significant responsibilities for the working environment we provide for our people.' (Severn Trent, 2004, p. 8).

The Stewardship report thus covers many areas of CSR, relating not only to the Group's approach to the protection of the natural environment, biodiversity and the efficient use of natural resources within its operations, but also to its role within society and local communities, its perceived CSR leadership role among its suppliers and customers in improving the performance of the entire supply chain, and its internal application of ethical principles in its HRM policies, for example. All of this is very much in line with Carroll's (1999) ideas of CSR, mentioned earlier.

Towards 'sustainable marketing'

Inextricably tied in with the concept and best practice of CSR in its widest sense is the idea of sustainable development. Sustainability was defined in the Brundtland Report of 1987 as:

> development that meets the needs of the present without compromising the ability of future generations to meet their own needs. (WCED, 1987)

Sustainability is not just concerned with environmental and ecological issues, as important as these are, but also with the social, economic and cultural development of society. The wider 'softer agenda' includes, therefore, the fair distribution of economic benefits, human rights, community involvement and product responsibility. This is taken seriously by business. Echoing the sentiments expressed in the Severn Trent example above, Jurgen Strube, the chairman of BASF, the large German chemical company, said that sustainable development in the areas of the economy, ecology and society will be the key to the success in the twenty-first century (as reported by Challener, 2001). Society cannot continue to enjoy economic growth without reference to the consequences for environmental protection and social stability (*OECD Observer, 2001*).

In the light of the whole CSR/sustainability debate, sustainable marketing is likely to become the next stage in the conceptual development of marketing as it focuses on some of the significant long-term challenges facing society in the twenty-first century. The challenge to marketing thinking is to broaden the concept of exchange to incorporate the longer-term needs of society at large rather than the short-term pursuit of individual gratification and consumption. It is not about marketers revising strategies to exploit new societal opportunities, it is about what society can afford to allow marketers to exploit and over what timescale. This sounds very idealistic: in a competitive world in which the customer is free to choose and, moreover, in which business operates on the principle of meeting customers' needs and wants, it sometimes requires courage for a business to change those principles if those changes precede customer concern and government legislation. Consumers within society will have to travel up a learning curve and that process is only just beginning.

We would, therefore, like to define sustainable marketing as:

> the establishment, maintenance and enhancement of customer relationships so that the objectives of the parties involved are met without compromising the ability of future generations to achieve their own objectives.

In short, consumers today, whatever the market imperative, cannot be allowed to destroy the opportunities for society tomorrow by taking out more than is being put back in. This not only embraces environmental and ecological issues but also the social and cultural consequences of a consumer society that equates 'more' with 'better'.

How does all this impact on the marketing process? The internalisation of costs (making the polluters pay), green taxes, legislation, support for cleaner technology, redesigned products to minimise resources and waste streams, reverse distribution channels to receive products for recycling and consumer education on sustainability are all an essential part of a new marketing agenda for the twenty-first century. To some it is not a choice, but a mandate that cannot be ignored (Fuller, 1999). Ecological and environmental agendas to date have had an impact on marketing strategy, but it has been patchy. The old adage 'reduce, recycle and reuse' has, for example, influenced the type of packaging materials used to ensure recyclability. Clothing manufacturers have produced plastic outdoor clothing that can be recycled; glue manufacturers have reduced the toxic emissions from their products; car manufacturers, in accordance with the EU's End-of-Life Vehicle Directive, now have to consider the recycling or other means of disposal of old cars. However, research often indicates that consumers given a free choice are reluctant to pay more for environmentally friendly products such as organic food and many find it hard to establish the link between their individual buying decision and its global impact. It will require a societal balance and adjustment period, but evidence is mounting that if change does not take place, the negative long-term impact on the environment and society could be irreversible.

Analysing the current situation

Introduction

'Our business is improving our customers' business', says CEO Henning Kagermann of SAP, based in Walldorf, Germany. As head of Europe's largest software company, Kagermann recognizes that customers want SAP to 'help them run their businesses smarter, cheaper and better'.[1] To satisfy customers while achieving corporate goals for growth and profitability, SAP's marketers track developments inside and outside the company, anticipate technological shifts and other environmental changes, then adjust internal capabilities and create a marketing plan to address the opportunities and threats they've identified.

Competition with Oracle, Microsoft and other rivals is one of the biggest external challenges for SAP. Another is the effect of changing customer preferences, which has prompted SAP to introduce new products such as 'on demand' online software. In addition, SAP wants to encourage positive media coverage by maintaining good relations with reporters and bloggers. Finally, to meet its goal of tripling the customer base by 2010, SAP would like to change the misperception that its software is for big corporations only. To do this, its marketing plan called for a multimedia campaign targeting the owners and technology managers of mid-sized companies.[2]

Like their counterparts at SAP, all marketing managers need a thorough understanding of the organization's current situation before they can create appropriate plans and programmes. This section describes Stage 1 of the marketing planning process, in which you collect and interpret data about the internal and external environment. The first part is an overview of environmental scanning and analysis for the marketing plan. The following part discusses particular environmental factors that can make a difference to marketing and performance. The final part looks at how to use the data collected to evaluate your organization's strengths, weaknesses, opportunities and threats for marketing planning purposes.

Environmental scanning and analysis

Early in the marketing planning process, you have to look at the organization's current situation, especially within the context of the mission, higher-level plans and higher-level goals. This is accomplished through environmental scanning and analysis, the systematic (and ongoing) collection and interpretation of data about both internal and external factors that may affect marketing and performance. When learning about the situation inside the organization, marketers use an internal audit; when learning about the situation outside the organization, they use an external audit.

All the relevant information is accumulated, evaluated and distilled into a critique reflecting the organization's primary strengths, weaknesses, opportunities and threats, known as the SWOT analysis. In addition, many marketers conduct a SWOT analysis of current or potential rivals to clarify the competitive situation. This understanding helps you develop a marketing plan to leverage your internal strengths, bolster your internal weaknesses, take advantage of competitors' main weaknesses and defend against competitors' strengths, as shown in Figure 4.2.

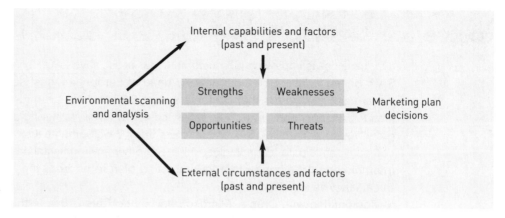

Figure 4.2 Environmental scanning and marketing planning

Details count in any environmental scan, but professional judgement plays a vital role as well. Use your best judgement (supported by other managers' insights, expert models and so on) to develop the most reasonable marketing plan under the circumstances. Over time, work on developing your ability to discern the combined influence of various environmental factors and trends on your firm and its marketing.[3]

Internal audit: identifying strengths and weaknesses

The internal audit covers the mission statement plus your organization's resources and capabilities, current offerings, previous performance, business relationships and key issues. These internal factors, individually and in combination, are instrumental in the way a company fulfils its mission, serves its customers and competes in the marketplace. And – just as important – they contribute to the organization's strengths and weaknesses in using marketing to deal with opportunities and threats.

A **strength** is an internal capability or factor that can help the organization achieve its objectives, making the most of opportunities or deflecting threats. For example, one of Nintendo's great strengths is its technical innovation, exhibited in products such as the Wii game console. Another is its sizeable cash position, which supports innovative new product development and other internal activities.

A **weakness** is an internal capability or factor that may prevent the organization from achieving its objectives or effectively handling opportunities and threats, especially within the competitive context. For instance, Sony had to postpone launching its PlayStation 3 game console until its engineers finalized the standards and technology for its Blu-ray DVD format. This delay was a weakness that opened opportunities for Nintendo's Wii and Microsoft's Xbox consoles. Also it was a setback to Sony's plan for polishing its image after recalling millions of laptop computer batteries.[4]

When auditing your internal strengths and weaknesses, search company records and databases for information such as current offerings, finances, personnel and skills, technological expertise, supplier relations, distributor connections, partnerships, previous marketing plans and results.

External audit: identifying opportunities and threats

The external audit covers political–legal factors, economic factors, social–cultural factors and technological factors (known as *PEST* or *STEP* if the order is rearranged) plus ecological and competitive factors that may present opportunities or pose threats. An opportunity is an external circumstance or factor that the organization can attempt to exploit for higher performance. For example, Cadbury Schweppes found that health-conscious consumers are interested in snacks with little fat and few calories. It also found that consumers now have very positive attitudes toward chewing gum. Therefore, by focusing on gum products like Trident, the firm is enjoying higher turnover and profit margins.[5]

A threat is an external circumstance or factor that could inhibit organizational performance, if not addressed. Cadbury Schweppes markets Dr Pepper, Mott's and other soft drinks, so competition from Coca-Cola and PepsiCo is a major threat. A threat for the company's chocolate and sweets business is the shift toward low-fat, low-calorie treats. Another threat is parents' concern about helping children choose healthier foods. This is why Cadbury Schweppes states: 'We do not vend our confectionery or carbonated beverages in primary schools and will only vend these products in secondary schools by invitation and in line with nutritional guidelines set by the school.'[6]

Sources for an external audit include internal information about customers, suppliers, partners, market share, technical standards; customer feedback through surveys, suggestions, complaints; government, academic or syndicated studies of the market, the industry, competition; industry groups; employees, suppliers, and other partners; media and online reports; special interest groups.

Analysing the internal environment

During an internal audit, you will scan and analyse five main factors: the organization's resources and capabilities; current offerings; previous performance; business relationships; and key issues. You're looking for information that can help you understand your organization's current situation and the strengths you can rely on when implementing a marketing plan.

Organizational resources and capabilities

Core competencies are internal capabilities that contribute to competitive superiority yet are not easily duplicated. Such capabilities are traced to the organization's human, financial, informational and supply resources (see Figure 4.3). One reason Wal-Mart de México has boosted its turnover and profit margin is its core competency in logistics management.

Human resources: Does your company have the people, skills, commitment, rewards to successfully implement your marketing plan?	**Informational resources:** Does your company have the data, tools and access to information to successfully implement your marketing plan?
Specifically examine: • Workforce knowledge, skills, morale, turnover • Top management support • Individual commitment, initiative, entrepreneurial spirit • Recruitment, training, rewards	*Specifically examine:* • Data capture, storage, reporting systems • Analysis tools • Access to timely, accurate, complete information
Financial resources: Does your company have the money to successfully implement your marketing plan?	**Supply resources:** Does your company have the supplies, supply systems and relationships to implement your marketing plan?
Specifically examine: • Funding for marketing activities • Funding for research • Funding for internal support • Anticipated funding for multi-year programmes	*Specifically examine:* • Ample availability of materials, parts, components and services • Supply chain relationships • Inventory management

Figure 4.3   Areas of focus in organizational resources

marketing in practice   Wal-Mart de México

Wal-Mart de México, a subsidiary of the world's largest retailer, has surpassed its local competitors and achieved enviable profitability through its expertise in planning inventory, warehousing goods and getting the right merchandise to the right stores. The retailer operates nearly 800 supermarkets, stores and supercentres.

Its marketing plan calls for tailoring the specific mix of goods and services in each store to the tastes and buying power of the surrounding area. Just as important, the company ensures that shelves are never empty and, in fact, the most popular products are available in abundance – at low, affordable prices.[7]

When planning for marketing, you and your managers must balance the investment and allocation of resources. The organization's values, ethical standards and social responsibility position also affect this balancing act. From a practical standpoint, the internal audit helps managers determine the resources they have, the resources they can obtain and where their resources are currently committed. This is the starting point for identifying any resource gaps and determining how best to allocate resources in support of the marketing plan.

Outsourcing, strategic alliances and supply chain realignment are three ways that organizations can gain or supplement resource arrangements to bridge any gaps for added strength. As an example, rather than devote internal resources to maintaining manufacturing facilities in every region, BMW, Skoda and other automakers serve South Asian markets by outsourcing some manufacturing to India. Fine-tuning the supply chain can help a firm boost on-time delivery and cut the lead time for obtaining supplies.[8]

Current offerings

In this part of the internal audit, you review and analyse the goods and services you currently offer so you know where you stand before making plans to move ahead. Also understand how your organization's offerings relate to the mission and to your resources. Companies generally examine the following, looking at historic and current trends:

- composition, sales and market share of product mix and lines
- customer needs satisfied by features and benefits
- product pricing and profitability, contribution to overall performance
- product age and position in product life cycle
- links to other products.

Previous performance

Although past performance is never a guarantee of future performance, looking at previous results can reveal insights about internal strengths and weaknesses. The purpose is to build on past marketing experience in planning new marketing activities. At a minimum, you will analyse these performance indicators:

- prior year sales (in units and monetary terms)
- prior year profits and other financial results
- historic trends in sales and profits by product, geographic region, customer segment, etc.
- results of previous marketing plans
- customer acquisition, retention and loyalty trends and costs.

Some companies use **data mining**, sophisticated analyses of database information to uncover customer behaviour patterns, to understand previous sales trends, customer loyalty, even the deals that got away. Samsung Electronics America scrutinized data from 10,000 distributors to see how many and what kind of orders it had lost to rivals. It learned that one rival had won 40 per cent of the health-care industry orders that Samsung did not get. As a result, Samsung resolved to strengthen ties with hardware firms serving the health-care field.[9] Similarly, Tesco used data mining of its sales records to identify customers who had not made recent purchases, then sent each a letter with a money-off coupon. Within three months, Tesco had won back 4,800 customers.[10]

Business relationships

As the Samsung example suggests, good business relationships can act as strengths, helping organizations make the most of opportunities or defend against threats and profitably satisfy customers. Among the areas of business relationships to be examined during an internal audit are:

- value added by suppliers, distributors and strategic alliance partners
- internal relationships with other units or divisions
- capacity, quality, service, commitment and costs of suppliers and channel members
- changes in business relationships over time
- level of dependence on suppliers and channel members.

The existence of a business relationship is not in and of itself a strength. Moreover, not having strong connections with vital suppliers or channel members can be a definite weakness when an organization is seeking aggressive growth or simply struggling to survive. On the other hand, close connections with internal divisions or channel members and suppliers can be an important competitive advantage.

Key issues

What specific issues could interfere with the organization's ability to move toward its mission and goals, and what are the warning signs of potential problems? What specific issues are pivotal for organizational success? Some organizations look at key issues more closely, according to customer segment, market or product.

You may need marketing research to get a more complete picture of certain issues. Consider what Unilever's researchers learned from a multinational study of women's attitudes toward beauty and self-image. Respondents said that media and advertising messages depict standards of beauty that most women – including themselves – cannot attain. Understanding this issue helped Unilever identify an opportunity that it pursued through a marketing plan to promote its Dove products with ads featuring women who don't look like supermodels. Younger women, in particular, are responding to Dove's message – which has reshaped Dove's brand image and boosted sales.[11]

Micro segmentation bases

Within a macro segment, a number of smaller micro segments may exist. To focus on these, the organisation needs to have a detailed understanding of individual members of the macro segment, in terms of their management philosophy, decision-making structures, purchasing policies and strategies, as well as their needs and wants. Such information can come from published sources, past experience of the potential buyer, sales force knowledge and experience, word of mouth within the industry, or at first hand from the potential buyer.

An overview of common bases for micro segmentation is given in Table 4.2.

Gathering, collating and analysing such depth of information is, of course, a time-consuming and sometimes difficult task, and there is always the question of whether it is either feasible or worthwhile. However, there are benefits in defining such small segments (even segments of one!) if it enables fine tuning of the marketing offering to suit specific needs. Given the volumes of goods and levels of financial

Table 4.2 Bases for micro segmentation in B2B markets

- Product
- Applications
- Technology
- Purchasing policies
- DMU structure
- Decision-making process
- Buyer–seller relationships

investment involved in some B2B markets, the effort is not wasted. An organisation that has a small number of very important customers would almost certainly treat each as a segment of one, particularly in a market such as the supply of organisation-wide computer systems where individual customer needs vary so much. In contrast, in a market such as office stationery, where standard products are sold to perhaps thousands of B2B customers, any segmentation is likely to centre around groups aggregating many tens of customers on the macro level.

Segmenting consumer markets

Segmenting consumer markets does have some similarities with B2B segmentation, as this section indicates. The main difference is that consumer segments are usually very much larger in terms of the number of potential buyers, and it is much more difficult, therefore, to get close to the individual buyer. Consumer segmentation bases also put more emphasis on the buyer's lifestyle and context, because most consumer purchases fulfil higher-order needs (see, for example, Maslow's hierarchy of needs, discussed in Chapter 3) rather than simply functional ones. The danger is, however, that the more abstract the segments become, the less easily understood they may become by those designing marketing strategies (Wedel and Kamakura, 1999). Each of the commonly used bases is now discussed in turn.

Geographic segmentation

Geographic segmentation defines customers according to their location. This can often be a useful starting point. A small business, for example, particularly in the retail or service sector, operating on limited resources, may look initially for custom within its immediate locale. Even multinationals, such as Heinz, often tend to segment geographically by dividing their global organisation into operating units built around specific geographic markets.

In neither case, however, is this the end of the story. For the small business, simply being there on the High Street is not enough. It has to offer something further that a significant group of customers want, whether it is attractively low prices or a high level of customer service. The multinational organisation segments geographically, partly for the sake of creating a manageable organisational structure, and partly in recognition that on a global scale, geographic boundaries herald other, more significant differences in taste, culture, lifestyle and demand. The Single European Market (SEM) may have created a market of some 450 million potential customers, yet the first thing that most organisations are likely to do is to segment the SEM into its constituent nations.

Example

> Take the marketing of an instant hot chocolate drink, made with boiling water. In the UK, virtually every household owns a kettle, and hot chocolate is viewed either as a bedtime drink or as a substitute through the day for tea or coffee. In France, however, kettles are not common, and hot chocolate is most often made with milk as a nourishing children's breakfast. Thus the benefits of speed, convenience and versatility that would impress the UK market would be less applicable in the French market. France would require a very different marketing strategy at best or, at worst, a completely different product.

Geographic segments are at least easy to define and measure, and information is often freely available from public sources. This kind of segmentation also has an operational advantage, particularly in developing efficient systems for distribution and customer contact, for example. However, in a marketing-oriented organisation, this is not sufficient. Douglas and Craig (1983), for example, emphasise the dangers of being too geographically focused and making assumptions about what customers in a region might have in common. Even within a small geographic area, there is a wide variety of needs and wants, and this method on its own tells you nothing about them. Heinz divides its global operation into geographically based subdivisions because it does recognise the effects of cultural diversity and believes in 'local marketing' as the best means of fully understanding and serving its various markets. It is also important to note that any organisation segmenting purely on geographic grounds would be vulnerable to competition coming in with a more customer-focused segmentation strategy.

Demographic segmentation

Demographic segmentation tells you a little more about the customer and the customer's household on measurable criteria that are largely descriptive, such as age, sex, race, income, occupation, socioeconomic status and family structure.

Demographics might even extend into classifications of body size and shape! It has been suggested that any male with a waist over 102 cm or female with a waist over 88 cm should consider it a warning of obesity. That amounts to an awful lot of people, especially in the UK, Germany and the USA, where the working classes are relatively affluent (Stuttaford, 2001). Over 9 million people in the UK alone are classified as clinically obese and are at risk of weight-related illness. That could be good news for some pharmaceutical and diet food manufacturers, but it presents a challenge to some other business sectors. Clothing retailers such as High and Mighty and Evans primarily target larger men and women respectively. Other retailers have to get their mix of stock sizes right to meet seasonal demand. Marks and Spencer, for example, undertook a survey of 2500 women and found that the average dress size is now a 14 whereas in 1980 it was a 12. Transport operators such as airlines and railways have even bigger problems. Economy-class seats on many aircraft are around 26 inches wide which is pretty cramped, even for those of us who are not built along the lines of a Sumo wrestler! The increasing size of travellers as well as the bad publicity about deep vein thrombosis being associated with sitting in cramped aircraft on long-haul flights is making airlines rethink their seating arrangements. Train operators are less concerned, however. In a push to cram more passengers into a carriage, modern rolling stock actually offers 6 inches less seat-room for commuters than carriages built in the 1970s (Bale, 2001).

marketing in action   An uplifting tale of a developing market

So, how do you segment the bra market? Clearly manufacturers are primarily (but not exclusively) (don't ask!) targeting women, but that is only the beginning. The British bra and lingerie company Gossard has found that a geographic approach to market segmentation can have some validity. The types of product that sell best in various countries are different, partly for the practical reason that women vary in average size across Europe, and partly because of cultural and lifestyle factors. Italian women want to be seductive and thus buy a lot of basques; the Germans are practical and look for support and quality; the French want to be fashionable and impress other women; and the Scandinavians want natural fibres. This is, of course, a grossly generalised survey, but the basic trends are there and give Gossard a basis for developing appropriate new products and strategies for different markets.

You might think that bra size is a useful segmentation variable that cuts across geographic boundaries, and indeed it is: the needs and priorities of larger women perhaps wanting to minimise the impact of their assets are very different from those of smaller women wanting to maximise them. The Wonderbra, for instance, was designed to target younger women, aged between 15 and 25, wanting a fashionable, fun, sexy bra that allows them to make the most of their assets. This appeal was reinforced by advertising slogans such as 'Hello, Boys', 'Mind If I Bring a Couple of Friends?' and 'In Your Dreams' alongside scantily clad, beautiful models. Even so, the marketers have to take into account more complex lifestyle issues as fashions change. Wonderbra's success is

not just about the proportion of smaller-breasted women within the population but also the trend towards more revealing clothes and the desirability of cleavage. The Deep Plunge range from Wonderbra launched in 2005 capitalises on that by being specifically designed to enhance current clothing fashions. Aiming at a slightly older, more sophisticated consumer, Gossard has launched the Super Smooth which, it claims, gives all the uplift of the Wonderbra but is unique because it has no seams, stitching or elastic. It is designed to be invisible under clothing so that the emphasis is on the effect of the bra rather than on the bra as a garment in its own right.

Marketing managers within this market do, however, need to keep an eye on how the

Lorna and her friends air their customised bras after undertaking the Playtex Moonwalk in London to raise money for breast cancer charities.

Source: © Lorna Young

consumer profile is changing. Industry research has indicated that over the last ten years or so, the average British bust size has increased from 34B to 36C or D, and nearly one-third of British women wear a D cup or larger. This is perhaps less than good news for Wonderbra, but excellent for companies like Bravissimo that specialise in larger sizes.

Nevertheless, underlying (or should that be underwiring?) all this is a remarkable consensus about the core features and benefits that women want from their bras. According to Gossard, 98 per cent want comfort (so what do the other 2 per cent want?!); 83 per cent consider underwear 'as a pleasure and enjoy the fancy and refined side of it'; 78 per cent want silhouette enhancement and 77 per cent want underwear that is invisible under clothing. So whatever you are looking for, whether it's frills, thrills, or functionality, the right bra is out there somewhere.

Sources: Baker (2004); Broadhead (1995); *Marketing Week* (2004a; 2004b); http://www.gossard.co.uk.

As with the geographic variable, demographics are relatively easy to define and measure, and the necessary information is often freely available from public sources. The main advantage, however, is that demographics offer a clear profile of the customer on criteria that can be worked into marketing strategies. For example, an age profile can provide a foundation for choice of advertising media and creative approach. Magazines, for instance, tend to have readerships that are clearly defined in terms of gender, age bands and socioeconomic groups. The under-35 female reader, for example, is more likely to go for magazines such as *Marie Claire*, *Bella* and *Cosmopolitan* than the over-35s who are more likely to read *Prima*, *Good Housekeeping* and *Family Circle*.

On the negative side, demographics are purely descriptive and, used alone, assume that all people in the same demographic group have similar needs and wants. This is not necessarily true (just think about the variety of people you know within your own age group).

Additionally, as with the geographic method, it is still vulnerable to competition coming in with an even more customer-focused segmentation strategy. It is best used, then, for products that have a clear bias towards a particular demographic group. For instance, cosmetics are initially segmented into male/female; baby products are primarily aimed at females aged between 20 and 35; school fee endowment policies appeal to households within a higher income bracket at a particular stage of the family lifecycle. In most of these cases, however, again as with the geographic method, the main use of demographic segmentation is as a foundation for other more customer-focused segmentation methods.

Geodemographic segmentation

Geodemographics can be defined as 'the analysis of people by where they live' (Sleight, 1997, p. 16) as it combines geographic information with demographic and sometimes even lifestyle data (see below) about neighbourhoods. This helps organisations to understand where their customers are, to develop more detailed profiles of how those customers live, and to locate and target similar potential customers elsewhere. A geodemographic system, therefore, will define types of neighbourhood and types of consumer within a neighbourhood according to their demographic

Table 4.3 Mosaic UK™ Group E: Urban Intelligence, Type E34: Town Gown Transition

- Older areas of large provincial cities close to universities, likely to consist of better quality early twentieth-century terraced housing with front gardens.
- Likely to be close to parks and strips of older shops, now including convenience stores, cheap restaurants and takeaways.
- Likely to be on bus routes and within easy cycling or walking distance of university campuses.
- Residents mainly aged around mid-20s and likely to be mature students, postgraduate or research students, or young lecturers. May also be young graduates working in professional jobs outside academia.
- Residents tend to be single and sociable, enjoying drinking, clubbing, cinema and generally 'hanging out' with their friends.
- They are idealistic and headstrong; concerned with international issues; sceptical of global corporations and brands; likely to sympathise with organisations such as Greenpeace and Friends of the Earth.
- They are likely to be *Guardian* readers.
- They are willing to recognise other cultures and are tolerant of immigrants.
- They are short of money, but not especially materialistic. They are not confident about financial management and they are not good at managing what money they do have.
- They are adventurous risk-takers who enjoy travel, and they are ambitious for their careers.
- They are at a transition stage of their lives and are likely to mature into lifestyles similar to those of their parents.

Source: © Experian Ltd, 2006. All rights reserved. The word 'Experian' is a registered trademark in the EU and other countries and is owned by Experian Ltd and/or its associated companies.

and lifestyle characteristics. Table 4.3 gives an example of how Experian's Mosaic UK™ profiles one of its neighbourhood types.

A number of specialist companies, including Experian, offer geodemographic databases. Most of them are generally applicable to a range of consumer markets, although some are designed for specific industries, and others have developed a range of variations on the main database to suit different industries or geographic regions.

Geodemographic systems are increasingly becoming available as multimedia packages. Mosaic™ is available on CD-ROM, giving the manager access to colour maps, spoken commentary on how to use the system, photographs and text. Experian and other providers are also working on customised geodemographic packages, tailored to suit a particular client's needs.

Example

Door-to-door marketing has evolved still further in its ability to target individual homes. Blanket drops of product samples or sales literature have been used for some time by consumer goods marketers, but the increasing refinement of databases has led to more sophisticated targeting. TNT Post (Doordrop Media) Ltd, a leading door-to-door drop company, has launched its *Personal Placement* service which can match a purchased or client-provided database with geodemographic neighbourhoods from ACORN, Mosaic™, etc. to identify those areas with a reasonable proportion of target households. Within each neighbourhood postcode there are around 2500 homes, and there are 8900 postcodes in the UK. By adopting a micro-targeting system, units as small as 700 households can be identified to reflect differences in housing types even within a neighbourhood. This, matched with mailing lists and databases, enables cost-effective, better targeted door-to-door delivery.

Experian's Mosaic™ geodemographic system is available on CD-ROM, thus enhancing its user-friendliness and flexibility.

Such systems are invaluable to the marketer across all aspects of consumer marketing, for example in planning sampling areas for major market research studies, or assessing locations for new retail outlets, or finding appropriate areas for a direct mail campaign or door-to-door leaflet drop.

Psychographic segmentation

Psychographics, or lifestyle segmentation, is an altogether more difficult area to define, as it involves intangible variables such as the beliefs, attitudes and opinions of the potential customer. It has evolved in answer to some of the shortcomings of the methods described above as a means of getting further under the skin of the customer as a thinking being. The idea is that defining the lifestyle of the consumer allows the marketer to sell the product not on superficial, functional features, but on benefits that can be seen to enhance that lifestyle on a much more emotional level. The term *lifestyle* is used in its widest sense to cover not only demographic characteristics, but also attitudes to life, beliefs and aspirations.

marketing in action   C'est la vie!

Mazzoli (2004) reports extensive market research that was undertaken in France to define and describe various lifestyle segments within the French youth market (aged 15–25). Six distinct 'tribes' emerged:

- *TV Addicts*: accounting for 39 per cent of the respondents, just over half the members of this tribe are female. They tend to live in small towns of fewer than 2000 inhabitants. As the label suggests, they like to watch television and they particularly enjoy series such as Charmed, Buffy the Vampire Slayer and Smallville. Not surprisingly, they identify with celebrities from the audio-visual world, such as Ben Affleck, Johnny Depp, Madonna, Robbie Williams, Tom Cruise, Brad Pitt and Steven Spielberg. Their favourite brands are Levis, Celio, Etam, Adidas and Hugo Boss.
- *Lolita Spirit*: accounting for 16 per cent of the respondents, 81 per cent of this tribe are female, and mostly aged between 20 and 25. They have mainly left the parental home and are living either alone or within a couple. Their favourite celebrities include Evelyne Thomas, Laura Pausini, Nolwenn and Séverinne Ferrer. Like the TV Addicts, Levis, Adidas and Etam are among their favourite brands along with Camaieu and Agnès B.
- *Electro Party*: comprising 8 per cent of the respondents, this tribe likes electronic music and its icons, such as Daft Punk, Carl Cox, Jeff Mills and Laurent Garnier. Members of this tribe are aged between 20 and 25, tend to live alone and are predominantly male. They tend to live in and around Paris. Their favoured brands are Mango, H&M, Dior, Diesel and Zara.
- *Noisy Provocation*: this tribe (5 per cent of respondents) is a little younger in profile, between 15 and 19 years old, and thus live in the parental home and are still in full-time education. Mostly male, this tribe likes provocative and/or strong celebrities such as Johnny Knoxville, Marilyn Manson, Björk and Kurt Kobain. Brands they like include Oxbow, Adidas, Decathlon, Quiksilver and Hugo Boss.
- *Hip Hop Fiction*: again young in profile, between 15 and 19 years old, this tribe (14 per cent of respondents) likes its Hip Hop. Artists and celebrities such as Eminem, Puff Daddy, Saian Supa Crew, Halle Berry, Will Smith and Djamel Debouzze appeal to them. Just over half this tribe is female, and their favoured brands include Levis, Adidas, Puma, Hugo Boss and Nike.
- *French Pride*: this tribe, 18 per cent of respondents, has a strong social conscience and a strong pride in 'Frenchness'. They admire the Dalai Lama, and French personalities such as Matthieu Kassovitz, Vincent Cassel and Olivier Besancenot. They live in large towns and cities (more than 100,000 inhabitants) and tend to be the oldest among the total sample surveyed. Their favoured brands include Zara, Levis, Dim, Hugo Boss and Diesel.

Plummer (1974) was an early exponent of lifestyle segmentation, breaking it down into four main categories: activities, interests, opinions and demographics.

Activities

The activities category includes all the things people do in the course of their lives. It therefore covers work, shopping, holidays and social life. Within that, the marketer will be interested in people's hobbies and their preferred forms of entertainment, as well as sports interests, club memberships and their activities within the community (voluntary work, for instance).

Interests

Interests refers to what is important to the consumer and where their priorities lie. It may include the things very close to them, such as family, home and work, or their interest and involvement in the wider community. It may also include elements of leisure and recreation, and Plummer particularly mentions areas such as fashion, food and media.

Opinions

The category of opinions comes very close to the individual's innermost thoughts, by probing attitudes and feelings about such things as themselves, social and cultural issues and politics. Opinion may also be sought about other influences on society, such as education, economics and business. Closer to home for the marketer, this category will also investigate opinions about products and the individual's view of the future, indicating how their needs and wants are likely to change.

Demographics

Demographic descriptors have already been extensively covered, and this category includes the kinds of demographic elements you would expect, such as age, education, income and occupation, as well as family size, lifecycle stage and geographic location.

By researching each of these categories thoroughly and carefully, the marketer can build up a very detailed and three-dimensional picture of the consumer. Building such profiles over very large groups of individuals can then allow the marketer to aggregate people with significant similarities in their profiles into named lifestyle segments. As you might expect, because lifestyles are so complex and the number of contributory variables so large, there is no single universally applicable typology of psychographic segments. Indeed, many different typologies have emerged over the years, emphasising different aspects of lifestyle, striving to provide a set of lifestyle segments that are either generally useful or designed for a specific commercial application.

In the USA, for example, advertising agencies have found the Values And Life Style (VALS-2) typology, based on Mitchell (1983), particularly useful. The typology is based on the individual's *resources*, mainly income and education, and *self-orientation*, i.e. attitude towards oneself, one's aspirations and the things one does to communicate and achieve them. The segments that emerge include, for example, *Achievers*, who fall within the category of 'status-oriented'. They have abundant resources and are career minded with a social life that revolves around work and family. They mind very much what other people think of them, and particularly crave the good opinion of those who they themselves admire. The implication is that Achievers have largely 'made it' in terms of material success, in contrast to *Strivers* (who are likely to be Achievers in the future) and *Strugglers* (who aspire to be Achievers, but may never make it). Both these segments are also status-oriented, but are less well endowed with resources and still have some way to go.

Schoenwald (2001) highlighted some of the dangers in taking psychographic segmentation so far that the relationship between segment characteristics and brand performance becomes lost. Although it may be useful for identifying broad trends, segment boundaries can change as the market changes and some individuals may not fit categories easily or neatly, for example being conservative on financial issues yet highly progressive when it comes to embracing high technology. Schoenwald reminds us that segmentation is a marketing tool for defining markets better and must, therefore, be actionable and not confusing.

Example

The 6 million vegetarians in the UK are members of an attractive segment defined in terms of the values that these consumers hold. Meat-free brand Quorn, with sales worth £95m per annum, has benefited not only from a demand for vegetarian meat substitutes, but also from demand for healthier food generally. The market as a whole was worth worth £626m in 2004, having increased by 38 per cent over five years.

Quorn's strapline 'It might just surprise you' reflects its repositioning as a mainstream healthy food brand rather than just appealing to vegetarians. The potential health dangers of red meat are increasingly being understood, so meat-free products are picking up new consumers who may not be fully vegetarian. It is these meat reducers and healthy eaters that have become the main target for meat-free foods. It has been estimated that 45 per cent of UK households are reducing their meat intake, so the potential market is very

'I can't believe it's not meat!' The wide variety of Quorn products now available indicates the broader customer base being targeted.

Source: © Quorn http://www.quorn.co.uk

large indeed as long as producers can overcome any consumer prejudices about vegetarian food being boring or 'cranky'. It is true that bean burgers, soya sausages and nut cutlets represent over half the sales in the category, but snacks and deli-type products are growing fast, with 16 per cent of sales. Ready meals, accounting for around 25 per cent of sales, have declined, however, but that is expected to change as manufacturers develop new varieties and taste appeals (*Campaign*, 2005; *Marketing Week*, 2005).

Within the SEM, many organisations have been trying to produce lifestyle-based psychographic segment profiles that categorise the whole of Europe. One such study, carried out by Euro Panel and marketed in the UK by AGB Dialogue, was based on an exhaustive 150-page questionnaire administered across the EU, Switzerland and Scandinavia. The main research areas covered included demographic and economic factors, as well as attitudes, activities and feelings. Analysis of the questionnaire data allowed researchers to identify sixteen lifestyle segments based on two main axes, innovation/conservatism and idealism/materialism. The results also identified twenty or so key questions that were crucial to matching a respondent with an appropriate segment. These key questions were then put to a further 20,000 respondents, which then allowed the definition of sixteen segments, including for example Euro-Citizen, Euro-Gentry, Euro-Moralist, Euro-Vigilante, Euro-Romantic and Euro-Business.

Despite the extent and depth of research that has gone into defining typologies such as these, they are still of somewhat limited use. When it comes to applying this material in a commercial marketing context, the marketer still needs to understand the underlying national factors that affect the buying decisions for a particular product.

Nevertheless, there are compelling reasons for such methods of segmentation being worth considering and persevering with, despite their difficulties. Primarily, they can open the door to a better-tailored, more subtle offering to the customer on all aspects of the marketing mix. This in turn can create a strong emotional bond between customer and product, making it more difficult for competitors to steal customers. Euro-segmentation adds a further dimension, in that it has the potential to create much larger and more profitable segments, assuming that the logistics of distribution allow geographically dispersed members of the segment to be reached cost effectively, and may thus create pan-European marketing opportunities.

The main problem, however, as we have seen, is that psychographic segments are very difficult and expensive to define and measure. Relevant information is much less likely to exist already in the public domain. It is also very easy to get the implementation wrong. For example, the organisation that tries to portray lifestyle elements within advertisements is depending on the audience's ability to interpret the symbols used in the desired way and to reach the desired conclusions from them. There are no guarantees of this, especially if the message is a complex one. Additionally, the user of Euro-segments has to be very clear about allowing for national and cultural differences when trying to communicate on lifestyle elements.

In summary, psychographic segmentation works well in conjunction with demographic variables to refine further the offering to the customer, increasing its relevance and defendability against competition. It is also valuable for products that lean towards psychological rather than functional benefits for the customer, for instance perfumes, cars, clothing retailers, etc. For such a product to succeed, the marketer needs to create an image that convinces consumers that the product can either enhance their current lifestyle or help them to achieve their aspirations.

Behaviour segmentation

All the categories of segmentation talked about so far are centred on the customer, leading to as detailed a profile of the individual as possible. Little mention has been made, however, of the individual's relationship with the product. This needs to be addressed, as it is quite possible that people with similar demographic and/or psychographic profiles may yet interact differently with the same product. Segmenting a market in these terms, therefore, is known as behaviour segmentation.

End use

What is the product to be used for? The answer to this question has great implications for the whole marketing approach. Think about soup, for instance. This is a very versatile product with a range of potential uses, and a wide variety of brands and product lines have been developed, each of which appeals to a different usage segment. A shopper may well buy two or three different brands of soup, simply because their needs change according to intended use, for example a dinner party or a snack meal. At this point, demographic and psychographic variables may become irrelevant (or at least secondary) if the practicalities of usage are so important to the customer. Table 4.4 defines some of the possible end uses of soup and gives examples of products available on the UK market to serve them.

Benefits sought

This variable can have more of a psychological slant than end usage and can link in very closely with both demographic and psychographic segments. In the case of a car, for example, the benefits sought may range from the practical ('reliable'; 'economic to run'; 'able to accommodate mum, dad, four kids, a granny, a wet dog and the remains of a picnic') to the more psychographically oriented ('environmentally friendly'; 'fast and mean'; 'overt status symbol'). Similarly, the benefits sought from a chilled ready meal might be 'ease of preparation', 'time saving', 'access to dishes I could not make myself', 'a reassuring standby in case I get home late one evening', and for the low-calorie and low-fat versions, 'a tasty and interesting variation on

Table 4.4 Usage segmentation in the soup market

Use	Brand examples
Dinner party starter	Baxter's soups; Covent Garden soups
Warming snack	Crosse & Blackwell's soups
Meal replacement	Heinz Wholesoups
Recipe ingredient	Campbell's Condensed soups
Easy office lunch	Batchelor's Cup-a-Soups

my diet!' It is not difficult to see how defining some of these *benefit segments* can also indicate the kinds of demographic or lifestyle descriptors that apply to people wanting those benefits.

> A new entrant in the chilled ready meals sector, Naked, is targeting those consumers who want healthy, tasty food without having to spend any significant time in preparation. The steamed meals and pan-fried dishes in exotic flavours within the Naked range are targeting professionals on the basis of the benefits being offered. Of course, the choice of brand name is purely incidental in that process! (*The Grocer*, 2005).

Usage rate

Not everyone who buys a particular product consumes it at the same rate. There will be heavy users, medium users and light users. Figure 4.4 shows the hypothetical categorisation of an organisation's customer base according to usage. In this case, 20 per cent of customers account for 60 per cent of the organisation's sales. This clearly raises questions for marketing strategies, for example should we put all our resources into defending our share of heavy users? Alternatives might be to make light users heavier; to target competitors' heavy users aggressively; or even to develop differentiated products for different usage rates (such as frequent-wash shampoo).

Again, this segmentation variable can best be used in conjunction with others to paint a much more three-dimensional picture of the target customer.

Loyalty

As with usage rate, loyalty could be a useful mechanism, not only for developing detail in the segment profile, but also for developing a better understanding of

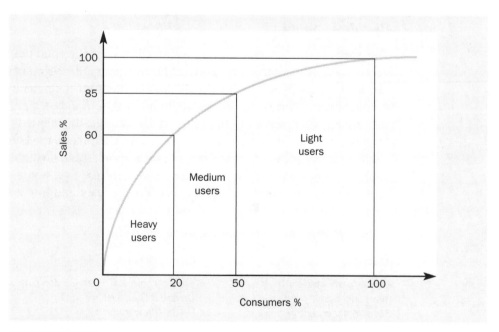

Figure 4.4   Consumer product usage categories

which segmentation variables are significant. For instance a carefully thought-out market research exercise might help an organisation to profile 'loyal to us', 'loyal to them' and 'switchers', and then discover what other factors seem to differentiate between each of these groups. More specifically, Wind (1982) identified six loyalty segments as follows:

1 Current loyal users who will continue to purchase the brand
2 Current customers who might switch brands or reduce consumption
3 Occasional users who might be persuaded to increase consumption with the right incentives
4 Occasional users who might decrease consumption because of competitors' offerings
5 Non-users who might buy the brand if it was modified
6 Non-users with strong negative attitudes that are unlikely to change.

What is certain is that brand loyalty can be a fragile thing, and is under increasing threat. This is partly as a result of the greater number of alternative brands available and incentives or promotions designed by competitors to undermine customer loyalty. The most serious threat in the UK, however, has come from supermarket own-brands, many of which look uncannily like the equivalent manufacturer brands but undercut them on price. Consumers thus believe that the own-brands are just as good, if not identical, and are thus prepared to switch to them and to be more price sensitive.

Assuming that loyalty does exist, even a simple combination of usage rate and loyalty begins to make a difference to the organisation's marketing strategy. If, for example, a large group of heavy users who are also brand switchers was identified, then there is much to be gained from investing resources in a tightly focused marketing mix designed to turn them into heavy users who are loyal to a particular company.

Attitude

Again, trespassing on the psychographic area, attitude looks at how the potential customer feels about the product (or the organisation). A set of customers who are already enthusiastic about a product, for example, require very different handling from a group who are downright hostile. A hostile group might need an opportunity to sample the product, along with an advertising campaign that addresses and answers the roots of their hostility. Attitude-based segments may be important in marketing charities or causes, or even in health education. Smokers who are hostile to the 'stop smoking' message will need different approaches from those who are amenable to the message and just need reassurance and practical support to put it into practice. Approaches aimed at the 'hostile' smoker have included fear ('look at these diseased lungs'), altruism ('what about your children?') and vanity (warning young women about the effect on their skin), but with little noticeable effect.

Buyer readiness stage

Buyer readiness can be a very valuable variable, particularly when one is thinking about the promotional mix. How close to purchasing is the potential customer? For

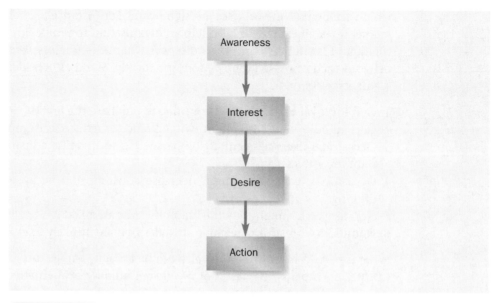

Figure 4.5　The AIDA response hierarchy model

example, at a very early stage the customer may not even be aware that the product exists, and therefore to get that customer moving closer to purchase, the organisation needs to generate *awareness* of the product. Then there is a need for information to stimulate *interest* in the product. The customer's ability to understand and interpret that information may lead to *desire* for the product, which in turn stimulates *action*: the purchase itself.

Figure 4.5 summarises this progression.

Behavioural segmentation, therefore, examines closely the relationship between the potential customer and the product, and there are a number of dimensions on which this can be done. Its main achievement is to bring the relationship between customer and product into sharper focus, thus providing greater understanding of the customer's specific needs and wants, leading to a better defined marketing mix. Another advantage of this kind of segmentation approach is that it provides opportunities for tailored marketing strategies to target brand switchers or to increase usage rates. All these benefits do justify the use of behavioural segmentation, as long as it does not lead to the organisation becoming product centred to the neglect of the customer's needs. The customer must still come first.

Multivariable segmentation

As has been hinted throughout the previous sections, it is unlikely that any one segmentation variable will be used absolutely on its own. It is more common for marketers to use a multi-variable segmentation approach, defining a 'portfolio' of relevant segmentation variables, some of which will be prosaic and descriptive while others will tend towards the psychographic, depending on the product and market in question. The market for adult soft drinks includes age segmentation along with some usage considerations (for example as a substitute for wine as a meal accompaniment), some benefit segmentation (healthy, refreshing, relaxing), and lifestyle elements of health consciousness, sophisticated imagery and a desire for exotic ingredients. Similarly, the banking sector is moving from traditional segmentation based upon corporate and retail customers to approaches aimed at creating segments based upon combinations of customer attitudes towards bank services and expected benefits. Simply grouping customers according to demographic criteria failed to reflect their attitudes towards technology and their readiness to use it, which could be strategically important as internet banking develops further (Machauer and Morgner, 2001).

The emergence of geodemographics in recent years, as discussed above, is an indicator of the way in which segmentation is moving, that is, towards multi-variable systems incorporating psychographics, demographics and geographics. These things are now possible and affordable because of increasingly sophisticated data collection mechanisms, developments in database creation and maintenance and cheaper, more accessible computing facilities. A properly managed database allows the marketer to go even further and to incorporate behavioural variables as the purchaser develops a trading history with a supplier. Thus the marketers are creeping ever closer to the individual consumer. The UK supermarkets that have developed and launched store loyalty cards that are swiped through the checkout so that the customer can accumulate points towards discounts, for example, are collecting incredibly detailed information about each individual shopper's profile. It tells them when we shop, how often, which branches of the store we tend to use, how much we spend per visit, the range of goods we buy, and the choices we make between own brands and manufacturer brands. The supermarkets can use this information to help them define meaningful segments for their own customer base, to further develop and improve their overall marketing mix or to make individually tailored offers to specific customers.

Implementation of segmentation

This section so far has very freely used the phrase 'segmenting the market', but before segmentation can take place, there has to be some definition of the boundaries of that market. Any such definition really has to look at the world through the consumer's eyes, because the consumer makes decisions based on the evaluation of alternatives and substitutes. Thus a margarine manufacturer cannot restrict itself to thinking in terms of 'the margarine market', but has to take a wider view of 'the spreading-fats market' which will include butter and vegetable oil based products alongside margarine. This is because, generally speaking, all three of these product groups are contending for the same place on the nation's bread, and the consumer will develop attitudes and feelings towards a selection of brands across all three groups, perhaps through comparing price and product attributes (for example taste, spreadability, cooking versatility and health claims). This opens up a much wider competitive scene, as well as making the margarine manufacturer think more seriously about product positioning and about how and why consumers buy it.

This whole issue of market definition and its implications for segmenta-tion comes back, yet again, to what should now be the familiar question of 'What business are we in?' It is a timely reminder that consumers basically buy solutions to problems, not products, and thus in defining market segments, the marketer should take into account any type of product that will provide a solution. Hence we are not in 'the margarine market', but in the 'lubricating bread' market, which brings us back full circle to the inclusion of butter and vegetable oil based spreads as direct competitors.

It is still not enough to have gone through the interesting exercise of segmenting a market, however it is defined. How is that information going to be used by the organisation to develop marketing strategies? One decision that must be made is how many segments within the market the organisation intends to target. We look first at targeting.

Targeting

There are three broad approaches available, summarised in Figure 4.6, and discussed in detail below.

Concentrated

The concentrated approach is the most focused approach of the three, and involves specialising in serving one specific segment. This can lead to very detailed knowledge of the target segment's needs and wants, with the added benefit that the organisation is seen as a specialist, giving it an advantage over its more mass-market

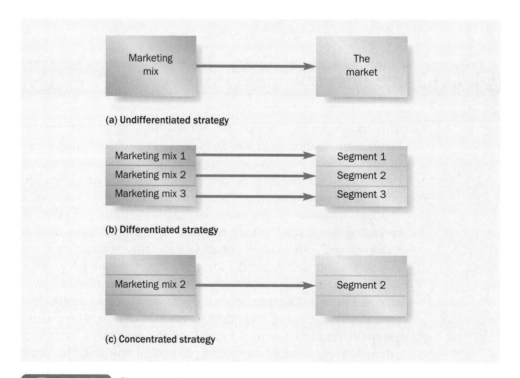

(a) Undifferentiated strategy

(b) Differentiated strategy

(c) Concentrated strategy

Figure 4.6   Segmentation targeting strategies

competitors. This, however, carries a risk of complacency, leaving the organisation vulnerable to competitive entry into the segment.

In terms of management, concentration is attractive because costs are kept down, as there is only one marketing mix to manage, and there is still the potential for economies of scale. Strategically, the concentration of resources into one segment may lead to a stronger, more defendable position than that achievable by competitors which are spreading their effort more thinly. However, being a niche specialist may make it more difficult for an organisation to diversify into other segments, whether through lack of experience and knowledge, or through problems of acceptance arising from being identified with the original niche.

The benefits also need to be weighed against the other potential risks. First, all the organisation's eggs are in one basket, and if that segment fails, then there is no fallback position. The second risk is that if competitors see a rival establishing and clearly succeeding in a segment like this, then they may try to take some of it.

Differentiated

As Figure 4.6 implies, a differentiated strategy involves the development of a number of individual marketing mixes, each of which serves a different segment. For example, Ford manufactures a range of cars, covering a number of different segments, from the Focus at the bottom end of the price range, generally intended for the younger female driver, to the Scorpio in the higher price bracket, intended for the status-seeking executive.

As with the concentrated strategy, this approach does allow the organisation to tailor its offerings to suit the individual segments, thus maintaining satisfaction. It also overcomes one of the problems of concentration by spreading risk across the market, so that if one segment declines, the organisation still has revenue from others.

To be implemented properly, this approach requires a detailed overview of the market and how it is developing, perhaps leading to the early detection of new opportunities or emerging segments. This knowledge is valuable for an organisation with a healthy curiosity about its environment, but is acquired at a cost (in terms of both finance and managerial time). It also leads to increased costs in trying to manage the marketing mixes for a number of products, with possible diseconomies of scale.

Overall, a differentiated strategy dilutes the organisation's efforts through the thin spreading of resources. The organisation must, therefore, be very careful not to overreach itself in the number of segments it attempts to cover. Nevertheless, it can help an organisation to survive in highly competitive markets.

Undifferentiated

The undifferentiated approach is the least demanding of the three approaches, in that it assumes that the market is one great homogeneous unit, with no significant differences between individuals within that market. Thus a single marketing mix is required that serves the needs of the entire market. The emphasis is likely, therefore, to be on developing mass communication, mass distribution and as wide an appeal as possible.

An undifferentiated approach does have some apparent advantages. It involves relatively low costs, as there is only one marketing mix that does not require the depth of research, fine tuning and updating that a concentrated or differentiated strategy would entail. It could also lead to the possible maximisation of economies of scale, because of having a single product in a potentially large market.

It is naive to hope that you can please everyone. What is likely to happen in reality is that some people will like your product offering more than others, and thus a segment (not of your own definition) will emerge by default. Because your product has not been tailored to that segment, it is unlikely to be exactly what that segment wants, and therefore any competitor who does target the segment more closely will attract those customers.

Example	At first glance it might be thought that the market for strawberries is largely undifferentiated. Market research, however, has revealed usage differences depending on the time of year, meal occasion and accompaniments. There are even different consumption patterns depending on the consumer's age. Around 40 per cent of strawberries are consumed in the summer and they feature in 619 million meals in the UK. Recent growth in strawberry consumption has been linked to its association with health. About 10 per cent of strawberries are consumed at breakfast, some with cereals, and 45 per cent are eaten with the evening meal. Consumers tend to be older, with the over-65s accounting for 28 per cent of consumption, but consumption among under-5s is also rising rapidly. Strawberries have a habit of popping up in fromage frais, in tub desserts and in dried fruit mixtures. All this data should give any marketer with a fertile imagination lots of ideas for promoting strawberries in different ways to meet different needs (Finn, 2005).

If an undifferentiated approach is possible at all, then it might best be suited for products with little psychological appeal. For example, petrol is essentially a very ordinary product that many of us purchase regularly but never even see (unless we are not very adept with a self-service pump). It makes the car go, regardless of whether it is a Rolls-Royce or a Lada and, traditionally, the only discriminating factor between brands has been price. Petrol retailers have now begun to create market segments, through the petrol itself (as with unleaded and petrols with extra additives), through the extended product (providing car washes, mini-supermarkets, etc.), and also through strong corporate images that create brands and engender loyalty. All of this is moving the petrol retailers away from undifferentiated strategies.

Quite apart from the advantages and disadvantages connected with each of the alternative approaches above, there are a number of factors influencing the choice of targeting strategy.

Marketing theory may well point to a particular strategy as being ideal, but if an organisation's resources cannot support and sustain that strategy, then an alternative must be found. A smaller organisation may, for example, need to adopt a concentrated strategy (perhaps based on a geographic segment in a consumer market, or on a specialist niche in a B2B market) to generate the growth required to allow a wider coverage of the market.

Table 4.5 Differentiation in the salt market

● Table salt	● Iodised salt
● Cooking salt	● Low-sodium salt
● Sea salt	● Garlic salt
● Rock salt	● Celery salt
● Alpine rock salt	et cetera!

It is also important to make the choice of strategy in the context of the product itself. As has already been indicated, certain types of product lend themselves more readily to certain approaches, for example a product with many potential variations that involve a high level of psychological relationship with the customer (such as clothing or cosmetics) is better suited to a differentiated or concentrated approach. Other products with a more functional bias can be treated in a more undifferentiated way.

It must be reiterated, though, that undifferentiated approaches are becoming increasingly rare. Salt used to be held up to marketing students as the prime example of a commodity product sold in an undifferentiated way. Table 4.5 demonstrates how all that has changed.

The product's lifecycle stage might also affect the choice of strategy. For example, an innovative new product, of which neither the industry nor the consumer has past experience, may first be marketed with an undifferentiated strategy in order to gain practical knowledge of the market's behaviour and reactions. It is very difficult to undertake meaningful market research in advance of launching such a new product, because the market may have problems conceptualising the product or putting it into context. It will be in the growth and maturity stages of the lifecycle that differentiated strategies will emerge as competitors enter the market and organisations learn from experience.

marketing in action   'As close to paradise as can be found'

Turtle Island represents for some the perfect holiday destination. The remote Fijian island in the Yasawa chain was purchased by Harvard graduate Richard Evanson in 1972 as a place to get away from it all, but also as the basis for a business so that his paradise could be shared. Development was needed before business was possible. A circular road was sympathetically built around the island, guest paths were established, Honduras mahogany trees were planted (some 300,000 trees over 26 years), to supplement the local species, and to encourage ecological diversity, stop soil erosion, create wind breaks and add to natural beauty. A three-acre organic vegetable garden was planted, extensive composting and recycling facilities were developed, and solar panel water heating installed to reflect a concern for ecology and the development of sustainable tourism.

The mission and values of the owner are to ensure that the marketing strategies fit with the culture and heritage to create sustainable tourism. Too many of the 'wrong' kind of tourists can soon degrade the local culture and environment. Turtle Island is at the opposite end of the spectrum from Benidorm or Blackpool. The capacity is just fourteen beachfront cottages on a private 500-acre estate and there are no plans to change that.

Guests wanting to lie on the beach drinking all day, or sleeping all day and clubbing all night, are certainly not welcome. Turtle Island is designed to appeal to English-speaking couples who can communicate and enjoy each other's company and humour. It's first-name terms as soon as you arrive and a key part of the experience is the interaction with staff and other guests.

The island resort is positioned as the nearest thing to paradise, and clearly to the targeted segment it is just that, as occupancy is high and many bookings cannot be fulfilled for the required dates. The climate, the lush vegetation, the activity programme ranging from snorkelling to mountain biking, the all-inclusive pricing policy, and the opportunity to 'get away from it all' appear highly attractive. The price structure is designed to keep the resort exclusive. Excluding airfares (you need a small seaplane to get to the island) the charge is over $2000 per couple per night and the minimum permitted booking is six nights to provide plenty of opportunity to unwind. Around 60 per cent of its guests are from the United States and 30 per cent from Australia and New Zealand. There is a 36 per cent rate of return visits which, considering its remote location, is exceptionally high.

What is important about Turtle Island is that the environmental responsibility and commitment demonstrated by the owner has been good for business and good for the island and its neighbouring community of over 6000 inhabitants. The concern with ecology, the deliberate attempt to restrict the number of tourists, the use of local materials (guests stay in traditional wood bures), the provision of medical facilities to the locals and a concern for monitoring, controlling and minimising the unfortunate impact of tourism, such as sewage, reef damage and social pollution, have given rise to international acclaim. Developed from an overgrazed and abused island with most of its trees cut down, the Turtle Island resort has won international recognition including a BA Environmental award. The package of experiences and the ecological orientation have proved to have a strong appeal to a specific market segment and the owner deliberately sought to reflect that when designing the tourist package. Built on a stance that the owner describes as 'destination

Targeting the desire for the perfect holiday on a desert island but with all the facilities and service that the consumer needs to have a relaxing, carefree holiday, the Turtle Island resort more than satisfies the customers willing to pay for the privilege.

Source: © Turtle Island, Fiji http://www.turtlefiji.com

stewardship', the values of Turtle Island aim to balance and respect the needs of the land, the resources, the people, the community, heritage and culture, while at the same time providing a unique and friendly environment beyond standard hotel star-ratings.

The island has not been without controversy, however. The *Lonely Planet 1997* guide suggested that the island was distinctly unfriendly to gays given its exclusive nature and priority to social mixing between the guests. This was strongly denied, countering that creating the ideal social mix is challenging. The comments in subsequent editions of Lonely Planet were modified, but it goes to show that near perfection on one dimension of CSR can still leave a company open to accusations, however unfounded, on another. Bookings do not appear to have been affected, however, and the careful segmentation and positioning strategy continues to bring success.

Sources: Berno (2004) Chesshyre (2000); Evanson (1999); Turtle Island (2003); http://www.turtlefiji.com.

That last comment is a reminder that strategic decisions cannot be taken in isolation from the activities of the competition. If competitors are clearly implementing differentiated strategies, then it is dangerous for you to adopt a more dilute, undifferentiated approach. It may make more sense to identify the segments within which the competition is strong and then to assess whether it would be possible to attack them head-on in those segments or to find a different niche and make that your own. Thus competition is affecting not only the choice of approach, but the actual choice of segment(s) to target.

Benefits of segmentation

The previous sections of this chapter should at least have served to show that market segmentation is a complex and dangerous activity, in the sense that the process of choosing variables, their measurement and their implementation leaves plenty of scope for poor management and disappointment. Nevertheless, there are few, if any, markets in which segmentation has no role to play, and it is important to remember the potential benefits to be gained, whether looking at the customer, the marketing mix or the competition.

The customer

The obvious gain to customers is that they can find products that seem to fit more closely with what they want. These needs and wants, remember, are not only related to product function, but also to psychological fulfilment. Customers may feel that a particular supplier is more sympathetic towards them, or is speaking more directly to them, and therefore they will be more responsive and eventually more loyal to that supplier. The organisation that fails to segment deeply enough on significant criteria will lose custom to competitors that do.

The marketing mix

This is a timely reminder that the marketing mix should itself be a product of understanding the customer. Market segmentation helps the organisation to target its marketing mix more closely on the potential customer, and thus to meet the customer's needs and wants more exactly. Segmentation helps to define shopping habits (in terms of place, frequency and volume), price sensitivity, required product benefits and features, as well as laying the foundations for advertising and promotional decisions. The customer is at the core of all decisions relating to the 4Ps, and those decisions will be both easier to make and more consistent with each other if a clear and detailed definition of the target segments exists.

In the same vein, segmentation can also help the organisation to allocate its resources more efficiently. If a segment is well defined, then the organisation will have sufficient understanding to develop very precise marketing objectives and an accompanying strategy to achieve them, with a minimum of wastage. The organisation is doing neither more nor less than it needs to do in order to satisfy the customer's needs and wants.

This level of understanding of segments that exist in the market also forms a very sound foundation for strategic decisions. The organisation can prioritise across segments in line with its resources, objectives and desired position within the market.

The competition

Finally, the use of segmentation will help the organisation to achieve a better understanding of itself and the environment within which it exists. By looking outwards, to the customer, the organisation has to ask itself some very difficult questions about its capacity to serve that customer better than the competition. Also, by analysing the competitors' offerings in the context of the customer, the organisation should begin to appreciate the competition's real strengths and weaknesses, as well as identifying gaps in the market.

Dangers of segmentation

The benefits of segmentation need to be balanced against the dangers inherent in it. Some of these, such as the risks of poor definition and implementation of psychographic segmentation, have already been mentioned.

Jenkins and McDonald (1997) raise more fundamental concerns with market segmentation processes that are not grounded in the capabilities of the organisation. To them, there needs to be more focus on how organisations should segment their markets rather than a focus on how to segment using the range of variables mentioned earlier in this section. To decide on the 'should' means having an understanding of the organisation, its culture, its operating processes and structure which all influence the view of the market and how it could be segmented (Piercy and Morgan, 1993).

Other dangers are connected with the essence of segmentation: breaking markets down into ever smaller segments. Where should it stop? Catering for the differing needs of a large number of segments can lead to fragmentation of the market, with additional problems arising from the loss of economies of scale (through shorter production runs or loss of bulk purchasing discounts on raw materials, for instance), as mentioned earlier in this section. Detail needs to be balanced against viability.

Within the market as a whole, if there are a number of organisations in direct competition for a number of segments, then the potential proliferation of brands may simply serve to confuse the customer. Imagine five competitors each trying to compete in five market segments. That gives the customer 25 brands to sort out. Even if customers can find their way through the maze of brands, the administration and marketing difficulties involved in getting those brands on to the supermarket shelves can be very costly.

Criteria for successful segmentation

Cutting through the detail of how to segment, and regardless of the complexities of segmentation in different types of market, are four absolute requirements for any successful segmentation exercise. Unless these four conditions prevail, the exercise will either look good on paper but be impossible to implement, or fail to deliver any marked strategic advantage.

Distinctiveness

Any segment defined has to be *distinctive*, that is, significantly different from any other segment. The basis of that difference depends on the type of product or the circumstances prevailing in the market at the time. It may be rooted in any of the segmentation variables discussed above, whether geographic, demographic or psychographic. Note too the use of the word *significant*. The choice of segmentation variables has to be relevant to the product in question.

Without a significant difference, segment boundaries become too blurred, and there is a risk that an organisation's offerings will not be sufficiently well tailored to attract the required customers.

Tangibility

It must be remembered that distinctiveness can be taken too far. Too much detail in segmentation, without sound commercial reasoning behind it, leads to fragmentation of effort and inefficiency. A defined segment must, therefore, be of a sufficient size to make its pursuit worthwhile. Again, the notion of size here is somewhat vague. For fmcg goods, viable *size* may entail many thousands of customers purchasing many tens of thousands of units, but in a B2B market, it may entail a handful of customers purchasing a handful of units.

Proving that a segment actually exists is also important. Analysis of a market may indicate that there is a gap that existing products do not appear to fill, whether defined in terms of the product itself or the customer profile. The next stage is to ask why that gap is there. Is it because no organisation has yet got round to filling it, or because the segment in that gap is too small to be commercially viable? Does that segment even exist, or are you segmenting in too much detail and creating opportunities on paper that will not work in practice?

Accessibility

As well as existing, a defined segment has to be *accessible*. The first aspect of this is connected with distribution. An organisation has to be able to find the means of delivering its goods and services to the customer, but this may not be so easy, for example, for a small organisation targeting a geographically spread segment with a low-priced infrequently purchased product. Issues of access may then become an extension of the segment profile, perhaps limiting the segment to those customers within a defined catchment area, or those who are prepared to order direct through particular media. Whatever the solution to problems of access, it does mean that the potential size of the segment has to be reassessed.

The second aspect of access is communication. Certain customers may be very difficult to make contact with, and if the promotional message cannot be communicated, then the chances of capturing those customers are much slimmer. Again, the segment profile may have to be extended to cover the media most likely to access those customers, and again, this will lead to a smaller segment.

Defendability

In talking about targeting strategies (see p. 526 above), one of the recurrent themes was that of the competition. Even with a concentrated strategy, targeting only one segment, there is a risk of competitors poaching customers. In defining and choosing segments, therefore, it is important to consider whether the organisation can develop a sufficiently strong differential advantage to defend its presence in that segment against competitive incursions.

B2B markets

Most of the above discussion has centred on consumer markets. With specific reference to B2B markets, Hlavacek and Ames (1986) propose a similar set of criteria for good segmentation practice. They suggest, for example, that each segment should be characterised by a common set of customer requirements, and that customer requirements and characteristics should be measurable. Segments should have identifiable competition, but be small enough to allow the supplier to reduce the competitive threat, or to build a defendable position against competition. In strategic terms, Hlavacek and Ames also propose that the members of a segment should have some logistical characteristic in common, for example that they are served by the same kind of distribution channel, or the same kind of sales effort. Finally, the critical success factors for each segment should be defined, and the supplier should ensure that it has the skills, assets and capabilities to meet the segment's needs, and to sustain that in the future.

Summary

This section has focused on the complexities and methods involved in dividing markets into relevant, manageable and targetable segments in order to allow better-tailored offerings to be developed.

- In B2B markets, segmentation techniques are divided into macro and micro variables or bases. Macro variables include both organisational characteristics, such as size, location and purchasing patterns, and product or service applications, defining the ways in which the product or service is used by the buyer. Micro segmentation variables lead to the definition, in some cases, of segments of one customer, and focus on the buyer's management philosophy, decision-making structures, purchasing policies and strategies, as well as needs and wants.

- In consumer markets, five main categories of segmentation are defined: geographic, demographic, geodemographic, psychographic and behaviour based. Between them, they cover a full range of characteristics, whether descriptive, measurable, tangible or intangible, relating to the buyer, the buyer's lifestyle and the buyer's relationship with the product. In practice, a multivariable approach to segmentation is likely to be implemented, defining a portfolio of relevant characteristics from all categories to suit the market under consideration.

- The implications of segmentation are wide-reaching. It forms the basis for strategic thinking, in terms of the choice of segment(s) to target in order to achieve internal and competitive objectives. The possibilities range from a niche strategy, specialising in only one segment, to a differentiated strategy, targeting two or more segments with different marketing mixes. The undifferentiated strategy, hoping to cover the whole market with only one marketing mix, is becoming increasingly less appropriate as consumers become more demanding, and although it does appear to ease the managerial burden, it is very vulnerable to focused competition.

- Segmentation offers a number of benefits to both the consumer and the organisation. Consumers get an offering that is better tailored to their specific needs, as well as the satisfaction of feeling that the market is offering them a wider range of products to choose from. The organisation is more likely to engender customer loyalty because of the tailored offering, as well as the benefits of more efficient resource allocation and improved knowledge of the market. The organisation can also use its segmentation as a basis for building a strong competitive edge, by understanding its customers on a deeper psychological level and reflecting that in its marketing mix(es). This forms bonds between organisation/product and customer that are very difficult for competition to break. There are, however, dangers in segmentation, if it is not done well. Poor definition of segments, inappropriate choice of key variables or poor analysis and implementation of the outcomes of a segmentation exercise can all be disastrous. There is also the danger that if competing marketers become too enthusiastic in trying to 'outsegment' each other, the market will fragment to an unviable extent and consumers will become confused by the variety of choice open to them.

- On balance, segmentation is a good and necessary activity in any market, whether it is a mass fmcg market of international proportions, or a select B2B market involving two or three well-known customers. In either case, any segment defined has to be distinctive (i.e. features at least one characteristic pulling it away from the rest that can be used to create a focused marketing mix), tangible (i.e. commercially viable), accessible (i.e. both the product and the promotional mix can reach it) and finally, defendable (i.e. against competition).

Questions for review and discussion

1 How might the market for personal computers, sold to B2B markets, be segmented?

2   Find examples of products that depend strongly on *demographic segmentation,* making sure that you find at least one example for each of the main demographic variables.

3   What is *psychographic segmentation* and why is it so difficult and so risky to do?

4   In what major way does *behavioural segmentation* differ from the other methods? Outline the variables that can be used in behavioural segmentation.

5   For each *targeting strategy,* find examples of organisations that use it. Discuss why you think they have chosen this strategy and how they implement it.

6   How can *market segmentation* influence decisions about the marketing mix?

case study   The pink pound

It is very difficult to estimate the size of the gay market in the UK. Although gay culture has increasingly become part of the mainstream, with many more openly gay celebrities and gay themes and characters featuring regularly in television dramas and comedies, Mintel (2000a, 2000b) has found that the gay market is largely a hidden population. Estimates of the size of the gay population vary between 3 per cent and 15 per cent of the total population but in Mintel's view it is likely to be towards the lower end of the scale overall with a higher concentration in urban areas. Estimates of its spending power also vary between £6bn and £8bn per annum in the UK and $464bn in the US.

There is some consensus on the characteristics of the gay market, however. Gay consumers are perceived to have a higher than average income, and almost 60 per cent of gay men are either single or not cohabiting. Those who are cohabiting are likely to be in dual-income households. In terms of spending patterns, therefore, the lack of dependants and responsibilities gives gay consumers more opportunities for lifestyle spending with a strong focus on leisure and socialising. *The Gay Times* has found that 80 per cent of its readership comes from the ABC1 socioeconomic groups, compared with 43 per cent of the general population.

There is plenty of opportunity for reaching the gay market. Mintel's (2000b) survey found that 77 per cent had internet access at home and/or at work which is much higher than the national average of 26 per cent. Research has also indicated that they spend up to ten times longer online than the average internet user, are more likely to buy the latest gadgets and are particularly appreciative of those organisations that reach out to communicate with them. The internet is important in that it allows gay people to build a stronger sense of community and it gives marketers a chance to locate and target the gay market efficiently and discreetly. The average household income of the gay internet user is £42,500. There are many ISPs and portals set up specifically for online gays (see, for example, http://uk.gay.com, http://www.rainbownetwork.com or http://www.pinklinks.co.uk). These sites attract mainstream advertisers, such as Tesco Direct, Marks and Spencer Financial, Virgin, British Airways, First Direct and IBM as well as companies specifically targeting the gay community.

There are also print media. In the UK, Chronos Publishing produces four national gay publications: *Boyz* (a free weekly magazine aimed at the younger end of the gay market), *The Pink Paper* (weekly newspaper sold via mainstream newsagents), *Fluid Magazine* (monthly style and listings magazine), and *Homosex* (free monthly glossy magazine focusing on sex and relationships). The other major media owner is the Millivres-Prowler Group which owns *The Gay Times* as well as a number of gay shops called Prowler. *The Gay Times* is a monthly, glossy publication which is one of Europe's best-selling gay magazines. Newsagent WH Smith classifies *The Gay Times* as a Tier One magazine, i.e. it must be stocked in every branch. Although the circulation figures for gay publications are not as high as those of mainstream media – *The Gay Times*, for example, has a circulation of around 70,000 – they do deliver a high quality affluent audience.

Many mainstream companies have still not realised the potential of the gay market. Market research has found that 86 per cent of companies have not communicated specifically with gay audiences. Many companies say that they target all groups, not just niche markets, and besides that, they can reach the same audience through mainstream media. In their view, many gays' purchasing decisions are made using the same criteria as those of heterosexual consumers. Companies could, however, be missing out. A phenomenal 92 per cent of gay consumers surveyed said that they were more likely to favour companies that acknowledge and support gay people, and 88 per cent said that it is important to them that a company is gay-friendly.

There are some product and service sectors in which gay consumers are explicitly targeted. The development of 'gay villages', particularly in London, Brighton and Manchester, has in turn led to many overtly gay pubs, bars, restaurants, clubs and shops opening close to each other. This creates a focal point for gay communities and indeed, gay pubs and clubs are important social venues. Mintel (2000b) found that 90 per cent of gay respondents were pub visitors (compared with 69 per cent of the general population) and 81 per cent had visited a club (compared with less than 30 per cent of the general population). Interestingly, club visiting does not decline with age among the gay community as dramatically as it does among the general population.

According to Mintel (2000b), the five most important factors which contribute towards enjoyment of a gay venue were cited as:

- Type of music (77 per cent)
- Not intense or intimidating (75 per cent)
- Have been before and liked it (68 per cent)
- Spacious with seating areas (62 per cent)
- Cheaper drinks and special offers (56 per cent).

The majority of gay bars and pubs are run by independents, although some mainstream breweries have committed themselves to the gay market. Bass, for example, runs 28 gay pubs across the UK while Scottish & Newcastle runs a number of gay pubs, mainly in London (six outlets) but with two in Manchester, purely due to their location on Canal Street at the heart of the 'gay village'. Some operators focus purely on the gay sector, such as the Manto Group (centred on Manchester) and Kudos Group (centred on London).

The holiday market too lends itself to gay targeting by both mainstream and specialised companies. VisitScotland targeted gay travellers, recognising the £72m that the pink pound brings to Scottish hotels every year. It hosted a number of visits by US tour operators that specialised in the gay market and launched a promotional campaign in magazines with high numbers of gay readers. It can be a struggle, however, when the industry sometimes attracts negative publicity such as that generated by the Highland B&B owner who turned away gay guests, describing them as 'deviants'.

Not all organisations actively target the pink pound but increasingly they are finding it difficult to discriminate on the grounds of sexual orientation. Sandals offers a number of all-inclusive adult-only and couples-only resorts in the Caribbean. However, there was considerable criticism when posters highlighted Sandals' resorts as a destination for 'romantic, mixed sex couples'. London Transport barred Sandals' advertisements from its trains after numerous complaints. Perhaps, in an open and non-discriminatory society, the pink pound as a concept may eventually become redundant and irrelevant as being gay becomes just another relatively minor consumer characteristic.

According to Mintel (2000a), respondents in its survey took an average of 2.07 holidays each per year, and 72 per cent of them had taken at least one holiday lasting a week or longer within the previous year. *The Gay Times* found that 41 per cent of its readership took two or more holidays per year. The beach/resort holiday destination is almost as popular with the gay community as with anyone else but gay holidaymakers are more likely to take city-based holidays (23 per cent of Mintel's respondents) than the general population (9 per cent). Mintel (2000a) points out that cities are more likely to have some form of gay infrastructure, in the form of bars and clubs, that would add value to a holiday.

Surprisingly, only 4 per cent of Mintel's respondents had been on a gay-themed holiday and only 3 per cent had booked their holiday using a gay travel agent or tour operator. Around 11 per cent had actually booked holidays over the internet, which is much higher than among the general population in which less than 2 per cent of holidays are booked on the internet. Via the gay websites mentioned earlier, it is easy to find gay-oriented travel agencies: http://www.throb.co.uk, for example, offers holidays to popular gay or gay-friendly resorts in Spain and offers incentives to encourage booking over the internet.

In summary, Mintel (2000a) says that gay holidaymakers want a more diverse array of gay travel products, targeting them with 'quality gay-friendly holidays, rather than gay-themed holidays'.

Sources: Fry (1998, 2000); Jamieson (2004); Lillington (2003); Mintel (2000a, 2000b); Muir (2003).

Questions

1 To what extent does the gay segment conform to the criteria for successful segmentation?
2 What segmentation bases are relevant to the gay pub/club and holiday markets?
3 What are the risks and rewards for a mainstream company targeting the gay segment?

References

Abratt, R. (1993), 'Market Segmentation Practices of Industrial Marketers', *Industrial Marketing Management*, 22, pp. 79–84.

Baker, L. (2004), 'Size Does Matter', *The Guardian*, 6 August, p. 6.

Bale, J. (2001), 'Seats Built for Those that Travel Light', *The Times*, 15 February.

Berno, T. (2004), *2004 World Legacy Awards: On-site Evaluation of Turtle Island, Yasawas, Fiji*, accessed via http:www.turtlefiji.com.

Broadhead, S. (1995), 'European Cup Winners', *Sunday Express*, 7 May, p. 31.

Campaign (2005), 'Quorn Awards Farm £8m Strategic Ad Brief', *Campaign*, 14 January, p. 8.

Chesshyre, T. (2000), 'Gay Can Be Green in Fiji', *The Times*, 19 February.

Douglas, S.P. and Craig, C.S. (1983), *International Marketing Research*, Prentice-Hall.

Evanson, R. (1999), 'A Global Icon in Sustainable Tourism', paper presented at the *2nd Annual Samoan Tourism Convention*, 24–25 February 1999.

Finn, C. (2005), 'Trends in the Consumption of Strawberries in the Home', *The Grocer*, 19 March, p. 55.

Fry, A. (1998), 'Reaching the Pink Pound', *Marketing*, 4 September, pp. 23–6.

Fry, A. (2000), 'Profits in the Pink', *Marketing*, 23 November, pp. 41–2.

Garrahan, M. (2004), 'Why Executives Will Always Be on the Move', *Financial Times*, 15 November, p. 1.

The Grocer (2005), 'Naked Gets its Kit on for the Chillers', *The Grocer*, 22 January, p. 64.

Hlavacek, J.D. and Ames, B.C. (1986), 'Segmenting Industrial and High Tech Markets', *Journal of Business Strategy*, 7 (2), pp. 39–50.

Jamieson, A. (2004), 'Death, Gambling and the Pink Pound: Is this Tourism's Future?', *The Scotsman*, 25 August, p. 19.

Jenkins, M. and McDonald, M. (1997), 'Market Segmentation: Organizational Archetypes and Research Agendas', *European Journal of Marketing*, 31 (1), pp. 17–32.

Johnson, K. (2005), Now Boarding: All Business-Class Flights', *Wall Street Journal*, 14 January, p. B1.

Lillington, K. (2003), 'Dream Ticket', *The Guardian*, 16 October, p. 25.

Machauer, A. and Morgner, S. (2001), 'Segmentation of Bank Customers by Expected Benefits and Attitudes', *International Journal of Bank Marketing*, 19 (1), pp. 6–18.

Marketing Week (2004a), 'Can Beattie Bring Subtlety to Gossard?', *Marketing Week*, 22 July, p. 25.

Marketing Week (2004b), 'Playtex Reveals Wonderbra Range Designed for Risqué Tops', *Marketing Week*, 5 August, p. 10.

Marketing Week (2005), 'Meat-free Food: the Pleasure Without the Flesh', *Marketing Week*, 26 May, p. 38.

Mazzoli, R. (2004), 'Les Jeunes, Leurs Tribus et Leurs Marques', *Marketing Magazine*, December, pp. 58–9.

McGill, A. (2004), Luxury Air Service Ready for Take-off', *The Belfast Newsletter*, 26 January, p. 5.

Mintel (2000a), 'The Gay Holiday Market, 8/11/00', accessed via http://sinatra2/mintel.com, October 2001.

Mintel (2000b), 'The Gay Entertainment Market, 12/12/00', accessed via http://sinatra2/mintel.com, October, 2001.

Mitchell, A. (1983), *The Nine American Lifestyles: Who Are We and Where Are We Going?*, Macmillan.

Moriarty, R. and Reibstein, D. (1986), 'Benefit Segmentation in Industrial Markets', *Journal of Business Research*, 14 (6), pp. 463–86.

Muir, H. (2003), 'Tube Bans "Anti-gay" Holiday Firm Adverts', *The Guardian*, 5 June, p. 13.

Piercy, N. and Morgan, N. (1993), 'Strategic and Operational Market Segmentation: a Managerial Analysis', *Journal of Strategic Marketing*, 1, pp. 123–40.

Plummer, J.T. (1974), 'The Concept and Application of Lifestyle Segmentation', *Journal of Marketing*, 38 (January), pp. 33–7.

Sarsfield, K. (2004), 'PrimeFlight Suspends its Belfast Operations', *Flight International*, 21 September.

Schoenwald, M. (2001), 'Psychographic Segmentation: Used or Abused', *Brandweek*, 22 January, pp. 34–8.

Sleight, P. (1997), *Targeting Customers: How to Use Geodemographic and Lifestyle Data in Your Business*, 2nd edn, NTC Publications.

Smith, W.R. (1957), 'Product Differentiation and Market Segmentation as Alternative Marketing Strategies', *Journal of Marketing*, 21 (July).

Smorszczewski, C. (2001), 'Corporate Banking', *Euromoney: The 2001 Guide to Poland*, May, pp. 4–5.

Stuttaford, T. (2001), 'The Heart Bears the Ultimate Burden', *The Times*, 15 February.

Turtle Island (2003), 'The Value Proposition of a Commitment to Environmental and Social Sustainability in Tourism', paper presented at the Small Luxury Hotels Annual Conference, Barbados, 27 May, accessed via http://www.turtlefiji.com.

Wedel, M. and Kamakura, W. (1999), *Market Segmentation: Conceptual and Methodological Foundations*, Dordrecht: Kluwer Academic Publishers.

Wind, Y. (1978), 'Issues and Advances in Segmentation Research', *Journal of Marketing Research*, 15 (3), pp. 317–37.

Wind, Y. (1982), *Product Policy and Concepts*, Methods and Strategy, Addison-Wesley.

Wind, Y. and Cardozo, R. (1974), 'Industrial Marketing Segmentation', *Industrial Marketing Management*, 3 (March), pp. 153–66.

Segmenting markets

Introduction

This section concerns a question that should be very close to any true marketer's heart: 'How do we define and profile our customer?' Until an answer is found, no meaningful marketing decisions of any kind can be made. It is not usually enough to define your customer as 'anyone who wants to buy our product' because this implies a product-oriented approach: the product comes first, the customer second. If marketing is everything we have claimed it to be, then the product is only a small part of a total integrated package offered to a customer. Potential customers must, therefore, be defined in terms of what they want, or will accept, in terms of price, what kind of distribution will be most convenient for them and through what communication channels they can best be reached, as well as what they want from the product itself.

Remember too that in a consumer-based society, possession of 'things' can take on a symbolic meaning. A person's possessions and consumption habits make a statement about the kind of person they are, or the kind of person they want you to think they are. The organisation that takes the trouble to understand this and produces a product that not only serves its functional purpose well, but also appears to reflect those less tangible properties of a product in the purchaser's eyes, will gain that purchaser's custom. Thus sport shoe manufacturers such as Reebok and Nike not only developed shoes for a wide range of specific sports (tennis, soccer, athletics, etc.), but also realised that a significant group of customers would never go near a sports facility and just wanted trainers as fashion statements. This meant that they served three distinctly different groups of customers: the professional/serious sports player, the amateur/casual sports player and the fashion victim. The R&D invested in state-of-the-art quality products, combined with the status connected with the first group and endorsement from leading sports icons, helped these companies to build an upmarket image that allowed them to exploit the fashion market to the full with premium-priced products. This in turn led to the expansion of product ranges to include branded sports and leisure clothing.

Example

The business traveller is an important market segment for travel industry operators, such as airlines, hotel chains and car rental companies. Although business travellers expect better service, as frequent travellers they tend to spend more money, more often. This group of customers, therefore, differs significantly from leisure- and economy-class customers. Business travellers sometimes need to book at short notice, travel to tight schedules, travel frequently and could need to change arrangements at the last minute. Airlines have adapted their service provision to meet the needs of this group. Fast check-in facilities, first- or business-class travel options and lounges, special boarding arrangements and loyalty schemes are all important for attracting these customers. Airlines also advertise specifically to the business traveller and keep their pricing competitive within the business flyer segment on competitive routes such as London–Brussels.

As time pressures become greater, the business traveller is demanding satellite airports with good connections and direct flights, better airport services and better on-board services. Those things alone are no guarantee of success, however, as Primeflight found. The price of private hire small (up to ten seats) jets opens up the possibility of targeted services from regional airports. Primeflight introduced a twice-daily non-stop service between Belfast International and Brussels. The service was direct, had fast-track check-in, access to the business lounge and first-class service for £695 return, compared with the average business-class price of about £670. The seven-seater aircraft were ideal for the loads expected. Within five months, however, flights were suspended due to, it was claimed, technical and operational hitches, although some experts argued that the aircraft's small capacity and lack of scale could not operate cost-effectively. Such setbacks have not deterred other airlines from focusing on the business traveller. Swiss International launched a Zurich to Geneva service, business class only, in a Boeing 737 with just over 50 seats that convert to beds. The price of a ticket was $2374. Lufthansa has launched three routes between Germany and the US that cost about $2245 one way and Air France has launched flights from Paris to oil-industry destinations such as Angola, Iran and Uzbekistan. Airlines with a focus on the business travel segment realise that this kind of service is limited to unusual routes with heavy business traffic and limited tourism. Often they land at smaller airports where there are no delays and the passenger can be in a taxi within fifteen minutes. All of this is in contrast to the low-cost, no-frills operators at the other end of the market forcing prices down to attract large numbers of leisure customers, and offering minimum service (Garrahan, 2004; Johnson, 2005; McGill, 2004; Sarsfield, 2004).

All this forms the basis of the concept of segmentation, first developed by Smith (1957). Segmentation can be viewed as the art of discerning and defining meaningful differences between groups of customers to form the foundations of a more focused marketing effort. The following part of this section looks at this concept in a little more depth, while the rest of the section will examine how the concept can be implemented and its implications for the organisation.

The concept of segmentation

The introductory part of this section has presented the customer-oriented argument for the adoption of the segmentation concept. There is, however, also a practical rationale for adopting it. Mass production, mass communication, increasingly sophisticated technology and increasingly efficient global transportation have all helped in the creation of larger, more temptingly lucrative potential markets. Few organisations, however, have either the resources or the inclination to be a significant force within a loosely defined market. The sensible option, therefore, is to look more closely at the market and find ways of breaking it down into manageable parts, or groups of customers with similar characteristics, and then to concentrate effort on serving the needs of one or two groups really well, rather than trying to be all things to all people. This makes segmentation a proactive part of developing a marketing strategy and involves the application of techniques to identify these segments (Wind, 1978).

It may help you to understand this concept better if you think of an orange. It appears to be a single entity, yet when you peel off the skin you find that it is made up of a number of discrete segments, each of which happily exists within the whole. Eating an orange is much easier (and much less wasteful and messy) if you eat it systematically, segment by segment, rather than by attacking the whole fruit at once. Marketers, being creative folk, have adopted this analogy and thus refer to the separate groups of customers that make up a market as market segments.

The analogy is misleading, however, in that each segment of an orange is more or less identical in size, shape and taste, whereas in a market, segments may be very different from each other in terms of size and character. To determine these things, each segment has its own distinct profile, defined in terms of a number of criteria, referred to as *bases* or *variables*, set by the marketer. The choice of appropriate criteria for subdividing the market is very important (Moriarty and Reibstein, 1986) and thus a significant proportion of this chapter is devoted to thinking about the bases by which segments might be defined in both consumer and B2B markets. Leading on from this, there is also the question of influences that might affect an organisation's choice of segmentation variables. Then, once an organisation has defined its market segments, what is it supposed to do with the information? This too is addressed in this section.

B2B and consumer markets, in general, tend to be segmented differently and will, therefore, be discussed separately, beginning with B2B markets.

Segmenting B2B markets

One major feature of B2B segmentation is that it can focus on both the organisation and the individual buyers within it. Additionally, there is the need to reflect group buying, that is, the involvement of more than one person in the purchasing decision (Abratt, 1993). All of this can be compared with a family buying situation in a consumer market, but operating on a much larger scale, usually within a more formalised process.

Wind and Cardozo (1974) suggest that segmenting a B2B market can involve two stages:

1 *Identify subgroups* within the whole market that share common general characteristics. These are called macro segments and will be discussed further below.
2 *Select target segments* from within the macro segments based on differences in specific buying characteristics. These are called micro segments.

Macro segmentation bases

Macro segments are based on the characteristics of organisations and the broader purchasing context within which they operate. Defining a macro segment assumes that the organisations within it will exhibit similar patterns and needs, which will be reflected in similar buying behaviour and responses to marketing stimuli.

The bases used for macro segmentation tend to be observable or readily obtained from secondary information (i.e. published or existing sources) and can be grouped into two main categories, each of which will now be discussed.

Organisational characteristics

There are three organisational characteristics: size, location and usage rate.

1 *Size.* The size of an organisation will make a difference to the way in which it views its suppliers and goes about its purchasing. A large organisation, for instance, may well have many people involved in decision-making; its decision-making may be very complex and formalised (because of the risks and level of investment involved), and it may require special treatment in terms of service or technical cooperation. In contrast, a small organisation may operate on a more centralised decision-making structure, involving one or two people and with simpler buying routines.

Similar segmentation strategies are now being employed in the modernising economies of Central Europe. Corporate banking hardly existed in Poland in the 1980s, but following economic reform, the number of companies in Poland has grown from 500,000 in 1990 to over 3 million in 2001. As well as this increase in the potential corporate customer base, the banks have been privatised and many have been taken over or have gone into partnership with Western European and US banks. This has led to a much more marketing-oriented attitude within the Polish banks and has started the process of client segmentation. Small and medium-sized enterprises, defined as those with a turnover of between Zloty 5–250m (€1.26–63.3m) have been targeted, initially for savings and loans products, but increasingly with cross-selling of factoring, leasing, trade finance and investment banking. This is changing the role of the banks from being simply lenders and deposit-takers to being financial advisers, and this has far-reaching implications for the type and level of communication required by existing and new customers. The next stage of development, internet banking, is still some way off, however, because of the need to create a stronger and more secure IT infrastructure for Polish businesses (Smorszczewski, 2001).

2 *Location.* Organisations may focus their selling effort according to the geographic concentration of the industries they serve. Such specialisation is, however, slowly breaking down as the old, heavy, geographically based industries, such as shipbuilding, mining and chemical production, become less predominant. Additionally, there is the emergence of smaller more flexible manufacturers, geographically dispersed in new technology parks, industrial estates and enterprise zones. Nevertheless, there are still examples of geographic segmentation, such as that of computer hardware and software sales, or in the financial sector, which is concentrated in London, Frankfurt, Zurich and the major capitals of the world. Organisations providing certain kinds of services might also look to geographic segments. A haulage company might specialise in certain routes and thus look for customers at specific points to make collection, delivery and capacity utilisation as efficient as possible.

3 *Usage rate.* The quantity of product purchased may be a legitimate means of categorising potential customers. A purchasing organisation defined as a 'heavy user' will have different needs from a 'light user', perhaps demanding (and deserving) different treatment in terms of special delivery or prices, for example. A supplier may define a threshold point, so that when a customer's usage rate rises above it, their status changes. The customer's account may be handed over to a more senior manager and the supplier may become more flexible in terms of

cooperation, pricing and relationship building. It is generally a better investment to make concessions in order to cultivate a relationship with a single heavy user than to try to attract a number of light users.

Product or service application

This second group of segmentation bases acknowledges that the same good can be used in many different ways. This approach looks for customer groupings, either within specific industries as defined by standard industrial classification (SIC) codes, each with its own requirements, or by defining a specific application and grouping customers around that.

The SIC code may help to identify sectors with a greater propensity to use particular products for particular applications. Glass, for example, has many industrial uses, ranging from packaging to architecture to the motor industry. Each of these application sectors behaves differently in terms of price sensitivity, ease of substitution, quality and performance requirements, for instance. Similarly, cash-and-carry wholesalers serve three broad segments: independent grocers, caterers and pubs. Each segment will purchase different types of goods, in different quantities and for different purposes.

The macro level is a useful starting point for defining some broad boundaries to markets and segments, but it is not sufficient in itself, even if such segmentation does happen too often in practice. Further customer-oriented analysis on the micro level is necessary.

Planning segmentation, targeting and positioning

The targeting process

To plan for targeting, you must consider the market coverage approach you want to take. As shown in Figure 4.7, you can use one of four coverage approaches: undifferentiated marketing, differentiated marketing, concentrated marketing or individualized marketing.

Undifferentiated marketing

Essentially a mass-marketing approach, undifferentiated marketing means targeting the entire market with the same marketing mix, ignoring any segment differences. This assumes that all customers in a particular market, regardless of any differences in characteristics or behaviour, will respond in the same way to the same marketing attention. Undifferentiated marketing is less expensive than other coverage strategies, due to the lower costs of developing and implementing only one marketing mix. However, today's markets are rarely so homogeneous; even slight differences can serve as clues to underlying needs in segments where an organization can gain competitive advantage, encourage customer loyalty and ultimately return profits.

Consider the increasingly fragmented market for salt. Industry giants Cargill (owner of the Diamond Crystal brand) and Morton (owned by Rohm & Haas) have segmented what was once assumed to be a homogeneous market according to type of customer (consumers, restaurants and institutional customers) and specific cooking uses and occasions. Now products such as sea salt, coarse crystal salt, natural mineral rock salt and other variations are marketed differently to different

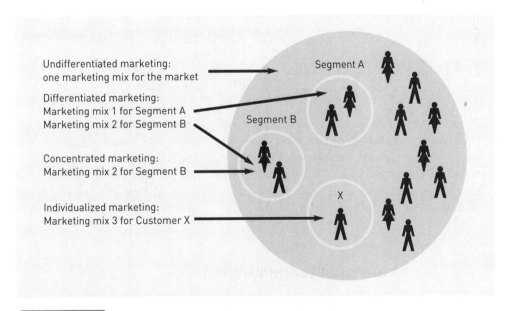

Figure 4.7   Segment targeting coverage strategies

segments. Meanwhile, brands such as La Baleine and small, family-owned businesses such as Quoddy Mist are marketing gourmet salts for smaller niches. Any marketer in this industry would avoid undifferentiated marketing because the mass market for salt no longer exists.[12]

Differentiated marketing

With **differentiated marketing**, you formulate a separate marketing mix for the two or more segments you choose to target. You may not target all segments in a given market, but for those you rank as priorities, you will need different marketing mixes geared to each segment's unique characteristics and behaviours. The assumption is that you can provoke a different response from each segment by using different marketing mixes. Customers benefit because their specific needs are being addressed, which increases satisfaction and encourages customer loyalty. Moreover, you can compete more effectively by tailoring the marketing mix for each segment, although this is much more costly than undifferentiated marketing and may overburden resources if not carefully managed.

Concentrated marketing

As you saw in Figure 4.7, **concentrated marketing** involves targeting one segment with one marketing mix. The idea is to compete more effectively and efficiently by understanding and satisfying one sizeable set of customers, rather than spreading organizational resources across multiple marketing activities for multiple segments. As long as the targeted segment remains attractive, this can be a profitable coverage approach. However, be aware that uncontrollable and unexpected factors such as new competition or changes in customer needs can make the targeted segment less attractive or even unfeasible over time.

Ryanair has profited from its concentrated marketing approach to targeting.

marketing in practice   Ryanair

Based in Dublin, Ryanair targets one big segment: price-sensitive customers who respond to low, low fares. 'You want luxury? Go somewhere else', states CEO Michael O'Leary. Ryanair saves money by using smaller airports, getting planes on the ground and into the air very quickly, flying limited schedules to selected European destinations and selling 98 per cent of all tickets online. Customers pay for every extra, from checked baggage to bottled water – even seat assignments carry a price tag. Ryanair's targeting is paying off with a healthy net profit margin of 18 per cent.[13]

Individualized marketing

You may be able to tailor marketing offers to individuals within certain targeted segments, a coverage approach known as **individualized** (or **customized**) **marketing**.

Airbus, for example, can identify all the potential buyers for passenger jets and cargo planes, get to know their needs and specifications, then develop a separate marketing mix for each. The markets for passenger jets and cargo planes are not so large that this is impractical, and the potential profit from each order is so great that individualized marketing makes sense for Airbus, especially in its competitive battle with arch-rival Boeing.[14]

If you have the right technology, you can opt for **mass customization** and create products and/or communications tailored to individual customers' needs on a larger scale. New Zealand, Canada and the United States are doing this with personalized postage stamps. Other products being marketed to individual customers through mass customization are personalized candies (such as M&Ms chocolates) and condiments in personalized bottles (such as Heinz catsup).[15]

Segment personas

Unilever and other marketers are adding a human dimension to targeting by constructing **personas,** fictitious yet realistic profiles representing how specific customers in targeted segments would typically buy, behave, and react in a marketing situation. The idea is to think about how customers actually interact with a product (and competing products), what influences and motivates those customers and how their needs and preferences affect their buying and consumption behaviour.

With assistance from its marketing agencies, Unilever constructed the persona of Katie, a 25-year-old single woman who represents a targeted consumer segment for its Sunsilk haircare products. Being able to envision Katie as a real person helped Sunsilk's marketers and agencies think about how specific marketing activities might fit into her life. What television programmes would Katie watch? How would she tend to react to marketing communications? 'It's about being in her world', explains the Sunsilk brand manager.[16]

The positioning process

With positioning, you use marketing to create a competitively distinctive position for your product in the minds of targeted customers. You need marketing research to understand how your targeted customers perceive your organization, product or brand and your competitors. Research can also help determine which attributes matter most to the targeted customers. Regardless of how you see your products, it is the customer's view that counts.

Altering a brand's positioning – even slightly – can be difficult. Consider the case of Montblanc, the German company famous worldwide for its premium writing instruments. In the early 1990s, Montblanc began **repositioning** – using its marketing plan to change the competitively distinctive positioning of its brand in the minds of the targeted customers. Montblanc wanted its brand perceived as super-luxury and it wanted to expand beyond pens. As a result, it needed to influence how customers thought and felt about its brand in relation to other super-luxury brands. One way Montblanc did this was by creating limited-edition pens embellished with precious metals and gems. Wealthy collectors took notice and soon were vying for the privilege of buying these very special pens, the world's most expensive. Montblanc's super-luxury positioning ultimately enabled the company to launch new products and enter new markets.[17]

Deciding on differentiation

Montblanc's experience illustrates the importance of deciding on a point of difference that is not only competitively distinctive but also relevant and believable. The limited-edition pens were nothing like ordinary pens – they were extremely high quality, beautifully designed and in quite short supply. Montblanc thus differentiated itself from rivals in ways that were credible, desirable and important to the targeted customer segment. Today Montblanc holds a solid 70 per cent of the world market for upmarket pens.[18]

In general, you can differentiate your offering along the lines of product, service, image, personnel or value. Whatever your choice, a product's positioning must be based on criteria that are meaningful and desirable from the customer's perspective yet competitively distinctive. Here are three examples of effective positioning based on desirable differentiation criteria:

- Mercedes-Benz: well-engineered, well-appointed luxury vehicles (product differentiation)
- Ryanair: low-cost, no-frills air travel (value differentiation)
- Vision Express: spectacles ready in one hour (service differentiation).

Applying positioning

In addition to satisfying the three desirability criteria, you must actually carry through the positioning in your product's marketing and performance. Determine first whether your organization can, realistically, develop and market a product that will live up to meaningful points of difference. Second, consider whether the points of difference can be communicated to the targeted segments. And third, determine whether you can sustain the product's performance and continue to communicate a meaningful point of difference over time. Montblanc has been so successful at repositioning itself as a super-luxury brand that it has been able to implement marketing plans for expanding into leather goods, wristwatches, eyewear and even fragrances.[19]

Positioning is basically the driver behind all the marketing activities you will include in your marketing plan. With differentiated marketing, you develop a positioning appropriate to each segment and apply that positioning through your marketing decisions for each segment. With concentrated marketing, you establish one positioning for the single segment you target. Remember that positioning is not a one-time decision: as markets and customers' needs change, you must be prepared to reposition a product, if necessary, for desirability and deliverability.

Summary

Segmentation helps marketers rule out inappropriate markets, identify specific segments for more study and better understand customers in those segments so the organization can more easily respond to their needs by providing value. Evaluating segments enables the organization to decide which to target and in what order. The process also provides a basis for creating a meaningful and competitively distinctive position in the minds of each target segment's customers.

Marketers can segment consumer markets by user-based characteristics (demographic, geographic, socioeconomic and lifestyle/personality) and product-related behavioural variables (user types, consumption patterns and usage frequency, brand loyalty, price sensitivity, perceived benefits and more). Business markets can be segmented using customer characteristics (industry type, geographic, industry position, company size and more) and product-related behavioural variables (consumption patterns/usage frequency, end use application, perceived benefits and more). Target-market coverage strategies include undifferentiated, differentiated, concentrated and individualized (customized) marketing. Effective positioning and repositioning must be competitively distinctive, relevant and credible as well as feasible, able to be communicated and sustainable.

case study   Groupe Danone: more than yoghurt

Although yoghurt, water and biscuits are entirely different products, Groupe Danone competes effectively in all three categories. The French company is the world's largest maker of yoghurt products. In addition, it markets bottled water (under Evian and other brands) and biscuits (under LU and other brands). Danone's marketers study the needs that drive consumer behaviour and reach out to targeted segments through differentiated marketing. The five geographic markets where they see the highest growth potential are China, India, Russia, Mexico and the United States.

In the yoghurt market, company marketers identified segments based on a diversity of needs and wants: some consumers want health benefits, some want a low-calorie snack, some prefer a fruity or creamy taste and so on. In response, Danone makes dozens of varieties of yoghurts with higher or lower levels of active cultures, sweetener, flavourings, fruits and other ingredients. Its yoghurt packages come in different sizes and shapes to accommodate buyers who want portable snacks, or eat yoghurt at home and who display other consumption behaviours.

Seeking growth, Danone bought a majority interest in China's Hangzhou Wahaha Group, which makes dairy drinks. With Danone's backing, Wahaha expanded capacity and used its brand and distribution system to break into the bottled water market. Now China is Danone's largest market for water, with annual purchases of more than four billion bottles.

Like their counterparts in other countries, some consumers in China prefer to support local businesses. This worked to Danone's advantage when the government asked the parent to assist Wahaha in developing a cola soft drink, Future Cola, positioned as 'the Chinese people's own cola'. The drink quickly became the number-three cola behind Coca-Cola and Pepsi-Cola, although its share is far less than the 24 per cent held by Coca-Cola. Danone's future marketing plans will continue to cover more than just yoghurt.[20]

Case question

1 How has positioning contributed to the success of Future Cola? What are the implications for Danone's future marketing plans in China?

Apply your knowledge

Research the segmentation, targeting and positioning of a particular company active in consumer or B2B marketing, using its products, advertising, website and other activities as clues. Prepare a brief written or oral report summarizing your conclusions.

- Based on the organization's marketing, what market(s) and segment(s) appear to be targeted?
- Is this company using differentiated, undifferentiated, concentrated or individualized marketing?
- What benefits are highlighted by the company's marketing, and what customer needs are they designed to satisfy?
- What product-related variables do you think this company is using to segment its market(s), apart from benefits sought?
- In one sentence, how would you describe the positioning of the firm or one of its products?

Build your own marketing plan

Proceed with the marketing plan you've been preparing. During the segmentation process for this organization, what markets would you eliminate from consideration, and why? What specific segmentation variables would you apply to the remainder of the market, and how would you expect them to create segments that make sense from a marketing perspective? What further research would support this segmentation? What criteria would you use to evaluate the segments you identify? Given the organization's overall goals, strengths and resources, what targeting approach would you choose? Finally, on what basis would you differentiate your offering for the customers in each targeted segment? Be sure that these ideas are appropriate in light of your earlier decisions, then document your choices in your marketing plan.

Planning direction, objectives and strategy

Introduction

Toyota believes in setting ambitious objectives. When planning the fuel-efficient Prius, the company pushed its engineers and designers to develop the car in only two years. An instant success, the Prius has polished Toyota's global image as an innovator. Toyota also set a goal of selling 1.2 million cars annually in Europe by 2010, despite competition from European, US, Japanese and Korean car manufacturers. To meet demand, Toyota's plant in Valenciennes, France, assembles small Yaris cars day and night. As a result, Toyota's European market share has risen to 5.7 per cent and it will reach its 2010 goal early, despite problems with vehicle recalls. Because sales in Japan are barely growing, Toyota's ability to reach future turnover targets depends on higher sales in Europe, Asia and the Americas.[21]

Toyota's marketing plans for each market are driven by its desire for rapid, profitable growth. This section discusses marketing plan objectives and direction, which make up the fourth stage in the marketing planning process. First, the section examines how direction and objectives guide the marketing plan and help the organization achieve longer-term goals. Next is a discussion of marketing plan direction, covering both growth and non-growth strategies. Finally, the section explains how to set effective marketing, financial and societal objectives.

Direction and objectives drive marketing planning

No marketing plan is developed in isolation. Toyota's marketing plan for Europe is influenced by its corporate priorities as well as top management's expectation of how the plan should contribute to achieving overall goals. Plans are made at three levels in the organization. Corporate-level plans are supported and implemented by business-level plans and, in turn, supported and implemented by functional-level plans for marketing, operations and so forth. As a marketer, you will formulate strategy, determine the optimal marketing-mix tools, and make programme-level decisions based on the direction and objectives of your marketing plan. The strategy pyramid illustrated in Figure 4.8 shows this linkage.

If the objectives in your marketing plan are explicit and clearly connected to higher-level objectives and long-term goals, the plan is more likely to produce the desired performance.[22] Thus, each objective, marketing strategy and marketing programme must be consistent with the plan's direction as well as with both organizational and business objectives. Consider how the UK telecommunications giant BT Group is using marketing to pursue growth after divesting underperforming businesses, reducing its debt and expanding its offerings.

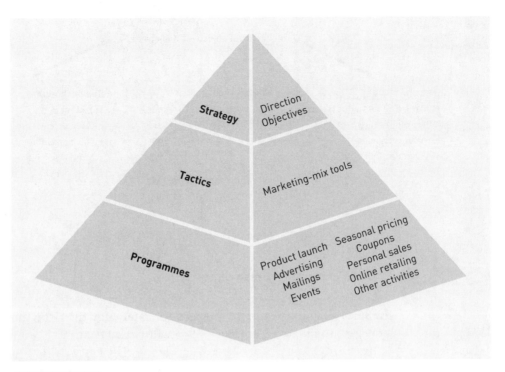

Figure 4.8   Strategy pyramid

Source: After Tim Berry and Doug Wilson, *On Target: The Book on Marketing Plans*, 2nd edn (Eugene, OR: Palo Alto Software, 2001), p. 107.

marketing in practice   BT Group

BT Group, with annual turnover of £19.5 billion and profit of £2 billion, has made broadband the centrepiece of its UK marketing plan for growth. In 2002, the telecommunications company set a goal of establishing 5 million broadband connections before 2007. Despite intense competition, the company's marketing focus on communicating broadband's ben-efits was so effective that the firm had 10 million broadband connections by the end of 2006. BT has also acquired technology service firms and expanded its electronic networking capabilities to better serve the lucrative corporate market. Now the marketing plan calls for doubling annual revenue from China-based multinational firms by 2010; it includes objectives for corporate philanthropy and eco-friendly activities, as well.[23]

Marketing plan direction

These days, BT has, like many companies, set growth as the direction for its marketing plans. Not all organizations pursue growth. Some seek to maintain their current position, postponing growth because of adverse economic conditions, fierce competition, financial problems or for other reasons. Others retrench by selling off units or products, exiting particular markets or downsizing in other ways – often

Figure 4.9   Choices of marketing plan direction

for survival purposes or to prepare for later growth. Growth and non-growth strategies, summarized in Figure 4.9, are discussed next.

Growth strategies

If your organization wants to grow, you will choose among the four main growth strategies proposed by H. Igor Ansoff: market penetration, product development, market development and diversification.[24] With **market penetration**, you offer existing products to customers in existing markets. This increases unit and/or monetary sales and simultaneously reinforces the brand or product's strength in each market. It also strengthens relationships by connecting customers to the organization with more product ties.

With **product development**, you market new products or product variations to customers in existing markets. This only works when you can develop a steady stream of product innovations appropriate for the needs of customers in those markets. Lamborghini has done this by designing new sports cars, offering limited-edition designer versions of its existing models and licensing its famous logo for clothing and accessories.[25]

With **market development**, you pursue growth by marketing existing products in new markets and segments. Such a strategy builds on the popularity of established products and allows firms to expand their customer base either geographically or by segment. Korea's LG, for example, has leveraged its strength in appliance technology and styling to market more washing machines and refrigerators to consumers in Europe and North America. As a result of higher efficiency, LG earns a higher profit margin on its appliances than its competitors earn on their appliances.[26]

The fourth growth strategy is **diversification**, which means marketing new products in new markets or segments. You can diversify by (1) distributing new products in new markets through existing channel arrangements, (2) initiating new marketing activities in new markets or (3) acquiring companies to gain access to new products and new markets. London-based Hanson, once part of a conglomerate, has been growing through diversification within the building materials industry. By buying brick companies in North America, cement companies in Australia and related businesses elsewhere, the company can offer a wider range of construction products in Europe, the Americas, Australia and the Pacific.[27]

Non-growth strategies

Sometimes growth is not an appropriate direction. Pressured by severe economic or competitive conditions, insufficient resources, ambitious expansion, lower demand or stagnant revenues and profits, organizations may follow a maintenance strategy or even retrench. You might therefore create a maintenance marketing plan to keep revenues, market share or profits at current levels, if possible, or at least defend against deterioration. Rather than invest in improving products, targeting new markets, developing new promotions or other marketing activities, your organization could try to harvest short-term profits from existing products and markets as a way of conserving resources and building a stronger foundation for later growth.

Organizations that cannot maintain their current levels may be forced into making marketing plans to retrench or, in the extreme, to shut down entirely. As shown in Figure 4.9, some common choices here are to withdraw from certain markets, eliminate particular products, downsize all marketing efforts, shrink distribution or go out of business. And, if the retrenchment goes well, the company will soon be able to start planning for a turnaround through a new growth strategy.

Brio's retrenchment strategy is a good example.

marketing in practice   Brio

Sweden's Brio has long been known for high-quality, expensive toys such as wooden trains as well as prams and other items for children. Besides designing and producing its own products, it eventually owned a regional toy chain, distributed toys in Scandinavian countries and marketed board games, among other activities. Then IKEA, Tesco and other large retailers began selling wooden trains at lower prices, just as the number of independent toy stores – a key distribution channel – plummeted in many markets. Brio's sales and profits suffered. Finally, management decided on retrenchment. By outsourcing production, divesting unprofitable subsidiaries, focusing product development and cutting costs, Brio planned to become, in a few years, 'a smaller company but profitable', said one of the company's owners.[28]

Clearly, the marketing plan for Brio's retrenchment strategy will be completely different from the marketing plan for any growth strategy. Guiding the organization in a particular direction requires specific marketing plan objectives keyed to that situation, which in turn will lead to different marketing strategies and programmes.

Marketing plan objectives

Marketing plan objectives are short-term targets that, when achieved through implementation of appropriate action programmes, will bring the organization closer to its longer-term goals. Some companies use the **Balanced Scorecard**, broad performance measures used to align strategy and objectives as a way to manage customer relationships, achieve financial targets, improve internal capabilities and attain sustainability. In such cases, the marketing plan objectives have to be structured appropriately to support these broader measures of performance.[29]

To be effective, your marketing plan objectives should be:

- *Relevant.* Be sure your objectives relate to the chosen direction and higher-level strategies and goals. Otherwise, the programmes you implement to achieve your plan's objectives will not support organizational needs. Although most businesses set objectives for revenues and profits, non-financial objectives such as those relating to corporate image are also important because they build and strengthen connections with other stakeholders.
- *Specific and measurable.* Vague targets will not help you determine what you need to accomplish and how. Simply calling for 'growth' is not enough. To be effective, your objectives should indicate, in quantitative terms, what the marketing plan is being developed to achieve.[30] To illustrate, HSBC Bank Malaysia's marketing plan for growth sets an objective of increasing the number of credit cards issued by 20 per cent each year, which means opening 500,000 new accounts. The bank's marketing managers can check progress toward this objective at any time by counting the number of accounts opened and cards issued.[31]
- *Time defined.* What is the deadline for achieving the objective? You will plan differently for objectives that must be achieved in six months compared with objectives to be achieved in 12 months. Setting an open-ended objective is like setting no objective at all, because you will lack a schedule for showing results – and will not be accountable. During one recent year, the Swiss food company Nestlé set an objective of raising annual sales volume by 4 per cent over the prior year. Knowing the deadline, the company had time to adjust its marketing plans when it found that six-month growth was 3.5 per cent.[32]
- *Realistic.* A marketing plan geared to attaining market dominance in six months is unlikely to be realistic for any business – especially for a start-up. Thus, your marketing plan objectives should be realistic to provide purpose for marketing and to keep organizational members motivated. One of LG's marketing objectives, for instance, is to increase its US appliance sales so quickly that it will hold a 10 per cent share of the US market for refrigerators and washing machines within three years.[33]
- *Challenging.* Realistic objectives need not be easy to attain. In fact, many marketers set aggressive yet realistic marketing plan objectives so they can expand more quickly than if their objectives resulted in incremental growth. Objectives that are too challenging, however, may discourage the marketing staff and tie up resources without achieving the desired result. LG's market-share objective is quite challenging because the company faces strong competition from Whirlpool, observes one of LG's US marketing managers.[34]

● *Consistent.* Is the objective consistent with the organization's mission, goals, strengths, core competencies and interpretation of external opportunities and threats? Are all objectives consistent with each other? Inconsistent objectives can confuse staff members and customers, detract from the marketing effort and result in disappointing performance. In the case of LG, its market-share objective makes sense in the context of the company's product development expertise, investment in customer service support and manufacturing capacity.

When G.R. Gopinath launched Air Deccan, he set specific, challenging and time-defined objectives to guide the new company's marketing.

marketing in practice   Air Deccan

'We're going to connect cities that are poorly connected by roads and trains', founder and managing director G.R. Gopinath said in introducing his no-frills airline, Air Deccan.[35] The company sees a profitable opportunity to serve India's growing middle-class segment of price-sensitive business travellers, families and sightseers. One of its first-year objectives was to attract 700,000 passengers. Three years after its founding, Air Deccan had exceeded its objectives and was carrying nearly 7 million passengers annually. Now Air Deccan has ambitious objectives for its new executive charter division. Will the airline reach its objectives and continue to fly high as competition intensifies?[36]

You can set marketing plan objectives in three categories. **Financial objectives** are targets for achieving financial results through marketing strategies and programmes. **Marketing objectives** are targets for achievements in marketing relationships and activities, which in turn directly support attainment of financial objectives. **Societal objectives** are targets for accomplishing results in areas related to social responsibility; such objectives indirectly influence both marketing and financial achievements. The choice of marketing plan objectives and specific targets will, of course, be different for every organization.

Financial objectives

Companies usually set objectives for external results such as unit, monetary, product and channel sales plus internal requirements such as profitability, return on investment and break-even deadlines. Figure 4.10 shows the focus and purpose of financial objectives commonly used by businesses. Non-governmental organizations (NGOs) typically set objectives for short-term and long-term fund-raising as well as other financial targets. To achieve the organization's financial objectives, you will need to coordinate other compatible objectives dealing with relationships between buyers and sellers as well as suppliers and distributors.

A company might set a financial objective for external results such as: *to achieve a minimum weekly sales volume of £1,000 for each new product.* Notice that this objective is relevant (for a profit-seeking organization); specific; time-defined; and measurable. Whether it is realistic, challenging and consistent depends on the

Focus of financial objective	Purpose and examples
External results	**To provide targets for outcomes of marketing activities such as:** • Increasing unit or monetary sales by geographic market • Increasing unit or monetary sales by customer segment • Increasing unit or monetary sales by product • Increasing unit or monetary sales by channel • Other objectives
Internal requirements	**To provide targets for managing marketing to meet organizational requirements such as:** • Achieving break-even status • Achieving profitability levels • Achieving return on investment levels • Other objectives

Figure 4.10   Focus and purpose of financial objectives

company's particular situation. A financial objective related to internal requirements might be: *to achieve an average annual profit margin of 13 per cent across all products.*

Because such objectives are measurable and time-defined, you can check progress, adjust your targets or change your marketing if necessary. Mercedes-Benz, for example, originally set an objective of selling 1,000 Maybach cars in its introductory year, at a price of €250,000 each. When unfavourable economic conditions dampened demand for super-luxury vehicles, the company lowered its first-year objective to 800 cars and set 1,000 cars as the second-year objective. Increased competition then became a factor. Two years later, Mercedes said annual sales of Maybachs stood at about 400.[37]

Marketing objectives

Connections with customers and channel members are particularly critical to organizational success, which is why every marketing plan should include objectives for managing these external relationships. Looking at the life cycle of a customer relationship, the organization would begin by approaching the customer to explore a possible relationship; establishing a relationship and adding more ties to strengthen it; reigniting customer interest if purchases plateau or loyalty wavers; saving the relationship if the customer signals intention to switch to another product or brand; and restarting the relationship if the customer is open to switching back. This life cycle applies to relations with channel members, as well.[38]

Consider Toyota's marketing objectives. Knowing that many car buyers begin to develop brand preferences years before they're old enough to drive or buy, the company has set objectives for starting relationships with young teens. Translating those objectives into action, it has become involved with Whyville.net, an online

Focus of marketing objective	Purpose and examples
External relationships	**To provide targets for managing relations with customers and other stakeholders such as:** • Enhancing brand, product, company image • Building brand awareness and preference • Stimulating product trial • Acquiring new customers • Retaining existing customers • Increasing customer satisfaction • Acquiring or defending market share • Expanding or defending distribution • Other relationship objectives
Internal activities	**To provide targets for managing specific marketing activities such as:** • Increasing output or speed of new product development • Improving product quality • Streamlining order fulfilment • Managing resources to enter new markets or segments • Conducting marketing research • Other objectives

Figure 4.11 Focus and purpose of marketing objectives

community. Participants are invited to use their avatars (the people or characters they create to depict themselves on the site) to 'drive' Toyota cars around the virtual world. The company hopes this will raise awareness of, and build preference for, its brand.[39]

Many businesses establish explicit objectives for building their customer base; enhancing customers' perceptions of the brand, product or company; holding on to existing customers; increasing customer loyalty; boosting or defending market share; strengthening ties with key distributors; improving customer satisfaction; and so on, as in Figure 4.11. The US conglomerate General Electric sets objectives for customer satisfaction and then examines the processes it must improve in order to meet those objectives. To boost satisfaction, GE's business financing division needed to process loan applications more quickly. After eliminating some steps in the process and working on some simultaneously instead of sequentially, GE was able to approve loans in just five days and improve its satisfaction ratings.[40]

In practice, you need to avoid conflicts between your marketing objectives and your financial objectives. It can be difficult to dramatically increase both market share and profitability at the same time, as one example. Therefore, marketers must determine the organization's priorities and formulate the marketing plan accordingly.

Non-profit organizations also set marketing objectives for attracting contributors, sponsors and other key relationships. For instance, the Canadian office of Doctors Without Borders set a one-year marketing objective of adding 1,000 new donors who would contribute at least once – and possibly more than once – to the organization's cause. The related financial objective was to break even on fund-raising costs within four months or less.[41]

In conjunction with objectives aimed at external relationships, you may formulate objectives covering internal activities such as increasing the accuracy or speed of order fulfilment; adjusting the focus, output or speed of new product development; and arranging the resources for entering new segments or markets. Planning for these activities helps lay the groundwork for achieving relationship objectives and the financial objectives that depend on those relationships.

Societal objectives

Because businesses are increasingly mindful of their responsibilities to society – and the way their actions are viewed by stakeholders – a growing number are setting societal objectives to be achieved through marketing. Such objectives are addressed in marketing plans because they indirectly help the company strengthen ties with customers (achieving marketing objectives) and increase or maintain sales (achieving financial objectives). As shown in Figure 4.12, societal objectives may relate to ecological protection or to social responsibility and stakeholder relations. The UK

Focus of societal objective	Purpose and examples
Ecological protection	**To provide targets for managing marketing related to ecological protection and sustainability:** • Reducing pollution with natural or 'greener' products, ecologically friendly processes • Doing business with 'greener' suppliers and channel members • Reducing waste by redesigning products and processes for recycling, other efficiencies • Conserving use of natural resources • Other objectives
Social responsibility and stakeholder relations	**To provide targets for managing marketing related to social responsibility and stakeholder relations:** • Building a positive image as a good corporate citizen • Supporting designated charities, community projects, human rights groups and others, with money and marketing • Encouraging volunteering among employees, customers, suppliers, channel members • Communicating with stakeholders to understand their concerns and explain societal activities • Other objectives

Figure 4.12   Focus and purpose of societal objectives

grocery chain Tesco, for example, has set an objective of reducing the average energy use in its facilities by 50 per cent within four years, part of its drive for environmentally friendly operations.[42]

Many businesses fulfil their societal objectives by donating money, goods or services to charities or good causes. This helps polish their image and demonstrates their commitment to the community and to society at large. Meralco (formerly the Manila Electric Co.) offers free computer literacy training to teachers in the Philippines. The company also sponsors an annual book drive in which employees donate reference books and other educational materials to local schools. Surveys confirm that customers notice and appreciate the energy company's activities. 'This definitely inspires us to work even harder and have more projects for social and national development', says CEO Manuel M. Lopez.[43]

Some companies set specific societal objectives for **cause-related marketing**, in which the brand or product is marketed through a connection to benefit a charity or other social cause. Experts say the chosen cause should have value for both stakeholders and the company.[44] Properly implemented social responsibility initiatives

Essential marketing plan checklist

Evaluating objectives

You must set appropriate objectives if you are to develop suitable marketing programmes for your organization's chosen direction and current situation. This checklist will help you evaluate the marketing, financial and societal objectives you have formulated for your marketing plan. Note your responses in the spaces provided, then put a tick mark next to the questions as you answer each one.[47]

☐ Is the objective relevant to the organization's direction and long-term goals?

_____

☐ Is the objective consistent with the organization's mission, strengths and core competencies?

_____

☐ Is the objective appropriate for the market's opportunities and threats?

_____

☐ Is the objective specific?

_____

☐ Is the objective time-defined?

_____

☐ Is the objective measurable?

_____

☐ Is the objective realistic yet challenging?

_____

☐ Is the objective in conflict with any other objective?

_____

have a positive effect on customer satisfaction and the company's market value, research shows.[45]

To communicate their societal objectives, activities and results to stakeholders, some companies distribute information to the media and post social responsibility and sustainability reports on their websites. For example, Royal Dutch/Shell posts its annual corporate social responsibility report on the corporate website, along with details about how it gathers data, the global principles and codes it follows and what external experts think of its sustainability reports. Shell has, in fact, been recognized for its management's use of external experts and the mechanisms it uses for fostering dialogue with stakeholders.[46]

Two starting points for more information about societal objectives are the UK government site on corporate social responsibility (www.csr.gov.uk/) and CSR Europe (www.csreurope.org/).

From objectives to marketing-mix decisions

The objectives you set during this stage of the marketing planning process are the targets to be achieved by implementing the decisions you make about the various marketing-mix elements. This is the point at which your earlier work comes together: on the basis of your situational analysis, your market and customer research and your segmentation, targeting and positioning decisions, you will be creating product, place, price and promotion strategies and action programmes for the who, what, when, where and how of marketing. Your objectives will also guide the development of customer service and internal marketing strategies to support the marketing mix.

Be aware that designing programmes to achieve some of your objectives may require marketing research support. To illustrate, Procter & Gamble, the US-based consumer packaged goods company, is already using social networking websites to promote certain brands. Its Herbal Essences shampoo page on MySpace.com invites consumers to upload photos of their latest hairstyles, for instance. Now P&G is sponsoring social networking sites such as Capessa (health.yahoo.com/capessa) to engage consumers and learn more about their concerns and preferences. The insights gained will help P&G set more appropriate objectives and plan programmes that more closely fit what its target markets want and need.[48]

Summary

Higher-level strategies and goals set the direction for marketing plans that outline objectives to be achieved through marketing strategies, tactics and programmes. Many organizations prepare marketing plans for growth through market penetration (offering existing products to existing markets), product development (offering new products or variations to existing markets), market development (offering existing products to new markets or segments) or diversification (offering new products to new markets or segments). Non-growth strategies include maintenance (to sustain current levels of revenues, share or profits) and retrenchment (to prepare for a turnaround into growth or to close down entirely).

Effective objectives must be relevant, specific, time-defined, measurable, realistic yet challenging, and consistent with the current situation. Financial objectives are targets for attaining financial results such as profitability through marketing strategies and programmes. Marketing objectives are targets for achievements in marketing relationships and activities. Societal objectives are targets for ecological protection or other areas of social responsibility. These objectives indirectly support the organization's ability to achieve financial and marketing objectives.

case study   Growth is on McDonald's marketing menu

In an ongoing quest to increase sales and market share, McDonald's has spread its red-and-yellow logo far and wide. Using marketing plans keyed to local conditions, the company encourages customers to try menu items as diverse as Ebi Filet-O shrimp burgers in Japan and Bigger Big Mac burgers in Britain. It also sets marketing objectives for building relationships with customers in a number of ways. For example, it invites people with mobile phones to sign up for special late-night offers delivered via text-message.

Responding to public interest in healthier foods, McDonald's now offers yoghurt, apple juice and other healthy foods in children's Happy Meals packages. The company has successfully introduced organic foods and reduced transfat levels in cooking oils. These initiatives also fit into McDonald's marketing plan for meeting societal objectives. Sustainability is a major focus, which is why all European McDonald's restaurants brew only coffee from Rainforest Alliance-certified growers and more than 30 per cent of the fish used in McDonald's menu items come from sustainable fisheries. In addition, the company sets societal objectives for charitable contributions and community-based efforts such as improving literacy.

Europe is a very lucrative market for McDonald's, contributing nearly 40 per cent of the company's annual profit. The marketing budget is far from unlimited, however. Thus, the company's marketers must decide on specific growth objectives for each year's marketing plan. Spending heavily to open new outlets has not produced the kind of profit impact that McDonald's expected. As a result, the CEO now has company marketers putting more emphasis on increasing the turnover of existing restaurants.[49]

Case questions

1 Not long ago, McDonald's decided to close 25 UK restaurants. How do you think this decision might have affected its UK marketing plan?

2 To set consistent and realistic yet challenging objectives, what internal and external factors should the marketers at McDonald's consider?

Apply your knowledge

Research the direction, marketing, financial and societal objectives of a particular company by examining its website, media coverage, products, advertising, packaging, financial disclosures, social responsibility reports and other aspects of its operation.

Based on your findings, write a brief report or make a brief oral presentation to the class.

- Is the company pursuing a growth, maintenance or retrenchment strategy? How do you know?
- Does the company disclose any specific objectives? If so, what are they and how do they relate to the company's direction?
- Identify one specific marketing, financial or societal objective that this company has set and compare it to the characteristics in this chapter's checklist. What changes would you recommend to make this objective more effective as a target for performance?
- Look for clues about whether the objective you have identified was actually achieved (and if not, why).

Build your own marketing plan

Continue working on your marketing plan. Looking at the organization's current situation, environment, markets, customers and mission statement, what is an appropriate direction for your marketing plan? What marketing, financial and societal objectives will you set to move in the chosen direction? If any of these objectives conflict, which should take priority, and why? How will these objectives guide your planning for the marketing mix and marketing support? What might cause you to rethink your objectives? Take a moment to consider how the direction and objectives fit with the information already in your marketing plan and how practical they are in terms of marketing implementation. Then record your thoughts in your marketing plan.

Planning for products and brands

Introduction

Trainers for toddlers? Germany's Adidas makes a wide variety of sports footwear, apparel and accessories for global markets. In addition to the Adidas brand, the company owns the Reebok, TaylorMade and Rockport brands. Now it has joined with Mattel, a well-known US toy manufacturer, to co-brand infant clothing and dolls. It is also testing some new product ideas online in Second Life, the virtual community that attracts consumers from all over the world. Although turnover is rising, will Adidas gain enough market share to overtake industry leader Nike?[50]

Adidas is seeking to achieve financial and marketing objectives through product and brand planning, part of stage 5 in the marketing planning process. This section opens with a discussion of product mix, product lines and the product life cycle, followed by an examination of new product development. Next, you will learn how to use different attributes in devising a tangible good or intangible service that will meet your customers' needs, your organizational targets and the marketplace realities. The final part of this section looks at planning for brands and brand equity.

Planning for products

At this point in the planning process, you understand your current situation and what each product means to the organization in financial and marketing terms. Now you're ready to plan your marketing mix, starting with the product. If you are creating a marketing plan for a company, your product may be a physical item (such as Adidas trainers), a service or a combination of tangible and intangible elements. If you work for a non-governmental organization, your product may be an idea such as better health; if you are marketing a geographic region, your product may be a place such as a tourist destination.

For any specific product you market or plan to market, look closely at:

- the customer segment being targeted
- the needs satisfied and value provided
- trends in pricing, unit sales, market share, revenues and profits
- age and performance over time, by segment, channel and geography
- sales connections between products
- current or potential opportunities and threats related to each product
- competitive strengths, weaknesses, position
- customers' perceptions of competing products.

The point of these analyses is to determine how each product provides value to customers and your organization. As a visual summary, you can create a grid matching each product to the intended target market, detail the need each product satisfies and indicate the value delivered from the customer's and organization's perspectives (see Figure 4.13). In addition, you may want to include information about each product's competitive position and strength.

	Customer segment A (briefly describe)	Customer segment B (briefly describe)	Customer segment C (briefly describe)
Product 1 (identify)	Customer need: Value to customer: Value to organization:	Customer need: Value to customer: Value to organization:	Customer need: Value to customer: Value to organization:
Product 2 (identify)	Customer need: Value to customer: Value to organization:	Customer need: Value to customer: Value to organization:	Customer need: Value to customer: Value to organization:
Product 3 (identify)	Customer need: Value to customer: Value to organization:	Customer need: Value to customer: Value to organization:	Customer need: Value to customer: Value to organization:

Figure 4.13   Product/segment analysis grid

Next you face decisions about managing the product mix and product lines; the product life cycle; new product development; and product attributes including quality and performance, features and benefits, design, packaging, labelling and brand. Figure 4.14 shows the four categories of product planning decisions.

Product mix and product line decisions

When planning for products, you will face choices about managing the **product mix** (the assortment of product lines offered by an organization), **product line length** (the number of individual items in each line of related products) and **product line depth** (the number of variations of each product within one line). Your marketing plan can cover one or more of the following:

- introduce new products in an existing line under the existing brand name (**line extensions** that lengthen the line)
- introduce variations of existing products in a product line (deepening the line)
- introduce new brand names in an existing product line or category (**multibrand strategy**)
- introduce new products under an existing brand (**brand extensions** that widen the mix)

Product mix and product lines	Product life cycle
• Change product line length or depth • Change product mix width • Manage product cannibalization	• Locate product in cycle by segment and market • Change progression through life cycle • Balance life cycles of multiple products
New product development	Product attributes
• Add new product categories • Expand existing lines or brands • Manage steps in process • Address ecological, ethical concerns	• Plan level of quality, performance • Provide valued benefits through features • Design for functionality, differentiation • Create packaging and labelling • Build brand equity

Figure 4.14 **Product planning decisions**

- introduce new lines in other product categories (**category extensions** that widen the mix)
- eliminate a product (shortening the line)
- eliminate or add a product line (narrowing or widening the mix).

Each decision about the product changes the way you satisfy customers in targeted segments, address opportunities, avert threats, allocate marketing resources and achieve marketing objectives. Consider the product decisions made by London-based Cadbury Schweppes.

marketing in practice   Cadbury Schweppes

Several years ago, Cadbury Schweppes' marketers noticed that more consumers were watching their weight and buying lower-calorie snacks. Until that time, the company's sales and profits had come primarily from chocolate sweets and soft drinks. Since then, Cadbury's marketers have invested heavily in lengthening and deepening chewing gum product lines to serve the needs of weight-conscious consumers. Recently Cadbury introduced sugar-free Trident gum, one of its most successful US gum brands, to European markets. It has also purchased gum brands in other countries to lengthen the gum product line and gain local customers. Despite a costly chocolate contamination scandal, Cadbury's timely product innovation and management have increased annual turnover beyond £6 billion and increased profit margins as well.[51]

Adding new products by extending a familiar, established line or brand can minimize the risk that customers and channel partners may perceive in trying something new. Because of this familiarity, the product's introductory campaign is likely to be more efficient and may even cost less than for an entirely new brand or product in a new category. Your development costs may also be lower if you base a new product on an existing product.

Extensions that are well received will reinforce the brand, capture new customers and accommodate the variety-seeking behaviour of current customers. Extensions are not without risk, however. If you extend a line or brand, customers or channel members may become confused about the different products you offer. For example, will a co-branded Adidas/Mattel doll be successful? Remember that channel members with limited shelf or storage space may be reluctant to carry additional products. And if the product does not succeed, perceptions of the brand or the remaining products in the line may be affected.[52]

In particular, look closely at whether you are spreading your resources too thinly and at how each product or line will contribute to organizational objectives. Be ready to cut products or lines that do not perform as desired, as Heinz did by eliminating a line of unusually coloured and flavoured frozen chips – even as its green catsup was gaining popularity. The company is also reducing the number of product variations offered in European markets to make better use of the shelf space stores allot to its brands.[53]

Also manage your products with an eye toward minimizing product **cannibalization**, which occurs when one of your products takes sales from another of your products. A line extension may attract customers who previously purchased other products in the same line, for example. Still, marketers sometimes decide they can attract new customers, retain current customers or achieve other objectives only by cannibalizing their own products rather than risk having competitors lure customers away.

Product life-cycle decisions

As you plan, you must make decisions about how to manage the **product life cycle**, a product's movement through the market as it passes from introduction to growth, maturity and eventual decline. Although no individual product's life cycle is entirely predictable or even necessarily sequential, the typical life cycle pictured in Figure 4.15 shows how sales and profitability can change in each part of the

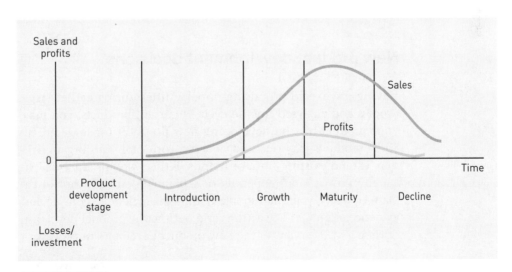

Figure 4.15   Product life cycle

Source: Philip Kotler, Veronica Wang, John Saunders and Gary Armstrong, *Principles of Marketing*, 4th edn (Harlow: Pearson Education, 2005), p. 604.

cycle. Corporate giants such as Heinz, Cadbury Schweppes and Unilever tend to have numerous products in targeted markets at one time, and each could very well be in a different part of its life cycle.

Analysing a product's life-cycle situation and using marketing activities actively to manage the cycle can help you plan to take advantage of anticipated ups and downs. Where is the product within its life cycle, how quickly is it progressing through each part of the cycle and what can marketers do either to alter the cycle or to get the most out of each part? As Figure 4.15 suggests, profitability is highest during the growth part of the life cycle and tends to decrease with maturity. This is why many companies plan strategies to extend or at least reinvigorate product growth.

Moreover, some products are reaching maturity much faster, compressing their life cycle. The DVD player, for instance, matured extremely quickly because of standardized components and technology; as more competitors entered the market and volume skyrocketed, the average price dropped to little more than 10 per cent of the introductory price in only six years. Now manufacturers are extending the life cycle by introducing high-definition DVD players, even as a standards battle rages between Blu-ray and HD-DVD technology. Looking ahead, will wider availability of downloadable movies and television programmes push DVD players into decline?[54]

Be aware that product life cycle can vary by segment and by market. For instance, research shows that sales of new household products and foods tend to increase more rapidly and reach maturity earlier in the United Kingdom and the Netherlands than in France and Spain. Knowing this, marketers targeting UK and Dutch consumers would push for wide distribution by the launch date to build growth momentum early in a product's introduction stage.[55] On the other hand, home appliances and consumer electronics products tend to move into the growth stage earlier in Denmark, Norway and Sweden – in about four years – than in France, the United Kingdom and Greece, where accelerating growth takes more than six years. Thus, marketers should consider launching products in markets where faster growth is possible early in the life cycle, and expect to wait longer for rapid growth in other markets.[56]

New product development decisions

Having discovered promising opportunities during earlier stages of the planning process and analysed the life cycle of current products, you may decide to change your product mix by developing new products for targeted customer segments. Some products may open up new categories for your organization; other products may extend existing lines or brands. Either way, product development details are usually shown in an appendix or separate document, not in the main marketing plan. However, your plan should outline the major decisions, include research or other evidence, highlight key actions and outline the product development schedule.

Here is an overview of the new product development process:

1 *Generate ideas* from inside the organization and from customers, sales representatives, channel partners, suppliers, competitive materials and other sources. To do this, IBM invites 100,000 employees, customers and consultants to join a yearly online Innovation Jam.[57]

2 *Screen ideas* to eliminate those that are inappropriate or not feasible, given the organization's strengths, core competencies and resources.

3 *Develop and test product concepts* to find out whether customers (and perhaps influential channel members) perceive value in the remaining ideas and respond positively to them.

4 *Develop the marketing strategy* to clarify targeting, positioning and specific marketing plan objectives for the new product. Also outline the proposed marketing mix and project sales and profits.

5 *Analyse the business case* for introducing each new product, including associated costs, sales and profits, to gauge the contribution toward achieving organizational objectives.

6 *Develop the product* to see whether the concept is practical, cost-effective and meets customers' needs and expectations.

7 *Test market the product*, with associated marketing strategies, to assess the likelihood of market acceptance and success. Try different marketing activities, evaluate customer response, anticipate competitors' reactions and adjust the product and marketing as needed.

8 *Launch the product commercially*, applying the lessons learned from test marketing and from previous product introductions.

New product development doesn't end with commercialization. You must monitor market response, including the reactions of customers, channel members and competitors. If you see that the product is not selling as well as projected, you will want to change the product or other elements of the marketing mix as needed. Research shows that the most successful new product innovations result from need identification, solution identification and marketing research. At the same time, the rate of new product failure is so high that you must carefully screen ideas to avoid investing in unpromising or unneeded products.[58]

Sweden's Electrolux approaches new product development from the perspective of meeting observed yet unstated consumer needs.

marketing in practice Electrolux

Known for household appliances such as dishwashers and cookers, Electrolux visits consumers at home to learn how, when and why they use appliances. Design chief Henrik Otto and his team use four personas to represent distinct customer segments defined by personality and lifestyle, benefits expected, usage patterns and similar elements. Working with marketing experts, sales staff and engineers, the designers create a new product and ask consumers to try out the prototype. Otto notes that 'people want their personalities to be reflected by their appliances', which is why Electrolux pays close attention to both aesthetics and functionality. As a result, its newer products earn higher profit margins than products that have been in the product mix much longer. The company also holds a yearly contest to honour creative appliance ideas from design students.[59]

Don't forget the ecological and ethical issues related to your product. Can ecofriendly supplies and processes be incorporated? Will the product's production or use adversely affect the natural environment? How will the new product serve

	Product 1	Product 2	Product 3
Quality (customers' view) and **performance** (objective measures)			
Features (and benefits delivered to satisfy customer needs)			
Design (for performance differentiation)			
Packaging (protect, store, facilitate use) and **labelling** (information, marketing communication)			
Brand (identity, differentiation, provoke response)			

Figure 4.16 Planning product attributes

your organization's societal objectives? What ethical questions might arise (such as whether to test products on animals) and how can you address these in a satisfactory way? Thinking about water conservation, Electrolux created countertop dishwashers that small families can use to clean a few dishes without wasting a lot of water.

Whether you are developing new products or improving existing ones, you will seek the optimal combination of quality and performance, features and benefits, design, packaging, labelling and brand (see Figure 4.16). You want your product to be competitively distinctive, attractive and valuable to customers while returning profits to the organization. Be sure your product is competitively superior on features and benefits valued by customers; also check that the product supports your marketing plan objectives. At W.L. Gore, a US company known for innovation, executives assess product ideas by asking: 'Is the opportunity real? Is there really somebody out there that will buy this? Can we win? What do the economics look like? Can we make money doing this? Is it unique and valuable? Can we have a sustained advantage [such as a patent]?'[60]

Quality and performance decisions

Quality means different things to different people; this is why you should define a product's **quality** in terms of how well it satisfies the needs of your customers. From this perspective, a high-quality product is one that satisfies needs better than a poor-quality product. You can certainly use objective performance measures to demonstrate a product's functionality, reliability, sturdiness and lack of defects. In the marketplace, however, customers are the final judges of quality and decide for themselves what level of quality they want and will pay for.

Extremely affluent consumers may be satisfied only by exceptionally high performance and quality. Or, as Hewlett-Packard found out, far superior quality may not be necessary.

marketing in practice   Hewlett-Packard

At one time, Hewlett-Packard, the US marketer of printers, computers and related equipment, routinely designed printers to exactingly high standards, even though this drove up costs and prices. As lower-priced competing printers gained popularity, however, HP's marketers realized they were missing the segment of customers who want reasonable quality at a reasonable price. They redesigned HP's printers to eliminate non-essential features and incorporate lighter materials. Now the expanded product line includes smaller and lower-priced printers based on innovative, cost-effective technologies that provide value to consumers and business buyers. Even the ink cartridge packages have been redesigned with earth-friendly recycled materials.[61]

B2B marketers know that quality is essential to products such as computer chips, which are the heart of many technology products. For example, Intel is aware that business customers require consistently high performance so it meticulously controls its manufacturing process to maintain the same high quality whether its chips are made in Ireland, Vietnam or Arizona.[62] Before you introduce or even begin developing a new product, you have to ensure that the entire organization is capable of consistently delivering the expected quality, given the available resources and schedule. This, too, is part of the marketing planning process.

Feature and benefit decisions

Customers buy a product not only for the **features**– specific attributes that contribute to functionality– but also for the **benefits**– the need-satisfaction outcomes they want or expect. Hewlett-Packard's customers want quickly printed, clear documents; some may even quantify the benefits sought in terms of number of pages printed per minute. Those customers would want to know that HP's product line includes inkjet printers that can produce 71 pages per minute. When evaluating competing printers, customers look at whether each model has the features that provide the benefits they value. In practice, you should plan for features that deliver the benefits that you know your customers value (based on marketing research).

As Hewlett-Packard discovered, not all customers want or are willing to pay for the benefits provided by a particular product's features. In fact, too many features can make a product too complex or expensive for the targeted audience.[63] Different segments often have different needs and different perceptions of the value of features and benefits. Figure 4.17 shows, in simplified form, how Groupe Michelin, the French tyre maker, might match features to benefits that satisfy the needs of

Customer segment and need	Feature and benefit
Lorry fleet owners who need to monitor tyre pressure and track the location of all tyres	Sensor patch on each tyre electronically transmits pressure and identification data to owners
Farmers who need to drive tractors over fields and in uneven terrain	Large, deep tyre patterns provide more secure road grip
Professional sports car drivers who seek winning performance	Special composition tyres for speed and handling

Figure 4.17 Matching features and benefits to needs

specific customer segments. You can see how Michelin could offer value and differentiate its tyres from those of competitors such as Goodyear.[64] Creating a similar matrix can help you pinpoint each segment's needs and identify features and benefits to satisfy those needs.

Features are as important for services as for physical goods. Jinjiang International, China's largest hotel chain, matches the features and furnishings of each of its 263 hotels with the needs of the targeted travellers, and then prices the accommodations accordingly. Before the Beijing Olympics and the Shanghai World Expo, Jinjiang opened new, no-frills, low-price hotels to accommodate thousands of budget-conscious travellers. It also renovated and updated its upmarket hotels for wealthy and executive travellers and raised the average room rate to 1,800 yuan (about €179).[65]

Design decisions

Directly or indirectly, customers' perceptions and buying choices are influenced to some degree by design. Moreover, your design decisions can affect the ecology as well as product performance. Therefore, as with all other product decisions, you should be sure that a product's design is consistent with your organization's marketing, financial and societal objectives and that it fits with your other marketing mix decisions. Ideally, design decisions should create a bridge to your future vision of how the product will benefit the target market. To illustrate, Nokia's senior consumer vision manager is responsible for guiding product designers toward a future in which consumers will use new-generation mobiles to connect, entertain and communicate at all times. Moreover, Nokia's designs are planned with fashion as well as functionality in mind.[66]

Your company may develop designs internally or hire outside design specialists. Denmark's Bang & Olufsen generates new product ideas and hires specialists to come up with designs that are aesthetically pleasing and technologically advanced as well as functional. 'If we have designers in-house, they tend to come too close to the technicians', explains the design and concepts director. 'That means they begin solving technical problems rather than focusing on the design.'[67] Bang & Olufsen also collaborates with other companies on product design; working with Korea's Samsung, it recently designed a stylish, premium-priced mobile for the luxury market.[68]

Product design has become such a prime point of differentiation, especially for mature products like household appliances, that everyday products need not be ordinary-looking. The sleek design lines of refrigerators made by China's Haier Group, for example, attract customers and help the company compete in the domestic market and internationally. In fact, the pressure of global competition has prompted many marketers to devote more time and resources to product design.[69]

Packaging and labelling decisions

Good packaging protects tangible goods, makes their use or storage more convenient for customers and, ideally, serves societal objectives such as ecological protection. For instance, Nike is reducing excess packaging and shipping costs by packaging some of its trainers in moulded cardboard containers that exactly fit the shoes, rather than in uniform rectangular shoeboxes.[70]

When planning for any product to be sold in a store, think carefully about how labelling can serve marketing functions. Labels are more than informative: they can capture the shopper's attention, describe how product features deliver benefits, differentiate the product from competing items and reinforce brand image.

Marketing functions aside, your labels must meet applicable laws and regulations. Cigarette marketers in the European Union, for instance, are required to devote 30 per cent of the front label and 40 per cent of the back label to health warnings. Also, labelling cannot use terminology implying that one type of cigarette is safer than others.[71] In Canada's Quebec province, multilingual labels must include a French equivalent for every word, printed in type that is as big as or bigger than the type used for other languages.

Use the following checklist as you proceed with product planning.

Essential marketing plan checklist

Planning for products

Now that you've set specific objectives for your marketing plan, you need to begin planning for your products. This checklist will help you think through the main issues and decisions. Write your answers in the spaces provided and put a tick mark next to the questions as you complete each one. If your marketing plan is for a product not yet on the market, use this checklist to consider the key decisions you'll face in planning for a successful introduction.

☐ What is the current situation of each product within its line and the overall product mix?

_____

☐ Would customers' needs and the organization's interests be served by changing the product mix, product lines or line depth?

_____

☐ Where is each product in its life cycle and what are the implications for product planning?

☐ What new products can be developed to take advantage of promising opportunities in targeted segments?

☐ If you're planning a new product, how can you improve the odds of success as you move through each step in the development process?

☐ How might cannibalization be minimized following new product introductions?

☐ What are the ecological and ethical considerations associated with each product?

☐ How can you change quality and performance, features and benefits, design, packaging or labelling to provide more value for customers and your organization?

Planning for brands

Branding is a pivotal aspect of product planning because it provides identity and competitive differentiation to stimulate customer response. An unbranded product is just a commodity, indistinguishable from competing products except in terms of price. A branded product may have the same attributes as competitors yet be seen as distinctly different (and provoke a different customer response) because of the rational or emotional value the brand adds in satisfying the customer's needs and wants.[72]

In planning for a brand, you should identify ways to increase brand equity, the extra value customers perceive in a brand that ultimately builds long-term loyalty. Higher brand equity contributes to sustained competitive advantage, attracts new channel partners and reinforces current channel relationships. It also enhances marketing power, allowing you to wring more productivity out of your marketing activities as customers (1) become aware of your brand and its identity, (2) know what the brand stands for, (3) respond to it and (4) want an ongoing relationship with it. The brand equity pyramid in Figure 4.18 illustrates these four levels leading to strong brand equity.

Be aware that customers in the targeted segment may know the brand, understand what it stands for and respond to it – but not want the kind of ongoing relationship that the organization would like. The ultimate objective of brand planning is to move customers upward through the levels of brand equity and encourage them to remain at the top. This raises the customer's lifetime value to the organization

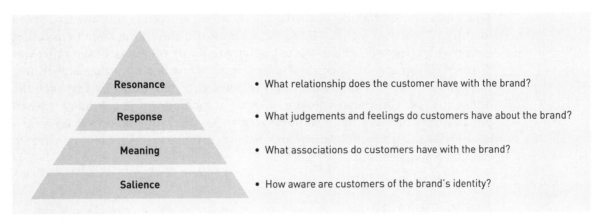

Figure 4.18   Brand equity pyramid

Source: After Kevin Lane Keller, *Strategic Brand Management*, 2nd edn (Upper Saddle River, NJ: Prentice Hall, 2003), p. 76.

and helps achieve your objectives. It is important to remember that companies benefit financially from brand equity, but the identity, meaning, response and relationships all derive from customer interaction with the brand.[73]

Brand identity

Here, you want to make customers in the targeted segment aware of your brand's identity. A brand can consist of words, numbers, symbols and/or graphics to add salience, such as the Nike name combined with its swoosh symbol or the Nestlé name combined with the nesting bird logo. You can develop or license a brand using one or more of the following approaches:

- *Company brand*. The company name becomes the brand, such as Sony and Starbucks. This associates the company's image with the product. If the company's image suffers, however, the brand is likely to feel the effect. Company brands are also known as *manufacturers' brands* or *national brands*.
- *Family or umbrella brand*. Each product in one or more lines or categories is identified as belonging to that particular brand family (or being under that brand umbrella). For example, Toyota puts the Lexus brand on a family of vehicles; Anheuser-Busch puts the Budweiser brand on a family of beers.
- *Individual brand*. A product is identified with a brand not shared by other products. The household lubricant WD-40 is a good example of an individual brand used only for that product.
- *Private brand*. Retailers and other channel members frequently brand their own products for differentiation from manufacturers' branded products. The supermarket chain Tesco uses Finest as its private brand; competitor Sainsbury uses Taste the Difference.
- *Co-brand*. Two companies put their brands on one product. An example is the MasterCard credit card co-branded by Barclays and Travelocity.

Bringing customers to this first level of brand equity involves decisions about the brand itself as well as other product attributes and marketing actions. For example, how can you use product packaging and labelling to convey a distinctive brand identity? Coca-Cola (ranked by some as the world's most valuable brand) uses hourglass bottles and red-and-white labelling to set its colas apart from other soft drinks. You can also build customers' awareness of the brand through advertising, in-store promotions, websites and other marketing activities that reinforce the differentiation. Customers who are unaware of a brand will not think of it when purchasing, which is why organizations often set marketing objectives for awareness. Establishing a brand identity and making customers aware of it is a prelude to creating brand meaning.

Brand meaning

The second level of brand equity is to shape the associations that customers have with your brand. What do you want the brand to stand for? What image or personality does the brand have, and is it the same as what you want to create? This is an especially important point when considering brand extensions. For example, the motorcycle manufacturer Harley-Davidson earns about 20 per cent of its revenues from extensions such as leather jackets. But experts doubt that its Xtreme Image cake-decorating kit reflects the brand's image of hard-driving independence, even though the kit is intended to appeal to women motorcycle riders.[74]

Once customers understand a brand's meaning, they come to rely on it as a shortcut when making buying choices, which expedites the buying process and reduces the perceived risk. You can mould brand meaning through positioning and through favourable associations backed up by product performance, features that deliver value through need satisfaction, distinctive design and so on. As with brand identity, other marketing activities are involved, as well.

Brand response

The third level of brand equity relates to customer response. Once customers are aware of the brand's identity and understand its meaning, they can make up their minds about the brand. Ideally, you want your customers to believe in your brand, trust it and perceive it as embodying positive qualities. You also want customers to see the brand as competitively superior and, just as important, have an emotional connection to it. Determining customer response requires marketing research, followed up by action steps either to reinforce positive responses or to turn negative (or neutral) responses into positive ones through marketing activities.

Marketers for Campbell's Soup recently faced the problem of a less enthusiastic response to the company's tinned condensed soups. 'I've got millions of households every week buying the product, despite the fact that we've priced too aggressively, that we haven't innovated, that we've allowed the quality gap between ourselves and alternatives to shrink', says Campbell's CEO.[75] To reignite brand perceptions of quality and competitive superiority, the company has devised new cooking methods, improved its recipes, created new easy-open packaging and added lower-sodium selections for health-conscious consumers.[76]

Brand relationship

The fourth level of brand equity deals with customers' relationship to the brand. They know about the brand, know what it means to them and how they feel about it. But are they sufficiently attached to remain loyal buyers? You want to encourage strong and enduring brand relationships because loyal customers tend to buy more, resist switching to competing brands and be willing to pay a premium for the brand and recommend it to others.[77] The issue is therefore how you can use your product plan, along with other marketing-mix activities, to reinforce customers' brand preference and loyalty.

One approach is to improve or at least maintain product quality and performance to avoid disappointing customers, tarnishing the brand and discouraging customer loyalty. Another is to add products or features that better satisfy current customers' needs. A third is to continue introducing innovative or upgraded product designs, packaging and labelling consistent with the brand image. Finally, your marketing plan should allow for research to see how effective you have been in moving customers up the brand equity pyramid toward sustained customer loyalty. Use the following checklist as you plan for your brand.

Essential marketing plan checklist

Planning for brands

Planning for brands must be carefully coordinated with planning for products. This brief checklist can help you think about your branding decisions and about how your product will support your brand. Note your answers in the spaces provided, putting a tick mark next to the questions as you answer them.

☐ How is the brand identified and what are the implications for its image?

☐ How is the brand positioned for competitive differentiation?

☐ How do product attributes support the brand image?

☐ Are customers aware of the brand? If so, what does it mean to them? How can brand awareness be expanded through marketing?

☐ What do customers think and feel about the brand? What relationship do they have or want with it?

☐ How can brand preference and loyalty be encouraged through marketing?

Source: Adapted from Kevin Lane Keller, *Strategic Brand Management*, 2nd edn (Upper Saddle River, NJ: Prentice Hall, 2003), Chapter 2.

Summary

Planning for products includes decisions about the product mix (the assortment of product lines being offered), product line length (the number of items in each line) and product line depth (the number of product variations within a line). The product life cycle is a product's market movement as it progresses from introduction to growth, maturity and decline. In new product development, marketers: (1) generate ideas; (2) screen ideas; (3) research customer reaction to ideas; (4) develop the marketing strategy; (5) analyse the business case; (6) develop the product to determine practicality; (7) test market the product; (8) commercialize it. Then they monitor market response.

Decisions must be made about product quality and performance, features and benefits, design, packaging and labelling, and branding. Quality should be seen in terms of how well a product satisfies customer needs. Features are attributes that contribute to product functionality and deliver benefits. Design is especially important for differentiation. Packaging protects products and facilitates their use or storage. Labels provide information, attract attention, describe features and benefits, differentiate products and reinforce brand image. Branding identifies a product and

case study — Philips refines its brand image

Philips Electronics, based in the Netherlands, is rethinking its brand image to compete more effectively in the consumer and business markets. Philips' product mix consists of consumer and professional lighting products; home appliances and home entertainment products; and medical systems for hospitals and clinics. In the past, many of the company's strongest brands were individual brands, such as Norelco. Now the company name is being added to some product lines, resulting in brands like Philips Norelco, to strengthen brand salience.

Although research indicates that the targeted segments have a positive image of the brand, Philips also wants to sharpen its differentiation by refining the brand's associations. 'Philips already has an image of being reliable and trustworthy, and that gives us a great base on which to build', notes the head of global management. 'But we're not perceived as exciting or innovative in the minds of our consumers, even though we are constantly innovating. So we need to change that perception.'[78]

At the same time, Philips' marketers recognize that many products are overburdened with features

that confuse customers. In response, the company is using customer-friendly design to heighten the 'sense and simplicity' of its products. Its four-member Simplicity Advisory Board, which consists of a fashion designer, an architect, a professor and a graphic designer, is on call to keep Philips focused on stylish yet easy-to-use functionality. Innovation is still a priority, but in the interest of simplicity rather than for the sake of new technology and complex features. The chief marketing officer explains: 'In the past, companies just developed the technology and hoped someone would buy it. Now we are starting from the point of discovering what exactly consumers want a product to do.'[79]

Case questions

1 What are the arguments for and against Philips adding the company brand to its individual brands (as in Philips Norelco)?

2 How is Philips integrating product and brand planning – and why?

differentiates it from competing products to stimulate customer response. Brand equity is the extra value customers perceive in a brand that builds long-term loyalty and boosts competitive advantage.

Apply your knowledge

Select an organization offering a branded good or service with which you are familiar and research its product and brand. Summarize your findings in a brief oral presentation or written report.

- From a customer's perspective, how would you describe the product's quality and performance? Do you think this perception of value matches what the marketer intended?
- How do the features deliver benefits to satisfy needs of the targeted customer segments?
- How do design, packaging and labelling contribute to your reaction, as a customer, to this product?
- Where does this product appear to be in its life cycle? How do you know?
- How would you describe this product's brand? What is the organization doing to build brand equity?

Build your own marketing plan

Going back to the marketing plan you've been preparing, is your product a tangible good or an intangible service? What level of quality is appropriate (and affordable) to meet the needs of the targeted customer segments? What needs do customers satisfy through products such as yours and what features must your product have in order to deliver the expected or desired benefits? What can you do with design, packaging and labelling to add value and differentiate your product? What brand image do you want to project? How do you want customers to feel about the brand and react toward it? What can you do to encourage brand loyalty? Think about your answers in the context of your earlier ideas and decisions, then draft the product and brand sections of your marketing plan.

Planning for pricing

Introduction

The global market leaders in personal computers are Hewlett-Packard, Dell, Lenovo and . . . Acer. Based in Taiwan, Acer has emphasized pricing in its marketing plan to boost turnover and spread its brand around the world. It's already the top-selling laptop brand in Europe but is seeking a higher share in China and other markets by pricing its PCs at least 5 per cent below competing PCs. Acer's success shows how price can be used to achieve such marketing objectives as increasing market share and strengthening competitive position. Price is also the key to achieving financial objectives such as sales and profitability targets. Despite its low prices, Acer is profitable, although its margins are much lower than those of the top three market leaders.[80]

Whereas the company spends money on other marketing-mix elements, it actually makes money through pricing. Nonetheless, ultimately it is the consumer or business customer who determines whether the price of an offer represents real value. Therefore, this section begins with a discussion of how customers perceive value and the difference between cost-based and value-based pricing, which is essential to planning for effective pricing. The next part of the section explains the various external and internal influences on pricing that you must consider when preparing a marketing plan. The final part of the section discusses how to handle specific pricing decisions, including setting pricing objectives, pricing new products, pricing multiple products and adapting prices.

Understanding price and value

Whether the price is a pound sterling, a euro or a bag of rice, customers will buy only when they perceive value – when a product's perceived benefits in meeting their needs outweigh the perceived price. Even when the price is collected in barter, customers will not complete a transaction if they perceive insufficient value. No matter what type of product you market, you cannot make planning decisions about price without looking at value from your customers' perspective.

Perceptions of value

A product's value is perceived by customers according to the total benefits they receive. An individual customer may consider one benefit more important than the others, but the combination of all benefits is what provides value. Customers form value perceptions in the context of competing or substitute products that might meet their needs, on the basis of benefits such as:

- *Performance.* Does the product perform as it should in meeting the customer's needs? Does it perform better than competing products?
- *Features.* Does the product have all the features expected or desired to meet current needs and future or unspoken needs? How do the features compare with those of competing products?
- *Quality.* Is the product defect-free, reliable and durable, compared with competing products?

- *Service*. Does the service meet customers' expectations? Is it faster, more convenient or more personalized than that offered by competitors?
- *Personal benefits*. Does the product deliver personal benefits such as status or self-expression?
- *Availability*. Is the product available whenever needed? Does the price change according to availability? How does this compare with that of competing products?

Against the total perceived benefits, customers weigh the total perceived costs (time and money) associated with the product, including:

- *Initial purchase price*. What time and money must the customer spend to obtain the product initially? How does the purchase price compare with competing products?
- *Maintenance and repair costs*. What is the estimated cost of maintenance over the product's life? How often is maintenance or repair generally required and how much time or money might the customer lose while waiting for repairs or maintenance?
- *Ongoing fees*. Does the product require an annual usage charge or other fees after the initial purchase? Must the customer pay a tax to continue using or possessing the product?
- *Installation*. Does the product require installation? What is the cost in time and money for installing this product compared with competing products?
- *Training*. Do customers need training to use the product properly and if so, what is the cost in time and money compared with competing products?
- *Ancillary products*. Does the product require the purchase of ancillary products, and at what cost? How does this compare with competing products?
- *Financing*. If applicable, what is the cost of financing the purchase of this product, what is the monthly payment (if any) and how do such costs compare with those of competing products?

Pricing based on value

Through research, you can determine how customers in your targeted segment(s) perceive the value of your product's total benefits and costs and the value of competing products. Then you can use this understanding of the customer's perspective to plan your pricing as well as your costs and your product design (see Figure 4.19a). This is not the way marketers have traditionally planned for pricing. In the past, most started with the product and its cost, developed a pricing plan to cover costs and then looked for ways to communicate value to customer (see Figure 4.19).[81]

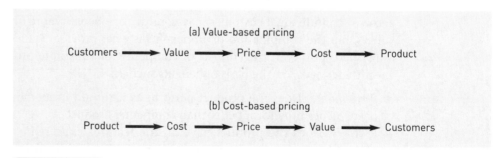

(a) Value-based pricing

Customers → Value → Price → Cost → Product

(b) Cost-based pricing

Product → Cost → Price → Value → Customers

Figure 4.19   Value-based pricing compared with cost-based pricing

Source: Adapted from Thomas T. Nagle and John E. Hogan, *The Strategy and Tactics of Pricing*, 4th edn (Upper Saddle River, NJ: Pearson Prentice Hall, 2006), p. 4.

Consider how IKEA uses value-based pricing.

marketing in practice   IKEA

Illustrating the trend toward value-based pricing, the Swedish furniture retailer IKEA starts by identifying a customer problem, such as the need for affordable, stylish, smaller-size furniture suitable for entertaining visitors in the kitchen. Its marketers examine value perceptions and competitive pricing, then set a target price lower than rivals. After estimating costs and setting product specifications appropriate for the target

price, they consult with suppliers and come to agreement on costs. Finally, they design the product, have it manufactured, then pack and ship the furniture to stores as inexpensively and expeditiously as possible. Thanks to careful pricing, IKEA has been able to expand to more than 250 stores in 34 nations and sell products online as well.[82]

Analysing influences on pricing decisions

Notice how IKEA looks closely at customer needs and at the competition (external influences) as well as its costs (an internal influence). As you prepare your marketing plan, you must consider a number of external and internal influences on pricing decisions.

External influences

Among the major external influences on pricing are: (1) customers; (2) market and demand; (3) competition; (4) channel members; and (5) legal, regulatory and ethical considerations.

Customers

Not all customers can or want to compare prices; not all customers are interested in buying the lowest-priced alternative. Research shows that consumers will accept a price if it is within what they consider an acceptable range for that good or service.[83] Customers may decide against buying a product that is priced unusually low because they suspect poor quality yet be willing to spend more if a product appears to offer value-added benefits, such as a prestige brand or special service.

Business buyers in particular may feel pressure to acquire raw materials, components or services at the lowest possible prices, which in turn affects their suppliers' pricing strategies. Some business buyers and consumers constantly switch brands or suppliers in search of bargains, especially now that they can quickly and easily compare prices online. Your challenge as a marketer is to communicate your product's benefits so customers recognize the differentiation and perceive the value in relation to the price.

If your product is particularly innovative or meets unspoken customer needs, you may have to go against long-established traditions of pricing and service levels.

Pricing decision	Inelastic demand	Elastic demand
Small decrease	Small increase in demand	Larger increase in demand
Small increase	Small decrease in demand	Larger decrease in demand

Figure 4.20   Pricing and elasticity of demand

For example, the founder of Japan's QB Net barbershops was accustomed to paying 3,000 yen or more for a traditional hour-long haircut with personal service. In a hurry during one such haircut, he wondered how many men shared his need for speed. When he asked people if they would be interested in a 10-minute haircut for 1,000 yen, he got such a positive reaction that he started QB Net. Today the chain has grown to 375 stores around Asia and serves 10 million customers annually in Japan alone.[84]

Market and demand

You also need to research the **demand** for your product in the target market – how many units are likely to be sold at different prices – and the effect of price sensitivity, or the **elasticity of demand**. When your research reveals **elastic demand**, a small percentage change in price will usually produce a large change in quantity demanded. On the other hand, if your research reveals **inelastic demand**, a small percentage change in price will usually produce a small percentage change in quantity demanded (*see* Figure 4.20).

Note that you can actually maintain or increase revenues by raising the price when demand is inelastic or by cutting the price when demand is elastic. Still, if you price a product excessively high you risk reducing demand; price it too low and you may spark strong demand that you cannot profitably satisfy. Yet it can be difficult to research the exact elasticity of demand for a particular product, even though you can conduct pricing experiments and analyse previous sales history to get data for estimating the elasticity of demand. Remember that elasticity of demand can vary widely from one segment to another and one market to another.

Competition

Whether the product is furniture or haircuts, competition exerts a strong influence on pricing decisions. Customers look at the costs and benefits of competing products when thinking about value, so be aware of what competitors are charging. However, it's risky to imitate another organization's pricing simply for competitive reasons, because your organization probably has very different costs, objectives and resources from those of your rival.

Should you become involved in a price war, your profit margins and prices will fall lower and lower. Another risk is that your product could face price competition from products that meet customers' needs in different ways, as when travellers can choose between air travel and train travel. In the planning process, therefore, you should consider any substitutes your customers might choose to meet their needs and how these choices could affect your pricing decisions.

Channel members

When making channel arrangements, you must ensure that wholesalers and retailers can buy at a price that will allow profitable resale to business customers or consumers. Channel members have to be able to cover the costs they incur in processing customer orders, repackaging bulk shipment lots into customer-size lots, product storage and other operations. To make this work, you have to think carefully about the costs and profit margins of all channel participants, along with the price perceptions of the targeted customer segment, when setting your product's price.

Even your choice of intermediaries depends on your product's price. If you market high-quality, high-priced products, you will have difficulty reaching your targeted segment through intermediaries known for stocking low-quality, low-priced products. If you market lower-quality, low-priced products, upmarket stores will not stock your products because of the mismatch with their target market. In short, carefully coordinate your channel decisions with your price decisions.

Legal, regulatory and ethical considerations

You will have to abide by local, national and regional laws and regulations when pricing your products. Among the issues are:

- *Price controls and price fixing.* Some countries control the prices of products such as prescription drugs, which limits pricing choices. Some areas also forbid the use of price fixing and other actions considered anti-competitive.
- *Resale maintenance.* Companies in the United Kingdom, the United States and some other nations are generally not allowed to insist that channel members maintain a certain minimum price on their products. This paves the way for more competition and reinforces the need to consider pricing throughout the channel.
- *Industry regulation.* Government regulators can affect pricing in some industries by allowing or blocking the sale of certain products or bundles.
- *Government requirements.* Legal and regulatory actions can affect pricing by mandating product standards, tests or labelling; these requirements add to the costs that you will seek to recoup through product pricing.
- *Taxes and tariffs.* Prices for products sold in certain countries must include value-added tax (VAT) or sales taxes, which vary from nation to nation. In addition, import tariffs also raise the price that customers pay for some products.

Going beyond legal and regulatory guidelines, look at the ethical implications. For example, is an airline or bank acting ethically when it promotes a special price without fully and prominently explaining any restrictions and extra fees? Is a pharmaceutical manufacturer acting ethically when it sets high prices for a life-saving drug that patients in some areas cannot afford? As challenging as such issues may be, building a reputation for ethical pricing ultimately enhances your brand's image and reinforces long-term customer loyalty.

Internal influences

Your pricing decisions will be affected by these major internal influences: (1) organizational and marketing plan objectives; (2) costs; (3) targeting and positioning; (4) product decisions and life cycle; and (5) other marketing-mix decisions.

Organizational and marketing plan objectives

Price and every other marketing-mix element must tie back to the objectives of the organization and the marketing plan. Because price generates revenue, it is a particularly important ingredient for achieving sales and profitability targets as well as for meeting societal objectives. If growth and market share are your key objectives, you might lower the product's price and reduce its perceived benefits or develop an entirely new product with fewer benefits that can be marketed at a lower price. Or you might develop a new product designed to sell for less as a way of meeting customer needs, as Nokia did by creating basic handsets for first-time mobile phone customers in India and other markets.[85]

Costs

Most companies price their products to cover costs, at least over the long run. In the short term, however, you may be willing to price for little or no profit when establishing a new product, competing with aggressive rivals or seeking to achieve another objective. When you have limited control over the **variable costs** that vary with production and sales, such as the cost of raw materials and parts, you will find pricing for profit even more challenging. For example, the sweets manufacturer Hershey recently experienced an increase in cocoa costs. Although the company had not raised the price of its chocolate candy bars for years, it finally decided on an 11 per cent increase. To pave the way for customer reception of this increase, the company promoted special 'limited edition' versions of Kit-Kat and other candy bars. As a result, sales increased 3 per cent during the three months following the price hike.[86]

If you compete primarily on the basis of price, you will be particularly concerned with managing variable costs and **fixed costs** (such as rent, insurance and other business expenses, which do not vary with production and sales). This keeps prices low and protects profit margins, as illustrated by Colruyt.

marketing in practice   Colruyt

Franz Colruyt, the Belgian discount food chain, looks for every possible way to minimize costs so it can keep grocery prices low. Its 165 stores have no fancy decorations, background music or shopping bags for customers to use. Instead of spending heavily on advertising, Colruyt invites customers to sign up to receive notices of forthcoming sales. To keep its prices competitive, 15 employees check prices at rival stores every day. The chain also publicizes a special hot-line number for customers to call if they find an item is being sold elsewhere for less. This reassures shoppers that Colruyt's prices are the lowest and encourages customer loyalty. Now Colruyt plans to open new stores in the Netherlands and Luxembourg.[87]

Although you may have difficulty determining a product's exact costs – especially if it has not yet been launched in the marketplace – you need cost information to calculate the **break-even point**. This is the point at which a product's revenues and costs are equal and beyond which the organization earns more profit as more units are sold. Unless you make some change in price (which will affect demand) or variable cost, your product will not become profitable until unit volume reaches the break-even point. The equation for this calculation is:

$$\text{break-even point} = \frac{\text{total fixed costs}}{\text{unit price} - \text{variable costs per unit}}$$

If, for example, a product's total fixed costs are €100,000, and one unit's variable costs are €2, the break-even point at a unit price of €6 is:

$$\frac{€100,000}{€6 - €2} = 25,000 \text{ units}$$

Using this break-even point, the organization will incur losses if it sells fewer than 25,000 units priced at €6. Above 25,000 units, however, the company can cover both variable and fixed costs and increase its profits as it sells a higher quantity. Figure 4.21 is a graphical depiction of break-even analysis, which does not take into account any changes in demand; how competitors might respond; how customers perceive the product's value; or other external influences on pricing. Nor does break-even analysis reflect how the cost per unit is likely to drop as you produce higher quantities and gain economies of scale. Still, it provides a rough approximation of the unit sales volume that you must achieve to cover costs and begin producing profit, which is important for planning purposes.

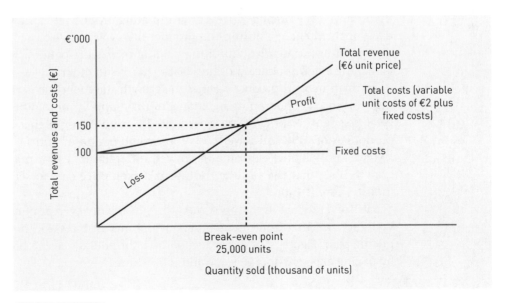

Figure 4.21   **Break-even analysis**

Targeting and positioning

Any pricing decisions should be consistent with your targeting and positioning decisions. For example, the grocery chain Aldi targets price-conscious consumers but positions itself as marketing good-quality food products for less. In line with this targeting and positioning, the retailer sets low prices and adjusts all its activities to keep costs as low as possible. When Aldi opened a city centre store in Manchester, its marketing plan targeted affluent shoppers in particular, because this segment is interested in upmarket foods at discount prices.[88]

Of course, if you're targeting non-price-sensitive customer segments and your positioning is upmarket, you will plan your pricing very differently.

---

marketing in practice   Vertu

Vertu, a division of Finland's Nokia, sells a line of expensive mobile phone handsets that are both chic and functional. The limited edition Signature Cobra, encrusted with rubies, diamonds and emeralds, carries a price tag of more than £160,000. Vertu handsets are positioned as upmarket fashion accessories for celebrities and other wealthy customers, with a special service component. Users can reach Vertu's concierge staff with one button and request help (in five languages) with restaurant reservations, airline tickets and other arrangements anywhere in the world. The high prices support the brand's luxury positioning and exclusivity.[89]

Product decisions and life cycle

As you can see in Figure 4.19a, pricing decisions are closely intertwined with product decisions. More companies are developing new products after they have determined customers' perceptions of value, set target costs and set a target price, rather than starting the pricing process after initiating production. Of course your pricing decisions will change during the product life cycle. As discussed below, you may start with either market-skimming pricing or market-penetration pricing when launching a new product and then make changes in other stages.

By the time your product reaches the growth stage where competition is increasing, you should choose pricing strategies that support more differentiation in targeted segments or pricing strategies geared to stimulating higher demand for more economies of scale and lower costs (or a combination of both).[90] As one example, BMW's Mini Cooper car remains so well differentiated as it matures through its growth stage that the car does not need drastic price cuts to sell, despite intense industry competition.[91]

Sales of a product in maturity will grow less rapidly even as more competitors are vying for the attention of customers, which necessitates another change in your pricing plan. Figure 4.22 shows five options for pricing mature products, suggested by pricing experts Thomas Nagle and John Hogan.

Pricing alternatives	Purpose
Unbundle and price products individually	Compete by pricing goods and services individually rather than as a bundle
Re-examine customer price sensitivity and change price accordingly	Maintain or improve revenue and profits
Set prices based on better understanding of costs and capacity	Reflect realistic costs and earn more profit at times when demand outstrips capacity
Add related products	Leverage success of an existing product by adding related goods or services at a profit
Change channel pricing	Expand channel coverage while reducing channel margins

Figure 4.22 **Pricing mature products**

Source: Adapted from Thomas T. Nagle and John E. Hogan, *The Strategy and Tactics of Pricing*, 4th edn (Upper Saddle River, NJ: Pearson Prentice Hall, 2006), pp. 275–7.

Use the following checklist as you consider pricing decisions during marketing planning.

Essential marketing plan checklist

Pricing through the product life cycle

Whether your marketing plan is for a new product or an existing product, you will face pricing decisions as it moves through its life cycle. The following questions are a good starting point for considering key issues in pricing at each point in the life cycle. Place a tick mark alongside the questions that apply to your situation as you note your answers in the space provided.

☐ At introduction, how can pricing be used to encourage channel acceptance of a new product?

_____

☐ At introduction, what pricing approach will stimulate product trial and repeat purchasing among customers?

_____

☐ At introduction, how can pricing be used to manage initial supply and demand?

_____

☐ During growth, how can pricing be used for competitive purposes?

_____

☐ During growth, what pricing approach will lead to break-even and profitability?

_____

☐ In maturity, how can pricing encourage customer loyalty and defend market share?

_____

☐ In maturity, what pricing approach will achieve sustained profitability and other objectives?

_____

☐ In maturity, what pricing approach will support expanded channel coverage?

_____

☐ In decline, what pricing approach might slow the slide of unit sales and protect profits?

_____

☐ In decline, how can pricing be used for profit as competitors withdraw from the market?

_____

Other marketing-mix decisions

In addition to product decisions and channel arrangements, planning for pricing is influenced by (and influences) planning for marketing communications. Obviously, many producers and channel members feature pricing in their promotions to attract customer attention and compete with direct rivals. Although marketers of luxury products may not make price as visible a part of their promotion activities, their pricing decisions will be affected by the benefits and value they emphasize in their marketing communications. In short, be sure your pricing fits with the other decisions you include in your marketing plan.

Making pricing decisions

Once you understand the external and internal influences on pricing, you can set pricing objectives for the period covered by the marketing plan. If your product is new, you will decide between market-skimming and market-penetration pricing. As your product line expands, you will face decisions about pricing multiple products and you may need to plan to adapt your product's price.

Setting pricing objectives

Your objectives for pricing will be based on your organization's objectives and those of the marketing plan. There are three categories of pricing objectives:

- *Financial objectives for pricing.* You may seek to maintain or improve profits; maintain or improve revenues; reach the break-even point by a certain date; support another product's revenues and profitability; or achieve a certain return.
- *Marketing objectives for pricing.* Here, you set relationship targets for pricing that will attract or retain customers; build or defend market share; build or change channel relations; or build brand image, awareness and loyalty.
- *Societal objectives for pricing.* You may set targets for covering the cost of using ecologically friendly materials and processes; providing reverse channels for recycling; generating cash for charitable contributions; or achieving other non-business objectives.

To illustrate, London is one of a growing number of cities that has set the societal objective of using pricing to reduce traffic jams and pollution. London charges drivers a fee of £8 to take their vehicles into central districts during weekdays. Local residents receive a discount, and certain vehicles (such as ambulances and taxis) pay nothing. The fee has cut traffic by 15 to 20 per cent, increased the average speed during peak times and raised money to pay for public transportation improvements.[92]

Pricing new products

A new product presents a special pricing challenge because you must decide whether to use **market-penetration pricing** and price relatively low for rapid acquisition of market share or use **market-skimming pricing**, setting a relatively high price to skim maximum revenues from the market, layer by layer. With market-penetration pricing, the price may be so low that the product is unprofitable and/or priced lower than competing products in the short term. Yet such pricing may be effective in the long run, if you are determined to boost volume and gain efficiencies that will lower costs as a foundation for future profitability.

Toyota, for example, introduced its Yaris subcompact car in Europe using market-penetration pricing. To build sales, the carmaker packed the car with extra features that enhance value perceptions and accepted smaller profit margins than it earns on luxury cars under the company's Lexus brand. Toyota sees the Yaris as competing with the top European brands (Volkswagen, Renault, Opel/Vauxhall and Ford) rather than with low-priced cars from Hyundai and Kia. In the growth stage of its life cycle, the Yaris has been redesigned and sells more than 250,000 units in Europe every year.[93]

Market-penetration pricing is not appropriate for every product, which is where internal and external influences come into play. Your customers may perceive less value in a luxury product that is launched with market-penetration pricing, for example. Also, market-penetration pricing may be inappropriate for the kinds of channel members you need to use to reach targeted customer segments. Finally, such pricing may not be consistent with your promotion decisions.

You should consider market-skimming pricing for innovative or top-quality products, to make an upmarket impression on selected customer segments that are less price-sensitive and place a premium on innovation. Market-skimming pricing is common with products employing new technology such as digital radio receivers, for example. Not only do you take in more money to help cover costs with this approach, you have the flexibility to lower prices as you monitor competitive response, attain volumes that yield economies of scale and shift to targeting more price-sensitive segments. On the other hand, if your initial price is too high, you may set customer expectations too high, slow initial sales and lower repeat sales if the product does not fulfil those expectations.

Pricing multiple products

Your plan for pricing should take into account more than one product in the line or mix, any optional or complementary products and any product bundles. The way you price each product sets it apart from other products in your mix, reflecting or reinforcing customer perceptions of each product's value. You can then balance prices within the product line or mix to reach your total revenue or profit objectives. As an example, price competition among lower-priced models of car may produce slimmer profits for a carmaker even as prices on upmarket vehicles boost profit margins for those products.[94] In services, a hotel company may market deluxe hotels, convention hotels and modestly priced tourist hotels, each with its own target market, pricing objectives and room rates in line with the perceived value.

If you offer a bundle of goods or services you must determine how to price that bundle, given the competition and customers' perceptions of the bundle's value. One advantage of bundling is that competitors can't easily duplicate every aspect of a unique, specially priced bundle. If customers do not want everything in your bundle at the price set, however, they may buy fewer products individually or look at competitive bundles. And later in a product's life cycle, you may get more benefit by unbundling and pricing each part separately.

Adapting prices

Your plan should allow for adapting prices when appropriate, either by increasing perceived value or by reducing perceived cost. Depending on local laws and regulations – and the rest of your marketing plan – some ways in which you can adapt prices include:

- *Discounts*. You can plan special discounts for customers who buy in large quantities or during non-peak periods; pay in cash; or assume logistical functions such as picking up products that would otherwise be delivered.
- *Allowances*. You can invite customers to trade-in older products and receive credit toward purchases of newer products; you may also offer customers refunds or rebates for buying during promotional periods.
- *Extra value*. To encourage intermediaries to carry your products, you may offer small quantities free when resellers place orders during a promotional period.

For consumers, you may temporarily increase the amount of product without increasing the price.

- *Periodic mark-downs.* Retailers, in particular, plan to mark down merchandise periodically, at the end of a selling season, to attract or reward shoppers or to stimulate new product trial.
- *Segmented pricing.* Depending on your segmentation decisions, your pricing can be adapted for customers of different ages (such as lower prices for children and older customers); members and non-members (such as lower prices for professional association members); different purchase locations (such as lower prices for products bought and picked up at the main plant); and time of purchase (such as lower prices for mobile phone service during non-peak periods).

Internal or external influences may prompt you to raise or lower a product's price. For example, you can use a price cut to stimulate higher demand or defend against competitive price reductions. You may want to use a price increase to deal with rising costs or product improvements that raise perceived quality and value. Whether such price adaptations achieve their objectives will depend on customer and competitor reaction.

Although you will usually fix most prices, the final price for a product is sometimes reached by negotiation with customers, as in the way consumers buy cars or airlines buy jet planes. And more organizations and consumers are allowing prices to be set through online auctions and *reverse auctions* (in which customers set the price at which they want to buy). Auction pricing can be a good way to market excess or out-of-date stock to price-sensitive customers without affecting the fixed price set for other segments.

Summary

Customers perceive a product's value according to the total benefits weighed against the total costs, in the context of competitive products and prices. During the planning process, marketers must research how customers perceive the value of their product and the value of competing products and, ideally, work backwards using the perceived value to make price, cost and product decisions. External influences on pricing decisions are: customers; market and demand; competition; channel members; and legal, regulatory and ethical considerations. Internal influences on pricing decisions are: organizational and marketing plan objectives; costs; targeting and positioning; product decisions and life cycle; and other marketing-mix decisions.

Two approaches to pricing new products are market-penetration pricing (to capture market share quickly) and market-skimming pricing (to skim maximum revenues from each market layer). Depending on local laws and regulations and the rest of the marketing plan, marketers can adapt prices using discounts, allowances, extra value, periodic mark-downs or segment pricing. Also, prices may be increased or decreased according to internal or external influences; negotiated; or influenced by customers in online or reverse auctions.

case study   Tata Group's 'one lakh' car

Is it possible to profit by marketing a car that sells for less than £1,600? India's Tata Group plans to find out. For several years, the company has been developing an ultra-low-priced compact car with a rear-mounted engine and room for four passengers. When first conceived, the car was to be priced at one lakh, which is 100,000 rupees (equivalent to approximately £1,120 at that time). Although the cost of materials has risen as the car moves through design and testing, Tata still targets a selling price of less than £ 1,600. But is this realistic?

Tata knows how to apply value-based pricing. It markets the Ace, a small lorry, for 1.1 lakh. Not surprisingly, the Ace has proven popular; within a year of its introduction, it had already generated sufficient revenue to cover all development costs. For now, the Ace is sold only in India because it would need substantial (and costly) changes to meet crash and emissions standards in other countries. Moreover, the Ace's profits are being squeezed by the same rising raw-materials costs that will affect the profitability of the 'one lakh' car. Yet through the Ace, Tata has gained design and manufacturing experience that it can use in

planning other affordable vehicles. It has also called on Fiat's small-car expertise.

In anticipation of the launch of the 'one lakh' car, Tata is building a new factory and test-driving prototypes of the new design. Despite the start-up expense, Tata believes that demand will be high enough to fuel significant sales, which is why its initial production target is 250,000 per year. Economies of scale will spread the development and production costs over more units, helping the profit picture. Yet Tata could face competition as companies such as Pakistan's Transmission Motor Company and India's Bajaj consider launching their own ultra-low-priced cars. Will the 'one lakh' car be both profitable and popular?[95]

Case questions

1 Why is market-penetration pricing appropriate for the marketing plan to launch Tata's 'one lakh' car?

2 If several competitors introduce ultra-low-priced cars, how would you suggest that Tata's marketers respond?

Apply your knowledge

Choose a particular business product (such as a tractor or specialized software) and research the marketer's approach to pricing. Then write up your ideas or give an oral presentation to the class.

- What benefits does this product appear to offer to business customers?
- What initial and ongoing costs would business customers perceive in connection with buying and maintaining this product?
- If the product is new, what pricing approach is the company using to launch it? Why is this approach appropriate for the product?
- How does the price reflect the product's positioning and other marketing mix decisions?
- How does the price of one competing or substitute product appear to reflect that product's value (from the customer's perspective)? If you were a customer, would you place a higher value on this competing product than on the product you have been researching? Why?

Build your own marketing plan

Continue developing your marketing plan by making pricing decisions about a new or existing product. What pricing objectives will you set for this product? If the product is new, will you use market-skimming pricing or market-penetration pricing – and why? Which external influences are most important to the pricing of this product? How do internal influences affect your pricing decision for this product? What price will you set for this one product and in what situations would you consider adapting the price? Consider how these pricing decisions fit in with earlier marketing decisions and with the objectives you've set, then document them in your marketing plan.

Planning for channels and logistics

Introduction

Zara, based in Spain, is known around the world for 'fast fashion'. Once its designers identify a new trend, they can have new styles manufactured and in company stores within five weeks. Knowing that today's most in-demand style may be unwanted tomorrow, Zara makes much of its clothing in Spain – close to its design centre – and speeds it by lorry to its European stores (by air to stores outside Europe). Yet by controlling supply and transportation costs, Zara has kept its gross profit margin well above 50 per cent.[96] Zara is a good example of the marketing-mix tool of 'place', how a company enables customers to take possession of a product in a convenient place and time, in a convenient form and quantity and at an acceptable price.

As basic as this may sound, planning for this part of the marketing mix is complex because these decisions must fit with your other marketing decisions while simultaneously meeting customers' needs and organizational objectives. Zara, for instance, must get new fashions to stores very quickly – without losing sight of its profit expectations. Focusing on 'place', this section opens with an overview of the value chain and its effect on marketing planning. Next, you'll learn about planning for flows and responsibilities within the value chain, followed by a discussion of channel levels and decisions about individual channel members. The closing part of the section examines some important logistics decisions to consider when preparing a marketing plan.

Analysing the value chain

The **value chain**, also known as the **value delivery network** or *supply chain*, is the succession of interrelated, value-added functions undertaken by the marketer with suppliers, wholesalers, retailers and other participants (including customers) to source supplies and ultimately deliver a product that fulfils customers' needs. Figure 4.23 shows a simplified value chain and explains the key areas to be analysed during the marketing planning process. The point is to understand how each participant in the chain adds value to the good or service that your customers buy and use. Then your marketing plan can reflect a 'performance' view of the chain, including activities to enhance the combined efficiency and effectiveness of all partners, where possible.

Imagine Zara as the central link of the value chain. In its role as producer, it's responsible for coordinating the transformation of inputs (fabric, for instance) into outputs (clothing) as well as inbound functions that occur upstream (bringing fabric to factories) and outbound functions that occur downstream (getting clothing to stores). The value added downstream occurs within a **marketing channel** (also known as a **distribution channel**), the set of functions performed by the producer or intermediaries, such as retailers, to make a particular product available to customers. Zara owns its own stores but other producers sell to wholesalers and/or retailers that resell to consumers.

The profitable flow of products, information and payments inbound and outbound to meet customer requirements is accomplished through **logistics**. One or

Decisions about adding value inbound:

- How to manage suppliers and obtain materials plus other needed inputs (locating suppliers, buying parts, printing product manuals, etc.)
- How to manage logistics (arranging physical, informational and financial flows related to inbound orders, supply availability, deliveries, etc.)

Decisions about adding value through the marketer's functions:

- How to manage flows in marketing (interpreting market data to understand customer needs, developing suitable products and distribution, communicating product differentiation, etc.)
- How to manage flows to transform inputs into outputs (manufacturing tangible items, delivering intangible services)
- How to manage flows through customer service and internal operations (responding to customer enquiries, managing materials, etc.)

Decisions about adding value outbound:

- How to manage product availability for convenient customer interactions (arranging direct or indirect channels, selecting and supervising channel members to handle transactions, etc.)
- How to manage logistics (arranging physical, informational and financial flows related to allocating quantities and assortments to meet demand, expedite transportation, manage inventory, etc.)

Customers

Figure 4.23   Areas of focus in a simplified value chain

more parties must handle inbound transportation of raw materials and components so Zara can produce its apparel; Zara or one of its suppliers must maintain raw materials inventory. Zara has to track production quantities, manage finished goods inventory and despatch finished goods outbound. Moreover, Zara's stores have to manage downstream transactions with buyers.

In planning for channel and logistics decisions, you should take into account the needs and behaviour of targeted customer segments; your SWOT analysis and competitive situation; your product's positioning; and your marketing plan objectives. Then consider which functions in the value chain must be accomplished and which participants should be responsible for each. These decisions lay the groundwork for adding value and meeting customers' needs at an acceptable cost to the customer and an acceptable profit to the organization. Because of the number of alternatives available to you, you should analyse a variety of channel and logistics arrangements before you make a final decision and document it in your marketing plan.

The value chain for services

If your marketing plan is for a service, be aware that your value chain should put particular focus on inbound activities, the service experience itself and outbound activities that involve the customer. Inbound functions cover supplies, information and payments related to providing the service; the service experience occurs in the central link (if delivered by your firm); and outbound functions cover service availability plus associated information and payments. Logistics for services are concerned with having the right supplies (and people) in the right place at the right time. Moreover, because services are perishable – they cannot be stored for future sale or consumption – your plan must carefully manage all flows to balance supply and demand.

The service experience, based on value-chain activities and logistics decisions, influences customer loyalty as well as costs, as the following example illustrates.

marketing in practice   British Airways and Austrian Airlines

British Airways and Austrian Airlines have made slightly different decisions about how to provide value to air travellers. Both are concerned about costs, especially when the price of fuel is sky high, but they also need to satisfy customers by delivering a comfortable experience. Although some low-fare competitors charge for all food and drink, these two carriers are not taking that route. British Airways recently substituted snacks and drinks for full meals on mid-morning and mid-afternoon flights; this lowered its costs and changed its inbound supply and inflight activities. In contrast, Austrian Airlines increased services for business-class passengers: it hired chefs to prepare gourmet meals on long flights and added several speciality coffees and desserts. This increased its costs and affected suppliers, inbound activities and the service experience itself. Still, the real question is: How will these changes affect long-term customer loyalty and profitability?[97]

Flows and responsibilities in the value chain

Your marketing plan should consider the need for a **reverse channel**, to return goods for service or when worn out and to reclaim products, parts or packaging for recycling. This is particularly important if you're marketing online and want to reassure customers that they can return or exchange what they buy. Amazon.com, for example, has arranged with a specialized company to handle any customer returns, which frees the retailer to concentrate on its retailing business.[98] In addition, look beyond immediate value-chain functions to see whether your suppliers' suppliers are providing the required quality or ecologically safe materials and, if selling to businesses, see how your customers' customers use the final product.

You face difficult trade-offs between value added and cost when making decisions about channels and logistics. Having a wide variety of products immediately available at all times in all locations (or ready to be despatched quickly on demand) is the most desirable situation but often too costly for your organization and for your customer. On the other hand, your customers are likely to be unsatisfied – and may turn to competitors – if you have too few products available; the wrong quantities or models available; and/or slow or expensive transactions.

There is a growing trend toward strengthening long-term relationships with value chain partners for mutual benefit. The Swedish furniture company IKEA forges long-term connections with its suppliers to ensure a steady stream of products designed to its specifications and cost guidelines. The company teaches suppliers to negotiate with their suppliers for the best price, quality materials and delivery schedules. 'When we buy fabric, for example, we have to compare the price from many, many suppliers', says a manager at the Binh Thanh Textile Factory in Vietnam, one of IKEA's suppliers.[99]

Planning for channels

Depending on your organization's situation and objectives, you can plan for a value chain that includes direct or indirect channels. With **direct channels**, you make products available directly to customers. For example, Dell uses direct channels, marketing its computers online, by phone and through catalogues. With **indirect channels**, you work through **intermediaries**, outside businesses or individuals that help producers make goods or services available to customers. Figure 4.24 shows

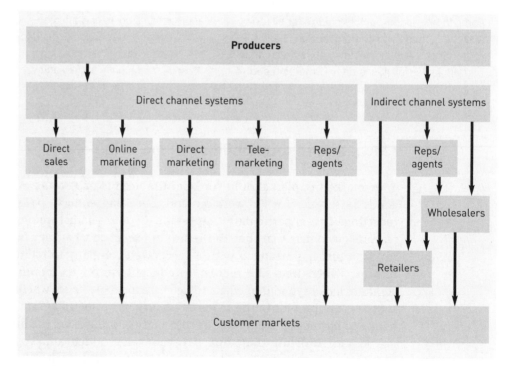

Figure 4.24 Marketing channel arrangements

Source: Adapted from Roger J. Best, *Market-Based Management*, 2nd edn (Upper Saddle River, NJ: Prentice Hall, 2000), p. 199.

how goods or services would reach customers through direct and indirect channels. It also shows the three major types of intermediaries, each of which adds value in a particular way:

- *Wholesalers* buy from producers, sort and store products, create smaller lots for buyer convenience and resell to other intermediaries or to business customers. Some take on duties normally handled elsewhere in the value chain, such as monitoring a customer's inventory.
- *Retailers* are companies such as IKEA and Tesco that resell products, giving consumers easy and convenient access to an array of products. Customers who buy from online retailers must wait for their purchases. Increasingly, however, online retailers such as Dixons in the United Kingdom offer installation and many other services offered by physical stores.[100]
- *Representatives, brokers and agents* (such as insurance agents) bring producers together with customers but generally do not take ownership of the products they market. These intermediaries add value through their knowledge of the market, customers and products.

In your marketing plan, you will have to specify the number of intermediary levels you want to use for each product – in other words, the length of the channel.

Channel length decisions

Longer channels have more intermediary levels separating the producer and its customers; shorter channels have fewer intermediaries. A direct channel is the shortest because there are no intermediaries and the producer deals directly with its customers through any or all of the methods shown at the left in Figure 4.24. This is appropriate when you want as much control as possible over dealings with customers and your organization can handle all outbound functions. If your markets and segments are not well defined or you lack the resources and knowledge to work directly with customers, however, using a direct channel can be inefficient at best and ineffective at worst.

The zero-level channel can work well for both business and consumer marketers, despite differences in products, customers, prices and markets. Nippon Steel, one of the world's largest steel producers, uses direct channels to sell to construction companies, carmakers, shipbuilders and other businesses in its home country of Japan and in other markets.[101]

Some organizations use a direct channel for certain segments (usually business customers) and an indirect channel with one level for other segments (usually consumers). This allows more control over the typically large-volume transactions with businesses and delegates responsibility for the higher number and smaller size of consumer transactions to intermediaries. Carmakers, for instance, use a direct channel when selling to government agencies so they can negotiate specifications, pricing and delivery, but use a separate single-level indirect dealer channel to sell to consumers. Here's a glimpse of Ford's value chain and dealer channel in Russia.

marketing in practice   Ford in Russia

Ford is the top-selling car brand in Russia, thanks to a forward-thinking marketing plan. Before any other foreign carmaker invested in local manufacturing, US-based Ford built a factory near St Petersburg and signed dealers to sell its Focus cars and wagons. Today it has 150 dealers in Russia; the southwestern Moscow dealer sells more Fords than any Ford dealer, anywhere.

Producing cars locally reduces import duties and transportation costs; it also gets cars to customers more quickly. Although Ford cars are more expensive than those made by local carmakers, customers are willing to pay more for extra features – and they like using Ford's affordable car loans to spread car payments over two or three years.[102]

Longer channels, such as the two- and three-level indirect channels illustrated at the right of Figure 4.24, send products through a series of representatives or agents, wholesalers or retailers before they reach the final customer. Such channel arrangements allow intermediaries to add value when your company is targeting multiple or geographically dispersed markets; you have limited resources or little customer knowledge; your customers have specialized needs; or your products require training, customization or service. Although the price paid by customers reflects a profit for intermediaries at all levels and covers the value they add, you may find that long channels are the best way to make certain products available. Many consumer products, such as packaged cereals and mouthwashes, move through longer channels.

Channel member decisions

If you decide to work with at least one level of intermediary, your marketing plan should indicate how many and what type of channel members you'll need for each level in each market. These decisions depend on the market, the product and its life cycle, customer needs and behaviour, product pricing and product positioning. Figure 4.25 summarizes the three broad choices in number of channel members.

If you use **exclusive distribution**, one intermediary will handle your product in a particular area. If you use **selective distribution**, a fairly small number of intermediaries will sell your product in the area. If you use **intensive distribution**, many intermediaries will handle your product in the area. How do you choose? You can enhance the luxury image of upmarket or specialized goods and services by using exclusive distribution. New products that require extensive customer education may be sold in exclusive or selective distribution. Also, products that require expert sales support or for which customers shop around are often marketed through selective distribution. Finally, consider intensive distribution for inexpensive, everyday products – especially impulse items – because of the opportunity to achieve higher sales volumes.

In addition, you have to choose specific intermediaries for each channel. In a marketing plan for an existing product or a new entry in an existing line, you may want to reassess the value each member is providing; add more channel members to expand market coverage if needed; and replace ineffective or inefficient members as necessary. As coverage increases, however, so does the possibility for conflict among channel members over customers, market coverage, pricing and other

	Exclusive distribution	Selective distribution	Intensive distribution
Value added for customer	• Individual attention • Knowledgeable sales help • Availability of training, other services	• Choice of outlets in each area • Some services available	• Convenient availability in many outlets • Competition among outlets may lower price
Value added for producer	• Positioning of expensive or technical product reinforced • Closer cooperation and exchange of information • More control over service quality, other aspects	• Ability to cover more of the market • Less dependent on a small number of channel members	• Higher unit sales • Ability to cover an area completely • Lower cost per unit
Concerns for producer	• Higher cost per unit • Potentially reach fewer customers	• Medium costs, medium control	• Less control over service quality, other aspects • More difficult to supervise • Possible conflict among channel members

Figure 4.25 Exclusive, selective and intensive distribution

issues. When preparing a marketing plan for a new or existing product, allow for educating channel members about the product's benefits; they should be induced to promote it actively. Also look ahead to think about whether a particular intermediary will be a strong partner in marketing the product (and possibly later products) now and in the future.

The following checklist will help you think about channel issues for your marketing plan.

Essential marketing plan checklist

Planning for marketing channels

☐ How do customers prefer to gain access to the product?

☐ What channels and channel members are best suited to the product, positioning and brand image?

☐ What are the organization's channel costs and will customers pay for access through these channels?

☐ Are the right assortments of products available at the right time and in the right quantities, with appropriate support?

☐ How much control does the organization want over channel functions?

_____

☐ How can channel decisions be used to manage the product life cycle?

_____

☐ What geographical, ecological, legal and regulatory considerations affect channel decisions?

_____

☐ How many channel levels and members are appropriate, given the organization's situation, objectives and targeting decisions?

_____

☐ Do channel members have capable sales and support staff, are they equipped to store and display the product and are they financially sound?

_____

Planning for logistics

A good logistics plan can help you compete by serving customers more effectively or by saving money. But details count. For example, Wal-Mart has built a highly profitable retail empire based on driving logistics costs ever lower (*see* the case study). Whatever your plan, you will need clear-cut, non-conflicting objectives. If your objective is to make more products available or get them to customers more quickly, expect your costs to be higher. If your objective is to cut the total cost of logistics, you might maintain lower inventory levels, raising the possibility that you might run out of some products. Your marketing plan must strike a balance between your customers' needs and your organization's financial, marketing and societal objectives.

A growing number of marketers, including Kaufhof's, are testing radio frequency identification (RFID) technology to improve inbound and outbound efficiency.

marketing in practice RFID at Kaufhof's

The Kaufhof department store chain in Germany has been testing radio frequency identification (RFID) technology since 2003. Each RFID tag attached to a package or product contains a computer chip, a tiny antenna and a unique identification number. The tags automatically send radio signals to indicate where they (and the items they identify) are located, whether in a warehouse, on a lorry or in the store. In Kaufhof's test, two apparel suppliers have been attaching RFID tags to each box they ship so the retailer can quickly and accurately track shipments in transit and receive the items into inventory at each store. As the chain expands its use of RFID, it will be in a better position to have the right merchandise in stock at the right store at the right time. However, RFID also raises ethical concerns about invasion of privacy. For instance, will the technology be used to track what individual customers buy or how they use certain products?[103]

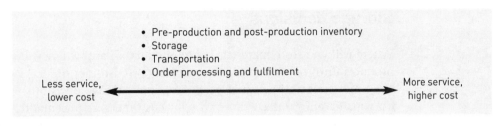

Figure 4.26 Implementing logistics objectives

As Figure 4.26 indicates, logistics decisions about pre- and post-production inventory, storage, transportation, order processing and fulfilment depend on whether your objectives are linked to less service (lower cost) or more service (higher cost).

Inventory decisions

Your decisions about inventory must be made even before the first product moves into the channel. Pre-production, you should identify the inventory level of parts and supplies required for the planned output. Post-production, think about how much inventory of a particular product is needed outbound to meet customer demand, balanced with organizational constraints of budgets, production and storage capacity. Zara, for example, produces limited quantities of each fashion, knowing it can get additional inventory to stores in just a few weeks, if needed. If your inventories are too low, customers will not find products when and where they want and your channel members will lose sales; if your inventories are too high, the organization's investment is tied up and you risk having some products go out of style, spoil or become obsolete.

Increasingly, producers, suppliers and channel members are collaborating to forecast demand and have the right amount of inventory when and were needed. Mistakes can be costly – resulting in empty shelves or, just as bad, warehouses full of obsolete or overpriced products, as Vizio well knows.

marketing in practice   Vizio

Vizio, based in southern California, captured 7 per cent of the North American market for LCD televisions in just three years. Its annual turnover exceeds $700 million, thanks to low-cost Asian production, low wholesale prices and fast response to market conditions. How does Vizio do it? In a word, logistics. It carefully monitors every detail, from the quality of the glass in its screens to the merchandise display patterns of its retail channel partners. But the most crucial element is inventory: because intense competition and improved production efficiency are lowering the retail price of LCD sets nearly every month, Vizio tracks stores' stock levels and maintains an on-hand inventory level equal to just two weeks of anticipated sales. This way, the company limits the damage to its profit margins in the event it must cut its wholesale prices unexpectedly.[104]

Storage decisions

Where will you store materials before production and where will you store finished products until needed to fill intermediary or customer orders? How long will you store materials and finished products? Such storage decisions are based, in part, on your inventory decisions and your customers' requirements. If you promise a business customer just-in-time stock replenishment, you might store products in a nearby warehouse or distribution centre for speedy delivery on schedule. Also examine how much space is needed for storing inventory at the site where customers actually gain access to the product.

Also look at the product itself and typical variations in demand when planning for product storage. Is your product perishable? Is it especially large (or small) or fragile? Does it have other physical characteristics that affect storage? Are large quantities needed quickly during periods of peak demand? Is demand erratic or steady? What are the implications for your marketing plan?

Transportation decisions

In the course of planning inbound and outbound logistics, choose the transportation modes that are appropriate for your product, your budget and your customers' needs and value perceptions. Choices include road transport by lorry (convenient for door-to-door shipments), rail transport (for bulky or heavy items), air transport (when time is a factor and budgets allow), water transport (when time is not a factor but cost is) and pipeline transport (for liquids and natural gases). Often products are despatched by more than one mode of transportation, such as lorry to water, rail or air and back to lorry. Figure 4.27 shows some of the key questions to ask when making transportation decisions for your marketing plan.

Question	Transportation choices
How quickly must products be at their destination?	Air is speediest; water is slowest
Is steady, predictable receipt of products desirable?	Pipeline allows for fairly steady transport of liquids and gases; water is least predictable
What level of transportation cost is acceptable to customers and organization?	Pipeline and water are least expensive; air is most expensive
Is transportation available from the point of despatch directly to the point of delivery?	Road transport offers the most convenient door-to-door delivery
What capacity is needed to transport this product?	Water and rail easily accommodate large, bulky products

Figure 4.27 Questions to ask when planning for transportation

Your flexibility in transportation choices depends, in part, on legal and regulatory rules governing competition in pricing and schedules, as well as your balance of cost and customer service. In many areas, transportation companies differentiate themselves through special product handling and convenience. In Canada, CN has invested heavily to increase capacity at its intermodal terminal in Brampton, where containers of merchandise arrive by rail, ready for transfer to lorries. Customers benefit from the CN's use of RFID to pinpoint the location of every container during its journey from point of origin (a railway terminal near a factory or seaport, for example) to Brampton and then on to the recipient's warehouse.[105]

Order processing and fulfilment decisions

Whether you're targeting business or consumer markets, you'll have to include order processing and fulfilment in your marketing plan, with decisions about the method and timing of:

- accepting orders and billing for purchases
- confirmation of order and available inventory
- picking and packing products for despatch
- documenting and tracking the contents of shipments
- handling returns, errors and damaged goods.

A growing number of organizations are planning better customer service through reduced order cycle time. This means your customers (whether consumers or businesses) will have as short a wait as possible between placing an order and receiving delivery. Gruma, Mexico's market-leading flour producer, has reduced cycle time for the tortillas it sells to KFC restaurants in China by building a manufacturing plant in Shanghai. Before the plant opened, Gruma exported frozen tortillas from North America to China for KFC. Now the tortillas are made fresh locally – and Gruma has a base from which to fulfil, quickly and profitably, orders from other Asian customers as well.[106]

You can use the following checklist as a guide to some of the key questions you need to ask when you plan for logistics.

Essential marketing plan checklist

Planning for logistics

☐ What logistics arrangements would enable customers to obtain products quickly, conveniently and at an acceptable price?

_____

☐ How can logistics add more value for the customer and the organization by boosting benefits or decreasing costs or both?

_____

☐ What influence are the organization's SWOT and resources likely to have on logistics decisions? Can any aspect of logistics be outsourced if necessary without compromising objectives or service?

☐ How can logistics be used for competitive advantage and to support positioning?

☐ What is the optimal balance of logistics costs and customer service, given the marketing plan objectives?

Summary

The value chain (also called the value delivery network or supply chain) is the succession of interrelated, value-added functions that enable a producer to create and deliver a product that fulfils customers' needs through connections with suppliers, wholesalers, retailers and other participants. The marketing (or distribution) channel refers to the set of functions performed by the producer or by intermediaries in making a product available to customers at a profit. Marketing channels are outbound functions downstream in the value chain, closer to the customer. Logistics refers to the flow of products, information and payments inbound and outbound to meet customer requirements.

Marketers can use direct channels – in which the organization deals directly with customers – and/or indirect channels – in which the organization works through other businesses or individuals (intermediaries). The three major types of intermediaries are wholesalers; retailers; and representatives, brokers and agents. In a channel with one or more levels, marketers can choose exclusive, selective or intensive distribution. The main functions involved in logistics are: pre- and post-production inventory; storage; transportation; order processing and fulfilment. Seeking to raise customer service levels generally raises logistics costs; seeking to reduce logistics costs generally reduces the level of customer service.

case study   Wal-Mart's retailing edge

How did Wal-Mart grow to become the largest retailer on the planet? The chain has several core competencies but perhaps the most important is its mastery of logistics. Think of the complexities of getting merchandise from 4,400 factories worldwide to the right place at the right time to satisfy the 138 million shoppers who visit Wal-Mart's 6,500 European, Asian and American stores every week. Thousands more click to buy on Walmart.com. Behind the scenes, the company maintains more than 150 distribution centres globally and uses RFID and other technology to receive and transfer merchandise quickly, plan inventory and – its hallmark – keep logistics costs down so retail prices are low.

Every new distribution centre represents an opportunity to hone efficiency by reducing the distance that merchandise must be transported inbound and outbound. With replenishment stock so close at hand – and one or more deliveries scheduled every day – Wal-Mart stores can carry lower inventory levels. Moreover, if a product unexpectedly sells out, it can be restocked in one day or even sooner. Inventory turns over so quickly that more than two-thirds of Wal-Mart's products are purchased by customers before the company is scheduled to pay the suppliers.

In fact, supplier collaboration is a critical component of Wal-Mart's logistics superiority. The retailer works directly with its major suppliers to forecast demand months in advance and plan inbound orders that will meet the needed inventory levels and merchandise assortments on a store-by-store basis. Because of this collaboration, suppliers are able to plan their production to meet Wal-Mart's specifications and arrange efficient despatch schedules. Sometimes Wal-Mart has its own fleet of lorries fetch merchandise from suppliers and plans deliveries so precisely that cartons of merchandise move non-stop from inbound lorries to outbound lorries and to the stores without being unloaded in a distribution centre.[107]

Case questions

1 If you were writing Wal-Mart's marketing plan, what would you include when planning for a reverse channel?

2 If you worked for a manufacturer trying to expand its retail distribution, what questions would you ask Wal-Mart before becoming one of its suppliers?

Apply your knowledge

Select a common consumer product, then research and analyse its value chain and its channel arrangements. Prepare a written report or an oral presentation summarizing your analysis.

- Draw a diagram to show a simplified value chain for this product. Is a reverse channel necessary or desirable? Why?
- Is this product available through direct channels such as by mail or from the producer's website? How does this channel arrangement benefit customers and the organization?
- Is the product available through indirect channels such as retailers? Why is this appropriate for the product, the market and the targeted customers?
- Is the product available through exclusive distribution? Through intensive distribution? Do you agree with this decision?

Build your own marketing plan

Continue developing your marketing plan by making decisions about channel arrangements and logistics. Should you market this product directly to customers or through indirect channels or a combination? How long should your channel be, and what value will each level add? Will you use intensive, selective or exclusive distribution, and why? What kinds of channel members would be most appropriate? Does your product require any special transportation, storage or post-purchase support? What specific customer needs should you take into account when planning logistics and how will you balance cost with customer service? Record your decisions and explain their implications in your marketing plan.

Planning for integrated marketing communication

Introduction

When the Beeb threw a party with music by Pink, Snow Patrol and other bands, it drew 36,000 people – 30,000 to Dundee, Scotland, and 6,000 to the Second Life website. Why would the British Broadcasting Corp., a UK television network, sponsor a concert in real life and online at the same time? The marketing objective was to engage its audience in new ways and showcase its mastery of digital delivery. In fact, the Second Life concert got Web-savvy opinion leaders talking about the Beeb and its high-tech capabilities, which is exactly what the network wanted.[108]

Even if you don't have the Beeb's money and technical ability to promote your products, you can still plan for effective communication, as this section explains. You'll learn the steps in the planning process for a communications campaign: define the target audience; set the objectives and determine the budget; consider legal, regulatory, social and ethical issues; choose tools, messages and media; plan for pre-tests and post-implementation analysis; and evaluate the campaign. The section also includes an overview of planning for advertising, sales promotion, personal selling, direct marketing and public relations – the most visible and creative aspects of many marketing plans.

Planning for integrated marketing communication

No matter what good or service you're marketing, you'll need some kind of communication to inform, influence and interact with customers and prospects. In most cases, you'll choose a combination of communication techniques. That's why your marketing plan must include **integrated marketing communication (IMC)**, the coordination of content and delivery of all the marketing messages in all media for an organization, product or brand to ensure consistency and support the positioning and objectives. Here's an example from the financial services industry.

marketing in practice   Capital One Bank Europe

Aggressive direct mail programmes highlighting low rates helped build Capital One's UK consumer credit business. However, facing intense competition and a difficult economy, the company recently repositioned itself on the basis of convenience. Its marketing plan called for coordinated IMC activities under the light-hearted theme 'We make changing easy'. The idea, said the head of the Capital One brand, was 'to make people smile, take notice and tackle those changes they've been putting off'. In addition to television commercials, some direct mail and free 'Lunch and Laugh' comedy events, the campaign included a website with advice about how to make changes in love, life and – of course – finances. Although consumers were the main audience, the company also previewed the new campaign for internal audiences before the public introduction.[109]

Understanding IMC tools

You can plan a communication campaign using one or more of five major IMC tools: advertising (such as Capital One's television commercials), sales promotion, personal selling, direct marketing (such as Capital One's direct mail packages) and public relations (such as its comedy events). These tools are briefly described here (and see Figure 4.28) and examined again later in the chapter.

Advertising

Advertising is non-personal promotion paid for by an identified sponsor like Capital One. This is a cost-effective way to inform large numbers of customers or channel members about a brand or product; persuade customers or channel members about a brand's or product's merits; encourage buying; and remind customers or channel members about the brand to encourage repurchase. Although television advertising remains popular, many companies see online advertising and social networking sites as less costly methods of communicating with more targeted audiences.[110]

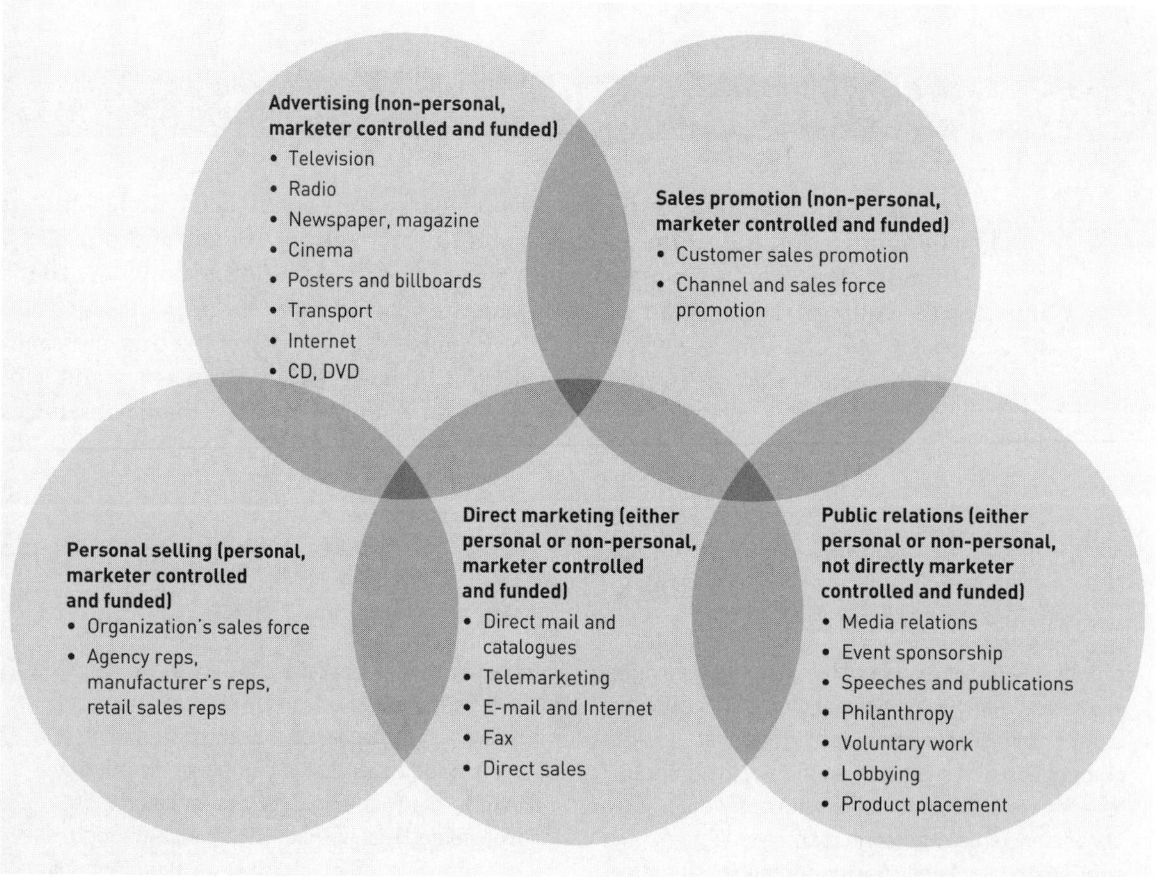

Advertising (non-personal, marketer controlled and funded)
- Television
- Radio
- Newspaper, magazine
- Cinema
- Posters and billboards
- Transport
- Internet
- CD, DVD

Sales promotion (non-personal, marketer controlled and funded)
- Customer sales promotion
- Channel and sales force promotion

Personal selling (personal, marketer controlled and funded)
- Organization's sales force
- Agency reps, manufacturer's reps, retail sales reps

Direct marketing (either personal or non-personal, marketer controlled and funded)
- Direct mail and catalogues
- Telemarketing
- E-mail and Internet
- Fax
- Direct sales

Public relations (either personal or non-personal, not directly marketer controlled and funded)
- Media relations
- Event sponsorship
- Speeches and publications
- Philanthropy
- Voluntary work
- Lobbying
- Product placement

Figure 4.28 IMC tools

Sales promotion

Sales promotion consists of incentives to enhance a product's short-term value and stimulate the target audience to buy soon (or respond in another way). Although advertising is an excellent way to build brand image and awareness and bring the audience to the brink of action, sales promotion provides impetus to take action right away. You can use sales promotion to induce customers to try a new product, for example, or to encourage channel members to stock and sell a new product. You can easily measure the results of most promotions by counting the number of coupons redeemed, the number of people who click on links in e-mail newsletters or on websites, and so on.

Personal selling

Personal selling – especially useful for two-way communication – can take many forms, including traditional in-person sales, Internet sales and telemarketing. Sending a sales representative to call on customers is extremely costly, whereas personal selling in most retail, telemarketing and Internet settings is less expensive. Still, companies marketing costly or complicated products to business markets may need sales reps to qualify customers, learn about their needs, recommend solutions, explain features and benefits, answer questions, demonstrate product use and complete sales transactions. Sales reps are also key players in learning about customers for marketing planning purposes, as well as for building trust and strengthening relationships.[111]

Direct marketing

With direct marketing, you use two-way communication to interact with targeted customers and stimulate direct responses that ultimately lead to an ongoing relationship. This communication may occur through letters and catalogues, television, radio, e-mail, Internet ads, newspaper ads, telemarketing, faxes, mobile phones or personal selling. The objective for an initial direct marketing contact might be to have a customer ask for product information or simply agree to receive further messages, launching a dialogue that ultimately culminates in a purchase. One of direct marketing's advantages is the ability to measure actual results (such as the number of credit card applications received in response to Capital One's direct mail programmes).

Public relations

Public relations (PR) activities promote dialogue to build understanding and foster positive attitudes between the organization and its publics. A marketing plan might call for a news conference to launch a new product, for example, or a special event to polish brand image. Because the firm does not directly control or pay for media mentions – and because the communication is not sales-directed – PR is very believable. However, there is no guarantee that the information will reach the intended audience in the preferred form or at the preferred time, if at all.

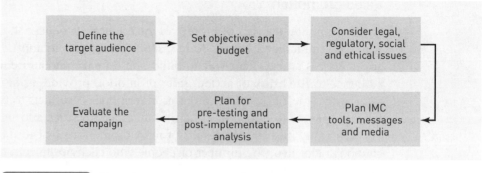

Figure 4.29 Planning an IMC campaign

Defining the target audience

As you can see in Figure 4.29, your first planning decision is to define the audience that you will target. This may be customers in a certain segment; people who influence buyers or users; people who are currently competitors' customers; current or potential channel members; members of the general public; media people; government officials or regulators; or other publics.

If you target intermediaries in an effort to move or *push* your product through the channel to customers, you're using a **push strategy** to stir channel interest using sales promotion, advertising or other communications techniques. An alternate approach is a **pull strategy**, which targets customers so they will request and buy the product from channel members. This *pulls* the product through the channel from producer to customer.

In your marketing plan, define who each IMC campaign should reach and, through research, indicate what audience members think or feel about the brand, product, organization or idea; their attitudes and behaviour toward competitors; what kind of message, appeal, delivery and timing would be most effective; what the message should contain and how it should be conveyed. For example, Unilever's recent marketing plan for Zhonghua, a toothpaste brand it markets in China, included research about brand perceptions. Zhonghua held a 16 per cent market share, yet wasn't popular with all ages. The brand director explained: 'We found the Zhonghua brand is weak on some attributes [such as] modernity, innovation, appeal to young consumers.' Therefore, Zhonghua planned advertising and sales promotion activities targeting young urban adults who were just entering the workforce and beginning to date.[112]

Setting the objectives and the budget

Your IMC campaign will aim to achieve marketing objectives that move the target audience through a hierarchy of cognitive, affective and behavioural responses. A **cognitive response** refers to a customer's mental reaction, including brand awareness and knowledge of product features and benefits. An **affective response** is a customer's emotional reaction, such as being interested in or liking a product.

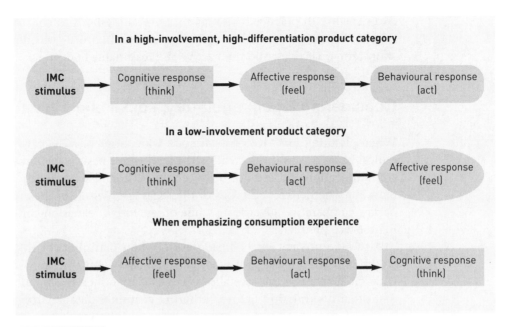

Figure 4.30   Using IMC to provoke audience response

Source: After Michael R. Solomon, *Consumer Behavior*, 5th edn (Upper Saddle River, NJ: Prentice Hall, 2002), pp. 200–2.

A **behavioural response** is how the customer acts, such as buying a product or applying for credit. Customers move through these responses in different order, depending on how involved they are in making that type of purchase; product differentiation in that category; and the influence of consumption experience (see Figure 4.30).

Usually your IMC objectives will relate to building long-term relationships by attracting customers' attention, communicating about the product or brand, persuading customers to seek out and buy the product once, supporting a positive attitude leading to repeat purchases and ultimately loyalty. Specific advertising objectives may be set to complement or support objectives for personal selling, direct marketing or other IMC tools in your plan. You may also set sales or profit objectives for IMC, particularly when you can measure and attribute the results to a particular campaign or message. Further, you may use IMC to enhance your firm's image or build brand awareness.

The IMC budget is developed and allocated in the context of your organization's overall marketing budgeting process and budget approval process, which may be driven from the floor up or the top down (or a combination).[113] One floor-up option is to allocate funding according to the IMC objectives and the cost of the tasks needed to achieve those objectives. This directly ties tasks and objectives for better accountability in terms of whether the tasks actually achieve the objectives. However, this method may lead to unrealistic budget requests and may complicate planning if particular tasks can't easily be linked to specific objectives.

Other budgeting methods include the affordability method (a top-down method based on how much the organization can afford to spend); percentage-of-sales method (spending a certain percentage of annual sales revenue or an average industry percentage of sales); competitive parity (budgeting according to what rivals spend). In practice, you may use several methods to construct a preliminary budget, look closely at costs and the market situation, consider both long- and short-term objectives, and then arrive at a reasonable budget.

Considering legal, regulatory, social and ethical issues

When planning for IMC, be aware of a wide range of legal, regulatory, social and ethical issues as you think creatively. On the most basic legal and ethical level, your communications should not be deceptive, distort facts or falsify product benefits. Find out whether certain types of messages are illegal; for instance, some nations outlaw comparative advertising while others forbid television commercials promoting tobacco products.

Also take privacy into consideration when planning for IMC. The European Union has strict rules about what personal data companies may collect and under what circumstances they are allowed to exchange such information. Retailers must first obtain permission before gathering customer data, sharing or selling it and using it for store marketing purposes. Companies must delete personal data after a set period, and they are forbidden to send personal data collected in the European Union to countries without equally strong privacy laws.[114] Such concerns about collection, storage, use and disclosure of personal data continue to make privacy a hot issue for marketers.

Planning IMC tools, messages and media

Most marketing plans employ more than one IMC tool to achieve their objectives. Your exact choices depend on your target audience; IMC objectives and budget; other marketing-mix decisions; and legal, regulatory, social and ethical considerations. They also depend on message and media strategy (discussed more fully later in this section). For instance, television advertising is generally more expensive than print advertising, so if you have a small budget or want to reach highly targeted audiences you may avoid television or use it sparingly. If your message involves an actual product demonstration, you will probably find radio inappropriate.

An unusually innovative or appealing IMC campaign can start a groundswell of **word of mouth** – people telling other people about the message, the product or another aspect of the marketing. Word of mouth has more credibility because it is not marketer controlled and it reflects what people in the market think, feel and do. Yet as word of mouth spreads, people may not get a complete or accurate message, and many outside the target audience may get the message (while some inside the target audience may not). You can certainly try to initiate positive word of mouth but you cannot control whether your audience picks up on the message and passes it along. In one recent study, the Toyota brand ranked highest on positive word of mouth, based on mentions in blogs, e-mails, phone calls and personal conversations.[115]

A more intense form of word of mouth is **buzz marketing**, in which you target opinion leaders to have them spread information to other people. Buzz marketing can spread product or brand information especially quickly on the Internet. However, buzz can fade quickly, because marketers can't control exactly what's being said, where and when the message spreads or how long it will circulate. Here's how Procter & Gamble has generated buzz through various marketing activities.

marketing in practice   Procter & Gamble

Procter & Gamble (P&G), with £35 billion in annual turnover, is a US-based marketer of household products that constantly experiments with buzz. For example, it enlisted 600,000 mothers to converse with friends and family about Dawn dishwashing liquid and other P&G products. The mothers receive free samples and a weekly message asking their opinions about marketing ideas. P&G has also got buzz from mobile marketing for its Max Factor cosmetics. When it invited women to use their mobile phones to register for a prize draw, the contest got people buzzing and drew 250,000 responses. Finally, P&G's humorous campaign for ThermaCare heat wraps, which combined newspaper ads and fake but funny websites, video clips and blog entries, caused enough buzz to bring 11 million consumers into contact with the company's communications.[116]

Planning for pre- and post-implementation analysis and evaluation

To get the information you need for making better IMC decisions, you should plan time and money for research to pre-test messages, creative approaches and use of media. The purpose is to gauge the target audience's response and have the opportunity to make changes, possibly pre-test additional elements and then launch the complete campaign. For example, you can conduct pre-tests to measure recognition (do a sample of the audience recognize what is being promoted?), recall (does the sample remember the message and what it communicated?), affective reaction (do the message, product and brand provoke positive reactions?) and behavioural intentions (are people likely to buy the product or take another action on the basis of the promotion?).

You should also plan for measuring and evaluating the results after full implementation. Specifically, determine whether the message or media failed to reach the target audience at times, and why; how well the audience understood the message; what the audience thought and felt about the product or brand, message and media; which messages and media were especially effective in provoking the desired audience response; and how well the IMC tools, messages and media are supporting the overall positioning and working with other marketing-mix strategies.

Planning advertising

Planning for advertising follows the general IMC planning pattern shown in Figure 4.28. Note that you'll generally wait to make detailed decisions until after your marketing plan is being implemented. Still, you have to plan the general direction of both message and media in order to allocate the overall budget among advertising and other IMC activities.

Planning messages

What will the message actually say? What will it look (and/or sound) like? These are the two main decisions in planning messages. Some messages follow a 'hard-sell' approach to induce the target audience to respond now; others take a more 'soft-sell' approach, persuading without seeming to do so. Capital One, for example, was using a 'soft-sell' approach in its messages.

Message planning is inseparable from media planning because the copy in the advertisement, the design and the creativity of its execution depend on media choice. A creative decision to show the product in action, for instance, can be executed through a visual medium such as television or the Web. Creativity is, in fact, crucial for attracting attention, building awareness and shaping positive attitudes.[117] Although all decision details need not be finalized until the marketing plan is actually implemented, you should have some idea of message and media strategy so you can plan IMC budgets, timing and marketing-mix coordination.

Planning media

Media planning has become more complex due to the multiplicity of media choices and vehicles and the resulting smaller audience sizes for each – **audience fragmentation**. You'll always have budget constraints as you seek to balance reach and frequency. **Reach** refers to the number or percentage of people in the target audience exposed to an advertisement in a particular media vehicle during a certain period. Capital One used television, for instance, to achieve high reach. Higher reach means the message gets to more people, but this usually comes at a cost. **Frequency** is the number of times the target audience is exposed to a message in a particular media vehicle during a certain period. Higher frequency means you expose more people to your message on more occasions, again at a cost.

Should you plan to spend more on reach or more on frequency? Which media and vehicles will get your message to the right people at the right time and in the desired frequency? An alternative to paying for high reach that may include people outside the target audience (which sometimes happens with television commercials, for example) is to use more precisely targeted media. The following checklist summarizes planning considerations for media.

Essential marketing plan checklist

Planning for media

Your marketing plan should explain the basic reasoning behind your choices of media and message, although it need not cover every detail of the IMC campaign. Based on the IMC tools you will use, your budget and objectives, the marketing environment and the profile of your target audience, think about each of the following aspects of media planning. Place a tick mark next to each question after you've entered your answers in the space provided.

- [ ] What media do the audience use and prefer? Are these media available in the geographic region being targeted?

- [ ] Can the media reach the right people in appropriate numbers to deliver messages during the customers' buying cycle?

- [ ] Will the audience consider some media excessively intrusive or annoying?

- [ ] What media are used by competitors and how might competing messages affect audience receptivity, understanding and response?

- [ ] Should media be used to deliver the message continuously, intermittently or seasonally?

- [ ] What are the creative possibilities, production requirements and costs for each medium?

- [ ] Will the IMC budget cover the projected media cost for the desired reach and frequency?

- [ ] What is the expected payback based on anticipated audience reaction?

Planning sales promotion

Include sales promotion in your marketing plan when you want to stimulate faster response from consumers and business customers, channel members (sometimes called *the trade*) and the sales force. Although such promotions add value for only a limited time, some marketers use them as part of a longer-term strategy to strengthen relationships with the target audience. Sales promotion spending now exceeds advertising spending in a number of industries, reflecting increased competitive pressure and the need to produce immediate results.

However, because sales promotion often adds value by reducing perceived cost – lowering the product's price, in effect – over-use may heighten price sensitivity among customers, diminish brand strength and hurt profitability. Moreover, says promotion specialist Stephen Callender, 'Promotions that go wrong make a brand's strategies appear ill-thought out. That leads to insidious damage to the brand's credibility.'[118] Thus, you should set clear objectives, understand applicable laws and regulations, choose your techniques carefully, monitor implementation and evaluate results to make your sales promotion programmes successful.

Planning for customer sales promotion

Figure 4.31 shows a variety of common sales promotion techniques you can use, depending on your objectives and your IMC strategy. Consider sales promotion to target consumers or business customers when you want to:

● *Encourage product trial.* Potential customers have to try a product at least once before they can form a definite opinion and decide to buy it again (and again). Sales promotion is therefore commonly used to introduce a product and to stimulate higher sales during the maturity stage.

● *Reinforce advertising for a product or brand.* An exciting sales promotion can help customers notice and remember your advertising messages.

● *Attract interest.* Simply getting customers to visit a store or contact a manufacturer about a product can be a challenge. Some marketers use coupons, samples or other techniques in an attempt to get customers to take the first step.

● *Encourage purchase of multiple products.* Depending on your product mix, you can use sales promotion to stimulate customer purchases of two, three or even more products.

● *Encourage continued product purchase and usage.* You want to build customer loyalty to increase sales and reduce customer acquisition costs. Airlines do this

Technique	Description
Sample	Free trial of a good or service
Coupon	Certificate redeemable for money off a product's price
Premium	A free or low-priced item offered to induce purchase of a product
Sweepstake or draw, contest, game	Chance to win cash or prizes through luck, knowledge or skill
Refund, rebate	Returning part or all of a product's price to the customer
Price pack	Special price marked by producer on the package or for multiple products bought together
Loyalty reward	Opportunity to earn gifts or cash for continuing to buy a certain product or from a certain company
Point-of-purchase display or demonstration	In-store materials promoting a product or in-store product demonstration
Branded speciality	Everyday item such as a calendar or T-shirt bearing the product name or brand, for reminder purposes

Figure 4.31 Sales promotion techniques targeting customers

with their frequent flyer programmes; supermarkets do this with their frequent shopper programmes.

Field marketing is becoming more popular as companies work with outside agencies to engage the target audience by bringing sales promotion to (and sometimes taking orders from) customers 'in the field' – in stores, shopping districts and city centres.[119] It can also be used to build reseller support, as Pernod Ricard has done.

---

marketing in practice   Pernod Ricard

Pernod Ricard, headquartered in Paris, has a €1 billion marketing budget to support its range of liquor products. It recently used field marketing to enlist new UK channel members for its Stolichnaya vodka and Havana Club rum beverages. To start, the company carefully researched the profile of the targeted customer segment for these brands. Then it hired a field marketing agency to visit hundreds of independent convenience stores in the areas where these targeted customers live. This effort added 157 new stores to Pernod Ricard's distribution channel in the first two weeks alone. Within three months, revenue from this expansion had covered all field marketing costs. Thanks to strong marketing support, Havana Club is the number-two rum in Europe.[120]

Planning for channel and sales force sales promotion

Particularly when using a push strategy, you may find sales promotion effective in enlisting the support of channel members and motivating sales representatives. Specifically, you can use channel and sales force promotions to:

- *Build channel commitment to a new product.* So many new products are introduced every year that channel members rarely have the space (or the money) to carry them all. Channel promotions can focus attention on a new product, encourage intermediaries to buy it, motivate the sales force to sell it and provide appropriate rewards.
- *Encourage more immediate results.* Sales promotion aimed at channel members and sales representatives offer inducements to take action during a specific time period.
- *Build relationships with channel members.* Keeping the ongoing support of major retail or wholesale businesses takes time and effort. Channel promotion offers opportunities for interactions that benefit the producer and its channel members.
- *Improve product knowledge.* Support the marketing effort by offering training and information through channel and sales force promotion.

Sales force promotions include contests (with cash or prizes as rewards), sales meetings (for training and motivation) and special promotional material (to supplement personal sales efforts). In planning a channel promotion, you may use monetary allowances (either discounts or payments for stocking or displaying a product); limited-time discounts (for buying early in the selling season or during other specified periods); free merchandise (extra quantities provided for buying a minimum quantity or a certain product); cooperative advertising (sharing costs when a channel member advertises a particular brand or product); or trade shows (setting up a booth or room at a convention centre to demonstrate products and interact with channel members or business buyers).

Planning personal selling

One of the most compelling reasons to include personal selling in a marketing plan is to establish solid relationships with new customers and maintain good relationships with the current customer base. Personal attention can make all the difference when your customers have unique problems, require customized solutions or place very large orders. Be sure to coordinate personal selling with all other marketing plan decisions to achieve the desired results. In addition, remind sales people to look beyond individual transactions and build long-term relationships with customers.

When planning for personal selling, consider:

- *Need*. Should your company have its own sales force or sell through retailers, agents or manufacturers' representatives? Some online businesses, such as Overstock.com, offer 'live chats' with reps who can answer questions and check on product specifications.[121]
- *Organization*. Will you organize reps according to geographic market, product, type of customer, size of customer or some other structure?
- *Size*. How many sales reps should you have, based on your objectives and current sales levels?
- *Compensation*. How will you determine sales force compensation?
- *Management*. How will you recruit, train, supervise, motivate and evaluate sales reps? How will sales reps be educated about legal, regulatory and ethical guidelines?
- *Process*. How will you generate sales leads? How will sales personnel access information about prospects and customers? What logistical activities must be coordinated with sales transactions, and who will be responsible?

Planning direct marketing

Although mail order and telemarketing are hardly new, a growing number of organizations now include these and other direct marketing techniques in their IMC plans. Why? With better technology, marketers can target audiences more precisely, adjust messages and timing according to audience need and form a dialogue to build relationships cost-effectively. Direct marketing costs more than advertising in mass media, yet its interactive quality, selectivity and customization potential may add enough flexibility to make the difference worthwhile. Just as important, you can easily measure customer response and modify the offer or the communication again and again to move customers in the desired direction and achieve your objectives.

In planning direct marketing, first decide what response you want to elicit from the target audience(s), in accordance with your objectives. Many marketers use direct marketing to generate leads for sales representatives; the desired response is to have a potential customer indicate interest in the product by calling, e-mailing or sending a reply by post. Banks and mobile phone companies frequently use direct marketing – especially mailings – to attract new customers, bring former customers back and encourage current customers to buy more.

Now you're ready to select appropriate media and formulate an appropriate offer, based on research into the target audience's media and buying patterns. Different audiences and markets require different media and offers. According to one specialist, Australian consumers are not as accustomed to catalogue shopping as US consumers, for example; another specialist observes that television is just gaining popularity as a direct marketing medium in Japan.[122] Be sure your direct marketing campaign fits with the product's positioning and allow time in the marketing plan schedule for testing the message and the mechanisms for response (such as a free-phone number, URL or postage-paid envelope). One of the advantages of direct marketing is that you can quickly see what actually works and use the results to refine your campaign or the overall marketing plan.

Planning public relations

At one time or another, nearly every organization has prepared news releases, arranged news conferences and answered questions from reporters. Yet media contact is only one aspect of this flexible and powerful IMC tool. You can use public relations not just to convey the organization's messages but also to build mutual understanding and maintain an ongoing dialogue between your organization and key members of the 'public'. Moreover, your message has more credibility when conveyed by media representatives than when communicated directly by your organization, as noted earlier.

Defining the 'public'

The 'public' in public relations may refer to people in any number of target audiences, such as customers and prospective customers, employees, channel members, suppliers, news reporters, investors and financial analysts, special interest groups, legislators and regulators, and community leaders. Each of these audiences can affect your plan's success and performance, but not all will be addressed in the same way; in fact, not all may be addressed in a single marketing plan.

In general, you can use PR to achieve one or more of the following objectives:

● *Identify and understand stakeholder concerns*. Through PR contacts such as community meetings, surveys and other methods, you can learn what your stakeholders think and feel about important issues such as your products, image, ecological record and so on. Kingfisher, a UK-based home products retailer, seeks out public opinion and government views on social and ecological issues such as buying timber sourced from endangered forests. The idea is to see how public concern is growing so the company can phase in changes over time.[123]

- *Convey the organization's viewpoint or important information.* Knowing your target audience's views, you can adapt your organization's position if appropriate. At the very least, you can use PR to explain your management's viewpoint or educate the public, especially vital in the midst of a crisis.
- *Correct misperceptions.* If one or more target audiences have misperceptions about some aspect of your organization – such as the quality of its products – you can plan to use PR to counteract the inaccuracies by providing more information, answering questions and allowing for periodic updates.
- *Enhance the organization's image.* Many organizations apply PR techniques to enhance their image. If an organization has been embroiled in controversy, PR can show what management is doing to improve and how it has gone beyond minimum requirements to satisfy its publics.
- *Promote products and brands.* You can use PR to communicate the features, benefits and value of your products and promote your brands.

Planning PR techniques

Your marketing plan may include a variety of PR techniques. One of the most commonly used is the news release, written and distributed to media representatives via printed document, e-mail, Web link or **podcasting** (distributing an audio or video file via the Internet). For more significant news, you may want to call a news conference, let media reps hear management speak and hold a question-and-answer session. Also consider whether you should seek publicity by sponsoring an event, the way the BBC sponsored a music festival in Dundee and online in Second Life.

This checklist will help you plan for consistency and a sense of unity in your IMC campaign.

Essential marketing plan checklist

Integrating marketing communications

To achieve your marketing plan objectives and communicate effectively with your target audience, you must integrate the messages and media in each campaign. Consider each of the following questions in turn, placing a tick mark next to each after you've noted your ideas in the space provided.

☐ Are the chosen IMC tools appropriate for the target audience(s), product, company image and IMC objectives?

_____

☐ Is the content of each message consistent with that of other messages, the brand image and the product's differentiating points?

_____

☐ Are the messages and media appropriate in the context of the overall marketing mix?

_____

☐ Is the campaign designed to foster customer receptivity, attention, interest and response?

_____

☐ Does the campaign support the product positioning and the marketing plan objectives?

_____

☐ Is your organization prepared to handle response to the messages?

_____

☐ How can you measure results to determine whether the campaign is effective?

_____

Summary

The purpose of integrated marketing communication (IMC) is to ensure that content and delivery of all the marketing messages in all media are coordinated and consistent, and that they support the positioning and objectives of the product, brand or organization. In IMC planning, first define the target audience and set objectives based on the responses desired from the target audience. Next, determine an appropriate budget and consider any applicable legal, regulatory, social and ethical issues that may affect messages, media or other aspects of IMC planning. Then select and plan for the use of specific IMC tools, messages and media; and plan pre- and post-implementation analysis to evaluate the campaign.

When planning advertising, consider message appeal, creativity and appropriateness for media; balance reach and frequency in the context of the budget. Use sales promotion to stimulate faster response from customers or channel members by adding value (or reducing perceived cost) for a limited time. If personal selling is appropriate, consider in-person sales, Internet sales or telemarketing. For more precise targeting, consider direct marketing to build relationships cost-effectively and have the ability to measure response compared with objectives. Plan for public relations to foster positive attitudes and an ongoing dialogue with key publics.

case study   Reckitt Benckiser reaches out to customers

Reckitt Benckiser is well known for household brands such as Dettol cleaning products, O'Cedar polishes, Finish dishwashing tabs and Calgon fabric care products. The UK company also offers personal care products in North America under brands such as Boots Healthcare and Clearasil. With annual turnover of £8 billion and a marketing budget exceeding £500,000, Reckitt has such a diverse product mix that its marketing plan calls for using every type of IMC tool.

Not long ago, for example, Reckitt's research found that furniture polish sales were declining because of the increased popularity of furniture that requires no polish and because more people are using household cleaning wipes. In response, the company launched a quirky advertising campaign to communicate how well its O'Cedar liquid polish protects furniture. The campaign reached millions of consumers, reinforced the positive brand image of O'Cedar and set the stage for additional promotions aimed at boosting purchases.

Another example: when Reckitt introduced new Optrex eye-care products, it raised awareness with television commercials and consumer brochures explaining Optrex's features and benefits. In addition, the firm offered training to employees in chemist's shops and provided point-of-purchase displays for store use. The advertising, sales promotion and personal selling worked together to reinforce the products' positioning as a soothing formulation for dry eyes.

Reckitt tailors its sales promotion activities to specific target segments. For instance, it has arranged for young teenagers to receive samples of Clearasil acne control products. And it invites visitors to its websites to subscribe to an e-mail newsletter with household tips, recipes, free samples, coupons and more. Watch for Reckitt's marketing plans to continue putting IMC tools to work as the company reaches out to communicate with consumers in more than 100 nations.[124]

Case questions

1 What kind of response (cognitive, affective or behavioural) do you think Reckitt Benckiser wanted to elicit by giving away Clearasil samples – and why?

2 Why would Reckitt support its Optrex product introductions with consumer brochures as well as point-of-purchase materials and store employee training?

Apply your knowledge

Choose a particular product; find two or more advertisements, promotions or other communications in which it is featured; and analyse the company's IMC activities. Then prepare a brief oral presentation or written report explaining your analysis.

- What target audience do you think these communications are designed to reach?
- What cognitive, affective or behavioural response(s) might these communications provoke?
- What objectives do you think the company has set for these communications and how would you recommend that it measure results?
- What legal, regulatory, social or ethical considerations are likely to influence this firm's IMC planning?

Build your own marketing plan

Plan your IMC decisions as you continue developing your marketing plan. What target audience(s) do you want to reach? What are your IMC objectives? What is an appropriate IMC budget, given the available resources, reach and frequency preferences and the chosen tools? Identify any legal, regulatory, social or ethical issues that would affect your IMC decisions. Will you use advertising, sales promotion, personal selling, direct marketing and/or public relations – and why? Outline one IMC campaign, indicating objectives, target audience, general message and media decisions, approximate budget and how results will be measured. Finally, document your ideas in a written marketing plan.

Services and non-profit marketing

Perspectives on service markets

Services are not a homogeneous group of products. There is wide variety within the services category, in terms of both the degree of service involved and the type of service product offered. Nevertheless, there are some general characteristics, common to many service products, that differentiate them as a genre from physical goods. This section, therefore, explores the criteria by which service products can be classified, and then goes on to look at the special characteristics of services and their implications for marketing.

Classifying services

There are few pure services. In reality, many product 'packages' involve a greater or lesser level of service. Products can be placed along a spectrum, with virtually pure personal service involving few, if any, props at one end, and pure product that involves little or no service at the other. Most products do have some combination of physical good and service, as shown in Figure 4.32. The purchase of a chocolate bar, for example, involves little or no service other than the involvement of a checkout or till operator. The purchase of a gas appliance will involve professional fitting, and thus is a combination of physical and service product. A new office computer system could similarly involve installation and initial training. A visit to a theme park or theatre could involve some limited support products, such as guides and gifts, while the main product purchased is the experience itself. Finally, a visit to a psychiatrist or a hairdresser may involve a couch, a chair and some minor allied props such as an interview checklist or a hair-dryer. The real product purchased here, however, is the personal service manufactured by the service deliverer, the psychiatrist or the hairdresser.

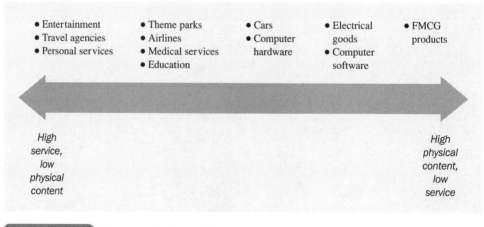

Figure 4.32   The product spectrum

Special characteristics of service markets

Five main characteristics have been identified as being unique to service markets (see, e.g., Sasser *et al.*, 1978; Cowell, 1984).

Lack of ownership

Perhaps the most obvious aspect of a service product is that no goods change hands, as such, and therefore there is no transfer of ownership of anything. A legal transaction does still take place; an insurance company agrees to provide certain benefits as long as the premiums are paid and the terms and conditions of the policy are met. A car rental company allows the customer full use of a vehicle for an agreed length of time, subject to some restraints on named drivers and type of usage, but the ownership of the vehicle remains with the rental company. A train seat can be reserved for a journey, but it is not owned. A subscription to the National Trust provides rights of access free of charge but no actual share in the ownership of its properties. The access, use or experience of the service is, therefore, often time-specific, usage-specific and subject to contractual terms and conditions.

The lack of ownership raises the issue of the transient nature of the purchase. Most service products involve some kind of 'experience' for the customer. This might be surrounded by props, for example a stage, lighting and sound systems, a lecture theatre, an insurance policy, a vehicle or a room, but these only serve to enhance or degrade the experience of the service. The faulty fuel gauge which means that the car hirer runs out of petrol in the most remote location, the hotel room next to the building site, the ineffective microphone at a concert all spoil the memory of the service consumed.

Intangibility

A visit to a retail store reveals an inviting display of products to purchase. These products can be examined, touched, tried on, sampled, smelt or listened to. All this can help the customer to examine what is on offer and to make choices between competing brands. The consumer regularly uses the whole range of senses to assist decision-making. This is especially important before the purchase is made, but even after the sale the product can be assessed in terms of its use, its durability and whether it lives up to general expectations. If there is a fault with a physical product, it can be returned or exchanged.

With service products, it is far more difficult to use the senses in the same way as a means of making a purchase decision because the actual service experience can only take place after that decision has been made. The heart of a service is the experience created for the customer, whether individually as with a personal service such as dentistry or hairdressing, or as a group experience, such as a lecture, a show or a flight. In many cases, once the purchase decision has been made, all the customer will receive is a ticket, a confirmation of booking or some promise of future benefit. The service experience itself is intangible, and is only delivered after the customer is committed to the purchase.

The Scottish Tourist Board ran a 'reawaken your senses' campaign to promote spring breaks. The campaign attempted to capture the intangible nature of the tourist experience by concentrating on visual imagery, such as fish, sea spray and scenery. The problem for this type of promotion is that it is difficult to distinguish the Scottish product offering from the many others available in equally scenic locations (http://www.visitscotland.com).

Despite the problem of intangibility, the potential customer can make some kind of prior assessment of the service product. Using available tangible cues, the customer can assess whether a particular service provider is likely to deliver what is wanted. The actual cues used and the priority given to them will vary according to the customer's particular needs at the time. In choosing a hotel, for example, a customer might look at the following:

1 *Location*. If the customer is on holiday, then perhaps a hotel near to the beach or other tourist attraction would be preferred, or one in a very peaceful scenic setting. A business traveller, in contrast, might look for one that is convenient for the airport or close to the client being visited.

2 *Appearance*. A customer's expectations about a hotel are likely to be affected by its appearance. Does it look shabby or well kept? Is it too big or too small? Does it look welcoming? What is the decor like, both internally and externally? Do the rooms seem spacious enough and well-appointed?

3 *Additional services*. The customer might be concerned about the peripheral aspects of the service on offer. The tourist who will be spending two weeks in a hotel might be interested in the variety of bars and restaurants provided, hairdressing, laundry or crèche facilities, shopping and postal services, or the nightlife. The business traveller might be more concerned about car parking, shuttle buses to the airport, or fax and telephone provision.

4 *Customer handling*. If the potential customer contacts the hotel for further information or to make a reservation, the quality of the handling they receive might affect the purchase decision. Courtesy and friendliness will make a good impression, as will a prompt and accurate response to the query. This kind of efficiency implies a commitment to staff training and good operating systems to assist easy access to relevant information and the speedy processing of bookings.

marketing in action   The multiplex: Oscar winner or turkey?

A visit to the cinema has been revolutionised over recent years, and further changes are still expected as efforts continue to be made to upgrade the customer experience. It is not very long ago that going to the cinema meant a choice of one main feature and a 'B' film and that was all. Stern-faced usherettes guided you with their torches towards a seat (usually the one you did not want), then they doubled up as ice-cream sellers during the interval (until they ran out of stock). Parking was usually non-existent, as cinemas were located in town centres, and queuing was the norm for more popular shows as no advance booking was possible. The seating was not particularly comfortable, and the whole episode was not very customer friendly. It is perhaps not surprising that cinema audiences declined over many years as people switched to new leisure pursuits. In the late 1940s, around 1.6 billion tickets were sold each year, but this had shrunk to 54 million by 1984 (Rushe, 2001). Television and video were thought to be the culprits behind the dramatic decline.

Since the opening of the first multiplex in Milton Keynes in 1985, the decline has stopped as marketing strategies have become far more oriented towards the modern consumer's needs. Cinema entered a second golden age that is still with us. This is very evident from a visit to a multiplex cinema, a format which has been a major influence in the rise in cinema attendances in the UK. A multiplex is a large building containing a number of small, individual cinemas around a central circulation area. A multiplex can thus show twelve or more different films at any one time and can seat up to 3500 customers in total. The size of the individual cinemas varies, so that, for example, blockbusting new releases can be put into bigger ones or even be shown in two cinemas at once, reflecting the expected popularity of the film. The seating in all the cinemas is invariably of a high standard.

Despite the undoubted success of the multiplex format in offering choice and an experience that cannot be replicated on a small screen, there is growing concern over how long the rapid development of new sites can continue. Between 1988 and 1991 around fourteen sites per year were added, stopped by the recession in the early 1990s. The period 1992–95 saw growth again, but at a rate of six sites per year. Between 1996 and 2001, however, the number of new multiplexes rose to 25 per year (Dodona, 2001). Cineworld (formerly UGC), Cine UK and Warner Village added the most, followed by Odeon, UCI and Showcase. There are now ten UK cities with more than 50 multiplex screens within a 15–20 minute drive of the city centres, although many smaller towns still have no provision.

The impact of multiplex cinemas might not yet have been fully played out, as they have become part of the property development business. The concept has expanded into multi-leisure parks (MLPs) that are now taking prime edge-of-town sites with plenty of parking, with the multiplex as the anchor tenant, a bowling alley and a choice of restaurants making the sites 'one-stop shop entertainment experiences'. Following the US lead, more sites are planned. Star City outside Birmingham, for example, has a 36-screen cinema, twelve restaurants and shops. These sites are attracting leisure trade that previously used the city centre. Town centres can attract between 15 and 20 per cent of their income from the night-time economy, so a competitive response is likely, probably through efforts to create a café, pub and club culture to draw people back.

There is an alternative view, however, that suggests that significant growth in demand for multiplex cinemas may be over. Already, poorly located cinemas have closed. The cinema market is not in decline, but it may be oversupplied, thus affecting individual site viability. Estimates vary about how many seats are needed to make a profit, some suggesting that a seat must be sold between 300 and 400 times a year to make money. Some multiplexes are struggling to reach 200 times. As most of the costs are fixed, an empty seat is lost revenue for ever but with the same cost of providing it. Dodona (2001) estimated that by 2005 there would be nearly 3400 screens, a growth of 1400 on 2001 levels, so it is critical for the multiplex operators that audiences should

For many film enthusiasts the multiplex is the only type of cinema they now visit.

Source: © VIEW Pictures Ltd/Alamy http://www.alamy.com
Photographer: Hufton + Crow.

continue to rise. The real victims could, however, be the remaining traditional cinemas and those multiplexes that are either poorly sited or not modernising further.

Marketing is therefore back on the agenda to build loyalty. Cinema audiences grew by 5 per cent in 2004 and box office revenues by 4 per cent, suggesting that despite the threats from DVD and other forms of entertainment, cinema-going remains a popular leisure pursuit. There were 175 million visits in 2004 and the prediction for 2008 is growth to 200 million. This perhaps reflects the fact that UK consumers, with an average of three visits per year per person, are attending the cinema a lot less often than their European counterparts and have some catching up to do.

The industry is still, however, heavily dependent upon the box office blockbusters. In 2004, the top ten film releases accounted for 40 per cent of box office revenues. What is needed is more creative marketing management to build upon an essentially undifferentiated cinema-going experience. Sophisticated service pricing systems could help, along with concepts borrowed from other sectors. For example, differentiation could be achieved through differential pricing, with earlier showings being cheaper, or pricing based on day of the week, month, location, seating position, service bundling (include meal), or even by specific film. Loyalty cards are also slowly being introduced, with UGC offering unlimited access to all of its 43 cinemas for a flat monthly fee. The idea has not been a great success to date.

Despite these challenges, service improvement has led to a trebling of cinema attendances at a time when many other visual media options are available, demonstrating the value of a strong customer focus in designing and delivering services.

Sources: Cox (2002); Dodona (2001); Kalsi and Napier (2005); *Marketing Week* (2005a); McCarthy (2002); Rushe (2001); http://www.ukfilmcouncil.org.uk.

In a wider sense, marketing and brand building are also important, of course. These help to raise awareness of a hotel chain's existence and positioning, and differentiate it from the competition. These communicate the key benefits on offer and thus help the customer to decide whether this is the kind of hotel they are looking for, developing their expectations. Advertising, glossy brochures and other marketing communications techniques can help to create and reinforce the potential customer's perception of location, appearance, additional services and customer handling, as well as the brand imagery. Strong marketing and branding also help to link a chain of hotels that might be spread worldwide, giving the customer some reassurance of consistency and familiarity. A business traveller in a strange city can seek out a known hotel name, such as Novotel, Holiday Inn, Sheraton, Campanile or Formule 1, and be fairly certain about what they are purchasing.

Example

Pizza Hut's menu, decor, servers, order processing, equipment, cooking procedures, etc., are all standardised (or allow minor variations and adaptations for local conditions), creating a consistent and familiar experience for the customer all over the world. Customers thus have a strong tangible impression of the character of Pizza Hut, what to expect of it, and what it delivers.

One of the greatest problems of intangibility is that it is difficult to assess quality both during and after the service has been experienced. Customers will use a combination of criteria, both objective and subjective, to judge their level of satisfaction, although it is often based on impressions, memories and expectations.

Different customers attach significance to different things. The frequent business traveller might be extremely annoyed by check-in delays or the noise from the Friday night jazz cabaret, while the holidaymaker might grumble about the beach being 20 minutes' walk away rather than the five minutes promised in the brochure. Memories fade over time, but some bad ones, such as a major service breakdown or a confrontation with service staff, will remain.

Perishability

Services are manufactured at the same time as they are consumed. A lecturer paces the lecture theatre, creating a service experience that is immediately either consumed or slept through by the students. Manchester United, Ajax or AC Milan manufacture sporting entertainment that either thrills, bores or frustrates their fans as they watch the match live. Similarly, audiences at Covent Garden or La Scala absorb live opera as it unfolds before them. With both sport and entertainment, it is likely that the customer's enjoyment of the 'product' is heightened by the unpredictability of live performance and the audience's own emotional involvement in what is going on. This highlights another peculiarity of service products: customers are often directly involved in the production process and the synergy between them and the service provider affects the quality of the experience. A friend might tell you, 'Yes, it was a brilliant concert. The band were on top form and the atmosphere was great!' To create such a complete experience, the band and their equipment do have to perform to the expected standard, the lighting and sound crews have to get it right on the night, and the venue has to have adequate facilities and efficient customer handling processes. The atmosphere, however, is created by the interaction between performer and audience and can inspire the performer to deliver a better experience. The customer therefore has to be prepared to give as well as take, and make their own contribution to the quality of the service product.

Perishability thus means that a service cannot be manufactured and stored either before or after the experience. Manufacture and consumption are simultaneous. A hotel is, of course, a permanent structure with full-time staff, and exists regardless of whether it has customers or not on a particular night. The hotel's service product, however, is only being delivered when there is a customer present to purchase and receive it. The product is perishable in the sense that if a room is not taken on a particular night, then it is a completely lost opportunity. The same is true of most service products, such as airline seats, theatre tickets, management consultancy or dental appointments. If a dentist cannot fill the appointment book for a particular day, then that revenue-earning opportunity is lost for ever. In situations where demand is reasonably steady, it is relatively easy to plan capacity and adapt the organisation to meet the expected demand pattern.

Even where demand does fluctuate, as long as it is fairly predictable managers can plan to raise or reduce service capacity accordingly. A larger plane or an additional performance might be provided to cater for short-term demand increases. It can be more difficult, however, if there are very marked fluctuations in demand that might result in facilities lying idle for a long time or in severe overcapacity. The profitability of companies servicing peak-hour transport demands can be severely affected because vehicles and rolling stock are unused for the rest of the day. Airlines too face seasonal fluctuations in demand.

Example

Attendance at soccer matches is a classic case of a perishable service. If missed, a match can never be experienced again, other than on film, and the revenue-earning capacity of the empty seat is lost for ever for that event. It has been argued that soccer clubs have become greedy when setting prices and that this is resulting in declining attendances at a number of clubs. Admission prices are so high that some of the traditional groups are being priced out of the market; the cheapest seat at a league match at Chelsea was £48 in August 2005. That's high compared with other forms of entertainment and staggeringly high compared to some of the low-cost airlines offering promotional fares. In 2003–04 occupancy levels at Premiership matches averaged 94.2 per cent. Many clubs have categories of fixtures according to their attractiveness, and categories are then priced in an attempt to avoid unfilled capacity (*Yorkshire Post*, 2005).

Example

The Kingdom Hotel in Zimbabwe is suffering from long-term decline, despite its great location at the Victoria Falls and catering for international tourists. This is just a part of the rapid decline of the tourism industry in Zimbabwe, caused largely by the policies of the Mugabe government. The revenue for tourism in Zimbabwe dropped from $700m in 1999 to just $60m in 2004. Meanwhile, the rooms remain empty, the facilities under-utilised, and the revenue lost for ever (Vasagar, 2005).

No matter how beautiful the setting, a hotel needs to promote itself to relevant customers in order to fill rooms and maintain revenue.

Source: © Kirk Pflaum http://www.sxc.hu

The concept of perishability means that a range of marketing strategies is needed to try to even out demand and bring capacity handling into line with it. These strategies might include pricing or product development to increase demand during quieter periods or to divert it from busier ones, or better scheduling and forecasting through the booking and reservation system. Similarly, the capacity and service delivery system can be adapted to meet peaks or troughs in demand through such strategies as part-time workers, increased mechanisation or cooperation with other service providers.

Inseparability

Many physical products are produced well in advance of purchase and consumption, and production staff rarely come into direct contact with the customer. Often, production and consumption are distanced in both space and time, connected only by the physical distribution system. Sales forecasts provide important guidelines for production schedules. If demand rises unexpectedly, opportunities might well exist to increase production or to reduce stockholding to meet customer needs.

As has already been said, with service products, however, the involvement of the customer in the service experience means that there can be no prior production and no storage and that consumption takes place simultaneously with production. The service delivery, therefore, cannot be separated from the service providers and thus the fourth characteristic of service products is inseparability. This means that the customer often comes into direct contact with the service provider(s), either individually, as with a doctor, or as part of a team of providers, as with air travel. The team includes reservations clerks, check-in staff, aircrew and perhaps transfer staff. In an airline, the staff team has a dual purpose. Clearly, they have to deliver their aspect of the service efficiently, but they also have to interact with the customer in the delivery of the service. An uncooperative check-in clerk might not provide the customer's desired seat, but in contrast, friendly and empathic cabin staff can alleviate the fear of a first-time flyer. The service provider can thus affect the quality of the service delivered and the manner in which it is delivered.

Example

> British Airways trains its cabin staff to be aware of other cultures. It carries people from many different nationalities, so it believes that it is important for cabin crew to think about these cultures and be able to handle them with sensitivity. Sensitivity was apparently the last thing on an air stewardess's mind on a Thomson holiday flight from the Canary Islands to Gatwick. With a flight just two-thirds full and the passengers all seated at the rear of the plane, the captain decided to ask some of the passengers to move to create a more even distribution. Unfortunately, the stewardess allegedly asked for eight fat people to move to the front of the plane. Any volunteers? Was she looking at you? Thomson denied that the stewardess used the word fat, and said that all such announcements were scripted (Yaqoob, 2005).

While the delivery of a personal service can be controlled, since there are fewer opportunities for outside interference, the situation becomes more complex when other customers are experiencing service at the same time. The 'mass service experience' means that other customers can potentially affect the perceived quality of that experience, positively or negatively. As mentioned earlier, the enjoyment of the atmosphere at a sporting event or a concert, for example, depends on the emotional charge generated by a large number of like-minded individuals. In other situations, however, the presence of many other customers can negatively affect aspects of the service experience. If the facility or the staff do not have the capacity or the ability to handle larger numbers than forecast, queues, overcrowding and dissatisfaction can soon result. Although reservation or prebooking can reduce the risk, service providers can still be caught out. Airlines routinely overbook flights deliberately, on the basis that not all booked passengers will actually turn up. Sometimes, however, they miscalculate and end up with more passengers than the flight can actually accommodate and have to offer free air miles, cash or other benefits to encourage some passengers to switch to a later flight.

What the other customers are like also affects the quality of the experience. This reflects the segmentation policy of the service provider. If a relatively undifferentiated approach is offered, there are all sorts of potential conflicts (or benefits) from mixing customers who are perhaps looking for different benefits. A hotel, for example, might have problems if families with young children are mixed with guests on an over-50s holiday. Where possible, therefore, the marketer should carefully target segments to match the service product being offered.

Finally, the behaviour of other customers can be positive, leading to new friends, comradeship and enjoyable social interaction, or it can be negative if it is rowdy, disruptive or even threatening. Marketers prefer, of course, to try to develop the positive aspects. Social evenings for new package holiday arrivals, name badges on coach tours, and warm-up acts to build atmosphere at live shows all help to break the ice. To prevent disruptive behaviour, the service package might have to include security measures and clearly defined and enforced 'house rules' such as those found at soccer matches.

Heterogeneity

With simultaneous production and consumption and the involvement of service staff and other customers, it can be difficult to standardise the service experience as planned. Heterogeneity means that each service experience is likely to be different, depending on the interaction between the customer and other customers, service staff, and other factors such as time, location and the operating procedures. The problems of standardising the desired service experience are greater when there is finite capacity and the service provided is especially labour intensive. The maxim 'when the heat is on the service is gone' reflects the risk of service breakdown when demand puts the system under pressure, especially if it is unexpected. This might mean no seats available on the train, delays in serving meals on a short-haul flight, or a queue in the bank on a Friday afternoon.

Some of the heterogeneity in the service cannot be planned for or avoided, but quality assurance procedures can minimise the worst excesses of service breakdown. This can be done by designing in 'failsafes', creating mechanisms to spot problems quickly and to resolve them early before they cause a major service breakdown. Universities, for example, have numerous quality assurance procedures to cover academic programmes, staffing and support procedures that involve self-assessment, student evaluation and external subject and quality assessment.

Example

Mystery shoppers are widely used to monitor service levels and the service experience provided. They eat at restaurants to check food, service and facilities, stay in hotels, drink in pubs, travel on planes, and visit cinemas, health clubs and garages. The lucky ones even get to go on expensive foreign holidays. The feedback provides front-line commentary and, however revealing, often shows companies the difference between the service promise and the reality of what is delivered. Most of the time, the focus is on the overall experience rather than individual performance, although at times staff are also the focus of attention. Normally, the mystery shopper is given a checklist of points to watch out for, and they have to be skilled in classifying and memorising elements of the delivered service. To be effective, the mystery shopper must be believable and natural and thus cannot go round with a checklist on a clipboard (McLuhan, 2002). So next time you are in Burger King or Pret à Manger, to name but two, you could be next to a shopper on a mission.

Management therefore has to develop ways of reducing the impact of heterogeneity. To help in that process, they need to focus on operating systems, procedures and staff training in order to ensure consistency. New lecturers, for example, might be required to undertake a special induction programme to help them learn teaching skills, preparing materials and handling some of the difficulties associated with disruptive students. Managers have to indicate clearly what they expect of staff in terms of the desired level of service. This must cover not only compliance with procedures in accordance with training, but also staff attitudes and the manner in which they deal with customers.

The next part of this section looks in more detail at the impact of the particular characteristics of service products on the design and implementation of the marketing programme.

Services marketing management

So far, this section has looked at the characteristics of service products in a very general way. We now look further at the implications of those characteristics for marketers in terms of formulating strategy, developing and measuring quality in the service product and issues of training and productivity.

Services marketing strategy

The traditional marketing mix consists of the 4Ps. For service products, however, additional elements of the marketing mix are necessary to reflect the special characteristics of services marketing. Shown in Figure 4.33, these are as follows:

● *People*: whether service providers or customers who participate in the production and delivery of the service experience

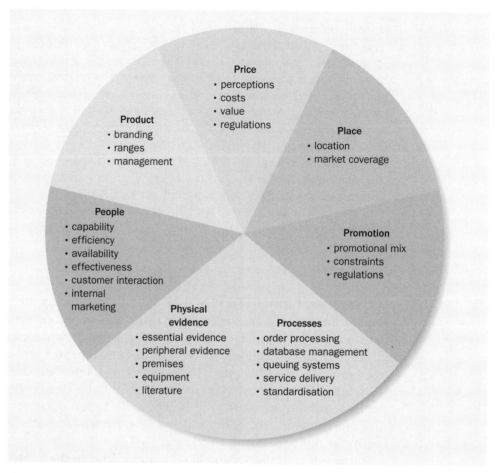

Figure 4.33 The services marketing mix

- *Physical evidence*: the tangible cues that support the main service product. These include facilities, the infrastructure and the products used to deliver the service
- *Processes*: the operating processes that take the customer through from ordering to the manufacture and delivery of the service.

Any of these extra marketing mix elements can enhance or detract from the customer's overall experience when consuming the service. However, despite the special considerations, the purpose of designing an effective marketing mix remains the same whether for services or physical products. The marketer is still trying to create a differentiated, attractive proposition for customers, ensuring that whatever is offered meets their needs and expectations.

All seven of the services marketing mix elements will now be considered in turn.

Product

From a supplier's perspective, many services can be treated like any other physical product in a number of ways. The supplier develops a range of products, each of which represents profit-earning opportunities. A hotel company might treat each of its hotels as a separate product with its own unique product management requirements arising from its location, the state of the building and its facilities, local competition and its strengths and weaknesses compared with others in the area. These products might, of course, be grouped into product lines and SBUs based on similarities and differences between them, just as physical products can be.

corporate social responsibilityin action

What do the Prince of Wales, the Catholic Church and environmental protesters have in common?

The answer: unanimous opposition to a Dracula theme park that was planned in Transylvania, an area of Romania renowned for its beauty, ancient oak forests and cultural heritage. Better-informed readers will know, of course, that Dracula never existed as such, but the character created by Bram Stoker was based on Vlad Tepes, a fifteenth-century ruler who shot to fame for impaling over 1000 Turks after a particularly nasty battle. His real name was Vlad Dracul, Dracul meaning Devil in Romanian. The 'Tepes' (impaler) was added later for obvious reasons. Hollywood added the fangs, blood drinking and associated niceties. Vlad was born in the medieval fortress city of Sighisoara, a UNESCO world heritage site which the Romanian government has undertaken to protect.

The original proposed project planned to develop 40 hectares of land initially, expanding to 60 in phase 2. It would have cost around £30m and was due to be ready for tourists by 2004. Castle Dracula would have been the centrepiece, housing a judgement chamber, vampire den and alchemy laboratory. Included would have been a mock torture room with stakes and knives, folk workshops for vampire protecting armour, a vampire fashion house, and rides with vampire themes, bringing a whole new meaning to 'The House of Horror'. The restaurants were going to offer such delicacies as 'blood pudding' and 'dish of brains' and for those who were brave enough, there would be motels on site. Linked to the park were a golf course, a campsite, a 700-bed hotel, souvenir shops, beer halls and a ballroom for 2000 dancers: something for everybody, but not eco-tourism (Moore Ede, 2002).

The park was expected to create around 3000 jobs and was planned to generate $21m per year

from 1 million visitors. It is in a poor region in a poor country with a quality of life that has been likened to that of Namibia and Libya (Douglas-Home, 2001). The theme park offered jobs in an area with 17 per cent unemployment, and the chance to buy shares in the venture, with 100 shares costing about £20, one-third the average monthly wage. The company created to develop the park, Fondul Pentru Dezvoltare Turistica Sighisoara (FPDTS), was 99 per cent owned by the Sighisoara municipality but was intended as a profit-making enterprise. It was also argued that the city would be restored after many years of neglect.

From a government perspective, what better way for the Ministry of Tourism to start to rebuild the brand image of Romania, which for many Europeans is off the tourism scale? Although the Transylvania region has much to offer, with fortified churches, castles, painted monasteries and unspoiled beauty, it is difficult to reach, about five hours by road from the capital Bucharest, it has little high-standard tourism infrastructure such as hotels and restaurants, no effective waste disposal system and no service tradition as a result of the Communist era. Dracula could have changed all that, however, even though Dracula films were not legal until 1989 and the Stoker book was not published in Romanian until 1992. A 1973 'Dracula: Truth and Legend' tour disappointed many foreigners as most of the time was spent tracing the life of Vlad, rather than the fangs and cape experience (George, 2002). The planned theme park would have addressed many of the issues of infrastructure and would have given the tourists what they really wanted.

There was a huge outcry across Europe and even from within Romania. Romania's Catholic and Orthodox bishops called for the abandonment of the park as they considered that it was an inappropriate symbol to offer visitors (Coppen, 2003). The Prince of Wales expressed concern (de Quetteville, 2004) and ecological protesters argued against the project on the grounds of the damage that it would do to the town of Sighisoara which was a world heritage site along with the surrounding natural environment. This wide variety of stakeholders formed a powerful and effective coalition (Jamal and Tanase, 2005). A stake was driven through the heart of the project and it was abandoned as being too controversial.

Within a year, however, the project was back, but this time bizarrely located nearer Bucharest at a farm once owned by executed dictator Nicolae Ceausescu. The connection between the new location at Snagov and Dracula is the claim that Vlad Tepes is buried nearby. Outside the Town Hall is a bust of the heavily armoured, thickly moustached Tepes. The park will include Disneyland style children's rides, a golf course, a horse racing circuit, and a housing development, and it is not likely to be opposed. The plan is to attract 1 million tourists annually with over 20 per cent coming from abroad, given the park's proximity to the international airport. It remains to be seen whether the development will be cheap and tacky or offer a true resort experience. The connection between evil and the glorification of death and happy family holidays appears to be regarded as incidental! Maybe Dracula should remain in Hollywood after all!

Sources: Coppen (2003); de Quetteville (2003, 2004); Douglas-Home (2001); George (2002); Jamal and Tanase (2005); Marinas (2004); Moore Ede (2002).

Many product concepts and the decisions concerning them apply equally to services and physical products. Positioning, branding, developing a mix, designing new services and managing the product lifecycle are all relevant.

Product development

Product development in some service situations can be complex as it involves 'packaging' otherwise separate elements into a service product. Therefore a holiday company may need to work with airlines, hotels and local tour companies to blend a package for the target segment. From a consumer perspective, any failure in any part of the system will be regarded as a criticism of the holiday company, even though air traffic delays or faulty plumbing may not be directly under the company's control. At a regional and national level, government and private companies may work together to develop new attractions and infrastructure for tourists.

Example

Hong Kong has adopted Disney in an effort to boost tourism. Although the smallest of the Disney theme parks, the Hong Kong park still has 1000 beds on site and hopes to attract 6 million visitors, one-third of whom will come from mainland China. An investment of that size and risk was only possible through a joint venture between Disney and the Hong Kong government. There will also be spin-off benefits for the whole economy, in terms of investment in infrastructure and employment in transportation, hospitality, catering and other related industries (Steiner, 2005).

Price

Because services are intangible, their pricing can be very difficult to set and to justify. The customer is not receiving anything that can be touched or otherwise physically experienced, so it can be hard for them to appreciate the benefits they have gained in return for their expenditure.

A solicitor's bill or the labour charges added to a repair bill can seem to be incredibly high to customers, because they do not stop to think about the training that has gone into developing professional skills nor of the peace of mind gained by having the job done 'properly'. As with any product, therefore, the customer's perception is central to assessing value for money.

The prices of some services are controlled by bodies other than the service provider. The amount that dentists charge for work under the National Health Service or that pharmacists charge to dispense a prescription is imposed by central government. Similarly, the BBC is funded by licence fees determined by government and charged to television owners. Other services price on a commission basis. An estate agent, for example, might charge the vendor a fee of 2 per cent of the selling price of the house, plus any expenses such as advertising.

Other service providers are completely free to decide their own prices, with due respect to competition and the needs, wants and perceptions of customers. In setting prices, however, service providers can find it very difficult to determine the true cost of provision, perhaps because of the difficulty of costing professional or specialist skills, or because the time and effort required to deliver a service vary widely between different customers, yet a standard price is needed. Perishability might also affect the pricing of professional services. A training provider, for example, who has little work on at the moment might agree to charge less than the normal daily rate, just to generate some income rather than none.

In service situations, price can play an important role in managing demand. By varying the price, depending on the time at which the service is delivered, service providers can try to discourage customers from purchasing at the busiest periods. Customers can also use price as a weapon. Passengers purchasing airline tickets shortly before the flight or visitors looking for a hotel room for the night might be able to negotiate a much lower price than that advertised. This is a result of the perishability of services: the airline would rather have a seat occupied and get something for it than let the flight take off with an empty one and, similarly, the hotel would rather have a room occupied than not.

The rail pricing system has changed considerably in the UK in recent years. Traditionally, the passenger bought a ticket, walked on to the train and found a seat. Few bothered to pay the additional charge for a seat reservation. The emphasis is now on encouraging advance booking so that capacity can be better planned. The price mechanism is used to achieve a spread of customers. Plans are now being considered, however, to introduce congestion charging on some overcrowded trains through the introduction of 'rail peak pricing' with passengers on the most popular services paying extra. With the use of smartcard technology it is becoming possible to charge by each train rather than generically by the time of day, although the main barrier is the difficulty of passengers knowing what price they have to pay before starting the journey. Something will have to be done on some of the commuter lines around London where on the one hand car passengers are being forced onto the trains because of road congestion charging, and yet rail investment is not keeping pace through more track, better carriages and better infrastructure. The conversion of the Waterloo to Reading trains from eight to ten carriages, for example, would increase passenger capacity by 25 per cent. Pricing is, however, one of the most powerful weapons for attracting customers to off-peak rather than peak-hour travel, provided work patterns allow it. The Great Anglia franchise, for example, offers passengers an early bird discount on their season ticket if they avoid arriving at Liverpool Street between 7.15 a.m. and 9.15 a.m. (*Modern Railways*, 2005; Webster, 2005).

Place

According to Cowell (1984), services are often supplied direct from the provider to the customer because production and consumption are simultaneous. Direct supply allows the provider to control what is going on, to differentiate through personal service, and to get direct feedback and interaction with the customer. Direct supply can take place from business premises, such as a hairdresser's salon, a solicitor's office or a university campus. Some services can also be supplied by telephone, such as insurance and banking services. Others are supplied by the service provider visiting the customer's home or premises, such as cleaning, repair of large appliances, equipment installation and servicing, or home hairdressing services.

Direct supply can cause problems for the service provider. It limits the number of customers that can be dealt with and the geographic coverage of the service. For sole traders or small businesses who particularly value the rapport and personal relationships built up with regular clients, this might be perfectly acceptable. Businesses that want to expand might find that direct supply involving the original proprietor of the business is no longer feasible. Professional service businesses, such as accountants or solicitors, might employ additional qualified staff to expand the customer base or to expand geographic coverage.

Example

A fitness-oriented society coupled with rising levels of obesity has been a major factor behind the rapid growth of the health and fitness sector since the mid-1990s. Participation among the adult population grew from 3.8 per cent in 1996 to 8 per cent in 2005, with an expected rise around 13.5 per cent by 2007 (Urquhart, 2005). This is further encouraged by the government's increased focus on health and fitness issues generally and obesity in particular. In the short term, however, the number of new members coming forward may have dropped in 2005.

There are 2403 publicly run fitness clubs in the UK and 1982 private clubs (Stevenson, 2005). Holmes Place has 76 clubs (50 in the UK) with a membership retention rate of 60 per cent, which is high compared to the rest of the industry. Its rival Fitness First has 166 clubs in the UK, a further 173 in the rest of Europe, and a total of 434 clubs generating 1.2 million members worldwide. David Lloyd actually reported lower membership numbers in 2005 compared with 2004, as users switch centres to obtain the latest facilities or just lose interest in the treadmill. The premium clubs are especially vulnerable as they need to invest in more and varied facilities such as swimming pools and indoor tennis courts. It is expected that some rationalisation will take place as users become ever more demanding (Stevenson, 2005).

The main means of growth for most clubs has been to open branches in new locations offering the same standard range of facilities. David Lloyd is trimming back its expansion plans and its new venues will feature racquet sports centres rather than traditional gyms. The question is whether growth can then continue, as there are already signs that saturation has been reached for the time being. In 2004, there were 796 new gyms being planned, 15 per cent down on 2003. Other marketing activities also involve extending the reach with, for example, tie-ins with local sports associations, corporate membership drives and joint initiatives such as LA Fitness's 'Wellness Centres' operated in conjunction with BUPA.

Other service businesses such as fast food outlets, domestic cleaners or debt collection agencies might opt to expand by franchising, while others will decide to move towards indirect supply through intermediaries paid on a commission basis. Thus the local pharmacist might act as an agent for a company that develops photographic film, a village shop might collect dry cleaning, insurance brokers distribute policies, travel agencies distribute holidays and business travel, and tourist information offices deal with hotel and guest house bookings. In some of these cases, the main benefit of using an intermediary is convenience for the customer and spreading the coverage of the service. In others, such as the travel agency and the insurance broker, the service provider gains the added benefit of having its product sold by a specialist alongside the competition.

Promotion

Marketing communication objectives, implementation and management for services are largely the same as for any other product. There are a few specific issues to point out, however. As with pricing, some professional services are ethically constrained in what marketing communication they are allowed to do. Solicitors in the UK, for example, are allowed to use print advertising, but only if it is restrained and factual. An advertisement can tell the reader what areas of the law the practice specialises in, but it cannot make emotive promises about winning vast amounts of compensation for you, for example.

Service products face a particularly difficult communications task because of the intangibility of the product. They cannot show you pretty pack shots, they cannot whet your appetite with promises of strawberry and chocolate-flavoured variants, they cannot show you how much of this amazing product you are getting for your money. They can, however, show the physical evidence, they can show people like you apparently enjoying the service, they can emphasise the benefits of purchasing this service. Testimonials from satisfied customers can be an extremely effective tool, because they reassure the potential customer that the service works and that the outcomes will be positive. Linked with this, word-of-mouth communication is incredibly important, especially for the smaller business working in a limited geographic area.

Finally, it must be remembered that many service providers are small businesses that could not afford to invest in glossy advertising campaigns even if they could see the point of it. Many can generate enough work to keep them going through word-of-mouth recommendation, websites and advertisements in the *Yellow Pages*. Much depends on the level of competition and demand in the local market for the kind of service being offered. If the town's High Street supports four different restaurants, then perhaps a more concerted effort might be justified, including, for example, advertising in local newspapers, door-to-door leaflet drops and price promotions.

Example

Ramada Jarvis Hotels (http://www.ramadaJarvis.co.uk) uses direct marketing to promote conference business in its 62 hotels in the UK. The information pack, which is targeted at potential business customers, includes a complete directory of locations, room configurations and prices along with a lot of visual imagery to show the standard of meeting rooms, food service and the range of staff who are employed to make the conference or meeting a success. The messages throughout stress quality and reliability.

It is important to remember, however, that customers are likely to use marketing communication messages to build their expectations of what the service is likely to deliver. This is true of any product but, because of intangibility, the judgement of service quality is much more subjective. It is based on a comparison of prior expectations with actual perceived outcomes. The wilder or more unrealistic the communication claims, therefore, the greater the chances of a mismatch that will lead to a dissatisfied customer in the end. The service provider does, of course, need to create a sufficiently alluring image to entice the customer, but not to the point where the customer undergoing the service experience begins to wonder if this is actually the same establishment as that advertised.

Example

The Australian Tourist Commission also makes heavy use of imagery to portray the natural and cultural delights of Australia to European audiences. Whether it is kangaroos, Ayers Rock, the Great Barrier Reef or Sydney Opera House, the visual message is the same: vibrant, exciting and surprising. The media advertisements and PR usually reinforce these themes, making full use of holiday programmes and travel shows as well as supporting Australia-themed national supplements in some of the daily newspapers. 'Brand Australia' campaigns are, however, targeted to attract different audiences and a number of campaigns are run simultaneously in different geographic markets.

The ATC has divided the 15 million potential visitors to Australia into five broad segments:

- Self challengers
- Comfort travellers
- Cocoon travellers
- Taste and try
- Pushing boundaries.

Each segment is distinguished by the travel experience sought, attitudes to travel, and the style of travel sought. For each segment, a media plan is developed to exploit the

Images of Aboriginal people in traditional dress encourage tourists seeking alternative cultural experiences to visit the Australian outback.

Source: © eyeubiquitous/hutchison http://www.eyeubiquitous.com

potential, and messages are tailor-made according to the attitudes held and benefits sought. There are unifying themes, however, such as overcoming the view that Australia is a remote, vast and 'once in a lifetime' destination to position it more as a 'liberating, civilised adventure' destination. A 'visiting journalist' programme, funded by the ATC, is especially important for stimulating more and better PR coverage, and around 1000 print and broadcast journalists are invited each year. It also helps to show Australia as being more than scenery and sun, with coverage of urban culture, food, wine, arts and cultural themes. An integrated campaign is important to overcome a concern, confirmed by research, that consumers are comfortable with Australia as a destination but lack an in-depth knowledge and sense of urgency to visit. The Brand Australia campaign aims to change that by strengthening the brand perception and presenting Australia as an experience destination for sophisticated travellers, not just a flop-on-the-beach paradise (Moldofsdky, 2005; http://www.atc.australia.com; http://www.australia).

People

Services depend on people and interaction between people, including the service provider's staff, the customer and other customers. As the customer is often a participant in the creation and delivery of the service product, there are implications for service product quality, productivity and staff training. The ability of staff to cope with customers, to deliver the service reliably to the required standard and to present an image consistent with what the organisation would want is of vital concern to the service provider. This is known as *internal marketing*. The role of the customer in the service is known as *interactive marketing*.

Physical evidence

Physical evidence comprises the tangible elements that support the service delivery, and offer clues about the positioning of the service product or give the customer something solid to take away with them to symbolise the intangible benefits they have received. Shostack (1977) differentiates between *essential evidence* and *peripheral evidence*. Essential evidence is central to the service and is an important contributor to the customer's purchase decision. Examples of this might be the type and newness of aircraft operated by an airline or of the car fleet belonging to a car hire firm, the layout and facilities offered by a supermarket or a university's lecture theatres and their equipment as well as IT and library provision. Peripheral evidence is less central to the service delivery and is likely to consist of items that the customer can have to keep or use.

Processes

Because the creation and consumption of a service are usually simultaneous, the production of the service is an important part of its marketing as the customer either witnesses it or is directly involved in it. The service provider needs smooth, efficient customer-friendly procedures. Some processes work behind the scenes, for example administrative and data processing systems, processing paperwork and information relating to the service delivery and keeping track of customers.

Systems that allow the service provider to send a postcard to remind customers that the next dental check-up or car service is due certainly help to generate repeat business, but also help in a small way to strengthen the relationship with the customer. Other processes are also 'invisible' to the customer, but form an essential part of the service package. The organisation of the kitchens in a fast food outlet, for example, ensures a steady supply of freshly cooked burgers available for counter staff to draw on as customers order. Well-designed processes are also needed as the service is delivered to ensure that the customer gets through with minimum fuss and delay and that all elements of the service are properly delivered. This might involve, for example, the design of forms and the information requested, payment procedures, queuing systems or even task allocation. At a hairdressing salon, for instance, a junior might wash your hair while the stylist finishes off the previous customer, and the receptionist will handle the payment at the end.

Example

Smartcards are revolutionising service delivery processes by cutting out human interaction, which can be slow, inconsistent and unreliable. Smartcards which are a similar size to a credit card have an embedded microprocessor and a memory that can be activated by either a reader or a signal-emitting device. The cards are especially popular with transport providers as a means of reducing queues at ticket offices and for travel authentication. The cards are not bound by travel zones and time restrictions as are normal season tickets and travel cards. The card reader at a station will automatically account for the journey time and distance, and the fare can be deducted from the previously topped-up card. Speed of processing is essential for keeping systems such as London Underground working. The Jubilee Line has the capacity to handle 39,000 people per hour and that's a lot of movement at its main stations in the peak periods.

Notes

1 Quoted in Megan Barnett, 'Taking on Tech's Titans', *SmartMoney*, April 2006, pp. 29–30.

2 Based on information from: Leila Abboud and Vauhini Vara, 'SAP Trails Nimble Start-Ups As Software Market Matures', *Wall Street Journal*, 23 January 2007, p. C1; 'SAP Intends to Triple Customer Base in Four Years', *InformationWeek*, 5 December, 2006, n.p.; 'New Campaigns', *B to B*, 11 December 2006, p. 14; Barnett, 'Taking on Tech's Titans'; 'Bloggers' Corner Proves Successful at SAP Event', *PR Week*, 20 November 2006, p. 19.

3 Craig S. Fleisher and Babette E. Bensoussan, *Strategic and Competitive Analysis* (Upper Saddle River, NJ: Prentice Hall, 2003), pp. 269–83.

4 Matt Richtel, 'Console Sales Beat Goals, Makers' Early Reports Say', *New York Times*, 8 January 2007, p. C4; 'Sony Keeps PS3 Targets Despite Headwind', *eWeek*, 14 December 2006, n.p.; 'Sony to Delay Release of PlayStation 3', *New York Times*, 15 March 2006, www.nytimes.com.

5 Melanie Warner, 'In Defense of Soda and Gum', *New York Times*, 4 March 2006, p. C3.

6 Quote from Cadbury Schweppes website (www.cadburyschweppes.com/EN/Environment-Society/Consumer/WhatWeAreDoing).

7 Jane Bussey, 'Wal-Mexico: Wal-Mart's Biggest Success', *Miami Herald*, 24 January 2006, www.herald.com; Kerry A. Dolan, 'It's Nice to Be Big', *Forbes*, 1 September 2003, pp. 84–5.

8 'Pacesetters Collaboration: Procter & Gamble', *BusinessWeek*, 21 November 2005, p. 92; 'India Emerges as New Auto Hub', *Asia Africa Intelligence Wire*, 30 August 2005, n.p.; 'Focusing on the Big Picture: What's the Real Deal with Global Supply Chains?', *World Trade*, February 2006, pp. 28ff.

9 Mitch Betts, 'Unexpected Insights', *Computerworld*, 14 April 2003, p. 34.

10 'Campaign Direct Awards 2006: The Ortus Award', *Campaign*, 7 April 2006, p. 8.

11 Quoted in Theresa Howard, 'Dove Ads Enlist All Shapes, Styles, Sizes', *USA Today*, 29 August 2005, p. 7B; Michelle Jeffers, 'Behind Dove's "Real Beauty"', *Adweek*, 12 September 2005, p. 34.

12 Sharon Kiley Mack, 'From the Sea: Salt from Maine Proving Itself in National Market', *Bangor Daily News*, 10 January 2007, www.bangordailynews.com; Allison Askins, 'Salt Has an Ancient History and a Bright Future', *The State* (Columbia, S.C.), 2 June 2003, www.thestate.com; Michael J. McCarthy, 'Little Umbrella Girl Watches Her Back in Kosher Salt War', *Wall Street Journal*, 10 June 2002, pp. A1ff.

13 Quote in Kerry Capell, '"Wal-Mart with Wings"', *Business Week Online*, 4 December 2006, www.businessweek.com. Also: 'Michael O'Leary', *Newsweek International*, 23 June 2003, pp. 64ff; 'Ryanair Blasted over Christmas Bags Cost', *Irish Post*, 10 January 2007, www.irishpost.co.uk.

14 David Gow, 'Boeing Sales Soar Ahead of Rival Airbus', *Guardian*, 5 January 2007, p. 27.

15 'New Zealand Post Tries Personalized Stamps', *ePostal News*, 10 October 2005, p. 2; Alicia Henry, 'You Oughta Be In . . . Stamps?', *Business Week*, 25 August 2003, p. 14; 'Heinz Anniversary Efforts Push Personalized Labels', *PR Week*, 11 September 2006, p. 2.

16 Todd Wasserman, 'Unilever, Whirlpool Get Personal with Personas', *Brandweek*, 18 September 2006, p. 13.

17 Pranay Gupte, 'Hand Candy', *Forbes Global*, 8 January 2007, p. 76; William George Shuster, 'Montblanc Celebrates Its Centenary', *Jewelers Circular Keystone*, May 2006, pp. 226ff.

18 Gupte, 'Hand Candy'.

19 Julie Bosman, 'Venerable Maker of Pens Turns to Young Designers', *New York Times*, 7 August 2006, p. C6.

20 Based on information from: David Gauthier-Villars, 'Water Fight in France Takes a Dirty Turn', *Wall Street Journal*, 1 February 2007, p. B7; Carol Matlack, 'Investors Like the Taste of Groupe Danone', *BusinessWeek Online*, 22 November 2006, www.businessweek.com; Julie Chao, 'China's Homegrown Cola Sees Future in "Fashionable" Drinks', *Taipei Times*, 20 June 2004, p. 12; David Haffenreffer, 'Danone Restructures Products Portfolio', *America's Intelligence Wire*, 30 July 2003; Hannah Booth, 'Bloom Researchers Yoghurt to Update Its Pack-Shape', *Design Week*, 6 February 2003, p. 5; Sherri Day, 'Yoghurt Makers Shrink the Cup, Trying to Turn Less into More', *New York Times*, 3 May 2003, pp. C1ff.

21 Ian Rowley, 'Even Toyota Isn't Perfect', *BusinessWeek*, 22 January 2007, p. 54; Micheline Maynard, 'Now Playing in Europe: The Future of Detroit', *New York Times*, 29 October 2006, sec. 3, p. 1; Yoshio Takahashi and Andrew Morse, 'Toyota Is Posed to Surpass GM as the Top Car Maker Next Year', *Wall Street Journal*, 23 December 2006, p. A4; Alex Taylor III, 'The Birth of the Prius', *Fortune*, 6 March 2006, pp. 111ff.

22 Tim Ambler, 'Set Clear Goals and See Marketing Hit Its Target', *Financial Times*, 29 August 2002, p. 8.

23 'British Telecommunications Beats Connectivity Goal by Double', *InformationWeek*, 3 January 2007, n.p.; 'BT Buys U.S. Anti-Hacking Specialist Counterpane', *eWeek*, 25 October 2006, www.eweek.com; 'BT Group PLC: U.K. Telecom Aims to Boost Annual Revenue from China', *Wall Street Journal*, 6 September 2006, n.p.; Dominic O'Connell, 'BT's 10-point Plan Becomes a Masterclass in Recovery', *Sunday Times*, 18 September 2005, p. 12.

24 H. Igor Ansoff, 'Strategies for Diversification', *Harvard Business Review*, September–October 1957, pp. 113–25; Philip Kotler, *Kotler on Marketing* (New York: Free Press, 1999), pp. 46–8.

25 Gail Edmondson, 'A Burst of Speed at Lamborghini', *BusinessWeek*, 15 January 2007, p. 44.

26 Moon Ihlwan, 'Korea: Red-Hot White Goods', *BusinessWeek*, 30 October 2006, p. 48.

27 'Hanson Charters New Business Unit', *Concrete Products*, 1 April 2006, n.p.; Abby Ellin, 'Building a Brand, One Brick at a Time', *New York Times*, 15 June 2003, sec. 3, p. 13.

28 Quote reported in Nicholas George, 'Brio's Toy Trains Hit the Buffers', *Financial Times*, 29 August 2003, www.ft.com; also: www.brio.net; 'BRIO AB Divests Polish Operations', *Nordic Business Report*, 19 December 2006, n.p.

29 For more about applying these performance measures, see Andrew Likierman, 'The Balanced Scorecard: Lots of Firms Have Got One, But Has It Done Them Any Good?', *Financial Management*, November 2006, pp. 29ff.

30 Tim Ambler, 'Awards Scheme Highlights the Need for Data-Driven Marketing', *Marketing*, 21 March 2002, p. 16.

31 Leon Harris, 'HSBC Targets More Than 20 pc Growth', *Business Times*, 18 August 2003, n.p.

32 'Nestlé: A Dedicated Enemy of Fashion', *The Economist*, 31 August 2002, pp. 47–8.

33 Ihlwan, 'Korea: Red-Hot White Goods.'

34 Ibid.

35 Quoted in Ray Marcelo, 'Deccan Aspires to Soar Above Rivals', *Financial Times*, 12 September 2003, www.ft.com.

36 'Deccan Lures India's New Jet Set with Executive Charters', *Flight International*, 17 October 2006, n.p.; Marcelo, 'Deccan Aspires to Soar Above Rivals'; Rasheed Kappan, 'Air Deccan to Link "Unconnected" Towns in South', *The Hindu*, 13 August 2003, www.thehindu.com; www.airdeccan.net.

37 'Mercedes Car Group Unit Sales Rise 3.2 pct in 2006', *Reuters*, 5 January 2007, www.reuters.com; Neal E. Boudette and Joseph B. White, 'Car Sales Get Chilly at Altitudes of $150,000', *Wall Street Journal*, 11 September 2003, www.wsj.com.

38 *See* Sandy D. Jap and Erin Anderson, 'Testing the Life-Cycle Theory of Inter-Organisational Relations: Do Performance Outcomes Depend on the Path Taken?', *Insead Knowledge*, February 2003, www.insead.edu.

39 Jean Halliday, 'Marketer of the Year: Toyota', *Advertising Age*, 13 November 2006, p. M-1.

40 Kathryn Kranhold, 'Theory & Practice: Client-Satisfaction Tool Takes Root', *Wall Street Journal*, 10 July 2006, p. B3; Craig Smith, 'Marketers Still Lost in the Metrics', *Marketing*, 10 August 2000, p. 15.

41 Tom Pope, 'Fundraising Ideas from North of the Border', *The Non-profit Times*, 15 January 2003, pp. 1ff.

42 David Pinto, 'Environment as a Retail Priority', *MMR*, 30 October 2006, p. 17.

43 Quoted in 'Power Distributor Cited for Social Responsibility', *Business World*, 23 July 2003, n.p.

44 Paul B. Brown, 'Strategic Corporate Altruism', *New York Times*, 23 December 2006, p. C5.

45 Xueming Luo and C.B. Bhattacharya, 'Corporate Social Responsibility, Customer Satisfaction and Market Value', *Journal of Marketing*, October 2006, pp. 1–18.

46 Telis Demos, 'Beyond the Bottom Line', *Fortune International*, 30 October 2006, p. 72; Howard Stock, 'U.K. Large Caps Hone Social Reporting Online', *Investor Relations Business*, 9 June 2003, n.p.

47 *Source*: After Marian Burk Wood, *The Marketing Plan Handbook, 3rd edn* (Upper Saddle River, NJ: Pearson Prentice Hall, 2008), Chapter 5.

48 Suzanne Vranica, 'P&G Boosts Social-Networking Efforts', *Wall Street Journal*, 8 January 2007, p. B4.

49 Kerry Capell, 'McDonald's Offers Ethics with Those Fries', *BusinessWeek Online*, 10 January 2007, www.businessweek.com; Janet Adamy, 'How Jim Skinner Flipped McDonald's', *Wall Street Journal*, 5 January 2007, p. B1; 'Will Ex-B.A. Chief Steer McDonald's Through Market Turbulence?', *Marketing Week*, 18 May 2006, p. 4; 'McD: Beresford Is Boss of Global Brand Strategy', *Nation's Restaurant News*, 8 May 2006, p. 124; Ian Rowley, 'Shrimp Burgers to the Rescue', *BusinessWeek*, 11 September 2006, p. 36.

50 'Mattel Dolls to Wear Adidas Brand', *Marketing Week*, 11 January 2007, p. 10; Christopher C. Williams, 'Barron's Insight: Adidas Is Pushing Its Game', *Wall Street Journal*, 12 November 2006, p. 2; Richard Siklos, 'A Virtual World But Real Money', *New York Times*, 19 October 2006, p. C1.

51 Matthew Boyle, 'Chew on This', *Fortune*, 4 September 2006, pp. 41ff; Kate Norton, 'A Bubbly 2007 for Cadbury Schweppes?', *BusinessWeek Online*, 6 December 2006, www.businessweek.com.

52 Kevin Lane Keller, *Strategic Brand Management*, 2nd edn (Upper Saddle River, NJ: Prentice Hall, 2003), pp. 582–91.

53 James Durston, 'Has Heinz Bottled It in Europe?', *Grocer*, 3 June 2006, pp. 32ff; Kevin O'Donnell, 'Green Ketchup Works, But Not on Blue Fries', *Brandweek*, 1 September 2003, p. 17; Sian Harrington, 'Sharper NPD at Heinz', *Grocer*, 21 June 2003, pp. 10ff.

54 Dylan McGrath, 'High-Def DVD War Is High-Stakes Fight', *Electronic Engineering Times*, 15 January 2007, pp. 1ff; Adam Lashinksy, 'Shootout in Gadget Land', *Fortune*, 10 November 2003, pp. 74ff.

55 Caroline Parry, 'New! Nouveau! Nieuw!', *Marketing Week*, 19 June 2003, p. 30.

56 'When Will It Fly?', *The Economist*, 9 August 2003, p. 51.

57 Jessi Hempel, 'Big Blue Brainstorm', *BusinessWeek*, 7 August 2006, p. 70.

58 'Expect the Unexpected', *The Economist*, 6 September 2003, p. 5.

59 Quoted in Ariane Sains and Stanley Reed, 'Electrolux Redesigns Itself', *BusinessWeek IN*, November 2006, pp. 12ff; also: Michael Rudnick, 'Electrolux's Sales in Major Appliances Slip 3.5 Percent in Third Quarter', *HFN*, 6 November 2006, p. 22; 'Electrolux Design Lab Announces Winning Product', *Appliance*, January 2007, p. S3.

60 Ann Harrington, 'Who's Afraid of a New Product?', *Fortune*, 10 November 2003, pp. 189ff.

61 Patrick Hoffman, 'HP Rolls Out Eco-Friendly Ink Cartridge Packaging', *eWeek*, 9 February 2007, http://www.eweek.com/article2/0,1759.2092886,00.asp; 'Hewlett-Packard Co.: Firm Unveils New Technology Allowing High-Volume Inkjets', *Wall Street Journal*, 4 October 2006, p. B18; Noshua Watson, 'What's Wrong with This Printer?', *Fortune*, 17 February 2003, pp. 120C–120H.

62 'The Problem with Made in China: Manufacturing in Asia', *The Economist (US)*, 13 January 2007, p. 68ff; Eric Pfeiffer, 'Chip Off the Old Block', *Business 2.0*, July 2003, pp. 54–5.

63 Roland T. Rust, Debora Viana Thompson and Rebecca W. Hamilton, 'Feature Bloat: The Product Manager's Dilemma', *Harvard Business School Working Knowledge*, 8 May 2006, hbswk.hbs.edu.

64 'In-Tire Sensor Redesigned', *Fleet Owner*, 1 December 2006, n.p.; Ian Morton, 'Michelin System Will Check, Inflate Tyres', *Automotive News*, 21 July 2003, p. 22; 'Keeping Michelin on a Roll', *Business Week*, 7 July 2003, p. 46.

65 'Jinjiang to Use IPO Funds for Hotel Facelift', *Business Daily Update*, 30 November 2006, n.p.; 'China's Budget Hotels Fill Up', *Wall Street Journal*, 27 November 2006, p. C8.

66 Cassell Bryan-Low, 'Nokia Aims at Rivals with Slimmer Phone', *Wall Street Journal*, 8 January 2007, p. A3; Jack Ewing, 'Staying Cool at Nokia', *BusinessWeek*, 17 July 2006, pp. 62–5.

67 Quoted in Poul Funder Larsen, 'Better Is . . . Better', *Wall Street Journal*, 22 September 2003, pp. R6, R11.

68 Evan Ramstad, 'The Cellphone Wears Prada', *Wall Street Journal*, 19 January 2007, p. B5.

69 Michael Rudnick, 'Sanyo Teams With Haier to Produce Refrigerators', *HFN*, 13 November 2006, p. 31; Michael Winnick, '5 Secrets to a Successful Launch', *Business 2.0*, September 2006, pp. 93ff; Frederick Balfour, 'China's Dream Team', *BusinessWeek*, 1 September 2003, pp. 50–1.

70 Nancy Einhart, 'Are Your Competitors Packing?', *Business 2.0*, July 2003, p. 52.

71 'EU's Tobacco Clamp Upheld', *Grocer*, 14 December 2002, p. 9.

72 This section draws on concepts discussed in Keller, *Strategic Brand Management*, Chapters 1 and 2 (see note 52).

73 Don E. Schultz, 'Branding Geometry', *Marketing Management*, September–October 2003, pp. 8–9.

74 Lucas Conley, 'When Brand Extensions Go Bad', *Fast Company*, October 2006, p. 38; Kenneth Hein, 'Brand Extensions Can Go Too Far', *Adweek*, 5 December 2005, p. 8.

75 Quoted in Sarah Ellison, 'Inside Campbell's Big Bet: Heating Up Condensed Soup', *Wall Street Journal*, 31 July 2003, pp. B1–B2.

76 Adrienne Carter, 'Lighting a Fire Under Campbell', *Business Week*, 4 December 2006, pp. 96ff; see note 26 – Ellison, 'Inside Campbell's Big Bet: Heating Up Condensed Soup'.

77 'New Customer Research on Customer Referrals, Commitment, Loyalty', *Report on Customer Relationship Management*, August 2003, pp. 2ff.

78 Quote reported in: Rina Chandran, 'Philips to Rework Brand Positioning', *Asia Africa Intelligence Wire*, 23 August 2003, n.p.

79 Quote reported in: Kerry Capell, 'Thinking Simple at Philips', *BusinessWeek*, 11 December 2006, p. 50. Also: Nelson D. Schwartz, 'Lighting Up Philips', *Fortune International*, 22 January 2007, p. 43ff; 'Cover Story: The Simple Life', *PR Week*, 29 January 2007, p. 15.

80 Bruce Einhorn, 'A Racer Called Acer', *BusinessWeek*, 29 January 2007, p. 48; 'Acer Talks Tough About Future PC Shipments', *PC Magazine Online*, 27 October 2006, www.pcmag.com, n.p.

81 This section draws on concepts in Thomas T. Nagle and John E. Hogan, *The Strategy and Tactics of Pricing*, 4th edn (Upper Saddle River, NJ: Pearson Prentice Hall, 2006).

82 'Swedish Home Furnisher Finds British Market Its Weakest Link', *Sunday Business (London)*, 3 January 2007, www.thebusinessonline.com; Lisa Margonelli, 'How Ikea Designs Its Sexy Price Tags', *Business 2.0*, October 2002, pp. 106–12.

83 Daniel J. Howard and Roger A. Kerin, 'Broadening the Scope of Reference Price Advertising Research', *Journal of Marketing*, October 2006, pp. 185–204; Wayne D. Hoyer and Deborah J. MacInnis, *Consumer Behaviour*, 3rd edn (Boston: Houghton Mifflin, 2004), p. 262.

84 'Barbers at the Gate', *The Economist*, 4 November 2006, p. 76; 'Low-Price Barber Operator QB Net to Boots Overseas Operations', *Jiji*, 30 October 2006, n.p.; 'Orix Acquires Low-Price Barbershop Operator QB Net', *Jiji*, 1 August 2006, n.p.; Jim Hawe, 'A New Style', *Wall Street Journal*, 22 September 2003, pp. R3, R7.

85 Leo Magno, 'Nokia Launches Entry-Level Phones for New Growth Markets', *Asia Africa Intelligence Wire*, 1 September 2003, n.p.

86 Michael V. Copeland, 'Hits & Misses: Lemons to "Limited Edition" Lemonade', *Business 2.0*, September 2003, p. 92.

87 'Colruyt to Enter Luxembourg, Dutch Market, Plans "One or Two Test Stores"', *Forbes.com*, 12 February 2007, www.forbes.com; Dan Bilefsky, 'Making the Cuts', *Wall Street Journal*, 22 September 2003, pp. R3, R7.

88 'Deep Discount Goes from Drab to Fab', *Grocer*, 11 November 2006, pp. 40ff.

89 'Call Waiting', *W*, December 2006, p. 96; 'The Origins of Vertu', *The Economist*, 22 February 2003, pp. 62–3.

90 This section draws on concepts in Thomas T. Nagle and John E. Hogan, *The Strategy and Tactics of Pricing*, 4th edn (Upper Saddle River, NJ: Pearson Prentice Hall, 2006).

91 Gina Chon and Stephen Power, 'Can an Itsy-Bitsy Auto Survive in the Land of the SUV?', *Wall Street Journal*, 9 January 2007, p. B1ff.; John Tagliabue, 'A Tale of 2 Carmakers and 2 Countries', *New York Times*, 16 May 2003, pp. W1ff.

92 Daniel Gross, 'What's the Toll? It Depends on the Time of Day', *New York Times*, 11 February 2007, sec. 3, p. 7; 'London Traffic Starts to See Benefits of Toll Levied on Motorists', *Wall Street Journal*, 6 May 2003, p. 1; 'Ken Livingstone's Gamble', *The Economist*, 15 February 2003, pp. 51–3.

93 Luca Ciferri, 'Toyota Ready for European Top League', *Automotive News Europe*, 20 March 2006, p. 5; 'The Asian Invasion Picks Up Speed', *BusinessWeek*, 6 October 2003, pp. 62–4.

94 Gail Edmondson, 'Classy Cars', *BusinessWeek*, 24 March 2003, pp. 62–6.

95 Based on information from Nandini Lakshman and Gail Edmondson, 'Tata and Fiat: Small Is Big in India', *Business Week Online*, 25 January 2007, www.businessweek.com; 'Carmaking in India: A Different Route', *The Economist*, 16 December 2006, p. 64; Peter Wonacott and Jason Singer, 'Ratan Tata Builds Indian Behemoth into Global Player', *Wall Street Journal*, 7 October 2006, pp. B1ff.

96 Sandy O'Loughlin, 'Is Uniqlo Unique Enough to Crash Fast Fashion Party? Japanese Upstart Aims for H&M/Zara Territory', *Brandweek*, 5 February 2007, p. 15; 'Shining Examples', *The Economist*, 17 June 2006, pp. 4–5; Thomas Mulier and Patrick Donahue, 'Inditex Goes One-Up on H&M', *International Herald Tribune*, 30 March 2006, p. 17.

97 Colin Bake, 'Cost-Cutting Efforts Continue', *Airline Business*, 1 January 2007, n.p.; Avery Johnson, 'Lean Cuisine: European Airlines Cut Perks', *Wall Street Journal*, 8 November 2006, pp. D1ff.

98 Brian Hindo, 'Outsourcing: What Happens to that Scarf You Really Hated', *BusinessWeek*, 15 January 2007, p. 36.

99 Quoted in Margo Cohen, 'IKEA Expects Vietnam Business, with Its Cheap Supplies, to Surge', *Wall Street Journal*, 24 September 2003, p. B13E.

100 Anita Likus, 'Online Retail Traffic Surges in Europe', *Wall Street Journal*, 13 December 2006, p. B3F.

101 'Nippon Steel Corp. Sales to Auto Makers Help Profit Rise by 33%', *Wall Street Journal*, 31 January 2007, online.wsj.com.

102 Jason Bush, 'They've Driven a Ford Lately', *BusinessWeek*, 26 February 2007, p. 52; Jason Stein, 'Ford Expands in Russia', *Automotive News Europe*, 22 January 2007, p. 3.

103 Jordan K. Speer, 'Kaufhof's Differentiating Factor RFID', *Apparel*, January 2007, pp. 24ff; Mark Roberti, 'RFID Is Fit to Track Clothes', *Chain Store Age*, May 2006, p. 158; Li Yuan, 'New Ways to Tell Where Your Kids Are; Tracking Gadgets, Services Can Pinpoint Exact Location; Weighing the Privacy Issue', *Wall Street Journal*, 27 April 2006, p. D1.

104 Pete Engardio, 'Flat Panels, Thin Margins', *BusinessWeek*, 26 February 2007, pp. 50–1; Tamara Chuang, 'Vizio Sales Strategy Is Highly Defined', *Orange County (Calif.) Register*, 3 October 2006, n.p.

105 'CN to Invest C$12 million in Major Capacity Improvements at Toronto-area Intermodal Terminal', *Canadian Corporate News*, 2 February 2007, n.p.

106 Geri Smith, 'Wrapping the Globe in Tortillas', *BusinessWeek*, 26 February 2007, p. 54.

107 Based on information from 'Prowess in Logistics Is Big Competitive Edge', *MMR*, 11 December 2006, p. 84; Anthony Bianco and Wendy Zellner, 'Is Wal-Mart Too Powerful?' *Business Week*, 6 October 2003, pp. 102–10; Mike Troy, 'Logistics Still Cornerstone of Competitive Advantage', *DSN Retailing Today*, 9 June 2003, pp. 209ff.; Michael Garry and Sarah Mulholland, 'Master of Its Supply Chain', *Supermarket News*, 2 December 2002, pp. 55ff.; Jerry Useem, 'One Nation Under Wal-Mart', *Fortune*, 3 March 2003, pp. 63–76.

108 Kerry Capell, 'BBC: Step Right into the Telly', *BusinessWeek*, 24 July 2006, pp. 51ff.

109 Carrick Mollenkamp and Ian McDonald, 'Outside Audit: Behind the British Debt Magic', *Wall Street Journal*, 31 October 2006, p. C1; 'Mark Ritson on Branding: How a Repositioning Should Be Done', *Marketing*, 13 September 2006, p. 21; 'Capital One Launches New UK Campaign', *Europe Intelligence Wire*, 26 September 2006, n.p.; 'Unloved Capital One Makes £9m Bid to Gain Popularity', *Marketing Week*, 7 September 2006, p. 8.

110 Ellen Sheng, 'Corporate Connections', *Wall Street Journal*, 29 January 2007, p. R8; Louise Story and Eric Pfanner, 'The Future of Web Ads Is in Britain', *New York Times*, 4 December 2006, www.nytimes.com.

111 See Sandy D. Jap and Erin Anderson, 'Testing the Life-Cycle Theory of Inter-Organisational Relations: Do Performance Outcomes Depend on the Path Taken?', *Insead Knowledge*, February 2003, www.insead.edu.

112 Normandy Madden, 'Global Highlight: Unilever's Zhonghua Toothpaste', *Advertising Age*, 19 February 2007, p. 55; 'Unilever Maintains Flexibility by Leasing', *Business Daily Update*, 9 October 2006, n.p.

113 See Nigel F. Piercy, 'The Marketing Budgeting Process: Marketing Management Implications', *Journal of Marketing*, October 1987, pp. 45–59.

114 David Scheer, 'Europe's New High-Tech Role: Playing Privacy Cop to the World', *Wall Street Journal*, 10 October 2003, pp. A1, A16.

115 'Stats: Keep Your Ear to the Ground', *Marketing News*, 1 September 2006, p. 4.

116 Emily Steel, 'Grabbing Older Consumers via Cellphone', *Wall Street Journal*, 31 January 2007, p. B3; Stuart Elliott, 'Online, P&G Gets a Little Crazy', *New York Times*, 14 December 2006, p. C3; Robert Berner, 'I Sold It Through the Grapevine', *BusinessWeek*, 29 May 2006, pp. 32–4.

117 See John Philip Jones, 'Is Advertising Still Salesmanship?', *Journal of Advertising Research*, May–June 1997, pp. 9ff.

118 Quoted in Belinda Gannaway, 'Hidden Danger of Sales Promotions', *Marketing*, 20 February 2003, pp. 31ff.; other sources: Liz Hamson, 'Measured Approach: There Is a Trade-Off Between Promotions and Profits and, Contrary to UK Marketers' Views, It Can Be Measured', *Grocer*, 19 April 2003, p. 38; Philip Kotler, *A Framework for Marketing Management*, 2nd edn (Upper Saddle River, NJ: Prentice Hall, 2003), pp. 318–19.

119 'Field Marketing: What Drives Engagement?', *Marketing*, 24 January 2007, p. 31.

120 Doreen Hemlock, 'Cuban Rum Rising', *Hartford Courant*, 24 February 2007, www.courant.com; 'Field Marketing Agency of the Year – Cosine', *Marketing*, 20 December 2006, p. 37.

121 Vauhini Vara, 'That Looks Great on You', *Wall Street Journal*, 3 January 2007, p. D1.

122 Doug McPherson, 'Riding the Wave of Opportunity', *Response*, November 2002, pp. 34ff.

123 Erin White, 'PR Firms Advise Corporations on Social-Responsibility Issues', *Wall Street Journal*, 13 November 2002, p. B10.

124 Based on information from 'The Work: New Campaigns – the World', *Campaign*, 26 January 2007, p. 32; Lisa Sanders, 'JWT Fails to Keep Up with Mr. Jones', *Advertising Age*, 3 July 2006, pp. 1ff; Jack Neff, 'Clearasil Marches into Middle-School Classes', *Advertising Age*, 13 November 2006, p. 8; 'Eye and Ear Care Product News', *Chemist & Druggist*, 5 August 2006, p. 34.

CHAPTER 5
Aspects of Contract and Negligence for Business

Unit 5: Aspect of Contract and Negligence for Business

Unit code: Y/601/0563

QCF level: 4

Credit value: 15 credits

Aim

The aim of this unit is to provide learners with an understanding of aspects of the law of contract and tort and the skill to apply them, particularly in business situations.

Unit abstract

The unit introduces the law of contract, with a particular emphasis on the formation and operation of business contracts. Learners are encouraged to explore the content of these agreements and then develop skills relating to the practical application of business contracts, including offer, acceptance, intention, consideration and capacity. Relevant case law examples will be covered. Learners will consider when liability in contract arises, the nature of the obligations on both sides of the contract, and the availability of remedies when a contract is not fulfiled in accordance with its terms.

Additionally, the unit will enable learners to understand how the law of tort differs from the law of contract and examine issues of liability in negligence relating to business and how to avoid it.

Learning outcomes

On successful completion of this unit a learner will:

1 Understand the essential elements of a valid contract in a business context
2 Be able to apply the elements of a contract in business situations
3 Understand Understand principles of liability in negligence in business activities
4 Be able to apply the principles of liability in negligence in business situations

Unit content

1 Understand the essential elements of a valid contract in a business context

Essential elements: offer and acceptance; intention to create legal relations; consideration; capacity; privity of contract (**note vitiating factors are included in *Unit 27: Further Aspects of Contract and Tort***)

Types of contract: facte to face; written; distance selling; impact

Types of terms: condition; warranty; innominate term; express; implied; exclusion clauses and their validity

2 Be able to apply the elements of a contract in business situations

Elements: application of relevant principles and case law to business scenarios

Specific terms: condition of standard form business contracts; analysis of express terms, implied terms and exclusion clauses in a given contract

Effect of terms: breach of condition, warranty and innominate terms; legality of exemption clauses; outline of remedies; damages

3 Understand principles of liability in negligence in business activities

Negligence: differences to contract; duty of care; breach of duty; damage – causation and remoteness of damage; personal injuries; damage to property; economic loss; occupier liability

Liability: employer's liability; vicarious liability; health and safety issues

4 Be able to apply principles of liability in negligence in business situations

Negligence: application of the legal principles of negligence and relevant statutory and case law to business scenarios including; personal injries, damage to property, economic loss, occupier liability; defences; contributory negligence; remedies

Learning outcomes and assessment criteria

Learning outcomes	Assessment criteria for pass
On successful completion of this unit a learner will:	The learner can:
LO1 Understand the essential elements of a valid contract in a business context	1.1 explain the importance of the essential elements require for the formation of a valid contract 1.2 discuss the impact of different types of contract 1.3 analyse terms in contracts with reference to their meaning and effect
LO2 Be able to apply the elements of a contract in business situations	2.1 apply the elements of contract in given business scenarios 2.2 apply the law on terms in different contracts 2.3 evaluate the effect of different terms in given contracts
LO3 Understand principles of liability in negligence in business activities	3.1 contrast liability in tort with contractual liability 3.2 explain the nature of liability in negligence 3.3 explain how a business can be vicariously liable
LO4 Be able to apply principles of liability in negligence in business situations	4.1 apply the elements of the tort of negligence and defences in diferent business situations 4.2 apply the elements of vicarious liability in given business situations

Guidance

Links

This unit links with all the law units in the BTEC Higher Nationals in Business.

Essential requirements

Learners will require access to law reports and contractual documents, such as existing business standard form contracts.

Employer engagement and vocational contexts

Centres should develop links with local businesses. Many businesses and chambers of commerce want to promote local business and are often willing to provide visit opportunities, guest speakers or information about their business and the local business context.

Offer and acceptance

Introduction

For a contract to exist, usually one party must have made an offer, and the other must have accepted it. Once acceptance takes effect, a contract will usually be binding on both parties, and the rules of offer and acceptance are typically used to pinpoint when a series of negotiations has passed that point, in order to decide whether the parties are obliged to fulfil their promises. There is generally no halfway house – negotiations have either crystallised into a binding contract, or they are not binding at all.

Unilateral and bilateral contracts

In order to understand the law on offer and acceptance, you need to understand the concepts of unilateral and bilateral contracts. Most contracts are bilateral. This means that each party takes on an obligation, usually by promising the other something – for example, Ann promises to sell something and Ben to buy it. (Although contracts where there are mutual obligations are always called bilateral, there may in fact be more than two parties to such a contract.)

By contrast, a unilateral contract arises where only one party assumes an obligation under the contract. Examples might be promising to give your mother £50 if she gives up smoking for a year, or to pay a £100 reward to anyone who finds your lost purse, or, as the court suggested in **Great Northern Railway Co v Witham** (1873), to pay someone £100 to walk from London to York. What makes these situations unilateral contracts is that only one party has assumed an obligation – you are obliged to pay your mother if she gives up smoking, but she has not promised in turn to give up smoking. Similarly, you are obliged to pay the reward to anyone who finds your purse, but nobody need actually have undertaken to do so.

A common example of a unilateral contract is that between estate agents and people trying to sell their houses – the seller promises to pay a specified percentage of the house price to the estate agent if the house is sold, but the estate agent is not required to promise in return to sell the house, or even to try to do so.

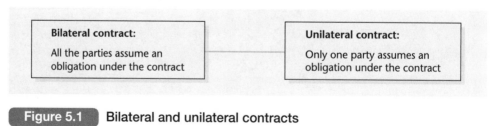

Bilateral contract:
All the parties assume an obligation under the contract

Unilateral contract:
Only one party assumes an obligation under the contract

Figure 5.1   Bilateral and unilateral contracts

Offer

The person making an offer is called the offeror, and the person to whom the offer is made is called the offeree. A communication will be treated as an offer if it

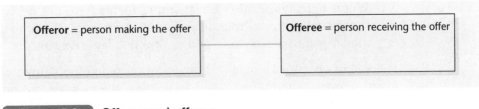

Figure 5.2 Offeror and offeree

indicates the terms on which the offeror is prepared to make a contract (such as the price of the goods for sale), and gives a clear indication that the offeror intends to be bound by those terms if they are accepted by the offeree.

An offer may be express, as when Ann tells Ben that she will sell her CD player for £200, but it can also be implied from conduct – a common example is taking goods to the cash desk in a supermarket, which is an implied offer to buy those goods.

Offers to the public at large

In most cases, an offer will be made to a specified person – as when Ann offers to sell her computer to Ben. However, offers can be addressed to a group of people, or even to the general public. For example, a student may offer to sell her old textbooks to anyone in the year below, or the owner of a lost dog may offer a reward to anyone who finds it.

key case

Offers can be addressed to the general public and are accepted when the offer is acted upon by a member of the general public. Advertisements for unilateral contracts are generally treated as offers.

In **Carlill** v **Carbolic Smoke Ball Co** (1893) the defendants were the manufacturers of 'smokeballs' which they claimed could prevent flu. They published advertisements stating that if anyone used their smokeballs for a specified time and still caught flu, they would pay that person £100, and that to prove they were serious about the claim, they had deposited £1,000 with their bankers.

Mrs Carlill bought and used a smokeball, but nevertheless ended up with flu. She therefore claimed the £100, which the company refused to pay. They argued that their advertisement could not give rise to a contract, since it was impossible to make a contract with the whole world, and that therefore they were not legally bound to pay the money. This argument was rejected by the court, which held that the advertisement did constitute an offer to the world at large, which became a contract when it was accepted by Mrs Carlill using the smokeball and getting flu. She was therefore entitled to the £100.

A more recent illustration is provided by the Court of Appeal in **Bowerman** v **Association of British Travel Agents Ltd** (1996). A school had booked a skiing holiday with a tour operator which was a member of the Association of British Travel Agents (ABTA). All members of this association display a notice provided by ABTA which states:

Where holidays or other travel arrangements have not yet commenced at the time of failure [of the tour operator], ABTA arranges for you to be reimbursed the money you have paid in respect of your holiday arrangements.

The tour operator became insolvent and cancelled the skiing holiday. The school was refunded the money they had paid for the holiday, but not the cost of the wasted travel insurance. The plaintiff brought an action against ABTA to seek reimbursement of the cost of this insurance. He argued, and the Court of Appeal agreed, that the ABTA notice constituted an offer which the customer accepted by contracting with an ABTA member.

A contract arising from an offer to the public at large, like that in **Carlill**, is usually a unilateral contract.

Invitations to treat

Some kinds of transaction involve a preliminary stage in which one party invites the other to make an offer. This stage is called an invitation to treat.

key case

Negotiations to enter into a contract can amount to an invitation to treat but not an offer.

In **Gibson** v **Manchester City Council** (1979) a council tenant was interested in buying his house. He completed an application form and received a letter from the Council stating that it 'may be prepared to sell the house to you' for £2,180. Mr Gibson initially queried the purchase price, pointing out that the path to the house was in a bad condition. The Council refused to change the price, saying that the price had been fixed taking into account the condition of the property. Mr Gibson then wrote on 18 March 1971 asking the Council to 'carry on with the purchase as per my application'. Following a change in political control of the Council in May 1971, it decided to stop selling Council houses to tenants, and Mr Gibson was informed that the Council would not proceed with the sale of the house. Mr Gibson brought legal proceedings claiming that the letter he had received stating the purchase price was an offer which he had accepted on 18 March 1971. The House of Lords, however, ruled that the Council had not made an offer; the letter giving the purchase price was merely one step in the negotiations for a contract and amounted only to an invitation to treat. Its purpose was simply to invite the making of a 'formal application', amounting to an offer, from the tenant.

Confusion can sometimes arise when what would appear, in the everyday sense of the word, to be an offer is held by the law to be only an invitation to treat. This issue arises particularly in the following areas.

Advertisements

A distinction is generally made between advertisements for a unilateral contract, and those for a bilateral contract.

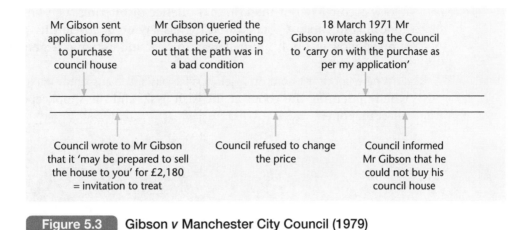

Figure 5.3   Gibson *v* Manchester City Council (1979)

Advertisements for unilateral contracts

These include advertisements such as the one in **Carlill *v* Carbolic Smoke Ball Co**, or those offering rewards for the return of lost property, or for information leading to the arrest or conviction of a criminal. They are usually treated as offers, on the basis that the contract can normally be accepted without any need for further negotiations between the parties, and the person making the advertisement intends to be bound by it.

Advertisements for a bilateral contract

These are the type of advertisements which advertise specified goods at a certain price, such as those found at the back of newspapers and magazines. They are usually considered invitations to treat, on the grounds that they may lead to further bargaining – potential buyers might want to negotiate about the price, for example – and that since stocks could run out, it would be unreasonable to expect the advertisers to sell to everybody who applied.

In **Partridge *v* Crittenden** (1968), an advertisement in a magazine stated 'Bramblefinch cocks and hens, 25s each'. As the Bramblefinch was a protected species, the person who placed the advertisement was charged with unlawfully offering for sale a wild bird contrary to the Protection of Birds Act 1954, but his conviction was quashed on the grounds that the advertisement was not an offer but an invitation to treat.

It was held in **Grainger & Sons *v* Gough** (1896) that the circulation of a price-list by a wine merchant was not an offer to sell at those prices but merely an invitation to treat.

Shopping

Price-marked goods on display on the shelves or in the windows of shops are generally regarded as invitations to treat, rather than offers to sell goods at that price. In **Fisher *v* Bell** (1960) the defendant had displayed flick knives in his shop window, and was convicted of the criminal offence of offering such knives for sale. On appeal, Lord Parker CJ stated that the display of an article with a price on it in a shop window was only an invitation to treat and not an offer, and the conviction was overturned.

Where goods are sold on a self-service basis, the customer makes an offer to buy when presenting the goods at the cash desk, and the shopkeeper may accept or reject that offer.

key case

Where goods are sold on a self-service basis, the customer makes an offer to buy when presenting the goods at the cash desk.

In **Pharmaceutical Society of Great Britain v Boots Cash Chemists (Southern) Ltd** (1953) Boots were charged with an offence concerning the sale of certain medicines which could only be sold by or under the supervision of a qualified pharmacist. Two customers in a self-service shop selected the medicines, which were price-marked, from the open shelves, and placed them in the shop's wire baskets. The shelves were not supervised by a pharmacist, but a pharmacist had been instructed to supervise the transaction at the cash desk. The issue was therefore whether the sale had taken place at the shelves or at the cash desk.

The Court of Appeal decided the shelf display was like an advertisement for a bilateral contract, and was therefore merely an invitation to treat. The offer was made by the customer when medicines were placed in the basket and presented at the cash desk, and was only accepted by the shop at the cash desk. Since a pharmacist was supervising at that point no offence had been committed.

There are two main practical consequences of this principle. First, shops do not have to sell goods at the marked price – so if a shop assistant wrongly marks a CD at £2.99 rather than £12.99, for example, you cannot insist on buying it at that price (though the shop may be committing an offence under the Trade Descriptions Act 1968). Secondly, a customer cannot insist on buying a particular item on display – so you cannot make a shopkeeper sell you the sweater in the window even if there are none left inside the shop. Displaying the goods is not an offer, so a customer cannot accept it and thereby make a binding contract.

Timetables and tickets for transport

The legal position here is rather unclear. Is a bus timetable an offer to run services at those times, or just an invitation to treat? Does the bus pulling up at a stop constitute an offer to carry you, which you accept by boarding the bus? Or, again, is even this stage just an invitation to treat, so that the offer is actually made by you getting on the bus or by handing over money for the ticket? These points may seem academic, but they become important when something goes wrong. If, for example, the bus crashes and you are injured, your ability to sue for breach of contract will depend on whether the contract had actually been completed when the accident occurred.

Although there have been many cases in this area, no single reliable rule has emerged, and it seems that the exact point at which a contract is made depends in each case on the particular facts. For example, in **Denton v GN Railway** (1856) it was said that railway company advertisements detailing the times at and conditions under which trains would run were offers. But in **Wilkie v London Passenger Transport Board** (1947) Lord Greene thought that a contract between bus company and passenger was made when a person intending to travel 'puts himself either on the platform or inside the bus'. The opinion was *obiter* but, if correct, it implies that the company makes an offer of carriage by running the bus or train and the passenger accepts when he or she gets properly on board, completing the contract. Therefore if the bus crashed, an injured passenger could have a claim against the bus company for breach of contract despite not having yet paid the fare or been given a ticket.

However, in **Thornton v Shoe Lane Parking Ltd** (1971) it was suggested that the contract may be formed rather later. If the legal principles laid down in **Thornton** are applied to this factual situation, it would appear that passengers asking for a ticket to their destination are making an invitation to treat. The bus company makes an offer by issuing the tickets, and the passengers accept the offer by keeping the tickets without objection. Fortunately, these questions are not governed solely by the law of contract as some legislation relevant to the field of public transport has since been passed.

There are other less common situations in which the courts will have to decide whether a communication is an offer or merely an invitation to treat. The test used is whether a person watching the proceedings would have thought the party concerned was making an offer or not.

How long does an offer last?

An offer may cease to exist under any of the following circumstances.

Specified time

Where an offeror states that an offer will remain open for a specific length of time, it lapses when that time is up (though it can be revoked before that – see p. 671).

Reasonable length of time

Where the offeror has not specified how long the offer will remain open, it will lapse after a reasonable length of time has passed. Exactly how long this is will depend upon whether the means of communicating the offer were fast or slow and on its subject matter – for example, offers to buy perishable goods, or a commodity whose price fluctuates daily, will lapse quite quickly. Offers to buy shares on the stock market may last only seconds.

In **Ramsgate Victoria Hotel** *v* **Montefiore** (1866) the defendant applied for shares in the plaintiff company, paying a deposit into their bank. After hearing nothing from them for five months, he was then informed that the shares had been allotted to him, and asked to pay the balance due on them. He refused to do so, and the court upheld his argument that five months was not a reasonable length of time for acceptance of an offer to buy shares, which are a commodity with a rapidly fluctuating price. Therefore the offer had lapsed before the company tried to accept it, and there was no contract between them.

Failure of a precondition

Some offers are made subject to certain conditions, and if such conditions are not in place, the offer may lapse. For example, a person might offer to sell their bike for £50 if they manage to buy a car at the weekend. In **Financings Ltd** *v* **Stimson** (1962) the defendant saw a car for sale at £350 by a second-hand car dealer on 16 March. He decided to buy it on hire-purchase terms. The way that hire purchase works in such cases is that the finance company buys the car outright from the dealer, and then sells it to the buyer, who pays in instalments. The defendant would therefore be buying the car from the finance company (the plaintiffs), rather than from the dealer. The defendant signed the plaintiffs' form, which stated that the agreement would be binding on the finance company only when signed on their behalf. The car dealer did not have the authority to do this, so it had to be sent to the plaintiffs for signing. On 18 March the defendant paid the first instalment of £70. On 24 March the car was stolen from the dealer's premises. It was later found, badly damaged and the defendant no longer wanted to buy it. Not knowing this, on 25 March the plaintiffs signed the written 'agreement'. They subsequently sued the defendant for failure to pay the instalments. The Court of Appeal ruled in favour of the defendant, as the so-called 'agreement' was really an offer to make a contract with the plaintiffs, which was subject to the implied condition that the car remained in much the same state as it was in when the offer was made, until that offer was accepted. The plaintiffs were claiming that they had accepted the offer by signing the document on 25 March. As the implied condition had been broken by then, the offer was no longer open so no contract had been concluded.

Rejection

An offer lapses when the offeree rejects it. If Ann offers to sell Ben her car on Tuesday, and Ben says no, Ben cannot come back on Wednesday and insist on accepting the offer.

Counter-offer

A counter-offer terminates the original offer.

key case

A counter-offer terminates the original offer.

In **Hyde** v **Wrench** (1840) the defendant offered to sell his farm for £1,000, and the plaintiff responded by offering to buy it at £950 – this is called making a counter-offer. The farm owner refused to sell at that price, and when the plaintiff later tried to accept the offer to buy at £1,000, it was held that this offer was no longer available; it had been terminated by the counter-offer. In this situation the offeror can make a new offer on exactly the same terms, but is not obliged to do so.

Requests for information

A request for information about an offer (such as whether delivery could be earlier than suggested) does not amount to a counter-offer, so the original offer remains open. In **Stevenson Jaques & Co** v **McLean** (1880) the defendant made an offer on a Saturday to sell iron to the plaintiffs at a cash-on-delivery price of 40 shillings, and stated that the offer would remain available until the following Monday. The plaintiffs replied by asking if they could buy the goods on credit. They received no answer. On Monday afternoon they contacted the defendant to accept the offer, but the iron had already been sold to someone else.

When the plaintiffs sued for breach of contract, it was held that their reply to the offer had been merely a request for information, not a counter-offer, so the original offer still stood and there was a binding contract.

Death of the offeror

The position is not entirely clear, but it appears that if the offeree knows that the offeror has died, the offer will lapse; if the offeree is unaware of the offeror's death, it probably will not (**Bradbury** v **Morgan** (1862)). So if, for example, A promises to sell her video recorder to B, then dies soon after, and B writes to accept the offer not knowing that A is dead, it seems that the people responsible for A's affairs after death would be obliged to sell the video recorder to B, and B would be obliged to pay the price to the executors.

However, where an offer requires personal performance by the offeror (such as painting a picture, or appearing in a film) it will usually lapse on the offeror's death.

Death of the offeree

There is no English case on this point, but it seems probable that the offer lapses and cannot be accepted after the offeree's death by the offeree's representatives.

Withdrawal of offer

The withdrawal of an offer is sometimes described as the revocation of an offer. The old case of **Payne** v **Cave** (1789) establishes the principle that an offer may be withdrawn at any time up until it is accepted. In **Routledge** *v* **Grant** (1828) the defendant made a provisional offer to buy the plaintiff's house at a specified price, 'a definite answer to be given within six weeks from date'. It was held that, regardless of this provision, the defendant still had the right to withdraw the offer at any moment before acceptance, even though the time limit had not expired.

A number of rules apply in relation to the withdrawal of offers.

Withdrawal must be communicated

It is not enough for offerors simply to change their mind about an offer; they must notify the offeree that it is being revoked.

> **key case**
>
> An offer can only be withdrawn if it is communicated.
>
> In **Byrne & Co** *v* **Leon Van Tienhoven** (1880) the defendants were a company based in Cardiff. On 1 October they posted a letter to New York offering to sell the plaintiffs 1,000 boxes of tinplates. Having received the letter on 11 October, the plaintiffs immediately accepted by telegram. Acceptances sent by telegram take effect as soon as they are sent (see p. 682 for details of the postal rule).
>
> In the meantime, on 8 October, the defendants had written to revoke their offer, and this letter reached the plaintiffs on 20 October. It was held that there was a binding contract, because revocation could only take effect on communication, but the acceptance by telegram took effect as soon as it was sent – in this case nine days before the revocation was received. By the time the second letter reached the plaintiffs, a contract had already been made.

The revocation of an offer does not have to be communicated by the offeror; the communication can be made by some other reliable source.

> **key case**
>
> The revocation of an offer can be made by the offeror or some other reliable source.
>
> In **Dickinson** *v* **Dodds** (1876) the defendant offered to sell a house to the plaintiff, the offer 'to be left open until Friday, June 12, 9 am'. On 11 June the defendant sold the house to a third party, Allan, and the plaintiff heard about the sale through a fourth man. Before 9 am on 12 June, the plaintiff
>
> handed the defendant a letter in which he said he was accepting the offer. It was held by the Court of Appeal that the offer had already been revoked by the communication from the fourth man, so there was no contract. By hearing the news from the fourth man, Dickinson 'knew that Dodds was no longer minded to sell the property to him as plainly and clearly as if Dodds had told him in so many words'.

An offeror who promises to keep an offer open for a specified period may still revoke that offer at any time before it is accepted, unless the promise to keep it open is supported by some consideration from the other party (by providing consideration the parties make a separate contract called an option).

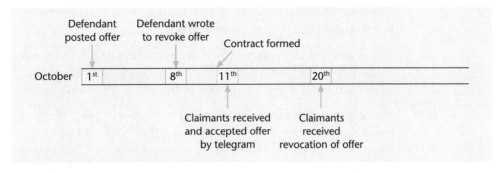

Figure 5.4   Byrne *v* Van Tienhoven (1880)

An exception to the rule that the withdrawal must be communicated to the offeree exists where an offeree moves to a new address without notifying the offeror. In these circumstances, a withdrawal which is delivered to the offeree's last known address will be effective on delivery to that address. In the same way, where a withdrawal reaches the offeree, but the offeree simply fails to read it, the withdrawal probably still takes effect on reaching the offeree (see *The Brimnes* (1975) p. 682). This would be the position where a withdrawal by telex or fax reached the offeror's office during normal business hours, but was not actually seen or read by the offeree or by any of their staff until some time afterwards.

Many offices receive a lot of post every day. This post may not go directly to the person whose name is on the envelope, but is received, opened and sorted by clerical staff and then distributed to the relevant people. In these situations there may be some difficulty in pinpointing when the information in the letter is communicated for these purposes. Is it when the letter is received within the company, when it is opened, or when it is actually read by the relevant member of staff? There is no authority on the point but the approach of the courts would probably be that communication occurs when the letter is opened, even though there may in those circumstances be no true communication.

In **Pickfords Ltd** *v* **Celestica Ltd** (2003) two offers were made by Pickfords, and the court had to decide whether the second offer had effectively withdrawn the first offer. Pickfords, the claimant, is a well-known furniture removal company.

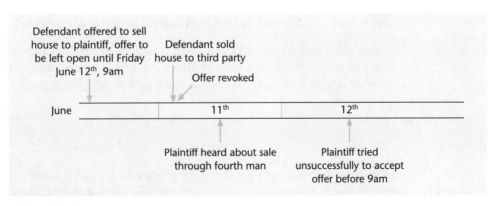

Figure 5.5   Dickinson *v* Dodds (1876)

Celestica, the defendant, is an IT company which wished to use Pickfords services to move premises. The court observed:

> It is as if the facts of this case have been devised for an examination question on the law of contract for first year law students. They raise some basic questions in relation to offer and acceptance in the law of formation of contract.

The litigation turned on the meaning and effect of three documents. The first document was a fax that was dated 13 September 2001 and which estimated the cost of the removal as being £100,000, though the final cost would depend on how many vehicle loads would be required. The second document was more detailed and was sent to the defendant on 27 September 2001. This contained a fixed quote for the removal of £98,760. The third document was a fax entitled 'Confirmation', which was sent by the defendant to the claimant and was dated 15 October 2001. This expressly referred to the fax dated 13 September 2001 and stated that the amount to be paid was 'not to exceed 100K'. The question for the court was whether the first offer on 13 September was capable of being accepted, or whether the second offer had withdrawn the first offer. The Court of Appeal concluded:

> In such a case, in my judgment, something more than the mere submission of the second quotation is required to indicate that [Pickfords] has withdrawn the first offer.

The question was whether the making of the second offer clearly indicated an intention on the part of the offeror to withdraw the first offer. The substantial differences between the two offers in this case went far beyond a mere difference in price which could have been explained as consistent with two alternative offers both being on the table for the defendant to choose which to accept. In the absence of any findings of fact as to the circumstances which gave rise to the second offer, the second offer superseded and revoked the first offer.

The fax was intended to be an acceptance of the first offer. Since the first offer had been revoked, the purported acceptance could not give rise to a contract. It was in law a counter-offer to accept the services offered by the claimant on the terms of the first offer, subject to the cap of £100,000. Since the work was carried out, this counter-offer must have been accepted by the claimant's conduct in carrying out the work.

Withdrawal of an offer to enter into a unilateral contract

There are a number of special rules that apply in relation to the revocation of an offer to enter into a unilateral contract. An offer to enter into a unilateral contract cannot be revoked once the offeree has commenced performance.

key case

An offer for a unilateral contract cannot be revoked once the offeree has commenced performance.	In **Errington** v **Errington** (1952) a father bought a house in his own name for £750, borrowing £500 of the price by means of a mortgage from a building

society. He bought the house for his son and daughter-in-law to live in, and told them that if they met the mortgage repayments, the house would be signed over to them once the mortgage was paid off. The couple moved in, and began to pay the mortgage instalments, but they never in fact made a promise to continue with the payments until the mortgage was paid off, which meant that the contract was unilateral.

When the father later died, the people in charge of his financial affairs sought to withdraw the offer. The Court of Appeal held that it was too late to do so. The part performance by the son and daughter-in-law prevented the offer from being withdrawn. The offer could only be withdrawn if the son and daughter-in-law ceased to make the payments.

In **Daulia Ltd *v* Four Millbank Nominees Ltd** (1978) the Court of Appeal stated that once an offeree had started to perform on a unilateral contract, it was too late for the offeror to revoke the offer. It should be noted that this statement was *obiter*, since the court found that the offeree in the case had in fact completed his performance before the supposed revocation.

There is an exception to this rule that part performance following an offer to enter into a unilateral contract prevents revocation of the offer. This exception applies in the context of unilateral offers to enter into a contract with an estate agent to pay commission for the sale of a property. In **Luxor (Eastborne) Ltd *v* Cooper** (1941) an owner of land had promised to pay an estate agent £10,000 in commission if the agent was able to find a buyer willing to pay £175,000 for the land. The arrangement was on the terms that are usual between estate agents and their clients, whereby the agent is paid commission if a buyer is found, and nothing if not. The House of Lords held that the owner in the case could revoke his promise at any time before the sale was completed, even after the estate agents had made extensive efforts to find a buyer or had stopped trying to do so.

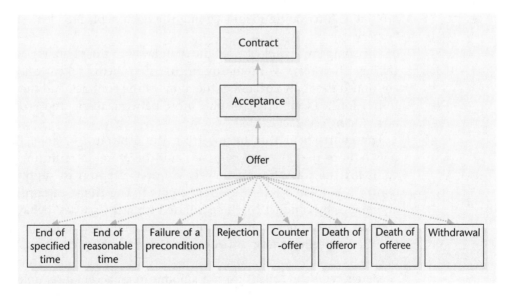

Figure 5.6   Termination of an offer

Where a unilateral offer is made to the world at large, to be accepted by conduct, it can probably be revoked without the need for communication if the revocation takes place before performance has begun. For example, if you place a newspaper advertisement offering a reward for the return of something you have lost, and then decide you might actually be better off spending that money on replacing the item, it would probably be impossible for you to make sure that everyone who knew about the offer knows you are withdrawing it – even if you place a notice of withdrawal in the newspaper, you cannot guarantee that everyone concerned will see it. It seems to be enough for an offeror to take reasonable steps to bring the withdrawal to the attention of such persons, even though it may not be possible to ensure that they all know about it. Thus, in the American case of **Shuey v United States** (1875) it was held that an offer made by advertisement in a newspaper could be revoked by a similar advertisement, even though the second advertisement was not read by all the offerees.

Acceptance

Acceptance of an offer means unconditional agreement to all the terms of that offer. Acceptance will often be oral or in writing, but in some cases an offeree may accept an offer by doing something, such as delivering goods in response to an offer to buy. The courts will only interpret conduct as indicating acceptance if it seems reasonable to infer that the offeree acted with the intention of accepting the offer.

In **Brogden v Metropolitan Rail Co** (1877) Brogden had supplied the railway company with coal for several years without any formal agreement. The parties then decided to make things official, so the rail company sent Brogden a draft agreement, which left a blank space for Brogden to insert the name of an arbitrator. After doing so and signing the document, Brogden returned it, marked 'approved'.

The company's employee put the draft away in a desk drawer, where it stayed for the next two years, without any further steps being taken regarding it. Brogden continued to supply coal under the terms of the contract, and the railway company to pay for it. Eventually a dispute arose between them, and Brogden denied that any binding contract existed.

The courts held that by inserting the arbitrator's name, Brogden added a new term to the potential contract, and therefore, in returning it to the railway company, he was offering (in fact counter-offering) to supply coal under the contract. But when was that offer accepted? The House of Lords decided that an acceptance by conduct could be inferred from the parties' behaviour, and a valid contract was completed either when the company first ordered coal after receiving the draft agreement from Brogden, or at the latest when he supplied the first lot of coal.

Merely remaining silent cannot amount to an acceptance, unless it is absolutely clear that acceptance was intended.

Merely remaining silent cannot amount to an acceptance, unless it is absolutely clear that acceptance was intended.

In **Felthouse** *v* **Bindley** (1862) an uncle and his nephew had talked about the possible sale of the nephew's horse to the uncle, but there had been some confusion about the price. The uncle subsequently wrote to the nephew, offering to pay £30 and 15 shillings and saying, 'If I hear no more about him, I consider the horse mine at that price.' The nephew was on the point of selling off some of his property in an auction. He did not reply to the uncle's letter, but did tell the auctioneer to keep the horse out of the sale. The auctioneer forgot to do this, and the horse was sold. It was held that there was no contract between the uncle and the nephew. The court felt that the nephew's conduct in trying to keep the horse out of the sale did not necessarily imply that he intended to accept his uncle's offer – even though the nephew actually wrote afterwards to apologise for the mistake – and so it was not clear that his silence in response to the offer was intended to constitute acceptance. This can be criticised in that it is hard to see how there could have been clearer evidence that the nephew did actually intend to sell, but, on the other hand, there are many situations in which it would be undesirable and confusing for silence to amount to acceptance.

It has been pointed out by the Court of Appeal in **Re Selectmove Ltd** (1995) that an acceptance by silence could be sufficient if it was the offeree who suggested that their silence would be sufficient. Thus in **Felthouse**, if the nephew had been the one to say that if his uncle heard nothing more he could treat the offer as accepted, there would have been a contract.

Acceptance of an offer to enter into a unilateral contract

Unilateral contracts are usually accepted by conduct. If I offer £100 to anyone who finds my lost dog, finding the dog will be an acceptance of the offer, making my promise binding – it is not necessary for anyone to contact me and say that they intend to take up my offer and find the dog.

There is no acceptance until the relevant act has been completely performed – so if Ann says to Ben that she will give Ben £5 if Ben washes her car, Ben would not be entitled to the money until the job is finished, and could not wash half the car and ask for £2.50.

Acceptance must be unconditional

An acceptance must accept the precise terms of an offer. In **Tinn** *v* **Hoffman** (1873) one party offered to sell the other 1,200 tons of iron. It was held that the other party's order for 800 tons was not an acceptance.

Negotiation and the 'battle of the forms'

Where parties carry on a long process of negotiation, it may be difficult to pinpoint exactly when an offer has been made and accepted. In such cases the courts will look at the whole course of negotiations to decide whether the parties have in fact reached agreement at all and, if so, when.

This process can be particularly difficult where the so-called 'battle of the forms' arises. Rather than negotiating terms each time a contract is made, many businesses try to save time and money by contracting on standard terms, which will be printed on company stationery such as order forms and delivery notes. The 'battle of the forms' occurs where one party sends a form stating that the contract is on their standard terms of business, and the other party responds by returning their own form and stating that the contract is on **their** terms.

The general rule in such cases is that the 'last shot' wins the battle. Each new form issued is treated as a counter-offer, so that when one party performs its obligation under the contract (by delivering goods for example), that action will be seen as acceptance by conduct of the offer in the last form. In **British Road Services v Arthur V Crutchley & Co Ltd** (1968) the plaintiffs delivered some whisky to the defendants for storage. The BRS driver handed the defendants a delivery note, which listed his company's 'conditions of carriage'. Crutchley's employee stamped the note 'Received under [our] conditions' and handed it back to the driver. The court held that stamping the delivery note in this way amounted to a counter-offer, which BRS accepted by handing over the goods. The contract therefore incorporated Crutchley's conditions, rather than those of BRS.

However, a more recent case shows that the 'last shot' will not always succeed. In **Butler Machine Tool Ltd v Ex-Cell-O Corp (England) Ltd** (1979) the defendants wanted to buy a machine from the plaintiffs, to be delivered ten months after

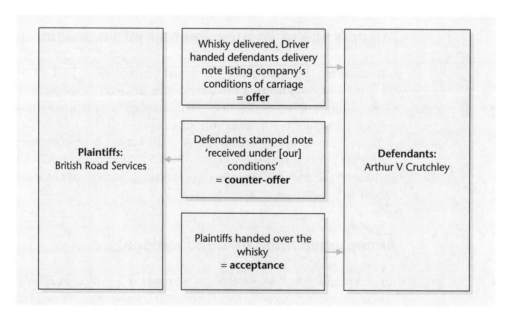

Figure 5.7 British Road Services *v* Arthur V Crutchley & Co Ltd (1968)

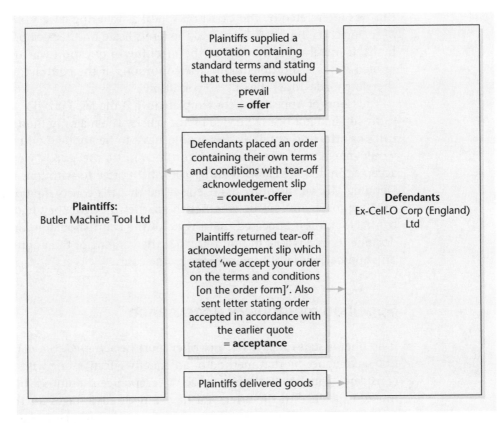

Figure 5.8   Butler Machine Tool Ltd *v* Ex-Cell-O Corp (England) Ltd (1979)

the order. The plaintiffs supplied a quotation (which was taken to be an offer), and on this document were printed their standard terms, including a clause allowing them to increase the price of the goods if the costs had risen by the date of delivery (known as a price-variation clause). The document also stated that their terms would prevail over any terms and conditions in the buyers' order. The buyers responded by placing an order, which was stated to be on their own terms and conditions, and these were listed on the order form. These terms did not contain a price-variation clause. The order form included a tear-off acknowledgement slip, which contained the words: 'we accept your order on the terms and conditions thereon' (referring to the order form). The sellers duly returned the acknowledgement slip to the buyers, with a letter stating that the order was being accepted in accordance with the earlier quotation. The acknowledgement slip and accompanying letter were the last forms issued before delivery.

When the ten months were up, the machine was delivered and the sellers claimed an extra £2,892, under the provisions of the price-variation clause. The buyers refused to pay the extra amount, so the sellers sued them for it. The Court of Appeal held that the buyers' reply to the quotation was not an unconditional acceptance, and therefore constituted a counter-offer. The sellers had accepted that counter-offer by returning the acknowledgement slip, which referred back to the buyers' conditions. The sellers pointed out that they had stated in their accompanying letter that the order was booked in accordance with the earlier quotation, but this was interpreted by the Court of Appeal as referring back to the type and price of the machine tool, rather than to the terms listed on the back of the sellers' document. It merely confirmed that the machine in question was the one originally quoted for, and did not modify the conditions of the contract. The contract was therefore made under the buyers' conditions.

The Court of Appeal also contemplated what the legal position would have been if the slip had not been returned by the sellers. The majority thought that the usual rules of offer and counter-offer would have to be applied, which in many cases would mean that there was no contract until the goods were delivered and accepted by the buyer, with either party being free to withdraw before that. Lord Denning MR, on the other hand, suggested that the courts should take a much less rigid approach and decide whether the parties thought they had made a binding contract, and if it appeared that they did, the court should go on to examine the documents as a whole to find out what the content of their agreement might be. This approach has not been adopted by the courts.

Specified methods of acceptance

If an offeror states that his or her offer must be accepted in a particular way, then only acceptance by that method or an equally effective one will be binding. To be considered equally effective, a mode of acceptance should not be slower than the method specified in the offer, nor have any disadvantages for the offeror. It was stated in **Tinn v Hoffman** (1873) that where the offeree was asked to reply 'by return of post', any method which would arrive before return of post would be sufficient.

Where a specified method of acceptance has been included for the offeree's own benefit, however, the offeree is not obliged to accept in that way. In **Yates Building Co Ltd v R J Pulleyn & Sons (York) Ltd** (1975) the sellers stated that the option they were offering should be accepted by 'notice in writing . . . to be sent registered

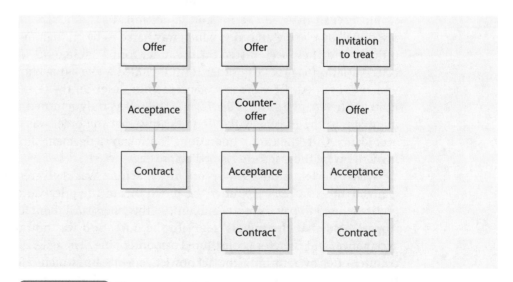

Figure 5.9 Three examples of how a contract can be made

or recorded delivery'. The purchaser sent his acceptance by ordinary letter post, but the court held that the acceptance was still effective. The requirement of registered or recorded delivery was for the benefit of the offeree rather than the offeror (as it ensured that their acceptance was received and that they had proof of their acceptance) and was not therefore mandatory.

The case of **Felthouse v Bindley** (see p. 677) shows that, although the offeror can stipulate how the acceptance is to be made, he or she cannot stipulate that silence shall amount to acceptance. In the same way, if the offeror states that the performance of certain acts by the offeree will amount to an acceptance, and the offeree performs those acts, there will only be an acceptance if the offeree was aware of the terms of the offer and objectively intended their acts to amount to an acceptance. In **Inland Revenue Commissioners v Fry** (2001) the Inland Revenue claimed over £100,000 of unpaid tax from Mrs Fry. Following negotiations, Mrs Fry wrote to the Inland Revenue enclosing a cheque for £10,000. In her letter she said that if the Inland Revenue accepted her offer of £10,000 in full and final settlement, it should present the cheque for payment. The Inland Revenue cashed the cheque but subsequently informed Mrs Fry that her offer was unacceptable. The High Court held that the Inland Revenue was entitled to the full amount of tax which it had claimed. The court explained that it was fundamental to the existence of a binding contract that there was a meeting of minds. An offer prescribing a mode of acceptance could be accepted by an offeree acting in accordance with that mode of acceptance. However, the Inland Revenue received thousands of cheques each day and there was no evidence that, when it cashed the cheque from Mrs Fry, it knew of the offer. The cashing of the cheque gave rise to no more than a rebuttable presumption of acceptance of the terms of the offer in the accompanying letter. On the evidence, that presumption had been rebutted, as a reasonable observer would not have assumed that the cheque was banked with the intention of accepting the offer in the letter.

An offeror who has requested the offeree to use a particular method of acceptance can always waive the right to insist on that method.

Acceptance must be communicated

An acceptance does not usually take effect until it is communicated to the offeror. As Lord Denning explained in **Entores Ltd v Miles Far East Corporation** (1955), if A shouts an offer to B across a river but, just as B yells back an acceptance, a noisy aircraft flies over, preventing A from hearing B's reply, no contract has been made. A must be able to hear B's acceptance before it can take effect. The same would apply if the contract was made by telephone, and A failed to catch what B said because of interference on the line; there is no contract until A knows that B is accepting the offer. The principal reason for this rule is that, without it, people might be bound by a contract without knowing that their offers had been accepted, which could obviously create difficulties in all kinds of situations.

Where parties negotiate face to face, communication of the acceptance is unlikely to be a problem; any difficulties tend to arise where the parties are communicating at a distance, for example by post, telephone, telegram, telex, fax or messenger.

Exceptions to the communication rule

There are some circumstances in which an acceptance may take effect without being communicated to the offeror.

Terms of the offer

An offer may state or imply that acceptance need not be communicated to the offeror, although, as **Felthouse v Bindley** shows, it is not possible to state that the offeree will be bound unless he or she indicates that the offer is not accepted (in other words that silence will be taken as acceptance). This means that offerors are free to expose themselves to the risk of unknowingly incurring an obligation, but may not impose that risk on someone else. It seems to follow from this that if the horse in **Felthouse v Bindley** had been kept out of the sale for the uncle, and the uncle had then refused to buy it, the nephew could have sued his uncle, who would have been unable to rely on the fact that acceptance was not communicated to him.

Unilateral contracts do not usually require acceptance to be communicated to the offeror. In **Carlill v Carbolic Smoke Ball Co** (1893) the defendants argued that the plaintiff should have notified them that she was accepting their offer, but the court held that such a unilateral offer implied that performance of the terms of the offer would be enough to amount to acceptance.

Conduct of the offeror

An offeror who fails to receive an acceptance through their own fault may be prevented from claiming that the non-communication means they should not be bound by the contract. In the **Entores** case (1955) it was suggested that this principle could apply where an offer was accepted by telephone, and the offeror did not catch the words of acceptance, but failed to ask for them to be repeated; and in *The Brimnes* (1975), where the acceptance is sent by telex during business hours, but is simply not read by anyone in the offeror's office.

The postal rule

The general rule for acceptances by post is that they take effect when they are posted, rather than when they are communicated. The main reason for this rule is historical, since it dates from a time when communication through the post was even slower and less reliable than it is today. Even now, there is some practical purpose for the rule, in that it is easier to prove that a letter has been posted than to prove that it has been received or brought to the attention of the offeror.

key case

An acceptance by post takes effect when it is posted, rather than when it is communicated.

The postal rule was laid down in **Adams** v **Lindsell** (1818). On 2 September 1817, the defendants wrote to the plaintiffs, who processed wool, offering to sell them a quantity of sheep fleeces, and stating that they required an answer 'in course of post'. Unfortunately, the defendants did not address the letter correctly, and as a result it did not reach the plaintiffs until the evening of 5 September. The plaintiffs posted their acceptance the same evening, and it reached the defendants on 9 September. It appeared that if the original letter had been correctly addressed, the defendants could have expected a reply 'in course of post' by 7 September. That date came and went, and they had heard nothing from the plaintiffs, so on 8 September they sold the wool to a third party. The issue in the case was whether a contract had been made before the sale to the third party on 8 September. The court held that a contract was concluded as soon as the acceptance was posted, so that the defendants were bound from the evening of 5 September, and had therefore breached the contract by selling the wool to the third party. (Under current law there would have been a contract even without the postal rule, because the revocation of the offer could only take effect if it was communicated to the offeree – selling the wool to a third party without notifying the plaintiffs would not amount to revocation. However, in 1818 the rules on revocation were not fully developed, so the court may well have considered that the sale was sufficient to revoke the offer, which was why an effective acceptance would have to take place before 8 September.)

Application of the postal rule

The traditional title 'postal rule' has become slightly misleading because the rule does not only apply to the post but could also potentially apply to certain other non-instantaneous modes of communication. The postal rule was applied to acceptance by telegram in **Cowan** v **O'Connor** (1888), where it was held that an acceptance came into effect when the telegram was placed with the Post Office. These days the Post Office in England no longer offers a telegram service, but the same rule will apply to the telemessage service which replaced it.

It is not yet clear whether the postal rule applies to faxes, e-mails and text messages. Professor Treitel suggests that the rule's application should depend on the circumstances of each case. He considers that the postal rule should only apply where the person accepting the offer is not in a position to know that their communication has been ineffective:

Fax messages seem to occupy an intermediate position. The sender will know at once if his message has not been received at all, and where this is the position the message should not amount to an effective acceptance. But if the message is received in such a form that it is wholly or partly illegible, the sender is unlikely to know this at once, and it is suggested an acceptance sent by fax might well be effective in such circumstances. The same principles should apply to other forms of electronic communication such as e-mail or website trading . . .

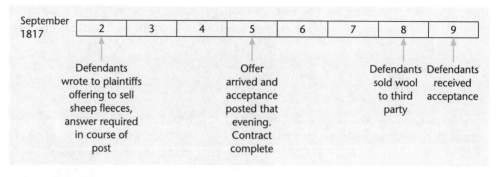

Figure 5.10   Adams *v* Lindsell (1818)

Use of the postal service must be reasonable. Only when it is reasonable to use the post to indicate acceptance can the postal rule apply. If the offer does not dictate a method of acceptance, appropriate methods can be inferred from the means used to make the offer. An offer made by post may generally be accepted by post, but it may be reasonable to accept by post even though the offer was delivered in some other way. In **Henthorn *v* Fraser** (1892) the defendant was based in Liverpool and the plaintiff lived in Birkenhead. The defendant gave the plaintiff in Liverpool a document containing an offer in Liverpool, and the plaintiff accepted it by posting a letter from Birkenhead. It was held that, despite the offer having been handed over in person, acceptance by post was reasonable because the parties were based in different towns.

Where an offer is made by an instant method of communication, such as telex, fax or telephone, an acceptance by post would not usually be reasonable.

Exceptions to the postal rule

Offers requiring communication of acceptance

An offeror may avoid the postal rule by making it a term of their offer that acceptance will only take effect when it is communicated to them. In **Holwell Securities Ltd *v* Hughes** (1974) the defendants offered to sell some freehold property to the plaintiffs but the offer stated that the acceptance had to be 'by notice in writing'. The plaintiffs posted their acceptance, but it never reached the defendants, despite being properly addressed. The court held that 'notice' meant communication, and therefore it would not be appropriate to apply the postal rule.

Instant methods of communication

When an acceptance is made by an instant mode of communication, such as telephone or telex, the postal rule does not apply. In such cases the acceptor will usually know at once that they have not managed to communicate with the offeror, and will need to try again.

In **Entores *v* Miles Far East Corporation** (1955) the plaintiffs were a London company and the defendants were an American corporation with agents in

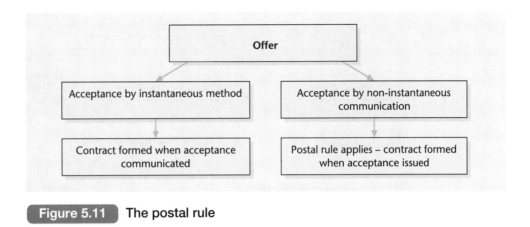

Figure 5.11   The postal rule

Amsterdam. Both the London company and the defendants' agents in Amsterdam had telex machines, which allow users to type in a message, and have it almost immediately received and printed out by the recipient's machine. The plaintiffs in London telexed the defendants' Amsterdam agents offering to buy goods from them, and the agents accepted, again by telex. The court case arose when the plaintiffs alleged that the defendants had broken their contract and wanted to bring an action against them. The rules of civil litigation stated that they could only bring this action in England if the contract had been made in England. The Court of Appeal held that because telex allows almost instant communication, the parties were in the same position as if they had negotiated in each other's presence or over the telephone, so the postal rule did not apply and an acceptance did not take effect until it had been received by the plaintiffs. Because the acceptance had been received in London, the contract was deemed to have been made there, and so the legal action could go ahead.

This approach was approved by the House of Lords in **Brinkibon** v **Stahag Stahl GmbH** (1983). The facts here were similar, except that the offer was made by telex from Vienna to London, and accepted by a telex from London to Vienna. The House of Lords held that the contract was therefore made in Vienna.

In both cases the telex machines were in the offices of the parties, and the messages were received inside normal working hours. In **Brinkibon** the House of Lords said that a telex message sent outside working hours would not be considered instantaneous, so the time and place in which the contract was completed would be determined by the intentions of the parties, standard business practice and, if possible, by analysing where the risk should most fairly lie.

Misdirected acceptance

Where a letter of acceptance is lost or delayed because the offeree has wrongly or incompletely addressed it through their own carelessness, it seems reasonable that the postal rule should not apply, although there is no precise authority to this effect. Treitel, a leading contract law academic, suggests that a better rule might be that if a badly addressed acceptance takes effect at all, it should do so at the time which is least advantageous to the party responsible for the misdirection.

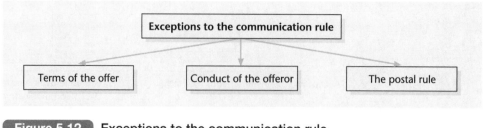

Figure 5.12   Exceptions to the communication rule

Effect of the postal rule

The postal rule has three main practical consequences:

1 A postal acceptance can take effect when it is posted, even if it gets lost in the post and never reaches the offeror. In **Household Fire Insurance _v_ Grant** (1879) Grant had applied for (and therefore offered to buy) shares in the plaintiff company. The shares were allotted to him and his name was put on the register of shareholders. The company did write to say that the shares had been allotted to Grant, but the letter was lost in the post and he never received it. Some time later the company went into liquidation, and the liquidator claimed from Grant the balance owing on the price of his shares. It was held that Grant was bound to pay the balance, because the contract had been completed when the company's letter was posted.

    It is likely that the same rule applies where the letter eventually arrives, but is delayed by postal problems.

2 Where an acceptance is posted after the offeror posts a revocation of the offer, but before that revocation has been received, the acceptance will be binding (posted acceptances take effect on posting, posted revocations on communication). This point is illustrated by the cases of **Byrne _v_ Van Tienhoven** (1880) and **Henthorn _v_ Fraser** (1892).

3 Where the postal rule applies, it seems unlikely that an offeree could revoke a postal acceptance by phone (or some other instant means of communication) before it arrives, though there is no English case on the point. A Scottish case, **Dunmore _v_ Alexander** (1830), does appear to allow such a revocation, but the court's views were only _obiter_ on this point.

Ignorance of the offer

It is generally thought that a person cannot accept an offer of which they are unaware, because in order to create a binding contract, the parties must reach agreement. If their wishes merely happen to coincide, that may be very convenient for both, but it does not constitute a contract and cannot legally bind them. Thus, if Ann advertises a reward for the return of a lost cat and Ben, not having seen or heard of the advertisement, comes across the cat, reads Ann's address on its collar and takes it back to Ann, is Ann bound to pay Ben the reward? No English case has clearly decided this point, and the cases abroad conflict with the main English case. On general principles Ben is probably unable to claim the reward.

In the American case of **Williams** *v* **Carwardine** (1833) the defendant offered a $20 reward for information leading to the discovery of the murderer of Walter Carwardine, and leaflets concerning the reward were distributed in the area where the plaintiff lived. The plaintiff apparently knew about the reward, but when she gave the information it was not in order to receive the money. She believed she had only a short time to live, and thought that giving the information might ease her conscience. The court held that she was entitled to the reward: she was aware of the offer and had complied with its terms, and her motive for doing so was irrelevant. A second US case, **Fitch** *v* **Snedaker** (1868), stated that a person who gives information without knowledge of the offer of a reward cannot claim the reward.

The main English case on this topic is **Gibbons** *v* **Proctor** (1891). A reward had been advertised for information leading to the arrest or conviction of the perpetrator of a particular crime and the plaintiff attempted to claim the reward, even though he had not originally known of the offer. He was allowed to receive the money, but the result does not shed much light on the problem because the plaintiff did know of the offer of reward by the time the information was given on his behalf to the person named in the advertisement.

Following the Australian case of **R** *v* **Clarke** (1927), it would appear that if the offeree knew of the offer in the past but has completely forgotten about it, they are treated as never having known about it. In that case a reward was offered by the Australian Government for information leading to the conviction of the murderers of two policemen. The Government also promised that an accomplice giving such information would receive a free pardon. Clarke was such an accomplice, who panicked and provided the information required in order to obtain the pardon, forgetting, at the time, about the reward. He remembered it later, but it was held that he was not entitled to the money.

Cross offers

These present a similar problem. If Ann writes to Ben offering to sell her television for £50, and by coincidence Ben happens to write offering to buy the television for £50, the two letters crossing in the post, do the letters create a contract between them? On the principles of offer and acceptance it appears not, since the offeree does not know about the offer at the time of the potential acceptance. The point has never been decided in a case but there are *obiter dicta* in **Tinn** *v* **Hoffman** (1873) which suggest there would be no contract.

Time of the formation of the contract

Normally a contract is formed when an effective acceptance has been communicated to the offeror. An exception to this is the postal rule, where the contract is formed at the time the acceptance is posted and there is no need for communication. A further exception to the general rule has been created by s. 11 of the Electronic Communications Act 2000. This establishes the precise time at which an electronic contract is made. Electronic contracts are concluded when the customer has both

- received an acknowledgement that their acceptance has been received, and
- confirmed their receipt of that acknowledgement.

These communications are taken to be effective when the receiving party is able to access them. Section 11 applies unless the parties agree otherwise. Thus electronic contracts will normally be formed at a later stage than other contracts.

Offer and acceptance implied by the court

Sometimes the parties may be in dispute as to whether a contract existed between them. They may never have signed any written agreement but one party may argue that the offer and acceptance had been made orally or through their conduct. Thus, in **Baird Textile Holdings Ltd** *v* **Marks & Spencer plc** (2001) Marks & Spencer had been in a business relationship with Baird Textile Holdings (BTH) for 30 years. BTH were based in the United Kingdom and had been a major supplier of clothes to Marks & Spencer over the years. In October 1999, Marks & Spencer advised BTH that it was ending all supply arrangements between them with effect from the end of the current production season. BTH brought a legal action against Marks & Spencer alleging that they had a contract with the company, and that a term of this contract had been breached by Marks & Spencer's terminating their supply arrangements in this way. The Court of Appeal held that there was no contract governing the relationship between the two litigants and that therefore Marks & Spencer were not in breach of a contract. It held that a contract should only be implied if it was necessary to do so 'to give business reality to a transaction and to create enforceable obligations between parties who are dealing with one another in circumstances in which one would expect that business reality and those enforceable obligations to exist'. It would not be necessary to imply such a contract if the parties might have acted in just the same way as they did without a contract. Marks & Spencer had preferred not to be bound by a contract so that they had maximum flexibility. For business reasons BTH had accepted this state of affairs.

In **West Bromwich Albion Football Club Ltd** *v* **El-Safty** (2006) the court held that there was no necessity to imply a contract between a football club and a doctor. In that case a footballer, Michael Appleton (known by his fans as 'Appy'), was signed by West Bromwich Albion Football Club for £750,000. Unfortunately, Appleton suffered a knee injury while training. The football club's physiotherapist said that he needed to see a surgeon. The football club telephoned the surgeon, El-Safty, who saw Appleton and recommended he undergo surgery. Appleton was unable to play football again after the surgery. It subsequently came to light that El-Safty's advice had been negligent and that the injury had only required minor treatment which would have allowed Appleton to be back on the football pitch within four months. The football club sued El-Safty. One argument put forward by the club was that the surgeon had been in breach of a contract with the football club. But the High Court held that, while there was a contract between the surgeon and the private insurance company BUPA which paid him, there was no contract between the football club and the surgeon. Such a contract could not be implied because the necessity test laid down in **Baird Textile Holdings Ltd** *v* **Marks & Spencer Plc** had not been satisfied.

Topical issue

Consumer's right to cancel

Usually, once an offer has been accepted the contract is binding, and the acceptor cannot withdraw their acceptance. An exception to this general rule has been created for certain consumers entering into contracts made at a distance. Under the Consumer Protection (Distance Selling) Regulations 2000 a consumer entering into a contract at a distance has a 'cooling-off' period after the formation of the contract, during which they can change their mind and withdraw from the contract. The relevant contract must have been made under an organised distance-selling arrangement, and there must have been no face-to-face contact between the consumer and the seller, for example in a shop. The contract is therefore likely to have been made over the telephone, through the post, on the internet or by using a catalogue. The cooling-off period allows the consumer to cancel the contract within seven working days of receiving the goods or concluding a contract for services. A large number of consumer contracts are excluded from this provision. Excluded contracts include those relating to financial services and the sale of land, vending machines, contracts for transport and leisure, and contracts to supply food for everyday consumption. Thus, if I buy an airplane ticket online or purchase some fast food from my local takeaway these contracts will not incorporate a cooling-off period during which I could withdraw from the contract.

Auctions, tenders and the sale of land

The above rules of offer and acceptance apply to the sale of land and to sales by tender and auction, but it is useful to know how those rules apply in practice in these fairly common situations.

Auction sales

The parties to an auction sale are the bidder and the owner of the goods. The auctioneer simply provides a service, and is not a party to the contract between buyer and seller. Under the Sale of Goods Act 1979 (s. 57(2)), the general rule is that the auctioneer's request for bids is an invitation to treat, and each bid is an offer. Each bidder's offer lapses as soon as a higher bid is made, and an offer is accepted by the auctioneer (on behalf of the seller) on the fall of the hammer. Any bidder may therefore withdraw a bid before the hammer falls, and the auctioneer may also withdraw the goods on behalf of the seller before that point.

Advertisement of an auction

An advertisement that an auction is to take place at a certain time is a mere declaration of intention and is not an offer which those who attend at the specified time thereby accept. This was decided in **Harris** *v* **Nickerson** (1873), where the plaintiff failed to recover damages for travelling to an auction which was subsequently cancelled.

Auction 'without reserve'

In many cases, sellers at an auction specify reserve prices – the lowest prices they will accept for their goods. If nobody bids at least that amount, the goods are not sold. An auction 'without reserve', on the other hand, means that the goods will be sold to the highest bidder, however low their bid. We have seen that an advertisement announcing that an auction will be held is an invitation to treat and not an offer, but in **Warlow** *v* **Harrison** (1859) it was held that if such an advertisement includes the words 'without reserve', it becomes an offer, from the auctioneers to the public at large, that if the auction is held they will sell to the highest bidder (though it does not oblige the auctioneers to hold the sale in the first place). The offer is accepted when a person makes a bid and when doing so assumes that there is no reserve. That acceptance completes a contract, which is separate from any contract that might be made between the highest bidder and the owner of the property being sold. An auctioneer who then puts a reserve price on any of the lots breaches this separate contract.

In **Barry** *v* **Davies** (2000) the defendant auctioneers were instructed to sell two engine analysers, which were specialist machines used in the motor trade. The claimant had been told the sale would be 'without reserve'. New machines would cost £14,000 each. The auctioneer attempted to start the bidding at £5,000, then £3,000, but the claimant was the only person interested in the machines and placed a bid of just £200 for each machine. The auctioneer refused to accept that bid and withdrew the machines from the sale. The claimant sought damages for breach of contract and he was awarded £27,600. The defendants' appeal was dismissed and the case of **Warlow** *v* **Harrison** was followed. A contract existed between the auctioneer and the bidder that the auction would be without reserve, and that contract had been breached.

Tenders

When a large organisation, such as a company, hospital, local council or government ministry, needs to find a supplier of goods or services, it will often advertise for tenders. Companies wishing to secure the business then reply to the advertisement, detailing the price at which they are willing to supply the goods or services, and the advertiser chooses whichever is the more favourable quotation. Tenders can also be invited for the sale of goods, in much the same way as bids are made at an auction.

As a general rule, a request for tenders is regarded as an invitation to treat (**Spencer v Harding** (1870)), so there is no obligation to accept any of the tenders put forward. The tenders themselves are offers, and a contract comes into existence when one of them is accepted.

In exceptional cases, however, an invitation for tenders may itself be an offer, and submission of a tender then becomes acceptance of that offer. The main example of this is where the invitation to tender makes it clear that the lowest tender (or the highest in the case of tenders to buy) will be accepted. In **Harvela Investments Ltd v Royal Trust Co of Canada (CI) Ltd** (1985) the defendants telexed two parties inviting them to submit tenders for the purchase of some shares, stating in the invitation 'we bind ourselves to accept the [highest] offer'. The House of Lords said that the telex was a unilateral offer to accept the highest bid, which would be followed by a bilateral contract with the highest bidder.

An invitation to tender may also be regarded as an offer to consider all tenders correctly submitted, even if it is not an undertaking actually to accept one. In **Blackpool and Fylde Aero Club Ltd v Blackpool Borough Council** (1990) the Council invited tenders from people wishing to operate leisure flights from the local airport. Those who wished to submit a tender were to reply to the Town Hall, in envelopes provided, by a certain deadline. The plaintiff returned his bid before the deadline was up, but the Council mistakenly thought it had arrived late. They therefore refused to consider it, and accepted one of the other tenders.

The plaintiff's claim for breach of contract was upheld by the Court of Appeal. Although the Council was not obliged to accept any of the tenders, the terms of their invitation to tender constituted an offer at least to consider any tender which was submitted in accordance with their rules. That offer was accepted by anyone who put forward a tender in the correct manner, and their acceptance would create a unilateral contract, obliging the Council to consider the tender. The Council was in breach of this unilateral contract.

In some cases a tenderer makes what is called a 'referential' tender, offering to top anyone else's bid by a specified amount. This occurred in **Harvela Investments Ltd v Royal Trust Co of Canada (CI) Ltd** (1985). Some shares were for sale, and the plaintiffs offered C\$2,175,000 for them. Another party offered to pay C\$2,100,000, or if this was not the highest bid, to pay C\$101,000 'in excess of any other offer'. The House of Lords made it clear that the type of 'referential' tender made by the second party was not legally an offer, and was not permissible in such a transaction. Therefore the first defendants were bound to accept the plaintiffs' bid. Their Lordships explained their decision on the grounds that the purpose of a sale by fixed bidding is to provoke the best price from purchasers regardless of what others might be prepared to pay, and that referential bids worked against this. Such bids would also present practical problems if allowed: if everyone made referential bids it would be impossible to define exactly what offer was being made, and if only some parties made bids in that way, the others would not have a valid opportunity to have their offers accepted.

Selection of tenders

The implications of choosing to accept a tender depend on what sort of tender is involved.

Specific tenders

Where an invitation to tender specifies that a particular quantity of goods is required on a particular date, or between certain dates, agreeing to one of the tenders submitted will constitute acceptance of an offer (the tender), creating a contract. This is the case even if delivery is to be in instalments as and when requested. If a company tenders to supply 100 wheelchairs to a hospital between 1 January and 1 June, their contract is completed when the hospital chooses the company's tender, and delivery must be made between those dates.

Non-specific tenders

Some invitations to tender are not specific, and may simply state that certain goods may be required, up to a particular maximum quantity, with deliveries to be made 'if and when' requested. For example, an invitation to tender made by a hospital may ask for tenders to supply up to 1,000 test tubes, 'if and when' required. In such a case, taking up one of the tenders submitted does not amount to acceptance of an offer in the contractual sense, and there is no contract. Once the tender is approved, it becomes what is called a standing offer. The hospital may order no test tubes at all, may spread delivery over several instalments, or may take the whole 1,000 test tubes at once. If the hospital does buy the test tubes or some of them, whether in instalments or all at once, then each time it places an order it accepts the test tube manufacturer's offer, and a separate contract for the amount required is made on each occasion. The result is that when the hospital places an order, the company is bound to supply within the terms of the offer as required, but the company can revoke the offer to supply at any time, and will then only be bound by orders already placed.

This kind of situation would not oblige the hospital to order its test tubes only from the company whose tender it approved. In **Percival v LCC** (1918) Percival submitted a tender to the LCC for the supply of certain goods 'in such quantities and at such times and in such manner' as the Committee required. The tender was approved, but the LCC eventually placed its orders with other suppliers. Percival claimed damages for breach of contract, but the court held that acceptance of the non-specific tender did not constitute a contract, and the LCC were not obliged to order goods – although Percival was obliged to supply goods which were ordered under the terms of the standing offer, so long as the offer had not been revoked.

The nature of a standing offer was considered in **Great Northern Railway Co v Witham** (1873). The plaintiffs had invited tenders for the supply of stores, and the defendant made a tender in these words: 'I undertake to supply the Company for twelve months with such quantities of [the specified articles] as the Company may order from time to time.' The railway company accepted this tender, and later placed some orders, which were met by the defendant. The court case arose when the railway company placed an order for goods within the scope of the tender, and the defendant refused to supply them. The court found that the supplying company was in breach of contract because the tender was a standing offer, which the

Invitation for tenders	
Containing general requirements	= invitation to treat
Containing conclusive criteria for selection	= offer
Selection of tenders	
Specific tender	= acceptance
Non-specific tender	= standing offer

Figure 5.13   Tenders

railway company could accept each time it placed an order, thereby creating a contract each time. The standing offer could be revoked at any time, but the tenderer was bound by orders already made, since these were acceptances of his offer and thereby completed a contract.

Sale of land

The standard rules of contract apply to the sale of land (which includes the sale of buildings such as houses), but the courts apply those rules fairly strictly, tending to require very clear evidence of an intention to be bound before they will state that an offer has definitely been made. The main reason for this is simply that land is expensive, and specific areas of land are unique and irreplaceable; damages are therefore often inadequate as a remedy for breach of contract in a sale of land, and it is better to avoid problems beforehand than put them right after a contract is made.

In **Harvey v Facey** (1893) the plaintiffs sent the defendants a telegram asking: 'Will you sell us Bumper Hall Pen? Telegraph lowest cash price.' The reply arrived, stating: 'Lowest price for Bumper Hall Pen, £900.' The plaintiffs then sent a telegram back saying: 'We agree to buy Bumper Hall Pen for £900 asked by you. Please send us your title deeds.' On these facts, the Privy Council held that there was no contract. They regarded the telegram from the defendants as merely a statement of what the minimum price would be if the defendants eventually decided to sell. It was therefore not an offer which could be accepted by the third telegram.

In practice, the normal procedure for sales involving land is as follows.

Sale 'subject to contract'

First, parties agree on the sale, often through an estate agent. At this stage their agreement may be described as 'subject to contract', and although the effect of these words depends on the intention of the parties, there is a strong presumption against there being a contract at this stage (**Tiverton Estates Ltd v Wearwell Ltd** (1975)). If the parties sign a document at this point, it will usually be an agreement to make a more formal contract in the future, rather than a contract to go through with the sale. It was held in **Alpenstow Ltd v Regalian Properties plc** (1985) that there were some circumstances in which the courts may infer that the parties intended to be legally bound when signing the original document, even though it was said to be 'subject to contract', but such cases would arise only rarely.

The idea of making an agreement 'subject to contract' is to allow the buyers to check thoroughly all the details of the land (to make sure, for example, that there are no plans to build a new airport just behind the house they are thinking of buying, or that the house is not affected by subsidence).

Exchange of contracts

The next stage is that the buyer and seller agree on the terms of the formal contract (usually through their solicitors, though there is no legal reason why the parties cannot make all the arrangements themselves). Both parties then sign a copy of the contract, and agree on a date on which the contracts will be exchanged, at which point the buyer usually pays a deposit of around 10 per cent of the sale price. Once the contracts are exchanged, a binding contract exists (though it is difficult to see this transaction in terms of offer and acceptance). However, if the contract is breached at this point the buyer can only claim damages – the buyer has no rights in the property itself.

After exchanging contracts, the parties may make further inquiries (checking, for example, that the seller really does own the property), and then the ownership of the land and house is transferred to the buyer, usually by means of a document known as a transfer. At this stage the buyer pays the balance of the purchase price to the seller. The buyer then has rights in the property – in the event of the seller breaching the contract, the buyer can have his or her property rights enforced in court, rather than just claiming damages.

These principles are illustrated by **Eccles v Bryant** (1947). After signing an agreement 'subject to contract', the parties consulted their solicitors, who agreed a draft contract. Each party signed the contract, and the buyer forwarded his copy to the seller's solicitor so that contracts could be exchanged. However, the seller changed his mind about the sale, and his solicitor informed the buyer's solicitor that the property had been sold to another buyer. The buyer tried to sue for breach of contract, but the Court of Appeal held that the negotiations were subject to formal contract, and the parties had not intended to be bound until they exchanged contracts. No binding obligations could arise before this took place. The court did not say when the exchange would be deemed to have taken place – that is, whether it was effective on posting of the contracts, or on receipt. In many cases a contract will specify when an exchange will be considered complete, by stating, for example, that the contract will be binding when the contracts are actually delivered.

How important are offer and acceptance?

Although offer and acceptance can provide the courts with a useful technique for assessing at what point an agreement should be binding, what the courts are really looking to judge is whether the parties have come to an agreement, and there are some cases in which the rules on offer and acceptance give little help.

An example of this type of situation is **Clarke _v_ Dunraven** (1897), which concerned two yacht owners who had entered for a yacht race. The paperwork they completed in order to enter included an undertaking to obey the club rules, and these rules contained an obligation to pay for 'all damages' caused by fouling. During the manoeuvring at the start of the race, one yacht, the _Satanita_, fouled another, the _Valkyrie_, which sank as a result. The owner of the _Valkyrie_ sued the owner of the _Satanita_ for the cost of the lost yacht, but the defendant claimed that he was under no obligation to pay the whole cost, and was only liable to pay the lesser damages laid down by a statute which limited liability to £8 for every ton of the yacht. The plaintiff claimed that entering the competition in accordance with the rules had created a contract between the competitors, and this contract obliged the defendant to pay 'all damages'.

Clearly it was difficult to see how there could be an offer by one competitor and acceptance by the other, since their relations had been with the yacht club and not with each other. There was obviously an offer and an acceptance between each competitor and the club, but was there a contract between the competitors? The House of Lords held that there was, on the basis that 'a contract is concluded when one party has communicated to another an offer and that other has accepted it or when the parties have united in a concurrent expression of intention to create a legal obligation'. Therefore responsibility for accidents was governed by the race rules, and the defendant had to pay the full cost of the yacht.

There are problems in analysing the contract between the entrants to the race in terms of offer and acceptance. It seems rather far-fetched to imagine that, on starting the race, each competitor was making an offer to all the other competitors and simultaneously accepting their offers – and in any case, since the offers and acceptances would all occur at the same moment, they would be cross offers and would technically not create a contract.

As we have seen, contracts for the sale of land are also examples of agreements that do not usually fall neatly into concepts of offer and acceptance. We will also see later that the problems arising from the offer and acceptance analysis are sometimes avoided by the courts using the device of collateral contracts.

Problems with offer and acceptance

Artificiality

Clearly there are situations in which the concepts of offer and acceptance have to be stretched, and interpreted rather artificially, even though it is obvious that the parties have reached an agreement. In **Gibson _v_ Manchester City Council** (1979) Lord Denning made it clear that he was in favour of looking at negotiations as a whole, in order to determine whether there was a contract, rather than trying to impose offer and acceptance on the facts, but his method has largely been rejected by the courts as being too uncertain and allowing too wide a discretion.

Revocation of unilateral offers

The problem of whether a unilateral offer can be accepted by part-performance has caused difficulties for the courts. It can be argued that since the offeree has not promised to complete performance, they are free to stop at any time, so the offeror should be equally free to revoke the offer at any time. But this would mean, for example, that if A says to B, 'I'll pay you £100 if you paint my living room', A could withdraw the offer even though B had painted all but one square foot of the room, and pay nothing.

This is generally considered unjust, and various academics have expressed the view that in fact an offer cannot be withdrawn once there has been substantial performance. American academics have contended that the offeror can be seen as making two offers: the main offer that the price will be paid when the act is performed, and an implied accompanying offer that the main offer will not be revoked once performance has begun. On this assumption, the act of starting performance is both acceptance of the implied offer, and consideration for the secondary promise that the offer will not be withdrawn once performance begins. An offeror who does attempt to revoke the offer after performance has started may be sued for the breach of the secondary promise.

In England this approach has been considered rather artificial. Sir Frederick Pollock has reasoned that it might be more realistic to say that the main offer itself is accepted by beginning rather than completing performance, on the basis that acceptance simply means agreement to the terms of the offer, and there are many circumstances in which beginning performance will mean just that. Whether an act counts as beginning performance, and therefore accepting the offer, or whether it is just preparation for performing will depend on the facts of the case – so, for example, an offer of a reward for the return of lost property could still be revoked after someone had spent time looking for the property without success, but not after they had actually found it and taken steps towards returning it to the owner. This principle was adopted in 1937 by the Law Revision Committee.

Revocation of offers for specific periods

The rule that an offer can be revoked at any time before acceptance even if the offeror has said it will remain open for a specified time could be considered unfairly biased in favour of the offeror, and makes it difficult for the offeree to plan their affairs with certainty.

In a Working Paper published in 1975, the Law Commission recommended that where an offeror promises not to revoke the offer for a specified time, that promise should be binding, without the need for consideration, and if it is broken the offeree should be able to sue for damages.

An 'all or nothing' approach

The 'all or nothing' approach of offer and acceptance is not helpful in cases where there is clearly not a binding contract under that approach, and yet going back on agreements made would cause great hardship or inconvenience to one party. The problems associated with house-buying are well known – the buyer may go to all the expense of a survey and solicitor's fees, and may even have sold their own house, only to find that the seller withdraws the house from sale, sells it to someone else, or demands a higher price – generally known as 'gazumping'. So long as all this takes place before contracts are exchanged, the buyer has no remedy at all (though the Government is proposing to legislate to deal with some of these specific problems). Similarly, in a commercial situation, pressure of time may mean that a company starts work on a potential project before a contract is drawn up and signed. They will be at a disadvantage if in the end the other party decides not to contract.

Objectivity

The courts claim that they are concerned with following the intention of the parties in deciding whether there is a contract, yet they make it quite clear that they are not actually seeking to discover what **was** intended, but what, looking at the parties' behaviour, an 'officious bystander' might assume they intended. This can mean that even though the parties were actually in agreement, no contract results, as was the case in **Felthouse** *v* **Bindley** – the nephew had asked for the horse to be kept out of the sale because he was going to sell it to his uncle, but because he did not actually communicate his acceptance, there was no contract.

Summary

For a contract to exist, usually one party must have made an offer, and the other must have accepted it. Once acceptance takes effect, a contract will usually be binding on both parties.

Unilateral and bilateral contracts

Most contracts are bilateral. This means that each party takes on an obligation, usually by promising the other something. By contrast, a unilateral contract arises where only one party assumes an obligation under the contract.

Offer

The person making an offer is called the offeror, and the person to whom the offer is made is called the offeree. A communication will be treated as an offer if it indicates the terms on which the offeror is prepared to make a contract, and gives a clear indication that the offeror intends to be bound by those terms if they are accepted by the offeree. An offer may be express or implied.

Offers to the public at large

In most cases, an offer will be made to a specified person, though offers can be addressed to a group of people, or even to the general public. A contract arising from an offer to the public at large, like that in **Carlill** *v* **Carbolic Smoke Ball Co** (1893), is usually a unilateral contract.

Invitations to treat

Some kinds of transaction involve a preliminary stage in which one party invites the other to make an offer. This stage is called an invitation to treat. Confusion can sometimes arise when what would appear, in the everyday sense of the word, to be an offer is held by the law to be only an invitation to treat. This issue arises particularly in the following areas.

Advertisements

Advertisements for unilateral contracts are usually treated as offers. Advertisements for a bilateral contract are generally considered invitations to treat.

Shopping

Price-marked goods displayed on the shelves or in the windows of shops are generally regarded as invitations to treat, rather than offers to sell goods at that price: **Pharmaceutical Society of Great Britain** *v* **Boots Cash Chemists (Southern) Ltd** (1953).

Timetables and tickets for transport

The legal position here is rather unclear; no single reliable rule has emerged, and it seems that the exact point at which a contract is made depends in each case on the particular facts.

How long does an offer last?

An offer may cease to exist under any of the following circumstances.

Specified time

Where an offeror states that an offer will remain open for a specific length of time, it lapses when that time is up.

Reasonable length of time

Where the offeror has not specified how long the offer will remain open, it will lapse after a reasonable length of time has passed.

Failure of a precondition

Some offers are made subject to certain conditions, and if such conditions are not in place, the offer may lapse.

Rejection

An offer lapses when the offeree rejects it.

Counter-offer

A counter-offer terminates the original offer: **Hyde** *v* **Wrench** (1840).

Requests for information

A request for information about an offer (such as whether delivery could be earlier than suggested) does not amount to a counter offer, so the original offer remains open.

Death of the offeror

The position is not entirely clear, but it appears that if the offeree knows that the offeror has died, the offer will lapse; if the offeree is unaware of the offeror's death, it probably will not.

Death of the offeree

There is no English case on this point, but it seems probable that the offer lapses and cannot be accepted after the offeree's death by the offeree's representatives.

Withdrawal of offer

The withdrawal of an offer is sometimes described as the revocation of an offer. The old case of **Payne** *v* **Cave** (1789) establishes the principle that an offer may be withdrawn at any time up until it is accepted. A number of rules apply in relation to the withdrawal of offers.

Withdrawal must be communicated

It is not enough for offerors simply to change their mind about an offer; they must notify the offeree that it is being revoked: **Byrne** *v* **Van Tienhoven** (1880). The revocation of an offer does not have to be communicated by the offeror; the communication can be made by some other reliable source: **Dickinson** *v* **Dodds** (1876).

Withdrawal of an offer to enter into a unilateral contract

There are a number of special rules that apply in relation to the revocation of an offer to enter into a unilateral contract. An offer to enter into such a contract cannot be revoked once the offeree has commenced performance: **Errington** *v* **Errington** (1952).

Acceptance

Acceptance of an offer means unconditional agreement to all the terms of that offer. Merely remaining silent cannot amount to an acceptance, unless it is absolutely clear that acceptance was intended: **Felthouse** *v* **Bindley** (1862).

Acceptance of an offer to enter into a unilateral contract

Unilateral contracts are usually accepted by conduct. There is no acceptance until the relevant act has been completely performed.

Acceptance must be unconditional

An acceptance must accept the precise terms of an offer.

Negotiation and the 'battle of the forms'

Where parties carry on a long process of negotiation, it may be difficult to pinpoint exactly when an offer has been made and accepted. In such cases the courts will look at the whole course of negotiations to decide whether the parties have in fact reached agreement at all and, if so, when. This process can be particularly difficult where the so-called 'battle of the forms' arises. The general rule in such cases is that the 'last shot' wins the battle. Each new form issued is treated as a counter-offer, so that when one party performs its obligation under the contract (by delivering goods, for example), that action will be seen as acceptance by conduct of the offer in the last form.

Specified methods of acceptance

If an offeror states that his or her offer must be accepted in a particular way, then only acceptance by that method or an equally effective one will be binding. Where a specified method of acceptance has been included for the offeree's own benefit, however, the offeree is not obliged to accept in that way.

Acceptance must be communicated

An acceptance does not usually take effect until it is communicated to the offeror.

Exceptions to the communication rule

There are some circumstances in which an acceptance may take effect without being communicated to the offeror.

Terms of the offer

An offer may state or imply that acceptance need not be communicated to the offeror.

Conduct of the offeror

An offeror who fails to receive an acceptance through their own fault may be prevented from claiming that the non-communication means they should not be bound by the contract.

The postal rule

The general rule for acceptances by post is that they take effect when they are posted, rather than when they are communicated: **Adams *v* Lindsell** (1818). The traditional title 'postal rule' has become slightly misleading because the rule does not only apply to the post but could also potentially apply to certain other non-instantaneous modes of communication. There are certain exceptions to the postal rule:

- offers requiring communication of acceptance;
- instant methods of communication;
- misdirected acceptance.

Ignorance of the offer

It is generally thought that a person cannot accept an offer of which they are unaware, because in order to create a binding contract, the parties must reach agreement. If their wishes merely happen to coincide, that may be very convenient for both, but it does not constitute a contract and cannot legally bind them.

Time of the formation of the contract

Normally, a contract is formed when an effective acceptance has been communicated to the offeree.

Questions

1 Alexander has four pet white rats which have been trained to dance together as a group. They escape from their cage. Alexander places an advertisement in the local newspaper describing the rats and promises to pay £1,000 for each rat to anyone who returns the rats to him. Beatrice, Alexander's neighbour, finds one of the rats. She keeps it warm and well fed in a shoe box overnight and then takes it to Alexander's house. Before she can reach the house, the rat escapes from the shoe box, runs away from her, and then wriggles through a hole back into Alexander's house. Charles searches diligently for the rats for two days. He spends £10 on bus fares travelling to different parts of the city. When he finds one of the rats, he takes it home with him and does not immediately return it. David finds another rat. Unfortunately, it has been savaged by a fox and is now dead. David takes the corpse to Alexander, who refuses to pay him anything. Ethel, Alexander's sister, finds another rat in her room. She gives the rat to Alexander, who

refuses to pay her anything. Alexander decides that, as one of the rats is dead, there is no point in reassembling them as a dancing group. Accordingly, he places leaflets about the city cancelling the promise of a reward. Charles does not see the leaflets and returns the rat he found to Alexander later that day. Alexander refuses to pay him anything.

Advise Alexander. *London External LL.B*

Alexander has made an offer to enter into a unilateral contract: **Carlill *v* Carbolic Smoke Ball Co**. Has this offer been accepted by Beatrice, Charles, David or Ethel?

Beatrice

Beatrice has failed to accept the offer because the rat ran away before she could return it to Alexander in accordance with the terms of his offer.

Charles

Before Charles returns the rat, Alexander purports to withdraw his offer. Following the cases of **Daulia Ltd *v* Four Millbank Nominees Ltd** (1978) and **Errington *v* Errington** (1952), once an offeree has started to perform the act of acceptance, the offeror cannot withdraw their offer. It is a question of fact whether Charles has done enough to amount to starting to perform the act of acceptance. It will depend on whether this required Charles to have started to return the rat (which he had not done) or simply find the rat. In addition, in order for Alexander to effectively withdraw the offer, the withdrawal must be made by a method which reaches substantially the same audience as the original offer (**Shuey *v* United States**). Again, this will be a question of fact whether the leaflets satisfy this requirement, when the original offer was made by an advertisement in a local newspaper.

David

David returns a dead rat. The advert makes no express statement that the rat had to be alive, but a court might be prepared to imply such a term.

Ethel

Ethel returns the rat before the offer is withdrawn. But Ethel is a family member, and there will therefore be an issue as to whether Alexander had an intention to contract with Ethel. On the facts, the court might be prepared to rebut the presumption against an intention to create legal relations between members of the family, because this was an offer to the world at large, with a general intention to create legal relations. In which case, Alexander would have to pay the reward to Ethel.

2 **At 9.00 am on Monday 13 August, Maurice, a car dealer, sends a telex to Austin offering to sell him a rare vintage car for £50,000. Austin receives the telex at 9.15 am and telexes his acceptance at 1.00 pm. Austin is aware that Maurice's office is closed for lunch between 1.00 and 2.00 pm. On his return to the office, Maurice does not bother to check whether he has received a telex from Austin and at 2.30 pm receives an offer for the car from Ford, which he accepts. At 4.00 pm Austin hears from another car dealer that Maurice has sold the car to Ford. He is advised that it will cost him an additional £2,000 to buy a similar car and he immediately sends Maurice another telex**

demanding that the original car be sold to him. Maurice receives this telex at 5.00 pm, at the same time as he reads the acceptance telex.

Advise Austin of his legal position and what remedies, if any, are open to him.
Oxford

Austin clearly wishes to establish that, at some point, he made a binding contract with Maurice; your task is to pinpoint when, if at all, that contract was made, using the rules of offer and acceptance. The clearest way to do this is to take each communication in turn, and consider its legal effect.

Maurice's first telex is clearly an offer; does Austin validly accept it? The general rule is that acceptance takes effect on communication; the application of this rule to telexed acceptances is contained in the cases of **Entores** and **Brinkibon**. Considering that the telex was sent outside working hours, when should it take effect, and considering the factors mentioned in **Brinkibon** – intentions of the parties, standard business practice – where should the risk lie? Obviously there is no clear answer, but in assessing where the risk should lie, you might take into account the fact that it seems reasonable for Austin to assume the telex would be read shortly after the lunch hour was finished, and to expect Maurice to check whether any reply had been received. This is relevant because in other cases on communication, the courts seem reluctant to bail out parties who fail to receive messages through their own fault (such as the requirement that telephone callers should ask for clarification if they cannot hear the other party – **Entores**). If Austin's telex acceptance is deemed to take effect when the telex is sent, a binding contract exists between them at that point, and this will take priority over the contract made with Ford. You should then consider the position if the rule that acceptance only takes effect on communication is strictly applied.

The next relevant communication is the other car dealer telling Austin that the car has been sold; **Dickinson v Dodds** makes it plain that information from a third party can amount to a revocation, and if this is the case, the offer ceases to be available and there is no contract between Austin and Maurice. However, in **Dickinson v Dodds** the message from the third party was such that the revocation was as clear as if the offeror had said it himself; if for any reason this was not the case here (if the dealer was known to be untrustworthy, for example), there would be no revocation, and the offer would still be available for acceptance at 5 pm, at which point the contract would be made.

Assuming a contract was made, Austin is likely to be limited to claiming damages. Maurice could only be forced to sell the car if the courts granted specific performance, and this is only done when damages would be an inadequate way of putting the plaintiff in the position they should have enjoyed if the contract had been performed as agreed. Here this could be done by allowing Austin to claim the difference between the car's price and the cost of a replacement.

3 Peter's car has been stolen. He places an advertisement in the Morriston *Evening News* stating that a reward of £1,000 will be given to any person who provides information leading to the recovery of the car – provided the reward is claimed by 1 January. Andrew, a policeman, finds the car, which has suffered severe accident damage. His best friend Kelvin tells him about the reward and Andrew applies for it by a letter posted on 30 December. The letter arrives at Peter's house on 2 January.

Advise Andrew whether he has a contractual right to the reward. *WJEC*

This question concerns the issue of offer and acceptance and consideration in unilateral contracts. You first need to consider whether Peter's advertisement is an offer. It is worth pointing out that not all advertisements are seen as offers, although in this case the issue is fairly straightforward as there are several cases in which advertisements proposing unilateral contracts, and specifically involving rewards, have been recognised as offers.

The fact that Andrew did not see the advertisement but was told about it by a friend seems to raise the issue of whether an offer can be accepted by someone who does not know about it. The cases on this matter are inconclusive, but the fact that Andrew does know about the reward by the time he applies for it would seem to avoid the problem.

The next issue is whether Andrew applies for the reward in time. As you know, acceptance does not usually take effect until it is communicated, but acceptances sent by post may take effect on posting – the postal rule. The postal rule will apply so long as it is reasonable to submit the application by post, and here there seems no reason why it should not be. This means that the offer is accepted in time, even though the letter arrives after the specified closing date.

However, there is another important issue to examine: consideration. Since Andrew is a policeman, it could be argued that finding the car and informing the owner of its whereabouts is no more than his public duty. In order to have provided consideration for the reward, he would need to have gone beyond this, as explained in cases such as **Glasbrook Brothers** *v* **Glamorgan County Council** (1925) and **Harris** *v* **Sheffield United**.

4 **Critically evaluate what in law will amount to an 'offer'.** *OCR*

Your introduction could start with a definition of an offer, which is stated at p. 664 to be a communication which indicates the terms on which the offeror is prepared to make a contract, and gives a clear indication that the offeror intends to be bound by those terms if they are accepted by the offeree. Your introduction could also put the concept of an offer into the wider context of the principle of freedom of contract. Contract law's emphasis on the requirement of an offer is an example of the belief that the parties should be free to make contracts on any terms they choose.

You could then move on to distinguishing the concept of an offer from an invitation to treat. You might start by looking at bilateral contracts and examine the approach of the courts to the specific scenarios of advertisements, shopping, timetables and tickets for transport, tenders (p. 690), auctions (p. 689) and the sale of land (p. 693). Offers for unilateral contracts could then be considered, and in particular the case of **Carlill** *v* **Carbolic Smoke Ball Co.**

The next stage of your answer could contain an examination of how long an offer lasts (p. 669).

The question requires you to 'critically evaluate' and it will therefore not be enough simply to describe the law. One of the problem areas has been the 'battle of the forms' (p. 678), and you could look closely at cases such as **Butler Machine Tool Ltd** *v* **Ex-Cell-O Corp**. The case of **Clarke** *v* **Dunraven** (p. 695) provides an example of the type of scenario which does not fit comfortably within the concept of offer (and acceptance). Other criticisms of the law on offers can be found at p. 695 under the subheading 'Problems with offer and acceptance'.

Reading list

Beale and Dugdale, 'Contracts between businessmen' (1975) 2 British Journal of Law and Society 45

Evans, 'The Anglo-American mailing rule: some problems of offer and acceptance in contracts by correspondence' (1966) 15 International and Comparative Law Quarterly 553

Gardner, 'Trashing with Trollope: a deconstruction of the postal rules in contract' (1992) 12 Oxford Journal of Legal Studies 170

Graw, 'Puff, Pepsi and "That Plane" – the John Leonard Saga' (2000) 15 Journal of Contract Law 281

Rawlings, 'The battle of the forms' (1979) 42 Modern Law Review 715

Reading on the internet

The Consumer Protection (Distance Selling) Regulations 2000 are available on the website of the Office of Public Sector Information at:

http://www.opsi.gov.uk/si/si2000/20002334.htm

The Office of Fair Trading provides a helpful guide to the distance-selling regulations on its website at:

http://www.oft.gov.uk/Business/Legal/DSR/default.htm

Negligence

Development of the duty of care

The neighbour principle

There is a duty in tort to take reasonable care to avoid acts or omissions which you can reasonably foresee would be likely to injure your neighbour.

The branch of law that we now know as negligence has its origins in one case: **Donoghue v Stevenson** (1932). The facts of **Donoghue v Stevenson** began when Mrs Donoghue and a friend went into a café for a drink. Mrs Donoghue asked for a ginger beer, which her friend bought. It was supplied, as was customary at the time, in an opaque bottle. Mrs Donoghue poured out and drank some of the ginger beer, and then poured out the rest. At that point, the remains of a decomposing snail fell out of the bottle. Mrs Donoghue became ill, and sued the manufacturer.

Up until this time, the usual remedy for damage caused by a defective product would be an action in contract, but this was unavailable to Mrs Donoghue, because the contract for the sale of the drink was between her friend and the café. Mrs Donoghue sued the manufacturer, and the House of Lords agreed that manufacturers owed a duty of care to the end consumer of their products. The ginger beer manufacturers had breached that duty, causing harm to Mrs Donoghue, and she was entitled to claim damages.

For the benefit of future cases, their Lordships attempted to lay down general criteria for when a duty of care would exist. Lord Atkin stated that the principle was that 'You must take reasonable care to avoid acts or omissions which you can reasonably foresee would be likely to injure your neighbour.' This is sometimes known as the neighbour principle. By 'neighbour', Lord Atkin did not mean the person who lives next door, but 'persons who are so closely and directly affected by my act that I ought to have them in contemplation as being so affected when I am directing my mind to the acts or omissions which are called in question'. The test of foreseeability is objective; the court asks not what the defendant actually foresaw, but what a reasonable person could have been expected to foresee.

The claimant does not have to be individually identifiable for the defendant to be expected to foresee the risk of harming them. In many cases, it will be sufficient if the claimant falls within a category of people to whom a risk of harm was foreseeable – for example, the end user of a product, as in **Donoghue v Stevenson**. The ginger beer manufacturers did not have to know that Mrs Donoghue would drink their product, only that someone would.

A two-stage test

The issue of reasonable foresight was never the only criterion for deciding whether a duty of care is owed. As time went on, and a variety of factual situations in which a duty of care arose were established, the courts began to seek precedents in which a similar factual situation had given rise to the existence of a duty of care. For example, it was soon well established that motorists owe a duty of care to other road users and employers owe a duty to their employees, but where a factual situation seemed completely new, a duty of care would only be deemed to arise if there were policy reasons for doing so. 'Policy reasons' simply mean that the judges take into account not just the legal framework, but also whether they believe society would benefit from the existence of a duty. This approach began to be criticised, and the apparent need to find such reasons was said to be holding back development of the law.

This view was addressed in **Anns v Merton London Borough** (1978), where Lord Wilberforce proposed a significant extension of the situations where a duty of care would exist, arguing that it was no longer necessary to find a precedent with similar facts. Instead, he suggested that whether a duty of care arose in a particular factual situation was a matter of general principle.

In order to decide whether this principle was satisfied in a particular case, he said, the courts should use a two-stage test. First, did the parties satisfy the neighbour test – in other words, was the claimant someone to whom the defendant could reasonably be expected to foresee a risk of harm? If the answer was yes, a *prima facie* duty of care arose. The second stage would involve asking whether there were any policy considerations that meant it would not be desirable to allow a duty of care in this situation. If there were no policy considerations that argued against establishing a duty of care, then a duty could be imposed.

This two-stage test changed the way in which the neighbour test was applied. Previously, the courts had used it to justify new areas of liability, where there were policy reasons for creating them. After **Anns v Merton London Borough**, the neighbour test would apply unless there were policy reasons for excluding it. This led to an expansion of the situations in which a duty of care could arise, and therefore in the scope of negligence. This expansion reached its peak in **Junior Books v Veitchi** (1983), where the House of Lords seemed to go one step further. The House appeared to suggest that what were previously good policy reasons for limiting liability should now not prevent an extension where the neighbour principle justified recovery. They therefore allowed recovery for purely economic loss (see p. 714) when previously this had not been permitted.

As the first stage was relatively easy to pass, it seemed likely that the bounds of liability would be extended beyond what was considered to be reasonable, particularly given the judiciary's notorious reluctance to discuss issues of policy – a discussion that was necessary if the second stage was to offer any serious hurdle. As a result, the growth in liability for negligence set all sorts of alarm bells ringing. Eventually, the problems of insuring against the new types of liability, and the way in which tort seemed to be encroaching on areas traditionally governed by contractual liability, led to a rapid judicial retreat and, in a series of cases, the judiciary began restricting new duties of care.

The judicial retreat

In 1990, the case of **Murphy v Brentwood District Council** came before a seven-member House of Lords. The House invoked the 1966 Practice Statement (which allows them to depart from their own previous decisions) to overrule **Anns**. They quoted the High Court of Australia in **Sutherland Shire Council v Heyman** (1985), a case in which the High Court of Australia had itself decided not to follow **Anns**:

It is preferable, in my view, that the law should develop novel categories of negligence incrementally and by analogy with established categories, rather than by a massive extension of a *prima facie* duty of care, restrained only by indefinable 'considerations which ought to negative, or to reduce or limit the scope of the duty or the class of person to whom it is owed'.

The broad general principle with its two-part test envisaged in **Anns** was thereby swept aside, leaving the courts to impose duties of care only when they could find precedent in comparable factual situations.

Rejection of the **Anns** test did not mean that the categories of negligence were closed, but the creation of new duties of care was intended to involve a much more gradual process, building step by step by analogy with previous cases involving similar factual situations. Issues of policy would still arise, as such consideration of policy is an inescapable result of the importance of the judge's position.

The law today

Over the years, case law has established that there are a number of factual situations in which a duty of care is known to be owed. For example, drivers owe a duty of care not to injure pedestrians, and employers owe a duty of care to take reasonable steps to protect their employees from injury. However, there are still situations in which it is not clear whether there is a duty of care, and following the moves towards a tighter test after **Anns** was overruled, the House of Lords set down a new test in **Caparo Industries plc v Dickman** (1990).

The case is explained in more detail below, but, essentially, it requires the courts, when faced with the question of whether a duty of care should be imposed, to ask:

● Was the damage caused reasonably foreseeable?
● Was there a relationship of proximity between claimant and defendant?
● Is it just and reasonable to impose a duty?

The **Caparo** test is now accepted as the basic test to be applied when a court is presented with a new factual situation in which it needs to decide whether a duty of care exists. However, the courts have developed more detailed, and more restrictive, rules which apply in certain types of case:

● where the damage caused is psychiatric, rather than physical, injury;
● where the damage caused is purely economic loss;
● where the damage was caused by a failure to act (known as liability for omissions);
● where the damage was caused by a third party, rather than the defendant;
● whether the defendant falls within a range of groups who have become subject to special rules on policy grounds.

We will look first at the basic **Caparo** test, and then afterwards at the special types of case.

Procedural issues

Before we move on to look at the rules surrounding where and when a duty of care will be found, there is one important procedural point which will help you make sense of some of the cases discussed in this section. Where a case raises an issue of law, as opposed to purely issues of fact, the defendant can make what is called a striking out application, which effectively argues that even if the facts of what the claimant says happened are true, this does not give them a legal claim against the defendant. Cases where it is not clear whether there is a duty of care are often the subject of striking out applications, where essentially the defendant is saying that even if they had caused the harm alleged to the claimant, there was no duty of care between them and so there can be no successful claim for negligence.

Where a striking out application is made, the court conducts a preliminary examination of the case, in which it assumes that the facts alleged by the claimant are true, and from there, decides whether they give rise to an arguable case in law – so in a case involving duty of care, they would be deciding whether, on the facts before them, the defendant may owe a duty of care to the claimant. If not, the case can be dismissed without a full trial. If the court finds that there is an arguable case, the striking out application will be dismissed, and the case can then proceed to a full trial (unless settled out of court). The claimant will still have to prove that the facts are true, and that the complete case is made out, so a case which is not struck out can still be lost at trial. Recent cases brought before the European Court of Human Rights have raised important questions about the use of striking out applications.

Duties of care: the Caparo test

key case

The basic test for a duty of care is whether the damage was reasonably foreseeable, whether there was a relationship of proximity between claimant and defendant, and whether it is just and reasonable to impose a duty.

As explained above, the basic test for a duty of care is now the one set down in **Caparo v Dickman** (1990). This will usually be applied to duty of care questions in cases involving physical injury and/or damage to property, and those which do not fall into any of the special categories listed above. In some cases, it is also applied alongside the special rules in those categories, and some

experts suggest that those special rules are in fact simply a more detailed application of the principles in the **Caparo** test.

The test requires the courts to ask three questions:

- Was the damage reasonably foreseeable?
- Was there a relationship of proximity between defendant and claimant?
- Is it just, fair and reasonable to impose a duty in this situation?

As we shall see from the cases in this section, in many situations one or more of these elements may overlap, and so the test is not always applied as a clear, three-step process.

Reasonable foreseeability

This element of the test has its foundations in the original 'neighbour principle' developed in **Donoghue v Stevenson** (see p. 707). Essentially, the courts have to ask whether a reasonable person in the defendant's position would have foreseen the risk of damage. A modern case which shows how this part of the test works is **Langley v Dray** (1998), where the claimant was a policeman who was injured in a car crash when he was chasing the defendant, who was driving a stolen car. The Court of Appeal held that the defendant knew, or ought to have known, that he was being pursued by the claimant, and therefore in increasing his speed he knew or should have known that the claimant would also drive faster and so risk injury. The defendant had a duty not to create such risks and he was in breach of that duty.

In order for a duty to exist, it must be reasonably foreseeable that damage or injury would be caused to the particular defendant in the case, or to a class of people to which he or she belongs, rather than just to people in general. In other words, the duty is owed to a person or category of persons, and not to the human race in general. A good, if old, example of this principle can be seen in **Palsgraf v Long Island Railroad** (1928). The case arose from an incident when a man was boarding a train, and a member of the railway staff negligently pushed him, which caused him to drop a package he was carrying. The box contained fireworks, which exploded, and the blast knocked over some scales, several feet away. They fell on the claimant and she was injured. She sued, but the court held that it could not reasonably be foreseen that pushing the passenger would injure someone standing several feet away. It was reasonably foreseeable that the passenger himself might be injured, but that did not in itself create a duty to other people.

That does not, however, mean that the defendant has to be able to identify a particular individual who might foreseeably be affected by their actions; it is enough that the claimant is part of a category of people who might foreseeably be affected. This was the case in **Haley v London Electricity Board** (1965). The defendants dug a trench in the street in order to do repairs. Their workmen laid a shovel across the hole to draw pedestrians' attention to it, but the claimant was blind, and fell into the hole, seriously injuring himself. It was agreed in court that the precautions taken would have been sufficient to protect a sighted person from injury, so the question was whether it was reasonably foreseeable that a blind person might walk by and be at risk of falling in. The Court of Appeal said that it was: the number of blind people who lived in London meant that the defendants owed a duty to this category of people.

Proximity

In normal language, proximity means closeness, in terms of physical position, but in law, it has a wider meaning which essentially concerns the relationship, if any, between the defendant and the claimant. In **Muirhead v Industrial Tank Specialities** (1985), Goff LJ pointed out that this does not mean that the defendant and claimant have to know each other, but that the situations they were both in meant that the defendant could reasonably be expected to foresee that his or her actions could cause damage to the claimant.

In this sense, proximity can be seen as simply another way of expressing the foreseeability test, as the case of **Caparo v Dickman** itself shows. The claimants, Caparo, were a company who had made a takeover bid for another firm, Fidelity, in which they already owned a large number of shares. When they were deciding whether to make the bid, they had used figures prepared by Dickman for Fidelity's annual audit, which showed that Fidelity was making a healthy profit. However, when the takeover was complete, Caparo discovered that Fidelity was in fact almost worthless. They sued Dickman, and the House of Lords had to decide whether Dickman owed them a duty of care. They pointed out that the preparation of an annual audit was required under the Companies Act 1985, for the purpose of helping existing shareholders to exercise control over a company. An audit was not intended to be a source of information or guidance for prospective new investors, and therefore could not be intended to help existing shareholders, like Caparo, to decide whether to buy more shares. The audit was effectively a statement that was 'put into more or less general circulation and may foreseeably be relied on by strangers to the maker of the statement, for any one of a variety of purposes which the maker of the statement has no reason to contemplate'. As a result, the House of Lords held that there was no relationship of proximity between Caparo and Dickman, and no duty of care.

Proximity may also be expressed in terms of a relationship between the defendant, and the activity which caused harm to the claimant, defined by Lord Brennan in **Sutradhar v Natural Environment Research Council** (2004) as 'proximity in the sense of a measure of control over and responsibility for the potentially dangerous situation'. An example of this kind of proximity can be seen in **Watson v British Boxing Board of Control** (2000), where the claimant was the famous professional boxer Michael Watson, who suffered severe brain damage after being injured during a match. He sued the Board, on the basis that they were in charge of safety arrangements at professional boxing matches, and evidence showed that if they had made immediate medical attention available at the ringside, his injuries would have been less severe. The Court of Appeal held that there was sufficient proximity between Mr Watson and the Board to give rise to a duty of care, because they were the only body in the UK which could license professional boxing matches, and therefore had complete control of and responsibility for a situation which could clearly result in harm to Mr Watson if the Board did not exercise reasonable care.

In **Sutradhar**, the claimant was a resident of Bangladesh, who had been made ill by drinking water contaminated with arsenic. The water came from wells near his home, and his reason for suing the defendants was that, some years earlier, they had carried out a survey of the local water system, and had neither tested for, nor revealed the presence of arsenic. The claimant argued that the defendants should have tested for arsenic, or made public the fact that they had not done so, so as not to lull local people into a false sense of security. The House of Lords, however, held that the defendants had no duty of care to users of the water system, because there was insufficient proximity. Mr Sutradhar himself had never seen the defendants' report, and so his claim had to be based on the idea that they owed a duty to the whole population of Bangladesh. The House of Lords said this could not be the case: the defendants had no connection with the project that had provided the wells, and no one had asked them to test whether the water was safe to drink. They had no duty to the people or the government of Bangladesh to test the water for anything, and were simply doing general research into the performance of the type of wells that happened to be used in that area. The fact that someone had expert knowledge of a subject did not impose on them a duty to use that knowledge to help anyone in the world who might require such help. Proximity required a degree of control of the source of Mr Sutradhar's injury, namely the drinking water supply of Bangladesh, and the defendants had no such control.

Justice and reasonableness

In practice, the requirement that it must be just and reasonable to impose a duty often overlaps with the previous two – in **Watson** and **Sutradhar**, for example, the arguments made under the heading of proximity could equally well be seen as arguments relating to justice and reasonableness. It was obviously more just and reasonable to expect the Boxing Board to supervise a match properly, since that was their job, than it was to expect the researchers in **Sutradhar** to take responsibility for a task that was not their job, and which they had never claimed to have done.

Where justice and reasonableness are specifically referred to, it is usually because a case meets the requirements of foreseeability and proximity, but the courts believe there is a sound public policy reason for denying the claim. An example is **McFarlane** v **Tayside Health Board** (1999). The claimant had become pregnant after her partner's vasectomy failed, and claimed for the costs of bringing up the child. The courts denied her claim, on the basis that it was not just and reasonable to award compensation for the birth of a healthy child – something most people, they said, would consider a blessing.

In **Commissioners of Customs and Excise** v **Barclays Bank plc** (2006), the government's Customs and Excise department was owed large sums in unpaid VAT by two companies, who had accounts with the defendant bank. Customs and Excise had gone to court and obtained what are called 'freezing' injunctions, which restricted the two companies' access to the money they had in the bank. The bank was notified of the orders, and should have prevented the companies from withdrawing money, but, apparently because of negligence, they failed to do so, which meant that the two companies were able to take out over £2 million, and Customs and Excise were unable to recover all the money owed. They sued the bank, claiming that it owed them a duty of care. The House of Lords held that it was foreseeable that Customs and Excise could lose money if the bank was negligent in handling the freezing injunction, and that this suggested there was also a degree of proximity. However, the decisive issue was whether it was just and reasonable to impose a duty. The House stated that where a court order was breached, the court had power to deal with that breach; this would usually be enough to ensure that banks complied with such orders, and there was nothing to suggest that the order created any extra cause of action. In addition, it was unjust and unreasonable that the bank should become exposed to a liability which could amount to very much more than the £2 million that was at stake in this case, when it had no way of resisting the court order, and got no reward for complying with it.

In **Rice and Thompson** v **Secretary of State for Trade & Industry and Stuntbrand Line** (2007), the claimants were a former dock worker, and the widow of another dock worker. Both the dockers had contracted the fatal illness asbestosis through unloading asbestos from ships. At the time, they were employed under a system which meant that they were taken on by the National Dock Labour Board, and would then be employed by various companies, via the Board, when they needed ships to be unloaded. The issue in the case was whether the Board had a duty to protect the workers from the asbestos risk, given that they were not actually the employer during unloading. The court held that it was just and reasonable to impose such a duty. The employment system via the Board had been set up by Parliament to keep the docks working efficiently, and part of the statute setting it up was clearly aimed at protecting the health of dock workers. The Board's relationship with the workers was comparable to that of an employer, and they knew, or should have known, of the risks in unloading asbestos without protection.

In **West Bromwich Albion Football Club v Medhat El-Safty** (2006), the case concerned a knee injury to a West Brom player, Michael Appleton. The club arranged for him to see the defendant, an orthopaedic consultant, who advised surgery. The operation was unsuccessful, and Mr Appleton could no longer play; it was established that the advice was negligent, as other treatment should have been tried first. As well as being a personal disaster, losing a player meant that the club lost money, and they sought to sue the defendant for their losses. The defendant clearly had a duty towards the player to take reasonable care to give competent medical advice, but the club could only claim if he also had a duty to take reasonable care not to damage their financial interest in the player. The Court of Appeal said that it was not just and reasonable to impose such a duty because there was nothing to suggest that the defendant should have realised he would be taking on that responsibility, and to take on this additional duty could have conflicted with his duty towards the player who was his patient, if, for example, aggressive treatment could have enabled him to play on, but led to problems later in life. The defendant was therefore not liable to the club.

Duties of care: pure economic loss

Many losses resulting from tort could be described as economic; if the claimant's house is burnt down because of the defendant's negligence, the loss is economic in the sense that the claimant no longer has an asset they used to have. Similarly, a claimant who suffers serious injury which makes them unable to work suffers a financial loss. The law of tort has always been willing to compensate for these losses with damages.

However, economic loss also has a more precise meaning in tort. The term is usually used to cover losses which are 'purely' economic, meaning those where a claimant has suffered financial damage that does not directly result from personal injury or damage to property – as when a product bought turns out to be defective, but does not actually cause injury or damage to other property. In cases of pure economic loss, the law of tort has been reluctant to allow a claim.

A case which illustrates the difference between the types of loss is **Spartan Steel v Martin** (1972). Here the defendants had negligently cut an electric cable, causing a power cut that lasted for 14 hours. Without electricity to heat the claimants' furnace, the metal in the furnace solidified, and the claimants were forced to shut their factory temporarily. They claimed damages under three heads:

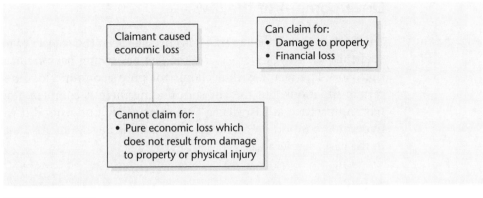

Figure 5.14   Negligence and economic loss

- damage to the metal that was in the furnace at the time of the power cut (physical damage to property);
- loss of the profit that would have been made on the sale of that metal (economic loss arising from damage to property); and
- loss of profit on metal which would have been processed during the time the factory was closed due to the power cut (pure economic loss).

A majority of the Court of Appeal held that the first two claims were recoverable but the third was not. The defendants owed the claimants a duty not to damage their property, and therefore to pay for any loss directly arising from such damage, as well as for the damage itself, but they did not owe them any duty with regard to loss of profit.

Economic loss and policy

There are two main reasons for the traditional reluctance to compensate pure economic loss. The first is that, traditionally, contract was the means by which economic loss was compensated, and the courts were reluctant to disturb this. Contract was seen as offering certainty; defendants could only be liable for losses caused by their own failure to fulfil a freely undertaken agreement, and this clearly had benefits in the commercial world.

The second reason, linked to the first, is the much-quoted 'floodgates' argument. This reasons that while, as a general rule, an act or omission can only cause personal injury or property damage to a limited number of people, the possible economic loss from the same act may be vast and in practice incalculable. In **Spartan Steel**, for example, had the defendants been liable to compensate for profit lost as a result of the power cut, the number and amount of claims might in theory have been astronomical. Although this does not provide much of a moral reason why such losses should not be compensated, an accepted part of law's role in a market economy like ours is to provide industry and commerce with a framework within which they can plan their activities, and preventing claims for economic loss obviously assists in this.

Development of the law

The issue of economic loss in negligence has been the subject of much legal activity over the past 40 years or so, and the law has swung backwards and forwards over the issue. The result is that claims for pure economic loss are now allowed in certain situations, but the law surrounding them is complex, fragmented and still has an unsettled air. However, it is more easily understood if we first look at the traditional position on economic loss, and the developments that have taken place in the past four decades.

Origins of the claim for economic loss

The initial position on pure economic loss in negligence was laid down in the case of **Candler** *v* **Crane, Christmas & Co** (1951). Here a firm of accountants had done some work for a client, knowing that the figures produced would also be considered by a third party. As a result of relying on the figures, the third party suffered financial loss, but the Court of Appeal held that the accountants owed no duty of care regarding economic loss to the third party; their responsibility was only to the client with whom they had a contractual relationship.

This remained the situation until 1963, when the extremely important case of **Hedley Byrne** *v* **Heller** provided that there were some situations in which negligence could provide a remedy for pure economic loss caused by things the defendant had said, or information they had provided; essentially, there needed to be a 'special relationship' between the parties, which would arise where the defendants supplied advice or information, knowing that the claimants would rely on it for a particular purpose. This is sometimes known as 'negligent misstatement'. (The case is discussed more fully below.)

Following this came the case of **Anns** *v* **Merton London Borough** (1978) which, as we discussed on p. 708, was part of the judicial expansion of negligence liability during the 1970s. The case concerned economic loss arising from the claimant's house being badly built; defective foundations had caused cracking in the walls. This might at first sight appear to be a case of damage to property, but the courts have traditionally been insistent that a defect is not the same thing as damage: where a product is defective in its manufacture, claims may be made for any personal injury caused as a result of the defect, or any damage to other property, but not for the defect itself, which is considered economic, since the loss arises from the reduced value of the object. In **Anns**, however, the House of Lords decided that the cracks in the walls could be viewed as damage to property rather than economic loss, and therefore compensated.

This was followed by the case which is generally viewed as forming the peak of the expansion in negligence liability, **Junior Books** *v* **Veitchi** (1983). The claimants in the case had had a factory built for them under a contract with the building firm. The factory needed a special type of floor in order to support the kind of machinery the claimants wanted to use, and the claimants requested that the builders use a particular flooring firm to provide this, which they did. After the floor was laid, it was found to be defective. If the factory owners had themselves contracted with the flooring company, they could have sued them in contract for the price of replacing the floor, but their only contract was with the builders; the builders had contracted with the flooring company. It was possible to make out a case that the builders had been negligent, but a potential stumbling block was that the factory owners' loss was purely economic: the defect in the floor posed no threat to safety, nor any risk of damage to the fabric of the building, and so the only loss was the cost of replacing it. However, a majority of the House of Lords held that there was nevertheless a duty of care between the builders and the factory owners with regard to the defect in the floor.

The situation after this was that claimants could recover for economic loss caused by statements under **Hedley Byrne**, and following **Anns** and then **Junior Books**, it was also possible to recover for economic loss caused by negligent acts. However, as we saw on p. 000, the general expansion of negligence liability was much criticised and it was at this point that the courts began to draw back, with the eventual overruling of **Anns** in **Murphy v Brentwood District Council** (see p. 708). Like **Anns**, **Murphy** concerned a defective building, and as well as laying down general principles for the way in which the law on negligence should develop, the House of Lords put a stop to the possibility that defects in products could be seen as damage to property; it reaffirmed that they were to be regarded as economic loss and that they could not be compensated in negligence.

Junior Books was not overruled in **Murphy**, but in a series of later cases on defective products the courts declined to follow it and eventually it was considered that **Junior Books** was to be regarded as unique to its facts, and in particular the idea that by specifying that the flooring company should be used, the claimants created a relationship of proximity between themselves and the defendants, even though there was no contract.

From there on, both the courts and academic commentators began to develop an approach to economic loss which distinguished between such loss when caused by negligent acts, and when caused by negligent statements or advice. Aside from the apparent anomaly of **Junior Books**, it appeared that economic loss arising from acts was not recoverable in negligence, whereas such loss arising from statements and advice was, if it could be fitted into the requirements of **Hedley Byrne**. This led to the rather bizarre situation in which surveyors or architects who negligently advise on the construction of a building that turns out to be defective are liable in negligence for economic loss caused as a result, but builders who are negligent in constructing such buildings are not.

The current position

During the 1990s, a new mood of cautious expansion was visible in a number of cases. These extended **Hedley Byrne** beyond liability for negligent statements or advice, and established that it can, in some circumstances, also cover negligent provision of services. This was specifically stated in **Henderson v Merrett Syndicates Ltd** (1995), and confirmed in **Williams and Reid v Natural Life Health Foods Ltd and Mistlin** (1998) (both cases are discussed below). The result now appears to be that when the **Hedley Byrne** principles are fulfilled, pure economic loss is recoverable both where it is caused by either negligent advice or information, or by negligent provision of services. There is also a category of cases where compensation has been given for economic loss caused by negligent provision of services, even though the requirements of **Hedley Byrne** were not entirely fulfilled – these are discussed on p. 724.

Economic loss is still not, however, recoverable where it is caused by defective products, where **Murphy** still applies. Nor is it recoverable when caused by negligent acts other than the provision of services. This was confirmed in **Londonwaste v AMEC Civil Engineering** (1997), a case similar to **Spartan Steel** in that the claimants, a company which burnt waste to provide electricity, lost profits as a result of being forced to close down when the defendant road menders severed a power cable. The waste company was allowed to recover for physical damage done to their power station, but not for loss of income from the sale of electricity, nor for the costs incurred from having to dispose of the waste elsewhere, since these were not the result of the physical damage done to the power station, although they were the results of the defendants' negligence.

We will now look in more detail at **Hedley Byrne** and its effects.

The Hedley Byrne principles

key case

There is a duty of care not to cause economic loss where there is a special relationship between the parties, the defendant voluntarily assumed a responsibility to the defendant, the claimant relied on the defendant's advice, and it was reasonable to do so.

The claimants in **Hedley Byrne v Heller** (1964) were an advertising agency, who had been asked by a firm called Easipower Ltd to buy substantial amounts of advertising space on their behalf. To make sure their clients were creditworthy, Hedley Byrne asked their own bank, the National Provincial, to check on them. National Provincial twice contacted Heller, who were Easipower's bankers and were backing them financially, to enquire about Easipower's creditworthiness. Heller gave favourable references on both occasions, but each time included a disclaimer stating that the information was being supplied 'without responsibility on the part of this Bank or its officials'.

The second enquiry asked whether Easipower was 'trustworthy, in the way of business, to the extent of £100,000 per annum', and Heller answered that Easipower was a respectably constituted company, considered good for its ordinary business engagements. This message was conveyed to Hedley Byrne, and, relying on that advice, they entered into a contract with Easipower Ltd. Easipower later went into

liquidation, leaving Hedley Byrne to pay the £17,000 due to companies from whom they had bought advertising space. Hedley Byrne claimed this amount from Heller.

In view of the words disclaiming liability, the House of Lords held that no duty of care was accepted by Heller, and none arose, so the claim failed. However, the House also considered what their conclusion would have been if no words of disclaimer had been used, and this is where the importance of the case lies. Their Lordships stated *obiter* that, in appropriate circumstances, there could be a duty of care to give careful advice, and that breach of that duty could give rise to liability for negligence. The fact that the sole damage was economic loss did not, they said, prevent this.

The House of Lords laid down a number of requirements which claimants would need to satisfy in order to establish a duty of care under **Hedley Byrne**. There must be:

- a 'special relationship' between the parties;
- a voluntary assumption of responsibility by the party giving the advice;
- reliance on that advice by the party receiving it; and
- it must be reasonable for that party to have relied on the advice.

The requirements are to a large extent interlinked, but some specific principles can be drawn out from the cases.

The 'special relationship'

This was described by Lord Reid in **Hedley** as arising where 'it is plain that the party seeking information or advice was trusting the other to exercise such a degree of care as the circumstances required, where it was reasonable for him to do that, and where the other gave the information or advice when he knew or ought to have known that the enquirer was relying on him'.

Lord Reid made it plain that the 'special relationship' requirement meant that **Hedley Byrne** only covers situations where advice is given in a business context:

> Quite careful people often express definite opinions on social or informal occasions, even when they see that others are likely to be influenced by them; and they often do that without taking the care which they would take if asked for their opinion professionally, or in a business connection . . . there can be no duty of care on such occasions.

Advice given off the cuff in a social setting will therefore not, as a rule, give rise to a duty of care. For example, both doctors and lawyers frequently complain that as soon as they disclose their profession at parties, fellow guests want to discuss backaches or boundary disputes; they can at least take comfort that, tedious though those conversations may be, they will not result in a negligence suit if the advice given is careless. Curiously, there is, however, one case in which a duty of care under **Hedley** was found in a purely friendly setting. In **Chaudry v Prabhakar** (1988), the defendant had advised the claimant, a friend, to buy a particular second-hand car, without noticing that it had been in an accident. It was in fact unroadworthy, and the claimant successfully sued for negligence. The case has, however, been heavily criticised, and is unlikely ever to be followed; it certainly appears wrong in the light of Lord Reid's statement.

An example of the special relationship can be seen in **Esso Petroleum Co Ltd v Mardon** (1976). Here the claimant had leased a petrol station on the strength of Esso's advice that he could expect to sell at least 200,000 gallons a year. In fact he only managed to sell 78,000 gallons in 15 months. The Court of Appeal held that in making the prediction, the petrol company had undertaken a responsibility to Mr Mardon, and he had relied on their skill in the petrol market; his claim was allowed.

The person giving the advice need not be a professional adviser. In **Lennon v Commissioner of the Metropolis** (2004), the claimant was an officer in the Metropolitan Police, who was changing jobs to go and work in the police force in Northern Ireland. He had been entitled to a housing allowance, and wanted to make sure this continued, so he asked an executive in the personnel department whether it would affect his housing allowance if he took time off between finishing one job and starting the other. She advised him that it would not. In fact, the time off counted as a break in service, which resulted in his losing entitlement to the housing allowance for ever. He sued the Metropolitan Police, who were vicariously liable for the personnel officer's acts. The Court of Appeal upheld his claim, stating that even though the personnel officer was not a professional adviser, she had a managerial job in the police service, and had, or had access to, special complex knowledge about the effects of transfers on police allowances of the kind in question. She had led the claimant to believe he could rely on her advice, rather than telling him the question was outside her sphere of experience and suggesting that he took advice from elsewhere.

Voluntary assumption of responsibility

As Lord Reid pointed out in **Hedley Byrne**, a person asked for advice in a business context has three choices: they can opt to give no advice; choose to give advice, but warn that it should not be relied on; or give the advice without giving any such warning. In general, someone who chooses the third option will be considered to have voluntarily assumed responsibility for that advice.

An example of where the courts will find such an assumption of responsibility can be seen in **Dean** *v* **Allin & Watts** (2001), where the Court of Appeal held that the defendant, a solicitor who had acted for clients who were borrowing money, had also assumed responsibility for the other party to the transaction – Mr Dean, the person lending the money. Mr Dean was a mechanic, and not widely experienced in business finance. He was approached by two borrowers seeking funding for their property company, and agreed to lend them £20,000, with a particular property being put up as security for the loan. The borrowers suggested that their solicitors draw up the necessary documentation, and met all the legal costs. Mr Dean made it clear that he would not be involving his own solicitor, and it was never suggested by the borrowers' solicitor that he should take independent legal advice.

The solicitor advised that the security could be dealt with by way of a deposit of the deeds to the property; this was in fact incorrect, and deposit of the deeds did not give Mr Dean any rights over the property. Eventually, the borrowers defaulted on the loan, and the mistake was discovered. Mr Dean now had neither his money, nor the property. He sued the solicitor, and the Court of Appeal held that, in knowing that Mr Dean was not taking independent advice, the solicitor knew that he was being relied on to ensure that there was effective security for the loan, and therefore in continuing to act, without recommending that Mr Dean take independent advice, he was assuming a responsibility to him. The court stressed the fact that the defendant knew Mr Dean was inexperienced in business matters, and also pointed out that there was no conflict of interest between his interests and those of the defendant's clients, who also wanted to put in place effective security for the loan. Had the solicitor advised Mr Dean to consult a solicitor of his own, the result would, the court said, have been different.

In **Calvert** *v* **William Hill Credit Ltd** (2008), the case concerned the question of how far a bookmaker could be liable for economic losses caused to a problem gambler. The claimant was a greyhound trainer who had initially made a lot of money from gambling, but whose gambling habits eventually became compulsive, leading to losses of over £2 million. Realising that he had a problem, he had asked the bookmaker, William Hill, to close his telephone betting account and not to allow him to open another one (an arrangement known as 'self-exclusion'). The bookmaker had in place procedures to do this, which were part of a social responsibility policy that was designed to protect problem gamblers, but in Mr Calvert's case the system failed and he was able to go on gambling with William Hill, as well as with other bookmakers.

He argued that there were two possible grounds on which it could be argued that William Hill owed him a duty of care. The first was that, by putting in place a social responsibility policy that was designed to protect problem gamblers, they had voluntarily assumed a responsibility towards such gamblers. The court rejected this idea, on the grounds that it was not reasonable to expect the bookmaker to identify all problem gamblers; that gamblers who signed up to the self-exclusion arrangement also agreed to a disclaimer absolving William Hill of legal responsibility for their economic losses; and that it was unfair to allow a situation in which problem gamblers could take their winnings if they were successful, but expect the bookmakers to compensate them if they were not.

The second argument was that, by agreeing to include Mr Calvert in the self-exclusion arrangement, the bookmaker assumed responsibility for carrying out that arrangement properly. The court found that he had identified himself to William Hill as a problem gambler, had asked for their help in excluding him from betting for six months, and had been told that he would get that help. That being the case, the court found that William Hill did have a duty of care to carry out the self-exclusion arrangement, and they had breached this duty. However, Mr Calvert's claim failed because the court found that William Hill's negligence did not ultimately cause his losses: even before he knew that the self-exclusion policy was not in place, he was still betting heavily through other bookmakers, and, given the extent of his gambling problem, the losses he sustained would have happened anyway.

Claimants not known to the defendant

More complex problems arise when the claimant is not known to the defendant, but claims to be, as Lord Bridge put it, 'a member of an identifiable class'. In **Goodwill v British Pregnancy Advisory Service** (1996), an attempt was made to use **Hedley Byrne** in a new factual context. The claimant, Ms Goodwill, had become pregnant by her boyfriend. Three years before their relationship began, he had undergone a vasectomy performed by the defendants. They had advised him after the operation that it had been successful and he would not need to use contraception in the future. He told Ms Goodwill this when they began their relationship, and she stopped using any contraception. In fact the vasectomy had reversed itself, and she became pregnant. She sued the defendants for negligence, claiming the cost of bringing up her daughter.

The Court of Appeal held that in order to claim successfully for pure economic loss arising from reliance on advice provided by the defendants, a claimant had to show that the defendants knew (either because they were told or because it was an obvious thing to assume) that the advice they supplied was likely to be acted on by the claimant (either as a specific individual or one of an ascertainable group), without independent enquiry, for a particular purpose which the defendants knew about at the time they gave the advice, and that the claimant had acted on the advice to his or her disadvantage.

In the case before them, the Court of Appeal held that at the time when the advice was given, the claimant was not known to the defendants, and was simply one of a potentially large class of women who might at some stage have a sexual relationship with the patient before them. They could not be expected to foresee that, years later, their advice to their patient might be communicated to and relied on by her for the purpose of deciding whether to use contraception; therefore the relationship between the defendants and Ms Goodwill was not sufficiently proximate to give rise to a duty of care. The court pointed out, however, that the situation might be different where a man and his partner were advised at the same time, or possibly even where their relationship was known to those giving the advice.

In common-sense terms, the distinction is a difficult one. Clearly, as Ms Goodwill pointed out, in this day and age it was not unlikely that a man of her boyfriend's age would have a sexual relationship with future partners, and while the class of possible future partners might be large, the number who would end up pregnant was not, given that once pregnancy had occurred, it would be known that the vasectomy had reversed itself. Furthermore, the purpose to which such partners would put the advice was exactly the same as the purpose for which the patient would use it: as a statement that if they had sexual relations, no pregnancy would result. What we see in cases like this one is the courts struggling to balance the need to compensate loss where justice demands it and no other means of redress is available, and yet avoid opening those much-mentioned floodgates and opening defendants to unreasonable liability. The theme is continued in the 'wills cases' discussed on p. 724.

The effect of disclaimers

Where a defendant has issued some kind of disclaimer (as in **Hedley Byrne** itself), this would appear to suggest that they are not accepting responsibility for their advice. However, the courts have stated that merely issuing a disclaimer will not always prevent liability under **Hedley Byrne**. Cases in this area are very fact-dependant, but the general approach seems to be that a disclaimer is more likely to prevent liability in cases where the claimant could reasonably be expected to understand what it meant, such as where the claimant is a business, or someone experienced in the kind of transaction taking place. This was the case in both **Omega Trust Co Ltd** v **Wright, Som & Pepper** (1997), where the case involved a valuation of commercial property, and **McCullagh** v **Lane Fox & Partners Ltd** (1996), which concerned information given by an estate agent to a purchaser at the upper end of the housing market; and, in both cases, the courts found that the disclaimer issued by the defendant could be taken to mean there was no assumption of responsibility under **Hedley Byrne**.

However, in **Smith** v **Eric S Bush** (1990), the case involved advice given by surveyors to the buyers of an ordinary family home and, in this case, the House of Lords found that the existence of a disclaimer did not mean there was no assumption of responsibility towards the buyers. The claimants' home had been negligently surveyed by the defendants, and was worth much less than they had paid for it. The survey had been commissioned by the building society from which the claimants had sought a mortgage, as part of its standard practice of ensuring that the property was worth at least the money that was being lent. However, such surveys were routinely relied upon by purchasers as well, and in fact purchasers actually paid the building society to have the survey done, although the surveyors' contract was always with the building society. The House of Lords held that in such situations surveyors assumed a duty of care to house purchasers; even though the surveys were not done for the purpose of advising home buyers, surveyors would be well aware that buyers were likely to rely on their valuation, and the surveyors only had the work in the first place because buyers were willing to pay their fees. An important factor was that this did not impose particularly wide liability: the extent of the surveyors' liability was limited to compensating the buyer of the house for up to the value of the house.

Reliance by the claimant

Reliance under **Hedley Byrne** requires that the claimant depended on the defendant using the particular skill or experience required for the task which the defendant had undertaken; it is not merely general reliance on the defendant exercising care.

The claimant must prove not only that they relied on the defendant, but that it was reasonable to do so, and the courts have held that this will not be the case where the claimant relies on information or advice for one purpose, when it was given for a different purpose. In **Caparo Industries plc** *v* **Dickman** (1990) (see p. 709 for full facts) Caparo relied on an auditor's report prepared by Dickman when deciding whether to invest in Fidelity. The House of Lords held that as auditors' reports were not prepared for the purpose of giving such guidance, Dickman were not liable.

Lord Bridge held that there was no special relationship between Caparo, as potential investors, and the auditors. He drew a distinction between situations where 'the defendant giving advice or information was fully aware of the nature of the transaction which the claimant had in contemplation' and those in which 'a statement is put into more or less general circulation and may foreseeably be relied upon by strangers to the maker of the statement, for any one of a variety of purposes which the maker of the statement has no specific reason to contemplate'.

This approach was followed in **Reeman** *v* **Department of Transport** (1997). Mr Reeman was the owner of a fishing boat that required an annual certificate of seaworthiness from the Department of Transport (DoT), without which it could not be used at sea. The boat was covered by such a certificate when Mr Reeman bought it, but it was later discovered that the surveyor who inspected it for the DoT had been negligent; the certificate should not have been issued and would not be renewed, making the boat practically worthless.

Mr Reeman sued for his economic loss, but the Court of Appeal held that, following **Caparo**, the provision of information for a particular purpose could not be taken as an assumption of responsibility for its use for a different purpose. The purpose of issuing the certificate was to promote safety, not to establish a boat's commercial value, even though the boat effectively had no commercial value without it. In addition, the class of person likely to rely on the statement had to be capable of ascertainment at the time the statement was made, and not merely capable of description; when the certificate was issued, there was no reason to identify Mr Reeman as someone who was likely to rely on it.

However, the courts are willing to look very closely at the circumstances in which advice was given, and there are cases where they have held that the fact that advice was given for one purpose does not mean it is unreasonable for the recipient to rely on it for another purpose at the same time. In **Law Society** *v* **KPMG Peat Marwick** (2000) the defendants were accountants to a firm of solicitors, and were asked by them to prepare the annual accounts which were required by the Law

Society. The accountants failed to uncover the fact that a senior partner in the firm was defrauding hundreds of clients. When the frauds eventually came to light, over 300 clients claimed compensation from a fund set up for this purpose by the Law Society, and the Law Society sued the accountants, claiming that the accounts had been prepared negligently. The accountants argued that their duty was only owed to the solicitors' firm; the Law Society held that the accountants owed a duty to them, by virtue of the Law Society's reliance on the information given in the accounts. The Court of Appeal analysed the situation using the three-step **Caparo** test. They held that if accountants' reports failed to highlight improprieties in the way a firm dealt with clients' money, it was clearly foreseeable that loss to the fund would result. There was sufficient proximity between the reporting accountant and the Law Society, and it was fair and reasonable to impose a duty. On this last point, the court made use of similar reasoning to that in **Smith** v **Eric S Bush**, pointing out that the imposition of a duty did not expose the accountants to unrestricted liability; the amount of compensation that could be claimed was restricted to the amount of clients' money that had been lost in the frauds, and the time within which it could be claimed was also limited, given that reports were delivered annually, so negligence in any one year could be uncovered by a non-negligent report the following year.

Recovery without reliance – the 'wills' cases

The 1980s and 1990s brought a crop of cases which have allowed compensation for economic loss caused by negligent advice or services, yet which do not sit quite comfortably within the principles of **Hedley Byrne**. In **Ross** v **Caunters** (1980), a solicitor had been negligent in preparing a client's will, with the result that it was in breach of probate law and the intended beneficiary was unable to receive her inheritance. She successfully sued the solicitor for the value of her loss. Although the loss was purely economic, and caused by an act rather than a statement, the case was not considered especially significant at the time, since it took place in the period after **Anns** v **Merton London Borough** (1978), when the wider approach to the issue of a duty of care was in place, and before **Murphy** v **Brentwood District Council** (1990) tightened up the requirements again. However, the significance comes from the fact that it was followed in the post-**Murphy** case of **White** v **Jones** (1995). Here, two daughters had had a quarrel with their father, and he cut them out of his will. The family was later reconciled, and the father instructed his solicitors to renew the £9,000 legacies to his daughters. A month later, he discovered that the solicitors had not yet done this, and reminded them of his instructions. Some time later, the father died, and it was found that the will had still not been changed, so the daughters could not receive their expected inheritance. They sued the solicitors, and the House of Lords allowed the claim, even though the loss was purely economic and the result of negligent work rather than a negligent misstatement.

White v **Jones** proved somewhat difficult to explain on **Hedley Byrne** principles. Wills are prepared in order to put into practice the wishes of the person making the will (the testator), and, as Lord Goff stated in **White** v **Jones**, in many cases, beneficiaries will not even be aware that they stand to gain, so it is hard to see how they can be said to rely on the solicitor's skill as required under **Hedley Byrne**.

Clearly the solicitors in both cases had assumed the responsibility for preparing the wills correctly for the testators, but could they also be said to have accepted a responsibility towards the beneficiaries? The House of Lords admitted that it was difficult to see how this could be argued, but, even so, they were prepared to allow a remedy.

What appears to have swayed them was the practical justice of the claimant's case: the solicitor had been negligent, yet the only party who would normally have a valid claim (the testator and his estate) had suffered no loss, and the party who had suffered loss had no claim. As Lord Goff pointed out, the result was 'a lacuna [loophole] in the law which needs to be filled'. The exact *ratio* of the case is difficult to discover, as the three judges were divided on how the assumption of responsibility problem was to be got over. Lords Browne-Wilkinson and Nolan argued that in taking on the job of preparing the will, the solicitor had voluntarily accepted responsibility for doing it properly, and it was for the law to decide the scope of that responsibility and in particular whether it included a duty to the claimants. Both held that it did. Lord Goff held that the solicitor had in fact assumed responsibility only to the testator, but that the law could and should deem that responsibility to extend to the intended beneficiaries.

However, even if the decision in **White v Jones** did no more than use practical justice to fill a loophole in the law, the case of **Carr-Glynn v Frearsons** (1998) extended it beyond this approach. Here a woman had made a will leaving the claimant her share in a property. The defendants, the solicitors who had drawn up the will, had advised her that there was a problem with the ownership of the property which could result in her share automatically passing to the other part-owners on her death, so that any bequest of it would be ineffective. They told her what to do to avoid the problem, but she died before taking the advice. The claimant therefore received nothing under the will, and the estate also suffered a loss since the share in the property passed to the co-owners.

The case was different from **Ross v Caunters** and **White v Jones**, where the estate had suffered no loss and the party who had suffered loss had no claim; here, allowing a duty of care to the disappointed beneficiaries might give rise to two claims for the same loss, one from the intended beneficiaries and one from the estate. However, the Court of Appeal held that although the estate had a claim, any damages it recovered by bringing that claim would not go to the claimant, who was therefore still left without a remedy unless the principle of **White v Jones** was extended to cover her. The court stated such an extension was reasonable; there was a duty of care, and it required that the solicitor should have taken action herself to ensure that the will would take effect as expected.

Limits of the 'wills' cases

Some limits to the extension of the wills cases have been laid down. In **Clarke v Bruce, Lance & Co** (1988), it was made clear that the duty of care to intended beneficiaries arises from the responsibility undertaken to the testator, and so cannot apply when the interests of the testator and the beneficiary differ. Here a solicitor had failed to advise his client that transactions he was planning to make would reduce the value of a legacy left in his will to the claimant. As a result, the claimant suffered some loss, but the case was held to fall outside the **Ross v**

Caunters principle; the interests of the claimant and the testator were not identical, and the solicitor's primary duty was to the interests of his client.

Further restrictions have been applied in **Worby v Rosser** (1999). Here the claimants were the wife and children of a Mr Worby. He had made a will in 1983, leaving most of his estate to them. Some time later, he fell under the influence of his accountant, a Mr Tuli, and made a new will which left a lot of money to Mr Tuli and reduced the amount left to the Worby family under the previous will. After Mr Worby died, the family were able to take action to prevent the second will being acted upon, on the ground that, essentially, Mr Worby had not really known what he was doing (this is known as lacking testamentary capacity and is part of the law on wills). However, the action proved quite expensive, and although the court in that action had awarded them costs, the Worbys were unable to actually get those costs paid by Mr Tuli. They therefore decided to sue Mr Rosser, the solicitor who had drawn up the second will, arguing that he owed them a duty of care to ensure that Mr Worby had testamentary capacity when he made the will, and that his breach of that duty had led to them incurring the legal costs.

The Court of Appeal rejected this argument. The aim of the courts in **White v Jones** had been to achieve practical justice for a category of beneficiaries who had no other remedy available to them. This was not the case for the claimants in Worby; they could sue the estate for their costs, and the estate could in turn sue the solicitor if it could be proved that he was negligent.

How far do the 'wills' cases go?

In the years since **White v Jones**, there has been great debate about how far the principles laid down in that case will go. It was no surprise to see them extended to will-making services offered by practitioners other than solicitors in **Esterhuizen v Allied Dunbar Assurance plc** (1998), but could they apply to agreements other than wills? The case of **Gorham v British Telecommunications plc** (2000) would seem to suggest that they can. The case involved a pension plan taken out by a Mr Gorham, on the advice of an insurance company. They told him he would be better off opting out of his employer's pension scheme and taking out his own pension instead; this was untrue. One of the advantages of the employer's scheme was the insurance benefits that would be paid to Mr Gorham's family if he died while working for the company. These were lost when he switched pensions, so when he did die, still an employee of the firm, his widow sued. The Court of Appeal found that the position of intended beneficiaries of an insurance policy was comparable to that of the intended beneficiaries to a will, and that the adviser had therefore undertaken a responsibility to the family, as well as to Mr Gorham himself.

Negligent misstatement and contract

Because contract was traditionally seen as the method for resolving disputes involving pure economic loss, it was originally thought that where two parties had made a contract, a negligence action could not be used to fill in any gaps in that contract. However, in **Henderson v Merrett Syndicates Ltd** (1995), it was established that the existence of a contract between the parties did not prevent a **Hedley**

Byrne special relationship arising. The case arose when the Lloyd's insurance organisation made considerable losses on many of its policies. The losses had to be borne by people who had invested in Lloyd's by underwriting the policies. Known as Lloyd's names, these people were grouped into syndicates and invested on the understanding that they were assuming unlimited liability; if big losses were made, the names could lose everything they had. They were willing to take on this liability because becoming a name was seen as a sure way of making money for those who were wealthy enough to be able to invest, and in previous years it had proved to be exactly that.

However, in the early 1990s, a series of natural and man-made disasters led to unusually big claims, and the names were called upon to pay; many were ruined financially as a result. They alleged that the agents who organised the syndicates had been negligent; many of the names had entered into contracts with these managers, but by the time the actions were brought, the three-year limitation period for a breach of contract action had expired. Could they then take advantage of the longer (six-year) limitation period for tort actions? The House of Lords held that they could; the syndicate managers had assumed responsibility for the names' economic welfare, and the existence of a contract could only prevent liability in tort if such liability would contradict the terms of the contract. Lord Goff explained:

> liability can, and in my opinion should, be founded squarely on the principle established in **Hedley Byrne** itself, from which it follows that an assumption of responsibility coupled with the concomitant reliance may give rise to a tortious duty of care irrespective of whether there is a contractual relationship between the parties, and in consequence, unless his contract precludes him from doing so, the plaintiff, who has available to him concurrent remedies in contract and tort, may choose that remedy which appears to him most advantageous.

Negligent misstatements often take place in a pre-contractual situation, where one party is trying to persuade the other to enter a contract. **Hedley Byrne** can apply in such situations, but in practice it has been made less important in this area by the Misrepresentation Act 1967, which imposes its own liability for false statements made during contractual negotiations.

Another case which, it has been suggested, reveals an expansion of liability for economic loss is **Spring *v* Guardian Assurance** (1994). The claimant, Mr Spring, had been employed by the defendant, but was sacked. When seeking a new job, he needed a reference, but the one supplied by the defendant said that Mr Spring was incompetent and dishonest. Not surprisingly, he failed to get the new job. He sued the defendant for negligence, claiming the economic loss caused by not getting the job. The trial judge found that Mr Spring was not dishonest, and that while the defendant had genuinely believed that what he had written was true, he had been negligent in the way he reached that conclusion. The House of Lords agreed that a duty of care existed, and the defendant had breached it.

Two key factors make **Spring** different from the usual **Hedley Byrne** case. First, the information which caused the loss was not given *to* the person who relied on it, as it was in **Hedley**, but was *about* him. Secondly, it is hard to see how there can be a truly voluntary assumption of responsibility where someone is asked to give an employment reference, because this is one situation where the three options outlined by Lord Reid in **Hedley** do not apply. Someone who refuses to give a reference is, effectively, giving a bad one, because the prospective new employer will assume there must be something to hide; equally, saying that the reference should not be relied on is likely to set alarm bells ringing. An ex-employer asked for a reference is therefore forced to assume responsibility, whichever option he or she chooses. A third issue is that claims involving damage to reputation would usually be considered to fall within the tort of defamation, which has its own rules; it was argued in the case that allowing a claim in negligence would subvert these rules. What swayed the House of Lords to allow the claim, however, seems to be very much, as in the wills cases, the practical justice of the situation.

Problems with the law on economic loss

Too many restrictions – or too few?

The case of **Spartan Steel** *v* **Martin** (1972) illustrates that the distinction between pure economic loss and other kinds of loss can be a very fine one – and one that in commonsense terms is difficult to justify. The defendants' negligence caused all three of the types of loss that resulted from the power cut, and all three types of loss were easily foreseeable, so why should they have been liable to compensate two sorts of loss but not the third? To the non-legal eye, distinguishing between them seems completely illogical – as indeed it must to a claimant who is left with a loss caused by someone else, and has no redress unless they have a contract. In many cases this can be seen as allowing a defendant to get away with seriously careless behaviour, regardless of the loss caused to others.

On the other hand, it can be argued that rather than not allowing sufficient redress for pure economic loss, the tort system in fact allows too much. In most cases of pure economic loss, what we are really talking about is not loss, but failure to make a gain. This is obvious in the wills cases, for example, but also applies to cases such as **Smith** *v* **Eric S Bush** (1990), where it can be argued that in buying the house the claimants were simply entering into a market transaction, and these always run the risk of creating loss as well as the possibility of making a gain. They did not have money taken from them, they simply bought a house which was worth less than they thought.

Traditionally, the role of tort law is to compensate those who have actually suffered loss; it can be argued that those who wish to protect their expectation of gain should do so through contract, and those who have given nothing in return for a service should not be compensated when that service lets them down financially. One answer to the latter view is that in most of the cases where claimants have not given anything in return for provision of advice or services, the defendants nevertheless gain a commercial benefit from the situation. This is most clear in **Smith** *v* **Eric Bush**, where the surveyors only had the work in the first place because house buyers were willing to pay for it, albeit indirectly, but it can also be found in less obvious situations. In **Hedley Byrne**, Lord Goff pointed out that in establishing whether the necessary special relationship existed in a particular case:

> [i]t may often be a material factor to consider whether the adviser is acting purely out of good nature or whether he is getting his reward in some indirect form. The service that a bank performs in giving a reference is not done simply

out of a desire to assist commerce. It would discourage the customers of the bank if their deals fell through because the bank had refused to testify to their credit when it was good.

Overlap with contract law

The issue of the relationship between contract and tort causes particular problems, and in particular, the assertion in **Henderson** that a claimant who has a contractual remedy as well as a possible action in negligence should be able to choose between them. As well as rendering the limitation period for contractual actions essentially meaningless in these situations, it allows the claimant to pick and choose in other ways. For example, in contract a loss will only be compensated if there was a very high degree of probability that it would result from the defendant's breach of contract; is it necessarily right that a claimant who cannot satisfy that requirement should get another bite of the cherry in tort, where liability can be allowed for even extremely unlikely losses if they were reasonably foreseeable?

Lack of clarity

Perhaps the most significant practical problem in this area is that in their anxiety to avoid opening the floodgates to massive liability, yet allow redress where justice seems to demand it, the courts have resorted to over-complex and not entirely logical arguments. The wills cases are an obvious example of this, and the result is uncertainty about their scope, and the possibility of further fragmentation in the way the law treats economic loss.

The same dilemma lies behind the curious situation that, as we said earlier, architects or surveyors who give negligent advice that leads to a defective building can be sued for the resulting economic loss, yet builders who construct defective buildings cannot. In practice, however, this particular situation has been addressed by introduction of legislation: the Defective Premises Act 1972 states that builders and others who take on work 'for or in connection with the provision of a dwelling-house' may be held liable to the owners of those dwellings if they fail to carry out the work properly, and the house becomes unfit for habitation. This contrasts with other Commonwealth jurisdictions, where the common law has allowed recovery in tort for defective buildings, most recently confirmed in New Zealand in **Invercargill City Council** *v* **Hamlin** (1996).

Duties of care: psychiatric injury or 'nervous shock'

It is well established that physical injury can give rise to a claim in tort, but what about psychiatric damage? The concept of a duty has been used to limit compensation claims for psychiatric damage (often called nervous shock), in the same way as it has been used to limit claims for economic loss. In the past, where there was no physical harm the courts were slow to accept claims for mental, rather than physical, injury caused by negligence. Such claims are now recognised but are subject to a number of restrictions.

What is 'nervous shock'?

Psychiatric injury has traditionally been known by the courts as 'nervous shock', a label which adds to the confusion surrounding this area of the law by being completely misleading. The term implies that claimants can seek damages because they are shocked at the result of a defendant's negligence, or perhaps upset, frightened, worried or grief-stricken. This is not the case. In order to claim for so-called 'nervous shock', a claimant must prove that they have suffered from a genuine illness or injury. In some cases, the injury or illness may actually be a physical one, brought on by a mental shock: cases include a woman who had a miscarriage as a result of witnessing the aftermath of a terrible road accident (**Bourhill v Young** (1943), though the woman's claim failed on other grounds), and a man who was involved in an accident but not physically injured in it, who later suffered a recurrence and worsening of the disease myalgic encephalomyelitis (ME), also known as chronic fatigue syndrome, as a result of the shock (**Page v Smith** (1995)).

If the shock has not caused a physical injury or illness, the claimant must prove that it has caused what Lord Bridge in **McLoughlin v O'Brian** (1983) (see below) described as 'a positive psychiatric illness'. Examples include clinical depression, personality changes, and post-traumatic stress disorder, an illness in which a shocking event causes symptoms including difficulty sleeping, tension, horrifying flashbacks and severe depression. It is important to be clear that this category does not include people who are simply upset by a shock, regardless of how badly; they must have a recognised psychiatric illness, and medical evidence will be needed to prove this. Consequently we will use the term psychiatric injury from now on, though 'nervous shock' is referred to in many judgments.

Claimants who can prove such injury can only claim in negligence if they can establish that they are owed a duty of care by the defendant, with regard to psychiatric injury (and of course that the defendant's negligence actually caused the injury). This will depend on their relationship to the event which caused the shock, and case law has developed different sets of rules, covering different categories of claimant. The number of categories has varied at different stages of the law's development, but since the most recent House of Lords case, **White and others v Chief Constable of South Yorkshire** (1998), there are now three:

- those who are physically injured in the event which the defendant has caused, as well as psychiatrically injured as a result of it;
- those who are put in danger of physical harm, but actually suffer only psychiatric injury. Victims who fall into this, or the previous category, are termed primary victims;
- those who are not put in danger of physical injury to themselves, but suffer psychiatric injury as a result of witnessing such injury to others; these are called secondary victims. A duty of care to secondary victims will arise only if they can satisfy very restrictive requirements.

Primary victims

An accident victim who suffers physical injury due to the negligence of another can recover damages not just for the physical injuries but also for any psychiatric injury as well. The ordinary rules of negligence apply to such cases. The category of primary victims also includes those who are put at risk of physical injury to themselves, but who actually suffer psychiatric injury as a result of the dangerous event. **White and others** (1998) confirms that if a person negligently exposes another to a risk of injury, they will be liable for any psychological injury that this may cause the other person, even if the threatened physical injury does not in fact happen.

This was originally established by the leading case of **Dulieu *v* White & Sons** (1901). The claimant was serving in a pub when one of the defendant's employees negligently drove his van and horses into the premises. The claimant feared for her safety, and although she was not actually struck she was badly frightened and suffered a miscarriage as a result. The defendant was found liable even though there was no physical impact, as he could have foreseen that the claimant would have suffered such shock.

The leading modern case on primary victims who are exposed to the risk of injury, but not actually physically hurt, is **Page *v* Smith** (1995). The claimant was involved in an accident which could have caused physical injury, but fortunately he escaped unhurt. Some years earlier, he had suffered from a serious illness called myalgic encephalomyelitis. He had had this illness for several years, but before the accident happened, it had gone into remission. After the accident, his old symptoms began to recur, and he claimed that this had been caused by the shock of being involved in the accident.

The House of Lords held that where it was reasonably foreseeable that a defendant's behaviour would expose the claimant to a risk of physical injury, there was a duty of care with regard to any injury that the claimant suffered, including psychiatric injury. It was not necessary that pyschiatric injury itself was foreseeable.

This approach was followed in **Simmons *v* British Steel plc** (2004). The claimant had been physically injured in a workplace accident, and as a result of his shock and anger at what had happened to him, he developed a severe skin condition. This led to him having to take a lot of time off work, and as a result of that, he developed a depressive illness. The House of Lords held that the employers were liable for the skin condition and the depressive illness, as well as the original injury. They had exposed him to a foreseeable risk of physical injury, and they were therefore liable for all the injuries that resulted from that risk. It did not matter that the actual type of the injuries was not foreseeable, nor that a victim who was more psychologically robust might not have been affected in this way (this refers to the rule that a defendant must take their victim as they find them).

Although a claimant can claim for psychiatric injury caused by fears for their own safety even though no physical injury actually occurred, there must be some basis for the fears. In **McFarlane *v* Wilkinson** (1997), the Court of Appeal held that the fear must be reasonable, given the nature of the risk and the claimant's situation. The case arose out of the terrible events on the *Piper Alpha* oil rig, when the rig caught fire and many people died as a result of the explosion. The claimant had been in a support boat about 50 yards from the rig and witnessed the disaster. His claim for the psychiatric injury suffered as a result was rejected by the Court of Appeal, on the ground that the boat he was on was clearly never in any danger, and so his fear for his safety was unreasonable (for reasons which will be obvious when we look at the witness cases below, merely seeing the disaster would not have been sufficient ground for this claimant's claim).

What is unclear is whether a claimant can be considered as a primary victim if they were not actually in physical danger, but had reasonable grounds for thinking that they might be. The two leading judgments in **White** differ slightly in this area: Lord Steyn says the claimant must have 'objectively exposed himself to danger or *reasonably believed* that he was doing so' (our italics); on the other hand Lord Hoffmann refers only to primary victims being 'within the range of foreseeable physical injury'. Of course, in the majority of cases the reasonable belief that the claimant was in danger will arise from the fact that they actually were, but in the throes of an emergency situation, it is not difficult to imagine making out a case for believing oneself to be in some danger when in fact there is no physical risk at all, and it is a pity that their Lordships did not make themselves clearer on this crucial point.

In **CJD Group B Claimants** *v* **The Medical Research Council** (1998), it was suggested that there might be a group which could not be considered primary victims in the usual sense, but who nevertheless should be treated in the same way. The claimants in the case had all had growth problems as children, and they had been treated with injections of growth hormone which, it was later discovered, may have been contaminated with the virus which causes Creutzfeldt–Jakob Disease (CJD), a fatal brain condition (this is the brain condition recognised as the human form of BSE or mad cow disease, but the events in this case have no link with the controversy over BSE-infected beef). It was established that those who had received the contaminated injections were at risk of developing CJD, but it was not possible to discover which batches had been contaminated, nor to test the recipients to discover whether a particular individual was harbouring the virus. As a result, the claimants were having to live with the fear of knowing that they might develop the disease, and some of them suffered psychiatric injury as a result of this.

It was established that the defendants had been negligent in allowing the injections to continue after the risk of contamination was suspected, and the claimants claimed that they were owed a duty as primary victims with regard to psychiatric injury, as the injections they were negligently given made them more than mere bystanders, and could be compared to the car accident in which the claimant in **Page** *v* **Smith** was involved. Morland J disagreed with this analysis, holding that they were not primary victims in the normal sense, because the psychiatric injury was not actually triggered by the physical act of the injections, but by the knowledge, which came later, that they might be at risk of developing CJD. Even so, he allowed their claim, on the basis that there was a relationship of proximity between the parties, that the psychiatric injuries were reasonably foreseeable, and there was no public policy reason to exclude them from compensation.

However, this approach was not followed in the key case of **Rothwell** *v* **Chemical and Insulating Co Ltd** (2007). The claimants in the case were a group of workers who had been negligently exposed to asbestos while working for the defendants. If asbestos gets into the lungs, it can cause one of a range of fatal diseases. At the time the case was brought, none of the defendants had any of these diseases, but they did have what are known as pleural plaques. These are a form of scarring on the lungs, which show that asbestos has been inhaled. The plaques do not cause any symptoms, or make it more likely that the person will get one of the asbestos-related illnesses, but because they are evidence that asbestos has entered the person's lungs, having them is a sign that that person may be at risk of asbestos-related illness. This naturally caused great anxiety among the claimants, but, as we have seen, this is not enough to make a claim for psychiatric injury. However, one of the claimants had gone on to develop clinical depression, which is a recognised psychiatric illness, as a result of the worry, and so the House of Lords had to consider whether the defendants owed him a duty of care with regard to psychiatric illness. They held that there was no duty of care in this case, stating that the question should be decided on the usual principles applicable to psychiatric illness caused at work. On this basis, the defendants could not reasonably have been expected to foresee that the claimant would suffer a psychiatric illness as a result of exposure to asbestos, so there was no duty of care and his claim failed.

Secondary victims

key case

A claimant who suffers psychiatric injury but is not physically injured or at risk of physical injury is a secondary claimant who must pass the tests set down in **Alcock**. This category includes rescuers and employees of the defendant.

White and others (1998) establishes that sufferers of psychiatric injury who are not either physically injured or in danger of being physically injured are to be considered secondary victims. Among the important cases which have fallen within this group are claims made by:

- people who have suffered psychiatric injury as a result of witnessing the death or injury of friends, relatives or work colleagues;
- those whose psychiatric injury has been caused by them unwittingly bringing about death or injury to others, where the ultimate cause was someone else's negligence;
- those who have suffered psychiatric injury as a result of acting as rescuers, both those who have voluntarily given assistance to others in danger, and those who have done so as a result of their jobs, such as police officers.

Until **White**, each of these groups had been subject to different treatment, but **White** establishes that they are all to be subject to the same rules, namely those developed in two key cases, **McLoughlin v O'Brian** (1982) and **Alcock v Chief Constable of Yorkshire** (1992). These cases established that secondary victims could only claim for psychiatric injury in very limited circumstances, and **White** confirms these limitations.

In **McLoughlin v O'Brian**, the claimant's husband and children were involved in a serious car accident, caused by the defendant's negligence. One of her daughters was killed and her husband and two other children badly injured. The claimant was not with her family when the accident happened, but was told about it immediately afterwards, and rushed to the hospital. There she saw the surviving members of her family covered in dirt and oil, and her badly injured son screaming in fear and pain. She suffered psychiatric injury as a result, including clinical depression and personality changes.

The House of Lords allowed her claim, even though up until then only witnesses who were actually present at the scene of a shocking incident had been allowed to recover for psychiatric injury. The decision itself was rather confused, in that Lord Bridge suggested that the sole criterion was still reasonable foresight, and the claimant could recover because her psychiatric injury was reasonably foreseeable, but Lords Wilberforce and Edmund-Davies favoured a different approach. They suggested that while psychiatric injury did have to be reasonably foreseeable, this in itself was not enough to create a duty of care towards secondary victims. Unlike other types of claimant, secondary victims would have to satisfy a series of other requirements, concerning their relationship to the primary victims of the shocking incident and their position with regard to that incident. This second approach is the one which has since found favour with the courts, and it was explained in detail in **Alcock** *v* **Chief Constable of South Yorkshire** (1992).

key case

Claimants who suffer psychiatric injury as a result of witnessing a shocking incident, but are not physically injured or at risk of physical injury, are owed a duty of care only if their psychiatric injury is caused by a sudden shock; they have a sufficiently close emotional tie to the primary victims; and they were sufficiently close in space and time to the shocking incident.

Alcock *v* **Chief Constable of Yorkshire** (1992) arose from the Hillsborough football stadium disaster in 1989. The events which gave rise to the case (and to **White and others** *v* **Chief Constable of South Yorkshire** (1998)) took place during the 1989 FA Cup Semi-Final match between Liverpool and Nottingham Forest. All tickets for the match had been sold, and it was being shown on live television. However, play had to be stopped after six minutes because so many spectators had been allowed onto the terraces that some were being crushed against the high fences that divided the terraces from the pitch. A total of 95 people died in the tragedy that followed, and another 400 needed hospital treatment for their injuries.

The South Yorkshire police were responsible for policing the ground, and it was widely thought that the incident was caused by a negligent decision on their part, which allowed too many people into the ground. Claims for physical injury and death were settled by the police, as were others for psychiatric injury which clearly fell within the accepted categories of those who could make a claim for this type of damage. This left two further groups who claimed psychiatric injury as a result of the tragedy: relatives and friends of those injured or killed, whose claims were examined in **Alcock**; and police officers on duty for the events of that day, who were represented in **White** (the fate of their claim is discussed later).

Alcock was a test case in that the specific claimants were chosen because between them they represented a range of relationships to the dead and injured, and positions in relation to the incident at the ground, which were held by around 150 other people who claimed to have suffered psychiatric injury as a result of the tragedy. They included parents, grandparents, brothers, brothers-in-law, fiancées and friends of the dead and injured, who had either been at the stadium when the disaster occurred and witnessed it at first hand, seen it live on the television, gone to the stadium to look for someone they knew, been told the news by a third party, or had to identify someone in the temporary mortuary at the ground.

The claimants argued that the test for whether they were owed a duty of care was simply whether their psychiatric injuries were reasonably foreseeable, as Lord Bridge had suggested in **McLoughlin**. The House of Lords took a different view, pointing out that while it was clear that deaths and injuries in traumatic accidents commonly caused suffering that went well beyond the immediate victims, it was generally the policy of the common law not to compensate third parties. They held that although some exceptions could be made, they should be subject to much stricter requirements than those which applied to primary victims.

The starting point, they said, was that a secondary victim must prove that psychiatric injury to secondary victims was a reasonably foreseeable consequence of the defendant's negligence. **White** confirms earlier cases in stating that this will only be established where a bystander of reasonable fortitude would be likely to suffer psychiatric injury; if the claimant only suffers psychiatric injury because they are unusually susceptible to shock, reasonable foreseeability is not proved. However, it was pointed out that this rule should not be confused with the 'eggshell skull' situation seen, for example, in **Page** v **Smith**, where as a result of psychiatric injury the damage is more serious than might be expected. So long as a bystander of normal fortitude would be likely to suffer

psychiatric injury, it does not matter that that psychiatric injury is made more serious by some characteristic personal to the claimant; but if the psychiatric injury would not have occurred at all to someone without the claimant's particular susceptibility, there is no claim.

Once reasonable foreseeability is established, there are three further tests which the courts must consider:

- the nature and cause of the psychiatric injury;
- the class of person into which the claimant falls, in terms of their relationship to the primary victim(s);
- the claimant's proximity to the shocking incident, in terms of both time and place.

The strength of restrictions which these tests place on claims can be seen in the fact that every single claimant in **Alcock** failed on at least one of them. Below we look at each in turn.

One further limitation on the duty of care in cases of psychiatric shock was added in **Greatorex** v **Greatorex** (2000), where it was held that a primary victim cannot owe a duty to secondary victims. The claimant in the case was a fire officer, who was called to a road accident, only to discover that his son was the driver, and had been seriously injured. He suffered post-traumatic stress disorder as a result, and brought a case against the son, whose negligence had caused the action (in practice he was suing not his son, but the Motor Insurance Bureau, who compensate victims of uninsured drivers; had the son been insured, the defendant would have been his insurance company). The unusual circumstances of the case meant that the father did fall within the **Alcock** requirements for a secondary victim, but the claim was dismissed on the ground that imposing a duty on people to take care of themselves so as not to shock others would impinge on the right of self-determination.

The nature and cause of the psychiatric injury

Like primary victims, secondary victims must prove that their psychiatric damage amounts to a recognised psychiatric illness. They are also subject to an additional requirement, that the psychiatric damage must have been caused by the claimant suffering a sudden and unexpected shock caused by a 'horrifying event'. This excludes, for example, cases in which people suffer psychiatric illness as a result of the grief of bereavement, or the stress and demands of having to look after a disabled relative injured by the negligence of another. In **Sion** v **Hampstead Health Authority** (1994), the claimant had developed a stress-related psychiatric illness as a result of watching his son slowly die in intensive care as a result of negligent medical treatment. It was held that as the father's psychiatric illness had not been caused by a sudden shock, he could not recover damages for it.

A contrasting case is **North Glamorgan NHS Trust** v **Walters** (2002). Here the claimant was the mother of a baby boy, who died after receiving negligent treatment for which the defendants were responsible. The little boy, Elliott, was ill in hospital. Unknown to his mother at the time, the hospital had misdiagnosed his illness. She woke up to find him choking and coughing blood, and was told by the doctors that he was having a fit, but that he was very unlikely to have suffered any serious damage. Later that day, he was transferred to another hospital, where she was told – correctly – that he had in fact suffered severe brain damage and was in a coma; she was asked to consider switching off his life support machine. She and her busband agreed to this on the following day.

The events caused her to suffer a psychiatric illness, but the hospital argued that they were not liable for this as it was not caused by a sudden shock, but by a sequence of events that took place over 36 hours. The Court of Appeal disagreed: it said that the 'horrifying event' referred to in **Alcock** could be made up of a series of events, in this case, witnessing the fit, hearing the news that her son was brain-damaged after being told that he was not, and then watching him die. Each had their own immediate impact, and could be distinguished from cases where psychiatric injury was caused by a gradual realisation that a child was dying.

The courts have held that shock can be the result, not just of injury or death to a loved one but also of damage to property. In **Attia** v **British Gas** (1988), British Gas were installing central heating into the claimant's house. She had spent many years decorating and improving her home and she was very attached to it. When she returned home in the afternoon she found her house on fire. It took the fire brigade four hours to get the blaze under control, by which time her house was seriously damaged. The fire was caused by the negligence of the defendants' employees. British Gas accepted their liability for the damage to the house but the claimant also sought damages for the nervous shock she had suffered as a result. The Court of Appeal accepted that she could make a claim for nervous shock resulting from the incident.

In many cases, causation will be difficult to prove, since in addition to the required shock, claimants will have experienced the grief of bereavement, which could equally well have caused their psychiatric injury. In **Vernon** v **Bosley (No 1)** (1996), it was made clear that so long as a sudden shock is at least partly responsible for the claimant's psychiatric injury, the fact that grief has also played a part in causing it will not prevent a claim. In that case, the claimant had witnessed his children drowning in a car that was negligently driven by their nanny. The Court of Appeal accepted that his psychiatric illness might have been partly caused by his grief at losing his children, but, since the shock of witnessing the accident had also played a part, it was not necessary to make minute enquiries into how much of his illness was attributable to each cause, if indeed it was even possible to find out.

The class of person

If a secondary victim can prove that, as a result of the defendant's negligence, they have suffered a recognisable psychiatric injury because of a sudden shock, the next hurdle they face is to prove that they fall within a class of people which the law allows to claim compensation for such injuries. The key cases have focused on four possible classes of people:

- relatives and friends of those killed or injured as a result of the defendant's negligence;
- rescuers at the scene of accidents;
- employees of the party causing the accident;
- 'unwitting agents' – people who cause death or injury to others, not through their own fault but as a result of someone else's negligence.

Relatives and friends

Alcock makes it clear that relatives are the people most likely to succeed in an action for psychiatric damage as a secondary victim. But there is no set list of relationships; whether or not a claim succeeds will depend on the facts of each particular case. In **McLoughlin** *v* **O'Brian** Lord Wilberforce said:

> As regards the class of persons, the possible range is between the closest of family ties – of parent and child, or husband and wife – and the ordinary bystander. Existing law recognizes the claims of the first; it denies that of the second, either on the basis that such persons must be assumed to be possessed of fortitude sufficient to enable them to endure the calamities of modern life, or that defendants cannot be expected to compensate the world at large . . . other cases involving less close relationships must be very carefully scrutinized. I cannot say that they should never be admitted. The closer the tie (not merely in relationship, but in care) the greater the claim for consideration. The claim, in any case, has to be judged in the light of the other factors, such as proximity to the scene in time and place, and the nature of the accident.

On the same subject, Lord Keith said in **Alcock**:

> As regards the class of persons to whom a duty may be owed . . . I think it sufficient that reasonable foreseeability should be the guide. I would not seek to limit the class by reference to particular relationships such as husband and wife or parent and child.

He said that friends and engaged couples could potentially be included, for, '[i]t is common knowledge that such ties exist, and reasonably foreseeable that those bound by them may in certain circumstances be at real risk of psychiatric illness if the loved one is injured or put in peril.'

Despite these liberal-sounding statements, on the actual facts of the case, brothers, brothers-in-law, grandparents, uncles and friends were all found not to have a sufficiently close relationship with the deceased or injured person to succeed in their action. This is partly because the House of Lords emphasised that a claimant would not only have to prove that the *type* of relationship was one that would generally be assumed to be close, such as brother and sister, but also that the relationship was *as a matter of fact* close: there also needed to be a close relationship in terms of love and affection. This point had merely been made in passing by Lord Wilberforce in **McLoughlin** *v* **O'Brian** when he said that ties had to be close 'not merely in relationship, but in care'.

The result in **Alcock** was that a claimant who was present at the stadium at the time of the disaster at which his brother was killed failed in his action because he had not supplied evidence to prove that he was as a matter of fact close to his brother. Lord Keith said that the closeness of the tie could be presumed in 'appropriate cases', giving as examples the relationship between parent and child and that between an engaged couple. But if the relationship of a brother is not an appropriate case it is difficult to imagine many other examples.

Rescuers

Until **White**, it had been assumed that rescuers, meaning people who suffered psychiatric injury as a result of helping the primary victims of a shocking incident, were a special case, on the ground of public policy – the theory being that such selfless behaviour should be encouraged and supported, and therefore not subjected to rules stricter than those of ordinary personal injury. This was generally viewed as the position taken in the classic rescuer case of **Chadwick v British Railways Board** (1967), where the claimant spent 12 hours helping victims of a terrible train disaster which occurred near his home, and in which over 90 people were killed. He successfully claimed for psychiatric injury which occurred as a result of the experience.

White, as stated earlier, arose from the Hillsborough disaster, and here the claimants were police officers who had been on duty at the ground on the day of the tragedy. Like **Alcock**, **White** was originally a test case in that the four claimants had performed different roles which between them represented the experiences of a number of other officers. Three of them had actually been at the scene of the crushing incident: PC Bevis had spent time attempting to resuscitate fans, who were in fact already dead, close to the fences; Inspector White had passed dead and injured fans from the fenced-in areas; as had PC Bairstow, who had also helped in giving a victim heart massage. The fourth officer, PC Glave, had moved bodies into a temporary morgue set up at the opposite end of the ground from the incident, and obtained first aid for some of the injured.

The claimants claimed on two alternative grounds: first, that the police force owed them a duty of care as employees, and this covered the psychiatric injuries they had suffered (this claim is discussed at p. 739); or secondly, that they were owed a duty of care as rescuers. They argued that either of these situations meant they were not secondary victims at all, and therefore not subject to the **Alcock** restrictions. The House of Lords rejected both arguments. It stated that only those who were in danger of physical injury (or, according to Lord Steyn, reasonably believed themselves to be so) could be viewed as primary victims; everyone else was a secondary victim. Rescuers were not to be considered as a special category of secondary victim either, but had to be subject to the normal rules on secondary victims, as stated in **Alcock**. This meant that none of the officers could have a claim on the basis of being rescuers, since they had no pre-existing close relationships with the primary victims.

In looking at the question of whether the officers could recover as rescuers, the House of Lords could easily have limited itself to considering whether professional rescuers should be treated in the same way as those who volunteer their help. It would have been easy to keep the special treatment of voluntary rescuers, yet deny the officers' claim on the grounds that the public policy reasons did not apply to them, since there should be no need to encourage them to act in ways that were already required by their jobs. However, the House chose to go further than this and consider the whole area of rescuers who suffer psychiatric shock. It stated that even voluntary rescuers were not, and should not be, a special category. Where acting as rescuer put a claimant in danger of physical injury, they could claim as a primary victim, but where no risk of physical injury was caused to the rescuer, they would be a secondary victim, and therefore subject to all the restrictions in **Alcock**.

Two main reasons were given by Lord Hoffmann for the ruling. First, that allowing rescuers to be a special case would sooner or later lead to difficult distinctions: once rescuers includes those who help without putting themselves in any physical danger, the line between rescuers and bystanders may become difficult to draw. How much help would someone have to give to be considered a rescuer? Lord Hoffmann's second reason was that allowing the claims of professional rescuers would appear unjust, given that the police officers' conditions of service provided for them to be compensated in other ways for the psychiatric injury they had suffered, while, on the other hand, the bereaved relatives in **Alcock** had been given nothing. While it is difficult to argue with the justice of this point, Lord Hoffmann's reasoning does not explain why volunteer rescuers should be treated in the same way as professional ones. Interestingly, Lord Hoffmann claimed that this was not a change in the law, stating that existing rescuer cases were merely examples of the standard rules on recovery for psychiatric shock, because the claimants in those cases were all at risk of physical injury to themselves and therefore primary victims. In the leading case of **Chadwick**, at least, this is debatable: while a theoretical risk of a wrecked train carriage collapsing on the claimant was mentioned in that case, it is by no stretch of the imagination a keystone of the judgment.

This reasoning makes the impact of the judgment less clear than it seems at first sight. If Mr Chadwick can be considered a primary victim on the facts of his case, it may be that what the decision actually does is to allow the courts to take a wide view of whether voluntary rescuers were subject to physical danger, and use that reasoning to allow or deny a claim, rather than explicitly mentioning public policy.

Employees

The second argument made by the police officers in **White** was that they were owed a duty of care as employees of the party whose negligence caused the shocking event. It is well established that employers owe a duty of care towards employees, which obliges them to take reasonable care to ensure that employees are safe at work, and, although police officers are not actually employed by their Chief Constable, the court accepted that, for the purposes of their argument, the relationship was sufficiently similar to the employer–employee relationship. The claimants in **White** argued that this meant they could not be considered secondary victims, and were not subject to the **Alcock** restrictions. This argument was rejected by the House of Lords.

The House stated that the employers' duty to employees was not a separate tort with its own rules, but an aspect of the law of negligence, and therefore subject to the normal rules of negligence. This meant that where a type of injury was subject to special restrictions on when a duty of care would exist, these rules applied where the injury was caused by an employer to an employee, just as they would normally. So, for example, just as there was no general duty not to cause economic loss to others, there was no duty for an employer not to cause economic loss to employees, by, for example, reducing opportunities to earn bonuses. In the same way, there was no special duty of care regarding psychiatric damage caused by employers to employees, just the normal rules.

An attempt to widen employers' liability for psychiatric injury caused by a shocking event was firmly rejected by the House of Lords in **French and others** *v* **Chief Constable of Sussex Police** (2005). The claimants were all police officers who had been involved in events leading up to a raid on a suspect's premises. The raid went wrong, and the suspect was fatally shot by one of the defendants' colleagues. None of the defendants were present at the time, but, after the shooting, four of the five faced criminal charges concerning their part in the raid. They were acquitted, but then internal disciplinary procedures were brought against them. These too were either dropped or dismissed, but the whole process lasted around five years, and the men alleged that, as a result of the stress it put them under, they had all suffered psychiatric injury. Their case was that the police force had failed to provide adequate training, and this failure had led to the shooting, and the subsequent consequences for the defendants. They held that the psychiatric injuries they had all suffered were a foreseeable consequence of the failure to provide proper training.

The House of Lords rejected this argument. The claimants were clearly not primary victims, and, since they had not witnessed the shooting, they were not even secondary victims, and had no sustainable claim in law. In addition, if the foreseeability argument were to succeed, it would mean that the Chief Constable should have foreseen that if the police force failed to offer adequate training, an event such as the shooting would occur, and criminal and/or disciplinary proceedings would be brought against the officers involved, and the stress of that process would cause psychiatric injury. The House of Lords held that this chain of events was not a foreseeable result of the original failure to provide training.

Employees are therefore only able to claim for psychiatric injury caused by a shocking event where they can satisfy the rules on claims by secondary victims, or where they can be considered primary victims. An example of the latter type of case is **Cullin** *v* **London Fire and Civil Defence Authority** (1999), where the claimant was a firefighter who suffered psychiatric injury after an incident in which two colleagues became trapped inside a burning building. The claimant was among those who went into the building to attempt a rescue which proved impossible; he later witnessed their bodies being carried out. The fire authority applied to have his action struck out on the ground that the situation was similar to those of the police officers in **White**, in that the claimant was a professional rescuer and the risk of psychiatric injury he had been exposed to was a normal part of his job. The court disagreed, and said that this approach was too narrow. Relying on remarks made *obiter* by Lord Goff in **White**, they said that a professional rescuer who could establish that they were exposed to danger and the risk of physical injury, or reasonably believed that they were, even if only in the aftermath of the event, could qualify as a primary victim. In this case it was at least arguable that the firefighter had been a primary victim and so the action could not be struck out.

There is also a category of cases in which employees sue for psychiatric injury caused not by accidents but by stress at work.

Unwitting agents

There remains one category of claimant whose position is left unclear in **White**, namely those who witness a shocking accident caused by someone else's negligence and, while they are in no physical danger themselves, might be considered more than mere bystanders because some action of theirs physically brings about death or injury to another. The best-known example is **Dooley v Cammell Laird** (1951). Here the claimant was operating a crane at the docks where he worked, when, through no fault of his, it dropped a load into the hold of the ship being unloaded. He successfully claimed for psychiatric injury caused through fearing for the safety of a colleague working below. Until **White**, the case, along with a couple of similar decisions, was viewed as establishing the right of an employee to recover for psychiatric injury caused by witnessing or fearing injury to colleagues as a result of their employers' negligence. In **White**, Lord Hoffmann maintains that there is no such right, and that the cases, all of which were first instance judgments, were decided on their facts, and before the **Alcock** control mechanisms were in place. However, he concedes that there may be grounds for treating unwitting agent cases as exceptional, and exempting them from the **Alcock** restrictions, though the point is *obiter* since, as Lord Hoffmann points out, the facts of **White** do not raise the issue.

The issue was examined in **Hunter v British Coal** (1998). Here the claimant was a driver in a coal mine, who accidentally struck a water hydrant while manoeuvring his vehicle. He went to try to find a hose to channel the water away safely, leaving behind a colleague, C. When the claimant was about 30 metres away, he heard the hydrant explode and rushed to find the valve to turn it off, which took about 10 minutes. During that time he heard a message over the tannoy that a man had been injured, and on his way back to the accident scene another colleague told him that it looked as though C was dead. This proved to be the case, and the claimant's belief that he was responsible for his colleague's death caused him to suffer clinical depression.

When it became clear that in fact the accident had occurred because of his employer's failure to put certain safety features in place, he sued. The Court of Appeal held that in order to be owed a duty of care of psychiatric injury, the claimant would have to have been at the scene of the accident when it happened, or seen its immediate aftermath; his depression had been caused by hearing about it and that was not sufficient. The case therefore seems to suggest that unwitting agents may have a claim if they satisfy the requirements of proximity in space and time.

Other bystanders

The cases make it clear that bystanders who have no relationship with the primary victims of an accident are very unlikely ever to be able to sue successfully for psychiatric injury experienced as a result. This approach approves the traditional position in cases such as **Bourhill v Young** (1943), where it was held that a woman who suffered psychiatric injury as a result of seeing the aftermath of a horrific motorcycle accident involving a stranger could not recover damages; the court held that an ordinary bystander could be expected to withstand the shock of such a sight, which meant that it was not reasonably foreseeable that the claimant would in fact suffer psychiatric damage as a result.

However, in **Alcock** the point was made that there might be very rare occasions when an incident was so horrific that psychiatric damage to even uninvolved bystanders was foreseeable, and there a duty of care would arise. The House of Lords gave the rather lurid and imaginative example of a petrol tanker crashing into a school playground full of children and bursting into flames.

Proximity

The third test which secondary victims must pass in order to have a claim concerns proximity, which in this case means how close they were to the shocking event, in terms of both time and place. In **Alcock** some claimants had seen the disaster from other stands inside the stadium; one of the claimants was watching the match on a television nearby and when he saw the disaster commence went to find his son (who had been killed); others saw the tragedy on the television at home or heard about it on the radio. **Alcock** established that to succeed in a claim for nervous shock, the witness must have been sufficiently proximate to the accident, which normally means that they must have been present at the scene of the accident or its immediate aftermath; hearing it on the radio or seeing it on the television will not usually be enough.

The House of Lords was not prepared to specify exactly what was the immediate aftermath, but the interpretation they give to the issue is narrower than that advocated in some of the *obiter dicta* in **McLoughlin v O'Brian**. Lord Keith appears to approve of the *dicta* in the Australian case of **Jaensch v Coffey** (1984), which stated that the aftermath continues for as long as the victim remains in the state caused by the accident, until they receive immediate post-accident treatment. **McLoughlin** was considered to be a borderline case by Lord Ackner and it was stated that identifying the body of a loved one at a temporary mortuary eight hours after the accident did not fall within seeing the immediate aftermath of the tragedy.

The House made it clear that merely being informed of the incident by a third party was not sufficiently proximate. This was confirmed in the very sad case of **Tan v East London and City Health Authority** (1999). The claimant was telephoned by a member of hospital staff and told that his baby had already died in its mother's womb, and would be stillborn. He went to the hospital for the birth, which took place around three hours later. He sued the hospital for psychiatric injury, but the court rejected his claim. It held that the shocking event that caused the psychiatric damage was the death of the baby before birth, rather than seeing it being born dead. The claimant had not witnessed the death itself, but been told about it over the phone, and therefore was not sufficiently proximate to the event.

In **Alcock**, the House also had to deal with the question of whether watching an incident on television could be sufficiently proximate to impose liability to secondary victims for nervous shock, as the Hillsborough disaster had been broadcast live on television to millions of people. The pictures did not pick out individuals, as broadcasting guidelines prevented the portrayal of death or suffering by recognisable individuals. On the facts, the House of Lords did not find that watching the television broadcasts was sufficiently proximate, though it did not rule out the possibility that sometimes television viewers could be sufficiently proximate. The House of Lords drew a distinction between recorded broadcasts and live ones. The former were never sufficiently proximate to give rise to a duty of care. With the latter they said that a claim was unlikely to arise because of the broadcasting guidelines which meant that normally even live broadcasts of disasters could not be equated with actually having been present at the scene of the tragedy. Lord Jauncey stated:

> I do not consider that a claimant who watches a normal television programme which displays events as they happen satisfies the test of proximity. In the first place a defendant could normally anticipate that in accordance with current television broadcasting guidelines shocking pictures of persons suffering and dying would not be transmitted. In the second place, a television programme such as that transmitted from Hillsborough involves cameras at different viewpoints showing scenes all of which no one individual would see, edited pictures and a commentary superimposed.

If pictures in breach of broadcasting guidelines were shown, their transmission would normally break the chain of causation as a *novus actus interveniens*. This would mean that the instigator of the incident would not be liable because they could not have foreseen that such pictures would be shown.

Occasionally the chain of causation would not be broken and liability on the original instigator could be imposed. The example the judges gave was of a publicity-seeking organisation arranging an event where a party of children were taken in a hot-air balloon, the event being shown live on television so that their parents could watch. If the basket suddenly burst into flames, the suddenness of the tragedy might mean that it was impossible for the broadcasters to shield the viewers from scenes of distress and this would be reasonably foreseeable to those whose negligence caused the accident.

Psychiatric injury not caused by accidents

Though most of the cases on psychiatric injury involve accidents, there are of course other ways in which negligence can cause such injury. The most significant area for litigation is psychiatric injury caused by prolonged exposure to stress at work, and the courts have treated this in a different way to psychiatric injury caused by accidents and sudden events, notably by not requiring that the illness be triggered by a sudden shock. This area is discussed more fully in the chapter on employers' liability.

In **W v Essex County Council (2000)**, the House of Lords was prepared to allow that there might be a claim for negligence causing psychiatric shock after the defendant council negligently placed a foster child who had a history of abusing other children into a family with four young children. He then abused those children, and both they and their parents suffered psychiatric injury as a result. Clearly there was no sudden shock, nor, certainly in the parents' case, any physical injury which would make them primary victims, nor did they directly witness the abuse. This would seem to set the case apart from other decisions on psychiatric injury, and the House of Lords did comment that the parents might well have difficulties making their claim, but they were not willing to strike the case out. However, it is important to note that the case took place shortly after **Osman** *v* **UK**, which put into question the use of striking out applications, and this may explain the courts' reluctance to dismiss the action. Whether it would have succeeded must now remain a mystery, as the case was settled out of court in January 2002, with the council paying £190,000 in compensation.

Statutory provision

In addition to the common law remedy for nervous shock, emotional distress can occasionally be compensated under statute. For example, there is a statutory award for bereavement contained in the Fatal Accidents Act 1976. There is no need to prove proximity to the incident that caused the death nor for evidence of a medically recognised mental illness. However, it has its own limitations as it is only awarded to a very small class of people, is for a fixed sum of money and is only available on death, not serious injury.

Problems with the law on psychiatric damage

The position of rescuers

As explained earlier, rescuers were traditionally thought to be a special case with regard to psychiatric shock, and a rescuer who suffered psychiatric shock as a result

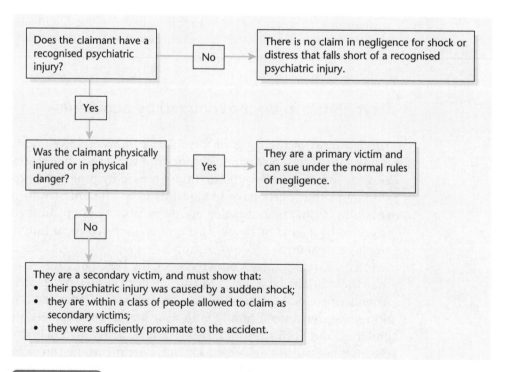

Figure 5.15 **Liability for psychiatric injury**

would not be subject to the same restrictions as a mere bystander. **White** of course changes this, and this aspect of the decision was comprehensively criticised in the dissenting judgments of Lords Goff and Griffiths in that case. Lord Hoffmann's claim that rescuers had never been a special case, and that the main authority, **Chadwick**, fitted in with his analysis because there was a danger of the train collapsing is disputed by Lord Goff. He points out that the trial judge in **Chadwick** treated the potential danger as irrelevant, and was right to do so, because it was clearly not the threat of danger to himself that caused Mr Chadwick's psychiatric injury, but the horror of spending hours surrounded by the terrible sights and sounds that were the aftermath of the accident.

Lord Goff also pointed out that making rescuers' claims dependent on whether they were at risk of physical injury could create unjust distinctions. He gave the example of two men going to help in the aftermath of a train crash, where the situation happened to be that helping victims in the front half of the train involved some threat of physical danger, and working in the back half did not. Each of the two men might perform the same service, suffer the same trauma and end up living with the same degree of psychiatric injury, yet if they happened to be helping at opposite ends of the train one would be able to claim compensation for his psychiatric injury and the other would not, a distinction which his Lordship said was 'surely unacceptable'.

The 'closeness of relationship' rules

As you will remember, it was established in **Alcock v Chief Constable of South Yorkshire** (1992) that one of the requirements for recovery by a secondary victim was that they should have a relationship with a primary victim that was 'close in care', meaning that it is not sufficient to establish, for example, that the primary and secondary victims were brothers; it must also be proved that the relationship between them was close in terms of the way they felt about each other.

The requirement must make the trial more traumatic for the claimant, yet quite how it contributes to the law is difficult to see. Clearly it would be ridiculous for a claimant who was the brother of a primary victim to claim damages if in fact they disliked each other intensely and rarely had any kind of contact – but in such cases, is it likely that the claimant would be able to prove that he had suffered a psychiatric illness as a result of his brother's death or injury? This requirement alone provides a limiting mechanism that makes the test of factual closeness unnecessary.

In addition, it is hard to see why this should affect the defendant's duty, which is still initially based on foreseeability; how can a defendant be said to foresee whether or not the person they injure will have a close relationship with their relatives, and therefore to owe a duty only if they do?

The proximity requirements

As you will recall, the decision in **Alcock** regarding proximity was that in order to claim for psychiatric injury, a secondary victim would have to have been present at the incident which endangered, injured or killed their loved one, or to have witnessed its 'immediate aftermath'.

In **McLoughlin**, the deciding factor seemed to be that the injured were in much the same state as when the accident happened, covered in oil and dirt, and so the implication seems to be that this made the sight of them more devastating, and therefore more likely to mentally injure Mrs McLoughlin. While it is clear that these factors could make a sight more distressing and shocking, it is difficult to make out why exactly the courts believe this should be the dividing line between experiences which can and cannot cause psychiatric injury. Sight is not the only way in which human beings perceive suffering: hearing about the circumstances of an accident, particularly when the outcome is not known, can surely be equally devastating. Similarly, the House of Lords in **Alcock** were emphatic that those seeing the incident on television could not be caused psychiatric injury by the experience, yet the claimants who saw the TV coverage would have known, right at the time when the incident was happening before their eyes, that their loved ones were there. Even if they could not identify them by sight, it is hard to see that this was less distressing than coming upon the aftermath of an accident, and if it was equally distressing, there seems no reason why it should be less likely to cause psychiatric injury.

Nor is the courts' emphasis on the time between the accident and the perception of it easy to justify. Among the **Alcock** claimants, for example, was one man who had gone to the ground and searched all night for the brother he knew had been at the match. It is difficult to see why those long hours of searching and worrying should be less likely to cause psychiatric injury than sight of a loved one immediately after an accident.

The 'sudden shock' requirement

As with the proximity requirements, it is difficult to find a rational basis for the line drawn between psychiatric injury caused by a sudden shock and the same injury caused by, for example, the stress of caring for a seriously injured relative, or the grief of being bereaved. So long as the psychiatric shock is a foreseeable result of the defendant's negligence, why should the precise aspect of the claimant's situation which triggered it off make any difference?

Take the case of **Sion v Hampstead Health Authority** (1994), for example (see p. 735). Had the son died suddenly of a fatal heart attack caused by his poor medical treatment, and his father been there to witness it, the father might very well have been able to secure compensation for any psychiatric illness he suffered as a result. Why should the fact that he watched his son die slowly, with all the stress and grief that must cause, change his situation? The defendant's treatment of his son is no less negligent; his own psychiatric injury is no less real, and nor is it less foreseeable. Furthermore, if sudden shock is a logical requirement, how are we to explain the decisions allowing claims for psychiatric injury after prolonged stress at work? Why is this stress coinsidered more harmful than the stress of caring for a relative injured by someone else's negligence? Clearly the law has to draw a line somewhere, but the justification for making a sudden shock the defining factor is hard to see.

Reform

The Law Commission has been looking at this area of the law for some time, and in 1995 began consulting with interested parties. The results of their consultations were published in 1998. The Commission argues that the current rules on compensation for secondary victims are too restrictive. They agree that the requirement for a close tie between primary and secondary victim is justified and should remain, but believe this alone would be sufficient; they recommend that the requirements of proximity (both in time and space, and in method of perception) should be abolished. They also suggest that the requirement for psychiatric injury to be caused by sudden shock should be abandoned.

Duties of care: omissions

As a general rule, the duties imposed by the law of negligence are duties not to cause injury or damage to others; they are not duties actively to help others. And if there is no duty, there is no liability. If, for example, you see someone drowning, you generally have no legal duty to save them, no matter how easy it might be to do so (unless there are special reasons why the law would impose such a duty on you in particular, such as under an employment contract as a lifeguard). This means tort law generally holds people liable for acts (the things people do), not omissions (the things they fail to do).

However, there are some situations in which the courts have recognised a positive duty to act, arising from the circumstances in which the parties find themselves. Although the categories are loose and at times overlap, the following are the main factors which have been taken into consideration.

Control exercised by the defendants

Where the defendants have a high degree of control over the claimant, they may have a positive duty to look after them which goes beyond simply taking reasonable steps to ensure that the defendants themselves do not cause injury. A key case in this area is **Reeves v Commissioner of Police for the Metropolis** (1999). The case was brought by the widow of a man who had committed suicide while in police custody. Although previous case law had accepted that the police had a duty of care to prevent suicide attempts by prisoners who were mentally ill, Mr Reeves was found to have been completely sane, and the police therefore argued that while clearly they had a duty of care not to cause his death, they could not be held responsible for the fact that he chose to kill himself, and had no duty to prevent him from doing so. However, the Court of Appeal held that their duty of care to protect a prisoner's health did extend to taking reasonable care to prevent him or her from attempting suicide; they accepted that to impose a positive duty like this was unusual, but explained that it was justified by the very high degree of control which the police would have over a prisoner, and the well-known high risk of suicide among suspects held in this way.

In **Orange v Chief Constable of West Yorkshire Police** (2001), the Court of Appeal emphasised that the duty established in **Reeves** did not amount to a general obligation to treat every prisoner as a suicide risk. The case involved the suicide of a married man with young children, who was arrested for being drunk and disorderly, and placed in a police cell. The custody officer who came to release him found that he had used his belt to hang himself from the horizontal bar of a grille inside the cell door. There had been no reason to suspect that he was a suicide risk, but his widow sued the police, claiming that they had been negligent in failing to take away his belt, or to monitor him properly, and in leaving him in a cell with a suspension point.

The Court of Appeal rejected this argument, stating that the duty laid down in **Reeves** was a duty to take reasonable steps to discover whether an individual prisoner was a suicide risk, and act accordingly. As there was no reason to suspect this prisoner might try to commit suicide, there was no duty to take steps to prevent him from doing so.

The 2001 prize for the cheekiest legal action must surely go to the claimant in another case in this area, **Vellino v Chief Constable of Greater Manchester** (2001). Mr Vellino was a career criminal, with an extensive record, and was well known to the local police. On several occasions the police had gone to his flat to arrest him, and he had tried to escape by jumping from the second floor windows to the ground floor below. On the occasion that gave rise to the case, the police arrived and Mr Vellino jumped, as usual, but this time he seriously injured himself, ending up with brain damage and paralysis, which made him totally dependent on others for his needs. He sued the police, arguing that they were under a duty to prevent him from escaping, and their failure to do so had caused his injuries. It was, his counsel argued, foreseeable that he would try to escape, and foreseeable injury could result.

The Court of Appeal rejected the argument entirely, pointing out that it would mean that arresting officers had a duty to hold a suspect in the lightest possible grip, just in case he or she wrenched a shoulder in struggling to break free. Equally, it would mean prisons could be sued if prisoners hurt themselves jumping off high boundary walls, since it was foreseeable that prisoners might try to escape and that jumping off high walls tends to cause injury.

In any case, the court said, Mr Vellino was not actually under the control of the police when he jumped. He was trying to escape police custody, which was a crime, and therefore the defence of illegality applied.

CHAPTER 6

Business Decision Making

Unit 6: Business Decision Making

Unit code: D/601/0578

QCF level: 5

Credit value: 15 credits

Aim

The aim of this unit is to give learners the opportunity to develop techniques for data gathering and storage, an understanding of the tools available to create and present useful information, in order to make business decisions.

Unit abstract

In business, good decision making requires the effective use of information. This unit gives learners the opportunity to examine a variety of sources and develop techniques in relation to four aspects of information: data gathering, data storage, and the tools available to create and present useful information.

ICT is used in business to carry out much of this work and an appreciation and use of appropriate ICT software is central to completion of this unit. Specifically, learners will use spreadsheets and other software for data analysis and the preparation of information. The use of spreadsheets to manipulate numbers, and understanding how to apply the results, are seen as more important than the mathematical derivation of formulae used.

Learners will gain an appreciation of information systems currently used at all levels in an organisation as aids to decision making.

Learning outcomes

On successful completion of this unit a learner will:

1 Be able to use a variety of sources for the collection of data, both primary and secondary
2 Understand a range of techniques to analyse data effectively for business purposes
3 Be able to produce information in appropriate formats for decision making in an organisational context
4 Be able to use software-generated information to make decisions in an organisation

Unit content

1 Be able to use a variety of sources for the collection of data, both primary and secondary

Primary sources: survey methodology; questionnarie design; sample frame; sampling methods; sample error

Secondary sources: internet research; government and other published data; by-product data

Storage: security of information; data protection issues; ethical issues

2 Understand a range of techniques to analyse data effectively for business purposes

Representative values: mean, median, mode; calculation from raw data and frequency distributions using appropriate software; using the results to draw valid conclusions

Measures of dispersion: standard deviation for small and large samples; typical uses (statistical process eg control, buffer stock levels)

Calculation: use of quartiles, percentiles, correlation coefficient

3 Be able to produce information in appropriate formats for decision making in an organisational context

Creation and interpretation of graphs using spreadsheets: line, pie, bar charts and histograms

Scatter (XY) graphs and linear trend lines: extrapolation for forecasting (reliability)

Presentations and report writing: use of appropriate formats; presentation software and techniques

4 Be able to use software-generated information to make decisions in an organisation

Management information systems: computers and information processing tools for operational, tactical and strategic levels of the organisation

Project management: networking and critical path analysis, Gantt and Pert charts

Financial tools: net present value; discounted cash flow; internal rates of return

Learning outcomes and assessment criteria

Learning outcomes	Assessment criteria for pass
On successful completion of this unit a learner will:	The learner can:
LO1 Be able to use a variety of sources for the collection of data, both primary and secondary	1.1 create a plan for the collection of primary and secondary data for a given business problem 1.2 present the survey methodology and sampling frame used 1.3 design a questionnaire for a given business problem
LO2 Understand a range of techniques to analyse data effectively for business purposes	2.1 create information for decision making by summarising data using representative values 2.2 analyse the results to draw valid conclusions in a business context 2.3 analyse data using measures of dispersion to inform a given business scenario 2.4 explain how quartiles, percentitles and the correlation coefficient are used to draw useful conclusions in a business context
LO3 Be able to produce information in appropriate formats for decision making in an organisational context	3.1 produce graphs using spreadsheets and draw valid conclusions based on the information derived 3.2 create trend lines in spreadsheet graphs to assist in forecasting for specified business information 3.3 prepare a business presentation using suitable software and techniques to disseminate information effectively 3.4 produce a formal business report
LO4 Be able to use software-generated information to make decisions in an organisation	4.1 use appropriate information processing tools 4.2 prepare a project plan for an activity and determine the critical path 4.3 use fiancial tools for decision making

Guidance

Links

This unit is linked to the other core units in the programme, in particular: *Unit 1: Business Environment, Unit 2: Meaning Financial Resources and Decisions; Unit 7: Business Strategy* and *Unit 8: Research Project.*

There are also links with the following specialist units: *Unit 9: Management Accounting Costing and Budgeting, Unit 15: Managing Business Activities to Achieve Results, Unit 16: Managing Communications, Knowledge and Information; Unit 19: Marketing Planning* and *Unit 34: Operations Management in Business.*

This unit also links to the Management and Leadership NOS as mapped in *Annexe B.*

Essential requirements

It is essential that learners have access to computers and the internet and specialist packages for statistical analysis and network planning.

Employer engagement and vocational contexts

Centres should try to develop link with local businesses. Many businesses and chambers of commerce are keen to promote local business and are often willing to provide visit opportunities, guest speakers, information about business and the local business context.

Collecting data

Introduction

Businesses need information to make decisions; part of this information will be 'statistical'.

A dictionary definition states that statistics are numerical facts collected systematically, arranged and studied.

For decision makers, the primary role of statistics is to provide them with the methods for obtaining and converting data (values, facts, observations, measurements) into useful information. Diagrammatically this can be seen in Figure 6.1.

Types of data

Data comes in different forms, each of which is dealt with slightly differently on conversion to information. The main groups are shown in Figure 6.2 and further defined below.

Categorical (qualitative) data

Nominal data

These are data which can be divided into *non-measurable* named categories, for example colours of eyes, type of accommodation, makes of car and so on. Or the colours of shoes worn by 10 students in a lecture:

blue, brown, black, black, white, brown, red, black, black, white

Here, the results are shown in their raw form, a simple list.

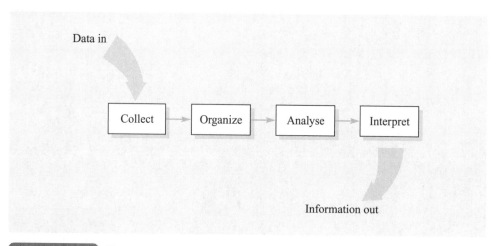

Figure 6.1   The process of data analysis

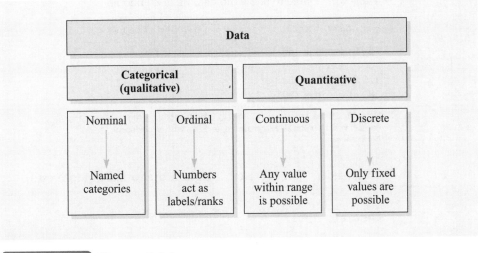

Figure 6.2   Types of data

Ordinal data

This is where numbers can act as labels or ranks. As the name suggests, it involves data representing some element of order. A year label would be a classic example. The classification of this type of data often causes confusion, as illustrated in the following example:

Levels of service are graded

1: Excellent   2: Good   3: Poor   4: Very poor

The words themselves (excellent, good etc.) are classified as nominal data. However, the accompanying codings are numbers specifically acting as ranks so these would be classified as ordinal data.

Note that there is a difference between ordering and coding. In the example opposite on shoe colours the colours could have been coded 1: black, 2: blue etc. but these numbers would *not* represent ordinal data because they do not give an order to the shoe colours.

Quantitative data

These are data which are measured, counted or quantified in some way. They can be divided into categories or classes according to their measurement. This type of data can be further subdivided into two types: continuous data and discrete data.

Continuous data

Continuous data are quantitative data for which any value within a continuous range of values is possible. It generally applies to data that are measured (e.g., heights, wages, times, weights). There is often debate about whether variables such as age and money should be classed as continuous data. In these cases common sense, with justification, prevails.

Table 6.1 A table to show the heights of 80 people

Height (cm)	Number* of people
150 to less than 160	12
160 to less than 170	24
170 to less than 180	28
180 to less than 190	16

Note: * The word 'frequency' is generally used to represent the number in each of the listed categories, and this term will be used from now on.

Consider Table 6.1. Here, height is the variable of interest.

Discrete data

These are quantitative data for which only certain fixed values (usually integers) are possible, for example counts, number of messages on an answerphone, number of visits to London and so on. Another example, with results shown in their raw form, follows:

Number of jewellery items worn by 15 students:

4, 5, 1, 0, 2, 3, 6, 2, 3, 0, 2, 4, 2, 0, 2

Table 6.2 shows the number of letters received each morning over a 30 day period. Here, the variable of interest is the number of letters.

Table 6.2 Number of letters received over a 30 day period

Number of letters each morning	Frequency
1	12
2	9
3	5
4	4

Activity 6.1

State whether the following data are discrete, continuous, nominal or ordinal.

(a) Daily temperatures in central Newcastle.
(b) Days of the week.
(c) Number of products sold by each shop in a chain of supermarkets.
(d) Position in the music charts of UK singles.

Working:

Answers at the end of the chapter on page 771.

Sources of information

There are two basic sources of information, primary and secondary.

Primary data

These are data which have been collected specifically for a particular purpose.

Everyone at some time or other will have taken part in a data collection process. Every form filled in provides primary data to someone somewhere.

Often the information provided (say from questionnaires, interviews and feedback forms) is only collected from a relatively small number of people. This is called a **sample**. In much rarer circumstances (for example the 10 yearly UK census) data may be collected from the population, or as many people in the country as it is possible to reach. A **population** need not be made up of every person living in the UK or even people themselves. Populations may be, for example, every chocolate bar produced by a factory using a batch of raw materials, salmon at a fish farm or all employees at a large firm.

The word **census** is used to describe the collection of data from the complete population.

The word **survey** describes the collection of data from a sample selected from a population. Samples are generally used as they are a more economical and practical method of data collection.

Data collected from a census or survey are known as **primary data**. The different ways in which such data are collected and how survey samples are determined will be discussed later in this chapter.

The gathering of primary data can be very costly and time consuming, particularly in the case of a census. Because of this census data is most commonly collected by governments or specialist market research companies who then make the information more widely available to others. It is at this stage that the data become known as **secondary data**.

Secondary data

These are data, originally collected for one project, but which then can be used for another purpose.

In the UK the Government Statistical Service holds most nationally published data. There are numerous government publications which include:

- *Social Trends*: an analysis and breakdown of many aspects of British life and work;
- *Financial Statistics*: key financial and monetary statistics within the UK;
- *Economic Trends*: a compilation of the main economic indicators.

Many other government publications are based on data which have been collected from surveys. Listed below are brief descriptions of some of these surveys.

- The *Family Expenditure Survey* (*FES*) investigates the income and spending patterns of about 7000 households in the UK. The population size is approximately 22 million and the survey is conducted annually.
- The *Survey of Retail Prices*, carried out by the Department of Employment, provides around 150,000 prices which are used in the calculation of the Retail Price Index (RPI). Population size is very difficult to estimate. The survey is conducted monthly.
- The *New Earnings Survey* (*NES*) collects information on the earnings of about 180,000 people. Population size is approximately 20 million and the survey is conducted annually.

Note that in the surveys where the population size is known the sample is less than 1% of the total population. The choice of sample size will be considered later in this chapter.

Other useful sources of secondary data include company and bank reviews, *The Employment Gazette*, *The Economist* and so on. Nowadays computing sources of secondary data are becoming ever more popular, for example Datastream, Prestel, the Internet and even Ceefax.

Of course secondary data can also be drawn from many other sources, and some of the spreadsheet exercises in this book will demonstrate that even a simple spreadsheet file can be a secondary data source.

Primary data collection methods

Data analysis often involves manipulation or work with data which have been collected from a survey: for that reason it is important to ensure that the collection of primary data is carried out in a statistically sound way, otherwise results may be biased. In the next sections, methods of collecting primary data will be examined.

Postal questionnaires

This is where a questionnaire is sent – usually through the post – to the desired sample. It is probably the most popular data collection method as it is very easy to make contact with respondents over a wide geographical area and is inexpensive to administer. Once the questionnaire has been received the respondents generally have a period of time in which to answer. This is particularly advantageous if 'non-instant recall' information is required. However, the method often results in very low return rates and, because there is no personal contact, it is impossible to probe for further information on interesting responses or to give clarification on any questions which may be misinterpreted.

Personal interviews

This procedure usually requires a trained interviewer going out and asking a pre-pared set of questions, either in a public place (for example stopping people on the street to take part in a political opinion poll) or at the respondent's home or place of work. Because of the involvement of a trained individual, some of the problems of postal questionnaires can be avoided. Ambiguous questions can be explained, interesting responses can be followed up and as the interviewer can encourage participation, the response rates are generally higher. But, because of the human contact, this method is very expensive (salary, training, transport), especially if a wide geographical cover is required. Also, accurate results rely heavily on the interviewer's expertise.

Telephone interview

This could be considered as almost a compromise between a postal questionnaire and a personal interview. There is still personal contact, with the added bonus of being able to directly enter responses on to a computer, if such facilities are available. But, in this case, there is an immediate bias as people who do not own a phone are excluded from the sample; also one is never sure who is responding at the other end of the telephone line.

Observation

This is the main method employed when the population of interest does not consist of people or require people's responses. An example of an observational survey is a traffic survey. Again, the method relies heavily on the skills of the observer, and owing to its nature can be the most time consuming (in terms of human participation) when observation of irregular events is required.

Estimation of sample size

As mentioned previously, the sample size may be very small in relation to the overall population. In fact there is no precise way in which an optimal sample size can be calculated for any particular survey. However, there are two useful statistical facts which should be kept in mind:

- the larger the size of the sample, the more *accurate* the information on the population will be;
- above a certain size, little *extra* information about a population can be gained yet costs in time and money increase.

Without becoming too technical, common sense is used in conjunction with any information already known and details about the information sought to estimate an appropriate sample size. This will be illustrated with some scenarios and suggestions of appropriate sample sizes.

Example

The IT resource manager of a large company wishes to do a quick market research exercise on employees' attitudes towards the printing facilities provided.

In this case, no particular specialist information is required, the results will probably have no major impact on the employees themselves and, knowing that they all use the IT facilities regularly, a sample size of, say, between 50 and 100 would be sufficient.

Example

A university is considering extending the teaching week to include Saturday mornings and wishes to receive some staff and student views on this.

In this case, the outcome of the survey could bring about a major change in the university's working environment. Because of this it would be advisable to find out the population size and select between 20% and 30% of the population (staff and students) to be canvassed.

Choosing a suitable, representative sample

In the same way as selecting a suitable sample size, common sense is the most important factor in ensuring a sample is representative.

Example

You are working for a building society and have been asked to find out the current average selling price for a three bedroom, semi-detached house in the north-east of England.

In this case you could *not* simply go into the nearest estate agent and pick up details on say 20 (or even 70) such houses and expect to have a representative sample for the whole of the area of interest.

Example

A students' union wishes to gauge students' opinions of the catering facilities provided in the union building.

In this case it would be reasonable to assume that asking, say, 50–100 students as they leave the union building would give a sufficiently representative sample as all would probably have an interest in the catering facilities.

Sampling methods

A number of methods are available to try and achieve a representative sample of the population and these are described below.

Simple random sampling

The key to this method is that every member of the population must have an equal chance of being included in the sample. For small populations, a method such as 'drawing from a hat' would achieve this. For larger populations, each member of the population is usually given a unique identification number and then random numbers are generated (often using a computer). The sample is then made up of the population members whose numbers match those generated. The method 'feels' fair, and has no bias. However, it might be difficult to contact all of the chosen sample (say if there is a wide geographical spread in the data) and (simply through chance) an unrepresentative sample may occur.

Stratified random sampling

This method is very similar to simple random sampling, but is used where it is thought that the population contains distinct groups who might have different views about the issues of interest (for example it might be thought that car owners and cyclists/pedestrians would have different views about the introduction of car control measures in a city centre). To overcome the danger of a sample accidentally being unrepresentative, the sample can be stratified according to these groups so that it has approximately the same proportions as the population (e.g., if there are 80% car owners and 20% cyclists/pedestrians in the population then the ratio of 4:1 should be reflected in the sample). For each 'stratum', the sample members are selected randomly (as above for simple random sampling). It is a comparatively unbiased sampling method and should give a representative sample. Again, however, it is necessary to have good access to the population of interest and stratification will add costs to the survey process.

Systematic sampling

Again this is similar to simple random sampling except that instead of picking a member of the sample by using a random number generator, the data are assumed to be in random order and every nth member is selected where n is given by

(population size) ÷ (desired sample size)

For example if a sample of 5 were required from a list of 30 people every 6th person could be chosen. Note that it is not necessary to start with the first person on the list – the start point should be chosen randomly. Thus the sample might contain the people numbered 1, 7, 13, 19 and 25 – or 2, 8, 14, 20 and 26 – or 3, 9, 15, 21 and 27 etc. It is an easy method to use, and can be useful if the exact population is not known (e.g., all users of a bank's cash machines on a particular day would be hard to define in advance, but every 15th customer could easily be questioned). Care must be taken to ensure that the sample is not biased (e.g., if every 5th item is taken from a production line with 5 machines, does that mean that the same machine is sampled each time?).

Cluster sampling

This method is frequently used when the population items of interest are widely spread and it is desirable to ensure that the sample elements are grouped together in some way (perhaps geographically or over a short period of time). For example, if a retailer wanted to interview a sample of shopkeepers it would make sense to randomly select two or three sales areas first. Every shopkeeper within those areas could then be interviewed: this would avoid the selection of a number of isolated shopkeepers scattered across the country. Clearly this is a useful method for widely spread geographical data where the population is not defined exactly. Again care must be taken to ensure that bias does not occur.

Quota sampling

Quota sampling is usually used where interviewing is the main method of data collection; the aim is similar to that for stratified sampling in that it is desirable to make sure the composition of the sample matches that in the population. The interviewer is given a 'predetermined' sample profile where the numbers of interviewees in each category are chosen to match the population proportions. The interviewer then selects people from the passing population to match the required numbers in each category. For example, on the basis of Table 6.3 an interviewer for a political opinion poll is required to sample 40 people in total: two of these will be professional females (social class A/B aged between 45 and 64, etc.). This will have been chosen so that the proportion in the sample ($^2/_{40}$ = 5%) is similar to that in the original population.

This method tends to have good response rates because the interviewer achieves the quota set – non-respondents are ignored and other people are chosen to replace them. However, it is very reliant on the interviewer, and bias could occur as it is a non-random technique.

Multistage sampling

Multistage sampling is a technique which is used for producing a representative sample from a widespread population – in similar situations to those discussed earlier for cluster sampling. However, in this case the process continues down to selection of the individual sampling units (rather than groups as for cluster sampling). This is done by splitting the sampling process into stages and using the most relevant of

Table 6.3 Interview quotas for a political opinion poll

Social class	A/B		C		D/E	
Age/Sex	M	F	M	F	M	F
18–29	0	0	3	1	2	2
30–44	1	1	2	1	4	3
45–64	2	2	3	1	2	2
65 or over	1	1	2	1	3	0

the sampling techniques already listed to each of these different stages. For example, a large food manufacturer wishing to conduct a national survey into the lifestyle and eating habits of consumers, to provide information for the possible launch of a pre-prepared food range, might use a three-stage survey to cover the whole of the country.

- *Stage 1* (*primary sampling units*): Split the UK into a number of regions (e.g. TV regions) and then randomly select a small number of these.
- *Stage 2* (*secondary sampling units*): Taking each of the selected regions, randomly sample sub-regions (perhaps parliamentary constituencies).
- *Stage 3* (*tertiary sampling units*): Individual households could then be selected by using systematic sampling from the electoral register.

This is another technique (like cluster sampling) which is very useful for widely spread data. Careful thought is necessary at the various sample stages to avoid the risk of bias.

Activity 6.2

Table 6.4 is a seminar group listing for students on the AR101 Introduction to Aromatherapy unit. With the aid of the list of random numbers below you are required to select a sample of 5 people, who will be given a free massage by the tutor, using:

(a) Simple random sampling.
(b) Stratified random sampling based on gender.
(c) Systematic random sampling.

Table 6.4 Seminar group listing for students on Aromatherapy unit

Surname	Forename	Surname	Forename
Black	Lynn	North	John
Kirk	Tim	Fox	Malcolm
Hughes	Jim	Peters	Sue
Hobson	Anne	Howe	Roy
Dixon	Patrick	Morris	Karen
Carr	Bill	Philipson	Gail
Murray	John	Plant	Vicki
Smith	Alan	Stewart	Angela
Thompson	Ivor	Ward	David
Swallow	Adam	Smith	Liz

Random numbers:

11	14	05	16	18	12	18	19	15	03	07
17	13	09	01	07	13	08	11	14	10	14
13	14	11	06	12	15	02	15	18	19	13

Working:

Answers at the end of the chapter on page 771.

Questionnaire design

Most primary data collection methods make use of questionnaires. Good questionnaire design is crucial to the success of a survey. Because of this it is very important to 'pilot' the questionnaire on a small number of respondents to check for inaccuracies in wording of a question, whether all possible answers of interest will be covered, etc.

Question types

There are three basic types of question used in questionnaires: dichotomous questions, multiple choice questions and open-ended questions. Here each will be examined in turn.

Dichotomous questions

These allow for two answers only. For example, yes or no; male or female; true or false; like or dislike.

Example

1. Are you living in halls of residence? Yes ☐   No ☐
2. Is your personal tutor: Male ☐   Female ☐ ?
3. 7 * 3 = 20   True ☐ or   False ☐ ?
4. Do you   Like ☐ or Dislike mathematics ☐ ?

It is important that questions of the type shown in (4) above are not overused where there may be 'middle ground', that is, they must allow for don't know; no opinion etc.

In such cases it is more appropriate to use multiple choice questions.

Multiple choice questions

Respondents can choose from several indicated possibilities. Included in this category are those questions which may ask the respondent to rank choices.

It is important to make sure that the possibilities are both 'comprehensive' and 'mutually exclusive' (that is every respondent should, unless otherwise stated, be able to pick one and only one of the possibilities).

Example

You never know – someone could be living in a tent!

What type of accommodation are you living in during this year of study?

Halls of residence ☐   Own/parents' house or flat ☐

Rented house/flat ☐   Lodgings ☐

Other (please specify) _____

The *other* category provides for any types which may have been missed, but care must be taken to make sure that this category does not end up being the most popular choice.

Example

Grey, green, violet and hazel eyes would all have to be put in the *other* category

What colour are your eyes?

Blue ☐

Brown ☐

Other (please specify) _____

When using questions which require a level of opinion, make sure there are the same number of potential answers 'for' as 'against'.

Example

3 choices on the 'for' side

Do you think the students' union catering facilities overall are:

Excellent ☐   OK ☐

Very good ☐   Bad ☐

Quite good ☐   Only 1 on the 'against'

Whenever it is appropriate, remember to account for the don't knows or the don't haves.

Example

How many doors does your car have?

(include the boot, if it is a hatchback)

One	☐	Four	☐
Two	☐	Five	☐
Three	☐	More than five	☐
Don't own a car	☐		

Open-ended questions

Respondents are left to answer these in any manner they choose.

The main advantage for this type of question is that it allows for an infinite number of divergent answers. This, however, is also their greatest disadvantage, as the responses to such questions are the hardest to process and analyse. Therefore, one needs to be wary not to use too many on any one questionnaire.

However, open-ended questions can be very useful in three particular areas:

1 On pilot surveys. Here they can be used to try and gauge all possible responses to a particular question so that this question can then become a well designed multiple choice question in the full survey.

Example

How do you get to and from work on an average day?

2 Probing – to get extra information depending on a choice made by a previous response.

Example

Was this university your first choice of place to study for your degree?

Yes ☐　　No ☐　　If No please briefly explain why _____

3 Used at the end of a questionnaire or section they can be a means of giving the respondent the chance to add anything they feel is important but is not covered by the questions given.

Note that open-ended questions can add weight and credibility to a final report by the use of actual responses as direct quotes.

In summary, when looking at the overall design of a questionnaire the following should be kept in mind:

- Questionnaires should be as short as possible.
- The questions themselves should:
  - avoid using complex words and phrases in their construction;
  - be meaningful;
  - not be too technical or involve too much calculation;
  - not be too personal or offensive;
  - not tax the memory;
  - be unambiguous.
- Questions should be arranged in a logical order.
- Questionnaires should be attractively laid out and constructed.
- How the responses will be analysed should be considered at the questionnaire design stage (i.e., appropriate coding should be considered).

Sources of error

No survey of any population can ever be 100% accurate. (One notable disaster was the predicted outcome of the 1992 general election when opinion polls stated that the Labour Party would win comfortably and, in fact, the Conservatives were returned to power.) There are several different ways in which errors can occur and there are steps which can be taken to try and avoid them.

Sampling errors

These errors arise from the sample not being representative of the population concerned. They are generally avoided by careful consideration of the sampling method to be used. With random samples, the size of these sampling errors can be usefully estimated.

Non-sampling errors

These arise from a variety of causes including:

- the incorrect recording of responses (e.g. by interviewers);
- transferring data incorrectly onto a computer for processing;
- sample members refusing to co-operate (non-respondents);
- failure to make initial contact with sample members (non-respondents);
- badly designed questions.

Non-sampling errors are generally avoided by good training of the individuals involved in the data collection and processing process; also, carrying out a pilot survey helps to minimize their occurrence.

Overall survey design

To summarize, here is a checklist of the main stages in survey design:

Planning

1 Define the survey aims.
2 Define the population.
3 Identify each member of the population.
4 Identify the sampling scheme (how to choose the sample and how large it should be).
5 Decide upon the method of data collection (postal questionnaire, interviews etc.).
6 Design a questionnaire (equally appropriate for personal interviews and observation).
7 Select and train any people involved in the data collection process.

Fieldwork

1 Select the sample.
2 Collect the data.
3 Follow up non-responses wherever possible.
4 Collate and code information (particularly if a computer is to be used for the analysis).

Analysis and interpretation

1 Screen data for recording errors and extreme values (known as outliers).
2 Carry out any statistical computations.
3 Identify and note any possible sources of error and/or bias.

Publication

Generally in two sections:

1 Written results and conclusions.
2 Detailed statistical section which includes:

   (a) details of the questionnaires used;
   (b) sampling details;
   (c) background statistical theory;
   (d) summary of data collected.

Activity 6.3

The following questions are taken from a questionnaire issued to new car owners by a local car showroom:

(a) What is the colour of your new car?
     Red   ☐   Blue   ☐   White   ☐   Other

(b) Did you use cash to pay for the car?
     Yes   ☐   No   ☐

(c) How much did you pay for the car?
     £5000–£7000   ☐   £7000–£9000   ☐   £9000–£11,000   ☐

(d) Do you feel that the service you received from our staff was
     Excellent   ☐   Very good   ☐   Good   ☐   Poor   ☐ ?

Considering each of the questions in turn state whether you think the question could be improved. If so suggest an alternative.

Working:

Answers at the end of the chapter on page 772.

Summary

1 Data may be defined as categorical (qualitative) or quantitative.
2 Categorical data can be further divided into nominal data and ordinal data.
3 Quantitative data can be further divided into continuous data and discrete data.
4 Data comes from either a primary or a secondary source.
5 A census involves collecting data from a population (all items/people of interest), while a survey collects data from a sample (a carefully chosen small group).
6 Primary data may be collected through a postal questionnaire, a personal interview, a telephone interview or by observation.
7 Common sense must be used to decide on a suitable sample size.

8 Samples may be chosen through the use of simple random sampling, stratified random sampling, systematic sampling, cluster sampling, quota sampling or multistage sampling.

9 Good questionnaire design is essential to the success of a survey.

10 The basic question types used in questionnaires are dichotomous, multiple choice and open-ended.

11 The categories in multiple choice questions should be comprehensive and mutually exclusive.

12 The answers to open-ended questions are difficult to process and analyse, hence care should be taken not to overuse these sorts of questions.

13 Sampling or non-sampling errors may arise from the survey process. Non-sampling errors are generally avoidable.

Exercises

1 The following are some commonly used sources of secondary data:

- Annual Abstract of Statistics
- Social Trends
- Economic Trends
- Regional Trends
- Family Spending
- Key Data
- Guide to Official Statistics.

Find a copy of one of these publications and prepare a summary of the information provided, giving appropriate examples. Can you think of managerial situations where such information could be valuable?

2 State whether the following data are discrete, continuous, nominal or ordinal.

(a) Petrol consumption rates for a range of cars.

(b) Exam grades (A, B, C etc.) for a group of students.

(c) Corresponding percentage exam marks for the same students.

(d) Types of cheese sold in a supermarket.

3 Suggest a suitable sampling method that could be used to obtain information on:

(a) The attitude of passengers to smoking on local bus services.

(b) The percentage of unsatisfactory components produced each week on a production line.

(c) The attitudes toward the provision of a workplace nursery in a large company.

(d) The views of car drivers to traffic calming measures on a residential road.

(e) The likely sales figures for a new type of tea bag.

4 You have been commissioned, by an independent national daily newspaper, to undertake a national survey of people's reactions to a number of issues including the government's recent handling of the economy. You have been instructed that for the survey to retain any credibility, it will be necessary to survey a representative cross-section of at least 5000 people. Consider, in detail, the sampling and data collection methods you would use to carry out this survey, paying particular attention to the requirements for a large, representative group of respondents.

5 A fast food company has many franchised outlets throughout the UK. An executive wants to survey the opinions of the franchise holders towards the current distribution system for raw materials. Suggest a sampling method the executive may use, giving reasons for your choice.

6 Table 6.5 is a seminar group listing for students on a first year Business Studies course. With the aid of the list of random numbers below you are required to select a sample of 4 people using:

(a) Simple random sampling.
(b) Stratified random sampling based on sex.
(c) Systematic random sampling.

Table 6.5 Seminar group listing for Business Studies students

First name	Surname	First name	Surname
Steven	Adams	Andrea	Cross
Clare	Anderson	John	Davidson
Graham	Buckley	Jacqui	Hobson
Glen	Burden	Iain	McLeod
Angela	Dean	Anne	Smith
Susan	Dixon	Elizabeth	Swift
Sarah	Gray	Stuart	Trainer
Joanne	Keane	Philip	Twist
Henry	Ross	Graham	West
David	Wright	Zoe	Wilkinson

Random numbers:

12	15	06	15	17	13	17	20	14	02
18	14	10	02	09	13	07	12	16	12
15	16	10	07	13	16	01	14	19	18

7 The deputy manager of a local department store has asked her marketing assistant to conduct a survey on the possibility of late night opening on Tuesdays and Thursdays. The deputy manager does not have a list of the store's customers but estimates there must be over 10,000 of them with 90% living locally. She does, however, have a breakdown of storecard holders based on age and gender and this is shown in Table 6.6.

Table 6.6 Estimated proportion of customers by age and gender

Age/Gender	Male	Female
Under 20	3	6
20–29	6	14
30–44	9	21
45–59	7	20
60 or over	4	10

Given that the marketing assistant only has a small budget for printing and stationery, and that the survey results are required in two weeks, suggest a suitable sample size and a sampling method. Give reasons for the choices made.

8 One hundred dairy farms in four European countries have been surveyed to collect information about their size, amount of livestock and number of employees.

(a) The intention is to use this survey as a pilot study, with the eventual survey covering farms across the EEC. Suggest a suitable sampling technique that could be used to decide which farms should take part in the larger study. Give reasons for your choice.

(b) In this wider study information on the *number* of different breeds of cows kept by the farmers is also to be collected. Suggest a question to be included in the study which would allow this.

Answers to activities

Activity 6.1

(a) Temperatures are generally stated to the nearest whole number, so the immediate reaction of most people is to say that these data are discrete. However, temperature can be *measured* very accurately so is therefore continuous.

(b) Nominal – as names are used.

(c) Discrete – the key word is number of products, so counts are dealt with.

(d) Ordinal – chart position is a number which represents the *ranking* of sales.

Activity 6.2

Note: As random numbers are involved there is no one right answer so the working below simply explains the correct methods to be used.

(a) Simple random sampling

The first column of names are allocated numbers 01 to 10 and the second column are allocated 11 to 20. Then the random number list provided is used starting at the first value (11) with every other number chosen subsequently (so that the random numbers chosen are 11, 05, 18 etc.). Those people whose allocated number matches up with the random number are then identified as the random sample.

(Note that it would be perfectly acceptable to choose numbers from anywhere else in the table given – this is just one way of doing it).

> 11 – John North
>
> 05 – Patrick Dixon
>
> 18 – Angela Stewart
>
> 18 – Ignore as already used
>
> 15 – Karen Morris
>
> 07 – John Murray

(b) Stratified random sampling (based on gender)

There are eight females and 12 males in the group, which means the ratio of male to female students is 3:2. So in a sample of 5 there should be three males and two females. In this particular sample the second row of random numbers is used (beginning at 17) ignoring those which would result in too many of either gender, i.e.,

> 17 – Vicki Plant (F)
>
> 13 – Sue Peters (F – now have two females as required)
>
> 09 – Ivor Thompson (M)

01 – Lynn Black (F so do not include)

07 – John Murray (M)

13 – Already used so ignore

08 – Alan Smith (M)

(c) Systematic random sampling

There are 20 people and a sample of 5 is required. Therefore pick every 20/5 = 4th person from the list i.e.,

Anne Hobson	Gail Philipson
Alan Smith	Liz Smith
Malcolm Fox	

(A random start point could have been chosen – it is not necessary to start with the 4th person.)

Activity 6.3

(a) The number of colours given as alternatives is very limited and it would be very likely that the Other category would have a high number of responses. In order to improve the questions a much greater variety of choices needs to be provided. However, it must also be recognized that it would be impossible to provide every possible shade.

What is the colour of your new car?

Red	☐	Blue	☐	White	☐
Green	☐	Yellow	☐	Gold	☐
Brown	☐	Black	☐	Silver	☐
Grey	☐	Purple	☐	Other	☐

(b) The two choices may be a bit restrictive – for instance it is possible that a part payment was made in cash (say a deposit). Rather than changing the question into multiple choice format the actual wording of the question can be changed to make it less ambiguous.

Was cash used for payment or part payment of the car ?

Yes ☐   No ☐

(c) This is a classic example of a question where the responses are not comprehensive and the categories are not mutually exclusive.

To illustrate these two points ask yourself if the car cost £4900 (or £11,500) which box would you tick? If the car cost exactly £9000 would you tick the second or third box?

The improved question should be:

How much did you pay for the car?

Less than £5000	☐	£5000 to less than £7000	☐
£7000 to less than £9000	☐	£9000 to less than £11,000	☐
£11,000 or over	☐		

(d) In this question there are more choices on the 'for' side than on the 'against' side.

Do you feel that the service you received from our staff was

Excellent ☐   Satisfactory ☐   Poor ☐ ?

CHAPTER 7

Business Strategy

Unit 7: Business Strategy

Unit code: A/601/0796

QCF level: 5

Credit value: 15 credits

Aim

The aim of this unit is to give learners the knowledge and understanding of how a business unit can strategically organise and plan for likely future outcomes in order to be successful.

Unit abstract

One of the aims of this unit is to build on learners' existing knowledge of the basic tools of business analysis such as PESTLE and draw it together so that the learners think strategically.

Learners will be introduced to further analysis tools needed for the process of strategic planning. They will be able to explain the significance of stakeholder analysis and carry out an environmental and organisational audit of a given organisation.

Learners will learn how to apply strategic positioning techniques to the analysis of a given organisation and prepare a strategic plan based on previous analysis. They will also learn how to evaluate possible alternative strategies (such as substantive growth, limited growth or retrenchment) and then select an appropriate future strategy for a given organisation.

Finally, learners will compare the roles and responsibilities for strategy implementation and evaluate resource requirements for the implementation of a new strategy for a given organisation. Learners will then be able to propose targets and timescales for implementation and monitoring of the strategy in a given organisation.

Learning outcomes

On successful completion of this unit a learner will:

1 Understand the process of strategic planning
2 Be able to formulate a new strategy
3 Understand approaches to strategy evaluation and selection
4 Understand how to implement a chosen strategy

Unit content

1 Understand the process of strategic planning

Strategic contexts and terminology: role of strategy; missions; visions; strategic intent; objectives; goals; core competencies; strategic architecture; strategic control

Strategic thinking: future direction of the competition; needs of customers; gaining and maintaining competitive advantage; Ansoff's growth-vector matrix; portfolio analysis

Planning systems: informal planning; top-down planning; bottom-up planning; behavioural approaches

Strategic planning issues: impact on managers; targets; when to plan; who should be involved; role of planning

Strategic planning techniques: BCG growth-share matrix; directional policy matrices; SPACE, PIMS

2 Be able to formulate a new strategy

Stakeholder analysis: stakeholder significance grid; stakeholder mapping

Environment auditing: political, economic, socio-cultural, technological, legal and environmental analysis (PESTLE); Porter's 5 force analysis; the threat of new entrants; the power of buyers; the power of suppliers; the threat of substitutes; competitive rivalry and collaboration

Strategic positioning: the Ansoff matrix; growth; stability; profitability; efficiency; market leadership; survival; mergers and acquisitions; expansion into the global marketplace

The organisational audit: benchmarking; SWOT analysis; product positions; value-chain analysis; demographic influences; scenario planning; synergy culture and values

3 Understand approaches to strategy evaluation and selection

Market entry strategies: organic growth; growth by merger or acquisition; strategic alliances; licensing; franchising

Substantive growth strategies: horizontal and vertical integration; related and unrelated diversification

Limited growth strategies: do nothing; market penetration; market development; product development; innovation

Disinvestment strategies: retrenchment; turnaround strategies; divestment; liquidation

Strategy selection: considering the alternatives; appropriateness; feasibility; desirability

4 Understand how to implement a chosen strategy

The realisation of strategic plans to operational reality: communication (selling the concepts); project teams; identification of team and individual roles, responsibilities and targets; programme of activities; benchmark targets at differing levels of the organisation

Resource allocation: finance; human resources; materials; time

Review and evaluation: an evaluation of the benchmarked outcomes in a given time period in relation to corporate, operational and individual targets

Learning outcomes and assessment criteria

Learning outcomes On successful completion of this unit a learner will:	Assessment criteria for pass The learner can:
LO1 Understand the process of strategic planning	1.1 explain strategic contexts and terminology – missions, visions, objectives, goals, core competencies 1.2 review the issues involved in strategic planning 1.3 explain different planning techniques
LO2 Be able to formulate a new strategy	2.1 produce an organisational audit for a given organisation 2.2 carry out an environmental audit for a given organisation 2.3 explain the significance of stakeholder analysis
LO3 Understand approaches to strategy evaluation and selection	3.1 analyse possible alternative strategies relating to substantive growth, limited growth or retrenchment 3.2 select an appropriate future strategy for a given organisation
LO4 Understand how to implement a chosen strategy	4.1 compare the roles and responsibilities for strategy implementation 4.2 evaluate resource requirements to implement a new strategy for a given organisation 4.3 discuss targets and timescales for achievement in a given organisation to monitor a given strategy

Guidance

Links

This unit should be linked with the other core units in the programme. It draws on the underpinning knowledge gained in the core and specialist units in the programme. Pre-requisites for this unit are core *Unit 1: Business Environment, Unit 2: Managing Financial Resources and Decisions, Unit 3: Organisations and Behaviour* and *Unit 4: Marketing Principles*.

Essential requirements

There are no essential or unique resources required for the delivery of this unit.

Employer engagement and vocational contexts

Centres should try to develop links with local businesses. Many businesses and chambers of commerce are keen to promote local business and are often willing to provide visit opportunities, guest speakers and information about business and the local business context.

Introducing strategy

Introduction

In November 2006 Yahoo! manager Brad Garlinghouse issued a memo that directly challenged the senior management of the internet giant. Leaked to the media as 'The Peanut Butter Manifesto', his memo accused Yahoo!'s leadership of lacking strategic direction. Growth had slowed, Google had overtaken Yahoo! in terms of on-line advertising revenues, and the share price had fallen by nearly a third since the start of the year. According to Brad Garlinghouse, Yahoo! was spread too thin, like peanut butter. It was time for strategic change.

All organisations are faced with the challenges of strategic direction: some from a desire to grasp new opportunities, others to overcome significant problems, as at Yahoo!. This book deals with why changes in strategic direction take place in organisations, why they are important, how such decisions are taken, and the concepts that can be useful in understanding these issues. This introductory chapter addresses particularly the meaning of 'strategy' and 'strategic management', why they are so important and what distinguishes them from other organisational challenges, tasks and decisions. The chapter will draw on the Yahoo! example in the Illustration on p. 779 to illustrate its points.

What is strategy?

Why were the issues facing Yahoo! described as 'strategic'?[1] What types of issues are strategic and what distinguishes them from operational issues in organisations?

The characteristics of strategic decisions

The words 'strategy' and 'strategic decisions' are typically associated with issues like these:

- *The long-term direction* of an organisation. Brad Garlinghouse explicitly recognised that strategic change in Yahoo! would require a 'marathon and not a sprint'. Strategy at Yahoo! involved long-term decisions about what sort of company it should be, and realising these decisions would take plenty of time.
- *The scope of an organisation's activities.* For example, should the organisation concentrate on one area of activity, or should it have many? Brad Garlinghouse believed that Yahoo! was spread too thinly over too many different activities.
- *Advantage* for the organisation over competition. The problem at Yahoo! was that it was losing its advantage to faster-growing companies such as Google. Advantage may be achieved in different ways and may also mean different things. For example, in the public sector, strategic advantage could be thought of as providing better value services than other providers, thus attracting support and funding from government.
- *Strategic fit with the business environment.* Organisations need appropriate *positioning* in their environment, for example in terms of the extent to which products

or services meet clearly identified market needs. This might take the form of a small business trying to find a particular niche in a market, or a multinational corporation seeking to buy up businesses that have already found successful market positions. According to Brad Garlinghouse, Yahoo! was trying to succeed in too many environments.

- *The organisation's resources and competences.*[2] Following 'the resource-based view' of strategy, strategy is about exploiting the strategic capability of an organisation, in terms of its resources and competences, to provide competitive advantage and/or yield new opportunities. For example, an organisation might try to leverage resources such as technology skills or strong brands. Yahoo! claims a brand 'synonymous with the Internet', theoretically giving it clear advantage in that environment.

- *The values and expectations* of powerful actors in and around the organisation. These actors – individuals, groups or even other organisations – can drive fundamental issues such as whether an organisation is expansionist or more concerned with consolidation, or where the boundaries are drawn for the organisation's activities. At Yahoo!, the senior managers may have pursued growth in too many directions, and been too reluctant to hold themselves accountable. But lower-level managers, ordinary employees, suppliers, customers and Internet users all have a stake in the future of Yahoo! too. The beliefs and values of these *stakeholders* will have a greater or lesser influence on the strategy development of an organisation, depending on the power of each. Certainly, Brad Garlinghouse was making a bold bid for influence over what seemed to be a failing strategy.

Overall, the most basic definition of strategy might be 'the long-term direction of an organisation'. However, the characteristics described above can provide the basis for a fuller definition:

> Strategy is the *direction* and *scope* of an organisation over the *long term*, which achieves *advantage* in a changing *environment* through its configuration of *resources and competences* with the aim of fulfilling *stakeholder* expectations.

illustration   Yahoo!'s peanut butter manifesto

Strategy can involve hard decisions about the scope of the business, its management and its organisation structure.

In November 2006, Brad Garlinghouse, MBA graduate and a Yahoo! senior vice president, wrote a memo to his top managers arguing that Yahoo!, the diversified Internet company, was spreading its resources too thinly, like peanut butter on a slice of bread. Edited extracts from the memo follow:

Three and half years ago, I enthusiastically joined Yahoo!. The magnitude of the opportunity was only matched by the magnitude of the assets. And an amazing team has been responsible for rebuilding Yahoo!. . . .

But all is not well. . . .

I imagine there's much discussion amongst the Company's senior-most leadership around the challenges we face. At the risk of being redundant, I wanted to share my take on our current situation and offer a recommended path forward, an attempt to be part of the solution rather than part of the problem.

Recognizing our problems

We lack a focused, cohesive vision for our company. We want to do everything and be everything – to everyone. We've known this for years, talk about it incessantly, but do nothing to fundamentally address it. We are scared to be left out. We are reactive instead of charting an unwavering course. We are separated into silos that far too frequently don't talk to each other. And when we do talk, it isn't to collaborate on a clearly focused strategy, but rather to argue and fight about ownership, strategies and tactics. . . .

I've heard our strategy described as spreading peanut butter across the myriad opportunities that continue to evolve in the online world. The result: a thin layer of investment spread across everything we do and thus we focus on nothing in particular.

I hate peanut butter. We all should.

We lack clarity of ownership and accountability. The most painful manifestation of this is the massive redundancy that exists throughout the organization. We now operate in an organizational structure – admittedly created with the best of intentions – that has become overly bureaucratic. For far too many employees, there is another person with dramatically similar and overlapping responsibilities. This slows us down and burdens the company with unnecessary costs.

There's a reason why a centerfielder and a left fielder have clear areas of ownership. Pursuing the same ball repeatedly results in either collisions or dropped balls. Knowing that someone else is pursuing the ball and hoping to avoid that collision – we have become timid in our pursuit. Again, the ball drops.

We lack decisiveness. Combine a lack of focus with unclear ownership, and the result is that decisions are either not made or are made when it is already too late. Without a clear and focused vision, and without complete clarity of ownership, we lack a macro perspective to guide our decisions and visibility into who should make those decisions. We are repeatedly stymied by challenging and hairy decisions. We are held hostage by our analysis paralysis.

We end up with competing (or redundant) initiatives and synergistic opportunities living in the different silos of our company. . . .

Solving our problems

We have awesome assets. Nearly every media and communications company is painfully jealous of our position. We have the largest audience, they are highly engaged and our brand is synonymous with the Internet.

If we get back up, embrace dramatic change, we will win.

I don't pretend there is only one path forward available to us. However, at a minimum, I want to be part of the solution and thus have outlined a plan here that I believe can work. It is my strong belief that we need to act very quickly or risk going further down a slippery slope. The plan here is not perfect; it is, however, FAR better than no action at all.

There are three pillars to my plan:

1 Focus the vision.
2 Restore accountability and clarity of ownership.
3 Execute a radical reorganization.

1 Focus the vision
a) We need to boldly and definitively declare what we are and what we are not.
b) We need to exit (sell?) non core businesses and eliminate duplicative projects and businesses.

My belief is that the smoothly spread peanut butter needs to turn into a deliberately sculpted strategy – that is narrowly focused. . . .

2 Restore accountability and clarity of ownership
a) Existing business owners must be held accountable for where we find ourselves today – heads must roll,
b) We must thoughtfully create senior roles that have holistic accountability for a particular line of business. . . .
c) We must redesign our performance and incentive systems.

I believe there are too many BU [Business Unit] leaders who have gotten away with unacceptable results and worse – unacceptable leadership. Too often they (we!) are the worst offenders of the problems outlined here. We must signal to both the employees and to our shareholders that we will hold these leaders (ourselves) accountable and implement change. . . .

3 Execute a radical reorganization
a) The current business unit structure must go away.

b) We must dramatically decentralize and eliminate as much of the matrix as possible.

c) We must reduce our headcount by 15–20%.

I emphatically believe we simply must eliminate the redundancies we have created and the first step in doing this is by restructuring our organization. We can be more efficient with fewer people and we can get more done, more quickly. We need to return more decision making to a new set of business units and their leadership. But we can't achieve this with baby step changes. We need to fundamentally rethink how we organize to win. . . .

I love Yahoo!. I'm proud to admit that I bleed purple and yellow. I'm proud to admit that I shaved a Y in the back of my head.

My motivation for this memo is the adamant belief that, as before, we have a tremendous opportunity ahead. I don't pretend that I have the only available answers, but we need to get the discussion going; change is needed and it is

needed soon. We can be a stronger and faster company – a company with a clearer vision and clearer ownership and clearer accountability.

We may have fallen down, but the race is a marathon and not a sprint. I don't pretend that this will be easy. It will take courage, conviction, insight and tremendous commitment. I very much look forward to the challenge.

So let's get back up.

Catch the balls.

And stop eating peanut butter.

Source: Extracts from Brad Garlinghouse's memo to Yahoo! managers, November 2006. Reprinted in *Wall Street Journal*, 16 November 2006.

Questions

1 Why were the issues facing Yahoo! described as strategic? Refer to the Exhibit on p. 782.

2 Identify examples of issues that fit each of the circles of the model in the Exhibit on p. 786.

The following exhibit summarises these characteristics of strategic decisions and also highlights some of the implications:

- *Complexity* is a defining feature of strategy and strategic decisions and is especially so in organisations with wide geographical scope, such as multinational firms, or wide ranges of products or services. For example, Yahoo! faces the complexity both of a fast-moving market environment and poorly-organised internal businesses.

- *Uncertainty* is inherent in strategy, because nobody can be sure about the future. For Yahoo!, the Internet environment is one of constant and unforeseeable innovation.

- *Operational decisions* are linked to strategy. For example, any attempt to coordinate Yahoo!'s business units more closely will have knock-on effects on web-page designs and links, career development and advertiser relationships. This link between overall strategy and operational aspects of the organisation is important for two other reasons. First, if the operational aspects of the organisation are not in line with the strategy, then, no matter how well considered the strategy is, it will not succeed. Second, it is at the operational level that real strategic advantage can be achieved. Indeed, competence in particular operational activities might determine which strategic developments might make most sense.

- *Integration* is required for effective strategy. Managers have to cross functional and operational boundaries to deal with strategic problems and come to agreements with other managers who, inevitably, have different interests and perhaps different priorities. Yahoo! for example needs an integrated approach to powerful advertisers such as Sony and Vodafone from across all its businesses.

Exhibit

Strategic decisions

Strategic decisions are about:

- The **long-term** direction of an organisation
- The **scope** of an organisation's activities
- Gaining **advantage** over competitors
- Addressing changes in the **business environment**
- Building on resources and competences (**capability**)
- **Values and expectations** of stakeholders

Therefore they are likely to:

- Be **complex** in nature
- Be made in situations of **uncertainty**
- Affect **operational** decisions
- Require an **integrated** approach (both inside and outside an organisation)
- Involve considerable **change**

- *Relationships and networks* outside the organisation are important in strategy, for example with suppliers, distributors and customers. For Yahoo!, advertisers and users are crucial sets of relationships.
- *Change* is typically a crucial component of strategy. Change is often difficult because of the heritage of resources and because of organisational culture. According to Brad Garlinghouse at least, Yahoo!'s barriers to change seem to include a top management that is afraid of taking hard decisions and a lack of clear accountability amongst lower-level management.

Levels of strategy

Strategies exist at a number of levels in an organisation. Taking Yahoo! again as an example, it is possible to distinguish at least three different levels of strategy. The top level is corporate-level strategy, concerned with the overall scope of an organisation and how value will be added to the different parts (business units) of the organisation. This could include issues of geographical coverage, diversity of products/services or business units, and how resources are to be allocated between the different parts of the organisation. For Yahoo!, whether to sell some of its existing businesses is clearly a crucial corporate-level decision. In general, corporate-level strategy is also likely to be concerned with the expectations of owners – the shareholders and the stock market. It may well take form in an explicit or implicit statement of 'mission' that reflects such expectations. Being clear about corporate-level strategy is important: determining the range of business to include is the *basis* of other strategic decisions.

The second level is business-level strategy, which is about how the various businesses included in the corporate strategy should compete in their particular markets (for this reason, business-level strategy is sometimes called 'competitive strategy'). In the public sector, the equivalent of business-level strategy is decisions about how units should provide best value services. This typically concerns issues such as pricing strategy, innovation or differentiation, for instance by better quality or a distinctive distribution channel. So, whereas corporate-level strategy involves decisions about the organisation as a whole, strategic decisions relate to particular strategic business units (SBU) within the overall organisation. A strategic business unit is a part of an organisation for which there is a distinct external market for goods or services that is different from another SBU. Yahoo!'s strategic business units include businesses such as Yahoo! Photos and Yahoo! Music.

Of course, in very simple organisations with only one business, the corporate strategy and the business-level strategy are nearly identical. None the less, even here, it is useful to distinguish a corporate-level strategy, because this provides the framework for whether and under what conditions other business opportunities might be added or rejected. Where the corporate strategy does include several businesses, there should be a clear link between strategies at an SBU level and the corporate level. In the case of Yahoo!, relationships with online advertisers stretch across different business units, and using, protecting and enhancing the Yahoo! brand is vital for all. The corporate strategy with regard to the brand should support the SBUs, but at the same time the SBUs have to make sure their business-level strategies do not damage the corporate whole or other SBUs in the group.

The third level of strategy is at the operating end of an organisation. Here there are operational strategies, which are concerned with how the component parts of an organisation deliver effectively the corporate- and business-level strategies in terms of resources, processes and people. For example, Yahoo! has web-page designers in each of its businesses, for whom there are appropriate operational strategies in terms of design, layout and renewal. Indeed, in most businesses, successful business strategies depend to a large extent on decisions that are taken, or activities that occur, at the operational level. The integration of operational decisions and strategy is therefore of great importance, as mentioned earlier.

The vocabulary of strategy

You will find a variety of terms used in relation to strategy, so it is worth devoting a little space to clarifying some of these. The following exhibit and illustration employ some of the terms that readers will come across in this and other books on strategy and in everyday business usage. The exhibit explains these in relation to a personal strategy readers may have followed themselves – improving physical fitness.

The vocabulary of strategy

Term	Definition	A personal example
Mission	Overriding purpose in line with the values or expectations of stakeholders	Be healthy and fit
Vision or strategic intent	Desired future state: the aspiration of the organisation	To run the London Marathon
Goal	General statement of aim or purpose	Lose weight and strengthen muscles
Objective	Quantification (if possible) or more precise statement of the goal	Lose 5 kilos by 1 September and run the marathon next year
Strategic capability	Resources, activities and processes. Some will be unique and provide 'competitive advantage'	Proximity to a fitness centre, a successful diet
Strategies	Long-term direction	Exercise regularly, compete in marathons locally, stick to appropriate diet
Business model	How product, service and information 'flow' between participating parties	Associate with a collaborative network (e.g. join running club)
Control	The monitoring of action steps to: • assess effectiveness of strategies and actions • modify as necessary strategies and/or actions	Monitor weight, kilometres run and measure times: if progress satisfactory, do nothing; if not, consider other strategies and actions

Not all these terms are always used in organisations or in strategy books: indeed, in this book the word 'goal' is rarely used. It will also be seen, through the many examples in this book, that terminology is not used consistently across organisations (see also the illustration). Managers and students of strategy need to be aware of this. Moreover, it may or may not be that mission, goals, objectives, strategies and so on are written down precisely. In some organisations this is done very formally; in others a mission or strategy might be implicit and, therefore, must be deduced from what an organisation is doing. However, as a general guideline the following terms are often used.

● A *mission* is a general expression of the overall purpose of the organisation, which, ideally, is in line with the values and expectations of major stakeholders and concerned with the scope and boundaries of the organisation. It is sometimes referred to in terms of the apparently simple but challenging question: *'What business are we in?'*
● A *vision* or *strategic intent* is the desired future state of the organisation. It is an aspiration around which a strategist, perhaps a chief executive, might seek to focus the attention and energies of members of the organisation.

illustration   The vocabulary of strategy in different contexts

All sorts of organisations use the vocabulary of strategy. Compare these extracts from the statements of communications giant Nokia and Kingston University, a public institution based in London with 20,000 students.

Nokia

Vision and Mission: Connecting is about helping people to feel close to what matters. Wherever, whenever, Nokia believes in communicating, sharing, and in the awesome potential in connecting the 2 billion who do with the 4 billion who don't.

If we focus on people, and use technology to help people feel close to what matters, then growth will follow. In a world where everyone can be connected, Nokia takes a very human approach to technology.

Strategy: At Nokia, customers remain our top priority. Customer focus and consumer understanding must always drive our day-to-day business behavior. Nokia's priority is to be the most preferred partner to operators, retailers and enterprises.

Nokia will continue to be a growth company, and we will expand to new markets and businesses. World leading productivity is critical for our future success. Our brand goal is for Nokia to become the brand most loved by our customers.

In line with these priorities, Nokia's business portfolio strategy focuses on five areas, with each having long-term objectives: create winning devices; embrace consumer Internet services; deliver enterprise solutions; build scale in networks; expand professional services.

There are three strategic assets that Nokia will invest in and prioritize: brand and design; customer engagement and fulfilment; technology and architecture.

Kingston University, London

Mission: The mission of Kingston University is to promote participation in higher education, which it regards as a democratic entitlement; to strive for excellence in learning, teaching and research; to realise the creative potential and fire the imagination of all its members; and to equip its students to make effective contributions to society and the economy.

Vision: Kingston University aims to be a comprehensive and community University. Our ambition is to create a University that is not constrained by present possibilities, but has a grander and more aspirational vision of its future.

Goals:

- To provide all our current and future students with equal opportunities to realise their learning ambition.
- To provide a comprehensive range of high-quality courses and a supportive environment that encourages critical learning and develops personal, social and employable skills.
- To create authority in research and professional practice for the benefit of individuals, society and the economy.
- To develop collaborative links with providers and stakeholders within the region, nationally and internationally.
- To make the University's organisation, structure, culture and systems appropriate for the delivery of its Mission and Goals.
- To manage and develop its human, physical and financial resources to achieve the best possible academic value and value-for-money.

Sources: www.nokia.com; Kingston University Plan, 2006–2010 (www.kingston.ac.uk).

Questions

1 How do the vocabularies of Nokia and Kingston University fit with each other and with the definitions given in the Exhibit on p. 782?

2 To what extent is strategy different for a commercial organisation such as Nokia and a public organisation like Kingston University?

3 Compare your university's (or employer's) strategic statements with Kingston's or Nokia's (use a web search with your organisation's name and terms such as 'strategy', 'vision' and 'mission'). What implications might there be for you from any similarities and differences?

- If the word *goal* is used, it usually means a general aim in line with the mission. It may well be qualitative in nature.
- On the other hand, an *objective* is more likely to be quantified, or at least to be a more precise aim in line with the goal. In this book the word 'objective' is used whether or not there is quantification.
- *Strategic capability* is concerned with the *resources and competences* that an organisation can use to provide value to customers or clients. *Unique resources* and *core competences* are the bases upon which an organisation achieves strategic advantage and is distinguished from competitors.
- The concept of *strategy* has already been defined. It is the long-term direction of the organisation. It is likely to be expressed in broad statements both about the direction that the organisation should be taking and the types of action required to achieve objectives. For example, it may be stated in terms of market entry, new products or services, or ways of operating.
- A *business model* describes the structure of product, service and information flows and the roles of the participating parties. For example, a traditional model for manufactured products is a linear flow of product from component manufacturers to product manufacturers to distributor to retailers to consumers. But information may flow directly between the product manufacturer and the final consumer (advertising and market research).
- *Strategic control* involves monitoring the extent to which the strategy is achieving the objectives and suggesting corrective action (or a reconsideration of the objectives).

The illustration on p. 782 compares strategy vocabulary from two organisations operating in very different *contexts*. Nokia is a private sector communications giant, competing against global corporations such as Motorola and Samsung. Profit is vital to Nokia, but still it sees its vision and mission in terms of connecting more people around the world. Kingston University, on the other hand, is a public university, with a commitment to increasing participation in higher education. But it too must earn revenues, and needs to make a surplus in order to be able to invest in the future. Kingston University is also competing for students and research funds, going head-to-head with similar universities in the UK and around the world. Corporate-level and business-level strategies are no less important for a public body such as Kingston University as a commercial one like Nokia.

Strategy vocabulary, therefore, is relevant to a wide range of contexts. A small entrepreneurial start-up will need a strategy statement to persuade investors and lenders of its viability. Public sector organisations need strategy statements not only to know what to do, but also to reassure their funders and regulators that what they do is what they should be doing. Voluntary organisations need to communicate exciting strategies in order to inspire volunteers and donors. If they are to prosper within the larger organisation, SBU managers need to propose clear strategies that are consistent with the objectives of their corporate owners and with the needs of other SBUs within the corporate whole. Even privately-held organisations need persuasive strategy statements to motivate their employees and to build long-term relationships with their key customers or suppliers. Strategy vocabulary, therefore, is used in many different contexts, for many different purposes. Strategy is part of the everyday language of work.

Strategic management

The term strategic management underlines the importance of managers with regard to strategy. Strategies do not happen just by themselves. Strategy involves people, especially the managers who decide and implement strategy. Thus this chapter uses strategic management to emphasise the human element of strategy.

The strategic management role is different in nature from other aspects of management. An operational manager is most often required to deal with problems of operational control, such as the efficient production of goods, the management of a salesforce, the monitoring of financial performance or the design of some new system that will improve the level of customer service. These are all very important tasks, but they are essentially concerned with effectively managing resources already deployed, often in a limited part of the organisation within the context of an existing strategy. Operational control is what managers are involved in for most of their time. It is vital to the success of strategy, but it is not the same as strategic management.

For managers, strategic management involves a greater scope than that of any one area of operational management. Strategic management is concerned with complexity arising out of ambiguous and non-routine situations with organisation-wide rather than operation-specific implications. This is a major challenge for managers who are used to managing on a day-to-day basis the resources they control. It can be a particular problem because of the background of managers who may typically have been trained, perhaps over many years, to undertake operational tasks and to take operational responsibility. Accountants find that they still tend to see problems in financial terms, IT managers in IT terms, marketing managers in marketing terms, and so on. Of course, each of these aspects is important, but none is adequate alone. The manager who aspires to manage or influence strategy needs to develop a capability to take an overview, to conceive of the whole rather than just the parts of the situation facing an organisation. This is often referred to as the 'helicopter view'.

Because strategic management is characterised by its complexity, it is also necessary to make decisions and judgements based on the *conceptualisation* of difficult issues. Yet the early training and experience of managers is often about taking action, or about detailed *planning* or *analysis*. This chapter is concerned with action related to the management of strategy. However, the major emphasis is on the importance of understanding the *strategic concepts* which inform this action.

Strategic management can be thought of as having three main elements: understanding *the strategic position* of an organisation, making *strategic choices* for the future and managing *strategy in action* (see the following exhibit). As this chapter is about the fundamentals of strategy, it concentrates on the first two elements, position and choice. Other issues to do with strategy in action – such as resourcing and the practice of strategy – are dealt with more fully in *Exploring Corporate Strategy*.[3] Nonetheless, it is important to understand why the three circles in the following exhibit have been drawn in this particular way.

This exhibit could have shown the three elements of strategic management in a linear sequence – first understanding the strategic position, then strategic choices and finally putting strategy in action. Indeed, many texts on the subject do just this. However, in practice, the elements of strategic management do not follow this

The fundamentals of the *Exploring Corporate Strategy* strategic management model

The
Strategic
Position

Strategic
Choices

Strategy
in Action

Source: Based on G. Johnson, K. Scholes and R. Whittington, *Exploring Corporate Strategy*, 8th edition, Pearson Education.

linear sequence – they are interlinked and feed back on each other. For example, in some circumstances an understanding of the strategic position may best be built up from the experience of trying a strategy out in practice. Test marketing a prototype would be a good example. Here strategy in action informs understanding of the strategic position.

The inter-connected circles of the above exhibit are designed to emphasise this non-linear nature of strategy. Position, choices and action should be seen as closely related, and in practice none has priority over another. It is only for structural convenience that this chapter starts with strategic position, continues with important choices such as diversification and internationalisation, and then concludes with strategy in action. This sequence is not meant to suggest that the process of strategic management must follow a neat and tidy path. Indeed, the evidence on how strategic management happens in practice suggests that it usually does not occur in tidy ways.

The strategic position

Understanding the strategic position is concerned with identifying the impact on strategy of the external environment, an organisation's strategic capability (resources and competences) and the expectations and influence of stakeholders. The sorts of questions this raises are central to future strategies:

- The *environment*. The organisation exists in the context of a complex political, economic, social, technological, environmental and legal world. This environment changes and is more complex for some organisations than for others. How this affects the organisation could include an understanding of historical and environmental effects, as well as expected or potential changes in environmental variables. Many of those variables will give rise to *opportunities* and others will exert *threats* on the organisation – or both.
- The *strategic capability* of the organisation – made up of *resources and competences*. One way of thinking about the strategic capability of an organisation is to consider its *strengths* and *weaknesses* (for example, where it is at a competitive advantage or disadvantage). The aim is to form a view of the internal influences – and constraints – on strategic choices for the future.
- The major influences of *stakeholder expectations* on an organisation's *purposes*. Purpose is encapsulated in an organisation's *vision*, *mission* and *values*. Here the issue of *corporate governance* is important: who *should* the organisation primarily serve and how should managers be held responsible for this? This raises issues of *corporate social responsibility* and *ethics*.
- *Cultural and historical influences* that can also influence strategy. Cultural influences can be *organisational*, *sectoral* or *national*. Historical influences can create *lock-in* on particular strategic trajectories. The impact of these influences can be *strategic drift*, a failure to create necessary change.

These positioning issues were all important for Yahoo! as it faced its crisis in 2006. The external environment offered the threat of growing competition from Google. Its strong Internet brand and existing audience were key resources for defending its position. The company was struggling with its purposes, with top management apparently indecisive. The company none the less had inherited a strong culture, powerful enough to make Brad Garlinghouse shave a Y on his head and believe that his blood bled in the corporate colours of his employer.

Strategic choices

Strategic choices involve the options for strategy in terms of both the directions in which strategy might move and the methods by which strategy might be pursued. For example, an organisation might have to choose between alternative diversification moves, for example entering into new products and markets. As it diversifies, it has different methods available to it, for example developing a new product itself or acquiring an organisation already active in the area.

- There are strategic choices in terms of how the organisation seeks to compete at the *business level*. Typically these involve pricing and differentiation strategies, and decisions about how to compete or collaborate with competitors.
- At the highest level in an organisation there are issues of *corporate-level strategy*, which are concerned with the scope, or breadth, of an organisation. These include *diversification* decisions about the portfolio of products and the spread of markets. For Yahoo!, being spread over too many businesses seems to be the major strategic problem. Corporate-level strategy is also concerned with the relationship between the separate parts of the business and how the corporate

'parent' adds value to these various parts. At Yahoo!, it is not clear how much the corporate parent is adding value to its constituent parts. These issues about the role of the centre and how it adds value are *parenting* issues.

- *International strategy* is a form of diversification, into new geographical markets. It is often at least as challenging as diversification. Organisations have to make choices about which geographical markets to prioritise and how to enter them, by export, licensing, direct investment or acquisition.
- Organisations have to make choices about the *methods* by which they pursue their strategies. Many organisations prefer to grow 'organically', in other words by building new businesses with their own resources. Other organisations might develop by mergers/acquisitions and/or strategic alliances with other organisations.

Strategy in action

Strategy in action is concerned with ensuring that chosen strategies are actually put into practice.

- *Structuring* an organisation to support successful performance. According to Brad Garlinghouse, structural silos, matrix organisation and bureaucracy were all big problems for Yahoo!.
- *Processes* are required to control the way in which strategy is implemented. Managers need to ensure that strategies are implemented according to plan, check on progress and make necessary adjustments on the way.
- Managing *strategic change* is typically an important part of putting strategy into action. This includes the need to understand how the context of an organisation should influence the approach to change and the different types of *roles* for people in managing change. It also looks at the *styles* that can be adopted for managing change and the *levers* by which change can be effected.

These issues, and related ones, are dealt with more extensively in *Exploring Corporate Strategy* 8th Edition by Gerry Johnson, Kevan Scholes and Richard Whittington.

Strategy development processes

The previous section introduced strategic position, strategic choices and strategy in action. Implicit so far is that strategies are the product of careful analysis and choices. However, this is not the only way that strategies develop in organisations. There are two broad explanations of strategy development:

- The *rational-analytic view* of strategy development is the conventional explanation. Here strategies are developed through rational and analytical processes, led typically by top managers. There is a linear sequence. First the strategic position is analysed; then, after weighing up the options, strategic choices are made; finally, structures, processes and change procedures are put in place to allow effective implementation. Often formal strategic planning systems are important to the analysis and formulation of the strategy. In this view, strategies are *intended*, in other words the product of deliberate choices.

- The *emergent strategy* view is the alternative broad explanation of how strategies develop. In this view, strategies often do not develop as intended or planned, but tend to emerge in organisations over time as a result of ad hoc, incremental or even accidental actions. Good ideas and opportunities often come from practical experience at the bottom of the organisation, rather than from top management and formal strategic plans. Even the best laid plans may need to be abandoned as new opportunities arise or the organisation learns from the marketplace.

The two views are not mutually exclusive. Intended strategies can often succeed, especially in stable markets where there are few surprises. Moreover, an organisation's key stakeholders – employees, owners, customers, regulators and so on – will typically want to see evidence of deliberate strategy-making: it is rarely acceptable to say that everything is simply emergent. But it is wise to be open as well to the possibilities of emergence. Inflexible plans can hinder learning and prevent the seizing of opportunities. Moreover, strategic choices do not always come about as a result of simple rational analysis: *cultural and political processes* in organisations can also drive changes in strategy.

This chapter allows for *both* the rational-analytical view and the emergent view. Indeed, the interconnected circles of the *Exploring Corporate Strategy* model in the exhibit on p. 788 deliberately underline the possibly non-linear aspects of strategy. It is not just a matter of putting strategic choices into action in a logical sequence leading from strategy formulation to strategy implementation. Strategy in action often creates the strategic choices in the first place, as new opportunities and constraints are discovered in practice. Implementation can lead to formulation as well.[4]

Summary

- Strategy is the *direction* and *scope* of an organisation over the *long term*, which achieves *advantage* in a changing *environment* through its configuration of *resources and competences* with the aim of fulfilling *stakeholder* expectations.
- Strategic decisions are made at a number of levels in organisations. *Corporate-level strategy* is concerned with an organisation's overall purpose and scope; *business-level (or competitive) strategy* with how to compete successfully in a market; and *operational strategies* with how resources, processes and people can effectively deliver corporate- and business-level strategies. Strategic management is distinguished from day-to-day operational management by the complexity of influences on decisions, the organisation-wide implications and their long-term implications.
- Strategic management has three major elements: understanding the *strategic position, strategic choices* for the future and *strategy in action*. The strategic position of an organisation is influenced by the external environment, internal strategic capability and the expectations and influence of stakeholders. Strategic choices include the underlying bases of strategy at both the corporate and business levels and the directions and methods of development. Strategy in action is concerned with issues of structure and processes for implementing strategy and the managing of change.

Recommended reading

It is always useful to read around a topic. As well as the specific references below, we particularly highlight:

- For general overviews of the evolving nature of the strategy discipline, R. Whittington, *What is strategy – and does it matter?* 2nd edition, International Thompson, 2000; and H. Mintzberg, B. Ahlstrand and J. Lampel, *Strategy Safari: a Guided tour through the wilds of Strategic Management*, Simon and Schuster, 2000.
- For contemporary developments in strategy practice, business newspapers such as the *Financial Times*, *Les Echos* and the *Wall Street Journal*, and business magazines such as *Business Week*, the *Economist*, *L'Expansion* and *Manager-Magazin*. See also the websites of the leading strategy consulting firms: www.mckinsey.com; www.bcg.com; www.bain.com.

Notes

1 The question 'What is strategy?' has been discussed in R. Whittington, *What is strategy – and does it matter?* (1993/2000), International Thompson; M. Porter, 'What is strategy?', *Harvard Business Review*, November–December (1996), pp. 61–78; and F. Fréry, 'The fundamental dimensions of strategy', *MIT Sloan Management Review*, vol. 48, no. 1 (2006), pp. 71–75.

2 The Harvard 'business policy' tradition is discussed in L. Greiner, A. Bhambri and T. Cummins, 'Searching for a strategy to teach strategy', *Academy of Management Learning and Education*, vol. 2, no. 4 (2003), pp. 401–420.

3 G. Johnson, K. Scholes and R. Whittington, *Exploring Corporate Strategy*, 8th edition (2008), Pearson.

4 The classic discussion of the roles of rational strategy formulation and strategy implementation is in H. Mintzberg, 'The design school: reconsidering the basic premises of strategic management', *Strategic Management Journal*, vol. 11 (1991), pp. 171–195 and H.I. Ansoff, 'Critique of Henry Mintzberg's The Design School', *Strategic Management Journal*, vol. 11 (1991), 449–461.

---

case example Electrolux

By 2005 Sweden's Electrolux was the world's largest producer of domestic and professional appliances for the kitchen, cleaning and outdoor use. Its products included cookers, vacuum cleaners, washing machines, fridges, lawn mowers, chain saws and also tools for the construction and stone industries. It employed about 70,000 people and sold about 40 million products annually in about 150 countries. Its annual sales in 2005 were 129 billion Swedish krona (~€14bn; ~£10bn) and profits about 3.9bn krona (~€420m). But 2005 saw two changes that would push the company into second place in the industry – behind the US company *Whirlpool*. First, Whirlpool completed its acquisition of *Maytag* – which gave it about 47 per cent market share in the USA and global sales of some $US19bn (~€15bn). Second, Electrolux announced that it was to demerge its outdoor products division (mowers, chain saws, etc.) as *Husqvarna*. This left Electrolux to focus on the indoor products for both the home and professional cooking and cleaning organisations.

So the 'new Electrolux' would have 57,000 employees and global sales of some SEK 104bn (~€11bn).

History

This was just the latest shift in strategy at Electrolux whose impressive growth and development started under the leadership of Alex Wenner-Gren in 1920s Sweden. The early growth was built around an expertise in industrial design creating the leading products in refrigeration and vacuum cleaning. By the mid-1930s the company had also established production outside Sweden in Germany, UK, France, USA and Australia.

The period following the Second World War saw a major growth in demand for domestic appliances and Electrolux expanded its range into washing machines and dishwashers. In 1967 Hans Werthén took over as president and embarked on a series of acquisitions that restructured the industry in Europe: 59 acquisitions were made in the 1970s alone followed by major acquisitions of Zanussi (Italy), White Consolidated Products (USA), the appliance division of Thorn EMI (UK) the outdoor products company Poulan/Weed Eater (USA) and AEG Hausgeräte (Germany). But the biggest acquisition of the 1980s was the Swedish Granges Group (this was a diversification into a metals conglomerate).

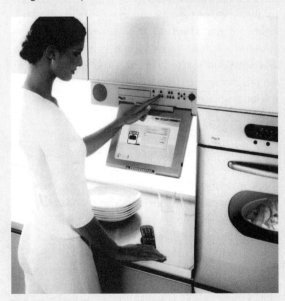

Photo: Electrolux

As a result of all these acquisitions, by 1990 75 per cent of Electrolux's sales were outside Sweden and this increased in the 1990s as Leif Johansson expanded into Eastern Europe, Asia (India and Thailand) and Central and South America (Mexico and Brazil). He then disposed of many of the 'non-core' industrial activities (particularly Granges). A major restructuring in the late 1990s created the shape of the group for the early 2000s – with about 85 per cent of sales in consumer durables and 15 per cent in related products for professional users (such as professional food service and laundry equipment).

The market

The 2005 annual report highlighted three critically important aspects of the company's markets that their strategies had to address:

Globalisation

'Electrolux operates in an industry with strong global competition. . . . Productivity within the industry has risen over the years, and consumers are offered increasingly better products at lower prices. More and more manufacturers are establishing plants in countries where production costs are considerably lower . . . and also purchasing more components there. In time, production costs for the major producers will essentially be at the same level. This will stimulate a shift of competitive focus to product development, marketing and brand-building.'

Market polarisation

'The combination of changing consumer preferences, the growth of global retail chains and greater global competition is leading to polarisation of the market. More consumers are demanding basic products. Companies that can improve efficiency in production and distribution will be able to achieve profitable growth in this segment. At the same time, demand for higher-price products is increasing.'

Consolidation of retailers

'The dealer structure in the household-appliances market [particularly in the USA] is being consolidated. Traditional dealers are losing market shares to large retail chains. The big chains benefit from high purchasing volumes and wide geographical coverage. This gives them greater opportunities to keep prices low. [But in turn, producers'] costs of serving large retailers is often lower than for traditional outlets, thanks to large volumes and efficient logistics.'

These three factors were also connected. For example, the rapid penetration of Asian producers (for example, LG and Samsung) into the US market was through securing big contracts with major US retailers (The Home Depot and Lowe's respectively).

Electrolux strategies

In the 2005 annual report the Chief Executive (Hans Stråberg) reflected on his first four years with the company and the challenges for the future: Four years ago I took over as President and CEO of Electrolux. My goal was to accelerate the development of Electrolux as a market-driven company, based on greater understanding of customer needs. . . . We [said that we] would achieve [our goals] by:

- Continuing to cut costs and drive out complexity in all aspects of operations
- Increasing the rate of product renewal based on consumer insight
- Increasing our investment in marketing, and building the Electrolux brand as the global leader in our industry.

He continued by describing the major changes in strategy that had occurred over those four years whilst looking forward to the continuing and new challenges after the demerger in 2006:

Managing under-performers

We have divested or changed the business model for units that could be considered as non-core operations or in which profitability was too low. [For example], instead of continuing production of air-conditioners in the US, which was not profitable, we out-sourced these products to a manufacturer in China. Our operations in motors and compressors have been divested.

Moving production to low-cost countries

Maintaining competitive production costs is a prerequisite for survival in our markets. We will work on improving profitability either by divesting specific units or by changing the business model. It is also important to continue relocating production from high-cost to low-cost countries. . . . We have shut down plants where costs were much too high, and built new ones in countries with competitive cost levels. For example, we moved production of refrigerators from Greenville in the US to Juarez in Mexico. This has enabled us to cut costs and at the same time open a state-of-the-art production unit for serving the entire North American market. The goal is for these activities to be largely completed by late 2008.

More efficient production and logistics

We have put a good deal of time and effort into making production and logistics more efficient. This has involved reducing the number of product platforms, increasing productivity, reducing inventory levels and increasing delivery accuracy.

More efficient purchasing

Purchasing is another area where we have implemented changes in order to improve our cost position, mainly through better coordination at the global level. We have launched a project designed to drastically reduce the number of suppliers. We have also intensified our cooperation with suppliers in order to cut the costs of components. [But] there is a good deal still to be done. Among other things, we are increasing the share of purchases from low-cost countries.

Intensified product renewal

Our future depends on how well we can combine a continued focus on costs with intensified product renewal and systematic development of both our brands and our personnel. . . . Our process for product development based on consumer insight reduces the risk of incorrect investment decisions. Achieving better impact in development of new products has involved making global coordination more efficient, which has given us a number of new global products. The result of our investments in product development over the past years is clearly reflected in the number of product launches for core appliances, which rose from about 200 in 2002 to about 370 in 2005. . . . Investment in product development has risen by SEK 500 million (~€77m) over the past three years. Our goal is to invest at least 2% of sales in product development. We will continue to launch new products at a high rate.

Access to competence

Over the past years we have established [talent management] processes and tools that ensure the Group of access to competence in the future. Active leadership development, international career opportunities and a result-oriented corporate culture enable us to successfully develop our human resources. In order to lead development in our industry, we will have to act fast and dare to do things differently. [We will also need] a strong environmental commitment and good relations with our suppliers.

Starting to build a strong global brand

When I took over as President and CEO in 2002 I stressed that we had to prioritise building of the Electrolux brand, both globally and across all product categories. A strong brand enables a significant price premium in the market, which leads to a sustainable long-term increase in margin. Work on building a strong brand has been very comprehensive. The share of products sold under the Electrolux brand has risen from 16% of sales in 2002 to almost 50% in 2005. We will continue to work on building the Electrolux brand as the global leader in our industry. Our goal is for our investment in brand-building to correspond to at least 2% of sales.

Looking ahead to the near future

Hans Stråberg concluded his review of the business by a look forward to the following year: We expect the Group to report higher profitability again in 2006. . . . In both North America and Europe we are going to launch a number of important new products. Professional Indoor

Products will improve its position in the North American market in 2006 by developing new distribution channels for food-service equipment. The success of our floor-care operation in the higher price segments will continue, among other things on the basis of higher volumes for cyclone vacuum cleaners.

There will be no change in the rate of relocation of production to low-cost countries. During the second half of 2006 we will see the full effect of the cost-savings generated by moving production from Greenville in the US to Juarez in Mexico. We expect that sales will be adversely affected by the strike at our appliance plant in Nuremberg, Germany [planned to close in 2007]. Continued reduction of purchasing costs is a very important factor for increasing our profitability in 2006.

The strategy that has been effectively implemented in recent years by everyone in our organisation is paying off. In 2006 we will continue this important work on strengthening the Electrolux brand, launching new products and reducing costs. Sources: Company website (www.electrolux.com); annual report 2005.

Questions

1 Refer to 'The characteristics of strategic decisions' on p. 778 and explain why the issues facing Electrolux were strategic. Try to find examples of all of the items cited in that section.

2 What levels of strategy can you identify at Electrolux? (Refer to 'Levels of strategy' on p. 782.)

3 Identify the main factors about the strategic position of Electrolux. List these separately under environment, capability and expectations (see 'The strategic position' on p. 788). In your opinion which are the most important factors?

4 Think about strategic choices for the company in relation to the issues raised in 'Strategic choices' on p. 789.

5 What are the main issues about strategy into action that might determine the success or failure of Electrolux's strategies? (Refer to 'Strategy in action' on p. 790.)

CHAPTER 8

Research Project

Unit 8: Research Project

Unit code: K/601/0941

QCF level: 5

Credit value: 20 credits

Aim

To develop learners' skills of independent enquiry and critical analysis by undertaking a sustained research investigation of direct relevance to their Higher Education programme and professional development.

Unit abstract

This unit is designed to enable learners to become confident using research techniques and methods. It addresses the elements that make up formal research including the proposal, a variety of research methodologies, action planning, carrying out the research itself and presenting the findings. To complete the unit satisfactorily, learners must also understand the theory that underpins formal research.

The actual research depends on the learner, the context of their area of learning, their focus of interest and the anticipated outcomes. The unit draws together a range of other areas from within the programme to form a holistic piece of work that will make a positive contribution to the learner's area of interest. Learners should seek approval from their tutors before starting their research project.

Learning outcomes

On successful completion of this unit a learner will:

1 Understand how to formulate a research specification
2 Be able to implement the research project within agreed procedures and to specification
3 Be able to evaluate the research outcomes
4 Be able to present the research outcomes.

Unit content

1 Understand how to formulate a research specification

Research formulation: aims and objectives; rationale for selection; methodology for data collection and analysis; literature review; critique of references from primary sources eg questionnaires, interviews; secondary sources eg books, journals, internet; scope and limitations; implications eg resources

Hypothesis: definition; suitability; skills and knowledge to be gained; aims and objectives; terms of reference; duration; ethical issues

Action plan: rationale for research question or hypothesis; milestones; task dates; review dates; monitoring/reviewing process; strategy

Research design: type of research eg qualitative, quantitative, systematic, original; methodology; resources; statistical analyses; validity; reliability; control of variables

2 Be able to implement the research project within agreed procedures and to specification

Implement: according to research design and method; test research hypotheses; considering test validity; reliability

Data collection: selection of appropriate tools for data collection; types eg qualitative, quantitative; systematic recording; methodological problems eg bias, variables and control of variables, validity and reliability

Data analysis and interpretation: qualitative and quantitative data analysis – interpreting transcripts; coding techniques; specialist software; statistical tables; comparison of variable; trends; forecasting

3 Be able to evaluate the research outcomes

Evaluation of outcomes: an overview of the success or failure of the research project planning, aims and objectives, evidence and findings, validity, reliability, benefits, difficulties, conclusion(s)

Future consideration: significance of research investigation; application of research results; implications; limitations of the investigation; improvements; recommendations for the future, areas for future research

4 Be able to present the research outcomes

Format: professional delivery format appropriate to the audience; use of appropriate media

Learning outcomes and assessment criteria

Learning outcomes On successful completion of this unit a learner will:	Assessment criteria for pass The learner can:
LO1 Understand how to formulate a research specification	1.1 formulate and record possible research project outline specifications 1.2 identify the factors that contribute to the process of research project selection 1.3 undertake a critical review of key references 1.4 produce a research project specification 1.5 provide an appropriate plan and procedures for the agreed research specification
LO2 Be able to implement the research project within agreed procedures and to specification	2.1 match resources efficiently to the research question or hypothesis 2.2 undertake the proposed research investigation in accordance with the agreed specification and procedures 2.3 record and collate relevant data where appropriate
LO3 Be able to evaluate the research outcomes	3.1 use appropriate research evaluation techniques 3.2 interpret and analyse the results in terms of the original research specification 3.3 make recommendations and justify areas for further consideration
LO4 Be able to present the research outcomes	4.1 use an agreed format and appropriate media to present the outcomes of the research to an audience

Guidance

Links

This unit may be linked to single or several units in the programme, depending on the research topic and the context of the area of learning. It can be linked to *Unit 49: Work-based Experience* and gives learners the opportunity to carry out research in the same organisation where they undertook their placement.

Essential requirements

Tutors will need to establish the availability of resources to support independent study before learners proceed with their proposal.

Employer engagement and vocational contexts

Centres should try to establish relationships with appropriate organisations in order to bring realism and relevance to learners' research projects.

Formulating and clarifying
the research topic

Introduction

Many students think that choosing their research topic is the most exciting part of their course. After all, this is something that they get to decide for themselves rather than having to complete a task decided by their tutors. We will stress in this chapter that it is important to choose something that will sustain your interest throughout the months that you will need to complete it. You may even decide to do some research that is something that forms part of your leisure activities!

Before you start your research you need to have at least some idea of what you want to do. This is probably the most difficult, and yet the most important, part of your research project. Up until now most of your studies have been concerned with answering questions that other people have set. This chapter is concerned with how to formulate and clarify your research topic and your research question. Without being clear about what you are going to research it is difficult to plan how you are going to research it. This reminds us of a favourite quote in *Alice's Adventures in Wonderland*. This is part of Alice's conversation with the Cheshire Cat. In this Alice asks the Cat (Carroll 1989:63–4):

> 'Would you tell me, please, which way I ought to walk from here?'
> 'That depends a good deal on where you want to get to', said the Cat.
> 'I don't much care where', said Alice.
> 'Then it doesn't matter which way you walk', said the Cat.

Formulating and clarifying the research topic is the starting point of your research project (Ghauri and Grønhaug 2005; Smith and Dainty 1991). Once you are clear about this, you will be able to choose the most appropriate research strategy and data collection and analysis techniques. The formulating and clarifying process is time consuming and will probably take you up blind alleys (Saunders and Lewis 1997). However, without spending time on this stage you are far less likely to achieve a successful project (Raimond 1993).

In the initial stages of the formulating and clarifying process you will be generating and refining research ideas (see 'Generating and refining research ideas', p. 805). It may be that you have already been given a research idea, perhaps by an organisation or tutor. Even if this has happened you will still need to refine the idea into one that is feasible. Once you have done this you will need to turn the idea into research questions and objectives (see 'Turning research ideas into research projects', p. 815) and to write the research proposal for your project (see 'Writing your research proposal', p. 824).

Mobile phone operators have high hopes that, following the success of text messaging, 'picture messaging', using camera phones will establish photos as a new genre in mobile communication. Although sales figures are good for camera phones, it's not clear to what extent people are using camera phones, to send picture messages. Recent media reports have described early results as disappointing. Possible explanations include obstacles such as cost, reliability and interface complexity. Alternatively, a camera phone's value might not lie in sending images but in using the captured images for other activities.

A team of researchers (Kindberg *et al.* 2005) decided to establish what users actually do with their camera phones. The research had two main objectives. The first was to explore the range and diversity of use to help broaden the team's outlook on current and future camera phone use. The second was to elucidate the characteristics and context of use for different activities to learn how such activities may be better supported.

The team recruited 34 subjects: 19 in the UK and 15 in the USA. The study consisted of two interviews with each subject, conducted two to five weeks apart. During each interview, researchers asked the subjects to show five images (photos or videos) from their camera phones. The images may have been either taken or received by the research subject.

The data collected enabled the research team to develop a six-part taxonomy that describes how people use camera phone images for social and personal purposes and affective and functional purposes. Reviewing the taxonomy reveals implications for future products and services.

Source: Nicholas Linton/Alamy

However, before you start the formulating and clarifying process we believe that you need to understand what makes a good research topic. For this reason we begin this chapter with a discussion of the attributes required for a good research topic.

Attributes of a good research topic

The attributes of a business and management research topic do not vary a great deal between universities (Raimond 1993), although there will be differences in the emphasis placed on different attributes. If you are undertaking your research project as part of a course of study the most important attribute will be that it meets the examining body's requirements and, in particular, that it is at the correct level. This means that you must choose your topic with care. For example, some universities require students to collect their own data as part of their research project whereas others allow them to base their project on data that have already been collected. Alternatively, some ask you to undertake an organisation-based piece of applied research, whilst others simply say that it must be within the subject matter of your course or programme. You, therefore, need to check the assessment criteria for your project and ensure that your choice of topic will enable you to meet these criteria. If you are unsure, you should discuss any uncertainties with your project tutor.

In addition, your research topic must be something you are capable of undertaking and one that excites your imagination. Capability can be considered in a variety of ways. At the personal level you need to feel comfortable that you have, or can develop, the skills that will be required to research the topic. We hope that you will develop your research skills as part of undertaking your project. However, some skills, for example foreign languages, may be impossible to acquire in the time you have available. As well as having the necessary skills we believe that you also need to have a genuine interest in the topic. Most research projects are undertaken over at least a six-month period. A topic in which you are only vaguely interested at the start is likely to become a topic in which you have no interest and with which you will fail to produce your best work.

Your ability to find the financial and time resources to undertake research on the topic will also affect your capability. Some topics are unlikely to be possible to complete in the time allowed by your course of study. This may be because they require you to measure the impact of an intervention over a long time period (Box 8.1). Similarly, topics that are likely to require you to travel widely or need expensive equipment should also be disregarded unless financial resources permit.

Box 8.1   Focus on student research

Turning ideas into a viable project

Zaynab was not short of ideas for her research. But she was much less sure about how she would move from a topic of interest for her research to a question that could be answered for her research project. It was emphasised to her by her tutors that ideas were easy, turning them into viable research projects was another matter altogether.

Having explored various websites and looked at some publications in the library, she drew up a plan of action which she was sure would give her the material necessary to write her research proposal.

Charting the ideas

At the start of her project, Zaynab got a huge sheet of paper to make a map of all of her ideas, questions, associations, sources and leads. She marked her most compelling thoughts in a red. Then she marked the main links to those ideas in that red too. She was careful not to throw out the weaker or isolated thoughts. She felt this map would help her know the place of all her thoughts. She thought that she could make another map later in the project if she felt there was too much information.

Archive the questions

Next Zaynab recorded who originally asked the question and left a space by each one to record answers or places to look for answers. Then she highlighted the questions that she found most challenging, the ones that really grabbed her attention. She thought that archiving questions would encourage her to articulate them well. Forming thoughts as questions helped her to be clear about what she needed to research.

Blog it

Zaynab was a keen blogger so she posted summaries of her ideas and questions on a weblog. She asked for site visitors to suggest further reading, new research methods or for answers to answer her questions. She received a healthy amount of feedback from which she made real progress in turning favourite idea into question that could be answered for her research project.

Thinking about the application of the findings

Zaynab knew that she would be expected to comment on the practical implications of her findings when writing up her research. Therefore, an important part of her plan of action at the outset was to ask herself what would be the implications for practice for the various outcomes that might be expected.

Capability also means you must be reasonably certain of gaining access to any data you might need to collect. Gill and Johnson (2002) argue that this is usually relatively straightforward to assess. They point out that many people start with ideas where access to data will prove difficult. Certain, more sensitive topics, such as financial performance or decision making by senior managers, are potentially fascinating. However, they may present considerable access problems. You, therefore, should discuss this with your project tutor.

For most topics it is important that the issues within the research are capable of being linked to theory (Raimond 1993). Initially, theory may be based just on the reading you have undertaken as part of your study to date. However, as part of your assessment criteria you are almost certain to be asked to set your topic in context (see 'Generating and refining research ideas', p. 805). As a consequence you will need to have a knowledge of the literature and to undertake further reading as part of defining your research questions and objectives (see 'Turning research ideas into research projects', p. 815).

Most project tutors will argue that one of the attributes of a good topic is clearly defined research questions and objectives (see 'Turning research ideas into research projects', p. 815). These will, along with a good knowledge of the literature, enable you to assess the extent to which your research is likely to provide fresh insights into the topic. Many students believe this is going to be difficult. Fortunately, as pointed out by Phillips and Pugh (2005), there are many ways in which such insight can be defined as 'fresh' (see 'Writing your research proposal', p. 824).

If you have already been given a research idea (perhaps by an organisation) you will need to ensure that your questions and objectives relate clearly to the idea (Kervin 1999). It is also important that your topic will have a **symmetry of potential outcomes**: that is, your results will be of similar value whatever you find out (Gill and Johnson 2002). Without this symmetry you may spend a considerable amount of time researching your topic only to find an answer of little importance. Whatever the outcome, you need to ensure you have the scope to write an interesting project report.

Finally, it is important to consider your career goals (Creswell 2002). If you wish to become an expert in a particular subject area or industry sector, it is sensible to use the opportunity to develop this expertise.

It is almost inevitable that the extent to which these attributes apply to your research topic will depend on your topic and the reasons for which you are undertaking the research. However, most of these attributes will apply. For this reason it is important that you check and continue to check any potential research topic against the summary checklist contained in Box 8.2.

Generating and refining research ideas

Some business and management students are expected both to generate and to refine their own research ideas. Others, particularly those on professional and post-experience courses, are provided with a research idea by an organisation or their university. In the initial stages of their research they are expected to refine this to a

Box 8.2   Checklist

Attributes of a good research topic

Capability: is it feasible?

- Is the topic something with which you are really fascinated?
- Do you have, or can you develop within the project time frame, the necessary research skills to undertake the topic?
- Is the research topic achievable within the available time?
- Will the project still be current when you finish your project?
- Is the research topic achievable within the financial resources that are likely to be available?
- Are you reasonably certain of being able to gain access to data you are likely to require for this topic?

Appropriateness: is it worthwhile?

- Does the topic fit the specifications and meet the standards set by the examining institution?
- Does your research topic contain issues that have a clear link to theory?
- Are you able to state your research question(s) and objectives clearly?
- Will your proposed research be able to provide fresh insights into this topic?
- Does your research topic relate clearly to the idea you have been given (perhaps by an organisation)?
- Are the findings for this research topic likely to be symmetrical: that is, of similar value whatever the outcome?
- Does the research topic match your career goals?

clear and feasible idea that meets the requirements of the examining organisation. If you have already been given a research idea we believe you will still find it useful to read the next subsection, which deals with generating research ideas. Many of the techniques which can be used for generating research ideas can also be used for the refining process.

Generating research ideas

If you have not been given an initial **research idea** there is a range of techniques that can be used to find and select a topic that you would like to research. They can be thought of as those that are predominantly **rational thinking** and those that involve more **creative thinking** (Table 8.1). The precise techniques that you choose to use and the order in which you use them are entirely up to you. However, like Raimond (1993), we believe you should use both rational and creative techniques, choosing those that you believe are going to be of most use to you and which you

Table 8.1 More frequently used techniques for generating and refining research ideas

Rational thinking	Creative thinking
- Examining your own strengths and interests	- Keeping a notebook of ideas
- Looking at past project titles	- Exploring personal preferences using past projects
- Discussion	- Relevance trees
- Searching the literature	- Brainstorming
- Scanning the media	

will enjoy using. By using one or more creative techniques you are more likely to ensure that your heart as well as your head is in your research project. In our experience, it is usually better to use a variety of techniques. In order to do this you will need to have some understanding of the techniques and the ways in which they work. We therefore outline the techniques in Table 8.1 and suggest possible ways they might be used to generate research ideas. These techniques will generate one of two outcomes:

- one or more possible project ideas that you might undertake;
- absolute panic because nothing in which you are interested or which seems suitable has come to mind (Jankowicz 2005).

In either instance, but especially the latter, we suggest that you talk to your project tutor. Box 8.3 illustrates how ideas are at the heart of business and management life.

Examining own strengths and interests

It is important that you choose a topic in which you are likely to do well and, if possible, already have some academic knowledge. Jankowicz (2005) suggests that one way of doing this is to look at those assignments for which you have received good grades. For most of these assignments they are also likely to be the topics in which you were interested (Box 8.1). They will provide you with an area in which to search and find a research idea. In addition, you may, as part of your reading, be able to focus more precisely on the sort of ideas about which you wish to conduct your research.

As noted in 'Attributes of a good research topic', p. 803, there is the need to think about your future. If you plan to work in financial management it would be sensible to choose a research project in the financial management field. One part of your course that will inevitably be discussed at any job interview is your research project. A project in the same field will provide you with the opportunity to display clearly your depth of knowledge and your enthusiasm.

Looking at past project titles

Many of our students have found looking at past projects a useful way of generating research ideas. For undergraduate and taught masters degrees these are often called dissertations. For research degrees they are termed theses. A common way of doing this is to scan your university's list of past project titles for anything that captures your imagination. Titles that look interesting or which grab your attention should be noted down, as should any thoughts you have about the title in relation to your own research idea. In this process the fact that the title is poorly worded or the project report received a low mark is immaterial. What matters is the fact that you have found a topic that interests you. Based on this you can think of new ideas in the same general area that will enable you to provide fresh insights.

Scanning actual research projects may also produce research ideas. However, you need to beware. The fact that a project is in your library is no guarantee of the quality of the arguments and observations it contains. In many universities all projects are placed in the library whether they are bare passes or distinctions.

Box 8.3   Focus on management research

What every leader needs to know about followers

Management studies courses and books usually contain plenty of material on leadership. Seemingly, everyone wants to understand just what makes a good leader. Followership, by contrast, is the stuff of the rarely mentioned. Most of the limited research and writing on subordinates has tended either to explain their behaviour in the context of leaders' development rather than followers', or mistakenly assume that followers are amorphous, all one and the same. As a result, we hardly notice, for example, that followers who follow mindlessly are altogether different from those who are deeply committed.

In a *Harvard Business Review* article Kellerman (2007) explores the behaviour of those in organisations whose role it is to follow. She argues that in an era of flatter, networked organisations and cross-cutting teams of knowledge workers, it's not always obvious who exactly is following (or, for that matter, who exactly is leading) and how they are going about it.

Kellerman develops a typology of followers using one metric – level of engagement of the follower. She categorises all followers according to where they fall along a continuum that ranges from 'feeling and doing absolutely nothing' to 'being passionately committed and deeply involved'.

Kellerman's typology specifies five types of followers: isolates, bystanders, participants, activist and diehards.

Isolates are completely detached. These followers are scarcely aware of what's going on around them. Moreover, they do not care about their leaders, know anything about them, or respond to them in any obvious way. Their alienation is, nevertheless, of consequence. By knowing and doing nothing, these types of followers passively support the status quo and further strengthen leaders who already have the upper hand. As a result, isolates can drag down their groups or organisations.

Bystanders observe but do not participate. These free riders deliberately stand aside and disengage, both from their leaders and from their groups or organisations. They may go along passively when it is in their self-interest to do so, but they are not internally motivated to engage in an active way. Their withdrawal also amounts to tacit support for whoever and whatever constitutes the status quo.

Participants are engaged in some way. Regardless of whether these followers clearly support their leaders and organisations or clearly oppose them, they care enough to invest some of what they have (time or money, for example) to try to make an impact.

Activists feel strongly one way or another about their leaders and organisations, and they act accordingly. These followers are eager, energetic and engaged. They invest heavily in people and processes, so they work hard either on behalf of their leaders or to undermine and even unseat them.

Diehards are prepared to go down for their cause – whether it's an individual, an idea, or both. These followers may be deeply devoted to their leaders, or they may be strongly motivated to oust their leaders by any means necessary. They exhibit an all-consuming dedication to someone or something they deem worthy.

Kellerman concludes by asserting that this typology has critical implications for the way leaders should lead and managers should manage.

It should be borne in mind that this article does not report a piece of original research. Kellerman points out in the piece that she has developed the typology 'after years of study and observation'. You may argue that this is worth little as it is based on impressions which are not substantiated by careful and systematic fieldwork. However, in our view this is just the sort of article that may stimulate ideas for a research project on, for example, differing patterns of 'followership' within different occupational groups.

Discussion

Colleagues, friends and university tutors are all good sources of possible project ideas. Often project tutors will have ideas for possible student projects, which they will be pleased to discuss with you. In addition, ideas can be obtained by talking to practitioners and professional groups (Gill and Johnson 2002). It is important that as well as discussing possible ideas you also make a note of them. What seemed like a good idea in the coffee shop may not be remembered quite so clearly after the following lecture!

Searching the literature

As part of your discussions, relevant literature may also be suggested. Sharp *et al.* (2002) discuss types of literature that are of particular use for generating research ideas. These include:

- articles in academic and professional journals;
- reports;
- books.

Of particular use are academic **review articles**. These articles contain both a considered review of the state of knowledge in that topic area and pointers towards areas where further research needs to be undertaken. In addition, you can browse recent publications, in particular journals, for possible research ideas. For many subject areas your project tutor will be able to suggest possible recent review articles, or articles that contain recommendations for further work. Reports may also be of use. The most recently published are usually up to date and, again, often contain recommendations that may form the basis of your research idea. Books by contrast are less up to date than other written sources. They do, however, often contain a good overview of research that has been undertaken, which may suggest ideas to you.

Searching for publications is only possible when you have at least some idea of the area in which you wish to undertake your research. One way of obtaining this is to re-examine your lecture notes and course textbooks and to note those subjects that appear most interesting (discussed earlier in this section) and the names of relevant authors. This will give you a basis on which to undertake a **preliminary search**. When the articles, reports and other items have been obtained it is often helpful to look for unfounded assertions and statements on the absence of research (Raimond 1993), as these are likely to contain ideas that will enable you to provide fresh insights.

Scanning the media

Keeping up to date with items in the news can be a very rich source of ideas. The stories which occur everyday in the 'broadsheet' or 'compact' newspapers (e.g. *The Times, financial Times, Guardian* and the *Daily Telegraph*), in both traditional print and online versions, may provide ideas which relate directly to the item (e.g. the extent to which items sold by supermarkets contravene the principles of 'green consumerism' by involving excessive 'food miles' in order to import them). The stories may also suggest other ideas which flow from the central story (e.g. the degree to which a company uses its claimed environmental credentials as part of its marketing campaign).

Keeping a notebook of ideas

One of the more creative techniques that we all use is to keep a notebook of ideas. All this involves is simply noting down any interesting research ideas as you think of them and, of equal importance, what sparked off your thought. You can then pursue the idea using more rational thinking techniques later. Mark keeps a notebook by his bed so he can jot down any flashes of inspiration that occur to him in the middle of the night!

Exploring personal preferences using past projects

Another way of generating possible project ideas is to explore your personal preferences using past project reports from your university. To do this Raimond (1993) suggests that you:

1 Select six projects that you like.
2 For each of these six projects, note down your first thoughts in response to three questions (if responses for different projects are the same this does not matter):
   a What appeals to you about the project?
   b What is good about the project?
   c Why is the project good?
3 Select three projects that you do not like.
4 For each of these three projects, note down your first thoughts in response to three questions (if responses for different projects are the same, or cannot be clearly expressed, this does not matter; note them down anyway):
   a What do you dislike about the project?
   b What is bad about the project?
   c Why is the project bad?

You now have a list of what you consider to be excellent and what you consider to be poor in projects. This will not be the same as a list generated by anyone else. It is also very unlikely to match the attributes of a good research project (Box 8.2). However, by examining this list you will begin to understand those project characteristics that are important to you and with which you feel comfortable. Of equal importance is that you will have identified those that you are uncomfortable with and should avoid. These can be used as the parameters against which to evaluate possible research ideas.

Relevance trees

Relevance trees may also prove useful in generating research topics. In this instance, their use is similar to that of mind mapping (Buzan 2006), in which you start with a broad concept from which you generate further (usually more specific) topics. Each of these topics forms a separate branch from which you can generate further, more detailed sub-branches. As you proceed down the sub-branches more ideas are generated and recorded. These can then be examined and a number selected and combined to provide a research idea (Sharp *et al.* 2002).

Brainstorming

The technique of **brainstorming** (Box 8.4), taught as a problem-solving technique on many business and management courses, can also be used to generate and refine research ideas. It is best undertaken with a group of people, although you can brainstorm on your own. To brainstorm, Moody (1988) suggests that you:

1 Define your problem – that is, the sorts of ideas you are interested in – as precisely as possible. In the early stages of formulating a topic this may be as vague as 'I am interested in marketing but don't know what to do for my research topic'.
2 Ask for suggestions, relating to the problem.
3 Record all suggestions, observing the following rules:
   ● No suggestion should be criticised or evaluated in any way before all ideas have been considered.
   ● All suggestions, however wild, should be recorded and considered.
   ● As many suggestions as possible should be recorded.
4 Review all the suggestions and explore what is meant by each.
5 Analyse the list of suggestions and decide which appeal to you most as research ideas and why.

Box 8.4   Focus on student research

Brainstorming

George's main interest was football. When he finished university he wanted to work in marketing, preferably for a sports goods manufacturer. He had examined his own strengths and discovered that his best marks were in marketing. He wanted to do his research project on some aspect of marketing, preferably linked to football, but had no real research idea. He asked three friends, all taking business studies degrees, to help him brainstorm the problem.

George began by explaining the problem in some detail. At first the suggestions emerged slowly. He noted them down on the whiteboard. Soon the board was covered with suggestions. George counted these and discovered there were over 100.

Reviewing individual suggestions produced nothing that any of the group felt to be of sufficient merit for a research project. However, one of George's friends pointed out that combining the suggestions of Premier League football, television rights and sponsorship might provide an idea which satisfied the assessment requirements of the project.

They discussed the suggestion further, and George noted the research idea as 'something about how confining the rights to show live Premiership football to paid-for satellite TV channels would impact upon the sale of Premiership club-specific merchandise'.

George arranged to see his project tutor to discuss how to refine the idea they had just generated.

Refining research ideas

The Delphi technique

An additional approach that our students have found particularly useful in refining their research ideas is the **Delphi technique** (Box 8.5). This involves using a group of people who are either involved or interested in the research idea to generate and choose a more specific research idea (Robson 2002). To use this technique you need:

1 to brief the members of the group about the research idea (they can make notes if they wish);
2 at the end of the briefing to encourage group members to seek clarification and more information as appropriate;
3 to ask each member of the group, including the originator of the research idea, to generate independently up to three specific research ideas based on the idea that has been described (they can also be asked to provide a justification for their specific ideas);
4 to collect the research ideas in an unedited and non-attributable form and to distribute them to all members of the group;
5 a second cycle of the process (steps 2 to 4) in which individuals comment on the research ideas and revise their own contributions in the light of what others have said;
6 subsequent cycles of the process until a consensus is reached. These either follow a similar pattern (steps 2 to 4) or use discussion, voting or some other method.

This process works well, not least because people enjoy trying to help one another. In addition, it is very useful in moulding groups into a cohesive whole.

Box 8.5   Focus on student research

Using a Delphi Group

Tim explained to the group that his research idea was concerned with understanding the decision-making processes associated with mortgage applications and loan advances. His briefing to the three other group members, and the questions that they asked him, considered aspects such as:

- the influences on a potential first-time buyer to approach a specific financial institution;
- the influence on decision making of face-to-face contact between potential borrowers and potential lenders.

The group then moved on to generate a number of more specific research ideas, among which were the following:

- the factors that influenced potential first-time house purchasers to deal with particular financial institutions;
- the effect of interpersonal contact on mortgage decisions;
- the qualities that potential applicants look for in mortgage advisers.

These were considered and commented on by all the group members. At the end of the second cycle Tim had, with the other students' agreement, refined his research idea to:

- the way in which a range of factors influenced potential first-time buyers' choice of lending institution.

He now needed to pursue these ideas by undertaking a preliminary search of the literature.

The preliminary study

Even if you have been given a research idea, it is still necessary to refine it in order to turn it into a research project. Some authors, such as Bennett (1991), refer to this process as a **preliminary study**. For some research ideas this will be no more than a review of some of the literature, including news items (Box 8.6). This can be thought of as the first iteration of your critical literature review. For others it may include revisiting the techniques discussed earlier in this section as well as informal discussions with people who have personal experience of and knowledge about your research ideas. In some cases **shadowing** employees who are likely to be

---

Box 8.6   Focus on research in the news

Many workers feel too qualified for jobs

More than half the workers in a huge swath of occupations think they are overqualified, research commissioned by the *Financial Times* shows. The figures reopen the debate about whether Britain is spending too much taxpayer money on churning out graduates. They could also be used against employers, accused by many economists of failing to adapt their business models to reap full benefit from the graduates in their workforces.

Two-thirds of people in 'customer service occupations', which include call centre workers, think their qualifications are more elevated than their job requires. For example, university graduates would count themselves overqualified if they were doing work they believed called for nothing more than A-levels.

Almost two-thirds of people in sales occupations also think they are overqualified, and more than 60 per cent in 'elementary administration and service occupations', which include junior clerical workers and postmen, feel this way.

Francis Green, an economist at Kent University who carried out the research, said the high figures were not surprising, since graduates were 'absolutely pouring into the labour market'. Professor Green said the proportion of workers who thought they were overqualified had increased by about five percentage points nationwide in five years.

Prime Minister Gordon Brown believes that Britain needs still more graduates to turn the country into a higher-skills economy, closing its productivity gap with competitors such as the

USA. More than 35 per cent of young people already have graduate-level qualifications in higher or further education, but the government's target is 50 per cent. However, critics regard the growth in graduate places, under both Labour and Conservative governments, as primarily designed to woo middle-class voters.

John Philpott, economist at the Chartered Institute of Personnel and Development, said that many people with qualifications were not being used well by employers 'still operating in low-quality, low-value markets that don't require high-quality people'. But Alex Bryson, research director at the Policy Studies Institute, said the high overqualification figures might partly reflect a 'trade-off' between convenience and salary. He pointed out that the occupations at the top of the list were 'customer-facing', with working hours designed to accommodate customers. By the same token, this wide variety of hours would also suit employees with other commitments, such as mothers.

Professor Green said the figures did not prove Britain was producing too many graduates. 'If someone goes to university and studies Picasso or Shakespeare', they make society better. 'We economists can't measure that, but it's absolutely absurd to discount it just because we can't do so'.

Professor Green's UK-wide figures are based on interviews with thousands of workers as part of long-term research into Britain's skills, part-financed by the former Department for Education and Skills.

Source: article by Turner, David (2007) *Financial Times*, 29 Oct.

important in your research may also provide insights. If you are planning on undertaking your research within an organisation it is important to gain a good understanding of your host organisation (Kervin 1999). However, whatever techniques you choose, the underlying purpose is to gain a greater understanding so that your research question can be refined.

At this stage you need to be testing your research ideas against the checklist in Box 8.2 and where necessary changing them. It may be that after a preliminary study, or discussing your ideas with colleagues, you decide that the research idea is no longer feasible in the form in which you first envisaged it. If this is the case, do not be too downhearted. It is far better to revise your research ideas at this stage than to have to do it later, when you have undertaken far more work.

Integrating ideas

The integration of ideas from these techniques is essential if your research is to have a clear direction and not contain a mismatch between objectives and your final project report. Jankowicz (2005:34–6) suggests an integrative process that our students have found most useful. This he terms 'working up and narrowing down'. It involves classifying each research idea first into its area, then its field, and finally the precise aspect in which you are interested. These represent an increasingly detailed description of the research idea. Thus your initial area, based on examining your course work, might be accountancy. After browsing some recent journals and discussion with colleagues this becomes more focused on the field of financial accounting methods. With further reading, the use of the Delphi technique and discussion with your project tutor you decide to focus on the aspect of activity-based costing.

You will know when the process of generating and refining ideas is complete as you will be able to say 'I'd like to do some research on . . .'. Obviously there will still be a big gap between this and the point when you are ready to start serious work on your research. The next subsections will ensure that you are ready to bridge that gap.

Refining topics given by your employing organisation

If, as a part-time student, your manager gives you a topic, this may present particular problems. It may be something in which you are not particularly interested. In this case you will have to weigh the advantage of doing something useful to the organisation against the disadvantage of a potential lack of personal motivation. You, therefore, need to achieve a balance. Often the research project your manager wishes you to undertake is larger than that which is appropriate for your course. In such cases, it may be possible to complete both by isolating an element of the larger organisational project that you find interesting and treating this as the project for your course.

One of our students was asked to do a preliminary investigation of the strengths and weaknesses of her organisation's pay system and then to recommend consultants to design and implement a new system. She was not particularly interested in this project. However, she was considering becoming a freelance personnel consultant. Therefore, for her course project she decided to study the decision-making process in relation to the appointment of personnel consultants. Her organisation's decision on which consultant to appoint, and why this decision was taken, proved to be a useful case study against which to compare management decision-making theory.

In this event you would write a larger report for your organisation and a part of it for your project report.

Other problems may involve your political relationships in he organisation. For example, there will be those keen to commission a project which justifies their particular policy position and see you as a useful pawn in advancing their political interests. It is important to have a clear stance with regards to what you want to do, and your personal objectives, and to stick to this.

finally, perhaps the biggest potential problem may be one of your own making: to promise to deliver research outcomes to your employer and not do so.

Turning research ideas into research projects

Writing research questions

Much is made in this book of the importance of defining clear **research questions** at the beginning of the research process. The importance of this cannot be overemphasised. One of the key criteria of your research success will be whether you have a set of clear conclusions drawn from the data you have collected. The extent to which you can do that will be determined largely by the clarity with which you have posed your initial research questions (Box 8.7).

Defining research questions, rather like generating research ideas (see p. 805), is not a straightforward matter. It is important that the question is sufficiently involved to generate the sort of project that is consistent with the standards expected of you (Box 8.2). A question that prompts a descriptive answer, for

Box 8.7	Focus on student research

Defining the research question

Imran was studying for a BA in Business Studies and doing his placement year in an advanced consumer electronics company. When he first joined the company he was surprised to note that the company's business strategy, which was announced in the company newsletter, seemed to be inconsistent with what Imran knew of the product market.

Imran had become particularly interested in corporate strategy in his degree. He was familiar with some of the literature that suggested that corporate strategy should be linked to the general external environment in which the organisation operated. He wanted to do some research on corporate strategy in his organisation for his degree dissertation.

After talking this over with his project tutor Imran decided on the following research question: 'Why does [organisation's name] corporate strategy not seem to reflect the major factors in the external operating environment?'

example 'What is the proportion of graduates entering the civil service who attended the old, established UK universities?', is far easier to answer than: 'Why are graduates from old, established UK universities more likely to enter the civil service than graduates from other universities?' More will be said about the importance of theory in defining the research question later in this section. However, beware of research questions that are too easy.

It is perhaps more likely that you fall into the trap of asking research questions that are too difficult. The question cited above, 'Why are graduates from old, established UK universities more likely to enter the civil service than graduates from other universities?' is a case in point. It would probably be very difficult to gain sufficient access to the inner portals of the civil service to get a good grasp of the subtle 'unofficial' processes that go on at staff selection which may favour one type of candidate over another. Over-reaching yourself in the definition of research questions is a danger.

Clough and Nutbrown (2002) use what they call the 'Goldilocks test' to decide if research questions are either 'too big', 'too small', 'too hot' or 'just right'. Those that are too big probably need significant research funding because they demand too many resources. Questions that are too small are likely to be of insufficient substance, while those that are too 'hot' may be so because of sensitivities that may be aroused as a result of doing the research. This may be because of the timing of the research or the many other reasons that may upset key people who have a role to play, either directly or indirectly, in the research context. Research questions that are 'just right', note Clough and Nutbrown (2002:34), are those that are 'just right for investigation at *this* time, by *this* researcher in *this* setting'.

The pitfall that you must avoid at all costs is asking research questions that will not generate new insights (Box 8.2). This raises the question of the extent to which you have consulted the relevant literature. It is perfectly legitimate to replicate research because you have a genuine concern about its applicability to your research setting (for example, your organisation). However, it certainly is not legitimate to display your ignorance of the literature.

McNiff and Whitehead (2000) make the point that the research question may not emerge until the research process has started and is therefore part of the process of 'progressive illumination'. They note that this is particularly likely to be the case in practitioner action research.

It is often a useful starting point in the writing of research questions to begin with one general focus research question that flows from your research idea. This may lead to several more detailed questions or the definition of research objectives. Table 8.2 has some examples of general focus research questions.

In order to clarify the research question Clough and Nutbrown (2002) talk of the Russian doll principle. This means taking the research idea and 'breaking down the research questions from the original statement to something which strips away the complication of layers and obscurities until the very essence – the heart – of the question can be expressed . . . just as the Russian doll is taken apart to reveal a tiny doll at the centre' (Clough and Nutbrown 2002:34).

Writing your research questions will be, in most cases, your individual concern but it is useful to get other people to help you. An obvious source of guidance is your project tutor. Consulting your project tutor will avoid the pitfalls of the questions that are too easy or too difficult or have been answered before. Discussing

Table 8.2 Examples of research ideas and their derived focus research questions

Research idea	General focus research questions
Advertising and share prices	How does the running of a TV advertising campaign designed to boost the image of a company affect its share price?
Job recruitment via the Internet	How effective is recruiting for new staff via the Internet in comparison with traditional methods?
The use of aromas as a marketing device	In what ways does the use of specific aromas in supermarkets affect buyer behaviour?
The use of Internet banking	What effect has the growth of Internet banking had upon the uses customers make of branch facilities?

your area of interest with your project tutor will lead to your research questions becoming much clearer.

Prior to discussion with your project tutor you may wish to conduct a brainstorming session with your peers or use the Delphi technique (see 'Generating and refining, research ideas', p. 805). Your research questions may flow from your initial examination of the relevant literature. As outlined in that section, journal articles reporting primary research will often end with a conclusion that includes the consideration by the author of the implications for future research of the work in the article. This may be phrased in the form of research questions. However, even if it is not, it may suggest pertinent research questions to you.

Writing research objectives

Your research may begin with a general focus research question that then generates more detailed research questions, or you may use your general focus research question as a base from which you write a set of research objectives. Objectives are more generally acceptable to the research community as evidence of the researcher's clear sense of purpose and direction. It may be that either is satisfactory. Do check whether your examining body has a preference.

We contend that research objectives are likely to lead to greater specificity than research or investigative questions. Table 8.3 illustrates this point. It summarises the objectives of some research conducted by one of our students. Expression of the first research question as an objective prompted a consideration of the objectives of the organisations. This was useful because it led to the finding that there often were no clear objectives. This in itself was an interesting theoretical discovery.

The second and third objectives operationalise the matching research questions by introducing the notion of explicit effectiveness criteria. In a similar way the fourth objective (parts a and b) and the fifth objective are specific about factors that lead to effectiveness in question 4. The biggest difference between the questions and objectives is illustrated by the way in which the fifth question becomes the fifth objective. They are similar but differ in the way that the objective makes clear that a theory will be developed that will make a causal link between two sets of variables: effectiveness factors and team briefing success.

This is not to say that the research questions could not have been written with a similar amount of specificity. They could. Indeed, you may find it easier to write

Table 8.3 Phrasing research questions as research objectives

Research question	Research objective
1 Why have organisations introduced team briefing?	1 To identify organisations' objectives for team briefing schemes
2 How can the effectiveness of team briefing schemes be measured?	2 To establish suitable effectiveness criteria for team briefing schemes
3 Has team briefing been effective?	3 To describe the extent to which the effectiveness criteria for team briefing have been met
4 How can the effectiveness of team briefing be explained?	4a To determine the factors associated with the effectiveness criteria for team briefing being met b To estimate whether some of those factors are more influential than other factors
5 Can the explanation be generalised?	5 To develop an explanatory theory that associates certain factors with the effectiveness of team briefing schemes

specific research questions than objectives. However, we doubt whether the same level of precision could be achieved through the writing of research questions alone. Research objectives require more rigorous thinking, which derives from the use of more formal language.

Maylor and Blackmon (2005) recommend that personal objectives may be added to the list of research objectives. These may be concerned with your specific learning objectives from completion of the research (e.g. to learn how to use a particular statistical software package or improve your word processing ability) or more general personal objectives such as enhancing your career prospects through learning about a new field of your specialism.

Maylor and Blackmon suggest that such personal objectives would be better were they to pass the well-known SMART test. That is that the objectives are:

- *Specific*. What precisely do you hope to achieve from undertaking the research?
- *Measurable*. What measures will you use to determine whether you have achieved your objectives? (e.g. secured a career-level first job in software design).
- *Achievable*. Are the targets you have set for yourself achievable given all the possible constraints?
- *Realistic*. Given all the other demands upon your time, will you have the time and energy to complete the research on time?
- *Timely*. Will you have time to accomplish all your objectives in the time frame you have set?

The importance of theory in writing research questions and objectives

Your consideration of theory should inform your definition of research questions and objectives.

Theory (Box 8.8) is defined by Gill and Johnson (2002:229) as 'a formulation regarding the cause and effect relationships between two or more variables, which may or may not have been tested'.

In a similar contribution to that of Sutton and Staw (1995), Whetten (1989) contends that if the presence of theory is to be guaranteed, the researcher must ensure that what is passing as good theory includes a plausible, coherent explanation for why certain relationships should be expected in our data.

There is probably no word that is more misused and misunderstood in education than the word 'theory'. It is thought that material included in textbooks is 'theory', whereas what is happening in the 'real world' is practice. Students who saw earlier drafts of this book remarked that they were pleased that the book was not too 'theoretical'. What they meant was that the book concentrated on giving lots of practical advice. Yet, the book is full of theory. Advising you to carry out research in a particular way (variable A) is based on the theory that this will yield effective results (variable B). This is the cause and effect relationship referred to in the

---

Box 8.8   Focus on management research

Clarifying what theory is not

Sutton and Staw (1995) make a useful contribution to the clarification of what theory is by defining what it is not. In their view theory is not:

1 *References*. Listing references to existing theories and mentioning the names of such theories may look impressive. But what is required if a piece of writing is to 'contain theory' is that a logical argument to explain the reasons for the described phenomena must be included. The key word here is 'why': why did the things you describe occur? What is the logical explanation?

2 *Data*. In a similar point to the one above, Sutton and Staw argue that data merely describe which empirical patterns were observed: theory explains why these patterns were observed or are expected to be observed. 'The data do not generate theory – only researchers do that' (Sutton and Staw 1995:372).

3 *Lists of variables*. Sutton and Staw argue that a list of variables which constitutes a logical attempt to cover the determinants of a given process or outcome do not comprise a theory. Simply listing variables which may predict an outcome is insufficient: what is

required for the presence of theory is an explanation of why predictors are likely to be strong predictors.

4 *Diagrams*. Boxes and arrows can add order to a conception by illustrating patterns and causal relationships but they rarely explain why the relationships have occurred. Indeed, Sutton and Staw (1995:374) note that 'a clearly written argument should preclude the inclusion of the most complicated figures – those more closely resembling a complex wiring diagram than a comprehensible theory'.

5 *Hypotheses or predictions*. Hypotheses can be part of a sound conceptual argument. But they do not contain logical arguments about why empirical relationships are expected to occur.

Sutton and Staw (1995:375) sum up by stating that 'theory is about the connections between phenomena, a story about why events, structure and thoughts occur. Theory emphasises the nature of causal relationships, identifying what comes first as well as the timing of events. Strong theory, in our view, delves into underlying processes so as to understand the systematic reasons for a particular occurrence or non-occurrence'.

definition of theory cited above and is very much the view of Kelly (1955). Kelly argues that the individual who attempts to solve the daily problems which we all face goes about this activity in much the same way as the scientist. Both continuously make and test hypotheses and revise their concepts accordingly. Both organise their results into what are called schemata and then into a system of broader schemata which are called theories. Kelly asserts that we need such schemata and theories in order to make sense of the complexity of the world in which we live. Without these organising frameworks we would be overwhelmed by the unconnected detail we would have to recall.

The definition demonstrates that 'theory' has a specific meaning. It refers to situations where, if A is introduced, B will be the consequence. Therefore, the marketing manager may theorise that the introduction of loyalty cards by a supermarket will lead to customers being less likely to shop regularly at a competitor supermarket. That is a theory. Yet, the marketing manager would probably not recognise it as such. He or she is still less likely to refer to it as a theory, particularly in the company of fellow managers. Many managers are very dismissive of any talk that smacks of 'theory'. It is thought of as something that is all very well to learn about at business school but bears little relation to what goes on in everyday organisational life. Yet, the loyalty card example shows that it has everything to do with what goes on in everyday organisational life.

Every purposive decision we take is based on theory: that certain consequences will flow from the decision. It follows from this that every managers' meeting that features a number of decisions will be a meeting that is highly **theory dependent** (Gill and Johnson 2002). All that will be missing is a realisation of this fact. So, if theory is something that is so rooted in our everyday lives it certainly is something that we need not be apprehensive about. If it is implicit in all our decisions and actions, then recognising its importance means making it explicit. In research the importance of theory must be recognised: therefore it must be made explicit.

Kerlinger and Lee (2000) reinforce Gill and Johnson's definition by noting that the purpose of examining relationships between two or more variables is to explain and predict these relationships. Gill and Johnson (2002:33) neatly tie these purposes of theory to their definition:

> . . . it is also evident that if we have the expectation that by doing A, B will happen, then by manipulating the occurrence of A we can begin to predict and influence the occurrence of B. In other words, theory is clearly enmeshed in practice since explanation enables prediction which in turn enables control.

In our example, the marketing manager theorised that the introduction of loyalty cards by a supermarket would lead to customers being less likely to shop regularly at a competitor supermarket. Following Gill and Johnson's (2002:33) point that 'explanation enables prediction which in turn enables control', the supermarket would be well advised to conduct research that yielded an explanation of why loyalty cards encourage loyalty. Is it a purely economic rationale? Does it foster the 'collector' instinct in all of us? Does it appeal to a sense of thrift in us that helps us cope with an ever more wasteful world? These explanations are probably complex and interrelated. Reaching a better understanding of them would help the marketing manager to predict the outcome of any changes to the scheme. Increasing the amount of points per item would be effective if the economic explanation was valid. Increasing the range of products on which extra points were offered might appeal to the 'collector' instinct. More accurate prediction would offer the marketing manager increased opportunities for control.

The explanations for particular outcomes are a concern for Mackenzie (2000a, 2000b). His argument is that much research (he used the example of employee opinion surveys) yield ambiguous conclusions because they only ask questions which reveal the state of affairs as they exist (in his example, the thinking of employees in regard to, say, their pay). What they do not ask is questions which help those using the research results to draw meaningful conclusions as to why the state of affairs is as it is. If meaningful conclusions cannot be drawn, then appropriate actions cannot be taken to remedy such deficiencies (or improve upon the efficiencies) that the research reveals. Usually such additional questions would involve discovering the key implementation processes (in the case of pay these may be the way in which managers make and communicate pay distribution decisions) which may shed light on the reasons why such deficiencies (or efficiencies) exist.

Mackenzie used the metaphor of the knobs on an old-fashioned radio to illustrate his argument. If the radio is playing a station and you are unhappy with what is being received, you will turn the volume knob to alter the volume or the tuning knob to change the station. He argues that the typical questionnaire survey is like the radio without knobs. You cannot make the results more useful, by knowing more about their causes, because you have no means to do so. All you have for your results is a series of what Mackenzie (2000a:136) terms 'knobless items', in which you are asking for respondents' opinions without asking for the reasons why they hold these opinions. What Mackenzie advocates is including '**knobs**' in the data collection process so that the causal relationship between a process and an outcome can be established.

Phillips and Pugh (2005) distinguish between research and what they call **intelligence gathering**, using what Mackenzie (2000a, 2000b) calls 'knobless items'. The latter is the gathering of facts (Box 8.9). For example, what is the relative proportion of undergraduates to postgraduates reading this book? What is the current spend

Box 8.9   Focus on research in the news

The e-sport revolution Korean-style

As Lee Yun-yeol limbered up in his tracksuit for the match of the year, hundreds of screaming girls in the Seoul stadium went wild. Against deafening heavy metal music, the fans screeched his name in high-pitched unison and waved signs proclaiming 'I want to cook you rice' – the Korean equivalent of 'Will you marry me?!' The commentators ran through the players' game histories and TV cameras panned across the audience. At home, some 10 million people were watching one of the eight cable channels ready to broadcast the match

live. In this high-octane atmosphere – somewhere between a rock concert and an soccer cup final – Mr Lee took his place. But he did not step into a boxing ring or on to a tennis court. He sat down before a computer screen, donned headphones, and prepared to bomb his opponent into oblivion in a computer game called Starcraft.

South Korea is the world's most wired country. Computer gaming has become mainstream and 'pro-gamers' are treated like pop stars and come armed with ultra-trendy hairstyles, lucrative sponsorship deals, burly bodyguards, and groupies. E-sports are not a niche pursuit in

Korea. Being a pro-gamer was named the most desired occupation in one survey of 1150 teenagers, and some private institutes even offer courses in online game strategies. Business also wants part of the action. Top companies such as Samsung Electronics, SK Telecom and Shinhan Bank all sponsor e-sports.

'Korea's great internet infrastructure has played a really big role in making e-sports so huge here', Je Hunho, general manager of the Korean E-sports Association, says. But he sees global potential: 'E-sports have started to spread across the world and we hope that one day it will be an Olympic sport.'

But the e-sports revolution has its darker side. In 2005 a South Korean man died after reportedly playing an online computer game for 50 hours with few breaks (BBC News Online 2005). The 28-year-old man collapsed after playing the game at an Internet café. The man had not slept properly, and had eaten very little during his marathon session, said police. The man only paused playing to go to the toilet and for short periods of sleep, said the police. 'We presume the cause of death was heart failure stemming from exhaustion', a provincial police official told the Reuters news agency. He was taken to hospital following his collapse, but died shortly after, according to the police. It is not known whether he suffered from any previous health conditions. They added that he had recently been dismissed from his job because he kept missing work to play computer games.

Players can easily get immersed in computer games and feel compelled to play for hours at a stretch, particularly in massively multiplayer online role playing games (MMORPGs) in which thousands of gamers play and interact in shared fantasy or science fiction worlds. Reports of gamers spending 10 to 15 hours a day in front of video games are becoming more frequent. Experts say gamers should take regular screen breaks.

According to the research of psychologist Professor Mark Griffiths, playing excessively is not problematic in any shape or form for the majority of gamers. However, his view is that online gaming addiction for a small minority is a real phenomenon and people suffer the same symptoms as traditional addictions. But this only applies to a small minority of gamers.

In one detailed survey of 540 gamers, Professor Griffiths and his team found that there were four playing more than 80 hours a week, which is considered 'excessive'. He explained many people liked to play MMORPGs for long periods of time because of the social aspect of the games. He explained that these are the types of games that completely engross the player. They are not games that you can play for 20 minutes and stop. 'If you are going to take it seriously, you have to spend time doing it', he said.

But he warned there was a difference between 'healthy enthusiasm' and 'unhealthy addiction'. People who sacrificed jobs, partners and loved ones were considered 'extreme players'. Unlike help for traditional addictions, such as gambling, there is very little help for computer game addiction, he said. 'It is not taken seriously yet – it is the same for internet addiction', he said. More than 15 million people, or 30% of the population, are registered for online gaming in South Korea. The country also host the annual World Cyber Games.

Sources: article by Fifield, Anna (2007) *Financial Times*, 15 Sept.; BBC News Online (2005).

per employee on training in the UK? What provision do small businesses make for bad debts? This is often called descriptive research and may form part of your research project. Descriptive research would be the first step in our example of supermarket loyalty card marketing. Establishing that there had been a change in customer behaviour following the introduction of supermarket loyalty cards would be the first step prior to any attempt at explanation.

Phillips and Pugh contrast such 'what' questions with 'why' questions. Examples of these 'why' questions are as follows: Why do British organisations spend less

Box 8.10   Focus on student research

Writing a research question based on theory

Justine was a final-year marketing undergraduate who was interested in the theory of cognitive dissonance (Festinger 1957). She wanted to apply this to the consumer purchasing decision in the snack foods industry (e.g. potato crisps) in the light of the adverse publicity that the consumption of such foods was having as a result of the 'healthy eating' campaign.

Justine applied Festinger's theory by arguing in her research project proposal that a consumer who learns that snack over-eating is bad for her health will experience dissonance, because the knowledge that snack over-eating is bad for her health is dissonant with the cognition that she continues to over-eat snacks. She can reduce the dissonance by changing her behaviour, i.e., she

could stop over-eating. (This would be consonant with the cognition that snack over-eating is bad for her health.) Alternatively, she could reduce dissonance by changing her cognition about the effect of snack over-eating on health and persuade herself that snack over-eating does not have a harmful effect on health. She would look for positive effects of snack over-eating, for example by believing that snack over-eating is an important source of enjoyment which outweighs any harmful effects. Alternatively, she might persuade herself that the risk to health from snack over-eating is negligible compared with the danger of car accidents (reducing the importance of the dissonant cognition).

Justine's research question was 'How does the adverse "healthy eating" campaign publicity affect the consumer's decision to purchase snack foods?'

per head on training than German organisations? Why are new car purchasers reluctant to take out extended warranties on their vehicles? Why do some travellers still prefer to use cross-channel ferries as opposed to the Channel Tunnel? Such questions go 'beyond description and require analysis'. They look for 'explanations, relationships, comparisons, predictions, generalisations and theories' (Phillips and Pugh 2005:48).

It is a short step from the 'why' research question to the testing of an existing theory in a new situation or the development of your own theory. This may be expressed as a hypothesis that is to be tested, or the eventual answer to your research question may be the development or amendment of a theory (Box 8.10).

Although intelligence gathering will play a part in your research, it is unlikely to be enough. You should be seeking to explain phenomena, to analyse relationships, to compare what is going on in different research settings, to predict outcomes and to generalise; then you will be working at the theoretical level. This is a necessary requirement for most research projects.

You may still be concerned that the necessity to be theory dependent in your research project means that you will have to develop a ground-breaking theory that will lead to a whole new way of thinking about management. If this is the case you should take heart from the threefold typology of theories summarised by Creswell (2002) (see Figure 8.1). He talks of 'grand theories', usually thought to be the province of the natural scientists (e.g. Darwin and Newton). He contrasts these with 'middle-range theories', which lack the capacity to change the way in which we think about the world but are nonetheless of significance. Some of the theories

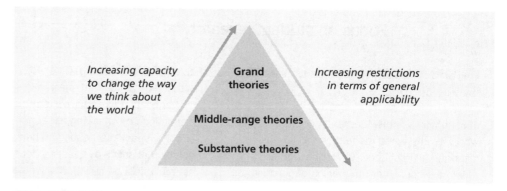

Figure 8.1   Grand, middle-range and substantive theories

of human motivation well known to managers would be in this category. However, most of us are concerned with 'substantive theories' that are restricted to a particular time, research setting, group or population or problem (Creswell 2002). For example, studying the reasons why a total quality initiative in a particular organisation failed would be an example of a substantive theory. Restricted they may be, but a host of 'substantive theories' that present similar propositions may lead to 'middle-range theories'. By developing 'substantive theories', however modest, we are doing our bit as researchers to enhance our understanding of the world about us. A grand claim, but a valid one!

This discussion of theory does assume that a clear theoretical position is developed prior to the collection of data (the **deductive approach**). This will not always be the case. It may be that your study is based on the principle of developing theory after the data have been collected (the **inductive approach**). This is a fundamental difference in research approach.

Writing your research proposal

At the start of all courses or modules we give our students a plan of the work they will be doing. It includes the learning objectives, the content, the assessment strategy and the recommended reading. This is our statement of our side of the learning contract. Our students have a right to expect this.

However, when we insist on a proposal for a research project that is often the equivalent of at least two other modules, there is often a marked reluctance to produce anything other than what is strictly necessary. This is unsatisfactory. It is unfair to your project tutor because you are not making entirely clear what it is you intend to do in your research. You are also being unfair to yourself because you are not giving yourself the maximum opportunity to have your ideas and plans scrutinised and subjected to rigorous questioning.

Writing a research proposal is a crucial part of the research process. If you are applying for research funding, or if your proposal is going before an academic research committee, then you will know that you will need to put a great deal of time into the preparation of your proposal. However, even if the official need for a proposal is not so vital it is still a process that will repay very careful attention.

The purposes of the research proposal

Organising your ideas

Writing can be the best way of clarifying our thoughts. This is a valuable purpose of the proposal. Not only will it clarify your thoughts but it will help you to organise your ideas into a coherent statement of your research intent. Your reader will be looking for this.

Convincing your audience

However coherent your ideas and exciting your research plan, it counts for little if the proposal reveals that what you are planning to do is simply not possible. As part of research methods courses many tutors ask students to draft a research proposal. This is then discussed with a tutor. What usually happens is that this discussion is about how the proposed research can be amended so that something more modest in scope is attempted. Initially work that is not achievable in the given timescale is proposed. The student's task is to amend initial ideas and convince the module tutor that the proposed research is achievable within the time and other resources available.

Contracting with your 'client'

If you were asked to carry out a research project for a commercial client or your own organisation it is unthinkable that you would go ahead without a clear proposal that you would submit for approval. Acceptance of your proposal by the client would be part of the contract that existed between you.

So it is with your proposal to your project tutor or academic committee. It may be necessary to obtain clearance from the relevant research ethics committee. For example, in one university the university's code of practice states that ethics committee perusal in necessary for all research involving human participants. It is important for all work that will be made public – for example, undergraduate dissertations, theses for higher degrees, externally funded research and 'unfunded' research (including undergraduate and postgraduate research) which produces reports or other publications. In another UK university, researchers have an obligation to spell out exactly what they mean by anonymity and confidentiality to research participants in advance of the research taking place. In this context anonymity refers to concealing the identity of the participants in all documents resulting from the research; and confidentiality is concerned with to the right of access to the data provided by individual participants and, in particular, the need to keep these data secret or private. In addition, researchers should clarify the steps they will take to ensure protection of respondents' identities and ensure that the information collected is stored securely.

Acceptance implies that your proposal is satisfactory. While this is obviously no guarantee of subsequent success, it is something of comfort to you to know that at least you started your research journey with an appropriate destination and journey plan. It is for you to ensure that you do not get lost!

The content of the research proposal

Title

This may be your first attempt at the title. It may change as your work progresses. At this stage it should closely mirror the content of your proposal.

Background

This is an important part of the proposal. It should tell the reader why you feel the research that you are planning is worth the effort. This may be expressed in the form of a problem that needs solving or something that you find exciting and has aroused your curiosity. The reader will be looking for evidence here that there is sufficient interest from you to sustain you over the long months (or years) ahead.

This is also the section where you will demonstrate your knowledge of the relevant literature. Moreover, it will clarify where your proposal fits into the debate in the literature. You will be expected to show a clear link between the previous work that has been done in your field of research interest and the content of your proposal. In short, the literature should be your point of departure. This is not the same as the critical literature review you will present in your final project report. It will just provide an overview of the key literature sources from which you intend to draw.

Research questions and objectives

The background section should lead smoothly into a statement of your research question(s) and objectives. These should leave the reader in no doubt as to precisely what it is that your research seeks to achieve. Be careful here to ensure that your objectives are precisely written and will lead to observable outcomes (look again at Table 8.3, e.g., 'to describe the extent to which the effectiveness criteria specified for the team briefing scheme have been met'). Do not fall into the trap of stating general research aims that are little more than statements of intent (e.g. 'to discover the level of effectiveness of the team briefing scheme').

Method

This and the background sections will be the longest sections of the proposal. It will detail precisely how you intend to go about achieving your research objectives. It will also justify your choice of method in the light of those objectives. These two aims may be met by dividing your method section into two parts: research design and data collection.

In the part on research design you will explain where you intend to carry out the research. If your earlier coverage has pointed out that your research is a single-organisation issue, perhaps a part of a piece of organisational consultancy, then this will be self-evident. However, if your research topic is more generic you will wish to explain, for example, which sector(s) of the economy you have chosen to research and why you chose these sectors. You will also need to explain the identity of your research population (e.g. managers or trade union officials) and why you chose this population.

This section should also include an explanation of the general way in which you intend to carry out the research. Will it be based, for example, on a questionnaire, interviews, examination of secondary data or use a combination of data collection techniques? Here again it is essential to explain why you have chosen your approach. Your explanation should be based on the most effective way of meeting your research objectives.

The research design section gives an overall view of the method chosen and the reason for that choice. The data collection section goes into much more detail about how specifically the data are to be collected. For example, if you are using a survey strategy you should specify your population and sample size. You should also clarify how the survey instrument such as a questionnaire will be distributed and how the data will be analysed. If you are using interviews, you should explain how many interviews will be conducted, their intended duration, whether they will be audio-recorded, and how they will be analysed. In short, you should demonstrate to your reader that you have thought carefully about all the issues regarding your method and their relationship to your research objectives. However, it is normally not necessary in the proposal to include precise detail of the method you will employ, for example the content of an observation schedule or questionnaire questions.

You will also need to include a statement about how you are going to adhere to any ethical guidelines. This is particularly important in some research settings, such as those involving medical patients or children.

Timescale

This will help you and your reader to decide on the viability of your research proposal. It will be helpful if you divide your research plan into stages. This will give you a clear idea as to what is possible in the given timescale. Experience has shown that however well the researcher's time is organised the whole process seems to take longer than anticipated (Box 8.11).

As part of this section of their proposal, many researchers find it useful to produce a schedule for their research using a **Gantt chart**. Developed by Henry Gantt in 1917, this provides a simple visual representation of the tasks or activities that make up your research project, each being plotted against a time line. The time we estimate each task will take is represented by the length of an associated horizontal bar, whilst the task's start and finish times are represented by its position on the time line. Figure 8.2 shows a Gantt chart for a student's research project. As we can see from the first bar on this chart, the student has decided to schedule in two weeks of holiday. The first of these occurs over the Christmas and New Year period, and the second occurs while her tutor is reading a draft copy of the completed project in April. We can also see from the second and fourth bar that, like many of our students, she intends to begin to draft her literature review while she is still reading new articles and books. However, she has also recognised that some activities must

Box 8.11 Worked example

Louisa's research timescale

As part of the final year of her undergraduate business studies degree, Louisa had to undertake an 8000–10 000-word research project. In order to assist her with her time management, she discussed the following outline timescale, developed using Microsoft Outlook's project planning tools 'Tasks', with her tutor.

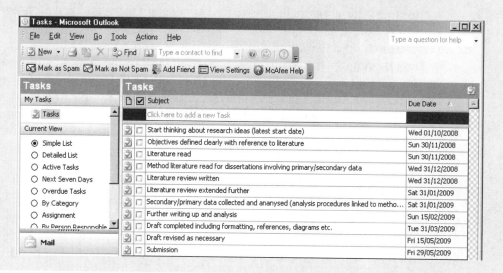

be undertaken sequentially. For example, bars 9 and 10 highlight that before she can administer her questionnaire (bar 10) she must complete all the revisions highlighted as necessary by the pilot testing (bar 9).

Resources

This is another facet of viability (Box 8.2). It will allow you and the reader to assess whether what you are proposing can be resourced. Resource considerations may be categorised as finance, data access and equipment.

Conducting research costs money. This may be for travel, subsistence, help with data analysis, or postage for questionnaires. Think through the expenses involved and ensure that you can meet these expenses.

Assessors of your proposal will need to be convinced that you have access to the data you need to conduct your research. This may be unproblematic if you are carrying out research in your own organisation. Many academic committees wish to see written approval from host organisations in which researchers are planning to conduct research. You will also need to convince your reader of the likely response rate to any questionnaire that you send.

It is surprising how many research proposals have ambitious plans for large-scale data collection with no thought given to how the data will be analysed. It is important that you convince the reader of your proposal that you have access to the necessary computer hardware and software to analyse your data. Moreover, it is necessary for you to demonstrate that you have either the necessary skills to perform the analysis or can learn the skills in an appropriate time, or you have access to help.

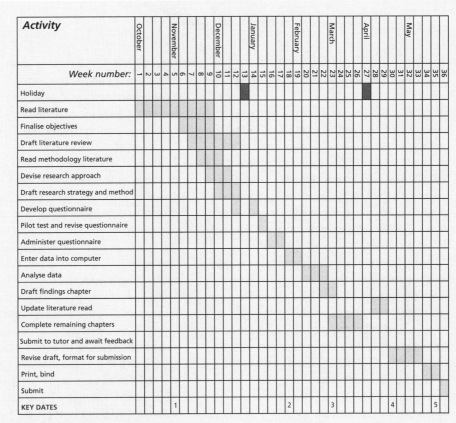

Figure 8.2   Gantt chart for a research project

References

It is not necessary to try to impress your proposal reader with an enormous list of references (Robson 2002). A few key literature sources to which you have referred in the background section and which relate to the previous work that is directly informing your own proposal should be all that is necessary.

Criteria for evaluating research proposals

The extent to which the components of the proposal fit together

Your rationale for conducting the research should include a study of the previous published research, including relevant theories in the topic area. This study should inform your research question(s) and objectives. Your proposed method should flow directly from these research question(s) and objectives (Box 8.12). The time that you have allocated should be a direct reflection of the methods you employ, as should the resources that you need.

Box 8.12 — Focus on student research

Fitting together the various components of the research proposal

Jenny was a middle manager in a large insurance company. She was very interested in the fact that electronic forms of communication meant that organisations could move information-based administrative work round different locations. Her company was scanning paper applications for insurance policies onto its computer system and delivering these into a central electronic bank of work. The company had employees in three different locations in the UK, and work was drawn from the bank on the basis of workload existing in each particular location. Recently, senior management had been considering developing work locations in South Asian cities, where it felt the standard of English meant that such functions could be fulfilled effectively. Jenny anticipated that this would pose certain logistical problems, for example, staff training and communications. Knowledge of these problems would give her a clear picture of the limit of complexity of the work that could be done. This was particularly important since the complexity range went from the simple to the technically complex. Research into the literature on cross-cultural training justified Jenny's concern. As a consequence of her thought and reading, she developed her research question as: 'What cross-cultural problems may be posed by international electronic work transfer in the insurance industry, and how may these problems limit the complexity of the work that may be transferred?'

Through her reading of the practitioner journals, Jenny was aware that some other financial-services organisations had been sending their work to Asia for some time. She decided that approaching these companies and interviewing their key personnel would be a fruitful approach. The main problem that Jenny would have with this research would be the time that the interview work would take, given that such companies were located all over the UK and North America. She was unsure how many interviews would be necessary. This would become clearer as she progressed in the research. However, it was unlikely that fewer than 10 companies would yield sufficient valuable data. She thought that she could collect the necessary data in a four-month period, which fitted in with her university deadline. There were no specific resources that Jenny needed other than finance and time. Since her research would be of immediate benefit to her employer she thought that neither would pose a problem.

The viability of the proposal

This is the answer to the question: 'Can this research be carried out satisfactorily within the timescale and with available resources?'

The absence of preconceived ideas

Your research should be an exciting journey into the unknown. Do not be like the student who came to Phil to talk over a research proposal and said, 'Of course, I know what the answer will be'. When asked to explain the purpose of doing the research if he already knew the answer, he became rather defensive and eventually looked for another supervisor and, probably, another topic.

If it is absolutely crucial that your proposal is of the highest quality then you may wish to use an **expert system** such as Peer Review Emulator™. This software is available either on its own or as part of the Methodologist's Toolchest™ suite of

Box 8.13   Focus on student research

A written research proposal

Puvadol was a student from Thailand who returned home from the UK to complete his MA dissertation. His proposed dissertation concerned the applicability of Western methods of involving employees in decision-making in Thai organisations.

An abbreviated version of Puvadol's proposal follows:

Title

The influences of Thai culture on employee involvement.

Background

Involving employees in the decision making of their employing organisations has been increasingly popular in Europe and North America in recent years. The influx of American organisations into Thailand has meant that similar approaches are being adopted. However, this assumes that Thai employees will respond to these techniques as readily as their European and American counterparts.

Doubts about the validity of these assumptions derive from studies of Thai national culture (Komin 1990). Using Rokeach's (1979) conceptual framework, Komin characterised Thai culture in a number of ways. I have isolated those that relate to employee involvement. These are that Thais wish to:

a save face, avoid criticism and show consideration to others;

b exhibit gratitude to those who have shown kindness and consideration;

c promote smooth, conflict-free interpersonal relations;

d interpret 'rules' in a flexible way with little concern for principles;

e promote interdependent social relations;

f be seen to be achieving success through good social relations rather than individual success.

I intend to demonstrate in this section that these six cultural values contradict the values of employee involvement (e.g. employee involvement may involve employees in openly criticising managers, which directly contradicts **a** above).

Research objectives

1 To examine the assumptions behind the management technique of employee involvement.

2 To establish the characteristics of the Thai national culture.

3 To identify the opinions of Thai employees and their managers, working in American-owned organisations in Thailand, towards values underpinning employee involvement.

4 To draw conclusions about the applicability of employee involvement to Thai employees.

Method

1 Conduct a review of the literatures on employee involvement and Thai national culture in order to develop research hypotheses.

2 Carry out primary research in three American-owned petrochemical and manufacturing organisations in Thailand to assess the opinions of Thai employees and their managers towards values underpinning employee involvement. Informal approval has been gained from three organisations. American-owned organisations are relevant because it is in these that employee involvement is most likely to be found and values underpinning employee involvement exhibited. Petrochemical and manufacturing organisations are chosen because the occupations carried out in these organisations are likely to be similar, thus ensuring that any differences are a function of Thai national culture rather than of occupational culture.

A questionnaire will be developed with questions based on the Thai values **a–f** in the Background section above. Each value will lead to a hypothesis (e.g. employee involvement may not be appropriate to Thai culture because it may mean that employees openly criticise their managers). The questions in the questionnaire will seek to test these hypotheses. The questionnaire will be distributed to a sample (size to be agreed) of employees and of managers across all three organisations.

Data analysis will use the SPSS software. Statistical tests will be run to ensure that results are a function of Thai cultural values rather than of values that relate to the individual organisations.

Timescale

January–March 2008: review of literature

April 2008: draft literature review

May 2008: review research methods literature and agree research strategy

June 2008: agree formal access to three organisations for collection of primary data

July–August 2008: compile, pilot and revise questionnaire

September 2008: administer questionnaire

October–November 2008: final collection of questionnaires and analysis of data

November 2008–February 2009: completion of first draft of project report

March–May 2009: final writing of project report

Resources

I have access to computer hardware and software. Access to three organisations has been negotiated, subject to confirmation. My employer has agreed to pay all incidental costs as part of my course expenses.

References

Komin, S. (1990) *Psychology of the Thai People: Values and Behavioral Patterns*. Bangkok, Thailand: National Institute of Development Administration (in Thai).

Rokeach, M. (1979) *Understanding Human Values: Individual and Society*. New York: The Free Press.

programs. It asks you a series of questions about your proposed research. The program then critiques these answers to ensure that common research standards are achieved (Idea Works 2008).

Summary

- The process of formulating and clarifying your research topic is the most important part of your research topic.
- Attributes of a research topic do not vary a great deal between universities. The most important of these is that your research topic will meet the requirements of the examining body.
- Generating and refining research ideas makes use of a variety of techniques. It is important that you use a variety of techniques, including those that involve rational thinking and those that involve creative thinking.
- The ideas generated can be integrated subsequently using a technique such as working up and narrowing down.
- Clear research questions, based on the relevant literature, will act as a focus for the research that follows.
- Research can be distinguished from intelligence gathering. Research is theory dependent.
- Writing a research proposal helps you to organise your ideas, and can be thought of as a contract between you and the reader.

- The content of the research proposal should tell the reader what you want to do, why you want to do it, what you are trying to achieve, and how you to plan to achieve it.

Self-check questions

Help with these questions is available at the end of the chapter.

1 For the workplace project for her professional course, Karen had decided to undertake a study of the effectiveness of the joint consultative committee in her NHS Trust. Her title was 'An evaluation of the effectiveness of the Joint Consultative Committee in Anyshire's Hospitals NHS Foundation Trust'. Draft some objectives which Karen may adopt to complement her title.
2 You have decided to search the literature to 'try to come up with some research ideas in the area of Operations Management'. How will you go about this?
3 A colleague of yours wishes to generate a research idea in the area of accounting. He has examined his own strengths and interests on the basis of his assignments and has read some review articles, but has failed to find an idea about which he is excited. He comes and asks you for advice. Suggest two techniques that your colleague could use, and justify your choice.
4 You are interested in doing some research on the interface between business organisations and schools. Write three research questions that may be appropriate.
5 How may the formulation of an initial substantive theory help in the development of a research proposal?
6 How would you demonstrate the influence of relevant theory in your research proposal?

Review and discussion questions

1 Together with your colleagues, decide on the extent to which a set of research topics constitute a 'good research topic' according to the checklist in Box 8.2. The set of topics you choose may be past topics obtained from your tutor which relate to your course. Alternatively, they may be those which have been written by you and your colleagues as preparation for your project(s).
2 Look through several of the academic journals which relate to your subject area. Choose an article which is based upon primary research. Assuming that the research question and objectives are not made explicit, infer from the content of the article what the research question and objectives may have been.
3 Watch the news on television. Most bulletins will contain stories on research which has been carried out to report the current state of affairs in a particular field. Spend some time investigating news sites on the Internet (e.g. http://www.news.google.com) in order to learn more about the research which relates to the news story. Study the story carefully and decide what further questions the report raises. Use this as the basis to draft an outline proposal to seek answers to one (or more) of these questions.

Progressing
your
research
project

From research ideas to a research proposal

- If you have not been given a research idea, consider the techniques available for generating and refining research ideas. Choose a selection of those with which you feel most comfortable, making sure to include both rational and creative thinking techniques. Use these to try to generate a research idea or ideas. Once you have got some research ideas, or if you have been unable to find an idea, talk to your project tutor.
- Evaluate your research ideas against the checklist of attributes of a good research project (Box 8.2).
- Refine your research ideas using a selection of the techniques available for generating and refining research ideas. Re-evaluate your research ideas against the checklist of attributes of a good research project (Box 8.2). Remember that it is better to revise (and in some situations to discard) ideas that do not appear to be feasible at this stage. Integrate your ideas using the process of working up and narrowing down to form one research idea.
- Use your research idea to write a general focus research question. Where possible this should be a 'why?' or a 'how?' rather than a 'what?' question.
- Use the general focus research question to write more detailed research questions and your research objectives.
- Write your research proposal making sure it includes a clear title and sections on:
  - the background to your research;
  - your research questions and objectives;
  - the method you intend to use;
  - the timescale for your research;
  - the resources you require;
  - references to any literature to which you have referred.

References

BBC News Online (2005) 'South Korean dies after games session'. Available at: http://news.bbc.co.uk/1/hi/technology/4137782.stm [Accessed 21 May 2008.]

Bennett, R. (1991) 'What is management research?', in N.C. Smith and P. Dainty (eds) *The Management Research Handbook*. London: Routledge: pp. 67–77.

Buzan, T. (2006) *The Ultimate Book of Mind Maps*. London: Harper Thorsons.

Carroll, L. (1989) *Alice's Adventures in Wonderland*. London: Hutchinson.

Clough, P. and Nutbrown, C. (2002) *A Student's Guide to Methodology*. London: Sage.

Creswell, J. (2002) *Qualitative, Quantitative, and Mixed Methods Approaches* (2nd edn). Thousand Oaks, CA: Sage.

Festinger, L. (1957) *A Theory of Cognitive Dissonance*. Stanford, CA: Stanford University Press.

Ghauri, P. and Grønhaug, K. (2005) *Research Methods in Business Studies: A Practical Guide* (3rd edn). Harlow: Financial Times Prentice Hall.

Gill, J. and Johnson, P. (2002) *Research Methods for Managers* (3rd edn). London: Sage.

Idea Works (2008) 'Methodologist's Toolchest features'. Available at: http://www.ideaworks.com/mt/index.html [Accessed 19 May 2008.]

Jankowicz, A.D. (2005) *Business Research Projects* (4th edn). London: Thomson Learning.

Kellerman, B. (2007) 'What Every Leader Needs to Know About Followers', *Harvard Business Review*, Vol. 85, No. 12. pp. 84–91.

Kelly, G.A. (1955) *The Psychology of Personal Constructs*. New York: Norton.

Kerlinger, F. and Lee, H. (2000) *Foundations of Behavioral Research* (4th edn). Fort Worth, TX: Harcourt College Publishers.

Kervin, J.B. (1999) *Methods for Business Research* (2nd edn). New York: HarperCollins.

Kindberg, T., Spasojevic, M., Fleck, R. and Sellen, A. (2005) *The Ubiquitous Camera: An In-Depth Study of Camera Phone Use*. Available at: http://www.informatics.sussex.ac.uk/research/groups/interact/publications/ubiquitousCamera.pdf [Accessed 19 May 2007.]

Mackenzie, K.D. (2000a) 'Knobby analyses of knobless survey items, part I: The approach', *International Journal of Organizational Analysis*, Vol. 8, No. 2. pp. 131–54.

Mackenzie, K.D. (2000b) 'Knobby analyses of knobless survey items, part II: An application', *International Journal of Organizational Analysis*, Vol. 8, No. 3, pp. 238–61.

Maylor, H. and Blackmon, K. (2005) *Researching Business and Management*. Basingstoke: Palgrave Macmillan.

McNiff, J. with Whitehead, J. (2000) *Action Research in Organizations*. London: Routledge.

Moody, P.E. (1988) *Decision Making: Proven Methods for Better Decisions* (2nd edn). Maidenhead, McGraw-Hill.

Phillips, E.M. and Pugh, D.S. (2005) *How to get a PhD* (4th edn). Maidenhead: Open University Press.

Raimond, P. (1993) *Management Projects*. London: Chapman & Hall.

Robson, C. (2002) *Real World Research* (2nd edn). Oxford: Blackwell.

Saunders, M.N.K. and Lewis, P. (1997) 'Great ideas and blind alleys? A review of the literature on starting research', *Management Learning*, Vol. 28, No. 3, pp. 283–99.

Sharp, J., Peters, J. and Howard, K. (2002) *The Management of a Student Research Project* (3rd edn). Aldershot: Gower.

Smith, N.C. and Dainty, P. (1991) *The Management Research Handbook*. London: Routledge.

Sutton, R. and Staw, B. (1995) 'What theory is not', *Administrative Science Quarterly*, Vol. 40, No. 3, pp. 371–84.

Whetten, D. (1989) 'What constitutes a theoretical contribution?', *Academy of Management Review*, Vol. 14, No. 4, pp. 490–5.

Further reading

Fisher, C. (2007) *Researching and Writing a Dissertation for Business Students* (2nd edn), Harlow: Financial Times Prentice Hall. Chapter 1 has some very practical tips on choosing your research topic.

Maylor, H. and Blackmon, K. (2005) *Researching Business and Management*. Basingstoke: Palgrave Macmillan. Chapter 3 covers similar ground to this chapter and has some useful ideas on generating research topics and some very interesting examples of student topics.

Sutton, R. and Staw, B. (1995) 'What theory is not', *Administrative Science Quarterly*, Vol. 40, No. 3, pp. 371–84. This is an excellent article which makes very clear what theory is by explaining what theory is not. The authors draw on their experience as journal editors who constantly have to examine articles submitted for publication. They report that the reason for refusals is usually that there is no theory in the article. This leads to some very clear and practical advice for us all to follow.

Whetten, D. (1989) 'What constitutes a theoretical contribution?', *Academy of Management Review*, Vol. 14, No. 4, pp. 490–5. Whetten also comments as a journal editor and covers similar ground to Sutton and Staw. Again, this is clear and straightforward advice and, read together with Sutton and Staw, gives a pretty clear idea of how to avoid criticisms of a lack of theory in research writing.

Media climate change reporting and environmental disclosure patterns in the low-cost airline industry in the twenty-first century

Emma was now at the start of her final year of her business and accounting degree. This was a four-year degree, with a placement year in the third year. Emma had been on placement in the finance and administration function of a budget airline company. Now, back at university, she was concerned that the project proposal form was due for submission in three weeks' time. The project proposal comprised a draft title, outline of the research topic including research question, aims and objectives, introduction to academic literature including the proposed theoretical base, research method and consideration of ethical issues, likely timescale and an assessment of the resources that would be needed. The proposal was the first formally assessed part of the research project and was the key document that would be used to allocate an appropriate project supervisor.

Emma reflected on her second year and final year modules and also what she had been involved with on her placement. During her placement Emma had mainly been helping in the production of the monthly management accounts and was responsible for checking the landing charges levied by airports against each inbound flight. The placement year had been very busy as the airline had enjoyed rapid growth and now flew to 24 destinations compared to 14 just two years ago. Emma thought about all of these but could only feel that this was a job and how could she turn any aspect of that into a research project. Emma now wished that she had done something different during that year that would give her a topic area. Although she knew people at the airline that she could interview or who would fill in questionnaires for her, the problem remained about what? Again, when she thought about her course and the modules she had studied, Emma could not really think of an area to turn into a suitable project and panic began to set in. Three weeks to think about and write a proposal now seemed impossible. She had performed very well in her second year modules, but all of the accounting modules

Source: Anthony Kay/Alamy

focused on technical aspects of accounting and financial reporting. Whilst Emma knew she was good at these aspects of accounting she wanted to try and identify a topic that was more in the news, and one that would link to both her placement experience and her course. She wanted to use the project in presentations for a job and was hoping to work in the airline or travel industry as a trainee accountant.

One of the final year modules that Emma was studying, 'Contemporary Issues in Accounting' covered aspects of corporate governance, social responsibility, whistle-blowing and ethics. There was a guest lecture that week given by a professor of ethics examining the issue of environmental accounting. The lecture highlighted the increased environmental disclosure that had taken place over the last decade as public companies sought to reassure stakeholders who were concerned about the adverse environmental impact caused by business. The lecture went into specific details, citing Deegan et al. (2000 and 2002), who had examined the oil and mining industries. This research showed how environmental disclosures had increased following adverse events such as oil spillages or pollution that had been widely reported in the media. The professor ended the lecture raising the issue of global warming and business responsibility, with the news that Prince Charles had not attended the World Future Energy Summit in Abu Dhabi due to the level of carbon waste from the associated flights for him and his entourage.[1]

Emma was pleased that she had attended the lecture, an obvious research topic was right in front of her! She thought of the airline industry and the problem of global warming and carbon omissions and wondered what companies in that industry were saying about those issues in their annual reports. She immediately looked up the annual reports for her placement company for the last five years which were all available as pdf documents on their corporate website. Quickly looking at the environmental section it was clear that there had been a significant increase in its content over that period. Emma was not surprised there had been an increase in disclosure as this was a common and already well observed trend. However it was a good starting point. She read the articles that the professor had referred to in his lecture, Deegan et al. (2000) and Deegan et al. (2002). From these articles she also referred to Patten (1992) and Gray et al. (1995). Looking on the electronic journal search she also found more recent articles on environmental disclosure such as Campbell et al. (2006) and Murray et al. (2006). They was certainly plenty of literature in the area. Emma focused on the earlier articles by Deegan et al. and Patten and arranged an appointment with one of the accounting tutors to discuss these and her ideas for the research proposal. The meeting was scheduled for the week before the proposal was due to be submitted, so Emma prepared some outline notes to take to the meeting from which she hoped to finalise her own proposal.

Emma had the following main points listed for the meeting:

- Increase in her placement company's environmental disclosure over the past five years.
- Look for same trends in all airline companies.
- Quantify levels of environmental disclosure.
- Relate to increase in disclosure trends from literature.
- Get news stories about omissions and carbon foot-printing.
- Interview placement company employees about their views.

---

[1] Borland, S. (2008) 'Prince Charles beamed all the way to Dubai', 23 Jan., www.telegraph.co.uk/news

The meeting with the tutor went well and the tutor was supportive of the general topic area, but Emma was surprised by how much further work she had still to do to formulate the proposal. Emma had told her tutor about the guest lecture, the annual report disclosures she already had identified, the articles and the link between the increased disclosure and global warming issues. The tutor asked Emma how she would be able to link the disclosure with the press stories and show that it was not just a coincidence. The only news stories Emma had so far collected all related to the past 12 months. Emma needed to think about this aspect in more depth. The tutor also asked Emma if she had any ideas about a possible theoretical base that could be relevant for the research. From the articles, Emma said that legitimacy theory would be used as this had been the theoretical framework within the articles. Again, the tutor raised concerns for Emma to think about to clearly establish that a legitimacy problem existed that could then be used to explain the increase in associated disclosure. Towards the end of the meeting the tutor also questioned Emma as to why she wanted to carry out interviews. Emma felt that having worked in the industry, she could get access to some of the management and that it would be useful for her research. The tutor acknowledged the possible access but questioned whether the interviews were really needed for the research and what value they were adding.

Over the next week, Emma tried to address the issues raised by the tutor. To show the increase in news stories associated with airlines and global warming, Emma had found out how to use one of the online media databases that would allow her to search for news stories by year by key words and groups of key words. Emma had already read one month's coverage and had coded the content into good, bad or neutral news. She had also started to collate the increased number of flights and destinations covered by the low-cost airlines over the years of her study. Emma had decided to narrow her focus onto this part of the industry rather than the whole airline industry. The biggest issue related to the need for interviews. It surprised her that she did not need to carry them out as she had always thought that doing this would be better for her research. She decided not to do them and to rely on desk-based research using the media coverage and annual report disclosures.

The topic area was now clear in her mind to investigate the change in environmental disclosure over time by low cost airlines. She was pleased to narrow the focus rather than have to research the whole industry, and due to the growth of such airlines this seemed a sensible approach. The most pleasing part of the process was that Emma also knew why she was looking at the disclosure and how she would try and explain its change over time. Having some idea of the theory base also filled Emma with confidence to proceed and she was now really looking forward to getting started for real.

The research topic and the proposal were handed in. The proposal was titled: Media Climate Change Reporting and Environmental Disclosure Patterns in the Low-Cost Airline Industry in the Twenty-First Century.

Questions

1 Why is it important that your research can be related to a relevant theory base, and when during the project does the theoretical framework need to be identified?

2 Do you think that Emma is right to restrict her project to only low-cost airlines, rather than the whole industry or a comparison with another sector? Give reasons for your answer.

3 Do you think Emma was correct in her decision not to carry out interviews? Give reasons for your answer.

If she were to change her mind, are there any ethical issues that would need to be addressed?

References

Campbell, D.J., Moore, G. and Shrives, P.J. (2006) 'Cross-sectional effects in community disclosure', *Accounting, Auditing and Accountability Journal*, Vol. 19, No. 1, pp. 96–114.

Deegan, C., Rankin, M. and Voght, P. (2000) 'Firms' disclosure reactions to major social incidents: Australian evidence', *Accounting Forum*, Vol. 24, No. 1, pp. 101–30.

Deegan, C., M. Rankin and Tobin J. (2002) 'An examination of the corporate social and environmental disclosures of BHP from 1983–1997: A test of legitimacy theory', *Accounting, Auditing and Accountability Journal*, Vol. 15, No. 3, pp. 312–43.

Gray, R.H., Kouhy, R. and Lavers, S. (1995) 'Corporate social and environmental reporting: a review of the literature and a longitudinal study of UK disclosure', *Accounting, Auditing & Accountability Journal*, Vol. 8, No. 2, pp. 47–77.

Murray, A., Sinclair, D. Power, D. and Gray, R. (2006) 'Do financial markets care about social and environmental disclosure? Further evidence from the UK', *Accounting, Auditing & Accountability Journal*, Vol. 19, No. 2, pp. 228–55.

Patten, D.M. (1992) 'Intra-industry environmental disclosure in response to the Alaskan oil spill: a note on legitimacy theory', *Accounting, Organisations and Society*, Vol. 17, pp. 471–75.

Self-check answers

1 These may include:
  a Identify the management and trade union objectives for the Joint Consultative Committee and use this to establish suitable effectiveness criteria.
  b Review key literature on the use of joint consultative committees.
  c Carry out primary research in the organisation to measure the effectiveness of the Joint Consultative Committee.
  d Identify the strengths and weaknesses of the Joint Consultative Committee.
  e Where necessary, make recommendations for action to ensure the effective function of the Joint Consultative Committee.

2 One starting point would be to ask your project tutor for suggestions of possible recent review articles or articles containing recommendations for further work that he or she has read. Another would be to browse recent editions of operations management journals such as the *International Journal of Operations & Production Management* for possible research ideas. These would include both statements of the absence of research and unfounded assertions. Recent reports held in your library or on the Internet may also be of use here. You could also scan one or two recently published operations management textbooks for overviews of research that has been undertaken.

3 From the description given, it would appear that your colleague has considered only rational thinking techniques. It would therefore seem sensible to suggest two creative thinking techniques, as these would hopefully generate an idea that would appeal to him. One technique that you could suggest is brainstorming, perhaps emphasising the need to do it with other colleagues. Exploring past

projects in the accountancy area would be another possibility. You might also suggest that he keeps a notebook of ideas.

4 Your answer will probably differ from that below. However, the sorts of things you could be considering include:

a How do business organisations benefit from their liaison with schools?

b Why do business organisations undertake school liaison activities?

c To what degree do business organisations receive value for money in their school liaison activities?

5 Let us go back to the example used in the chapter of the supermarket marketing manager who theorises that the introduction of a loyalty card will mean that regular customers are less likely to shop at competitor supermarkets. This could be the research proposal's starting point, i.e. a hypothesis that the introduction of a loyalty card will mean that regular customers are less likely to shop at competitor supermarkets. This prompts thoughts about the possible use of literature in the proposal and the research project itself. This literature could have at least two strands. First, a practical strand which looks at the research evidence which lends credence to the hypothesis. Second, a more abstract strand that studies human consumer behaviour and looks at the cognitive processes which affect consumer purchasing decisions.

This ensures that the proposal and resultant research project are both theory driven and also ensures that relevant theory is covered in the literature.

6 Try including a subsection in the background section that is headed 'How the previous published research has informed my research questions and objectives'. Then show how, say, a gap in the previous research that is there because nobody has pursued a particular approach before has led to you filling that gap.